GREGG
College Keyboarding & Document Processing

**9th Edition
Lessons 1-120**

Ober
Johnson
Rice
Hanson

Scot Ober
Ball State University

Jack E. Johnson
State University of West Georgia

Arlene Rice
Los Angeles City College

Robert N. Hanson
Northern Michigan University

Visit the *College Keyboarding* Web site at **www.gdp.glencoe.com**

 **Glencoe
McGraw-Hill**

New York, New York   Columbus, Ohio   Woodland Hills, California   Peoria, Illinois

REVIEWERS

Peggy Burrus
Red Rocks Community College
Lakewood, CO

Judy Ehresman
Mercer County Community College
Trenton, NJ

Aida Galvan-De La Rosa
Steve Szymoniak
Texas State Technical College
Harlingen, TX

Mary Hanson
Northwest Technical College
East Grand Forks, MN

Rebecca Jones
Bladen Community College
Dublin, NC

Patricia King
Blackhawk Technical College
Janesville, WI

Barb Muchnok
Westmoreland County Community College
Youngwood, PA

Carolyn Seefer
Diablo Valley College
Pleasant Hill, CA

Pam Strong
Shelton State Community College
Tuscaloosa, AL

All brand names and product names are trademarks or registered trademarks of their respective companies.

Glencoe/McGraw-Hill
A Division of The McGraw-Hill Companies

Gregg College Keyboarding & Document Processing Lessons 1–120, 9th Edition

Send all inquiries to:
Glencoe/McGraw-Hill
21600 Oxnard Street, Suite 500
Woodland Hills, CA 91367

ISBN 0-07-824176-6

Printed in the United States of America.

5 6 7 8 9   071   06 05 04 03

CONTENTS

PART ONE:
The Alphabet,
Number, and
Symbol Keys

PART TWO:
Basic Business Documents

**PART FOUR:
Advanced
Formatting**

**PART FIVE:
Specialized
Applications**

**PART SIX:
Using and
Designing
Business
Documents**

SKILLBUILDING

APPENDIX

INDEX

About Keyboarding

Each day the world becomes more and more technologically advanced. As a result, learning new skills for the world of work is even more important.

One such skill that can prepare you for virtually any job in the world is keyboarding. From accountants to zoologists and every occupation in between, the ability to quickly and accurately type information is an essential skill that can increase your chances of being hired (or getting your dream job).

Formerly referred to as "typing," keyboarding is the act of entering data by means of designated computer keys. Today, as we rely more and more on computers to handle everyday work and leisure activities, the art of accurately conveying information is a necessity. So whether you are emailing a relative, developing a class presentation, or downloading map directions, keyboarding knowledge can make the job easier.

Preface

Gregg College Keyboarding & Document Processing Lessons 1–120, 9th Edition, is a multi-component instructional program designed to give the student and the instructor a high degree of flexibility and a high degree of success in meeting their respective goals. For student and instructor convenience, the core components of this instructional system are available in either a kit format or a book format. *Gregg College Keyboarding Lessons 1–20, 5th Edition*, is also available for the development of touch-typing skills for use in shorter computer keyboarding classes.

THE KIT FORMAT

Gregg College Keyboarding & Document Processing Lessons 1–120, 9th Edition, provides a complete kit of materials for both courses in the keyboarding curriculum generally offered by colleges. Each kit, which is briefly described below, contains a softcover textbook and a student word processing manual.

Kit 1: Lessons 1–60. This kit provides the text and word processing manual for the first course. Since this kit is designed for the beginning student, its major objectives are to develop touch control of the keyboard and proper typing techniques, to build basic speed and accuracy, and to provide practice in applying those basic skills to the formatting of letters, reports, tables, memos, and other kinds of personal and business communications.

Kit 2: Lessons 61–120. This kit provides the text and word processing manual for the second course. This course continues the development of basic typing skills and emphasizes the formatting of various kinds of business correspondence, reports, tables, electronic forms, and desktop publishing projects from unarranged and rough-draft sources.

THE BOOK FORMAT

For the convenience of those who wish to obtain the core instructional materials in separate volumes, *Gregg College Keyboarding & Document Processing Lessons 1–120, 9th Edition*, offers textbooks for the first course: *Gregg College Keyboarding & Document Processing Lessons 1–60, 9th Edition*, or *Gregg College Keyboarding Lessons 1–20, 5th Edition*. For the second course, *Gregg College Document Processing Lessons 61–120* is offered, and for the two-semester course, *Gregg College Keyboarding & Document Processing Lessons 1–120* is available. In each instance, the content of the textbooks is identical to that of the corresponding textbooks in kit format. Third semester instruction is available in *Gregg College Document Processing Lessons 121–180*.

SUPPORTING MATERIALS

Gregg College Keyboarding & Document Processing Lessons 1–120, 9th Edition, includes the following additional components:

Instructional Materials. Supporting materials are provided for instructor use with either the kits or the textbooks. The special Instructor Wraparound Edition offers lesson plans and reduced-size student pages to enhance classroom instruction. Distance learning tips, instructional methodology, adult learner strategies, and special needs features are also included in this wraparound edition. Solution keys for all of the formatting exercises in Lessons 1–180 are contained in separate booklets used with this program. Finally, test booklets are available with the objective test formats and alternative document processing tests for each part.

Computer Software. IBM-compatible computer software is available for the entire program. The computer software provides a complete instructional system.

STRUCTURE

Gregg College Keyboarding & Document Processing, 9th Edition, opens with a two-page part opener that introduces students to the focus of the instruction. Objectives are presented, and opportunities within career clusters are highlighted. The unit opener familiarizes students with the lesson content to be presented in the five lessons for the unit.

Every lesson begins with a *Warmup* that should be typed as soon as students are settled at the keyboard. In the *New Keys* section, all alphabet, number, and symbol keys are introduced in the first 20 lessons. Drill lines in this section provide the practice necessary to achieve keyboarding skills.

An easily identifiable *Skillbuilding* section can be found in every lesson. Each drill presents to the student a variety of different activities designed to improve speed and accuracy. Skillbuilding exercises include Technique Timings, Diagnostic Practices, Paced Practices, MAP (Misstroke Analysis and Prescription), and Timings that progress from 1 to 5 minutes in length.

Many of the skillbuilding sections also include a *Pretest, Practice,* and *Posttest* routine. This routine is designed to build speed and accuracy skills as well as confidence. The Pretest helps identify speed and accuracy needs. The Practice activities consist of a variety of intensive enrichment drills. Finally, the Posttest measures improvement.

Introduction

STARTING A LESSON

Each lesson begins with the goals for that lesson. Read the goals carefully so that you understand the purpose of your practice. In the example at the left, the goals for the lesson are to type 28wpm (words per minute) on a 2-minute timing with no more than 5 errors and to format simple reports.

BUILDING STRAIGHT-COPY SKILL

Warmups. Each lesson begins with a warmup that reinforces learned alphabet, number, and/or symbol keys.

Skillbuilding. The skillbuilding portion of each lesson includes a variety of drills to individualize your keyboarding speed and accuracy development. Instructions for completing the drills are always provided beside each activity.

Additional skillbuilding drills are included in the back of the textbook. These drills are used to help you meet your individual goals.

MEASURING STRAIGHT-COPY SKILL

Straight-copy skill is measured in wpm (words per minute). All timings are the exact length needed to meet the speed goal for the lesson. If you finish a timing before time is up, you have automatically reached your speed goal for the lesson.

Counting Errors. Specific criteria are used for counting errors. Count an error when:
1. Any stroke is incorrect.
2. Any punctuation after a word is incorrect or omitted. Count the word before the punctuation as incorrect.
3. The spacing after a word or after its punctuation is incorrect. Count the word as incorrect.
4. A letter or word is omitted.
5. A letter or word is repeated.
6. A direction about spacing, indenting, and so on, is violated.
7. Words are transposed.

(**Note:** Only one error is counted for each word, no matter how many errors it may contain.)

Determining Speed. Typing speed is measured in words per minute (wpm). To compute wpm, count every 5 strokes, including spaces, as 1 "word." Horizontal word scales below an activity divide lines into 5-stroke words. Vertical word scales beside an activity show the number of words in each line cumulatively totaled. For example, in the illustration shown, if you complete a line, you have typed 8 words. If you complete 2 lines, you have typed 16 words. Use the bottom word scale to determine the word count of a partial line. Add that number to the cumulative total for the last complete line.

```
23  Ada lost her letter; Dee lost her card.      8
24  Dave sold some of the food to a market.      16
25  Alva asked Walt for three more matches.      24
26  Dale asked Seth to watch the last show.      32
    |  1  |  2  |  3  |  4  |  5  |  6  |  7  |  8  |
```

CORRECTING ERRORS

As you learn to type, you will probably make some errors. To correct an error, press **BACKSPACE** (shown as ← on some keyboards) to delete the incorrect character. Then type the correct character.

If you notice an error on a different line, use the up, down, left, or right arrows to move the insertion point immediately to the left or right of the error. Press **BACKSPACE** to delete a character to the left of the insertion point or **DELETE** to delete a character to the right of the insertion point.

TYPING TECHNIQUE

Correct position at the keyboard enables you to type with greater speed and accuracy and with less fatigue. When typing for a long period, rest your eyes occasionally by looking away from the screen. Change position, walk around, or stretch when your muscles feel tired. Making such movements and adjustments may help prevent your body from becoming too tired. Additionally, long-term bodily damage, such as carpal tunnel syndrome, can be prevented.

If possible, adjust your workstation as follows:

Chair. Adjust the height so that your upper and lower legs form a 90-degree angle and your lower back is supported by the back of the chair.

Keyboard. Center your body opposite the J key, and lean forward slightly. Keep your forearms horizontal to the keyboard.

Screen. Position the monitor so that the top of the screen is just below eye level and about 18 to 26 inches away.

Text. Position your textbook or other copy on either side of the monitor as close to it as vertically and horizontally possible to minimize head and eye movement and to avoid neck strain.

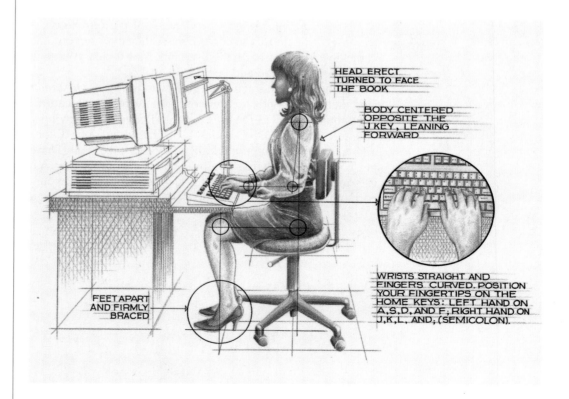

HEAD ERECT
TURNED TO FACE
THE BOOK

BODY CENTERED
OPPOSITE THE
J KEY, LEANING
FORWARD

FEET APART
AND FIRMLY
BRACED

WRISTS STRAIGHT AND
FINGERS CURVED. POSITION
YOUR FINGERTIPS ON THE
HOME KEYS: LEFT HAND ON
A, S, D, AND F; RIGHT HAND ON
J, K, L, AND; (SEMICOLON).

Before You Begin

USING MICROSOFT WINDOWS

If you are using *Gregg College Keyboarding & Document Processing Lessons 1–120, 9th Edition*, you must know how to use a mouse, and you must know some basic information about Microsoft Windows.

Before you begin Lesson 1, turn to the Introduction section in your word processing manual and read the information presented there. Note: If you are using the book with Lessons 1–20, then use Windows Help to familiarize yourself with Windows. You will learn how to navigate within a program and learn the skills you will need to use Windows.

Moving around, or navigating, within a program with a mouse involves pointing, clicking, double-clicking, and dragging.

Through Windows Help, you will learn the names and functions of the different parts of a window. You will want to pay close attention to the menu bar and command names as well as how to select options in a dialog box.

STARTING YOUR PROGRAM

Once you have completed the Introduction, you are ready to begin Lesson 1. If you are using the *Gregg College Keyboarding & Document Processing Lessons 1–120, 9th Edition,* software that is correlated with this textbook, you must first start Windows. To start the *Gregg College Keyboarding & Document Processing Lessons 1–120* software, in the Program Manager, locate the Glencoe Keyboarding group icon. Double-click the icon to open the group window. If you will be saving your data to a disk, insert your data disk into the correct drive before you continue.

In the Glencoe Keyboarding group window, if there is a *Gregg College Keyboarding & Document Processing Lessons 1–120, 9th Edition* icon, double-click that icon to start the program. Choose the correct class; then choose your name from the class list. If your name does not appear on the list, click *New* to add your name to the list. Then follow the instructions to log in and begin Lesson 1.

If there is no *Gregg College Keyboarding & Document Processing* icon, select the icon that corresponds to your course name and the location of your data. For example, if your course is called *Lessons 1–60* and you will be saving your data to a disk in drive A, double-click the GDP Lessons 1–60 (Drive A) icon. If you will be saving your data to a disk in drive B, double-click the GDP Lessons 1–60 (Drive B) icon. If you will be saving your data to a hard drive or network drive, you may have an icon specified for your use only. (If you are unsure of which icon to use, ask your instructor.) Double-click the correct program icon, and follow the on-screen directions to log in and begin Lesson 1.

About Your Book

Each **Part Opener** is a two-page spread that provides a list of the part objectives and a special feature that focuses on the use of your keyboarding skills in various career clusters.

KEYBOARDING IN HEALTH SERVICES

Within the health services job cluster, there is an enormous range of job opportunity in the medical and health care industry. Hundreds of different occupations exist in health care practice, including business-oriented positions. In fact, career opportunities within this cluster are among the fastest growing in the national marketplace. The current job outlook is quite positive as managed care has significantly increased opportunities for doctors and other health professionals, particularly in the area of preventative care. Additionally, the aging population requires more highly skilled medical workers.

Opportunities in Health Careers

Consider health care jobs, medical careers, health care management, and medical management. Various job possibilities exist in these areas, and work as a medical transcriber, clinical technician, nurse, medical analyst, surgical technician or surgeon, physical therapist, orderly, pharmacist, or medical researcher can most likely be easily found. Interestingly, keyboarding skill is important for all of these positions.

49

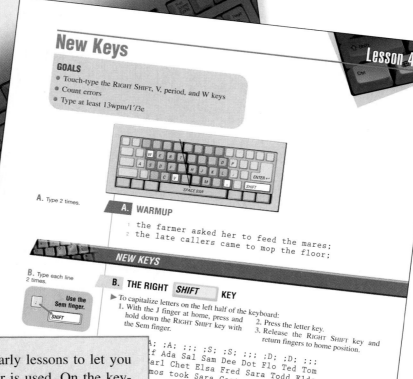

Unit 1
Keyboarding: The Alphabet

LESSON 1
A S D F J K L ;
Enter Space Bar

LESSON 2
H E O R

LESSON 3
M T P C

LESSON 4
Right Shift V . W

LESSON 5
Review

The **Unit Opener** helps you organize your study of unit concepts. The visual listing previews what will be taught in the unit.

New Keys

Lesson 4

GOALS
- Touch-type the RIGHT SHIFT, V, period, and W keys
- Count errors
- Type at least 13wpm/1'/3e

A. Type 2 times.

A. WARMUP

```
1  the farmer asked her to feed the mares;
2  the late callers came to mop the floor;
```

NEW KEYS

B. Type each line 2 times.

Use the Sem finger.
SHIFT

B. THE RIGHT SHIFT KEY

▶ To capitalize letters on the left half of the keyboard:
1. With the J finger at home, press and hold down the RIGHT SHIFT key with the Sem finger.
2. Press the letter key.
3. Release the RIGHT SHIFT key and return fingers to home position.

```
;A; ;A; ;;; ;S; ;S; ;;; ;D; ;D; ;;;
f Ada Sal Sam Dee Dot Flo Ted Tom
arl Chet Elsa Fred Sara Todd Elda
mos took Sara Carter to the races
```

KEY

```
fvf vfv fff fvf fvf vfv fff fvf
Eva vet Ava vat Eve ova Vel vee
e Vera ever vast Reva dove vest
ed for Vassar; Val voted for me
```

KEY

```
.l. .l. lll l.l l.l .l. lll l.l
ea. ea. sr. sr. Dr. Dr. Sr. Sr.
. A.D. p.m. Corp. amt. Dr. Co.
ma left. Dave left. Sarah came home.
```

Use the L finger.

Color Coding is used in the early lessons to let you easily differentiate which finger is used. On the keyboard chart shown at the beginning of each new-key lesson, new keys are highlighted, previously learned keys are labeled but not highlighted, and unlearned keys are blank. You will have a sense of progress as you move through the 20 new-key lessons.

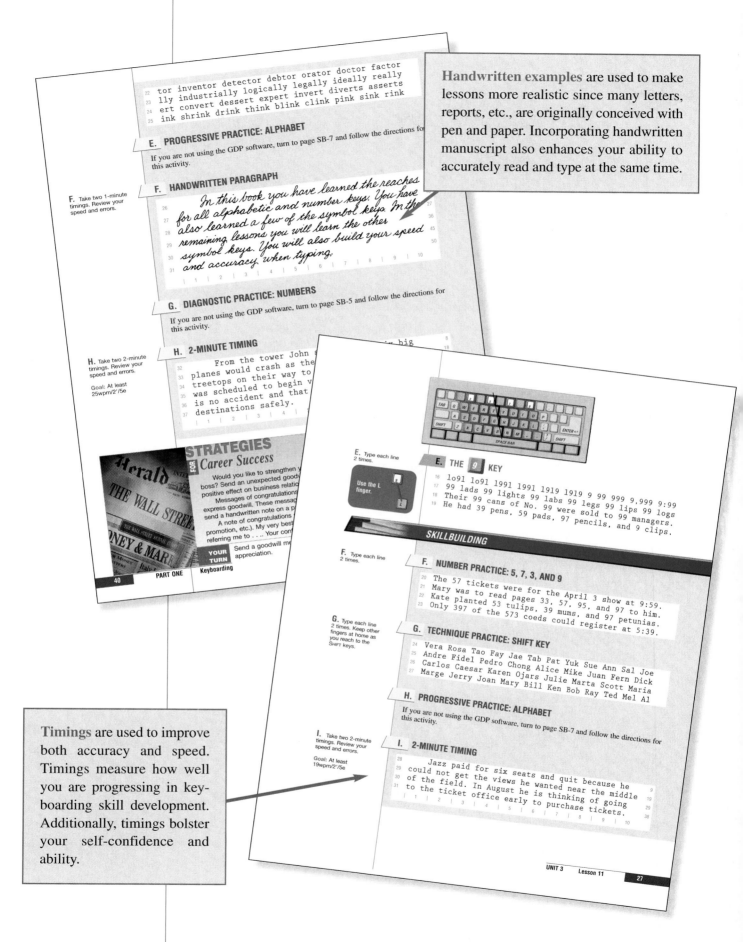

If you are not using the GDP software, turn to page SB-7 and follow the directions for this activity.

22 tor inventor detector debtor orator doctor factor
23 lly industrially logically legally ideally really
24 ert convert dessert expert invert diverts asserts
25 ink shrink drink think blink clink pink sink rink

E. PROGRESSIVE PRACTICE: ALPHABET

F. HANDWRITTEN PARAGRAPH

F. Take two 1-minute timings. Review your speed and errors.

In this book you have learned the reaches for all alphabetic and number keys. You have also learned a few of the symbol keys. In the remaining lessons you will learn the other symbol keys. You will also build your speed and accuracy when typing.

G. DIAGNOSTIC PRACTICE: NUMBERS

If you are not using the GDP software, turn to page SB-5 and follow the directions for this activity.

H. 2-MINUTE TIMING

H. Take two 2-minute timings. Review your speed and errors.

Goal: At least 25wpm/2'/5e

32 From the tower John s... big
33 planes would crash as the
34 treetops on their way to
35 was scheduled to begin v
36 is no accident and that
37 destinations safely.

STRATEGIES for Career Success

Would you like to strengthen y... boss? Send an unexpected goody... positive effect on business relatio...
Messages of congratulations... express goodwill. These message... send a handwritten note on a p...
A note of congratulations... promotion, etc.). My very best... referring me to . . . Your con...

YOUR TURN Send a goodwill me... appreciation.

40 PART ONE Keyboarding

Handwritten examples are used to make lessons more realistic since many letters, reports, etc., are originally conceived with pen and paper. Incorporating handwritten manuscript also enhances your ability to accurately read and type at the same time.

E. THE 9 KEY

Use the L finger.

16 lo9l lo9l 1991 1991 1919 1919 9 99 999 9,999 9:99
17 99 lads 99 lights 99 labs 99 legs 99 lips 99 logs
18 Their 99 cans of No. 99 were sold to 99 managers.
19 He had 39 pens, 59 pads, 97 pencils, and 9 clips.

SKILLBUILDING

F. Type each line 2 times.

F. NUMBER PRACTICE: 5, 7, 3, AND 9

20 The 57 tickets were for the April 3 show at 9:59.
21 Mary was to read pages 33, 57, 95, and 97 to him.
22 Kate planted 53 tulips, 39 mums, and 97 petunias.
23 Only 397 of the 573 coeds could register at 5:39.

G. Type each line 2 times. Keep other fingers at home as you reach to the SHIFT keys.

G. TECHNIQUE PRACTICE: SHIFT KEY

24 Vera Rosa Tao Fay Jae Tab Pat Yuk Sue Ann Sal Joe
25 Andre Fidel Pedro Chong Alice Mike Juan Fern Dick
26 Carlos Caesar Karen Ojars Julie Marta Scott Maria
27 Marge Jerry Joan Mary Bill Ken Bob Ray Ted Mel Al

H. PROGRESSIVE PRACTICE: ALPHABET

If you are not using the GDP software, turn to page SB-7 and follow the directions for this activity.

I. Take two 2-minute timings. Review your speed and errors.

Goal: At least 19wpm/2'/5e

I. 2-MINUTE TIMING

28 Jazz paid for six seats and quit because he
29 could not get the views he wanted near the middle
30 of the field. In August he is thinking of going
31 to the ticket office early to purchase tickets.

Timings are used to improve both accuracy and speed. Timings measure how well you are progressing in keyboarding skill development. Additionally, timings bolster your self-confidence and ability.

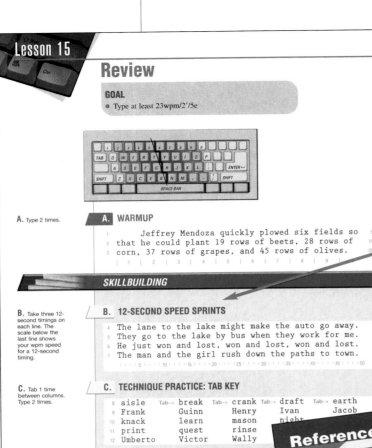

Lesson 15

Review

GOAL
● Type at least 23wpm/2'/5e

A. Type 2 times.

A. WARMUP

```
1      Jeffrey Mendoza quickly plowed six fields so     9
2   that he could plant 19 rows of beets, 28 rows of    19
3   corn, 37 rows of grapes, and 45 rows of olives.     28
    | 1 | 2 | 3 | 4 | 5 | 6 | 7 | 8 | 9 |
```

SKILLBUILDING

B. Take three 12-second timings on each line. The scale below the last line shows your wpm speed for a 12-second timing.

B. 12-SECOND SPEED SPRINTS

```
4   The lane to the lake might make the auto go away.
5   They go to the lake by bus when they work for me.
6   He just won and lost, won and lost, won and lost.
7   The man and the girl rush down the paths to town.
    | | 5 | | | 10 | | | 20 | | | 30 | | | 40 | | | 50
```

C. Tab 1 time between columns. Type 2 times.

C. TECHNIQUE PRACTICE: TAB KEY

```
8   aisle   Tab→ break  Tab→ crank  Tab→ draft  Tab→ earth
9   Frank        Guinn       Henry       Ivan        Jacob
10  knack        learn       mason       night
11  print        quest       rinse
12  Umberto      Victor      Wally
```

D. Type each line 2 times. Try not to slow down for the capital letters.

D. TECHNIQUE PRACTICE: SHIFT KEY

```
13  Sue, Pat, Ann, and Gail left for
14  The St. Louis Cardinals and New Y
15  Dave Herr took Flight 481 for Mem
16  An address for Karen Cook is 5 Ba
17  Harry Truman was born in Missouri
```

34   **PART ONE**   Keyboarding

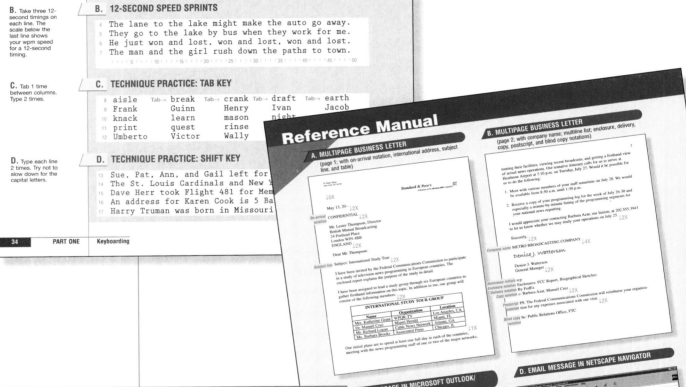

Reference Manual

A. MULTIPAGE BUSINESS LETTER
(page 1: with on-arrival notation, international address, subject line, and table)

B. MULTIPAGE BUSINESS LETTER
(page 2: with company name; multiline list; enclosure, delivery, copy, postscript, and blind copy notations)

C. EMAIL MESSAGE IN MICROSOFT OUTLOOK/INTERNET EXPLORER

D. EMAIL MESSAGE IN NETSCAPE NAVIGATOR

R-5   REFERENCE MANUAL

Skillbuilding practice in every lesson offers an individualized plan for speed and accuracy development. A variety of skill-building exercises, including Technique Practice, Pretest/Practice/Posttest, Sustained Practice, 12-Second Speed Sprints, Diagnostic Practice, Progressive Practice, Paced Practice, and Number Practice, provides the foundation for progress in your skill development.

Reference Manual material found in the front of the book enables you to easily locate information regarding the proper way to format business letters, reports, email messages, memoranda, and other forms of written communication. Elements such as line spacing, placement of letterhead and body text, etc., are all illustrated in detail for your instructional support. Additionally, 50 "must-know" rules for language arts in business contexts are included with examples in the Reference Manual to help improve writing skills.

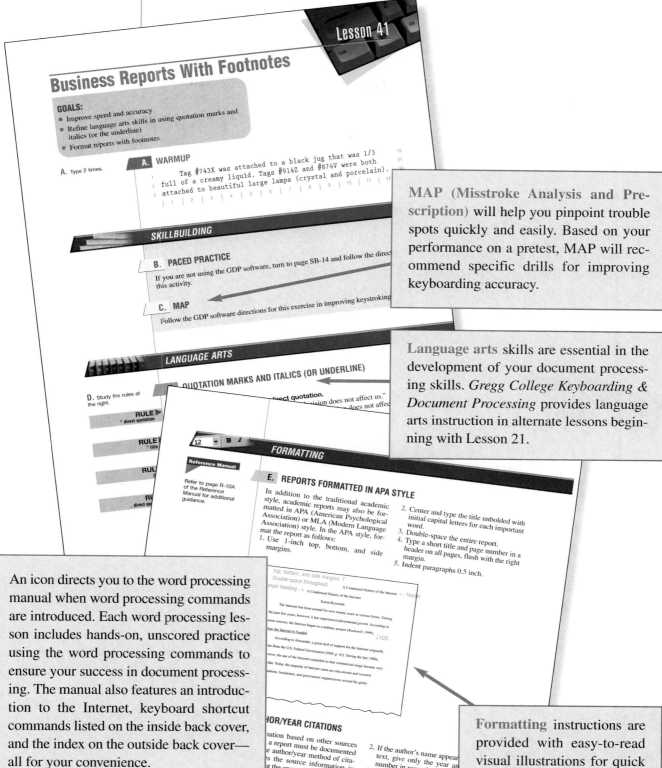

MAP (Misstroke Analysis and Prescription) will help you pinpoint trouble spots quickly and easily. Based on your performance on a pretest, MAP will recommend specific drills for improving keyboarding accuracy.

Language arts skills are essential in the development of your document processing skills. *Gregg College Keyboarding & Document Processing* provides language arts instruction in alternate lessons beginning with Lesson 21.

An icon directs you to the word processing manual when word processing commands are introduced. Each word processing lesson includes hands-on, unscored practice using the word processing commands to ensure your success in document processing. The manual also features an introduction to the Internet, keyboard shortcut commands listed on the inside back cover, and the index on the outside back cover—all for your convenience.

Formatting instructions are provided with easy-to-read visual illustrations for quick and efficient study. Model documents help you move from the simple to the complex in developing document processing skills.

The last document processing exercise in most units is designated as a Progress Check/Proofreading Check. Make it your goal to have zero typographical errors when the GDP software first scores the document.

Correspondence 50-35 ▶

Personal-Business Letter With Single-Line Numbered List, Enclosure, and Copy Notations

Current Date | Ms. Karen Shalicky | Lincoln Travel Center | 2384 Longdale Avenue | Suite 4113 | Boston, MA 02134-3489 | Dear Ms. Shalicky:

¶ I am interested in taking a cruise in one of the following regions:

- Alaska Inland Passageway
- Caribbean Islands
- Greek Isles

¶ Could you please send me some promotional materials for these cruises. My financial resources are such that I would like to limit my cruise package to $5,000 and would prefer a cruise no longer than ten days in length. I will be accompanied by my friend, Bonnie Davis, and I assume that any quotes you give me could apply to both of us. ¶ We would like to do sightseeing in some of these locations. Do you have special excursions available to passengers? I am enclosing a list of the sites we would like to visit in each of these regions. ¶ The best time for us to travel is between June 1 and June 20, and we would like you to schedule our trip around those dates. I hope to hear from you soon.

Yours truly, | Rita Wright | 678 Ardale Avenue | Milton, MA 02186-2190 | Enclosure | c: Bonnie Davis

☑ **Progress Check / Proofreading Check**

Documents designated as Proofreading Checks serve as a check of your proofreading skill. Your goal is to have zero typo-graphical errors when the GDP software first scores the document.

Special features are designed to enhance your study of keyboarding. The *Keyboarding Connection* features illustrate the importance of keyboarding skills outside of the classroom. The *Strategies for Career Success* features offer an employment-related connection with useful hints for succeeding in any career.

Keyboarding CONNECTION

Avoid Email Flame Wars

Don't fan the flames! A flame is an offensive email that expresses anger, criticism, or insults. If flames are transmitted to a mailing list, they can produce a long list of flames and counter flames known as flame wars.

You may be tempted to join in, but this is a waste of everyone's time. Often the initial offense was merely a poorly worded email that a reader interpreted as an insult. The ___ those who intentionally send inflammatory emails called flame bait. Resis___ send a cutting response, and consider if the writer's intent was to ___

___judges something you wrote and becomes offended, just ___ology can thwart a potential fire. Avoid miscommunication by ___ your emails.

___een insulted by an email? What was your response?

Appendix
Ten-Key Numeric Keypad

GOAL:
- To control the ten-key numeric keypad keys.

Some computer keyboards have a separate ten-key numeric keypad located to the right of the alphanumeric keyboard. The arrangement of the keypad enables you to type numbers more rapidly than using the top row of the alphanumeric keyboard.

To input numbers using the ten-key numeric keypad, you must activate the Num Lock (Numeric Lock) key. Usually, an indicator light signals that the Num Lock is activated.

On the keypad, 4, 5, and 6 are the home keys. Place your fingers on the keypad home row as follows:

- First finger (J finger) on 4
- Second finger (K finger) on 5
- Third finger (L finger) on 6

The keypad keys are controlled as follows:

- First finger controls 1, 4, and 7
- Second finger controls 2, 5, and 8
- Third finger controls 3, 6, 9, and decimal point

- Right thumb controls 0
- Fourth finger controls ENTER

Since different computers have different arrangements of ten-key numeric keypads, study the arrangement of your keypad. The illustration shows the most common arrangement. If your keypad is arranged differently from the illustration, check with your instructor for the correct placement of your fingers on the keypad.

The Appendix contains instructions for the ten-key numeric keypad. Students practice entering numerical data using touch-typing techniques.

NEW KEYS

A. THE 4, 5, AND 6 KEYS

A. Use the first finger to control the 4 key, the second finger to control the 5 key, and the third finger to control the 6 key.

Keep your eyes on the copy.

Before beginning, check to be sure the Num Lock Key is activated.

Type first column from top to bottom. Next, type the second column; then type the third column. Press ENTER after typing the final digit of each number.

444	456	454
555	654	464
666	445	546
455	446	564
466	554	654
544	556	645
566	664	666
644	665	555
655	456	444
456	654	456

22wpm

What is the difference between a job and a career?
Think carefully. A job is work that people do for money. A
career is a sequence of related jobs built on a foundation
of interests, knowledge, training, and experiences.

24wpm

Learn more about the world of work by looking at the
sixteen career clusters. Most jobs are included in one of
the clusters that have been organized by the government.
During your exploration of careers, list the clusters that
interest you.

26wpm

Once you identify your career clusters of interest,
look at the jobs within each cluster. Find out what skills
and aptitudes are needed, what education and training are
required, what the work environment is like, and what is
the possibility for advancements.

28wpm

Use your career center and school or public libraries
to research career choices. Search the Internet. Consult
with professionals for another perspective of a specific
career. As you gather information about career options,
you may discover other i   career possibilities.

30wpm

Gain insights int
participating in an i
temporary job within
familiar with a spec
You'll gain valuabl
career or not.

32wpm

Whichever pa
pride in yoursel
what you believ
how you view y
in yourself. I
your self-con

The back-of-the book skillbuilding routines are designed with YOU in mind. The Paced Practice skillbuilding paragraphs use an upbeat, motivational storyline with guidance in career choices. The Supplementary Timings relate critical thinking skills to careers.

Supplementary Timing 9

One of the most important decisions we all have to
face is choosing a career. The possibilities can appear
overwhelming. Fear not! Your critical thinking skills will
save you! Start your career planning today. Begin with
self-assessment. What are your interests? Do you enjoy
working indoors or outdoors? Do you prefer working with
numbers or with words? Are you the independent type or
would you rather work with a group? What are your favorite
academic studies? Think about these questions and then
create a list of your interests, skills, aptitudes, and
values. What you discover about yourself will help you in
finding the career that is right for you.

After you have explored your personal interests, look
at the sixteen career clusters for a wide range of job
prospects. Most jobs are included in one of these clusters
that have been organized by the government. During your
exploration, make a note of the clusters that interest you
and investigate these clusters.

Gather as much information as possible by using all
available resources. Scan the Help Wanted section in the
major Sunday newspapers for job descriptions and salaries.
Search the Net. The Internet provides electronic access to
worldwide job listings. If you want to know more about a
specific company, access its home page. Go to your college
placement office. Sign up for interviews with companies
that visit your campus. Visit your local school or county
library and ask the reference librarian for occupational
handbooks. Talk with people in your field of interest to
ask questions and get advice. Attend chapter meetings of
professional organizations to network with people working
in your chosen profession. Volunteer, intern, or work a
part-time or temporary job within your career choice for
valuable, first-hand insight. Taking an initiative in your
job search will pay off.

A career search requires the use of critical thinking
skills. These skills will help you to choose the career
that will match your skills and talents.

10
21
33
44
55
66
77
89
100
111
123
131
142
153
165
176
188
194
205
216
228
240
251
263
274
286
297
308
319
331
342
353
365
370
381
392
400

1 | 2 | 3 | 4 | 5 | 6 | 7 | 8 | 9 | 10 | 11 | 12

Reference Manual

A. MAJOR PARTS OF A MICROCOMPUTER SYSTEM

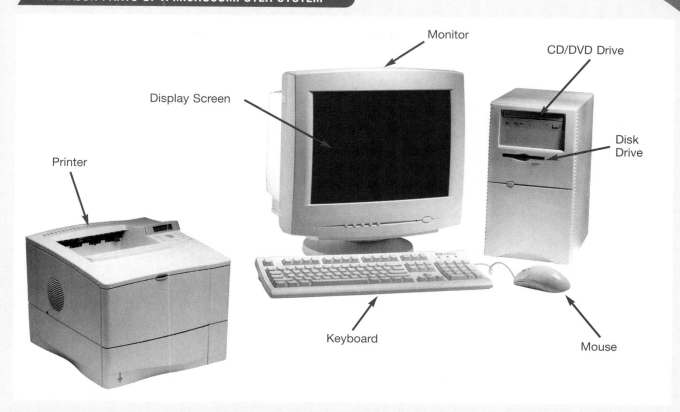

Monitor

CD/DVD Drive

Display Screen

Disk Drive

Printer

Keyboard

Mouse

B. THE COMPUTER KEYBOARD

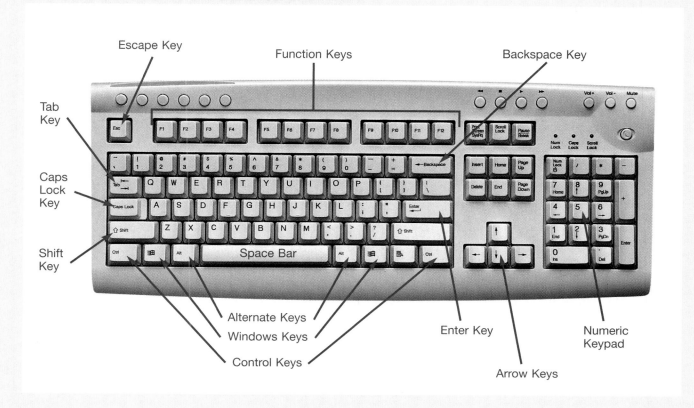

Escape Key

Function Keys

Backspace Key

Tab Key

Caps Lock Key

Shift Key

Alternate Keys

Windows Keys

Control Keys

Enter Key

Arrow Keys

Numeric Keypad

A. BUSINESS LETTER
(in block style with standard punctuation)

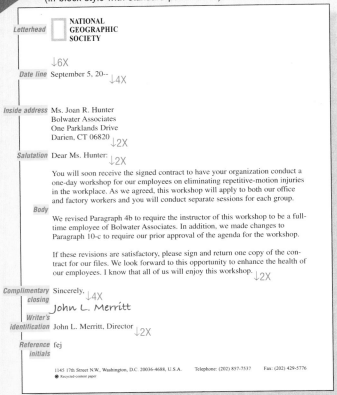

Letterhead — **NATIONAL GEOGRAPHIC SOCIETY**

↓6X

Date line — September 5, 20-- ↓4X

Inside address — Ms. Joan R. Hunter
Bolwater Associates
One Parklands Drive
Darien, CT 06820 ↓2X

Salutation — Dear Ms. Hunter: ↓2X

Body — You will soon receive the signed contract to have your organization conduct a one-day workshop for our employees on eliminating repetitive-motion injuries in the workplace. As we agreed, this workshop will apply to both our office and factory workers and you will conduct separate sessions for each group.

We revised Paragraph 4b to require the instructor of this workshop to be a full-time employee of Bolwater Associates. In addition, we made changes to Paragraph 10-c to require our prior approval of the agenda for the workshop.

If these revisions are satisfactory, please sign and return one copy of the contract for our files. We look forward to this opportunity to enhance the health of our employees. I know that all of us will enjoy this workshop. ↓2X

Complimentary closing — Sincerely, ↓4X

John L. Merritt

Writer's identification — John L. Merritt, Director ↓2X

Reference initials — fej

1145 17th Street N.W., Washington, D.C. 20036-4688, U.S.A.   Telephone: (202) 857-7537   Fax: (202) 429-5776
♻ Recycled-content paper

B. BUSINESS LETTER IN MODIFIED-BLOCK STYLE
(with open punctuation, multiline list, and enclosure notation)

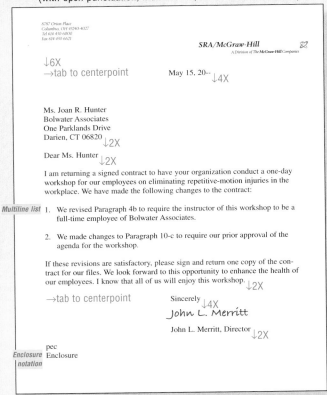

8787 Orion Place
Columbus, OH 43240-4027
Tel 614 430 6000
Fax 614 430 6621

SRA/McGraw-Hill
A Division of The *McGraw-Hill* Companies

↓6X
→tab to centerpoint   May 15, 20-- ↓4X

Ms. Joan R. Hunter
Bolwater Associates
One Parklands Drive
Darien, CT 06820 ↓2X

Dear Ms. Hunter ↓2X

I am returning a signed contract to have your organization conduct a one-day workshop for our employees on eliminating repetitive-motion injuries in the workplace. We have made the following changes to the contract:

Multiline list — 1. We revised Paragraph 4b to require the instructor of this workshop to be a full-time employee of Bolwater Associates.

2. We made changes to Paragraph 10-c to require our prior approval of the agenda for the workshop.

If these revisions are satisfactory, please sign and return one copy of the contract for our files. We look forward to this opportunity to enhance the health of our employees. I know that all of us will enjoy this workshop. ↓2X

→tab to centerpoint   Sincerely ↓4X

John L. Merritt

John L. Merritt, Director ↓2X

Enclosure notation — pec
Enclosure

C. BUSINESS LETTER IN SIMPLIFIED STYLE
(with single-line list, enclosure notation, and copy notation)

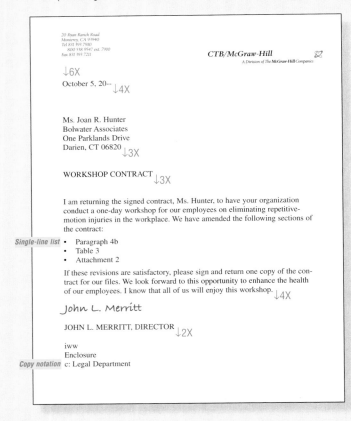

20 Ryan Ranch Road
Monterey, CA 93940
Tel 831 393 7910
800 538 9547 ext. 7910
Fax 831 393 7211

CTB/McGraw-Hill
A Division of The *McGraw-Hill* Companies

↓6X
October 5, 20-- ↓4X

Ms. Joan R. Hunter
Bolwater Associates
One Parklands Drive
Darien, CT 06820 ↓3X

WORKSHOP CONTRACT ↓3X

I am returning the signed contract, Ms. Hunter, to have your organization conduct a one-day workshop for our employees on eliminating repetitive-motion injuries in the workplace. We have amended the following sections of the contract:

Single-line list — • Paragraph 4b
• Table 3
• Attachment 2

If these revisions are satisfactory, please sign and return one copy of the contract for our files. We look forward to this opportunity to enhance the health of our employees. I know that all of us will enjoy this workshop. ↓4X

John L. Merritt

JOHN L. MERRITT, DIRECTOR ↓2X

iww
Enclosure

Copy notation — c: Legal Department

D. PERSONAL-BUSINESS LETTER
(in modified-block style and with international address and standard punctuation)

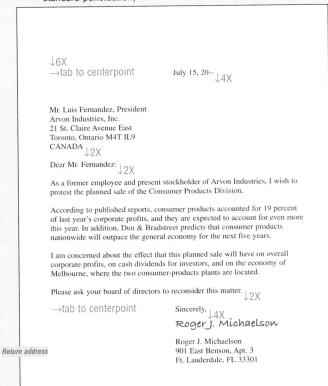

↓6X
→tab to centerpoint   July 15, 20-- ↓4X

Mr. Luis Fernandez, President
Arvon Industries, Inc.
21 St. Claire Avenue East
Toronto, Ontario M4T IL9
CANADA ↓2X

Dear Mr. Fernandez: ↓2X

As a former employee and present stockholder of Arvon Industries, I wish to protest the planned sale of the Consumer Products Division.

According to published reports, consumer products accounted for 19 percent of last year's corporate profits, and they are expected to account for even more this year. In addition, Dun & Bradstreet predicts that consumer products nationwide will outpace the general economy for the next five years.

I am concerned about the effect that this planned sale will have on overall corporate profits, on cash dividends for investors, and on the economy of Melbourne, where the two consumer-products plants are located.

Please ask your board of directors to reconsider this matter. ↓2X

→tab to centerpoint   Sincerely, ↓4X

Roger J. Michaelson

Roger J. Michaelson

Return address — 901 East Benson, Apt. 3
Ft. Lauderdale, FL 33301

A. BUSINESS LETTER ON EXECUTIVE STATIONERY

(7¼″ × 10½″; 1-inch side margins; with delivery notation)

Two Penn Plaza
10th Floor
New York, NY 10121-2298
Tel 212 904 2500
Fax 212 904 6630

Sweet's Group
McGraw-Hill Construction Information Group
A Division of The **McGraw-Hill** Companies

↓6X

July 18, 20-- ↓4X

Mr. Rodney Eastwood
BBL Resources
52A Northern Ridge
Fayetteville, PA 17222 ↓2X

Dear Rodney: ↓2X

I see no reason that we should continue to consider the locality around Geraldton for our new plant. Even though the desirability of this site from an economic view is undeniable, there is insufficient housing readily available for our workers.

In trying to control urban growth, the city has been turning down the building permits for new housing or placing so many restrictions on foreign investment as to make it too expensive.

Please continue to seek out other areas of exploration where we might form a joint partnership. ↓2X

Sincerely, ↓4X

Arlyn J. Bunch

Arlyn J. Bunch
Vice President for Operations ↓2X

mme
Delivery notation By Fax

B. BUSINESS LETTER ON HALF-PAGE STATIONERY

(5½″ × 8½″; 0.75-inch side margins)

1221 Avenue of the Americas
New York, NY 10020-1095

↓4X

July 18, 20-- ↓4X

Business Week
A Division of The **McGraw-Hill** Companies

Mr. Rodney Eastwood
BBL Resources
52A Northern Ridge
Fayetteville, PA 17222 ↓2X

Dear Rodney: ↓2X

We should continue considering Geraldton for our new plant. Even though the desirability of this site from an economic view is undeniable, there is insufficient housing readily available.

Please continue to seek out other areas of exploration where we might form a joint partnership. ↓2X

Sincerely, ↓4X

Arlyn J. Bunch

Arlyn J. Bunch
Vice President for Operations ↓2X

adk

C. BUSINESS LETTER FORMATTED FOR A WINDOW ENVELOPE

AMERICAN PRINTING HOUSE FOR THE BLIND, INC.

↓6X

July 18, 20-- ↓3X

Mr. Rodney Eastwood
BBL Resources
52A Northern Ridge
Fayetteville, PA 17222 ↓3X

Dear Rodney: ↓2X

I see no reason that we should continue to consider the locality around Geraldton for our new plant. Even though the desirability of this site from an economic view is undeniable, there is insufficient housing readily available for our workers.

In trying to control urban growth, the city has been turning down the building permits for new housing or placing so many restrictions on foreign investment as to make it too expensive.

Please continue to seek out other areas of exploration where we might form a joint partnership. ↓2X

Sincerely, ↓4X

Arlyn J. Bunch

Arlyn J. Bunch
Vice President for Operations ↓2X

woc

1839 Frankfort Avenue   P.O. Box 6389   Louisville, Kentucky 40206-0389   502-895-2405   Fax: 502-899-2350

D. MEMO

(with table and attachment notation)

↓6X

→tab

MEMO TO: Nancy Price, Executive Vice President ↓2X

FROM: Arlyn J. Bunch, Operations *ajb* ↓2X

DATE: July 18, 20-- ↓2X

SUBJECT: New Plant Site ↓2X

As you can see from the attached letter, I've informed BBL Resources that I see no reason why we should continue to consider the locality around Geraldton for our new plant. Even though the desirability of this site from an economic standpoint is undeniable, there is insufficient housing available. In fact, as of June 25, the number of appropriate single-family houses listed for sale within a 25-mile radius of Geraldton was as follows: ↓2X

Agent	Units
Belle Real Estate	123
Castleton Homes	11
Red Carpet	9
Geraldton Homes	5

↓1X

In addition, in trying to control urban growth, Geraldton has been either turning down building permits for new housing or placing excessive restrictions on them.

Because of this deficiency of housing for our employees, we have no choice but to look elsewhere. ↓2X

llw
Attachment notation Attachment

A. MULTIPAGE BUSINESS LETTER

(page 1; with on-arrival notation, international address, subject line, and table)

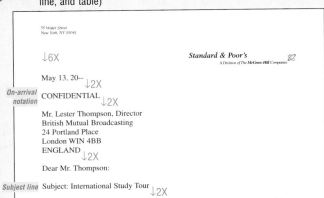

55 Water Street
New York, NY 10041

↓6X

Standard & Poor's
A Division of The McGraw-Hill Companies

May 13, 20-- ↓2X

On-arrival notation CONFIDENTIAL ↓2X

Mr. Lester Thompson, Director
British Mutual Broadcasting
24 Portland Place
London WIN 4BB
ENGLAND ↓2X

Dear Mr. Thompson:

Subject line Subject: International Study Tour ↓2X

I have been invited by the Federal Communications Commission to participate in a study of television news programming in European countries. The enclosed report explains the purpose of the study in detail.

I have been assigned to lead a study group through six European countries to gather firsthand information on this topic. In addition to me, our group will consist of the following members: ↓2X

INTERNATIONAL STUDY TOUR GROUP		
Name	**Organization**	**Location**
Mrs. Katherine Grant	WPQR-TV	Los Angeles, CA
Dr. Manuél Cruz	Miami Herald	Miami, FL
Mr. Richard Logan	Cable News Network	Atlanta, GA
Ms. Barbara Brooks	Associated Press	Chicago, IL

↓1X

Our initial plans are to spend at least one full day in each of the countries, meeting with the news programming staff of one or two of the major networks,

B. MULTIPAGE BUSINESS LETTER

(page 2; with company name; multiline list; enclosure, delivery, copy, postscript, and blind copy notations)

2

touring their facilities, viewing recent broadcasts, and getting a firsthand view of actual news operations. Our tentative itinerary calls for us to arrive at Heathrow Airport at 7:10 p.m. on Tuesday, July 27. Would it be possible for us to do the following:

1. Meet with various members of your staff sometime on July 28. We would be available from 8:30 a.m. until 1:30 p.m.

2. Receive a copy of your programming log for the week of July 26-30 and especially a minute-by-minute listing of the programming segments for your national news reporting.

I would appreciate your contacting Barbara Azar, our liaison, at 202.555.3943 to let us know whether we may study your operations on July 25. ↓2X

Sincerely, ↓2X

Company name METRO BROADCASTING COMPANY ↓4X

Denise J. Watterson

Denise J. Watterson
General Manager ↓2X

Reference initials rcp
Enclosure notation Enclosures: FCC Report, Biographical Sketches
Delivery notation By FedEx
Copy notation c: Barbara Azar, Manuél Cruz ↓2X

Postscript notation PS: The Federal Communications Commission will reimburse your organization for any expenses associated with our visit. ↓2X

Blind copy notation bc: Public Relations Office, FTC

C. EMAIL MESSAGE IN MICROSOFT OUTLOOK/ INTERNET EXPLORER

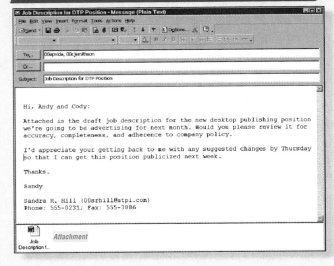

Job Description for DTP Position - Message (Plain Text)

File Edit View Insert Format Tools Actions Help

To... 00apvida, 00cjsmithson
Cc...
Subject: Job Description for DTP Position

Hi, Andy and Cody:

Attached is the draft job description for the new desktop publishing position we're going to be advertising for next month. Would you please review it for accuracy, completeness, and adherence to company policy.

I'd appreciate your getting back to me with any suggested changes by Thursday so that I can get this position publicized next week.

Thanks.

Sandy

Sandra R. Hill (00srhill@atpi.com)
Phone: 555-0231; Fax: 555-3886

Job Description f... *Attachment*

D. EMAIL MESSAGE IN NETSCAPE NAVIGATOR

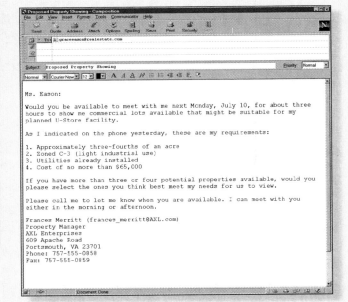

Proposed Property Showing - Composition

File Edit View Insert Format Tools Communicator Help

Send Quote Address Attach Options Spelling Save Print Security

To: graceeason@realestate.com

Subject: Proposed Property Showing   Priority: Normal

Normal Courier New 12

Ms. Eason:

Would you be available to meet with me next Monday, July 10, for about three hours to show me commercial lots available that might be suitable for my planned U-Store facility.

As I indicated on the phone yesterday, these are my requirements:

1. Approximately three-fourths of an acre
2. Zoned C-3 (light industrial use)
3. Utilities already installed
4. Cost of no more than $65,000

If you have more than three or four potential properties available, would you please select the ones you think best meet my needs for us to view.

Please call me to let me know when you are available. I can meet with you either in the morning or afternoon.

Frances Merritt (frances_merritt@AXL.com)
Property Manager
AXL Enterprises
609 Apache Road
Portsmouth, VA 23701
Phone: 757-555-0858
Fax: 757-555-0859

Document Done

A. FORMATTING ENVELOPES

A standard large (No. 10) envelope is 9½ by 4⅛ inches. A standard small (No. 6¾) envelope is 6½ by 3⅝ inches. Although either address format shown below is acceptable, the format shown for the large envelope (all capital letters and no punctuation) is recommended by the U.S. Postal Service for mail that will be sorted by an electronic scanning device.

Window envelopes are often used in a word processing environment because of the difficulty of aligning envelopes correctly in some printers. A window envelope requires no formatting, since the letter is formatted and folded so that the inside address is visible through the window.

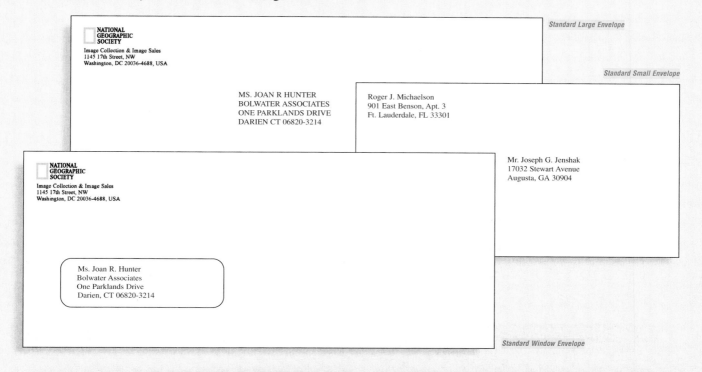

Standard Large Envelope

NATIONAL
GEOGRAPHIC
SOCIETY
Image Collection & Image Sales
1145 17th Street, NW
Washington, DC 20036-4688, USA

MS. JOAN R HUNTER
BOLWATER ASSOCIATES
ONE PARKLANDS DRIVE
DARIEN CT 06820-3214

Standard Small Envelope

Roger J. Michaelson
901 East Benson, Apt. 3
Ft. Lauderdale, FL 33301

Mr. Joseph G. Jenshak
17032 Stewart Avenue
Augusta, GA 30904

NATIONAL
GEOGRAPHIC
SOCIETY
Image Collection & Image Sales
1145 17th Street, NW
Washington, DC 20036-4688, USA

Ms. Joan R. Hunter
Bolwater Associates
One Parklands Drive
Darien, CT 06820-3214

Standard Window Envelope

B. FOLDING LETTERS

To fold a letter for a large envelope:
1. Place the letter *face up* and fold up the bottom third.
2. Fold the top third down to 0.5 inch from the bottom edge.
3. Insert the last crease into the envelope first, with the flap facing up.

To fold a letter for a small envelope:
1. Place the letter *face up* and fold up the bottom half to 0.5 inch from the top.
2. Fold the right third over to the left.
3. Fold the left third over to 0.5 inch from the right edge.
4. Insert the last crease into the envelope first, with the flap facing up.

To fold a letter for a window envelope:
1. Place the letter *face down* with the letterhead at the top and fold the bottom third of the letter up.
2. Fold the top third down so that the address shows.
3. Insert the letter into the envelope so that the address shows through the window.

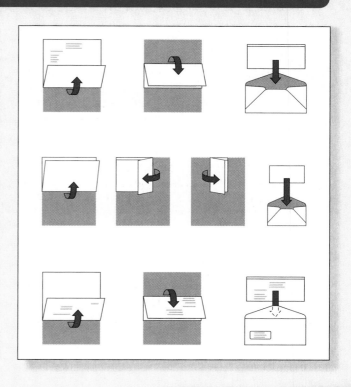

Reference Manual

A. OUTLINE

Set right tab at 0.3; left tabs at 0.4 and 0.7.

↓6X

14 pt **AN ANALYSIS OF THE SCOPE AND EFFECTIVENESS**
OF ONLINE ADVERTISING ↓2X

12 pt↓ **The Status of Point-and-Click Selling** ↓2X

tab **Jonathan R. Evans** ↓2X

January 19, 20-- ↓2X

I. INTRODUCTION ↓2X

II. SCOPE AND TRENDS IN INTERNET ADVERTISING
    A. Internet Advertising
    B. Major Online Advertisers
    C. Positioning and Pricing
    D. Types of Advertising ↓2X

III. ADVERTISING EFFECTIVENESS
    A. The Banner Debate
    B. Increasing Advertising Effectiveness
    C. Measuring ROI ↓2X

IV. CONCLUSION

B. TITLE PAGE

center page↓

14 pt **AN ANALYSIS OF THE SCOPE AND EFFECTIVENESS**
OF ONLINE ADVERTISING ↓2X

12 pt↓ **The Status of Point-and-Click Selling** ↓12X

Submitted to ↓2X
Luis Torres
General Manager
ViaWorld, International ↓12X

Prepared by ↓2X
Jonathan R. Evans
Assistant Marketing Manager
ViaWorld, International ↓2X

January 19, 20--

C. TRANSMITTAL MEMO

(with 2-line subject line and attachment notation)

↓6X

→ tab
MEMO TO: Luis Torres, General Manager ↓2X

FROM: Jonathan R. Evans, Assistant Marketing Manager *jre* ↓2X

DATE: January 19, 20-- ↓2X

SUBJECT: An Analysis of the Scope and Effectiveness of Online
Advertising ↓2X

Here is the report analyzing the scope and effectiveness of Internet Advertising that you requested on January 5, 20--.

The report predicts that the total value of business-to-business e-commerce market will reach $1.3 trillion by 2003, up from $190 billion in 1999. New technologies aimed at increasing Internet ad interactivity and the adoption of standards for advertising response measurement and tracking will contribute to this increase. Unfortunately, as discussed in this report, the use of "rich media" and interactivity in Web advertising will create its own set of problems.

I enjoyed working on this assignment, Luis, and learned quite a bit from my analysis of the situation. Please let me know if you have any questions about the report. ↓2X

urs
Attachment

D. TABLE OF CONTENTS

Set left tab at 0.5; right dot-leader tab at 6.

↓6X

14 pt **CONTENTS** ↓2X

A. REPORT IN BUSINESS STYLE

(page 1; with footnotes and single-line list)

↓6X

Title 14 pt **AN ANALYSIS OF THE SCOPE AND EFFECTIVENESS OF ONLINE ADVERTISING**
↓2X

Subtitle 12 pt↓ **The Status of Point-and-Click Selling**
↓2X

Byline **Jonathan R. Evans**
↓2X

Date **January 19, 20--**
↓2X

Side hd **INTRODUCTION**
↓2X

Over the past three years, the number of American households online has tripled, from an estimated 15 million in 1996 to 45 million in 1999. Jupiter Communications, predicts that by the year 2003, 70 million households, representing about 62% of all U.S. households, will be online. Online business has grown in tandem with the expanding number of Internet users. Forrester Research Inc. predicts that the total value of business-to-business e-commerce will reach $109 billion in 1999 and is likely to reach $1.3 trillion by 2003.[1]
↓2X

Para hd **Uncertainty**. The uncertainties surrounding advertising on the Internet remain one of the major impediments to the expansion. Dating from just 1994 when the first banner ads appeared on the Hotwired home page, the young Internet advertising industry is today in a state of flux.
↓2X

Some analysts argue that advertising on the Internet can and should follow the same principles as advertising on television and other visual media. Others contend that advertising on the Internet should reflect the unique characteristics of this new medium.
↓2X

Reasons for Not Advertising Online. A recent Association of National Advertisers survey found two main reasons cited for not advertising online:[2]
↓2X

1. The difficulty of determining return on investment
2. The lack of reliable tracking and measurement data

Footnotes
[1] George Anders, "Buying Frenzy," *Wall Street Journal*, July 12, 1999, p. R6.
[2] "eStats: Advertising Revenues and Trends," *eMarketer Home Page*, August 11, 1999, http:www.emarketer.com/estats/ad (January 7, 2000).

B. REPORT IN BUSINESS STYLE

(page 3; with long quotation and table)

3

who argue that banners have a strong potential for advertising effectiveness point out that it is not the banner format itself which presents a problem to advertising effectiveness, but rather the quality of the banner and the attention to its placement. According to Mike Windsor, president of Ogilvy Interactive:
↓2X

indent 0.5"→ Long quotation It's more a case of bad banner ads, just like there are bad television ads. The space itself has huge potential. As important as using the space within the banner creatively is to aim it effectively. Unlike broadcast media, the Web offers advertisers the opportunity to reach a specific audience based on data gathered about who is surfing at a particular site and what their interests are.[1] ← indent 0.5"

Thus, while some analysts continue to argue that the banner advertisement is passé, there is little evidence of its abandonment. Instead ad agencies are focusing on increasing the banner's effectiveness.
↓2X

SCOPE AND TRENDS IN ONLINE ADVERTISING
↓2X

Starting from zero in 1994, analysts agree that the volume of Internet advertising spending has risen rapidly. However, as indicated in Table 3, analysts provide a wide range of the exact amount of such advertising.
↓2X

TABLE 3. INTERNET ADVERTISING 1998 Estimates	
Source	**Estimate**
Internet Advertising Board	$1.92 billion
Forester	1.30 billion
IDC	1.20 billion
Burst! Media	560 million
Source: "Advertising Age Teams with eMarketer for Research Report," *Advertising Age*, May 3, 1999, p. 24.	

↓1X

The differences in estimates of total Web advertising spending is generally attributed to the different methodologies used by the research agencies to

[1] Lisa Napoli, "Banner Ads Are Under the Gun—And On the Move," *New York Times*, June 17, 1999, p. D1.

C. REPORT IN ACADEMIC STYLE

(page 1; with endnotes and multiline list)

↓3DS

14 pt **AN ANALYSIS OF THE SCOPE AND EFFECTIVENESS OF ONLINE ADVERTISING**
↓1DS

The Status of Point-and-Click Selling
↓1DS

12 pt↓ **Jonathan R. Evans**
↓1DS

January 19, 20--
↓1DS

INTRODUCTION

Over the past three years, the number of American households online has tripled, from an estimated 15 million in 1996 to 45 million in 1999. Jupiter Communications, predicts that by the year 2003, 70 million households, representing about 62% of all U.S. households, will be online. Online business has grown in tandem with the expanding number of Internet users. Forrester Research Inc. predicts that the total value of business-to-business e-commerce will reach $109 billion in 1999 and is likely to reach $1.3 trillion by 2003.[i]

Reasons for Not Advertising Online. A recent Association of National Advertisers survey found two main reasons cited for not advertising online:[ii]

1. The difficulty of determining return on investment, especially in terms of repeat business.

2. The lack of reliable tracking and measurement data

Some analysts argue that advertising on the Internet can and should follow the same principles as advertising on television.[iii] Other visual media

D. REPORT IN ACADEMIC STYLE

(last page; with long quotation and endnotes)

14

advertising effectiveness, but rather the quality of the banner and the attention to its placement. According to Mike Windsor, president of Ogilvy Interactive:

indent 0.5"→ Long quotation It's more a case of bad banner ads, just like there are bad television ads. The space itself has huge potential. As important as using the space within the banner creatively is to aim it effectively. Unlike broadcast media, the Web offers advertisers the opportunity to reach a specific audience based on data gathered about who is surfing at a particular site and what their interests are.[vii] ← indent 0.5"

From the advertiser's perspective, the most effective Internet ads do more than just deliver information to the consumer and grab the consumer's attention—they also gather information about consumers (e.g., through "cookies" and other methodologies). From the consumer's perspective, this type of interactivity may represent an intrusion and an invasion of privacy. There appears to be a shift away from the ad-supported model and toward the transaction model, wherein users pay for the content they want and the specific transactions they perform.

Endnotes
[i] George Anders, "Buying Frenzy," *Wall Street Journal*, July 12, 1999, p. R6.
[ii] "eStats: Advertising Revenues and Trends," *eMarketer Home Page*, August 11, 1999, http:www.emarketer.com/estats/ad (January 7, 2000).
[iii] Bradley Johnson, "Nielsen/NetRatings Index Shows 4% Rise in Web Ads," *Advertising Age*, July 19, 1999, p. 18.
[iv] Tom Hyland, "Web Advertising: A Year of Growth," *Internet Advertising Board Home Page*, November 13, 1999, http:www.iab.net/advertise (January 8, 2000).
[v] Adrian Mand, "Click Here: Free Ride Doles Out Freebies to Ad Surfers," *Brandweek*, March 8, 1999, p. 30.
[vi] Andrea Petersen, "High Price of Internet Banner Ads Slips Amid Increase in Web Sites," *Wall Street Journal*, March 2, 1999, p. B20.
[vii] Lisa Napoli, "Banner Ads Are Under the Gun—And On the Move," *New York Times*, June 17, 1999, p. D1.

Reference Manual

A. LEFT-BOUND REPORT IN BUSINESS STYLE

(page 1; with endnotes and single-line list)

left margin: 1.75″   right margin: *default* (1.25″)

↓6X

14 pt

**AN ANALYSIS OF THE SCOPE AND
EFFECTIVENESS OF ONLINE ADVERTISING** ↓2X

12 pt↓

The Status of Point-and-Click Selling ↓2X

Jonathan R. Evans ↓2X

January 19, 20-- ↓2X

INTRODUCTION ↓2X

Over the past three years, the number of American households online has tripled, from an estimated 15 million in 1996 to 45 million in 1999. Jupiter Communications, predicts that by the year 2003, 70 million households, representing about 62% of all U.S. households, will be online. Online business has grown in tandem with the expanding number of Internet users. Forrester Research Inc. predicts that the total value of business-to-business e-commerce will reach $109 billion in 1999 and is likely to reach $1.3 trillion by 2003.[i] ↓2X

Uncertainty. The uncertainties surrounding advertising on the Internet remain one of the major impediments to the expansion. Dating from just 1994 when the first banner ads appeared on the Hotwired home page, the young Internet advertising industry is today in a state of flux. ↓2X

Some analysts argue that advertising on the Internet can and should follow the same principles as advertising on television and other visual media. Others contend that advertising on the Internet should reflect the unique characteristics of this new medium. ↓2X

Reasons for Not Advertising Online. A recent Association of National Advertisers survey found two main reasons cited for not advertising online:[ii] ↓2X

1. The difficulty of determining return on investment
2. The lack of reliable tracking and measurement data

B. BIBLIOGRAPHY

(For business or academic style using either endnotes or footnotes)

↓6X

hanging indent

12 pt↓   14 pt **BIBLIOGRAPHY** ↓2X

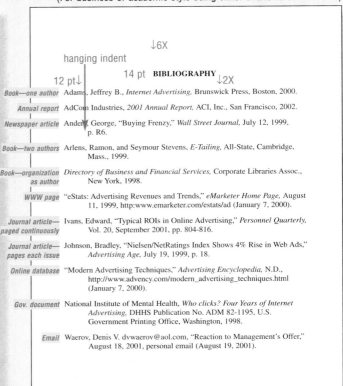

Book—one author Adams, Jeffrey B., *Internet Advertising*, Brunswick Press, Boston, 2000.

Annual report AdCom Industries, *2001 Annual Report*, ACI, Inc., San Francisco, 2002.

Newspaper article Andrew, George, "Buying Frenzy," *Wall Street Journal*, July 12, 1999, p. R6.

Book—two authors Arlens, Ramon, and Seymour Stevens, *E-Tailing*, All-State, Cambridge, Mass., 1999.

Book—organization as author *Directory of Business and Financial Services*, Corporate Libraries Assoc., New York, 1998.

WWW page "eStats: Advertising Revenues and Trends," *eMarketer Home Page*, August 11, 1999, http:www.emarketer.com/estats/ad (January 7, 2000).

Journal article—paged continuously Ivans, Edward, "Typical ROIs in Online Advertising," *Personnel Quarterly*, Vol. 20, September 2001, pp. 804-816.

Journal article—pages each issue Johnson, Bradley, "Nielsen/NetRatings Index Shows 4% Rise in Web Ads," *Advertising Age*, July 19, 1999, p. 18.

Online database "Modern Advertising Techniques," *Advertising Encyclopedia*, N.D., http://www.advency.com/modern_advertising_techniques.html (January 7, 2000).

Gov. document National Institute of Mental Health, *Who clicks? Four Years of Internet Advertising*, DHHS Publication No. ADM 82-1195, U.S. Government Printing Office, Washington, 1998.

Email Waerov, Denis V. dvwaerov@aol.com, "Reaction to Management's Offer," August 18, 2001, personal email (August 19, 2001).

C. MEMO REPORT

(page 1, with single-line list)

↓6X

→tab

MEMO TO: Luis Torres, General Manager ↓2X

FROM: Jonathan R. Evans, Assistant Marketing Manager *jre* ↓2X

DATE: January 19, 20-- ↓2X

SUBJECT: An Analysis of the Scope and Effectiveness of Online Advertising ↓2X

According to a July 12, 1999, *Wall Street* Journal article, over the past three years, the number of American households online has tripled, from an estimated 15 million in 1996 to 45 million in 1999. Jupiter Communications, predicts that by the year 2003, 70 million households, representing about 62% of all U.S. households, will be online. Online business has grown in tandem with the expanding number of Internet users. Forrester Research Inc. predicts that the total value of business-to-business e-commerce will reach $109 billion in 1999 and is likely to reach $1.3 trillion by 2003.

UNCERTAINTY

The uncertainties surrounding advertising on the Internet remain one of the major impediments to the expansion. Dating from just 1994 when the first banner ads appeared on the Hotwired home page, the young Internet advertising industry is today in a state of flux.

Some analysts argue that advertising on the Internet can and should follow the same principles as advertising on television and other visual media. Others contend that advertising on the Internet should reflect the unique characteristics of this new medium.

A recent Association of National Advertisers survey found two main reasons cited for not advertising online:

1. The difficulty of determining return on investment
2. The lack of reliable tracking and measurement data

D. REPORTS: SPECIAL FEATURES

MARGINS AND SPACING. Use a 2″ top margin for the first page of each section of a report (for example, the table of contents, first page of the body, and bibliography page) and a 1″ top margin for other pages. Use default side margins (1.25″) and bottom margins (1″) for all pages. If the report is going to be bound on the left, add 0.5″ to the left margin. Single-space business reports and double-space academic reports.

HEADINGS. Center the report title in 14-point font (press **ENTER** to space down before switching to 12-point font). Single-space multiline report titles in a single-spaced report and double-space multiline titles in a double-spaced report. Leave 1 blank line before and after all parts of a heading block (consisting of the title, subtitle, author, and/or date) and format all lines in bold.

Leave 1 blank line before and after side headings and format in bold, beginning at the left margin. Format paragraph headings in bold; begin at the left margin for single-spaced reports and indent for double-spaced reports. The text follows on the same line, preceded by a period and 1 space.

CITATIONS. For business and academic reports, format citations using your word processor's footnote (or endnote) feature. For reports formatted in APA or MLA style, use the format shown on page R-10.

Reference Manual

A. REPORT IN APA STYLE

(page 3; with author/year citations)

top, bottom, and side margins: 1″
Double-space throughout.

An Analysis of the Scope and Effectiveness

of Online Advertising

Jonathan R. Evans

main hd. Introduction

Over the past three years, the number of American households online has tripled, from an estimated 15 million in 1996 to 45 million in 1999. Jupiter Communications, predicts that by the year 2003, 70 million households, representing about 62% of all U.S. households, will be online (Napoli, 1999). Online business has grown in tandem with the expanding number of Internet users. Forrester Research Inc. predicts that the total value of business-to-business e-commerce will reach $109 billion in 1999 and is likely to reach $1.3 trillion by 2003 (Arlens & Stevens, 1999).

↓1DS

subhd. <u>Uncertainty</u>

The uncertainties surrounding advertising on the Internet remain one of the major impediments to the expansion. Dating from just 1994 when the first banner ads appeared on the Hotwired home page, the young Internet advertising industry is today in a state of flux.

Some analysts argue that advertising on the Internet can and should follow the same principles as advertising on television and other visual media ("eStats," 1999). Others contend that advertising on the Internet should reflect

B. REFERENCES IN APA STYLE

top, bottom, and side margins: 1″
Double-space throughout.

References

→tab Adams, J. B. (2000). *Internet advertising.* Boston: Brunswick Press.

AdCom Industries. (2002). *2001 annual report.* San Francisco: ACI, Inc.

Anders, G. (1999, July 12). Buying frenzy. *Wall Street Journal,* p. R6.

Arlens, R., & Stevens, S. (1999). *E-tailing.* Cambridge, MA: All-State.

Directory of business and financial services. (1998). New York: Corporate Libraries Association.

eStats: Advertising revenues and trends. (n.d.). New York: eMarketer. Retrieved August 11, 1999 from the World Wide Web: http:www.emarketer. com/estats/ad.

Ivans, E. (2001). Typical ROIs in online advertising. *Personnel Quarterly, 20,* 804-816.

Johnson, B. (1999, July 19). Nielsen/NetRatings Index shows 4% rise in Web ads. *Advertising Age, 39,* 18.

Napoli, L, (1999, June 17). Banner ads are under the gun—And on the move. *New York Times,* p. D1.

National Institute of Mental Health. (1998). *Who clicks? Four years of Internet advertising* (DHHS Publication No. ADM 82-1195). Washington,

C. REPORT IN MLA STYLE

(page 1; with author/page citations)

top, bottom, and side margins: 1″
Double-space throughout.

Jonathan R. Evans

Professor Inman

Management 302

19 January 20--

An Analysis of the Scope and Effectiveness

of Online Advertising

Over the past three years, the number of American households online has tripled, from an estimated 15 million in 1996 to 45 million in 1999. Jupiter Communications, predicts that by the year 2003, 70 million households, representing about 62% of all U.S. households, will be online (Napoli D1). Online business has grown in tandem with the expanding number of Internet users. Forrester Research Inc. predicts that the total value of business-to-business e-commerce will reach $109 billion in 1999 and is likely to reach $1.3 trillion by 2003 (Arlens & Stevens 376-379).

The uncertainties surrounding advertising on the Internet remain one of the major impediments to the expansion. Dating from just 1994 when the first banner ads appeared on the Hotwired home page, the young Internet advertising industry is today in a state of flux.

Some analysts argue that advertising on the Internet can and should follow the same principles as advertising on television and other visual media ("eStats"). Others contend that advertising on the Internet should reflect the

D. WORKS CITED IN MLA STYLE

top, bottom, and side margins: 1″
Double-space throughout.

Works Cited

Adams, Jeffrey B. *Internet Advertising.* Boston: Brunswick Press, 2000.

AdCom Industries. *2001 Annual Report.* San Francisco: ACI, Inc., 2002.

Anders, George. "Buying Frenzy," *Wall Street Journal,* July 12, 1999, p. R6.

hanging indent Arlens, Ramon, and Seymour Stevens. *E-Tailing.* Cambridge, MA: All-State, 1999.

Corporate Libraries Association. *Directory of Business and Financial Services.* New York: Corporate Libraries Association, 1998.

"eStats: Advertising Revenues and Trends." *eMarketer Home Page.* 11 Aug. 1999. 7 Jan. 2000. http:www.emarketer.com/estats/ad.

Ivans, Edward. "Typical ROIs in Online Advertising." *Personnel Quarterly* Sep. 2001: 804-816.

Johnson, Bradley. "Nielsen/NetRatings Index Shows 4% Rise in Web Ads." *Advertising Age* 19 Jul. 1999: 18.

Napoli, Lisa. "Banner Ads Are Under the Gun—And On the Move." *New York Times* 17 Jun. 1999: D1.

National Institute of Mental Health. *Who Clicks? Four Years of Internet Advertising.* DHHS Publication No. ADM 82-1195. Washington, DC: GPO, 1998.

Reference Manual

A. MEETING AGENDA

First type list unformatted; then apply numbering feature.

↓6X

14 pt   **MILES HARDWARE EXECUTIVE COMMITTEE** ↓2X

12 pt↓   **Meeting Agenda** ↓2X

   June 7, 20--, 3 p.m. ↓2X

1. Call to order ↓2X
2. Approval of minutes of May 5 meeting
3. Progress report on building addition and parking lot restrictions (Norman Hodges and Anthony Pascarelli)
4. May 15 draft of five-Year Plan
5. Review of National Hardware Association annual convention
6. Employee grievance filed by Ellen Burrows (John Landstrom)
7. New expense-report forms (Anne Richards)
8. Announcements
9. Adjournment

B. MINUTES OF A MEETING

Format body as a two-column open table; manually adjust column widths as needed.

↓6X

14 pt   **RESOURCE COMMITTEE** ↓2X

12 pt↓   **Minutes of the Meeting** ↓2X

   March 13, 20-- ↓2X

ATTENDANCE	The Resource Committee met on March 13, 20--, at the Airport Sheraton in Portland, Oregon, with all members were present. Michael Davis, chairperson, called the meeting to order at 2:30 p.m. ↓2X
APPROVAL OF MINUTES	The minutes of the January 27 meeting were read and approved.
OLD BUSINESS	The members of the committee reviewed the sales brochure on electronic copyboards and agreed to purchase one for the conference room. Cynthia Giovanni will secure quotations from at least two suppliers.
NEW BUSINESS	The committee reviewed a request from the Purchasing Department for three new computers. After extensive discussion regarding the appropriate use of the computers and software to be purchased, the committee approved the request.
ADJOURNMENT	The meeting was adjourned at 4:45 p.m. ↓2X

Respectfully submitted, ↓4X

D. S. Madsen

D. S. Madsen, Secretary

C. ITINERARY

Format body as a two-column open table; manually adjust column widths as needed.

↓6X

14 pt   **ITINERARY** ↓2X

12 pt↓   **For Arlene Gilsdorf** ↓2X

   March 12-15, 20-- ↓2X

THURSDAY, MARCH 12 ↓2X

5:10 p.m.-7:06 p.m.	Flight from Detroit to Portland; Northwest 83 (Phone: 800-555-1212); e-ticket; Seat 8D; nonstop; dinner ↓2X
	Jack Weatherford (Home: 503-555-8029; Office: 503-555-7631) will meet your flight on Thursday, provide transportation during your visit, and return you to the airport on Saturday morning. ↓2X
	Airport Sheraton (503-555-4032) King-sized bed, nonsmoking room; late arrival guaranteed (Reservation No. 30ZM6-02) ↓2X

FRIDAY, MARCH 13

9 a.m.-5:30 p.m.	Portland Sales Meeting 1931 Executive Way, Suite 10 Portland (503-555-7631)
Evening	On your own

SATURDAY, MARCH 14

7:30 a.m.-2:47 p.m.	Flight from Portland to Detroit; Northwest 360; e-ticket; Seat 9a; nonstop; breakfast

D. LEGAL DOCUMENT

Set left tabs at 1″ and 3″.

↓3DS

14 pt   **POWER OF ATTORNEY** ↓1DS

12 pt↓   KNOW ALL MEN BY THESE PRESENTS that I, ATTORNEY LEE FERNANDEZ, of the City of Tulia, County of Swisher, State of Texas, do hereby appoint my son, Robert Fernandez, of this City, County, and State as my attorney-in-fact to act in my name, place, and stead as my agent in the management of my business operating transactions.

I give and grant unto my said attorney full power and authority to do and perform every act and thing requisite and necessary to be done in the said management as fully, to all intents and purposes, as I might or could do if personally present, with full power of revocation, hereby ratifying all that my said attorney shall lawfully do.

IN WITNESS WHEREOF, I have hereunto set my hand and seal this thirteenth day of April, 20--. ↓2DS

→tab to centerpoint   _____ (L.S.) ↓1DS

SIGNED and affirmed in the presence of: ↓2DS

_____ ↓2DS

_____

A. RESUME

Format body as a two-column open table; manually adjust column widths as needed.

↓6X

14 pt   **TERRY M. MARTINA** ↓2X

12 pt ↓   **250 Maxwell Avenue, Boulder, CO 80305**
       Phone: 303-555-9311; email: tmartina@ecc.edu
                     ↓1X ↓1X

OBJECTIVE	Position in resort management anywhere in Colorado ↓2X
EDUCATION	A. A. in hotel management to be awarded May 2001 Edgewood Community College, Boulder, CO
EXPERIENCE	*Assistant Manager, Burger King Restaurant* Boulder, CO: 1999-Present • Achieved grade point average of 3.1 (on 4.0 scale). • Received Board of Regent tuition scholarship. • Financed all college expenses through savings, scholarships, and part-time work. *Student Intern, Ski Valley Haven* Aspen, CO: September-December 2000 • Worked as an assistant to the night manager of 200-room ski resort. • Gained practical experience in operating First-Guest management system. • Was in charge of producing daily occupancy reports.
PERSONAL	• Speak and write fluent Spanish • Competent in Microsoft Office 2000 • Secretary of ECC Hospitality Services Association • Special Olympics volunteer: Summer 2000
REFERENCES	Available upon request

B. APPLICATION LETTER

↓6X

March 1, 20-- ↓4X

Mr. Lou Mansfield, Director
Human Resources Department
Rocky Resorts International
P.O. Box 1412
Denver, CO 80214 ↓2X

Dear Mr. Mansfield: ↓2X

Please consider me an applicant for the position of concierge for Suite Retreat, as advertised in last Sunday's *Denver Times.*

I will receive my A.A. degree in hotel administration from Edgewood Community College in May and will be available for full-time employment immediately. In addition to my extensive coursework in hospitality services and business, I've had experience in working for a ski lodge similar to Suite Retreats in Aspen. As a lifelong resident of Colorado and an avid skier, I would be able to provide your guests with any information they request.

After you've reviewed my enclosed resume, I would appreciate having an opportunity to discuss with you why I believe I have the right qualifications and personality to serve as your concierge. I can be reached at 303-555-9311. ↓2X

Sincerely, ↓4X

Terry M. Martina

Terry M. Martina
250 Maxwell Avenue, Apt. 8
Boulder, CO 80305 ↓2X

Enclosure

C. PLACING INFORMATION ON PRINTED LINES

Because of the difficulty of aligning copy on a printed line with a computer and printer, lined forms such as job-application forms are most efficiently completed on a typewriter.

When typing on a lined form, use the typewriter's variable line spacer to adjust the paper so that the line is in the position that a row of underlines would occupy. (On many machines, this is accomplished by pressing in the left platen knob.)

Do not leave any lines for requested information blank; use *N/A* ("not applicable") if necessary. Because of space limitations, it may be necessary to abbreviate some words.

Because first impressions are important, ensure that all your employment documents are in correct format, are neat in appearance, and are free from errors.

D. JOB-APPLICATION FORM

(first page)

ROCKY RESORTS INTERNATIONAL
P.O. Box 1412   Denver, CO 80218

Employment Application

POSITION APPLIED FOR Concierge   DATE OF APPLICATION 3/18/02

TYPE OF EMPLOYMENT DESIRED ☒ Full-time   ☐ Part-time   ☐ Temporary   ☐ Co-op/Internship

NAME Martina   Terry   M
      LAST   FIRST   MI

ADDRESS 250 Maxwell Avenue, Apt. B   Boulder   CO   80305
          STREET   CITY   STATE   ZIP

TELEPHONE 303-555-9331   SOCIAL SECURITY NO. 247-72-8431

If you are under 18, can you furnish a work permit? .... N/A .... ☐ Yes .. ☐ No

Have you ever worked here before? .... ☒ Yes .. ☐ No

Are you legally eligible for employment in this country? .... ☒ Yes .. ☐ No

Have you been convicted of a felony within the past seven years? .... ☐ Yes .. ☒ No

If yes, please explain _____ N/A _____

EDUCATION (most recent first)

Institution	City/State	Degree/Major	Dates
Edgewood Community College, Boulder, CO		A.A.—Hotel Admin.	2000-02
Durango High School, Durango, CO		Diploma	1997-2000

WORK EXPERIENCE (most recent first)

Organization	City/State	Position	Dates (inclusive)
Burger King Restaurant	Boulder, CO	Asst. Mgr.	1999-present
Ski Valley Haven	Aspen, CO	Intern	Sep-Dec 1999

AN EQUAL OPPORTUNITY EMPLOYER

A. BOXED TABLE *(Default Style)*

(with subtitle, braced headings, total line, and table note.)

center page ↓

		Year-to-Date Sales		Prior-Year Sales	
Title	**12 pt ↓ AUSTIN-REEVES PRINTER DEPOT**				
Subtitle	**Sales Through September 2001**				
	(000s omitted) ↓1X				
Column hds	↓1X **Product**	**2002**	**2001**	**2000**	**1999**
	Dot matrix	$ 5	$ 14	$ 19	$ 28
	Ink-jet: color	188	423	569	841
	Ink-jet: color portable	4	7	6	24
Body	Ink-jet: black and white	146	200	273	588
	Printer and copier combination	1,000	1,184	1,622	2,054
	Black-and-white laser: standard	144	316	389	507
	Black-and-white laser: premium	2,591	1,636	2368	87
	Color laser	6	0	0	0
Total line	Totals	$4,084	$3,780	$5,246	$4,129
Table note	Note: Year-to-date sales have increased 7.4%.				

Braced column hd

B. OPEN TABLE

(with subtitle, blocked column headings, and 2-line heading)

First, format the table in default (boxed) style. Then delete all borders.

center page ↓

	12 pt ↓ **SUITE RETREAT**		
	New Lodging Rates ↓1X		
↓1X **Location**	**Rack Rate**	**Discount Rate**	**Saving**
Bozeman, Montana	$ 95.75	$ 91.50	4.4%
Chicago, Illinois	159.00	139.50	12.3%
Dallas, Texas	249.50	219.00	12.2%
Las Vegas, Nevada	98.50	89.95	8.7%
Los Angeles, California	179.00	139.00	22.3%
Minneapolis, Minnesota	115.00	95.00	17.4%
New York City, New York	227.50	175.00	23.1%
Orlando, Florida	105.75	98.50	6.3%
Portland, Maine	93.50	93.50	0.0%
Seattle, Washington	143.75	125.75	12.5%

C. RULED TABLE

(with table number and centered column headings)

2

an effort to reduce errors and provide increased customer support, we have recently added numerous additional telephone support services, some of which are available 24 hours a day and others available during the work day. These are shown in Table 2. ↓2X

12 pt↓ **Table 2. COMPUTER SUPPLIES SUPPORT SERVICES** ↓1X

Support Service	Telephone	Hours
Product literature	800-555-3867	6 a.m. to 5 p.m.
Replacement parts	303-555-3388	24 hours a day
Technical documentation	408-555-3309	24 hours a day
Troubleshooting	800-555-8277	10 a.m. to 5 p.m.
Printer drivers	800-555-2377	6 a.m. to 5 p.m.
Software notes	800-555-3496	24 hours a day
Technical support	800-555-1205	24 hours a day
Hardware information	303-555-4289	6 a.m. to 5 p.m.

↓1X

We hope you will take advantages of these additional services to ensure that the computer hardware and software you purchase from Computer Supplies continues to provide you the quality and service you have come to expect from our company.

Sincerely,

Douglas Pullis

Douglas Pullis
General Manager

cds

First, format the table in default (boxed) style. Then delete all borders. Finally, add borders to the top and bottom of the column-heading row and to the bottom of the last row of the body of the table.

D. TABLES: SPECIAL FEATURES

VERTICAL PLACEMENT. Vertically center a table that appears on a page by itself. Leave 1 blank line before and after a table appearing with other text.

TITLE BLOCK. Center and bold all lines of the title block, typing the title in all caps and the subtitle in upper- and lowercase. If a table has a number, type the word *Table* in upper- and lowercase. Follow the table number with a period and 1 space.

COLUMN HEADINGS. Center column headings if *all* columns consist of text (e.g., words, phone numbers, or years). Block column headings if columns consist of text (left-aligned) and quantities (right-aligned). Regardless of the type of column, center braced headings. If the column headings do not take the same number of lines, align the headings at the bottom (by choosing the *bottom alignment* option). Use bold upper- and lowercase.

COLUMN CAPITALIZATION. Capitalize only the first word and proper nouns in column entries.

PERCENTAGES AND DOLLARS. Repeat the % sign for each number in a column (unless the heading identifies the data as percentages). Insert the $ sign only before the first amount and before a total amount. Align the $ sign with the longest amount in the column, inserting spaces after the $ sign as needed (leaving 2 spaces for each digit and 1 space for each comma).

TOTAL LINE. Add a border above a total line. Use the word *Total* or *Totals* as appropriate.

A. FORMATTING BUSINESS FORMS

Many business forms can be created and filled in by using templates that are provided within commercial word processing software. Template forms can be used "as is" or they can be edited. Templates can also be used to create customized forms for any business.

When a template is opened, the form is displayed on screen. The user can then fill in the necessary information, including personalized company information. Data is entered into cells or fields and you can move quickly from field to field with a single keystroke—usually by pressing TAB or ENTER.

B. U.S. POSTAL SERVICE ABBREVIATIONS

(for States, Territories, and Canadian Provinces)

States and Territories

Alabama	AL
Alaska	AK
Arizona	AZ
Arkansas	AR
California	CA
Colorado	CO
Connecticut	CT
Delaware	DE
District of Columbia	DC
Florida	FL
Georgia	GA
Guam	GU
Hawaii	HI
Idaho	ID
Illinois	IL
Indiana	IN
Iowa	IA
Kansas	KS
Kentucky	KY
Louisiana	LA
Maine	ME
Maryland	MD
Massachusetts	MA
Michigan	MI
Minnesota	MN
Mississippi	MS
Missouri	MO
Montana	MT
Nebraska	NE
Nevada	NV
New Hampshire	NH
New Jersey	NJ
New Mexico	NM
New York	NY
North Carolina	NC
North Dakota	ND
Ohio	OH
Oklahoma	OK
Oregon	OR
Pennsylvania	PA
Puerto Rico	PR
Rhode Island	RI
South Carolina	SC
South Dakota	SD
Tennessee	TN
Texas	TX
Utah	UT
Vermont	VT
Virgin Islands	VI
Virginia	VA
Washington	WA
West Virginia	WV
Wisconsin	WI
Wyoming	WY

Canadian Provinces

Alberta	AB
British Columbia	BC
Labrador	LB
Manitoba	MB
New Brunswick	NB
Newfoundland	NF
Northwest Territories	NT
Nova Scotia	NS
Ontario	ON
Prince Edward Island	PE
Quebec	PQ
Saskatchewan	SK
Yukon Territory	YT

C. PROOFREADERS' MARKS

Proofreaders' Marks		Draft	Final Copy
⌒	Omit space	data base	database
∨ or ∧	Insert	if hes going	if he's not going,
≡	Capitalize	Maple street	Maple Street
ℒ	Delete	a final draft	a draft
#	Insert space	allready to	all ready to
when	Change word	and if you	and when you
/	Use lowercase letter	our President	our president
⁋	Paragraph	⁋ Most of the	Most of the
•••	Don't delete	a true story	a true story
○	Spell out	the only ①	the only one
∽	Transpose	they all see	they see all

Proofreaders' Marks		Draft	Final Copy
SS	Single-space	ss [first line / second line	first line / second line
ds	Double-space	ds [first line / second line	first line / second line
⎤	Move right	Please send	Please send
⎣	Move left	May I	May I
∿	Bold	Column Heading	**Column Heading**
ital	Italic	ital Time magazine	*Time* magazine
u/l	Underline	u/l Time magazine	Time magazine readers
♂	Move as shown	readers will see	will see

Language Arts for Business
(50 "must-know" rules)

PUNCTUATION

COMMAS

RULE 1 ▶
, direct address
(L. 21)

Use commas before and after a name used in direct address.
Thank you, John, for responding to my email so quickly.
Ladies and gentlemen, the program has been canceled.

RULE 2 ▶
, independent clause
(L. 27)

Use a comma between independent clauses joined by a coordinate conjunction (unless both clauses are short).
Ellen left her job with IBM, and she and her sister went to Paris.
But: Ellen left her job with IBM and went to Paris with her sister.
But: John drove and I navigated.

Note: An independent clause is one that can stand alone as a complete sentence. The most common coordinate conjunctions are *and, but, or,* and *nor.*

RULE 3 ▶
, introductory expression
(L. 27)

Use a comma after an introductory expression (unless it is a short prepositional phrase).
Before we can make a decision, we must have all the facts.
But: In 2000 our nation elected a new president.

Note: An introductory expression is a group of words that come before the subject and verb of the independent clause. Common prepositions are *to, in, on, of, at, by, for,* and *with.*

RULE 4 ▶
, direct quotation
(L. 41)

Use a comma before and after a direct quotation.
James said, "I shall return," and then left.

RULE 5 ▶
, date
(L. 57)

Use a comma before and after the year in a complete date.
We will arrive on June 2, 2001, for the conference.
But: We will arrive on June 2 for the conference.

RULE 6 ▶
, place
(L. 57)

Use a comma before and after a state or country that follows a city (but not before a ZIP Code).
Joan moved to Vancouver, British Columbia, in May.
Send the package to Douglasville, GA 30135, by Express Mail.
But: Send the package to Georgia by Express Mail.

RULE 7 ▶

, series

(L. 61)

Use a comma between each item in a series of three or more.

> We need to order paper, toner, and font cartridges for the printer.
>
> They saved their work, exited their program, and turned off their computers when they finished.

Note: Do not use a comma after the last item in a series.

RULE 8 ▶

, transitional expression

(L. 61)

Use a comma before and after a transitional expression or independent comment.

> It is critical, therefore, that we finish the project on time.
>
> Our present projections, you must admit, are inadequate.
>
> *But:* You must admit our present projections are inadequate.

Note: Examples of transitional expressions and independent comments are *in addition to, therefore, however, on the other hand, as a matter of fact,* and *unfortunately.*

RULE 9 ▶

, nonessential expression

(L. 71)

Use a comma before and after a nonessential expression.

> Andre, who was there, can verify the statement.
>
> *But:* Anyone who was there can verify the statement.
>
> Van's first book, *Crisis of Management,* was not discussed.
>
> Van's book *Crisis of Management* was not discussed.

Note: A nonessential expression is a group of words that may be omitted without changing the basic meaning of the sentence. Always examine the noun or pronoun that comes before the expression to determine whether the noun needs the expression to complete its meaning. If it does, the expression is *essential* and does *not* take a comma.

RULE 10 ▶

, adjacent adjectives

(L. 71)

Use a comma between two adjacent adjectives that modify the same noun.

> We need an intelligent, enthusiastic individual for this job.
>
> *But:* Please order a new bulletin board for our main conference room.

Note: Do not use a comma after the second adjective. Also, do not use a comma if the first adjective modifies the combined idea of the second adjective and the noun (for example, *bulletin board* and *conference room* in the second example above).

SEMICOLONS

RULE 11 ▶

; no conjunction

(L. 97)

Use a semicolon to separate two closely related independent clauses that are *not* joined by a conjunction (such as *and, but, or,* or *nor*).

> Management favored the vote; stockholders did not.
>
> *But:* Management favored the vote, but stockholders did not.

RULE 12 ▶

; series

(L. 97)

Use a semicolon to separate three or more items in a series if any of the items already contain commas.

> Staff meetings were held on Thursday, May 7; Monday, June 7; and Friday, June 12.

Note: Be sure to insert the semicolon *between* (not within) the items in a series.

HYPHENS

RULE 13
- number
(L. 57)

Hyphenate compound numbers between twenty-one and ninety-nine and fractions that are expressed as words.

Twenty-nine recommendations were approved by at least three-fourths of the members.

RULE 14
- compound adjective
(L. 67)

Hyphenate compound adjectives that come before a noun (unless the first word is an adverb ending in –ly).

We reviewed an up-to-date report on Wednesday.
But: The report was up to date.
But: We reviewed the highly rated report.

Note: A compound adjective is two or more words that function as a unit to describe a noun.

APOSTROPHES

RULE 15
' singular noun
(L. 37)

Use 's to form the possessive of singular nouns.

The hurricane's force caused major damage to North Carolina's coastline.

RULE 16
' plural noun
(L. 37)

Use only an apostrophe to form the possessive of plural nouns that end in s.

The investors' goals were outlined in the stockholders' report.
But: The investors outlined their goals in the report to the stockholders.
But: The women's and children's clothing was on sale.

RULE 17
' pronoun
(L. 37)

Use 's to form the possessive of indefinite pronouns (such as *someone's* or *anybody's*); do not use an apostrophe with personal pronouns (such as *hers, his, its, ours, theirs,* and *yours*).

She could select anybody's paper for a sample.
It's time to put the file back into its cabinet.

COLONS

RULE 18 ▶
: explanatory material
(L. 91)

Use a colon to introduce explanatory material that follows an independent clause.

> The computer satisfies three criteria: speed, cost, and power.
>
> *But:* The computer satisfies the three criteria of speed, cost, and power.
>
> Remember this: only one coupon is allowed per customer.

Note: An independent clause can stand alone as a complete sentence. Do not capitalize the word following the colon.

PERIODS

RULE 19 ▶
. polite request
(L. 91)

Use a period to end a sentence that is a polite request.

> Will you please call me if I can be of further assistance.

Note: Consider a sentence a polite request if you expect the reader to respond by doing as you ask rather than by giving a yes-or-no answer.

QUOTATION MARKS

RULE 20 ▶
" quotation
(L. 41)

Use quotation marks around a direct quotation.

> Harrison responded by saying, "Their decision does not affect us."
>
> *But:* Harrison responded by saying that their decision does not affect us.

RULE 21 ▶
" title
(L. 41)

Use quotation marks around the title of a newspaper or magazine article, chapter in a book, report, and similar terms.

> The most helpful article I found was "Multimedia for All."

ITALICS (OR UNDERLINE)

RULE 22 ▶
title
(L. 41)

Italicize (or underline) the titles of books, magazines, newspapers, and other complete published works.

> Grisham's *The Brethren* was reviewed in a recent *USA Today* article.

SENTENCES

RULE 23 ▶
fragment
(L. 21)

Avoid sentence fragments.

Not: She had always wanted to be a financial manager. But had not had the needed education.

But: She had always wanted to be a financial manager but had not had the needed education.

Note: A fragment is a part of a sentence that is incorrectly punctuated as a complete sentence. In the first sentence above, "but had not had the needed education" is not a complete sentence because it does not contain a subject.

RULE 24 ▶
run-on
(L. 21)

Avoid run-on sentences.

Not: Mohamed is a competent worker he has even passed the MOUS exam.

Not: Mohamed is a competent worker, he has even passed the MOUS exam.

But: Mohamed is a competent worker; he has even passed the MOUS exam.

Or: Mohamed is a competent worker. He has even passed the MOUS exam.

Note: A run-on sentence is two independent clauses that run together without any punctuation between them or with only a comma between them.

AGREEMENT

RULE 25 ▶
agreement singular
agreement plural
(L. 67)

Use singular verbs and pronouns with singular subjects; use plural verbs and pronouns with plural subjects.

I <u>was</u> happy with <u>my</u> performance.

<u>Janet and Phoenix</u> <u>were</u> happy with <u>their</u> performance.

Among the items discussed <u>were</u> our <u>raises and benefits</u>.

RULE 26 ▶
agreement pronoun
(L. 81)

Some pronouns *(anybody, each, either, everybody, everyone, much, neither, no one, nobody,* and *one)* are always singular and take a singular verb. Other pronouns *(all, any, more, most, none,* and *some)* may be singular or plural, depending on the noun to which they refer.

<u>Each</u> of the employees <u>has</u> finished <u>his or her</u> task.

<u>Much</u> <u>remains</u> to be done.

<u>Most</u> of the pie <u>was</u> eaten, but <u>most</u> of the cookies <u>were</u> left.

RULE 27 ▶
agreement intervening words
(L. 81)

Disregard any intervening words that come between the subject and verb when establishing agreement.

The <u>box</u> containing the books and pencils <u>has</u> not been found.

<u>Alex</u>, accompanied by Tricia, <u>is</u> attending the conference and taking <u>his</u> computer.

RULE 28 ▶
agreement nearer noun
(L. 101)

If two subjects are joined by *or, either/or, neither/nor,* or *not only/but also,* make the verb agree with the subject nearer to the verb.

Neither the coach nor the <u>players</u> <u>are</u> at home.

Not only the coach but also the <u>referee</u> <u>is</u> at home.

But: <u>Both</u> the coach and the referee <u>are</u> at home.

PRONOUNS

RULE 29
nominative pronoun
(L. 107)

Use nominative pronouns (such as *I, he, she, we, they,* and *who*) as subjects of a sentence or clause.

The programmer and <u>he</u> are reviewing the code.

Barb is a person <u>who</u> can do the job.

RULE 30
objective pronoun
(L. 107)

Use objective pronouns (such as *me, him, her, us, them,* and *whom*) as objects of a sentence, clause, or phrase.

The code was reviewed by the programmer and <u>him</u>.

Barb is the type of person <u>whom</u> we can trust.

ADJECTIVES AND ADVERBS

RULE 31
adjective/adverb
(L. 101)

Use comparative adjectives and adverbs (*-er, more,* and *less*) when referring to two nouns or pronouns; use superlative adjectives and adverbs (*-est, most,* and *least*) when referring to more than two.

The <u>shorter</u> of the <u>two</u> training sessions is the <u>more</u> helpful one.

The <u>longest</u> of the <u>three</u> training sessions is the <u>least</u> helpful one.

WORD USAGE

RULE 32
accept/except
(L. 117)

***Accept* means "to agree to"; *except* means "to leave out."**

All employees <u>except</u> the maintenance staff should <u>accept</u> the agreement.

RULE 33
affect/effect
(L. 117)

***Affect* is most often used as a verb meaning "to influence"; *effect* is most often used as a noun meaning "result."**

The ruling will <u>affect</u> our domestic operations but will have no <u>effect</u> on our Asian operations.

RULE 34
farther/further
(L. 117)

***Farther* refers to distance; *further* refers to extent or degree.**

The <u>farther</u> we drove, the <u>further</u> agitated he became.

RULE 35
personal/personnel
(L. 117)

***Personal* means "private"; *personnel* means "employees."**

All <u>personnel</u> agreed not to use email for <u>personal</u> business.

RULE 36
principal/ principle
(L. 117)

***Principal* means "primary"; *principle* means "rule."**

The <u>principle</u> of fairness is our <u>principal</u> means of dealing with customers.

Reference Manual

CAPITALIZATION

RULE 37 ▶
≡ sentence
(L. 31)

Capitalize the first word of a sentence.

Please prepare a summary of your activities.

RULE 38 ▶
≡ proper noun
(L. 31)

Capitalize proper nouns and adjectives derived from proper nouns.

Judy Hendrix drove to Albuquerque in her new Pontiac convertible.

Note: A proper noun is the official name of a particular person, place, or thing.

RULE 39 ▶
≡ time
(L. 31)

Capitalize the names of the days of the week, months, holidays, and religious days (but do not capitalize the names of the seasons).

On Thursday, November 25, we will celebrate Thanksgiving, the most popular holiday in the fall.

RULE 40 ▶
≡ noun #
(L. 77)

Capitalize nouns followed by a number or letter (except for the nouns *line, note, page, paragraph,* and *size).*

Please read Chapter 5, which begins on page 94.

RULE 41 ▶
≡ compass point
(L. 77)

Capitalize compass points (such as *north, south,* or *northeast)* only when they designate definite regions.

From Montana we drove south to reach the Southwest.

RULE 42 ▶
≡ organization
(L. 111)

Capitalize common organizational terms (such as *advertising department* and *finance committee)* only when they are the actual names of the units in the writer's own organization and when they are preceded by the word *the.*

The report from the Advertising Department is due today.

But: Our advertising department will submit its report today.

RULE 43 ▶
≡ course
(L. 111)

Capitalize the names of specific course titles but not the names of subjects or areas of study.

I have enrolled in Accounting 201 and will also take a marketing course.

NUMBER EXPRESSION

RULE 44 ▶
general
(L. 41)

In general, spell out numbers zero through ten, and use figures for numbers above ten.

We rented two movies for tonight.

The decision was reached after 27 precincts sent in their results.

RULE 45
 # figure
(L. 41)

Use figures for

- **Dates. (Use *st, d,* or *th* only if the day comes before the month.)**
  The tax report is due on April 15 *(not* April 15<u>th</u>)
  We will drive to the camp on the 23d (or *23rd* or *23ʳᵈ*) of May.

- **All numbers if two or more *related* numbers both above and below ten are used in the same sentence.**
  Mr. Carter sent in 7 receipts, and Ms. Cantrell sent in 22.
  But: The 13 accountants owned three computers each.

- **Measurements (time, money, distance, weight, and percent).**
  The $500 statue we delivered at 7 a.m. weighed 6 pounds.

- **Mixed numbers.**
  Our sales are up 9½ (or *9 1/2)* percent over last year.

RULE 46
 # word
(L. 57)

Spell out

- **A number used as the first word of a sentence.**
  Seventy-five people attended the conference in San Diego.

- **The shorter of two adjacent numbers.**
  We have ordered 3 two-pound cakes and one 5-pound cake for the reception.

- **The words *million* and *billion* in even amounts (do not use decimals with even amounts).**
  A $5 ticket can win $28 million in this month's lottery.

- **Fractions.**
  Almost one-half of the audience responded to the question.

Note: When fractions and the numbers twenty-one through ninety-nine are spelled out, they should be hyphenated.

ABBREVIATIONS

RULE 47
abbreviate none
(L. 67)

In general business writing, do not abbreviate common words (such as *dept.* or *pkg.),* compass points, units of measure, or the names of months, days of the week, cities, or states (except in addresses).
Almost one-half of the audience indicated they were at least 5 feet 8 inches tall.

Note: Do not insert a comma between the parts of a single measurement.

RULE 48
abbreviate measure
(L. 87)

In technical writing, on forms, and in tables, abbreviate units of measure when they occur frequently. Do not use periods.
14 oz   5 ft 10 in   50 mph   2 yrs 10 mo

RULE 49
abbreviate lowercase
(L. 87)

In most lowercase abbreviations made up of single initials, use a period after each initial but no internal spaces.
a.m.   p.m.   i.e.   e.g.   e.o.m.
Exceptions: mph   mpg   wpm

RULE 50
abbreviate ≡
(L. 87)

In most all-capital abbreviations made up of single initials, do not use periods or internal spaces.
OSHA   PBS   NBEA   WWW   VCR   MBA
Exceptions: U.S.A.   A.A.   B.S.   Ph.D.   P.O.   B.C.   A.D.

PART 1

The Alphabet, Number, and Symbol Keys

OBJECTIVES

KEYBOARDING

▶ Operate by touch the letter, number, and symbol keys.

▶ Demonstrate proper typing technique.

▶ Use the correct spacing with punctuation.

▶ Type at least 28 words per minute on a 2-minute timing with no more than 5 errors.

TECHNICAL

▶ Answer correctly at least 90 percent of the questions on an objective test.

BUSINESS AND ADMINISTRATIVE SERVICES

Opportunities in business and administrative careers

Occupations in the business and administrative services cluster focus on providing management and support services for various companies. The many positions found in this cluster include receptionist, bookkeeper, administrative assistant, claim examiner, accountant, word processor, office manager, and chief executive officer.

Managers and administrators are in charge of planning, organizing, and controlling businesses. Management support workers gather and analyze data to help company executives make decisions. Administrative support workers perform a variety of tasks, such as record keeping, operating office equipment, managing their own projects and assignments, and developing high-level integrated software skills as well as Internet research skills. Ideally, everyone in business should be patient, detail-oriented, and cooperative. Excellent written and oral communication skills are definitely an asset as well.

Many companies have been revolutionized by technological improvements in the computer. As a result, keyboarding skill provides a definite advantage for those who work in business and administrative services. Now, more than ever, success in the business world is dependent upon adaptability and education.

Unit 1

Keyboarding: The Alphabet

LESSON 1
A S D F J K L ;
Enter Space Bar

LESSON 2
H E O R

LESSON 3
M T P C

LESSON 4
Right Shift V . W

LESSON 5
Review

Home Keys

GOALS

- Touch-type the home keys (A S D F J K L ;)
- Touch-type the SPACE BAR
- Touch-type the ENTER key
- Type at least 10wpm/1'/3e

LEFT HAND			RIGHT HAND
First Finger	F	J	First Finger
Second Finger	D	K	Second Finger
Third Finger	S	L	Third Finger
Fourth Finger	A	;	Fourth Finger
		Space Bar	Thumb

NEW KEYS

A. Follow the directions to become familiar with the home keys.

A semicolon (;) is commonly called the sem key.

A. THE HOME KEYS

▶ The **A S D F J K L ;** keys are known as the home keys.

1. Place the fingers of your left hand on the home keys as follows: first finger on **F**; second finger on **D**; third finger on **S**; fourth finger on **A**.
2. Place the fingers of your right hand on the home keys as follows: first finger on **J**; second finger on **K**; third finger on **L**; and fourth finger on **;**.
3. Curve your fingers.
4. Using the correct fingers, type each character as you say it to yourself: a s d f j k l ;.
5. Remove your fingers from the keyboard and replace them on the home keys.
6. Press each home key again as you say each character: a s d f j k l ;.

B. THE *SPACE* BAR

The SPACE BAR, located beneath the letter keys, is used to space between words and after marks of punctuation.

1. With fingers held motionless on the home keys, poise your right thumb about a half inch above the SPACE BAR.
2. Type the characters, then press the SPACE BAR 1 time. Bounce your thumb off.
3. Type the characters a s d f, press the SPACE BAR 1 time, then type the characters j k l ;.

C. Type each line 1 time, pressing the SPACE BAR where you see a space and pressing the ENTER key at the end of a line.

C. THE *ENTER*↵ KEY

The ENTER key moves the insertion point to the beginning of a new line. Reach to the ENTER key with the fourth finger of your right hand. Keep your J finger at home. Lightly press the ENTER key. Practice using the ENTER key until you can do so with confidence and without looking at your hands.

```
asdf jkl; asdf jkl; ↵
asdf jkl; asdf jkl; ↵
```

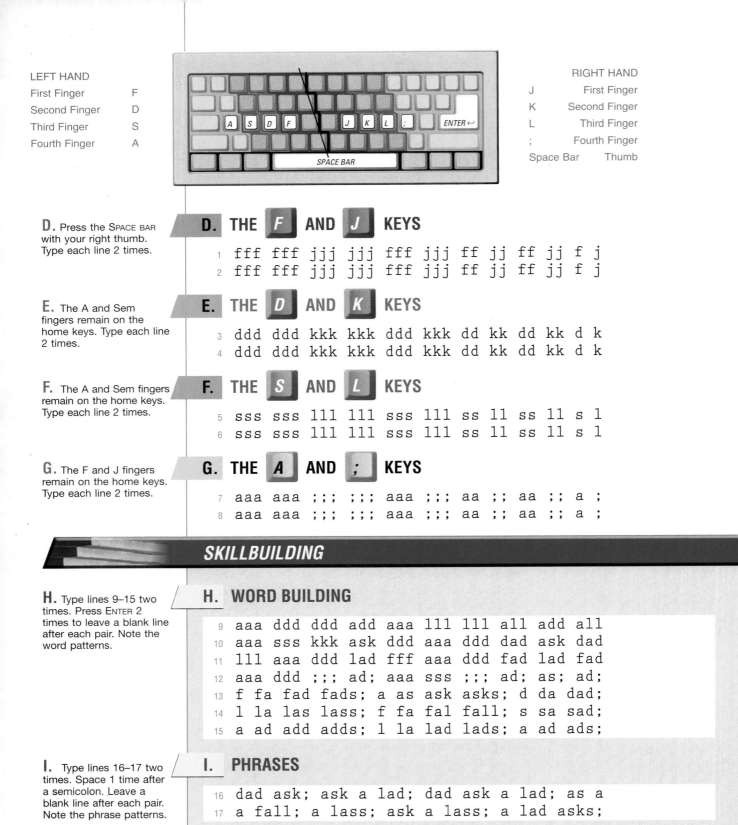

LEFT HAND

First Finger	F
Second Finger	D
Third Finger	S
Fourth Finger	A

RIGHT HAND

J	First Finger
K	Second Finger
L	Third Finger
;	Fourth Finger
Space Bar	Thumb

D. Press the SPACE bar with your right thumb. Type each line 2 times.

D. THE F AND J KEYS

```
1  fff fff jjj jjj fff jjj ff jj ff jj f j
2  fff fff jjj jjj fff jjj ff jj ff jj f j
```

E. The A and Sem fingers remain on the home keys. Type each line 2 times.

E. THE D AND K KEYS

```
3  ddd ddd kkk kkk ddd kkk dd kk dd kk d k
4  ddd ddd kkk kkk ddd kkk dd kk dd kk d k
```

F. The A and Sem fingers remain on the home keys. Type each line 2 times.

F. THE S AND L KEYS

```
5  sss sss lll lll sss lll ss ll ss ll s l
6  sss sss lll lll sss lll ss ll ss ll s l
```

G. The F and J fingers remain on the home keys. Type each line 2 times.

G. THE A AND ; KEYS

```
7  aaa aaa ;;; ;;; aaa ;;; aa ;; aa ;; a ;
8  aaa aaa ;;; ;;; aaa ;;; aa ;; aa ;; a ;
```

SKILLBUILDING

H. Type lines 9–15 two times. Press ENTER 2 times to leave a blank line after each pair. Note the word patterns.

H. WORD BUILDING

```
9   aaa ddd ddd add aaa lll lll all add all
10  aaa sss kkk ask ddd aaa ddd dad ask dad
11  lll aaa ddd lad fff aaa ddd fad lad fad
12  aaa ddd ;;; ad; aaa sss ;;; ad; as; ad;
13  f fa fad fads; a as ask asks; d da dad;
14  l la las lass; f fa fal fall; s sa sad;
15  a ad add adds; l la lad lads; a ad ads;
```

I. Type lines 16–17 two times. Space 1 time after a semicolon. Leave a blank line after each pair. Note the phrase patterns.

I. PHRASES

```
16  dad ask; ask a lad; dad ask a lad; as a
17  a fall; a lass; ask a lass; a lad asks;
```

J. Take two 1-minute timings. Try to complete both lines each time.

Goal: At least 10wpm/1'/3e

J. 1-MINUTE TIMING

```
18  ask a sad lad; a fall fad; add a salad;
19  ask a dad;
    |  1  |  2  |  3  |  4  |  5  |  6  |  7  |  8  |
```

New Keys

GOALS

- Touch-type the H, E, O, and R keys
- Type at least 11wpm/1'/3e

Fingers are named for home keys. (Example: The second finger of the left hand is the D finger.)

A. Type 2 times.

A. WARMUP

1 fff jjj ddd kkk sss lll aaa ;;; fff jjj
2 a salad; a lad; alas a fad; ask a lass;

NEW KEYS

B. Type each line 2 times. Space 1 time after a semicolon.

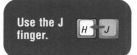

Use the J finger.

B. THE H KEY

3 jjj jhj jhj hjh jjj jhj jhj hjh jjj jhj
4 has has hah hah had had aha aha ash ash
5 hash half sash lash dash hall shad shah
6 as dad had; a lass has half; add a dash

C. Type each line 2 times. Keep your eyes on the copy as you type.

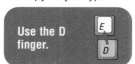

Use the D finger.

C. THE E KEY

7 ddd ded ded ede ddd ded ded ede ddd ded
8 lea led see he; she eke fed sea lee fee
9 feed keel ease heal held seal lead fake
10 he fed a seal; she held a lease; a keel

D. Type each line 2 times. Keep fingers curved.

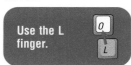

Use the L finger.

D. THE O KEY

11 lll lol lol olo lll lol lol olo lll lol
12 doe off foe hod oh; oak odd ode old sod
13 shoe look kook joke odes does solo oleo
14 he held a hook; a lass solos; old foes;

E. Type each line 2 times. Keep the A finger at home.

E. THE R KEY

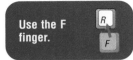

Use the F finger.

```
15  fff frf frf rfr fff frf frf rfr fff frf
16  red ark ore err rah era rod oar her are
17  oars soar dear fare read role rare door
18  a dark red door; he read a rare reader;
```

SKILLBUILDING

F. Type each line 2 times.

F. WORD PATTERNS

```
19  dale kale sale hale|fold sold hold old;
20  feed deed heed seed|dash sash lash ash;
21  lake rake sake fake|dear sear rear ear;
```

G. Take two 1-minute timings. Try to complete both lines each time. Press ENTER only at the end of line 23.

Goal: At least 11wpm/1'/3e

G. 1-MINUTE TIMING

```
22  she asked for a rare old deed; she held
23  a red door ajar;
```
| 1 | 2 | 3 | 4 | 5 | 6 | 7 | 8 |

Keyboarding CONNECTION

What Is the Internet?

What is the easiest way to go to the library? Try using your fingertips! The Internet creates a "virtual library"—a library with no walls. Nothing can match the Internet as a research device. It is not just one computer but an immense connection of computers talking to each other, organizing and exchanging information.

The Internet is synonymous with "cyberspace," a word describing the power and control of information. The Internet has been called "a network of networks" linked together to deliver information to users. The Internet connects more than 200 million people to over 3 million computer networks.

The Internet is considered a Wide Area Network (WAN) because the computers on it span the entire world. Each day the Net increases at about 1000 new users every hour.

YOUR TURN List some ways the Internet, as a "virtual library," enhances your research activities.

New Keys

A. Type 2 times.

A. WARMUP

```
1 aa ;; ss ll dd kk ff jj hh ee oo rr aa;
2 he held a sale for her as she had asked
```

NEW KEYS

B. Type each line 2 times.

Use the J finger.

B. THE M KEY

```
3 jjj jmj jmj mjm jjj jmj jmj mjm jjj jmj
4 mad mom me; am jam; ram dam ham mar ma;
5 arms loam lame roam make fame room same
6 she made more room for some of her ham;
```

C. Type each line 2 times.

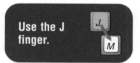
Use the F finger.

C. THE T KEY

```
7 fff ftf ftf tft fff ftf ftf tft fff ftf
8 tar tam mat hot jot rat eat lot art sat
9 told take date late mart mate tool fate
10 he told her to set a later date to eat;
```

D. Type each line 2 times.

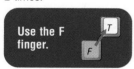
Use the Sem finger.

D. THE P KEY

```
11 ;;; ;p; ;p; p;p ;;; ;p; ;p; p;p ;;; ;p;
12 pat pal sap rap pet par spa lap pad mop
13 pale palm stop drop pelt plea slap trap
14 please park the red jeep past the pool;
```

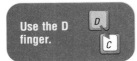
E. THE  C KEY

15 ddd dcd dcd cdc ddd dcd dcd cdc ddd dcd
16 cot cod sac act car coo arc ace cop cat
17 pack tack chat coat face aces deck cost
18 call her to race cool cars at the track

SKILLBUILDING

F. Sit in the correct position as you type these drills. Refer to the illustration on page xiii in the Introduction. Type each line 2 times.

F. SHORT PHRASES

19	as so	she had	has met	let her	fast pace
20	to do	ask her	for the	had pop	look past
21	do as	lap top	her pad	let pat	halt them
22	as he	had for	red cap	she let	fast plot

G. Take two 1-minute timings. Try to complete both lines each time. Use word wrap. Press ENTER only at the end of line 24.

Goal: At least 12wpm/1'/3e

G. 1-MINUTE TIMING

23 the old store at home had lots of cheap
24 stools for the sale;
| 1 | 2 | 3 | 4 | 5 | 6 | 7 | 8 |

STRATEGIES
FOR *Career Success*

Being a Good Listener

Silence is golden! Listening is essential for learning, getting along, and forming relationships.

Do you tend to forget people's names after being introduced? Do you look away from the speaker instead of making eye contact? Do you interrupt the speaker before he or she finishes talking? Do you misunderstand people? Answering yes can indicate poor listening skills.

To improve your listening skills, follow these steps. *Hear the speaker clearly.* Do not interrupt, let the speaker develop his or her ideas before you speak. *Focus on the message.* At the end of a conversation, identify major items discussed. Mentally ask questions to help you assess the points the speaker is making. *Keep an open mind.* Do not judge. Developing your listening skills benefits everyone.

YOUR TURN Assess your listening behavior. What techniques can you use to improve your listening skills? Practice them the next time you have a conversation with someone.

New Keys

GOALS

- Touch-type the RIGHT SHIFT, V, period, and W keys
- Count errors
- Type at least 13wpm/1′/3e

A. Type 2 times.

A. WARMUP

1 the farmer asked her to feed the mares;
2 the late callers came to mop the floor;.

NEW KEYS

B. Type each line 2 times.

Use the Sem finger.

SHIFT

B. THE RIGHT *SHIFT* KEY

▶ To capitalize letters on the left half of the keyboard:

1. With the J finger at home, press and hold down the RIGHT SHIFT key with the Sem finger.

2. Press the letter key.

3. Release the RIGHT SHIFT key and return fingers to home position.

3 ;;; ;A; ;A; ;;; ;S; ;S; ;;; ;D; ;D; ;;;
4 Art Alf Ada Sal Sam Dee Dot Flo Ted Tom
5 Amos Carl Chet Elsa Fred Sara Todd Elda
6 Carl Amos took Sara Carter to the races

C. Type each line 2 times.

Use the F finger.

C. THE *V* KEY

7 fff fvf fvf vfv fff fvf fvf vfv fff fvf
8 Val eve Eva vet Ava vat Eve ova Vel vee
9 have vase Vera ever vast Reva dove vest
10 Dave voted for Vassar; Val voted for me

D. Type each line 2 times. Space 1 time after a period following an abbreviation; do not space after a period within an abbreviation; space 1 time after a period ending a sentence.

Use the L finger.

D. THE *.* KEY

11 111 1.1 1.1 .1. 111 1.1 1.1 .1. 111 1.1
12 dr. dr. ea. ea. sr. sr. Dr. Dr. Sr. Sr.
13 a.m. acct. A.D. p.m. Corp. amt. Dr. Co.
14 Selma left. Dave left. Sarah came home.

E. Type each line 2 times.

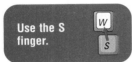

Use the S finger.

E. THE W KEY

15 sss sws sws wsw sss sws sws wsw sss sws
16 wow sow war owe was mow woe few wee row
17 wake ward wart wave wham whom walk what
18 Wade watched Walt Shaw walk for a week.

SKILLBUILDING

F. Type each line 2 times.

F. BUILD SKILL ON SENTENCES

19 Amos Ford saw Emma Dale feed the mares.
20 Dr. Drake called Sam; he asked for Ted.
21 Vera told a tale to her old classmates.
22 Todd asked Cale to move some old rakes.

G. Type each line 1 time. After typing all the lines, count your errors. Refer to page xviii in the Introduction if you need help.

G. COUNTING ERRORS IN SENTENCES

23 Ada lost her letter; Dee lost her card.
24 Dave sold some of the food to a market.
25 Alva asked Walt for three more matches.
26 Dale asked Seth to watch the last show.

H. Take two 1-minute timings. Try to complete both lines each time.

Goal: At least 13wpm/1'/3e

H. 1-MINUTE TIMING

27 Val asked them to tell the major to see
28 Carla at the local farm.

| 1 | 2 | 3 | 4 | 5 | 6 | 7 | 8 |

Review

GOALS
- Reinforce new-key reaches
- Type at least 14wpm/1'/3e

A. Type 2 times.

A. WARMUP

1 Dave called Drew to ask for a road map.
2 Elsa took three old jars to her mother.

SKILLBUILDING

B. Type each line 2 times.

B. WORD PATTERNS

3 feed seed deed heed|fold cold mold told
4 fame tame lame same|mate late date fate
5 lace face mace race|vast last cast fast
6 park dark hark mark|rare dare fare ware

C. Type each line 2 times.

C. PHRASES

7 at the|he has|her hat|for the|come home
8 or the|he had|her top|ask the|late date
9 to the|he met|her mop|ask her|made more
10 of the|he was|her pop|ask too|fast pace

D. Type each line 2 times.

D. BUILD SKILL ON SENTENCES

11 She asked Dale to share the jar of jam.
12 Cal took the tools from store to store.
13 Darel held a sale to sell some clothes.
14 Seth watched the old cat chase the car.

E. Take a 1-minute timing on each line. Review your speed and errors.

E. SENTENCES

15 Carl loved to talk to the tall teacher.
16 She dashed to take the jet to her home.
17 Walt asked her to deed the farm to Ted.

| 1 | 2 | 3 | 4 | 5 | 6 | 7 | 8 = Number of 5-stroke words

F. Take two 1-minute timings on the paragraph. Press ENTER only at the end of the paragraph. Review your speed and errors.

F. PARAGRAPH

CUMULATIVE WORDS

18 Rachael asked Sal to take her to school   8
19 for two weeks. She had to meet Freda or   16
20 Walt at the school to work on the maps.   24

| 1 | 2 | 3 | 4 | 5 | 6 | 7 | 8 |

G. Take two 1-minute timings. Review your speed and errors.

Goal: At least 14wpm/1'/3e

G. 1-MINUTE TIMING

21 Dot Crews asked Al Roper to meet her at   8
22 the tree to look for the jacket.   14

| 1 | 2 | 3 | 4 | 5 | 6 | 7 | 8 |

Keyboarding CONNECTION

Using Search Engines

How can you most efficiently find information on the Web? Use a search engine! A search engine guides you to the Web's resources. It analyzes the information you request, navigates the Web's many networks, and retrieves a list of relevant documents. Popular search engines include Lycos, Excite, Alta Vista, and Yahoo.

A search engine examines electronic databases, newswires, journals, article summaries, articles, home pages, and user group lists. It can access material found in as many as 30 million Web sites. When you request a specific keyword search, a search engine scans its large database and searches the introductory lines of text, as well as the title, headings, and subheadings of a Web page. The search engine displays the information that most closely matches your request.

YOUR TURN Try different search engines and see which ones you like best. Choose three of your favorite search engines. Then conduct a search using the keywords *apple pie*. Compare the results for each search engine.

Unit 2

Keyboarding: The Alphabet

New Keys

GOALS

- Touch-type the I, LEFT SHIFT, hyphen, and G keys
- Type at least 15wpm/1'/3e

A. Type 2 times.

A. WARMUP

1 The major sold three wool hats at cost.
2 Dale took her cats to the vet at three.

NEW KEYS

B. Type each line 2 times.

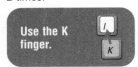

Use the K finger.

B. THE *I* KEY

3 kkk kik kik iki kkk kik kik iki kkk kik
4 aid did fir him kid lid mid pit sip tip
5 chip dice itch film hide iris kite milk
6 This time he left his tie at the store.

C. Type each line 2 times.

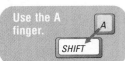

Use the A finger.

C. THE LEFT *SHIFT* KEY

▶ To capitalize letters on the right half of the keyboard:

1. With the F finger at home, press and hold down the LEFT SHIFT key with the A finger.
2. Press the letter key.
3. Release the LEFT SHIFT key and return fingers to the home position.

7 aaa Jaa Jaa aaa Kaa Kaa aaa Laa Laa aaa
8 Joe Kip Lee Hal Mat Pat Jim Kim Les Pam
9 Jake Karl Lake Hope Mark Jack Kate Hale
10 Les Lee rode with Pat Mace to the park.

D. Type each line 2 times. Do not space before or after a hyphen; keep the J finger in home position.

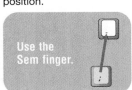

Use the Sem finger.

D. THE _ KEY

11 ;;; ;p; ;-; ;-; -;- ;;; ;-; -;- ;;; ;-;
12 two-thirds two-fifths trade-off tip-off
13 look-alike jack-of-all-trades free-fall
14 I heard that Ms. Lee-Som is well-to-do.

E. THE G KEY

15 fff fgf fgf gfg fff fgf fgf gfg fff fgf
16 age cog dig fig hog jog lag peg rag sag
17 gold rage sage grow page cage gate wage
18 Gail G. Grove greeted the great golfer.

SKILLBUILDING

F. Type each line
2 times.

F. TECHNIQUE PRACTICE: SPACE BAR

19 Vic will meet. Ed is here. Ava is here.
20 See them. Do it. Make these. Hold this.
21 See Lester. See Kate. See Dad. See Mom.
22 Take this car. Make the cakes. Hide it.

G. Type each line
2 times.

G. TECHNIQUE PRACTICE: HYPHEN KEY

23 Two-thirds were well-to-do look-alikes.
24 Jo Hames-Smith is a jack-of-all-trades.
25 Phil saw the trade-offs at the tip-off.
26 Two-fifths are packed for Jo Mill-Ross.

H. Take two
1-minute timings.
Review your
speed and errors.

Goal: At least
15wpm/1'/3e

H. 1-MINUTE TIMING

WORDS

27 Al Hall left the firm two weeks ago. I   8
28 will see Al at the park at three.   15

| 1 | 2 | 3 | 4 | 5 | 6 | 7 | 8 |

New Keys

GOALS

- Touch-type the U, B, colon, and X keys
- Type at least 16wpm/1'/3e

A. Type 2 times.

A. WARMUP

1 Evette jogged eight miles with Christi.
2 Philip gave Shari the award for spirit.

NEW KEYS

B. Type each line 2 times. Keep your other fingers at home as you reach to U.

Use the J finger.

B. THE U KEY

3 jjj juj juj uju jjj juj juj uju jjj juj
4 cue due hue put rut cut dug hut pup rum
5 cult duet fuel hulk just lump mule pull
6 Hugh urged us to put out the hot fires.

C. Type each line 2 times.

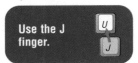

Use the F finger.

C. THE B KEY

7 fff fbf fbf bfb fff fbf fbf bfb fff fbf
8 bag cab bad lab bat rib bar tab beg web
9 bake back bead beef bath bail beam both
10 Bart backed Bill for a big blue bumper.

D. The colon is the shift of the semicolon key. Type each line 2 times. Space 1 time after a period following an abbreviation and 1 time after a colon.

Use the Sem finger.

D. THE ; KEY

11 ;;; ;;; ;;; ;:; ;;; ;:; ;:; ;:; ;;; ;:;
12 Dr. Poole: Ms. Shu: Mr. Rose: Mrs. Tam:
13 Dear Ed: Dear Flo: Dear James: Dear Di:
14 Date: To: From: Subject: for the dates:

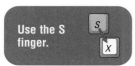

Use the S finger.

E. THE X KEY

```
15  sss sxs sxs xsx sss sxs sxs xsx sss sxs
16  box fox hex lax lux mix six tax vex wax
17  apex axle exam flax flex flux taxi text
18  Max asked six pals to fix a sixth taxi.
```

SKILLBUILDING

F. TECHNIQUE PRACTICE: COLON KEY

```
19  as follows: these people: this example:
20  Dear Sirs: Dear Madam: Dear Mrs. Smith:
21  Dear Di: Dear Bo: Dear Peter: Dear Mom:
22  for this part: as listed: the projects:
```

G. WORD PRACTICE

Top row

```
23  We were told to take our truck to Hugo.
24  There were two tired people at the hut.
25  Please write to their home to tell Tom.
```

Home row

```
26  Jake asked his dad for small red flags.
27  Sara added a dash of salt to the salad.
28  Dale said she had a fall sale at Drake.
```

Bottom row

```
29  He came to the mall at five to meet me.
30  Victoria came to vote with ample vigor.
31  Mable Baxter visited via the Marta bus.
```

H. Take two 1-minute
timings. Review your
speed and errors.

Goal: At least
16wpm/1'/3e

H. 1-MINUTE TIMING

WORDS

```
32  Dear Jack: Fred would like to take Pam        8
33  Hall to the home game at five tomorrow.       16
    |  1  |  2  |  3  |  4  |  5  |  6  |  7  |  8  |
```

Lesson 8

New Keys

GOALS
- Touch-type the Y, comma, Q, and slash keys
- Type at least 17wpm/1'/3e

A. Type 2 times.

A. WARMUP

1 Jack asked Philip if Charlie came home.
2 Kim had a short meal with Victor Baker.

NEW KEYS

B. Type each line 2 times.

Use the J finger.

B. THE Y KEY

3 jjj jyj jyj yjy jjj jyj jyj yjy jjj jyj
4 boy cry day eye fly guy hay joy key may
5 yard year yelp yoke yolk your yule play
6 Peggy told me that she may try to stay.

C. Type each line 2 times.

Use the K finger.

C. THE , KEY

7 kkk k,k k,k ,k, kkk k,k k,k ,k, kkk k,k
8 as, at, do, if, is, it, of, oh, or, so,
9 if so, if it is, what if, what of, too,
10 Dale, Barbra, Sadie, or Edith left too.

D. Type each line 2 times.

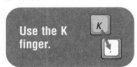

Use the A finger.

D. THE Q KEY

11 aaa aqa aqa qaq aaa aqa aqa qaq aaa aqa
12 quip quit quack quail quake quart quash
13 quest quick quilts quotes quaver queasy
14 Four quiet squires quilted aqua quilts.

E. Type each line 2 times. Do not space before or after a slash.

Use the Sem finger.

E. THE / KEY

15 ;;; ;/; ;/; /;/ ;;; ;/; ;/; /;/ ;;; ;/;
16 his/her him/her he/she either/or ad/add
17 do/due/dew hale/hail fir/fur heard/herd
18 Ask him/her if he/she chose true/false.

SKILLBUILDING

F. Type each line 2 times.

F. PHRASES

19 if it is|she will do|will he come|he is
20 he said so|who left them|will she drive
21 after all|he voted|just wait|to ask her
22 some said it|for that firm|did she seem

G. Type each line 2 times.

G. TECHNIQUE PRACTICE: SHIFT KEY

23 Ada, Idaho; Kodiak, Alaska; Lima, Ohio;
24 Lula, Georgia; Sully, Iowa; Alta, Utah;
25 Mr. Ray Tims; Mr. Ed Chu; Mr. Cal York;
26 Ms. Vi Close; Ms. Di Ray; Ms. Sue Ames;

H. Take two 1-minute timings. Review your speed and errors.

Goal: At least 17wpm/1'/3e

H. 1-MINUTE TIMING

27 George predicted that Lu will have five   8
28 boxed quilts. David Quayles was to pack   16
29 a mug.   17
      | 1 | 2 | 3 | 4 | 5 | 6 | 7 | 8 |

Lesson 9

New Keys

GOALS

- Touch-type the N, Z, question mark, and TAB keys
- Type at least 18wpm/1'/3e

A. Type 2 times.

A. WARMUP

1 I quit the sales job at Huber, Georgia.
2 Alice packed two boxes of silver disks.

NEW KEYS

B. Type each line 2 times.

B. THE [N] KEY

3 jjj jnj jnj njn jjj jnj jnj njn jjj jnj
4 and ban can den end fan nag one pan ran
5 aunt band chin dent find gain hang lawn
6 Al and Dan can enter the main entrance.

C. Type each line 2 times. Keep the F finger at home as you reach to the Z.

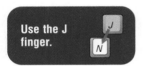

C. THE [Z] KEY

7 aaa aza aza zaz aaa aza aza zaz aaa aza
8 zap zig buzz gaze haze jazz mazes oozes
9 zip zoo zinc zing zone zoom blaze craze
10 The size of the prized pizza amazed us.

D. The question mark is the shift of the slash. Space 1 time after a question mark at the end of a sentence. Type each line 2 times.

D. THE [?] KEY

11 ;;; ;/? ;/? ?;? ;;; ;/? ;/? ?;? ;;; ;?;
12 Can John go? If not Jane, who? Can Ken?
13 Who will see? Can this be? Is that you?
14 Why not quilt? Can they go? Did he ask?

E. The word counts in this book credit you with 1 stroke for each paragraph indention in a timing. Press the TAB key after the timing starts.

E. THE `TAB` KEY

The TAB key is used to indent paragraphs. Reach to the TAB key with the A finger. Keep your other fingers on the home keys as you quickly press the TAB key. Pressing the TAB key moves the insertion point 0.5 inch (the default setting) to the right.

Use the `TAB` A finger.

F. Type each paragraph 2 times. Press ENTER only at the end of the paragraph.

F. PRACTICE THE `TAB` KEY

```
15  Each   Tab→  day   Tab→  set   Tab→  your   Tab→  goal
16  to           type        with        more         speed.

17  You          will        soon        reach        your
18  goal         if          you         work         hard.
```

SKILLBUILDING

G. Type each line 2 times.

G. TECHNIQUE PRACTICE: QUESTION MARK

```
19  Who? Why? How? When? What? True? False?
20  Is it Mo? Why not? What for? Which one?
21  Did Mary go? Is Clinton ready? Why not?
22  Who competed with me? Dana? James? Kay?
```

H. Type each line 2 times.

H. PHRASES

```
23  and the|for the|she is able|can they go
24  for him|ask him|they still|did they fly
25  of them|with us|can he send|ought to be
26  has been able|they need it|he will call
```

I. TECHNIQUE PRACTICE: HYPHEN

Hyphens are used:
- To show that a word is divided (lines 27 and 31).
- To make a dash using two hyphens with no space before or after, (lines 28 and 31).
- To join words in a compound word (lines 29, 30, and 32).

```
27      Can Larry go to the next tennis tourna-
28 ment? I am positive he--like Lane--will find
29 the event to be a first-class sports event.
30 If he can go, I will get first-rate seats.
31      Larry--like Ella--enjoys going to tourna-
32 ments that are always first-rate, first-class
33 sporting events.
```

J. Space 1 time after a
semicolon, colon, and
comma and 1 time after a
period and question mark
at the end of a sentence.
Type each line 2 times.

J. PUNCTUATION PRACTICE

```
34 Kate writes; John sings. Are they good?
35 Send these items: pens, pencils, clips.
36 Hal left; she stayed. Will they attend?
37 Wes made these stops: Rome, Bern, Kiev.
```

K. Take two 1-minute
timings. Review your
speed and errors.

Goal: At least
18wpm/1'/3e

K. 1-MINUTE TIMING

```
38      Zelik judged six typing contests        7
39 that a local firm held in Piqua. Vick       14
40 Bass was a winner.                           18
   |  1  |  2  |  3  |  4  |  5  |  6  |  7  |  8  |
```

STRATEGIES FOR *Career Success*

Preparing a Job-Interview Portfolio

Don't go empty-handed to that job interview! Take a portfolio of items with you. Definitely include copies of your resume and your list of references, with at least three professional references. Your academic transcript is useful, especially if you are asked to complete a company application form. Appropriate work samples and copies of certificates and licenses are also helpful portfolio items.

The interview process provides you the opportunity to interview the organization. Include a list of questions you want to ask during the interview.

A comprehensive portfolio of materials will benefit you by giving you a measure of control during the interview process.

YOUR TURN Start today to compile items for your interview portfolio. Include copies of your resume, your reference list, and copies of certificates and licenses. Begin developing a list of interview questions. Think about appropriate work samples to include in your portfolio.

Review

GOAL

- Type at least 19wpm/1'/3e

A. Type 2 times.

A. WARMUP

1 She expects to work hard at her job.
2 Keith had a very quiet, lazy afternoon.

SKILLBUILDING

B. Take a 1-minute timing on each paragraph. Review your speed and errors.

B. SHORT PARAGRAPHS

3 You can utilize your office skills   7
4 to complete tasks. Some types of jobs   15
5 require more skills.   19

6 You will be amazed at how easily   7
7 and quickly you complete your task when   15
8 you can concentrate.   19

| 1 | 2 | 3 | 4 | 5 | 6 | 7 | 8 |

C. Type each line 2 times.

C. WORD PATTERNS

9 banister minister adapter filter master
10 disable disband discern discord discuss
11 embargo emerge embody empty employ emit
12 enforce endure energy engage engine end
13 precept precise predict preside premier
14 subtract subject subsist sublime subdue
15 teamster tearful teaches teak team tear
16 theater theirs theory thefts therm them
17 treason crimson season prison bison son
18 tribune tribute tripod trial tribe trim

D. Type each line 2 times. Keep fingers curved and wrists low but not resting on the keyboard as you practice these lines.

D. ALPHABET REVIEW

19 Alda asked Alma Adams to fly to Alaska.
20 Both Barbara and Bill liked basketball.
21 Carl can accept a classic car in Cairo.
22 David dined in a dark diner in Detroit.
23 Elmo said Eddie edited the entire text.
24 Five friars focused on the four fables.
25 Guy gave a bag of green grapes to Gina.
26 Haughty Hugh hoped Hal had helped Seth.
27 Irene liked to pickle pickles in brine.
28 Jon Jones joined a junior jogging team.
29 Kenny kept a kayak for a trek to Koyuk.
30 Lowell played a well-planned ball game.
31 Monica made more money on many markups.
32 Ned knew ten men in a main dining room.
33 Opal Orem opened four boxes of oranges.
34 Pat paid to park the plane at the pump.
35 Quincy quickly quit his quarterly quiz.
36 Robin read rare books in their library.
37 Sam signed, sealed, and sent the lease.
38 Todd caught trout in the little stream.
39 Uncle Rubin urged Julie to go to Utica.
40 Viva Vista vetoed the five voice votes.
41 Walt waited while Wilma went to Weston.
42 Xu mixed extra extract exactly as told.
43 Yes, your young sister played a cymbal.
44 Zesty zebras zigzagged in the Ohio zoo.

E. Take two 1-minute timings. Review your speed and errors.

Goal: At least 19wpm/1'/3e

E. 1-MINUTE TIMING

45   Zoe expected a quiet morning to do   7
46 all of her work. Joy Day was to bring   15
47 five of the tablets.   19

| 1 | 2 | 3 | 4 | 5 | 6 | 7 | 8 |

Unit 3
Keyboarding: The Numbers

Number Keys

GOALS

- Touch-type the 5, 7, 3, and 9 keys
- Type at least 19wpm/2'/5e

A. Type 2 times.

A. WARMUP

1   The law firm of Quayle, Buster, Given, and   9
2 Rizzo processed all the cases last June and July;   19
3 however, we will seek a new law firm next summer.   29

   | 1 | 2 | 3 | 4 | 5 | 6 | 7 | 8 | 9 | 10

NEW KEYS

B. Type each line 2 times.

Use the F finger.

B. THE 5 KEY

4 fr5f fr5f f55f f55f f5f5 f5f5 5 55 555 5,555 5:55
5 55 fury 55 foes 55 fibs 55 fads 55 furs 55 favors
6 The 55 students read the 555 pages in 55 minutes.
7 He found Item 5 that weighed 55 pounds, 5 ounces.

C. Type each line 2 times.

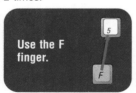

Use the J finger.

C. THE 7 KEY

8 ju7j ju7j j77j j77j j7j7 j7j7 7 77 777 7,777 7:77
9 77 jigs 77 jobs 77 jugs 77 jets 77 jars 77 jewels
10 The 77 men bought Items 77 and 777 for their job.
11 Joe had 57 books and 77 tablets for a 7:57 class.

D. Type each line 2 times.

Use the D finger.

D. THE 3 KEY

12 de3d de3d d33d d33d d3d3 d3d3 3 33 333 3,333 3:33
13 33 dots 33 died 33 dine 33 days 33 dogs 33 drains
14 The 33 vans moved 73 cases in less than 33 hours.
15 Add 55 to 753; subtract 73 to get a total of 735.

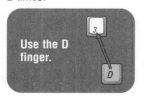

E. Type each line 2 times.

Use the L finger.

E. THE 9 KEY

16 lo9l lo9l 1991 1991 1919 1919 9 99 999 9,999 9:99
17 99 lads 99 lights 99 labs 99 legs 99 lips 99 logs
18 Their 99 cans of No. 99 were sold to 99 managers.
19 He had 39 pens, 59 pads, 97 pencils, and 9 clips.

SKILLBUILDING

F. Type each line 2 times.

F. NUMBER PRACTICE: 5, 7, 3, AND 9

20 The 57 tickets were for the April 3 show at 9:59.
21 Mary was to read pages 33, 57, 95, and 97 to him.
22 Kate planted 53 tulips, 39 mums, and 97 petunias.
23 Only 397 of the 573 coeds could register at 5:39.

G. Type each line 2 times. Keep other fingers at home as you reach to the SHIFT keys.

G. TECHNIQUE PRACTICE: SHIFT KEY

24 Vera Rosa Tao Fay Jae Tab Pat Yuk Sue Ann Sal Joe
25 Andre Fidel Pedro Chong Alice Mike Juan Fern Dick
26 Carlos Caesar Karen Ojars Julie Marta Scott Maria
27 Marge Jerry Joan Mary Bill Ken Bob Ray Ted Mel Al

H. PROGRESSIVE PRACTICE: ALPHABET

If you are not using the GDP software, turn to page SB-7 and follow the directions for this activity.

I. Take two 2-minute timings. Review your speed and errors.

Goal: At least 19wpm/2'/5e

I. 2-MINUTE TIMING

28 Jazz paid for six seats and quit because he   9
29 could not get the views he wanted near the middle   19
30 of the field. In August he is thinking of going   29
31 to the ticket office early to purchase tickets.   38
    | 1 | 2 | 3 | 4 | 5 | 6 | 7 | 8 | 9 | 10

Review

GOAL

● Type at least 20wpm/2'/5e

A. Type 2 times.

A. WARMUP

```
1       Rex played a very quiet game of bridge with      9
2   Zeke. In March they played in competition with       18
3   39 players; in January they played with 57 more.     28
```
| 1 | 2 | 3 | 4 | 5 | 6 | 7 | 8 | 9 | 10

SKILLBUILDING

B. Take three 12-second timings on each line. The scale below the last line shows your wpm speed for a 12-second timing.

B. 12-SECOND SPEED SPRINTS

```
4   A good neighbor paid for these ancient ornaments.
5   Today I sit by the big lake and count huge rocks.
6   The four chapels sit by the end of the old field.
7   The signal means help is on its way to the child.
```
| 5 | 10 | 15 | 20 | 25 | 30 | 35 | 40 | 45 | 50

C. Take a 1-minute timing on the first paragraph to establish your base speed. Then take four 1-minute timings on the remaining paragraphs. As soon as you equal or exceed your base speed on one paragraph, advance to the next, more difficult paragraph.

C. SUSTAINED PRACTICE: SYLLABIC INTENSITY

```
8        People continue to rent autos for personal      9
9    use and for their work, and car rental businesses   19
10   just keep growing. You may want to try one soon.     29

11       It is likely that a great deal of insurance      9
12   protection is part of the standard rental cost to    19
13   you. You may, however, make many other choices.      28

14       Perhaps this is not necessary, as you might      9
15   already have the kind of protection you want in a    19
16   policy that you currently have on the automobile.    29

17       Paying separate mileage charges could evolve     9
18   into a very large bill. This will undoubtedly be     19
19   true if your trip involves distant destinations.     29
```

D. Type each line
2 times.

D. ALPHABET PRACTICE

20 Packing jam for the dozen boxes was quite lively.
21 Fay quickly jumped over the two dozen huge boxes.
22 We vexed Jack by quietly helping a dozen farmers.
23 The quick lynx from the zoo just waved a big paw.
24 Lazy brown dogs do not jump over the quick foxes.

E. Type each line
2 times.

E. NUMBER PRACTICE

25 Mary was to read pages 37, 59, 75, and 93 to Zoe.
26 He invited 53 boys and 59 girls to the 7:35 show.
27 The 9:37 bus did not come to our stop until 9:55.
28 Purchase Order 53 listed Items 35, 77, 93, and 9.
29 Flight 375 will be departing Gate 37 at 9:59 p.m.

F. Type each sentence
on a separate line. Type
2 times.

F. TECHNIQUE PRACTICE: ENTER KEY

30 Can he go? If so, what? We are lost. Jose is ill.
31 Did she type the memos? Tina is going. Jane lost.
32 Max will drive. Xenia is in Ohio. She is tallest.
33 Nate is fine; Ty is not. Who won? Where is Nancy?
34 No, she cannot go. Was he here? Where is Roberta?

G. Type each line 2
times. Space without
pausing.

G. TECHNIQUE PRACTICE: SPACE BAR

35 a b c d e f g h i j k l m n o p q r s t u v w x y
36 an as be by go in is it me no of or to we but for
37 Do you go to Ada or Ida for work every day or so?
38 I am sure he can go with you if he has some time.
39 He is to be at the car by the time you get there.

H. Take two
2-minute timings.
Review your speed
and errors.

Goal: At least
20wpm/2′/5e

H. 2-MINUTE TIMING

40   Jack and Alex ordered six pizzas at a price   9
41 that was quite a bit lower than for the one they   9
42 ordered yesterday. They will order from the same   29
43 place tomorrow for the party they are planning   38
44 to have.   40

| 1 | 2 | 3 | 4 | 5 | 6 | 7 | 8 | 9 | 10

Lesson 13

Number Keys

GOALS
- Touch-type the 8, 2, and 0 keys
- Type at least 21wpm/2′/5e

A. Type 2 times.

A. WARMUP

```
1      Mary, Jenny, and Quinn packed 79 prizes in      9
2  53 large boxes for the party. They will take all    19
3  of the boxes to 3579 North Capitol Avenue today.    29
   |  1  |  2  |  3  |  4  |  5  |  6  |  7  |  8  |  9  |  10
```

NEW KEYS

B. Type each line 2 times.

Use the K finger.

B. THE 8 KEY

```
4  ki8k ki8k k88k k88k k8k8 k8k8 8 88 888 8,888 8:88
5  88 inks 88 inns 88 keys 88 kits 88 kids 88 knives
6  Bus 38 left at 3:38 and arrived here at 8:37 p.m.
7  Kenny called Joe at 8:38 at 883-7878 or 585-3878.
```

C. Type each line 2 times.

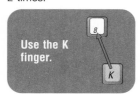

Use the S finger.

C. THE 2 KEY

```
8  sw2s sw2s s22s s22s s2s2 s2s2 2 22 222 2,222 2:22
9  22 seas 22 sets 22 sons 22 subs 22 suns 22 sports
10 The 22 seats sold at 2:22 to 22 coeds in Room 22.
11 He added Items 22, 23, 25, 27, and 28 on Order 2.
```

D. Type each line 2 times.

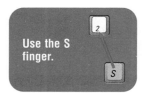

Use the Sem finger.

D. THE 0 KEY

```
12 ;p0; ;p0; ;00; ;00; ;0;0 ;0;0 0 00 000 0,000 0:00
13 20 pads 30 pegs 50 pens 70 pins 80 pits 900 parks
14 You will get 230 when you add 30, 50, 70, and 80.
15 The 80 men met at 3:05 with 20 agents in Room 90.
```

E. Type each line 2 times.

E. NUMBER PRACTICE

16 Jill bought 55 tickets for the 5:50 or 7:50 show.
17 Maxine called from 777-7370 or 777-7570 for Mary.
18 Sally had 23 cats, 23 dogs, and 22 birds at home.
19 Items 35, 37, 38, and 39 were sent on October 30.
20 Did Flight 2992 leave from Gate 39 at 9:39 today?
21 Sue went from 852 28th Street to 858 28th Street.
22 He sold 20 tires, 30 air filters, and 200 wipers.

F. Type each sentence on a separate line. For each sentence, press TAB, type the sentence, then press ENTER. After you have typed all 11 sentences, leave a blank line and type them all a second time.

F. TECHNIQUE PRACTICE: TAB KEY

23   Casey left to go home. Where is John? Did
24 Susan go home with them?

25   Isaiah drove my car to work. Sandy parked
26 the car in the lot. They rode together.

27   Pat sold new cars for a new dealer. Dana
28 sold vans for the same dealer.

29   Nick bought the nails to finish the job.
30 Chris has the bolts. Dave has the wood.

G. PACED PRACTICE

If you are not using the GDP software, turn to page SB-14 and follow the directions for this activity.

H. DIAGNOSTIC PRACTICE: ALPHABET

If you are not using the GDP software, turn to page SB-2 and follow the directions for this activity.

I. Take two 2-minute timings. Review your speed and errors.

Goal: At least 21wpm/2'/5e

I. 2-MINUTE TIMING

31   Jim told Bev that they must keep the liquid   9
32 oxygen frozen so that it could be used by the new   9
33 plant foreman tomorrow. The oxygen will then be   28
34 moved quickly to its new location by transport or   38
35 rail next evening.   42

| 1 | 2 | 3 | 4 | 5 | 6 | 7 | 8 | 9 | 10 |

Lesson 14

Number Keys

GOALS
- Touch-type the 4, 6, and 1 keys
- Type at least 22wpm/2'/5e

A. Type 2 times.

A. WARMUP

1   We quickly made 30 jars of jam and won a big   9
2 prize for our efforts on March 29. Six of the jam 19
3 jars were taken to 578 Culver Drive on April 28. 29

| 1 | 2 | 3 | 4 | 5 | 6 | 7 | 8 | 9 | 10

NEW KEYS

B. Type each line 2 times.

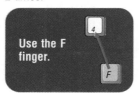

Use the F finger.

B. THE 4 KEY

4 fr4f fr4f f44f f44f f4f4 f4f4 4 44 444 4,444 4:44
5 44 fans 44 feet 44 figs 44 fins 44 fish 44 flakes
6 The 44 boys had 44 tickets for the games at 4:44.
7 Matthew read 4 books, 54 articles, and 434 lines.

C. Type each line 2 times.

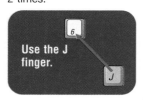

Use the J finger.

C. THE 6 KEY

8 jy6j jy6j j66j j66j j6j6 j6j6 6 66 666 6,666 6:66
9 66 jabs 66 jams 66 jobs 66 join 66 jots 66 jewels
10 Tom Lux left at 6:26 on Train 66 to go 600 miles.
11 There were 56,640 people in Bath; 26,269 in Hale.

D. Type each line 2 times.

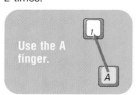

Use the A finger.

D. THE 1 KEY

12 aq1a aq1a a11a a11a a1a1 a1a1 1 11 111 1,111 1:11
13 11 aces 11 adds 11 aims 11 arts 11 axes 11 arenas
14 Sam left here at 1:11, Sue at 6:11, Don at 11:11.
15 Eric moved from 1661 Main Street to 1116 in 1995.

E. NUMBER PRACTICE

E. Type each line 2 times. Focus on accuracy rather than speed as you practice the number drills.

16 Adding 10 and 20 and 30 and 40 and 70 totals 170.
17 Al selected Nos. 15, 16, 17, 18, and 19 to study.
18 The test took Sam 10 hours, 8 minutes, 3 seconds.
19 Did the 39 men drive 567 miles on Route 23 or 27?
20 The 18 shows were sold out by 8:37 on October 18.
21 On April 29-30 we will be open from 7:45 to 9:30.

F. PROGRESSIVE PRACTICE: NUMBERS

If you are not using the GDP software, turn to page SB-11 and follow the directions for this activity.

G. HANDWRITTEN PARAGRAPH

G. Take two 1-minute timings. Review your speed and errors.

22 *Good writing skills are critical for success*   9
23 *in business. Numerous studies have shown*   18
24 *that these skills are essential for job advancement.*   27

| 1 | 2 | 3 | 4 | 5 | 6 | 7 | 8 | 9 | 10 |

H. DIAGNOSTIC PRACTICE: ALPHABET

If you are not using the GDP software, turn to page SB-2 and follow the directions for this activity.

I. 2-MINUTE TIMING

I. Take two 2-minute timings. Review your speed and errors.

Goal: At least 22wpm/2'/5e

25   James scheduled a science quiz next week for   9
26 George, but he did not let him know what time the   19
27 exam was to be taken. George must score well on   29
28 this exam in order to be admitted to the class   38
29 at the Mount Garland Academy.   44

| 1 | 2 | 3 | 4 | 5 | 6 | 7 | 8 | 9 | 10 |

Review

GOAL
- Type at least 23wpm/2'/5e

A. Type 2 times.

A. WARMUP

1   Jeffrey Mendoza quickly plowed six fields so   9
2 that he could plant 19 rows of beets, 28 rows of   19
3 corn, 37 rows of grapes, and 45 rows of olives.   28

    | 1 | 2 | 3 | 4 | 5 | 6 | 7 | 8 | 9 | 10

SKILLBUILDING

B. Take three 12-second timings on each line. The scale below the last line shows your wpm speed for a 12-second timing.

B. 12-SECOND SPEED SPRINTS

4 The lane to the lake might make the auto go away.
5 They go to the lake by bus when they work for me.
6 He just won and lost, won and lost, won and lost.
7 The man and the girl rush down the paths to town.

         5   10   15   20   25   30   35   40   45   50

C. Tab 1 time between columns. Type 2 times.

C. TECHNIQUE PRACTICE: TAB KEY

8   aisle   Tab→ break   Tab→ crank Tab→ draft   Tab→ earth
9   Frank   Guinn   Henry   Ivan   Jacob
10 knack   learn   mason   night   ocean
11 print   quest   rinse   slide   title
12 Umberto   Victor   Wally   Xavier   Zenger

D. Type each line 2 times. Try not to slow down for the capital letters.

D. TECHNIQUE PRACTICE: SHIFT KEY

13 Sue, Pat, Ann, and Gail left for Rome on June 10.
14 The St. Louis Cardinals and New York Mets played.
15 Dave Herr took Flight 481 for Memphis and Toledo.
16 An address for Karen Cook is 5 Bar Street, Provo.
17 Harry Truman was born in Missouri on May 8, 1884.

E. Type each line 2 times.

E. PUNCTUATION PRACTICE

18 Jan Brooks-Smith was a go-between for the author.
19 The off-the-record comment led to a free-for-all.
20 Louis was a jack-of-all-trades as a clerk-typist.
21 Ask Barbara--who is in Central Data--to find out.
22 Joanne is too old-fashioned to be that outspoken.

PRETEST → PRACTICE → POSTTEST

F. PRETEST: Vertical Reaches

PRETEST
Take a 1-minute timing. Review your speed and errors.

23   A few of our business managers attribute the   9
24 success of the bank to a judicious and scientific 19
25 reserve program. The bank cannot drop its guard. 29

| 1 | 2 | 3 | 4 | 5 | 6 | 7 | 8 | 9 | 10 |

G. PRACTICE: Up Reaches

PRACTICE
Speed Emphasis:
If you made 2 or fewer errors on the Pretest, type each *individual* line 2 times.
Accuracy Emphasis:
If you made 3 or more errors, type each *group* of lines (as though it were a paragraph) 2 times.

26 at atlas plate water later batch fatal match late
27 dr draft drift drums drawn drain drama dress drab
28 ju jumpy juror junky jumbo julep judge juice just

H. PRACTICE: Down Reaches

29 ca cable cabin cadet camel cameo candy carve cash
30 nk trunk drink prank rinks brink drank crank sink
31 ba batch badge bagel baked banjo barge basis bank

I. POSTTEST: Vertical Reaches

POSTTEST
Repeat the Pretest timing and compare performance.

J. PROGRESSIVE PRACTICE: ALPHABET

If you are not using the GDP software, turn to page SB-7 and follow the directions for this activity.

K. 2-MINUTE TIMING

K. Take two 2-minute timings. Review your speed and errors.

Goal: At least 23wpm/2'/5e

32   Jeff Malvey was quite busy fixing all of the   9
33 frozen pipes so that his water supply would not 19
34 be stopped. Last winter Jeff kept the pipes from 29
35 freezing by wrapping them with an insulated tape 39
36 that protected them from the cold. 46

| 1 | 2 | 3 | 4 | 5 | 6 | 7 | 8 | 9 | 10 |

Unit 4

Keyboarding: The Symbols

Symbol Keys

GOALS
- Touch-type $ ( ) ! keys
- Type at least 24wpm/2'/5e

A. Type 2 times.

A. WARMUP

```
1      Gill was quite vexed by that musician who        9
2  played 5 jazz songs and 13 country songs at the     18
3  fair. He wanted 8 rock songs and 4 blues songs.      28
   |  1  |  2  |  3  |  4  |  5  |  6  |  7  |  8  |  9  |  10
```

NEW KEYS

B. DOLLAR is the shift of 4. Do not space between the dollar sign and the number. Type each line 2 times.

B. THE $ KEY

```
4  frf fr4f f4f f4$f f$$f f$$f $44 $444 $4,444 $4.44
5  I quoted $48, $64, and $94 for the set of chairs.
6  Her insurance paid $150; our insurance paid $175.
7  Season concert seats were $25, $30, $55, and $75.
```

C. PARENTHESES are the shifts of 9 and 0. Do not space between the parentheses and the text within them. Type each line 2 times.

Use the L finger on (. Use the Sem finger on).

C. THE (AND) KEYS

```
8  lo9l lo9l lo(l lo(l l((l ;p0; ;p0; ;p); ;p); ;));
9  Please ask (1) Al, (2) Pat, (3) Ted, and (4) Dee.
10 Sue has some (1) skis, (2) sleds, and (3) skates.
11 Mary is (1) prompt, (2) speedy, and (3) accurate.

12 Our workers (Lewis, Jerry, and Ty) were rewarded.
13 The owner (Ms. Parks) went on Friday (August 18).
14 The Roxie (a cafe) had fish (salmon) on the menu.
15 The clerk (Ms. Fay Green) will vote yes (not no).
```

D. THE ! KEY

D. EXCLAMATION is the shift of 1. Space 1 time after an exclamation point at the end of a sentence. Type each line 2 times.

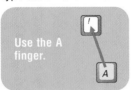

Use the A finger.

16 aqa aqla aq!a a!!a a!!a Where! Whose! What! When!
17 Put those down! Do not move them! Leave it there!
18 He did say that! Jake cannot take a vacation now!
19 You cannot leave at this time! Janie will go now!

SKILLBUILDING

E. Type the paragraph 2 times.

E. TECHNIQUE PRACTICE: SPACE BAR

20 　　　We will all go to the race if I win the one
21 I am going to run today. Do you think I will be
22 able to run at the front of the pack and win it?

F. Take three 12-second timings on each line. The scale below the last line shows your wpm speed for a 12-second timing.

F. 12-SECOND SPEED SPRINTS

23 Walking can perk you up if you are feeling tired.
24 Your heart and lungs can work harder as you walk.
25 It may be that a walk is often better than a nap.
26 If you walk each day, you may have better health.

| | | | 5 | | | | 10 | | | | 15 | | | | 20 | | | | 25 | | | | 30 | | | | 35 | | | | 40 | | | | 45 | | | | 50

G. PACED PRACTICE

If you are not using the GDP software, turn to page SB-14 and follow the directions for this activity.

H. Take two 2-minute timings. Review your speed and errors.

Goal: At least 24wpm/2'/5e

H. 2-MINUTE TIMING

27 　　　Katie quit her zoo job seven days after she　　9
28 learned that she was expected to travel to four　　19
29 different zoos in the first year of employment.　　28
30 After quitting that job, she found an excellent　　38
31 job that required her to travel less frequently.　　48

| 1 | 2 | 3 | 4 | 5 | 6 | 7 | 8 | 9 | 10

Review

GOAL

- Type at least 25wpm/2'/5e

A. Type 2 times.

A. WARMUP

1   Yes! We object to the dumping of 25 toxic   9
2 barrels at 4098 Nix Street. A larger number (36)   19
3 were dumped on the 7th, costing us over $10,000.   28

   | 1 | 2 | 3 | 4 | 5 | 6 | 7 | 8 | 9 | 10

SKILLBUILDING

B. Type each line 2 times.

B. NUMBER PRACTICE

4 we 23 pi 08 you 697 row 492 tire 5843 power 09234
5 or 94 re 43 eye 363 top 590 quit 1785 witty 28556
6 up 70 ye 63 pit 085 per 034 root 4995 wrote 24953
7 it 85 ro 49 rip 480 two 529 tour 5974 quite 17853
8 yi 68 to 59 toy 596 rot 495 tier 5834 queue 17373
9 op 90 qo 19 wet 235 pet 035 rope 4903 quote 17953

C. Type each line 2 times.

C. WORD BEGINNINGS

10 tri trinkets tribune trifle trick trial trip trim
11 mil million mileage mildew mills milky miles mild
12 spo sponsor sponge sports spore spoon spool spoke
13 for forgiving forbear forward forbid forced force

14 div dividend division divine divide diving divers
15 vic vicinity vicious victory victims victor vices
16 aff affliction affiliates affirms affords affairs
17 tab tablecloth tabulates tableau tabloids tablets

D. Type each line 2 times.

D. WORD ENDINGS

18 ive repulsive explosive alive drive active strive
19 est nearest invest attest wisest nicest jest test
20 ply supply simply deeply damply apply imply reply
21 ver whenever forever whoever quiver waiver driver

```
22   tor inventor detector debtor orator doctor factor
23   lly industrially logically legally ideally really
24   ert convert dessert expert invert diverts asserts
25   ink shrink drink think blink clink pink sink rink
```

E. PROGRESSIVE PRACTICE: ALPHABET

If you are not using the GDP software, turn to page SB-7 and follow the directions for this activity.

F. Take two 1-minute timings. Review your speed and errors.

F. HANDWRITTEN PARAGRAPH

```
26   In this book you have learned the reaches      9
27   for all alphabetic and number keys. You have   18
28   also learned a few of the symbol keys. In the  27
29   remaining lessons you will learn the other     36
30   symbol keys. You will also build your speed    45
31   and accuracy when typing.                      50
     |  1  |  2  |  3  |  4  |  5  |  6  |  7  |  8  |  9  |  10
```

G. DIAGNOSTIC PRACTICE: NUMBERS

If you are not using the GDP software, turn to page SB-5 and follow the directions for this activity.

H. Take two 2-minute timings. Review your speed and errors.

Goal: At least 25wpm/2'/5e

H. 2-MINUTE TIMING

```
32        From the tower John saw that the six big    8
33   planes would crash as they zoomed quickly over  18
34   treetops on their way to the demonstration that 27
35   was scheduled to begin very soon. We hope there 37
36   is no accident and that the pilots reach their  46
37   destinations safely.                            50
     |  1  |  2  |  3  |  4  |  5  |  6  |  7  |  8  |  9  |  10
```

STRATEGIES FOR *Career Success*   Goodwill Messages

Would you like to strengthen your relationship with a customer, coworker, or boss? Send an unexpected goodwill message! Your expression of goodwill has a positive effect on business relationships.

Messages of congratulations or appreciation provide special opportunities to express goodwill. These messages can be quite brief. If your handwriting is good, send a handwritten note on a professional note card. Otherwise, send a letter or email.

A note of congratulations might be "I just heard the news about your (award, promotion, etc.). My very best wishes." An appreciation note could be "Thank you for referring me to . . .. Your confidence and trust are sincerely appreciated."

YOUR TURN Send a goodwill message to someone to express congratulations or appreciation.

Symbol Keys

GOALS

- Touch-type * # ' keys
- Type at least 26wpm/2'/5e

A. Type 2 times.

A. WARMUP

```
 1        Bill Waxmann quickly moved all 35 packs of      9
 2 gear for the Amazon trip (worth $987) 26 miles       18
 3 into the jungle. The move took 14 days in all.       27
   |  1  |  2  |  3  |  4  |  5  |  6  |  7  |  8  |  9  |  10
```

NEW KEYS

B. ASTERISK is the shift of 8. Type each line 2 times.

Use the K finger.

B. THE [*] KEY

```
 4 kik ki8k k8*k k8*k k**k k**k This book* is great.
 5 Use an * to show that a table source is included.
 6 Asterisks keyed in a row (*******) make a border.
 7 The article quoted Hanson,* Pyle,* and Peterson.*
```

C. NUMBER (if before a figure) or POUNDS (if after a figure) is the shift of 3. Type each line 2 times.

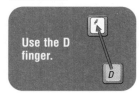

Use the D finger.

C. THE [#] KEY

```
 8 de3d de3#d d3#d d3#d d##d d##d #3 #33 #333 #3,333
 9 Al wants 33# of #200 and 38# of #400 by Saturday.
10 My favorite seats are #2, #34, #56, #65, and #66.
11 Please order 45# of #245 and 13# of #24 tomorrow.
```

D. Apostrophe is to the right of the semicolon. Type each line 2 times.

Use the Sem finger.

D. THE ' KEY

12 ;'; ';' ;'; ';' Can't we go in Sue's or Al's car?
13 It's Bob's job to cover Ted's work when he's out.
14 What's in Joann's lunch box for Sandra's dessert?
15 He's gone to Ty's banquet, which is held at Al's.

SKILLBUILDING

E. PACED PRACTICE

If you are not using the GDP software, turn to page SB-14 and follow the directions for this activity.

F. DIAGNOSTIC PRACTICE: ALPHABET

If you are not using the GDP software, turn to page SB-2 and follow the directions for this activity.

G. Take two 1-minute timings. Review your speed and errors.

G. HANDWRITTEN PARAGRAPH

16 You have completed the first segment of   8
17 your class. You have learned to type all of   17
18 the alphabetic keys, the number keys, and some 26
19 of the symbol keys. Next you will learn the   35
20 remaining symbol keys on the top row.   42

| 1 | 2 | 3 | 4 | 5 | 6 | 7 | 8 | 9 | 10

H. Take two 2-minute timings. Review your speed and errors.

Goal: At least 26wpm/2'/5e

H. 2-MINUTE TIMING

21   Max had to make one quick adjustment to his   9
22 television set before the football game began.   18
23 The picture during the last game was fuzzy and   27
24 hard to see. If he cannot fix the picture, he may   37
25 have to purchase a new television set; and that   47
26 may not be possible today.   52

| 1 | 2 | 3 | 4 | 5 | 6 | 7 | 8 | 9 | 10

Symbol Keys

GOALS

- Touch-type & % " @ keys
- Type at least 27wpm/2'/5e

A. Type 2 times.

A. WARMUP

```
1       The teacher (James Quayle) gave us some work      9
2  to do for homework for 11-28-00. Chapters 3 and 4      19
3  from our text* are to be read for a hard quiz.         28
   |  1  |  2  |  3  |  4  |  5  |  6  |  7  |  8  |  9  |  10
```

NEW KEYS

B. AMPERSAND (sign for *and*) is the shift of 7. Space before and after the ampersand. Type each line 2 times.

Use the J finger.

B. THE & KEY

```
4  juj ju7j j7j j7&j j&&j j&&j Max & Dee & Sue & Ken
5  Brown & Sons shipped goods to Crum & Lee Company.
6  Johnson & Loo brought a case against May & Green.
7  Ball & Trump vs. Vens & See is being decided now.
```

C. PERCENT is the shift of 5. Do not space between the number and the percent sign. Type each line 2 times.

Use the F finger.

C. THE % KEY

```
8  ft5f ft5%f f5%f f5%f f%%f f%%f 5% 55% 555% 5,555%
9  Robert quoted rates of 8%, 9%, 10%, 11%, and 12%.
10 Pat scored 82%, Jan 89%, and Ken 90% on the test.
11 Only 55% of the students passed 75% of the exams.
```

D. Quotation is the shift of the apostrophe. Do not space between the quotation marks and the text they enclose. Type each line 2 times.

Use the Sem finger.

D. THE " KEY

12 ;'; ";" ;"; ";" "That's a super job," said Mabel.
13 The theme of the meeting is "Improving Your Job."
14 John said, "Those were good." Sharon said, "Yes."
15 Allison said, "I'll take Janice and Ed to Flint."

E. At is the shift of 2. Space before and after @ except when used in an email address. Type each line 2 times.

Use the S finger.

E. THE @ KEY

16 sws sw2s s2@s s2@s s@@s s@@s Buy 15 @ $5 in June.
17 You can email us at this address: projec@edu.com.
18 Order 12 items @ $14 and another 185 items @ $16.
19 Lee said, "I'll buy 8 shares @ $6 and 5 @ $7.55."

FORMATTING

F. Read these rules about the placement of quotation marks. Then type lines 20–23 two times.

F. PLACEMENT OF QUOTATION MARKS

1. The closing quotation mark is always typed *after* a period or comma but *before* a colon or semicolon.

2. The closing quotation mark is typed *after* a question mark or exclama-

tion point if the quoted material is a question or an exclamation; otherwise, the quotation mark is typed *before* the question mark or exclamation point.

20 "Hello," I said. "My name is Hal; I am new here."
21 Zack read the article "Can She Succeed Tomorrow?"
22 James said, "I'll mail the check"; but he didn't.
23 Did Amy say, "We lost"? She said, "I don't know."

G. Type each line
2 times.

G. ALPHABET AND SYMBOL PRACTICE

24 Gaze at views of my jonquil or red phlox in back.
25 Jan quickly moved the six dozen big pink flowers.
26 Joe quietly picked six razors from the woven bag.
27 Packing jam for the dozen boxes was quite lively.

28 Mail these "Rush": #38, #45, and #67 (software).
29 No! Joe's note did not carry a rate of under 9%.
30 Lee read "The Computer Today." It's here Monday.
31 The book* cost us $48.10; 12% higher than yours.

H. Take a 1-minute
timing on the first
paragraph to establish
your base speed. Then
take four 1-minute timings
on the remaining
paragraphs. As soon as
you equal or exceed your
base speed on one
paragraph, advance to the
next, more difficult
paragraph.

H. SUSTAINED PRACTICE: NUMBERS AND SYMBOLS

32   We purchased several pieces of new computer   9
33 equipment for our new store in Boston. We were   19
34 amazed at all the extra work we could get done.   28

35   For our department, we received 5 printers,   9
36 12 computers, and 3 fax machines. We heard that   19
37 the equipment cost us several thousand dollars.   28

38   Next week 6 computers (Model ZS86), 4 old   9
39 copiers (drums are broken), and 9 shredders will   18
40 need to be replaced. Total cost will be high.   28

41   Last year $150,890 was spent on equipment   9
42 for Iowa's offices. Breaman & Sims predicted a   18
43 17% to 20% increase (*over '95); that's amazing.   28

| 1 | 2 | 3 | 4 | 5 | 6 | 7 | 8 | 9 | 10

I. Take two 2-minute
timings. Review your
speed and errors.

Goal: At least
27wpm/2'/5e

I. 2-MINUTE TIMING

44   Topaz and onyx rings were for sale at a   8
45 reasonable price last week. When Mavis saw the   17
46 rings with these stones, she quickly bought them   27
47 both for her sons. These jewels were difficult to   37
48 find, and Mavis was happy that she could purchase   47
49 the rings before someone else did.   54

| 1 | 2 | 3 | 4 | 5 | 6 | 7 | 8 | 9 | 10

Lesson 20

Review

GOAL

● Type at least 28wpm/2'/5e

A. Type 2 times.

A. WARMUP

```
1       Vin went to see Exhibits #794 and #860. He        9
2  had quickly judged these zany projects that cost      19
3  $321 (parts & labor)--a 5% markup from last year.     29
   |  1  |  2  |  3  |  4  |  5  |  6  |  7  |  8  |  9  |  10
```

SKILLBUILDING

B. Type each line 2 times.

B. PUNCTUATION PRACTICE

period
comma
semicolon
colon, hyphen
exclamation point

question mark
colon, apostrophe
dash
quotation marks
parentheses

```
4  Go to Reno. Drive to Yuma. Call Mary. Get Samuel.
5  We saw Nice, Paris, Bern, Rome, Munich, and Bonn.
6  Type the memo; read reports. Get pens; get paper.
7  Read the following pages: 1-10, 12-22, and 34-58.
8  No! Stop! Don't look! Watch out! Move over! Jump!

9  Can you wait? Why not? Can he drive? Where is it?
10 I have these reports: Susan's, Bill's, and Lou's.
11 It's the best--and cheapest! Don't lose it--ever.
12 "I can," she said, "right now." Val said, "Wait!"
13 Quint called Rome (GA), Rome (NY), and Rome (WI).
```

PRETEST ➡ PRACTICE ➡ POSTTEST

C. PRETEST: Alternate- And One-hand Words

PRETEST
Take a 1-minute timing.
Review your speed and
errors.

```
14       The chairman should handle the tax problem        9
15 downtown. If they are reversed, pressure tactics      19
16 might have changed the case as it was discussed.      28
   |  1  |  2  |  3  |  4  |  5  |  6  |  7  |  8  |  9  |  10
```

PRACTICE
Speed Emphasis:
If you made 2 or fewer errors on the Pretest, type each *individual* line 2 times.
Accuracy Emphasis:
If you made 3 or fewer errors, type each *group* of lines (as though it were a paragraph) 2 times.

D. PRACTICE: Alternate-hand Words

17	the	with	girl	right	blame	handle	antique	chairman
18	for	wish	town	their	panel	formal	problem	downtown
19	pan	busy	they	flair	signs	thrown	signals	problems

E. PRACTICE: One-hand Words

20	lip	fact	yolk	poplin	yummy	affect	reverse	pumpkin
21	you	cast	kill	uphill	jumpy	grease	wagered	opinion
22	tea	cage	lump	limply	hilly	served	bravest	minimum

POSTTEST
Repeat the Pretest timing and compare performance.

F. POSTTEST: Alternate- And One-hand Words

G. Take three 12-second timings on each line. The scale below the last line shows your wpm speed for a 12-second timing.

G. 12-SECOND SPEED SPRINTS

23 Paul likes to work for the bank while in college.
24 They will make a nice profit if the work is done.
25 The group of friends went to a movie at the mall.
26 The man sent the forms after she called for them.

` ' ' ' 5 ' ' '10 ' ' '15 ' ' '20 ' ' '25 ' ' '30 ' ' '35 ' ' '40 ' ' '45 ' ' '50`

H. Take two 1-minute timings. Review your speed and errors.

H. HANDWRITTEN PARAGRAPH

27 *In your career, you will use the* 7
28 *skills you are learning in this course.* 15
29 *However, you will soon discover that you* 23
30 *must also possess human relations skills.* 31

I. MAP

Follow the GDP software directions for this exercise in improving keystroking accuracy.

J. DIAGNOSTIC PRACTICE: NUMBERS

If you are not using the GDP software, turn to page SB-5 and follow the directions for this activity.

K. Take two 2-minute timings. Review your speed and errors.

Goal: At least 28wpm/2'/5e

K. 2-MINUTE TIMING

31   Jake or Peggy Zale must quickly fix the fax 9
32 machine so that we can have access to regional 18
33 reports that we think might be sent within the 28
34 next few days. Without the fax, we will not be 37
35 able to complete all our monthly reports by the 47
36 deadline. Please let me know of any problems. 56

`| 1 | 2 | 3 | 4 | 5 | 6 | 7 | 8 | 9 | 10`

PART 2

Basic Business Documents

OBJECTIVES

KEYBOARDING

▶ Operate the keyboard by touch.

▶ Type at least 36 words per minute on a 3-minute timing with no more than 4 errors.

LANGUAGE ARTS

▶ Develop proofreading skills and correctly use proofreaders' marks.

▶ Use capitals, commas, and apostrophes correctly.

▶ Develop composing and spelling skills.

WORD PROCESSING

▶ Use the word processing commands necessary to complete the document processing activities.

DOCUMENT PROCESSING

▶ Format email, business and academic reports, block-style business letters, envelopes, memos, and tables.

TECHNICAL

▶ Answer at least 90 percent of the questions correctly on an objective test.

KEYBOARDING IN HEALTH SERVICES

Within the health services job cluster, there is an enormous range of job opportunity in the medical and health care industry. Hundreds of different occupations exist in health care practice, including business-oriented positions. In fact, career opportunities within this cluster are among the fastest growing in the national marketplace. The current job outlook is quite positive as the growth in managed care has significantly increased opportunities for doctors and other health professionals, particularly in the area of preventative care. Additionally, the aging population requires more highly skilled medical workers.

Opportunities in Health Careers

Consider health care jobs, medical careers, health care management, and medical management. Various job possibilities exist in these areas, and work as a medical transcriber, clinical technician, nurse, medical analyst, surgical technician or surgeon, physical therapist, orderly, pharmacist, or medical researcher can most likely be easily found. Interestingly, keyboarding skill is important for all of these positions.

Unit 5
Email and Word Processing

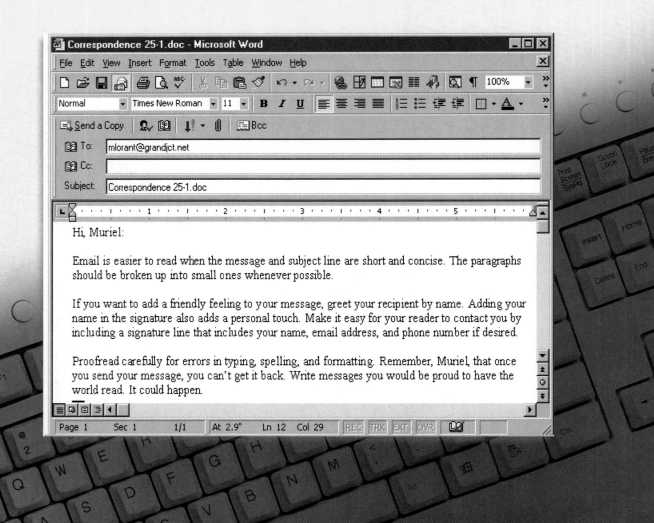

Hi, Muriel:

Email is easier to read when the message and subject line are short and concise. The paragraphs should be broken up into small ones whenever possible.

If you want to add a friendly feeling to your message, greet your recipient by name. Adding your name in the signature also adds a personal touch. Make it easy for your reader to contact you by including a signature line that includes your name, email address, and phone number if desired.

Proofread carefully for errors in typing, spelling, and formatting. Remember, Muriel, that once you send your message, you can't get it back. Write messages you would be proud to have the world read. It could happen.

Orientation to Word Processing: A

GOALS
- Improve speed and accuracy
- Refine language arts skills in punctuation and grammar
- Practice basic word processing commands

A. Type 2 times.

A. WARMUP

```
1        Juan Valdez will lead 10 managers during this sales      10
2   period; his expert input has always been valuable. Will      21
3   Quentin earn 8% commission ($534) after order #K76 arrives?   32
    |  1  |  2  |  3  |  4  |  5  |  6  |  7  |  8  |  9  |  10  |  11  |  12
```

SKILLBUILDING

B. PROGRESSIVE PRACTICE: NUMBERS

If you are not using the GDP software, turn to page SB-11 and follow the directions for this activity.

C. PACED PRACTICE

If you are not using the GDP software, turn to page SB-14 and follow the directions for this activity.

LANGUAGE ARTS

D. Study the rules at the right.

D. COMMAS AND SENTENCES

Note: The callout signals in the left margin indicate which language arts rule has been applied.

RULE ▶
, direct address

Use commas before and after a name used in direct address.
> Thank you, John, for responding to my email so quickly.
> Ladies and gentlemen, the program has been canceled.

RULE ▶
fragment

Avoid sentence fragments.
> *Not:* She had always wanted to be a financial manager. But had not had the needed education.
> *But:* She had always wanted to be a financial manager but had not had the needed education.

Note: A fragment is a part of a sentence that is incorrectly punctuated as a complete sentence. In the first sentence above, "but had not had the needed education" is not a complete sentence because it does not contain a subject.

Avoid run-on sentences.

Not: Mohamed is a competent worker he has even passed the MOUS exam.

Not: Mohamed is a competent worker, he has even passed the MOUS exam.

But: Mohamed is a competent worker; he has even passed the MOUS exam.

Or: Mohamed is a competent worker. He has even passed the MOUS exam.

Note: A run-on sentence is two independent clauses that run together without any punctuation between them or with only a comma between them.

Edit the paragraph to insert any needed punctuation and to correct any errors in grammar.

4   You must be certain, Sean that every email message is
5 concise. And also complete. In addition, Sean, use a clear
6 subject line the subject line describes briefly the principal
7 content of the email message. You should use a direct style of
8 writing, use short lines and paragraphs. The recipient of your
9 email message will be more likely to read and respond to a
10 short message. Than a long one. Your reader will be grateful
11 for any writing techniques. That save time. Another thing you
12 should do Sean is to include an appropriate closing, your
13 reader should know immediately who wrote the message.

FORMATTING

Go To
Word Processing Manual

E. WORD PROCESSING

Study Lesson 21 in your word processing manual. Complete all of the shaded steps while at your computer.

Keyboarding
CONNECTION   Defining the Email Address

With most email software, a header at the top of each email message contains the sender's address. What is the meaning of the strange configuration of an email address?

An email address contains three parts: anyname@email.com. First is the email user's name (before the @ sign). Next is the name of the host computer the person uses (before the period). The third part is the zone, or domain, for the type of organization or institution to which the host belongs (e.g., *edu* = education; *gov* = government; *com* = company).

Be careful to include each part of an email address and punctuate the address completely and correctly. Even a small error will prevent your message from reaching the recipient.

YOUR TURN Have you ever sent an email that did not reach its recipient because of an address error? What type of error did you make?

Orientation to Word Processing: B

GOALS
- Practice hyphenation
- Type at least 28wpm/3'/5e
- Practice basic word processing commands

A. Type 2 times.

A. WARMUP

```
1        Zenobia bought 987 reams of 16# bond paper from V & J    11
2  Co. @ $5/ream. Part of this week's order is usable. About    23
3  24 percent is excellent quality; the rest cannot be used.    34
   | 1 | 2 | 3 | 4 | 5 | 6 | 7 | 8 | 9 | 10 | 11 | 12
```

SKILLBUILDING

B. Type each line 2 times.

B. HYPHEN PRACTICE

Hyphens are used:
1. To show that a word is divided (lines 4 and 8).
2. To make a dash by typing two hyphens with no space before or after (lines 5 and 8).
3. To join words in a compound (lines 6, 7, and 9).

```
4  Can Larry possibly go with us next week to the golf tourna-
5  ment? I am positive that he--like you--would enjoy the game
6  and realize that it is a first-class sporting event. If you
7  think he can go, I will get first-class reservations on the
8  next plane. Larry--just like Tom and I--always likes every-
9  thing to be first-class and first-rate. Money is no object.
```

Note: In your word processing program, when you type text followed by two hyphens (--) followed by more text and then a space, an em dash (—) will automatically be inserted.

C. PROGRESSIVE PRACTICE: ALPHABET

If you are not using the GDP software, turn to page SB-7 and follow the directions for this activity.

D. Take two 3-minute timings. Review your speed and errors.

Goal: At least 28wpm/3'/5e

D. 3-MINUTE TIMING

```
10      Once you learn to use a variety of software programs,    11
11  you will feel confident and comfortable when you are using   23
12  a computer. All you have to do is take the first step and    35
13  decide to strive for excellence.                             42
14      Initially, you might have several questions as you       52
15  gaze up at a screen that is filled with icons. If you try    64
16  learning to use just one or two commands each day, you will  76
17  discover that using software is exciting.                    84
    | 1 | 2 | 3 | 4 | 5 | 6 | 7 | 8 | 9 | 10 | 11 | 12
```

FORMATTING

Go To
Word Processing Manual

E. WORD PROCESSING

Study Lesson 22 in your word processing manual. Complete all of the shaded steps while at your computer.

STRATEGIES FOR *Career Success*

Preparing to Conduct a Meeting

Do you want to conduct a successful meeting? Meetings tend to fail because they last too long and attendees do not stay focused. First, determine the meeting's purpose (e.g., to make a decision or obtain/provide information).

Decide who needs to attend the meeting. Include those who can significantly contribute, as well as decision-makers. Prepare an agenda, that is, a list of items to be discussed. Distribute it to attendees a few days before the meeting.

Choose where you will conduct the meeting and schedule the room. Determine if you will be teleconferencing, videoconferencing, or needing audio-visual equipment. If appropriate, arrange for refreshments. Check the room temperature, acoustics, and lighting. Attention to these details will increase your chances for a successful outcome.

YOUR TURN Think about a meeting you attended that was a failure. What could the meeting leader have done to better prepare for the meeting?

Orientation to Word Processing: C

GOALS

- Improve speed and accuracy
- Refine language arts skills in composing
- Practice basic word processing commands

A. Type 2 times.

A. WARMUP

```
1        We expect the following sizes to be mailed promptly      11
2   on January 8: 5, 7, and 9. Send your payment quickly so       22
3   that the items will be sure to arrive before 2:35* (*p.m.)!    34
    |  1  |  2  |  3  |  4  |  5  |  6  |  7  |  8  |  9  | 10  | 11  | 12
```

SKILLBUILDING

B. Take a 1-minute timing on the first paragraph to establish your base speed. Then take four 1-minute timings on the remaining paragraphs. As soon as you equal or exceed your base speed on one paragraph, advance to the next, more difficult paragraph.

B. SUSTAINED PRACTICE: CAPITALS

```
4        The insurance industry will undergo major changes due    11
5   to the many natural disasters the United States has seen in    23
6   the last few years in places like California and Florida.      34

7        The major earthquakes in San Francisco, Northridge,       11
8   and Loma Prieta cost thousands of dollars. Faults like         22
9   the San Andreas are being watched carefully for activity.      33

10       Some tropical storms are spawned in the West Indies       11
11  and move from the Caribbean Sea into the Atlantic Ocean.       22
12  They could affect Georgia, Florida, Alabama, and Texas.        33

13       Some U.S. cities have VHF-FM radio weather stations.      11
14  NASA and NOAA are agencies that launch weather satellites      23
15  to predict the locations, times, and severity of storms.       34
```

C. DIAGNOSTIC PRACTICE: ALPHABET

If you are not using the GDP software, turn to page SB-2 and follow the directions for this activity.

LANGUAGE ARTS

D. Answer each question with a complete sentence.

D. COMPOSING: SENTENCES

16 What word processing software do you prefer?
17 What is your favorite search engine on the Internet?
18 What Web browser do you like to use when you access the Internet?
19 What class are you taking now that is effectively preparing you for the workplace?
20 If you could work in any foreign country, which one would you choose?
21 What documents do you type most frequently as a student?

FORMATTING

Go To

Word Processing Manual

E. WORD PROCESSING

Study Lesson 23 in your word processing manual. Complete all of the shaded steps while at your computer.

Physicians and other health care professionals use keyboarding skills on a frequent basis.

Orientation to Word Processing: D

GOALS
- Type at least 29wpm/3'/5e
- Practice basic word processing commands

A. Type 2 times.

A. WARMUP

1 The experts quickly realized that repairs could cost 11
2 "$985 million" and might exceed 60% of their budget. Will 23
3 Valdez & Co. begin work before 12 or just wait until 4:30? 35

| 1 | 2 | 3 | 4 | 5 | 6 | 7 | 8 | 9 | 10 | 11 | 12

SKILLBUILDING

B. Take three 12-second timings on each line. The scale below the last line shows your wpm speed for a 12-second timing.

B. 12-SECOND SPEED SPRINTS

4 Mary will be able to go home when she can run fast and far.
5 Sam can come to the store if he is able to stop for a soda.
6 Suzy knows that she must send the mail out by noon or else.
7 Only a few good desks will be made by the end of this week.

I I I I 5 I I I I 10 I I I I 15 I I I I 20 I I I I 25 I I I I 30 I I I I 35 I I I I 40 I I I I 45 I I I I 50 I I I I 55 I I I I 60

PRETEST → PRACTICE → POSTTEST

C. PRETEST: Common Letter Combinations

PRETEST
Take a 1-minute timing. Review your speed and errors.

8 He tried to explain the delay in a logical way. The 11
9 man finally agreed to insure the package and demanded to 22
10 know why the postal worker did not record the total amount. 34

| 1 | 2 | 3 | 4 | 5 | 6 | 7 | 8 | 9 | 10 | 11 | 12

D. PRACTICE: Word Beginnings

PRACTICE
Speed Emphasis:
If you made 2 or fewer errors on the Pretest, type each *individual* line 2 times.
Accuracy Emphasis:
If you made 3 or more errors, type each *group* of lines (as though it were a paragraph) 2 times.

11 re reuse react relay reply return reason record results red
12 in inset inept incur index indeed intend inning insured ink
13 de dents dealt death delay detest devote derive depicts den

E. PRACTICE: Word Endings

14 ly lowly dimly apply daily barely unruly deeply finally sly
15 ed cured tamed tried moved amused tasted billed creamed fed
16 al canal total equal local postal plural rental logical pal

POSTTEST
Repeat the Pretest timing and compare performance.

F. POSTTEST: Common Letter Combinations

G. Take two 3-minute timings. Review your speed and errors.

Goal: At least 29wpm/3′/5e

G. 3-MINUTE TIMING

```
17      If you ever feel tired when you are typing, you should   11
18   take a rest. Question what you are doing that is causing     22
19   your muscles to be fatigued. You will realize that you       33
20   can change the fundamental source of your anxiety.           43
21      Take a deep breath, and enjoy the relaxing feeling as     54
22   you exhale slowly. Check your posture to be sure that        65
23   you are sitting up straight with your back against your      76
24   chair. Stretch your neck and back for total relaxation.      87
     | 1  | 2  | 3  | 4  | 5  | 6  | 7  | 8  | 9  | 10 | 11 | 12
```

FORMATTING

Go To

Word Processing Manual

H. WORD PROCESSING

Study Lesson 24 in your word processing manual. Complete all of the shaded steps while at your computer.

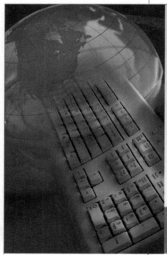

Keyboarding CONNECTION

Business Email Style Guide

Watch those email p's and q's! Even though email is relatively informal, you need to be succinct and clear. Greet your reader with a formal "Dear..." or an informal "Hi...", etc. Put the most important part of your message first. Watch the length of your paragraphs; four to five lines per paragraph won't put off your reader.

Use asterisks, caps, dashes, etc., for emphasis. Avoid unfamiliar abbreviations, slang, or jargon. Not everyone who receives your business email may know a particular catchword or phrase. Proofread your email. Be concerned about grammar, punctuation, and word choice. Use your email's spell checker.

End your business email politely. Expressions of appreciation (e.g., Thanks) or goodwill (e.g., Best wishes) let your reader know you are finishing your message.

YOUR TURN In Lesson 25 you will learn how to format and compare email messages. Create an email message to send to a coworker, colleague, or friend. Review the email for adherence to the guidelines listed above.

Email Basics

GOALS
- Improve speed and accuracy
- Refine language arts skills in proofreading
- Format and compose a basic email message

A. Type 2 times.

A. WARMUP

```
1        Exactly 610 employees have quit smoking! About 2/3      10
2 of them just quit recently. They realized why they can't      21
3 continue to smoke inside the buildings and decided to stop.   33
   | 1  | 2  | 3  | 4  | 5  | 6  | 7  | 8  | 9  | 10 | 11 | 12
```

SKILLBUILDING

B. Tab 1 time between columns. Type 2 times.

B. TECHNIQUE PRACTICE: TAB KEY

```
4 A. Uyeki    B. Vorton    C. Wetzel   D. Xenios    E. Young
5 F. Zeller   G. Ambrose   H. Brown    I. Carter    J. Denney
6 K. Elmer    L. Fraser    M. Greene   N. Hawkins   O. Irvin
7 P. Jarvis   Q. Krueger   R. Larkin   S. Majors    T. Norris
8 U. Vassar   V. Hagelin   W. Wesley   X. Bernet    Y. Robins
```

C. PROGRESSIVE PRACTICE: ALPHABET

If you are not using the GDP software, turn to page SB-7 and follow the directions for this activity.

D. MAP

Follow the GDP software directions for this exercise in improving keystroking accuracy.

LANGUAGE ARTS

E. Study the proofreading techniques at the right.

E. PROOFREADING YOUR DOCUMENTS

Proofreading and correcting errors are essential parts of document processing. To become an expert proofreader:
1. Use the spelling feature of your word processing software to check for spelling errors; then read the copy aloud to see if it makes sense.
2. Proofread for all kinds of errors, especially repeated, missing, or transposed words; grammar and punctuation; and numbers and names.
3. Check for formatting errors such as line spacing, tabs, margins, and use of bold.

F. Compare these lines with lines 4–7 in the 12-second speed sprints on page 57. Edit the lines to correct any errors.

F. PROOFREADING

9 Mary will be able to go when she can run fast and far.
10 Sam can come to the store if she is able to stop for soda.
11 Suzy know that she must send the mail out by noon or else.
12 Only a few good disks will be made by the end of this week.

FORMATTING

G. BASIC PARTS OF AN EMAIL MESSAGE

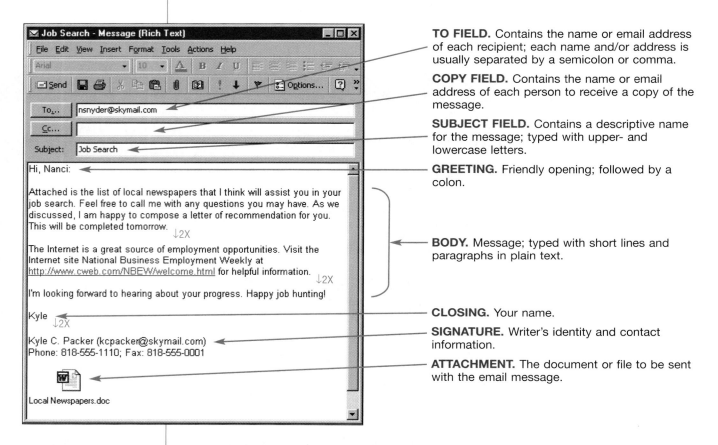

TO FIELD. Contains the name or email address of each recipient; each name and/or address is usually separated by a semicolon or comma.

COPY FIELD. Contains the name or email address of each person to receive a copy of the message.

SUBJECT FIELD. Contains a descriptive name for the message; typed with upper- and lowercase letters.

GREETING. Friendly opening; followed by a colon.

BODY. Message; typed with short lines and paragraphs in plain text.

CLOSING. Your name.

SIGNATURE. Writer's identity and contact information.

ATTACHMENT. The document or file to be sent with the email message.

H. FORMATTING AND COMPOSING AN EMAIL MESSAGE

1. Use the address book feature or type the email address of each recipient in the *To, Cc,* or *Bcc* boxes. A semicolon or comma is usually automatically inserted to separate several names.
2. If you use the reply feature, include the original message if it helps the reader remember the topic(s) more easily.
3. Use a descriptive, concise subject line with upper- and lowercase letters.

    Example: Items for Meeting Agenda

4. Use the attachment feature if you need to attach a file or document.
5. Use a friendly greeting. Follow the greeting with a colon. Use the recipient's first name or a courtesy title and last name for a more business-like greeting.

    Example: Hi, Jim: or Dear Jim:
    Example: Jim: or Mr. Andrews:

6. Use short lines (about 60 characters) with plain text, or let the lines word wrap if your email program supports word wrap.

7. Keep paragraphs short and type them with normal capitalization and punctuation in plain text. Typing in all caps is considered shouting.

8. Type paragraphs single-spaced and blocked at the left with 1 blank line between them.

9. A closing is optional. Type your name in the closing, and leave 1 blank line above and below the closing.

   Example: Sandy Hill or Sandy

10. Use a signature line so the recipient clearly knows your identity and contact information.

    Example:

    Sandra R. Hill (srhill@email.com)

    Phone: 661-555-1223

    Fax: 661-555-1205

11. Revise and proofread your message carefully before sending it. You can't get it back!

Go To

Word Processing Manual

I. WORD PROCESSING: EMAIL A DOCUMENT

Study Lesson 25 in your word processing manual. Complete all of the shaded steps while at your computer. Then format the jobs that follow.

DOCUMENT PROCESSING

Correspondence 25-1

Email Message

1. In the *To* box, send the email message to yourself.
2. Type the subject line: `Effective Email`
3. Type the greeting, using your first name and then type the body as shown below.
4. Type your closing and first name.
5. Proofread your email message when you finish for typing, spelling, and formatting errors.

Hi, First Name: ↓2X

Email is easier to read when the message and subject line are short and concise. The paragraphs should be broken up into small ones whenever possible. ↓2X

If you want to add a friendly feeling to your message, greet your recipient by name. Adding your name in the signature also adds a personal touch. Make it easy for your reader to contact you by including a signature line that includes your name, email address, and phone number if desired. ↓2X

Proofread carefully for errors in typing, spelling, and formatting. Remember, First Name, that once you send your message, you can't get it back. Write messages you would be proud to have the world read. It could happen.

Correspondence 25-2

Email Message

1. In the *To* box, send the email message to yourself, your teacher, or a friend.
2. Type the subject line: `Effective Email Format`
3. Type an appropriate greeting.
4. Compose a short, appropriate message.
5. Type a closing and signature line to identify yourself.
6. Proofread your email message when you finish for typing, spelling, and formatting errors.

Unit 6

Reports

**AN ANALYSIS OF CORPORATE
SICK-LEAVE POLICIES**

Recent Trends in the Business World

Linda C. Motonaga

April 5, 20--

Corporate sick-leave policies must be studied carefully in order to maximize employee productivity and minimize excessive absenteeism. The reasons for absences and the responsiveness of employers to the needs of the employees must be examined in order to determine some practical alternatives to current policies.

REASONS FOR ABSENCE

There are many reasons employees are absent from work. Illness and personal emergency are common reasons for absenteeism. However, recent surveys have shown that about 28% of reported sick time isn't due to illness. This percentage is on the rise. Recent studies have also shown that absences due to personal needs and stress are increasing. Also, many workers believe that they are "entitled" to a day off now and then. Perhaps it is time for employers to revamp their sick-leave policies and make these policies more responsive to the needs of the employees.

RESPONSIVENESS OF EMPLOYERS

If employees are finding it necessary to take sick days when they are not ill, it makes sense to conclude that possibly employers are either not aware of why absenteeism exists or have chosen not to respond to their employees' needs. One thing is certain—ignoring the problem will not make it go away.

POSSIBLE SOLUTIONS

Flexible scheduling is one creative way in which employers can respond to the needs of employees. If workers are given the opportunity for a flexible working schedule, stress levels should go down, and personal needs can be handled during the time they are off. Another solution might be to give employees a fixed number of days off each year for reasons other than illness. This gives workers a legitimate reason for a planned absence and gives employers some advance notice so that absences do not hurt productivity.

ENDING PROCRASTINATION

Judy Baca

Everyone at one time or another has put off some task, goal, or important plan at work for any number of reasons. Perhaps you think time is too short or the task isn't really that important. Either way, procrastination can lead to a stalled life and career.

EVALUATE YOUR SITUATION

Joyce Winfrey of Time Management Incorporated has some very good advice that will help you begin to move forward. She says that you should ask yourself two very basic questions about why you are procrastinating:

1. Am I procrastinating because the task at hand is not really what I want?

2. Is there a valid reason for my procrastination?

After you have asked yourself these questions, Ms. Winfrey suggests that you do the following:

Look deep within yourself. If you are looking for excuses, then the process of asking these questions will be a waste of your time. However, if you answer these questions honestly, you might find answers that surprise you and that will help clarify your situation.

She also recommends several techniques that can help you get back on task and put an end to procrastination.

PRACTICE NEW TECHNIQUES

Identifying and understanding the techniques that follow is the first step. Once you know what to do, you can begin to practice these steps daily.

2

Take Baby Steps. Don't make any task bigger than it really is by looking at the whole thing at once. Break it down into baby steps that are manageable.

Don't Strive for Perfectionism. If you are waiting for the perfect solution or the perfect opportunity, you will be immobilized. Accept the fact that no one and nothing is perfect. Then accept your mistakes and move on.

Enjoy the Task. Enjoy the task at hand and find something in it that is positive and rewarding. Confront your fears with a plan of action.

Remind yourself of all these techniques daily. Post them by your telephone, by your desk, or in your car. You will find that your personal life and career will gain momentum, and success will soon be yours.

One-Page Business Reports

GOALS
- Type at least 30wpm/3'/5e
- Format one-page business reports

A. Type 2 times.

A. WARMUP

```
1        Mr. G. Yoneji ordered scanners* (*800 dots per inch)     11
2   in vibrant 24-bit color! He quickly realized that exactly    23
3   31% of the work could be scanned in order to save money.     34
    |  1  |  2  |  3  |  4  |  5  |  6  |  7  |  8  |  9  |  10 |  11 |  12
```

SKILLBUILDING

B. Take three 12-second timings on each line. The scale below the last line shows your wpm speed for a 12-second timing.

B. 12-SECOND SPEED SPRINTS

```
4   She went to the same store to find some good books to read.
5   Frank will coach eight games for his team when he has time.
6   Laura sent all the mail out today when she left to go home.
7   These pages can be very hard to read when the light is dim.
    I I I I 5 I I I I 10 I I I I 15 I I I I 20 I I I I 25 I I I I 30 I I I I 35 I I I I 40 I I I I 45 I I I I 50 I I I I 55 I I I I 60
```

C. DIAGNOSTIC PRACTICE: ALPHABET

If you are not using the GDP software, turn to page SB-2 and follow the directions for this activity.

D. Take two 3-minute timings. Review your speed and errors.

Goal: At least 30wpm/3'/5e

D. 3-MINUTE TIMING

```
8        Holding a good business meeting may require a great     10
9   deal of planning and preparing. The meeting must be well     21
10  organized and an agenda must be prepared. It may be hard     32
11  to judge how long a meeting may take or how many people     43
12  will discuss the raised issues.                              49
13       A good moderator is needed to execute the agenda. He    60
14  or she must know when to move on to the next topic and       71
15  when to continue debate on a topic. After a productive       82
16  meeting, a leader should be very pleased.                    90
    |  1  |  2  |  3  |  4  |  5  |  6  |  7  |  8  |  9  |  10 |  11 |  12
```

Reference Manual

Refer to page R-8C of the Reference Manual for an illustration of a report in academic style.

E. BASIC PARTS OF A REPORT

There are two basic styles of reports: business and academic. The illustration that follows is for a business report.

↓6X

14 pt **AN ANALYSIS OF CORPORATE**
SICK-LEAVE POLICIES ↓2X

12 pt ↓ **Recent Trends in the Business World**
↓2X

Linda C. Motonaga ↓2X

April 5, 20-- ↓2X

Corporate sick-leave policies must be studied carefully in order to maximize employee productivity and minimize excessive absenteeism. The reasons for absences and the responsiveness of employers to the needs of the employees must be examined. ↓2X

REASONS FOR ABSENCE ↓2X

There are many reasons employees are absent from work. Illness and personal needs are among the top reasons. ↓2X

Illness. Illness is often caused by all the stress in the workplace. Employees may have to care for parents and children. ↓2X

Personal Needs. Recent studies have also shown that absences due to personal needs are increasing. Two important questions must be addressed:

1. Should employers rethink their sick-leave policies?
2. How can a new sick-leave policy be more responsive to the needs of the employee? ↓2X

POSSIBLE SOLUTIONS ↓2X

If employees are finding it necessary to take more sick days, it makes sense to conclude that possibly employers are either not aware of why absenteeism exists or have chosen not to respond to their employees' needs. Flexible scheduling is one creative way to respond to the needs of employees. A four-day workweek might be a practical solution that would solve problems for both sides. Another solution might be to give employees a fixed number of days off each year for reasons other than illness. This gives workers a legitimate reason for a planned absence.

TITLE. Subject of the report; centered; typed about 2 inches from the top of the page in bold and all caps, with a 14-point font size; 2-line titles single-spaced.

SUBTITLE. Secondary or explanatory title; centered; typed 1 blank line below the title, in bold, with upper- and lowercase letters.

BYLINE. Name of the writer; centered; typed 1 blank line below the previous line, in bold.

DATE. Date of the report; centered; typed 1 blank line below the previous line, in bold.

BODY. Text of the report; typed 1 blank line below the previous line, single-spaced at the left margin, with 1 blank line between paragraphs.

SIDE HEADING. Major subdivision of the report; typed 1 blank line below the previous line at the left margin, in bold and all caps.

PARAGRAPH HEADING. Minor subdivision of the report; typed 1 blank line below the previous line at the left margin, in bold, with upper- and lowercase letters; followed by a period (also in bold).

LIST. Numbered or bulleted items in a report; typed at the left margin, single-spaced, with 1 blank line above and below the list.

F. BUSINESS REPORTS

To format a business report:
*   Single-space business reports.
*   Press ENTER 6 times to begin the first line of the report approximately 2 inches from the top of the page.
*   Change the font size to 14 points, and type the title in all caps, centered, in bold, and single-spaced. Single-space a 2-line title.
*   Press ENTER 2 times and change the font size to 12 points.

*   If the report includes a subtitle, byline, or date, type each item centered and in bold upper- and lowercase letters.
*   Press ENTER 2 times after each line in the heading block.
*   Insert 1 blank line after all paragraphs.
*   Do not number the first page.

G. REPORTS WITH SIDE HEADINGS

To format side headings:
- Insert 1 blank line before and after side headings.
- Type side headings at the left margin, in bold, and in all caps.

Go To

Word Processing Manual

H. WORD PROCESSING: ALIGNMENT AND FONT SIZE

Study Lesson 26 in your word processing manual. Complete all of the shaded steps while at your computer. Then format the jobs that follow.

DOCUMENT PROCESSING

Report 26-1

Business Report

Type this report in standard format for a business report with side headings.

Type the actual current year in place of 20--.

In your word processor, when you type text followed by two hyphens (--), followed by more text and then a space, an em dash (—) will automatically be inserted.

↓6X

14 pt. **AN ANALYSIS OF CORPORATE SICK-LEAVE POLICIES** ↓1X ↓2X

12 pt. ↓ **Recent Trends in the Business World** ↓2X

Linda C. Motonaga ↓2X

April 5, 20-- ↓2X

Corporate sick-leave policies must be studied carefully in order to maximize employee productivity and minimize excessive absenteeism. The reasons for absences and the responsiveness of employers to the needs of the employees must be examined in order to determine some practical alternatives to current policies. ↓2X

REASONS FOR ABSENCE ↓2X

There are many reasons employees are absent from work. Illness and personal emergency are common reasons for absenteeism. However, recent surveys have shown that about 28 percent of reported sick time isn't due to illness. This percentage is on the rise. Recent studies have also shown that absences due to personal needs and stress are increasing. Also, many workers believe that they are "entitled" to a day off now and then. Perhaps it is time for employers to revamp their sick-leave policies and make these policies more responsive to the needs of the employees. ↓2X

RESPONSIVENESS OF EMPLOYERS ↓2X

If employees are finding it necessary to take sick days when they are not ill, it makes sense to conclude that possibly employers either are not aware of why absenteeism exists or have chosen not to respond to their employees' needs. One thing is certain—ignoring the problem will not make it go away. ↓2X

(Continued on next page)

POSSIBLE SOLUTIONS ↓2X

Flexible scheduling is one creative way in which employers can respond to the needs of employees. If workers are given the opportunity for a flexible working schedule, stress levels should go down and personal needs can be handled during the time they are off. Another solution might be to give employees a fixed number of days off each year for reasons other than illness. This gives workers a legitimate reason for a planned absence and gives employers some advance notice so that absences do not hurt productivity.

Report 26-2 ▶

Business Report

Open the file for Report 26-1 and make the following changes:

1. Delete the subtitle, and change the date to October 23.
2. Change the byline to Amy Ho, and change the second side heading to EMPLOYER RESPONSIVENESS.
3. Delete the last two sentences in the last paragraph at the end of the report. Add these sentences to the end of the last paragraph:

Employees will not feel the need to invent elaborate reasons for their absences. They will feel like they are in control of their schedule outside of work so that they can determine the best way to schedule their time off. When they return to work, they will feel relaxed and ready to work.

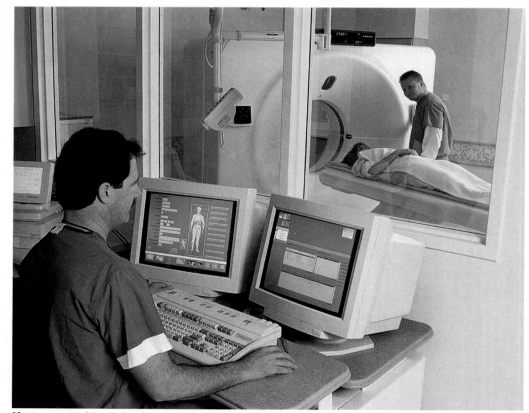

Many opportunities in health careers rely on keyboarding input to perform diagnostic tests.

Multipage Rough-Draft Business Reports

GOALS

- Improve speed and accuracy
- Refine language arts skills in punctuation
- Identify and apply basic proofreaders' marks
- Format multipage rough-draft business reports

A. Type 2 times.

A. WARMUP

```
1       On 7/23 the office will convert to a new phone system.   11
2  A freeze on all toll calls is requested for July. Account    23
3  #GK95 has a balance of $68 and isn't expected to "pay up."    35
   |  1  |  2  |  3  |  4  |  5  |  6  |  7  |  8  |  9  |  10  |  11  |  12
```

SKILLBUILDING

B. Take a 1-minute timing on the first paragraph to establish your base speed. Then take four 1-minute timings on the remaining paragraphs. As soon as you equal or exceed your base speed on one paragraph, advance to the next, more difficult paragraph.

B. SUSTAINED PRACTICE: PUNCTUATION

```
4       Anyone who is successful in business realizes that the   11
5  needs of the customer must always come first. A satisfied     23
6  consumer is one who will come back to buy again and again.    35

7       Consumers must learn to lodge a complaint in a manner    11
8  that is fair, effective, and efficient. Don't waste time      22
9  talking to the wrong person. Go to the person in charge.      33

10      State your case clearly; be prepared with facts and      11
11 figures to back up any claim--warranties, receipts, bills,    23
12 and checks are all very effective. Don't be intimidated.      34

13      If the company agrees to work with you, you're on the    11
14 right track. Be specific: "I'll expect a check Tuesday,"      22
15 or "I'll expect a replacement in the mail by Saturday."       33
```

C. PROGRESSIVE PRACTICE: ALPHABET

If you are not using the GDP software, turn to page SB-7 and follow the directions for this activity.

D. Study the rules at the right.

D. COMMAS AND SENTENCES

Note: The callout signals in the margin indicate which language arts rule has been applied.

RULE ▶
, independent

The underline calls attention to a point in the sentence where a comma might mistakenly be inserted.

Use a comma between independent clauses joined by a coordinate conjunction (unless both clauses are short.)

Ellen left her job with IBM, and she and her sister went to Paris.
But: Ellen left her job with IB**M** and went to Paris with her sister.
But: John drov**e** and I navigated.

Note: An independent clause is one that can stand alone as a complete sentence. The most common coordinate conjunctions are *and*, *but*, *or*, and *nor*.

RULE ▶
, introductory

Use a comma after an introductory expression (unless it is a short prepositional phrase).

Before we can make a decision, we must have all the facts.
But: In 20**00** our nation elected a new president.

Note: An introductory expression is a group of words that come before the subject and verb of the independent clause. Common prepositions are *to, in, on, of, at, by, for,* and *with.*

Edit the paragraph to insert any needed punctuation and to correct any errors in grammar.

```
16      All business reports should be single-spaced and all lines
17  in the heading block should be typed in bold. If the report
18  title has two lines it should be single-spaced and typed in
19  all caps. Below the title you might want to include a subtitle.
20  Type the subtitle one blank line below the title and use both
21  upper- and lowercase letters. Most reports include a byline and
22  include a date. After the date begin typing the report body.
23  If the report has a side heading type it in all caps in bold.
```

FORMATTING

E. BASIC PROOFREADERS' MARKS

Proofreaders' marks are used to indicate changes or corrections to be made in a document (called a *rough draft*) that is being revised for final copy. Study the chart to learn what each proofreaders' mark means.

Proofreaders' Marks		Draft	Final Copy
⌒	Omit space	data base	database
∨ or ∧	Insert	if he̯s going	if he's not going,
≡	Capitalize	Maple street	Maple Street
⟡	Delete	a final draft	a draft
# ∧	Insert space	allready to	all ready to

(Continued on next page)

Proofreaders' Marks	Draft	Final Copy
⊥ꞵ *when* Change word	and ⊥f *when* you	and when you
/ Use lowercase letter	our ₽resident	our president
⌣ Transpose	they all see	they see all
SS Single-space	SS ⎡ first line ⎣ second line	first line second line

F. MULTIPAGE BUSINESS REPORTS

To format a multipage report:

- Use the same side margins for all pages of the report.
- Leave an approximate 2-inch top margin on page 1.
- Leave an approximate 1-inch bottom margin on all pages.

Note: When you reach the end of a page, your word processing software will automatically insert a soft page break. If a soft page break separates a side heading from the paragraph that follows it, insert a hard page break just above the side heading to keep them together.

- Leave a 1-inch top margin on continuing pages.
- Do not number the first page. However, number all continuing pages at the top right.

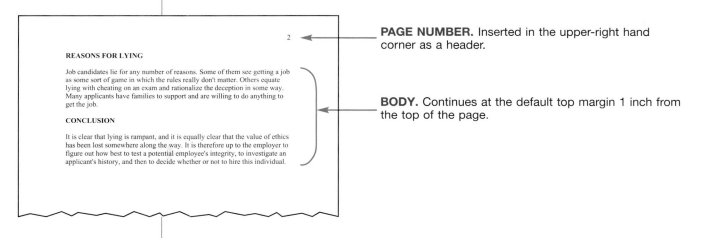

PAGE NUMBER. Inserted in the upper-right hand corner as a header.

BODY. Continues at the default top margin 1 inch from the top of the page.

G. BUSINESS REPORTS WITH PARAGRAPH HEADINGS

To format paragraph headings:

- Type paragraph headings at the left margin in bold and in upper-and lower-case letters.
- Follow the paragraph heading by a bold period and 1 space.

Go To

Word Processing Manual

H. WORD PROCESSING: PAGE NUMBERING AND PAGE BREAK

Study Lesson 27 in your word processing manual. Complete all of the shaded steps while at your computer. Then format the jobs that follow.

Note: The report lines are shown with extra spacing to accommodate the proof-readers' marks. Use standard business report spacing when you type the report.
1. Type the report using standard business report format.
2. Type any paragraph headings at the left margin in bold and in upper- and lower-

case letters, followed by a bold period and 1 space.
3. Insert a page number at the top right, and suppress the page number on the first page.
4. Spell-check, preview, and proofread your document for spelling and formatting errors before printing it.

THE INTEGRITY AND ~~MORALS~~ ETHICS
OF JOB APPLICANTS

~~By~~ Elizabeth Reddix

April 5, 20--

INTRODUCTION

¶ Some studies have found that about ~~9 out of 10~~ 90 percent of job applicants have lied in someway in order to land a job. The lies range from small exaggerations to blatant and completely fraudulent information such as lying about a degree or perhaps about ones history of earnings. After tallying the results of a survey to a large group of College students, one psychologist found that ~~approximately~~ about 90 out of 100 of them were willing to lie ~~in order~~ to land a job.

¶ One way to help screen out the deceptions from the truth is to identify the most common deceptions. Another way is to try to understand why applicants feel the need to lie. After these factors are identified and understood, it will be easier to make some judgment calls on the ethical integrity of an applicant.

COMMON DECEPTIONS

¶ There are ~~a great~~ many areas in which job applicants are willing to make false statements in order to get a job. These could include verbal statements or written ones.

School activities. Many ~~job~~ applicants are willing to exaggerate or totally falsify ~~totally~~ their participation in school activities. In order to prove leadership ability, an applicant might be willing to say that he was president of a nonexistent club or perhaps organized some type of fictional fund-raising activity.

(Continued on next page)

The ¶ symbol indicates the start of a new paragraph.

, introductory

, introductory

, introductory

, introductory

Former Job titles. Another area rampant with deception is the list of previous Job Titles. In order to make a ~~previous~~ *former* job sound more impressive, a job contender might add a word or two to the title or perhaps rename the title al together.

, introductory

Computer Experience. Since we live in an age of computer technology, most employers are looking for people with computer experience. Usually, the more *computer* experience a ~~person~~ *candidate* has, the better off he will be in terms of competing with others for the same position.

REASONS FOR LYING

¶ Job Candidates lie for any number of reasons. Some of them see getting a job as some sort of game in which the rules don't really matter. Others equate lying with cheating on an exam and rationalize the deception in some way. Many applicants have families to support and are willing to do any thing to get the job.

Conclusion

, independent

¶ It is clear that lying is ~~quite~~ rampant, and it is equally clear that the value of ethics has been lost some where along the way. It is therefore up to the employer to figure out how best to test a potential employee's integrity, to investigate an applicant's history, and then to decide whether *or not* to hire this individual.

Report 27-4 ▶

Multipage Business Report

Open the file for Report 27-3 and make the following changes:
1. Change the byline to Diane Jackson.
2. Change the date to July 7.
3. Change the last side heading to COMMON REASONS FOR LYING.

4. Add this sentence to the end of the last paragraph:

   The importance of ethics in a future employee should never be underestimated.

Business Reports With Lists

GOALS

- Type at least 31wpm/3'/5e
- Format business reports with bulleted and numbered lists

A. Type 2 times.

A. WARMUP

```
1      At 8:30, Horowitz & Co. will fax Order #V546 to us for    11
2  immediate processing! Just how many additional orders they    23
3  will request isn't known. About 7% of the orders are here.    35
   | 1  | 2  | 3  | 4  | 5  | 6  | 7  | 8  | 9  | 10 | 11 | 12
```

SKILLBUILDING

B. Take three 12-second timings on each line. The scale below the last line shows your wpm speed for a 12-second timing.

B. 12-SECOND SPEED SPRINTS

```
4  Mary will not be able to meet them at the game later today.
5  The class is not going to be able to meet if they are gone.
6  They could not open that old door when the chair fell over.
7  This very nice piece of paper may be used to print the job.
   5     10     15     20     25     30     35     40     45     50     55     60
```

PRETEST → PRACTICE → POSTTEST

PRETEST
Take a 1-minute timing. Review your speed and errors.

C. PRETEST: Close Reaches

```
8       The growth in the volume of company assets is due to    11
9  the astute group of twenty older employees. Their answers    23
10 were undoubtedly the reason for the increase in net worth.    35
   | 1  | 2  | 3  | 4  | 5  | 6  | 7  | 8  | 9  | 10 | 11 | 12
```

PRACTICE
Speed Emphasis:
If you made 2 or fewer errors on the Pretest, type each *individual* line 2 times.

Accuracy Emphasis:
If you made 3 or more errors, type each *group* of lines (as though it were a paragraph) 2 times.

D. PRACTICE: Adjacent Keys

```
11 as ashes cases class asset astute passes chased creased ask
12 we weave tweed towed weigh wealth twenty fewest answers wet
13 rt worth alert party smart artist sorted charts turtles art
```

E. PRACTICE: Consecutive Fingers

```
14 un undue bunch stung begun united punish outrun untie funny
15 gr grand agree angry grade growth egress hungry group graph
16 ol older solid tools spool volume evolve uphold olive scold
```

POSTTEST
Repeat the Pretest timing and compare performance.

F. POSTTEST: Close Reaches

G. Take two 3-minute timings. Review your speed and errors.

Goal: At least 31wpm/3'/5e

G. 3-MINUTE TIMING

```
17        Credit cards can make shopping very convenient, and      11
18  they frequently help you record and track your spending.       22
19  However, many card companies impose high fees for using        33
20  their credit cards.                                            37
21        You must realize that it may be better to pay in cash    48
22  and not use a credit card. Examine all your options. Some      60
23  card companies do not charge yearly fees. Some may offer       71
24  you extended warranties on goods you buy with their credit     83
25  cards. Judge all the details; you may be surprised.            93
```
| 1 | 2 | 3 | 4 | 5 | 6 | 7 | 8 | 9 | 10 | 11 | 12

FORMATTING

H. BULLETED AND NUMBERED LISTS

- Numbers or bullets call attention to items in a list. If the sequence of the items is important, use numbers rather than bullets.
- Numbers and bullets appear either at the left margin or are indented to the same point as the paragraphs in the document.
- The numbers and bullets themselves are followed by an indent, and carry-over lines are indented automatically to align with the text in the previous line, not the bullet or number.

I. BUSINESS REPORTS WITH LISTS

To format a list in a business report:
- Press ENTER 2 times to insert 1 blank line above the list.
- Type the list *unformatted* (without the bullets or numbers) at the left margin.
- If all the items in the list are 1 line long, single-space the entire list.
- If any items in the list are multiline, single-space each item in the list but insert a blank line between the items for readability.
- Press ENTER 2 times to insert 1 blank line below the list.
- Select all lines of the list and apply the number or bullet feature to the selected lines of the list only.

J. WORD PROCESSING: BULLETS AND NUMBERING

Go To

Word Processing Manual

Study Lesson 28 in your word processing manual. Complete all of the shaded steps while at your computer. Then format the jobs that follow.

Report
28-5

Business Report
With Lists

Type the actual date in
place of Current Date.

1. Type the report using standard business report format.

2. Use the bullet and numbering feature to add bullets or numbers to the list after typing the list unformatted.

INCREASING YOUR ENERGY
Shannon Wahlberg
Current Date

When your energy level is running high, you are more creative, happier, and more relaxed. Some people believe that we are born with a personality that is innately either energetic, lethargic, or somewhere in between. However, we are all capable of generating more energy in our lives at home or at work.

CREATING MORE ENERGY

There are many ways in which you can generate more energy before you leave for work. These two methods are simple and can be practiced without a great deal of planning:

1. Wake up to natural light by opening your curtains before you go to bed. The light coming in signals your body to stop releasing melatonin, a hormone that tells your body to continue sleeping.
2. Play music that is lively and upbeat. This will set the tone for the day.

MAINTAINING MORE ENERGY

Once you have raised your energy level at home, you can also learn to maintain your energy level at work.

- Remain positive throughout the day.
- Avoid people who are negative and have low energy. Instead, seek out those who are cheerful and positive. They will boost your energy level.
- Avoid high-fat foods, sweets, and heavy meals during the working day.
- Accept your periods of low energy as natural rhythms, knowing that they will pass. This will help you relax.

If you practice these methods to create and maintain your energy levels, you will find that these techniques will become a natural part of your daily life. Enjoy the change and experiment with your own techniques!

Open the file for Report 28-5 and make the following changes:

1. Change the first side heading to HOW TO CREATE MORE ENERGY.
2. Change the second side heading to HOW TO MAINTAIN MORE ENERGY.

3. Change the third bulleted item to this:
   Avoid foods with caffeine, such as sodas and coffee.
4. Change the fourth bulleted item to this:
   Monitor your sleep. Sleeping too long can make you just as tired as sleeping too little.

Academic Reports

GOALS
- Improve speed and accuracy
- Refine language arts skills in proofreading
- Format academic reports

A. Type 2 times.

A. WARMUP

```
1       Will the package arrive at 9:45 or 11:29? The exact        11
2  answer to this question could mean the difference between      23
3  losing or saving their account; Joyce also realizes this.      34
   |  1  |  2  |  3  |  4  |  5  |  6  |  7  |  8  |  9  |  10  |  11  |  12
```

SKILLBUILDING

B. Type each paragraph 1 time. Change every masculine pronoun to a feminine pronoun. Change every feminine pronoun to a masculine pronoun.

B. TECHNIQUE PRACTICE: CONCENTRATION

```
4       She will finish composing the report as soon as he has
5  given her all the research. Her final draft will be turned in
6  to her boss; he will submit it to the company president.

7       His new job with her company was fascinating. When the
8  chance to join her firm came up, he jumped at it immediately.
9  I wonder if she will give him a promotion anytime soon?
```

C. PACED PRACTICE

If you are not using the GDP software, turn to page SB-14 and follow the directions for this activity.

STRATEGIES FOR Career Success

Turning Negative Messages Positive

Accentuate the positive. When communicating bad news (e.g., layoffs, product recalls, price increases, personnel problems), find the positive.

People respond better to positive rather than negative language, and they are more likely to cooperate if treated fairly and with respect. Avoid insults, accusations, criticism, or words with negative connotations (e.g., failed, delinquent, bad). Focus on what the reader can do rather than on what you won't or can't let the reader do. Instead of "You will not qualify unless..." state "You will qualify if you are...."

Assuage your audience's response by providing an explanation to support your decision and examples of how they might benefit. Analyze your audience, and decide whether to give the negative news in the beginning, middle, or end of your message. Regardless of your approach, always maintain goodwill.

YOUR TURN Review some of your written documents and observe if they have a positive tone.

D. Type these frequently misspelled words, paying special attention to any spelling problems in each word.

D. SPELLING

```
10  personnel information its procedures their committee system
11  receive employees which education services opportunity area
12  financial appropriate interest received production contract
13  important through necessary customer employee further there
14  property account approximately general control division our
```

Edit the sentences to correct any misspellings.

```
15  All company personel will receive important information.
16  Are division has some control over there financial account.
17  There comittee has received approximately three contracts.
18  The employe and the customer have an oportunity to attend.
19  We have no farther interest in the property or it's owner.
20  When it is necessary, apropriate proceedures are followed.
```

E. MORE PROOFREADERS' MARKS

1. Review the most frequently used proofreaders' marks introduced in Lesson 27.

2. Study the additional proofreaders' marks presented here.

Proofreaders' Marks	Draft	Final Copy
d͢s Double-space	d͢s ⌈first line ⌊second line	first line second line
...... Don't delete	a ~~true~~ story	a true story
◯ Spell out	the only ①	the only one
⌷ Move right	Please send	Please send
⌷ Move left	May 1	May 1
∿ Bold	Column Heading	**Column Heading**
ital Italic	ital Time magazine	*Time* magazine
u/l Underline	u/l Time magazine	<u>Time</u> magazine readers
↗ Move as shown	(readers) will see	will see
¶ New paragraph	¶ Most of the	Most of the

F. ACADEMIC REPORTS

To format an academic report:

1. Double-space academic reports.
2. After you have set the line spacing to double, press ENTER 3 times to begin the first line of the academic report about 2 inches from the top of the page.
3. Type the title in all caps, centered, in bold, and change the font size to 14 points. Double-space a 2-line title.
4. Press ENTER 1 time and change the font size to 12 points.
5. If the report includes a subtitle, byline, or date, type each item centered, in bold and upper- and lowercase letters; press ENTER 1 time after each line in the heading block.
6. Type side headings at the left margin, in bold and all caps.
7. Press TAB 1 time at the start of paragraphs and paragraph headings to indent them 0.5 inch.
8. Type paragraph headings in bold and in upper- and lowercase letters, and follow the paragraph heading with a bold period and 1 space.
9. Leave an approximate 1-inch bottom margin on all pages, and leave a 1-inch top margin on continuing pages.
10. Do not number the first page. However, number all continuing pages at the top right.

Go To

Word Processing Manual

G. WORD PROCESSING: LINE SPACING

Study Lesson 29 in your word processing manual. Complete all of the shaded steps while at your computer. Then format the jobs that follow.

DOCUMENT PROCESSING

Report 29-7

Multipage Academic Report

Reference Manual

See page R-8C and R-8D of the Reference Manual for an illustration of a multipage report in academic style.

1. Type this report in standard format for an academic report.
2. Type the 2-line title double-spaced, and use standard format for the rest of the heading block.
3. Insert a page number at the top right, and suppress the page number on the first page.
4. Spell-check, preview, and proofread your document for spelling and formatting errors before printing it.

ELECTRONIC SAFEGUARDS IN THE DIGITAL WORLD

Trends in Technology

Kevin Nguyen

July 13, 20--

More and more people are using computers and the Internet for a wide variety of reasons, both personal and professional. Most of the technology requires the use of passwords, usernames, pin numbers, and miscellaneous other important codes to access their accounts. Unfortunately at times it seems like the number of codes that necessary is increasing in geometric proportions. The problem is how to maintain accurate records of these various security codes and still preserve a secure environment, technologically speaking.

Highlighted words are spelling words from the language arts activities.

(Continued on next page)

SECURITY CODE OVERLOAD

People need ① or sometimes ② security codes just to log-on to their computers. Several more are needed to access web sites, trade stocks, and shop and bank online, just to name a few. In addition, most people need to remember codes for their home phones, work phones, cell phones, and voice mail. Banks require codes to withdraw money and use credit cards and ATMs. With so many security codes proliferating on a daily basis, its no wonder that we are often frustrated and frazzled as we move through our daily lives going about our personal and professional business. To add insult to injury, we are often being asked to change our passwords and codes on a regular basis.

MANAGING SECURITY CODES

Several things can be done to help manage this ever-growing list of security codes. Try to choose passwords that are in some way meaningful to you but that cannot be guessed at by an intruder. Use a combination of letters and numbers. An article in the magazine Technology Bytes suggests using using street addresses or names of pets that can be easily remembered but that have no logical association with anything else.

If you decide to keep a list of security codes, make sure to protect the file in an appropriate way. If you must write down your passwords, physically lock them up. You must control and manage these important and necessary security codes to protect your personal and financial information.

Report 29-8 ▶

Multipage
Academic Report

Open the file for Report 29-7 and make the following changes:

1. Change the byline to your name.
2. Add this paragraph below the last paragraph at the end of the report:

A number of Web sites are available to help you remember your passwords and usernames. However, these sites can help you do much more than simply manage your security codes. Some sites can provide instant registration at new sites with just one click. They also offer price comparisons while you shop anywhere on the Web, and they bring together the best search engines all in one place for easier searching. They can also filter email to help you eliminate cluttered email boxes full of junk.

Academic Reports With Displays

GOALS

- Type at least 32wpm/3'/5e
- Format rough-draft academic reports with indented lists and displays

A. Type 2 times.

A. WARMUP

```
1      Did Zagorsky & Sons charge $876 for the renovation?     11
2  An invoice wasn't quite right; the exact amount charged in  23
3  July can be found in an email message to zagsons@post.com.  35
   |  1  |  2  |  3  |  4  |  5  |  6  |  7  |  8  |  9  |  10  |  11  |  12
```

SKILLBUILDING

B. MAP

Follow the GDP software directions for this exercise in improving keystroking accuracy.

C. DIAGNOSTIC PRACTICE: NUMBERS

If you are not using the GDP software, turn to page SB-5 and follow the directions for this activity.

D. Take two 3-minute timings. Review your speed and errors.

Goal: At least 32wpm/3'/5e

D. 3-MINUTE TIMING

```
4      If you want to work in information processing, you     10
5  must realize that there are steps that you must take to    21
6  plan for such an exciting career. First, you must decide   32
7  whether or not you have the right personality traits.      43
8      Then you must be trained in the technical skills you   54
9  will need in such an important field. The technology is    65
10 changing each day. You must stay focused on keeping up     76
11 with these changes. Also, you must never quit wanting to   87
12 learn new skills each day you are on the job.              96
   |  1  |  2  |  3  |  4  |  5  |  6  |  7  |  8  |  9  |  10  |  11  |  12
```

E. ACADEMIC REPORTS WITH LISTS

To format a list in an academic report:
- Press ENTER 1 time to begin the list.
- Type the list *unformatted* at the left margin, double-spaced.
- Press ENTER 1 time after the last line in the list.
- Select all lines of the list and apply the number or bullet feature to the selected lines of the list only. Do not include the blank lines above and below the list in your selection.
- Increase or decrease the indent of the list as needed so that the list begins at the same point of indention as the paragraphs in the report.

F. ACADEMIC REPORTS WITH INDENTED DISPLAYS

A paragraph having 4 lines or more that are quoted or having lines that need special emphasis should be formatted so that the paragraph stands out from the rest of the report. To format academic reports with indented displays:

- Type the paragraph single-spaced and indented 0.5 inch from both the left and the right margins (instead of enclosing it in quotation marks).
- Use the indent command in your word processing software to format a displayed paragraph.

Go To

Word Processing Manual

G. WORD PROCESSING: INCREASE INDENT AND CUT, COPY, AND PASTE

Study Lesson 30 in your word processing manual. Complete all of the shaded steps while at your computer. Then format the jobs that follow.

DOCUMENT PROCESSING

Report 30-9

Multipage Academic Report With Displayed Paragraph

Reference Manual

See page R-8D of the Reference Manual for an illustration of a multipage report in academic style with a displayed paragraph.

1. Type the report using standard academic report format.
2. Type the list using standard format for lists in an academic report. Use the number feature to add numbers to the list after you have typed the list unformatted. Use the cut and paste feature to move the second numbered item.
3. Type the display using standard format for indented displays in an academic report.
4. Type paragraph headings indented 0.5 inch, in bold, and in upper-and lower-case letters, and follow the paragraph heading with a bold period and 1 space.
5. Insert a page number at the top right, and suppress the page number on the first page.

ENDING PROCRASTINATION

Judy Baca

Every one at one time or another has put of some task, goal or important plan at work for any number of reasons. perhaps you think time is too short or the task isn't really that important. Either way, procrastination can lead to a stalled life and career.

(Continued on next page)

EVALUATE YOUR SITUATION

Joyce Winfrey, of Time Management Incorporated, has some very good advice that will help you ~~to~~ begin to move forward. She says that you should ask yourself 2 very basic questions about why you are procrastinating:

1. Is there a valid reason for my procrastination?
2. Am I procrastinating because the task at hand is not really what I want?

After you have asked yourself these questions, ms. Winfrey suggests that you do the following:

Look deep within yourself. If you are looking for excuses, then the process of asking these questions will be a waste of your time. However, if you answer these questions honestly, you might find answers that surprise you and that will help clarify your situation.

She also recommends several techniques that can help you get back on task and put an end to procrastination.

PRACTICE NEW TECHNIQUES

Identifying and understanding the techniques ~~which~~ that follow is the first step. Once you know what to do, you can begin to practice these steps daily.

Take Baby Steps. Don't make any task bigger than it really is by looking at the whole thing at once. Break it down into baby steps that are manageable.

Don't Strive for Perfectionism. If you are waiting for the perfect solution or the perfect opportunity, you will be immobilized. Accept the fact that no one and nothing is perfect. Then accept your mistakes and move on.

Enjoy the Task. Enjoy the task at hand and find something in it that is positive and rewarding. Confront your fears with a plan of action.

Remind yourself of all these techniques daily. Post them by your telephone, by your desk, or in your car. You will find that your personal life and career will gain momentum, and success will soon be yours.

Report 30-10 ▶

Multipage Academic Report With List

Progress Check
Proofreading Check

Documents designated as Proofreading Checks serve as a check of your proofreading skill. Your goal is to have zero typographical errors when the GDP software first scores the document.

1. Type the report using standard academic report format for a multipage academic report with a list.

2. Make all changes as indicated by the proofreaders' marks.

MEN AND WOMEN ^IN^ THE CORPORATE WORKPLACE

Betty Goldberg

June 8, 20--

have you ever observed a little boy and a ~~young~~ _little_ girl playing together? You are likely to notice the little girl following the rules and being polite and the little boy making the rules as he goes along and _being_ focused on winning the game. These patterns of behavior that have been practiced since childhood tend to stay with us and influence our behavior in the ¢orporate Ⱳorkplace.

Competition and Cooperation

Men are more competitive (generally) and want to win at any cost. Winning in the work place could mean landing the better job, getting the raise, or putting a plan into effect. Women tend to want to problem solve through cooperation. They tend to look at modesty and politeness as virtues, while males tend to look at these traits as weaknesses. Women generally want to be accepted and liked, where as men might prefer to make their point and be aggressive in wielding power to get what they want.

BEING EFFECTIVE AT WORK

There are several ways in which Ⱳomen can be effective at work without giving up behavior that is more comfortable for them. Once these ③ methods have been (identified clearly, they can be put into practice with ease.

1. Find a forum that allows you to publicize your accomplishments. A status report on a project might be a good place to note your achievements.
2. Practice stating your goals in a public way at least once a day. This will help you to feel comfortable expressing your ideas.
3. Concentrate on the issues that are most important to you and drop the ones that arent really critical.

After you have practiced these techniques, you will find that they begin to become a habit. As you find a comfort level with these strategies, you will find that you are accomplishing more at work and feeling better about your self and your new sense of ~~power and~~ control.

Unit 7

Correspondence

LESSON 31
Business Letters

LESSON 32
Business Letters With Enclosure Notations

LESSON 33
Envelopes and Labels

LESSON 34
Memos

LESSON 35
Correspondence Review

MEMO TO: All Salaried Employees

FROM: Amy Vigil, Human Resources

DATE: November 2, 20--

SUBJECT: Health Care Benefit Plan

Effective January 1, Allied Aerospace Industries will contract with MedNet to begin a new health benefits program for all eligible salaried personnel. A brochure outlining important program information will be mailed to you soon.

An open enrollment period will be in effect during the entire month of January. If you and your family are interested in one of the MedNet health plan options, you may transfer yourself and your dependents into any appropriate plan. All applications must be received no later than midnight, January 31. You may also access your plan over the Internet at www.mednet.com if it is more convenient.

If you have any questions or need any help understanding your options, please call me at Ext. 134. I will be happy to help you select the plan that is best for you.

urs

April 3, 20--

Ms. Linda Lopez
Account Manager
The Internet Connection
7625 Fay Avenue
La Jolla, CA 92037

Dear Ms. Lopez:

Our company is interested in hosting an educational seminar this spring that will focus on meeting the growing need for information industry professionals to keep abreast of emerging new technologies and trends. We are specifically interested in information on high-speed Internet connections.

I understand that The Internet Connection specializes in these seminars and will also help businesses analyze their needs and choose an appropriate solution. I am in the process of contacting several companies similar to yours who might be interested in conducting these seminars. Please contact me by Thursday or Friday at the latest so that we can discuss this matter further.

I appreciate the fine service we have always received from you in the past, Ms. Lopez, and I look forward to hearing from you.

Sincerely,

Ruzanna Aleksanyan
Technology Specialist

urs

Trend Electronics
2206 31st Street
Minneapolis, MN 55407-1911

Mr. Charles Goldstein
Software Solutions
2981 Canwood Street
Roselle, IL 60172

Lesson 31

Business Letters

GOALS
- Improve speed and accuracy
- Refine language arts skills in capitalization
- Format a business letter in block style

A. Type 2 times.

A. WARMUP

```
1        You can save $1,698 when you buy the 20-part video     10
2   series! Just ask for Series #MX5265 in the next 7 days;     21
3   ordering early qualified you for a sizable discount of 5%.  33
    |  1  |  2  |  3  |  4  |  5  |  6  |  7  |  8  |  9  | 10  | 11  | 12
```

SKILLBUILDING

B. Take three 12-second timings on each line. The scale below the last line shows your wpm speed for a 12-second timing.

B. 12-SECOND SPEED SPRINTS

```
4   Mary will be able to go home when she can run fast and far.
5   Sam can come to the store if he is able to stop for a soda.
6   Suzy knows that she must send the mail out by noon or else.
7   Only a few good desks will be made by the end of this week.
     I I I I 5 I I I I 10 I I I I 15 I I I I 20 I I I I 25 I I I I 30 I I I I 35 I I I I 40 I I I I 45 I I I I 50 I I I I 55 I I I I 60
```

C. PROGRESSIVE PRACTICE: ALPHABET

If you are not using the GDP software, turn to page SB-7 and follow the directions for this activity.

D. PROGRESSIVE PRACTICE: NUMBERS

If you are not using the GDP software, turn to page SB-11 and follow the directions for this activity.

LANGUAGE ARTS

E. Study the rules at the right.

E. CAPITALIZATION

RULE ▶
= sentence

Capitalize the first word of a sentence.
    Please prepare a summary of your activities.

RULE ▶
= proper

Capitalize proper nouns and adjectives derived from proper nouns.
    Judy Hendrix drove to Albuquerque in her new Pontiac convertible.

Note: A proper noun is the official name of a particular person, place, or thing.

(Continued on next page)

RULE ▶
= time

Capitalize the names of the days of the week, months, holidays, and religious days (but do not capitalize the names of the seasons).

On Thursday, November 25, we will celebrate Thanksgiving, the most popular holiday in the fall.

Edit the paragraph to insert or delete capitalization.

```
 8      The american flag can be seen flying over the White
 9  House in Washington. Our Country's flag is often seen
10  flying over Government buildings on holidays like July 4,
11  independence day. Memorial Day signals the end of spring
12  and the start of Summer. Most Americans consider Labor day
13  the beginning of the fall season. In december many people
14  observe christmas and Chanukah. most government holidays are
15  scheduled to fall on either a Monday or a friday. Sometimes
16  the birthdays of Historical figures are also celebrated.
```

FORMATTING

F. BASIC PARTS OF A BUSINESS LETTER

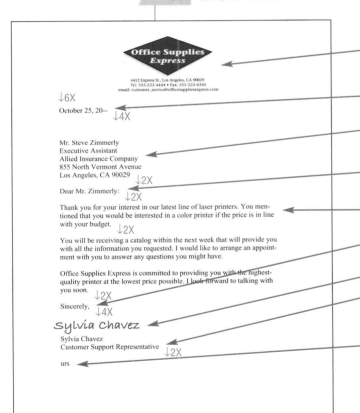

LETTERHEAD. Printed name, address, and telephone number (and/or fax number and email address) of the company.

DATE LINE. Month, day, and year of the letter; typed about 2 inches from the top of the page.

INSIDE ADDRESS. Name and address of the party to whom the letter is written; typed 4 lines below the date.

SALUTATION. Opening greeting; typed 2 lines below the inside address.

BODY. Text or message of the letter; typed 2 lines below the salutation.

COMPLIMENTARY CLOSING. Closing farewell; typed 2 lines below the body.

SIGNATURE. Handwritten signature of the writer.

WRITER'S IDENTIFICATION. Name, or title, or both of the writer; typed 4 lines below the complimentary closing.

REFERENCE INITIALS. Initials of the typist; typed 2 lines below the writer's identification.

G. BUSINESS LETTERS IN BLOCK STYLE

1. Type all lines beginning at the left margin.
2. Press ENTER 6 times to begin the first line of the letter about 2 inches from the top of the page, and then type the date.

3. After the date, press ENTER 4 times and type the inside address. Leave 1 space between the state and the ZIP Code.

(Continued on next page)

4. After the inside address, press ENTER 2 times, and type the salutation. For standard punctuation, type a colon after the salutation. Press ENTER 2 times after the salutation.
5. Single-space the body of the letter, but press ENTER 2 times between paragraphs. Do not indent paragraphs.
6. Press ENTER 2 times after the last paragraph, and type the complimentary clos-ing. For standard punctuation, type a comma after the complimentary closing.
7. Press ENTER 4 times after the complimentary closing, and type the writer's identification.
8. Press ENTER 2 times after the writer's identification, and type your reference initials in lowercase letters with no periods or spaces.

Go To

Word Processing Manual

H. WORD PROCESSING: INSERT DATE

Study Lesson 31 in your word processing manual. Complete all of the shaded steps while at your computer. Then format the jobs that follow.

DOCUMENT PROCESSING

Correspondence 31-3

Business Letter in Block Style

1. Type the letter using standard business letter format for a block-style letter.
2. Use standard punctuation: a colon after the salutation and a comma after the complimentary closing.
3. Use word wrap for the paragraphs. Press ENTER only at the end of each paragraph. Your lines may end differ-ently from those shown in the illustra-tion.
4. Type your initials for the reference ini-tials.
5. Always spell-check, preview, and proof-read your letter when you finish for typ-ing, spelling, and formatting errors.

↓6X

Current Date ↓4X

≡ proper

Ms. Linda Lopez
Account Manager
The Internet Connection
7625 Fay Avenue
La Jolla, CA 92037 ↓2X

≡ proper

Dear Ms. Lopez: ↓2X

≡ sentence ≡ time

Our company is interested in hosting an educational seminar this spring that will focus on meeting the growing need for information industry professionals to keep abreast of emerging new technologies and trends. We are specifically

≡ proper

interested in information on high-speed Internet connections. ↓2X

I understand that The Internet Connection specializes in these seminars and will also help businesses analyze their needs and choose an appropriate solution. I am in the process of contacting several companies similar to yours

≡ sentence

≡ time

who might be interested in conducting these seminars. Please contact me by Thursday or Friday at the latest so that we can discuss this further. ↓2X

(Continued on next page)

I appreciate the fine service we have always received from you in the past, Ms. Lopez, and look forward to hearing from you. ↓2X

Sincerely, ↓4X

Ruzanna Aleksanyan
Technology Specialist ↓2X

urs

Open the file for Correspondence 31-3 and make the following changes:
1. Change the date to May 8.

2. Change the writer's identification to: Gail Madison and her job title to Technology Engineer.

Note: The | symbol indicates the end of a line. The ¶ symbol indicates the start of a new paragraph.
1. Type the letter using standard business letter format for a block-style letter.

2. Spell-check, preview, and proofread your letter when you finish for typing, spelling, and formatting errors.

May 25, 20-- | Ms. Linda Lopez | Account Manager | The Internet Connection | 7625 Fay Avenue | La Jolla, CA 92037 | Dear Ms. Lopez:

¶ Thank you so much for hosting the educational seminar last Tuesday that focused on the topic of high-speed Internet connections. Our company and our employees are now well prepared to make a decision about the best type of Internet connection for their particular needs.

¶ Because this seminar was so successful, I have been authorized to contract with The Internet Connection for a continuing series of seminars on any topics related to emerging new technologies and trends as they apply to the needs of our company and our employees. I will call you on Monday so that we can arrange for a meeting to finalize some contractual issues.

¶ Once again, thank you for a very successful and productive seminar!

Sincerely, | Ruzanna Aleksanyan | Technology Specialist |

urs

Business Letters With Enclosure Notations

GOALS

- Type at least 33wpm/3'/5e
- Format a business letter with an enclosure notation

A. Type 2 times.

A. WARMUP

```
1        Sales by two travel agencies (Quill, Virgil, & Johnson    11
2   and Keef & Zane) exceeded all prior amounts. Total sales       22
3   for that year were as follows: $1,540,830 and $976,233.        33
    |  1  |  2  |  3  |  4  |  5  |  6  |  7  |  8  |  9  | 10 | 11 | 12
```

SKILLBUILDING

B. Type each line 2 times.

Technique Tip: Press the BACKSPACE key with the sem finger without looking at your keyboard.

B. TECHNIQUE PRACTICE: BACKSPACE KEY

1. Type each letter (or group of letters) as shown.
2. When you reach the backspace sign (←), backspace 1 time to delete the last keystroke.
3. Type the next group of letters. The result will be a new word. For example, if you see "hi← at," you would type "hi," backspace 1 time, and then type "at," resulting in the new word "hat" instead of the original word "hit."

```
4   p←cat c←tab b←peg p←but p←tie t←pop m←pat f←sit m←but t←cub
5   t←mop b←fib r←fat w←fin p←tin c←top p←ban f←can y←get m←let
6   di←ye be←ag ge←um ri←ob mu←ad la←id fi←an bi←ad to←ip ro←id
7   pa←it ti←on fi←un ra←un pi←an ge←ot ba←it fa←it ma←it sa←it
8   bin←t any←t new←t was←r sea←t tap←n fan←t lap←d for←x fin←x
9   pin←t ham←d sod←n rid←p rap←n tap←n dip←n sin←p lip←d put←n
```

PPP

PRETEST → PRACTICE → POSTTEST

C. PRETEST: Discrimination Practice

PRETEST
Take a 1-minute timing. Review your speed and errors.

PRACTICE
Speed Emphasis:
  If you made 2 or fewer errors on the Pretest, type each *individual* line 2 times.
Accuracy Emphasis:
  If you made 3 or more errors, type each *group* of lines (as though it were a paragraph) 2 times.

```
10       Steven saw the younger, unruly boy take flight as he      11
11  threw the coin at the jury. The brave judge stopped the        22
12  fight. He called out to the youth, who recoiled in fear.       33
    |  1  |  2  |  3  |  4  |  5  |  6  |  7  |  8  |  9  | 10 | 11 | 12
```

D. PRACTICE: Left Hand

```
13  vbv verb bevy vibes bevel brave above verbal bovine behaves
14  wew west weep threw wedge weave fewer weight sewing dewdrop
15  fgf gulf gift fight fudge fugue flags flight golfer feigned
```

E. PRACTICE: Right Hand

```
16  uyu buys your usury unity youth buoys unruly untidy younger
17  oio coin lion oiled foils foist prior recoil iodine rejoice
18  jhj jury huge enjoy three judge habit adjust slight jasmine
```

POSTTEST
Repeat the Pretest timing and compare performance.

F. POSTTEST: Discrimination Practice

G. Take two 3-minute timings. Review your speed and errors.

Goal: At least 33wpm/3′/5e

G. 3-MINUTE TIMING

```
19        Be zealous in your efforts when you write business     10
20  letters. Your business communications must convey clearly     22
21  the information and ideas you want the receivers to read.     34
22  Your letters should be formatted neatly in acceptable         45
23  business letter formats.                                      50
24        Before sending letters, quickly read them just to       60
25  make sure that your letters explain your position very        71
26  clearly. Proofread your letters for correct formatting,       82
27  grammar, and spelling. Use your communication skills to       93
28  enhance your professional image.                              99
      |  1  |  2  |  3  |  4  |  5  |  6  |  7  |  8  |  9  |  10  |  11  |  12
```

FORMATTING

H. ENCLOSURE NOTATION

- To indicate that an item is enclosed with a letter, type the word *Enclosure* on the line below the reference initials.

- If more than one item is being enclosed, type the word *Enclosures*.

Example: urs

Enclosure

DOCUMENT PROCESSING

Correspondence 32-6

Business Letter in Block Style with Enclosure Notation

Reference Manual

See page R-3B and R-3C of the Reference Manual for an illustration of a business letter with an enclosure notation.

The | symbol indicates the end of a line.

1. Type the letter using standard business letter format.

2. Spell-check, preview, and proofread your document for spelling and formatting errors before printing it.

Current Date | Ms. Denise Bradford | Worldwide Travel, Inc. | 1180 Alvarado, SE | Albuquerque, NM 87108 | Dear Ms. Bradford:
¶ Our company has decided to hold its regional sales meeting in Scottsdale, Arizona, during the second week of January. I need information on a suitable conference site.

(Continued on next page)

¶ We will need a meeting room with the following items: 30 computer workstations with an Internet connection, copy stands, mouse pads, and adjustable chairs; an LCD projector with a large screen; and a microphone and podium. The hotel should have a fax machine and on-site secretarial services. We might also need a messenger service.

¶ A final decision on the conference site must be made within the next two weeks. Please send me any information you have available for a suitable location in Scottsdale immediately. I have enclosed a list of conference attendees and their room preferences. Thank you for your help.

Sincerely yours, | Bill McKay | Marketing Manager | urs | Enclosure

---

Correspondence 32-7 ▶

Business Letter in Block Style with Enclosure Notation

1. Open the file for Correspondence 32-6.
2. Change the inside address to 1032 San Pedro, SE.
3. Change the first sentence as follows:
   Our company has decided to hold its annual national sales meeting during the first week of February in Scottsdale, Arizona.
4. In the first sentence of the second paragraph, change the information after the colon as follows:
   30 computer workstations, an LCD projector with a large screen, and a microphone and podium.

Correspondence 32-8 ▶

Business Letter in Block Style with Enclosure Notations

Current Date | Mr. Bill McKay | Marketing Manager | Viatech Communications | 9835 Osuna Road, NE | Albuquerque, NM 87111 | Dear Mr. McKay:

¶ Thank you for your inquiry regarding a conference site in Scottsdale, Arizona, for 35 people during the second week of January.

¶ I have enclosed the following brochures with detailed information on some properties in Scottsdale that provide exclusive service to businesses like yours: Camelback Resorts, Shadow Pines Suites, and Desert Inn Resorts and Golf Club. All these properties have meeting rooms that will accommodate your needs and also offer additional services you might be interested in using.

(Continued on next page)

¶ Please call me when you have reached a decision. I will be happy to make the final arrangements as well as issue any airline tickets you may need. Yours truly, | Ms. Denise Bradford | Travel Agent | urs | Enclosures

When keyboarding input is not convenient, palm-held organizers can help you schedule meetings and plan conferences.

Lesson 33

Envelopes and Labels

GOALS

- Improve speed and accuracy
- Refine language arts skills in composing sentences
- Format envelopes and labels and fold letters

A. Type 2 times.

A. WARMUP

```
1        Does Quentin know if 1/2 of the January order will be    11
2   ready? At 5:30 about 46% of the orders still hadn't been      22
3   mailed! Mr. Gray expects a very sizable loss this month.      33
    |  1  |  2  |  3  |  4  |  5  |  6  |  7  |  8  |  9  |  10 |  11 |  12
```

SKILLBUILDING

B. Take three 12-second timings on each line. The scale below the last line shows your wpm speed for a 12-second timing.

B. 12-SECOND SPEED SPRINTS

```
4   Today we want to find out if our work will be done on time.
5   Doug will be able to drive to the store if the car is here.
6   Jan will sign this paper when she has done all of the work.
7   This time she will be sure to spend two days with her sons.
    I I I I 5 I I I I 10 I I I I 15 I I I I 20 I I I I 25 I I I I 30 I I I I 35 I I I I 40 I I I I 45 I I I I 50 I I I I 55 I I I I 60
```

C. PACED PRACTICE

If you are not using the GDP software, turn to page SB-14 and follow the directions for this activity.

LANGUAGE ARTS

D. Answer each question with a complete sentence.

D. COMPOSING: SENTENCES

8   What are your best traits that you will bring to your job when you graduate?

9   What are the best traits that you will want to see in your new boss?

10   Would you rather work for a large or a small company?

11   How much money do you expect to earn on your first job?

12   Would you like your first job to be in a small town or a large city?

13   What do you see yourself doing in ten years?

14   What types of benefits do you think you would like to have?

E. ENVELOPES

The envelope feature of your word processor simplifies your task of addressing a No. 10 envelope. The standard size for business envelopes is 9½ by 4⅛ inches. A business envelope should include the following:

• **Return Address.** If necessary, type the sender's name and address in upper- and lowercase style in the upper left corner. Business stationery usually has a printed return address. Use the default placement and the default font of your word processor for the return address.

• **Mailing Address.** Type the recipient's name and address in upper- and lowercase style (or in all-capital letters without any punctuation) toward the center of the envelope. Use the default placement and the default font of your word processor for the mailing address.

Note: Postal scanners read addresses more efficiently if they are typed in all-capital letters without any punctuation.

Trend Electronics
2206 31st Street
Minneapolis, MN 55407-1911

Mr. Charles R. Harrison
Reliable Software, Inc.
5613 Brunswick Avenue
Minneapolis, MN 55406

Standard large envelope, No. 10, is $9^{1}/_{2} \times 4^{1}/_{8}$ inches.

F. LABELS

The label feature of your word processor simplifies the task of preparing various labels. You can use different label settings to print a full sheet of labels or to print a single label. You may want to use a mailing label as an alternative to printing an envelope.

When preparing labels, test the label settings by printing your labels on a blank page before you print them on the actual label form.

G. FOLDING LETTERS

To fold a letter for a No. 10 envelope:
1. Place the letter face up, and fold up the bottom third of the page.
2. Fold the top third of the page down to about 0.5 inch from the bottom edge of the page.

3. Insert the last crease into the envelope first with the flap facing up.

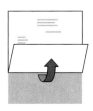 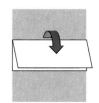 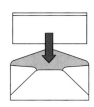

Go To

Word Processing Manual

H. WORD PROCESSING: ENVELOPES AND LABELS

Study Lesson 33 in your word processing manual. Complete all of the shaded steps while at your computer. Then format the jobs that follow.

DOCUMENT PROCESSING

Correspondence 33-9

Envelope

1. Prepare an envelope with the following mailing address:
   Mr. Charles Goldstein | Software Solutions | 2981 Canwood Street | Roselle, IL 60172.

2. Insert the following return address:
   Shannon Stone | Data Systems, Inc. | 2201 South Street | Racine, WI 53404.
3. Add the envelope to a blank document.

Correspondence 33-10

Envelope

1. Open the file for Correspondence 31-3 and prepare an envelope for the letter.

2. Do not insert a return address.
3. Add the envelope to the letter.

Correspondence 33-11

Mailing Labels

1. Select an address label product about 1 inch deep, large enough to fit a 4-line address. Label choices will vary; however, Avery standard, 5160, Address is a good choice for laser and ink jet printers. Avery standard, 4010, Address is a good choice for dot matrix printers.

2. Prepare address labels for the names and addresses that follow.
3. Type the addresses in order from left to right as you see them displayed below in the first group.
4. Move to the second group of labels and type them again from left to right.

Purchasing Dept.
Abbott Laboratories
Abbott Park
Chicago, IL 60064

Frank Zimmerly
Cartridges, Etc.
1220 Charleston Rd.
Oso Park, CA 90621

John Sanchez
Adobe Systems
1585 Charleston Rd.
Los Angeles, CA 90029

Mike Rashid
Internet Services
901 Thompson Place
Sunnyvale, CA 94088

Jennifer Reagan
Aetna Life
151 Farmington Avenue
Hartford, CT 06156

Bob Patterson
Affiliated Publishing
135 Morrisey Blvd.
Boston, MA 02107

1. Select an address label product about 1 inch deep, large enough to fit a 4-line address. Label choices will vary; however, Avery standard, 5160, Address is a good choice for laser and ink jet printers. Avery standard, 4010, Address is a good choice for dot matrix printers.

2. Prepare a full page of the same label with the following address:
   Shipping and Receiving | E-Office Outlet | 1122 N. Highland St. | Arlington, VA 22201

1. Open the file for Correspondence 32-6 and prepare an envelope for the letter.
2. Insert the following return address:
   Bill McKay | The Office Connection | 6909 Oso Circle | Buena Park, CA 90621.

3. Add the envelope to the letter.

Keyboarding skills are important for the preparation of shipping labels in distribution centers.

Lesson 34

Memos

GOALS
- Type at least 34wpm/3′/5e
- Format interoffice memos

A. Type 2 times.

A. WARMUP

```
1        This series* (*6 films, 28 minutes) by J Zeller goes    11
2  beyond the "basics" of computers. Viewers keep requesting     23
3  an extension on the dates; this includes 3/2, 5/5, and 8/9.   35
   |  1  |  2  |  3  |  4  |  5  |  6  |  7  |  8  |  9  |  10  |  11  |  12
```

SKILLBUILDING

B. DIAGNOSTIC PRACTICE: ALPHABET

If you are not using the GDP software, turn to page SB-2 and follow the directions for this activity.

C. PROGRESSIVE PRACTICE: ALPHABET

If you are not using the GDP software, turn to page SB-7 and follow the directions for this activity.

D. Take two 3-minute timings. Review your speed and errors.

Goal: At least 34wpm/3′/5e

D. 3-MINUTE TIMING

```
4         Companies providing services over the Internet use a    11
5  process called data mining. They look for patterns in the      23
6  quantities of information they gather from visitors to         34
7  company Web sites.                                             38
8         Data mining tracks purchasing habits of customers and   49
9  targets advertisements to them based on their current and      61
10 past buying patterns. Data mining is also used to forecast     73
11 consumer behavior and to look for trends. First, customers     85
12 complete surveys. The results are gathered and stored in a     97
13 database to be analyzed.                                      102
   |  1  |  2  |  3  |  4  |  5  |  6  |  7  |  8  |  9  |  10  |  11  |  12
```

E. INTEROFFICE MEMOS

An interoffice memo is usually sent from one person to another in the same organization. To format a memo on plain paper or on letterhead stationery:

1. Press ENTER 6 times for a top margin of about 2 inches.
2. Type the headings (including the colons) in all caps and bold: MEMO TO:, FROM:, DATE:, and SUBJECT:.
3. Press TAB 1 time after typing the colon to reach the point where the heading entries begin.
4. Insert 1 blank line between the heading lines and between the heading lines and the memo body.
5. Insert 1 blank line between paragraphs. Most memos are typed with blocked paragraphs (no indentions).
6. Insert 1 blank line between the body and the reference initials.

DOCUMENT PROCESSING

Correspondence 34-14

Interoffice Memo

Reference Manual

Refer to page R-7C of the Reference Manual for an illustration of a memo.

1. Type the memo using standard memo format.
2. Spell-check, preview, and proofread your document for spelling and formatting errors before printing it.

↓6X

MEMO TO: All Salaried Employees ↓2X

FROM: Amy Vigil, Human Resources ↓2X

DATE: November 2, 20-- ↓2X

SUBJECT: Health Care Benefit Plan ↓2X

Effective January 1, Allied Aerospace Industries will contract with MedNet to begin a new health benefits program for all eligible salaried personnel. A brochure outlining important program information will be mailed to you soon. ↓2X

An open enrollment period will be in effect during the entire month of January. If you and your family are interested in one of the MedNet health plan options, you may transfer yourself and your dependents into any appropriate plan. All applications must be received no later than midnight, January 31. You may also access your plan over the Internet at www.mednet.com if it is more convenient. ↓2X

If you have any questions or need any help understanding your options, please call me at Ext. 134. I will be happy to help you select the plan that is best for you. ↓2X

urs

Correspondence
34-15 ▶

Interoffice Memo

MEMO TO: Amy Vigil, Human Resources | **FROM:** Dan Westphal | **DATE:** November 23, 20-- | **SUBJECT:** MedNet Benefit Plan

¶ Thank you for the brochure detailing the various options for employees under the MedNet plan. I would like clarification on some of the services included in the plan.

¶ Because both my wife and I are employees of Allied Aerospace Industries, do we have the choice of enrolling separately under different options? In our present plan, I know that this is possible.

¶ We have two dependents. Is it possible to enroll both dependents under different options of the plan, or do they both fall under either one option or the other? I know that in the past you have asked for evidence of dependent status and dates of birth.

¶ If you need any further information, please let me know. Thank you very much for your help.

urs

Correspondence
34-16 ▶

Interoffice Memo

Open the file for Correspondence 34-14 and make the following changes:
1. Send the memo to All Allied Aerospace Industries Employees.
2. Change the date to December 2.
3. Change the subject line to Health Care Open Enrollment Period.

Keyboarding CONNECTION

Searching the Web

Research projects on the World Wide Web! Access up-to-date information from all over the world.

To conduct a search, specify keywords and certain relationships among them. Many search engines use arithmetic operators to symbolize Boolean relationships. A plus sign (+) is used instead of AND, a minus sign (−) instead of NOT, and no sign instead of OR.

Simple document searches match a single keyword (e.g., *cherry*). Advanced searches might match any of the words (e.g., *cherry pie*); all words (e.g., *+cherry +pie*); a phrase (e.g., *"cherry pie"*); or some words and not others (e.g., *+cherry +pie −tree*). There is no space between the plus or minus sign and its word.

YOUR TURN From your Web browser, open a Web search engine site. Type various searches in the entry box of the search engine and start the search. Compare the results.

Correspondence Review

GOALS

- Improve speed and accuracy
- Refine language arts skills in proofreading
- Format various types of correspondence with an attachment notation
- Practice italicizing and underlining

A. Type 2 times.

A. WARMUP

1   Item #876 won't be ordered until 9/10. Did you gather   11
2 all requests and input them exactly as they appeared? Zack   23
3 will never be satisfied until he contacts jack@orders.com.   35

| 1 | 2 | 3 | 4 | 5 | 6 | 7 | 8 | 9 | 10 | 11 | 12

SKILLBUILDING

B. MAP

Follow the GDP software directions for this exercise in improving keystroking accuracy.

C. Take a 1-minute timing on the first paragraph to establish your base speed. Then take four 1-minute timings on the remaining paragraphs. As soon as you equal or exceed your base speed on one paragraph, advance to the next, more difficult paragraph.

C. SUSTAINED PRACTICE: ALTERNATE-HAND WORDS

4   When eight of them began a formal discussion on some   11
5 of the major issues, the need for a chair was very evident.   23
6 A chair would be sure to handle the usual work with ease.   35

7   The eight people in that group decided that the work   11
8 would be done only if they selected one person to be chair   23
9 of their group. They began to debate all the major issues.   35

10   One issue that needed to be settled right up front was   11
11 the question of how to handle proxy votes. It seemed for a   23
12 short time that a fight over this very issue would result.   35

13   The group worked diligently in attempting to solve the   11
14 issues that were being discussed. All of the concerns that   23
15 were brought to the group were reviewed in depth by them.   34

| 1 | 2 | 3 | 4 | 5 | 6 | 7 | 8 | 9 | 10 | 11 | 12

D. Edit this paragraph to correct any typing or formatting errors.

D. PROOFREADING

16   It doesnt matter how fast you can type or how well
17 you now a software program if you produce documents taht
18 are filled with errors. You must learn to watch for errors
19 in spelling punctuation, and formatting. Look carefully
20 between words and sentences.Make sure that after a period
21 at the end of a sentence, you see one space. Sometime it
22 helps to look at the characters in the sentence justabove
23 the one you are proofreading to ensure accuracy.

FORMATTING

E. ATTACHMENT NOTATION

The word *Attachment* (rather than *Enclo-sure*) is typed below the reference initials when material is physically attached (stapled or clipped) to a memo.

Example: urs
           Attachment

Word Processing Manual

F. WORD PROCESSING: ITALIC AND UNDERLINE

Study Lesson 35 in your word processing manual. Complete all of the shaded steps while at your computer. Then format the jobs that follow.

DOCUMENT PROCESSING

Correspondence 35-17

Interoffice Memo with Attachment Notation

MEMO TO: All Executive Assistants | **FROM:** Barbara Azar, Staff Development Coordinator | **DATE:** Current Date | **SUBJECT:** Standardizing Document Formats

¶ Last month we received our final shipment of new laser printers. The installation of these printers in your offices marked the final phase out of all ink jet printers.

¶ Because all of us can now use a variety of standardized fonts in our correspondence, please note the following change: <u>From now on, all book and journal titles should be set in Arial Narrow</u>. This new formatting change will help us to standardize our correspondence.

¶ The latest edition of the book *Quick Reference for the Automated* Office has two pages of helpful information on laser printers, which I have attached. Please read these pages carefully, and we will discuss them at our next meeting.

urs | Attachment

MEMO TO: Barbara Azar, Staff Development Coordinator | **FROM:** Sharon Hearshen, Executive Assistant | **DATE:** Current Date | **SUBJECT:** Laser Printer Workshop

¶ The new laser printers we received are <u>fabulous</u>! I know that you worked very hard to get these printers for us, and all of us in the Sales and Marketing Department certainly appreciate your effort.

¶ Several of us would be very interested in seeing the printers demonstrated. Would it be possible to have a workshop with some hands-on training? We are particularly interested in learning about font selection, paper selection, and envelopes and labels.

¶ I have attached an article on laser printers from the latest issue of *Office Technology*. It is very informative, and you might like to include it as a part of the workshop. Please let me know if I can help you in any way.

urs | Attachment

**Progress Check
Proofreading Check**

Documents designated as Proofreading Checks serve as a check of your proofreading skill. Your goal is to have zero typographical errors when the GDP software first scores the document.

1. Type the following business letter, and then prepare an envelope for the document.
2. Do not include a return address.
3. Add the envelope to the letter.

October 1, 20-- | Mrs. Elizabeth McGraw | 844 Lincoln Boulevard | Santa Monica, CA 90403 | Dear Mrs. McGraw:

¶ The League of Women Voters is looking for volunteers to work at the various polling places during the upcoming elections. If you think you will be able to volunteer your time, please fill out and mail the following enclosed items: registration form, schedule of availability, and insurance waiver form.

¶ After I receive these items, I will contact you to confirm a location, time, and date.

¶ Your efforts are greatly appreciated, Mrs. McGraw. Concerned citizens like you make it possible for the public to have a convenient place to vote. Thank you for your interest in this very worthy cause!

Sincerely yours, | Ashley Abbott | Public Relations Volunteer | urs | Enclosures

Unit 8

Tables

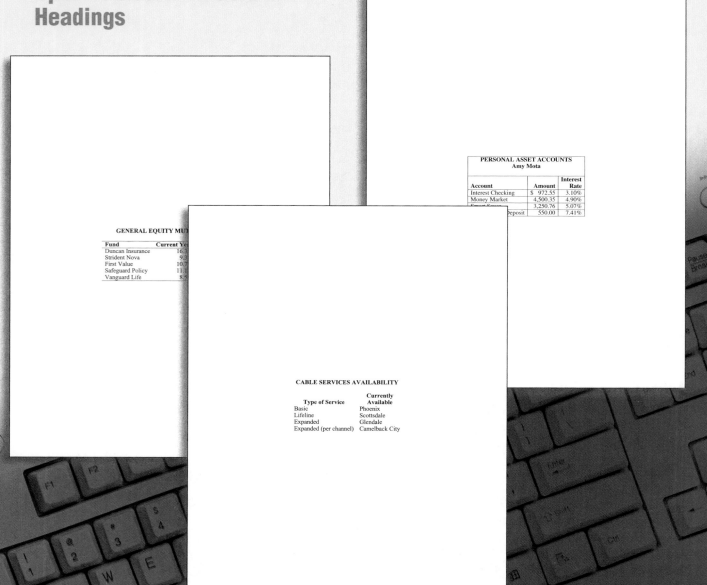

PERSONAL ASSET ACCOUNTS
Amy Mota

Account	Amount	Interest Rate
Interest Checking	$ 972.55	3.10%
Money Market	4,500.35	4.90%
Smart Saver	3,250.76	5.07%
Deposit	550.00	7.41%

GENERAL EQUITY MUT...

Fund	Current Ye...
Duncan Insurance	16.3
Strident Nova	9.3
First Value	10.7
Safeguard Policy	11.1
Vanguard Life	8.5

CABLE SERVICES AVAILABILITY

Type of Service	Currently Available
Basic	Phoenix
Lifeline	Scottsdale
Expanded	Glendale
Expanded (per channel)	Camelback City

Boxed Tables

GOALS

- Type at least 35wpm/3'/4e
- Format boxed tables

A. Type 2 times.

A. WARMUP

```
1        A plain paper reader/printer must be ordered; it must    11
2    accept jackets and have a footprint of 15 x 27* (*inches).    23
3    Please ask Gary to request Model Z-340 whenever he arrives.   35
     |  1  |  2  |  3  |  4  |  5  |  6  |  7  |  8  |  9  |  10  |  11  |  12
```

SKILLBUILDING

B. Take three 12-second timings on each line. The scale below the last line shows your wpm speed for a 12-second timing.

B. 12-SECOND SPEED SPRINTS

```
4    The book that is on top of the big desk will be given away.
5    Bill must pay for the tape or he will have to give it back.
6    They left the meeting after all of the group had gone away.
7    The third person to finish all of the work today may leave.
     I I I I 5 I I I I 10 I I I I 15 I I I I 20 I I I I 25 I I I I 30 I I I I 35 I I I I 40 I I I I 45 I I I I 50 I I I I 55 I I I I 60
```

C. DIAGNOSTIC PRACTICE: ALPHABET

If you are not using the GDP software, turn to page SB-2 and follow the directions for this activity.

D. Take two 3-minute timings. Review your speed and errors.

Goal: At least 35wpm/3'/4e

D. 3-MINUTE TIMING

```
8        Technology that tracks eye movements is used by some     11
9    Web designers to judge how customers interact with Web       22
10   pages. The technology determines which zone of the Web       33
11   page is seen first, which feature is viewed most often,      44
12   and how quickly information is located on the Web page.      55
13       Eye movements are tracked using a combination of         65
14   hardware and data analysis software. Customers wear cameras  77
15   that record eye movements. The pupil dilations and scanning  89
16   patterns of their eyes are measured to record the amount     100
17   of mental strain exerted.                                    105
     |  1  |  2  |  3  |  4  |  5  |  6  |  7  |  8  |  9  |  10  |  11  |  12
```

E. BASIC PARTS OF A TABLE

- Tables have vertical columns (identified by a letter) and horizontal rows (identified by a number).
- A cell, or "box," is created where a column and a row intersect.
- Tables formatted with borders all around (as shown in the illustration) are called boxed tables.
- Tables formatted with no borders are called open tables.

- Center a table vertically when it appears alone on the page.
- Center a table horizontally if the cell widths have been adjusted automatically to fit the contents.

Note: You will learn to center tables vertically and horizontally in Lesson 38.

↓center page

ALASKAN VACATIONS			
Sailing Dates and Prices ↓1X			
↓1X Northern Departures	Interior Stateroom	Ocean View Stateroom	↓1X Guest
January 12	$599	$699	$ 99
February 14	599	699	99
March 11	699	799	199
April 2	699	799	199
May 11	699	799	299
June 6	799	899	399
July 1	799	899	399
August 21	799	899	399

Row 1
Row 2
Row 3
Row 4
Row 5
Row 6
Row 7
Row 8
Row 9
Row 10

Column A   Column B   Column C   Column D

TITLE. Center and type in all caps and bold. If there is no subtitle, insert 1 blank line after the title.

SUBTITLE. Center on the line below the title, and type in upper- and lowercase letters and bold. Press ENTER 1 time to insert a blank line below the subtitle.

HEADING BLOCK. Title and subtitle.

COLUMN HEADINGS. Center or left-align (for text), or right-align (for numbers). Align vertically at the bottom. Type in upper- and lowercase letters and bold.

COLUMN ENTRIES. Align text entries at the left; align number entries at the right. Capitalize only the first word and proper nouns. Add spaces after the dollar sign to align with widest column entry below.

Go To

Word Processing Manual

F. WORD PROCESSING: TABLE—CREATE AND AUTOFIT TO CONTENTS

Study Lesson 36 in your word processing manual. Complete all of the shaded steps while at your computer. Then format the jobs that follow.

DOCUMENT PROCESSING

Table 36-1

Three-Column Boxed Table

Simple tables often do not have titles, subtitles, or column headings.

1. Insert a boxed table with 3 columns and 3 rows.
2. Left-align all column entries.
3. Automatically adjust the column widths for all columns.

Mary Spangler	President	Administration
Joyce Moore	Dean	Jefferson Hall
Thelma Day	Chairperson	Da Vinci Hall

Table 36-2 ▶

Two-Column
Boxed Table

1. Insert a boxed table with 2 columns and 4 rows.
2. Left-align all column entries.

3. Automatically adjust the column widths for all columns.

Marie Covey, Executive Editor	Santa Clarita, California
Albert Russell, Associate Editor	Newport, Rhode Island
Bob Harris, Contributing Writer	St. Louis, Missouri
Sylvestra Zimmerly, Art Director	Albuquerque, New Mexico

Table 36-3 ▶

Two-Column
Boxed Table

1. Open the file for Table 36-2.
2. Change the name and title in Row 4, Column A to `Theodore Easton, Film Editor.`

3. Change the city and state in Row 4, Column B to `Socorro, New Mexico.`

Table 36-4 ▶

Three-Column
Boxed Table

Barbara Azar	Professor	Computer Technologies
Ken Kennedy	Professor	Foreign Languages
Bonnie Marquette	Instructor	Computer Technologies
Kevin Nguyen	Assistant	Social Sciences

STRATEGIES FOR *Career Success*

Nonverbal Communication

"It's not what he said, but how he said it." More than 90 percent of your spoken message contains nonverbal communication that expresses your feelings and desires. People respond to this nonverbal language.

Posture can convey your mood. For example, leaning toward a speaker indicates interest. Leaning backward suggests dislike or indifference. Your handshake, an important nonverbal communicator, should be firm but not overpowering.

Your head position provides many nonverbal signals. A lowered head usually expresses shyness or withdrawal. An upright head conveys confidence and interest. A tilted head signifies curiosity or suspicion. Nodding your head shows positive feeling, while left-right headshakes signify negative feeling. Your face strongly expresses your emotions. Narrow, squinting eyes signify caution, reflection, or uncertainty. Wide-open eyes convey interest and attention.

YOUR TURN Turn off the sound on a television program. How much of the plot can you understand just from the nonverbal communication signals?

Lesson 37

Open Tables With Titles

GOALS
- Improve speed and accuracy
- Refine language arts skills in punctuation
- Format open tables with titles

A. Type 2 times.

A. WARMUP

```
1    The check for $432.65 wasn't mailed on time! Late      10
2  charges of up to 10% can be expected. To avoid a sizable  21
3  penalty, just send an email message to quickpay@epay.com. 32
   |  1  |  2  |  3  |  4  |  5  |  6  |  7  |  8  |  9  |  10  |  11  |  12
```

SKILLBUILDING

B. Take a 1-minute timing on the first paragraph to establish your base speed. Then take four 1-minute timings on the remaining paragraphs. As soon as you equal or exceed your base speed on one paragraph, advance to the next, more difficult paragraph.

B. SUSTAINED PRACTICE: ROUGH DRAFT

```
4      Various human responses are asymmetrical. This means    11
5  that we ask more from one side of the body than the other   23
6  each time we wave, wink, clap our hands, or cross our legs.  35

7      Each one of these actions demands a clear deçision,      11
8  usually unconscious and instantaneous, to start the course  23
                                          begin
9  of moving two parts of the body in different directions.     34

10 All children go though remarkably involved steps as they     12
       kids
11 develop their preferried. As children grows she or he may    23
                 ence      a child
12 favor the right hand, the left, or both the same at times.   35

13 When most kids are eihgt or seven, stability ocurrs,         11
14 and one hand is permanently dominent over the other. For     22
15 some unnown reason, choose the right hand.                   34
        nine out of ten
   |  1  |  2  |  3  |  4  |  5  |  6  |  7  |  8  |  9  |  10  |  11  |  12
```

C. PACED PRACTICE

If you are not using the GDP software, turn to page SB-14 and follow the directions for this activity.

D. Study the rules at the right.

D. APOSTROPHE

RULE ▶
' singular

Use 's to form the possessive of singular nouns.

The hurricane's force caused major damage to North Carolina's coastline.

RULE ▶
' plural

Use only an apostrophe to form the possessive of plural nouns that end in s.

The investors' goals were outlined in the stockholders' report.

But: The investors outlined their goals in the report to the stockholders.

But: The women's and children's clothing was on sale.

RULE ▶
' pronoun

Use 's to form the possessive of indefinite pronouns (such as *someone's* or *anybody's*); do not use an apostrophe with personal pronouns (such as *hers, his, its, ours, their,* and *yours*).

She could select anybody's paper for a sample.

It's time to put the file back into its cabinet.

Edit the sentences to insert any needed punctuation.

16 The womans purse was stolen as she held her childs hand.
17 If the book is yours, please return it to the library now.
18 The girls decided to send both parents donations to school.
19 The childs toy was forgotten by his mothers good friend.
20 The universities presidents submitted the joint statement.
21 The four secretaries salaries were raised just like yours.
22 One boys presents were forgotten when he left the party.
23 If these blue notebooks are not ours, they must be theirs.
24 The plant was designed to recycle its own waste products.

FORMATTING

E. TABLE HEADING BLOCK

Note: The title and subtitle (if any) make up the table heading block.

To format a table heading block:

- Type the title centered in all caps and bold. If the table does not have a subtitle, insert 1 blank line after the title.
- Type the subtitle (if any) centered on the line below the title in upper- and lowercase letters in bold.
- Insert 1 blank line below the subtitle.

Go To
Word Processing Manual

F. WORD PROCESSING: TABLE—MERGE CELLS AND BORDERS

Study Lesson 37 in your word processing manual. Complete all of the shaded steps while at your computer. Then format the jobs that follow.

Table 37-5 ▶

Two-Column Open Table With Title

'singular

1. Insert a table with 2 columns and 5 rows.
2. Merge the cells in Row 1; then center and type the title in bold and all caps.
3. Press ENTER once to insert 1 blank line after the title.
4. Left-align all column entries.
5. Automatically adjust the column widths for all columns.
6. Remove the table borders.

PC CONNECTION'S LOCATIONS

Valencia Mall	Santa Clarita, California
Town Center Square	Stevenson Ranch, California
Northridge Mall	Northridge, California
Granary Square	Valencia, California

Table 37-6 ▶

Three-Column Open Table With Title and Subtitle

' singular
'plural

1. Insert a table with 3 columns and 5 rows.
2. Merge the cells in Row 1; then center and type the title in bold and all caps.
3. Press ENTER 1 time and type the subtitle centered in bold.
4. Press ENTER 1 time to insert 1 blank line after the subtitle.
5. Left-align all column entries.
6. Automatically adjust the column widths for all columns.
7. Remove the table borders.

NEWHALL DISTRICT'S REGISTRATION
Seniors' Schedule

Meadows	Monday, February 14	11 a.m.
Stevenson Ranch	Monday, February 21	10 a.m.
Old Orchard	Monday, February 28	11 a.m.
Wiley Canyon	Monday, March 7	10 a.m.

Table 37-7 ▶

Two-Column Open Table With Title and Subtitle

' singular

1. Insert a table with 2 columns and 6 rows.
2. Use standard table format for an open table with a title and subtitle.

MAR VISTA REALTY'S TOP SELLERS
First Quarter

James Kinkaid	Santa Clarita
Deborah Springer	Northbridge
Patricia Morelli	Woodland Hills
Jan McKay	Malibu
Daniel Aboud	San Luis Obispo

Open Tables With Column Headings

GOALS

- Type at least 35wpm/3'/4e
- Format open tables with column headings

A. Type 2 times.

A. WARMUP

```
1        Jerry wrote a great article entitled "Interviewing      10
2   Techniques" on pp. 23 and 78! A&B@bookstore.com expected a    22
3   sizable number of requests; thus far, 65% have been sold.     33
    |  1  |  2  |  3  |  4  |  5  |  6  |  7  |  8  |  9  |  10  |  11  |  12
```

SKILLBUILDING

B. Take three 12-second timings on each line. The scale below the last line shows your wpm speed for a 12-second timing.

B. 12-SECOND SPEED SPRINTS

```
4   Blake was paid to fix the handle on the bowls that he made.
5   Alan led the panel of four men until the work was all done.
6   Jan will sign this paper when she has done all of the work.
7   They will focus on their main theme for the last six weeks.
    I I I I 5 I I I I 10 I I I I 15 I I I I 20 I I I I 25 I I I I 30 I I I I 35 I I I I 40 I I I I 45 I I I I 50 I I I I 55 I I I I 60
```

C. PROGRESSIVE PRACTICE: ALPHABET

If you are not using the GDP software, turn to page SB-7 and follow the directions for this activity.

D. Take two 3-minute timings. Review your speed and errors.

Goal: At least 35wpm/3'/4e

D. 3-MINUTE TIMING

```
8         Telecommuting is a word you may have heard before but   11
9    don't quite understand. Very simply, it means working at     22
10   home instead of driving in to work. Many people like the     33
11   convenience of working at home. They realize they can save   45
12   money on expenses like gas, clothing, and child care.        56
13        Most home office workers use a computer in their job.   67
14   When their work is completed, they can just fax or email     78
15   it to the office. If they need to communicate with other     89
16   employees, they can use the phone, fax, or computer and      100
17   never have to leave home.                                    105
     |  1  |  2  |  3  |  4  |  5  |  6  |  7  |  8  |  9  |  10  |  11  |  12
```

E. COLUMN HEADINGS

Column headings describe the information contained in the column entries. Refer to page R-13A in the Reference Manual for an illustration of column headings.

To format column headings:
- Type the column headings in upper- and lowercase letters and bold.
- If a table has a combination of 1- and 2-line column headings, press ENTER 1 time before typing the 1-line column heading to push the heading down so it aligns vertically at the bottom of the cell.
- Center column headings in tables with all-text columns.
- Left-align column headings in a column with all text.
- Right-align column headings in a column with all numbers.

Go To

Word Processing Manual

F. WORD PROCESSING: TABLE—CENTER HORIZONTALLY AND CENTER PAGE

Study Lesson 38 in your word processing manual. Complete all of the shaded steps while at your computer. Then format the jobs that follow.

DOCUMENT PROCESSING

Table 38-8

Two-Column Open Table With Column Headings

Note: Center all tables horizontally and vertically from now on.
1. Insert a table with 2 columns and 6 rows.
2. Type the title block in standard table title block format.
3. Type the column headings centered in upper- and lowercase letters and bold.
4. Left-align the column entries.
5. Automatically adjust the column widths for all columns.
6. Center the table horizontally and vertically.
7. Remove all table borders.

↓center page
VENDOR LIST
July 1, 20-- ↓1x

Product	Vendor
Laser printers	Office Supplies Unlimited
Workstations	PC Junction, Inc.
Cellular phones	Satellite Communications
Scanners	Atlantic-Pacific Digital

Table
38-9

Two-Column
Open Table With
Column Headings

1. Insert a table with 2 columns and 6 rows.
2. Type the title block in standard table title block format.
3. Type the column headings centered in upper- and lowercase letters and bold.
4. In Column B, press ENTER 1 time before typing the 1-line column heading to push the heading down so it aligns vertically at the bottom of the cell.

5. Left-align the column entries.
6. Automatically adjust the column widths for all columns.
7. Center the table horizontally and vertically.
8. Remove all table borders.

COMMITTEE ASSIGNMENTS

Academic Committee Assignments	Professor
Institutional Integrity	Anne McCarthy
Educational Programs	Bill Zimmerman
Student Services	John Yeh
Financial Resources	Steve Williams

Table
38-10

Two-Column
Open Table With
Column Headings

1. Open the file for Table 38-8.
2. Change the date to the current date.
3. Change the 4 products in Column A as follows:

```
Copiers
Processors
Controller cards
Modems
```

Table
38-11

Two-Column
Open Table With
Column Headings

CABLE SERVICES AVAILABILITY ↓1x

Type of Service	Currently Available
Basic	Phoenix
Lifeline	Scottsdale
Expanded	Glendale
Expanded (per channel)	Camelback City

Lesson 39

Ruled Tables With Number Columns

GOALS
- Improve speed and accuracy
- Refine language arts skills in spelling
- Format ruled tables with number columns

A. Type 2 times.

A. WARMUP

```
1       Does Xavier know that around 8:04 a.m. his July sales    11
2   quota was realized? Invoice #671 indicates a 9% increase!    23
3   Several of the employees weren't able to regain their lead.  35
    | 1 | 2 | 3 | 4 | 5 | 6 | 7 | 8 | 9 | 10 | 11 | 12
```

SKILLBUILDING

B. Type the paragraph 2 times. Use the CAPS LOCK key to type a word or series of words in all caps. Tap the CAPS LOCK key with the A finger.

B. TECHNIQUE PRACTICE: SHIFT KEY AND CAPS LOCK

```
4       The new computer has CD-ROM, PCI IDE HDD controller,
5   and an SVGA card. Mr. J. L. Jones will order one from PC
6   EXPRESS out of Orem, Utah. IT ARRIVES NO LATER THAN JULY.
```

PPP

PRETEST → PRACTICE → POSTTEST

C. PRETEST: Horizontal Reaches

PRETEST
Take a 1-minute timing. Review your speed and errors.

```
7       The chief thinks the alarm was a decoy for the armed    11
8   agent who coyly dashed away. She was dazed as she dodged    22
9   a blue sedan. He lured her to the edge of the high bluff.   33
    | 1 | 2 | 3 | 4 | 5 | 6 | 7 | 8 | 9 | 10 | 11 | 12
```

D. PRACTICE: In Reaches

PRACTICE
Speed Emphasis:
If you made 2 or fewer errors on the Pretest, type each *individual* line 2 times.
Accuracy Emphasis:
If you made 3 or more errors, type each *group* of lines (as though it were a paragraph) 2 times.

```
10  oy foyer loyal buoys enjoy decoy coyly royal cloy ploy toys
11  ar argue armed cared alarm cedar sugar radar area earn hear
12  lu lucid lunch lured bluff value blunt fluid luck lush blue
```

E. PRACTICE: Out Reaches

```
13  ge geese genes germs agent edges dodge hinge gear ages page
14  da daily dazed dance adapt sedan adage panda dash date soda
15  hi hints hiked hired chief think ethic aphid high ship chip
```

POSTTEST
Repeat the Pretest timing and compare performance.

F. POSTTEST: Horizontal Reaches

G. Type these frequently misspelled words, paying special attention to any spelling problems in each word.

 **G. SPELLING**

16 prior activities additional than faculty whether first with
17 subject material equipment receiving completed during basis
18 available please required decision established policy audit
19 section schedule installation insurance possible appreciate
20 benefits requirements business scheduled office immediately

Edit the sentences to correct any misspellings.

21 We requierd the office to schedule all prior activities.
22 The business scheduled the instalation of the equipment.
23 The decision established the basis of the insurance policy.
24 Please audit any additionl material available to faculty.
25 If possible, they would appreciate recieving them soon.
26 Section requirements to receive benefits were completed.

FORMATTING

H. RULED TABLES WITH NUMBER COLUMNS

 Review the use of borders in Lesson 37 as needed.

To format a ruled table with number columns:
1. Remove all table borders.
2. Apply borders to the top and bottom of Row 2 and to the bottom of the last row.
3. Right-align column headings and column entries with numbers.
4. If the column entry includes a dollar sign, add spaces after the dollar sign to align the dollar sign just to the left of

the widest column entry below it as follows: add 2 spaces for each number and 1 space for each comma. In the example below, 3 spaces were added after the dollar sign.

Example:

$ 375
2,150
49

I. WORD PROCESSING: TABLE—ALIGN TEXT IN A COLUMN

Go To
Word Processing Manual

Study Lesson 39 in your word processing manual. Complete all of the shaded steps while at your computer. Then format the jobs that follow.

Table 39-12 ▶

Three-Column Ruled Table With Number Columns

1. Insert a ruled table with 3 columns and 5 rows.
2. Type the heading block and table in standard table format.
3. Add spaces after the dollar sign as needed to align the dollar sign just to the left of the widest column entry below it.
4. Center the table horizontally and vertically.
5. Remove all table borders and apply borders to the top and bottom of Row 2 and to the bottom of the last row.

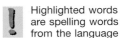

Highlighted words are spelling words from the language arts activity.

↓center page
NORTHERN BELL PHONES
Inside Wire Repair Service ↓1X

Per-Month Plan	Today's Rates	1995 Rates
Residence	$ .60	$1.00
Business	1.30	1.30
Private Line	3.50	4.50

Table 39-13 ▶

Four-Column Ruled Table With Number Columns

1. Insert a ruled table with 4 columns and 7 rows.
2. Type the heading block and table in standard table format.
3. Add spaces after the dollar sign to align the dollar sign just to the left of the widest column entry below it.
4. Center the table horizontally and vertically.
5. Remove all table borders; then apply borders to the top and bottom of Row 2 and to the bottom of the last row.

↓center page
HOLIDAY RESORT SUITES
Available Rates ↓1X

Hotel	Rack Rate	Club Rate	3-Night Savings
Porter Ranch Inn	$ 92.00	$36.00	$ 68.00
Jamaican Inn	119.00	59.50	178.50
Casitas Suites	120.00	60.00	180.00
The Desert Inn Resort	135.00	75.50	178.50
Sannibel Courtyard	150.00	75.00	225.00

Table 39-14 ▶

Three-Column Ruled Table With Number Columns

GENERAL EQUITY MUTUAL FUNDS

Fund	Current Year	Previous Year
Duncan Insurance	16.3%	2.0%
Strident Nova	9.3%	3.5%
First Value	10.7%	12.1%
Safeguard Policy	11.1%	9.7%
Vanguard Life	8.5%	10.1%

Formatting Review

GOALS

- Type at least 36wpm/3'/4e
- Format tables with a variety of features
- Format documents with a variety of features

A. Type 2 times.

A. WARMUP

```
1       On July 15, a check for exactly $329.86 was mailed to    11
2  Zak & Quinn, Inc.; they never received Check #104. Does       22
3  Gary know if the check cleared the company's bank account?     34
   |  1  |  2  |  3  |  4  |  5  |  6  |  7  |  8  |  9  |  10  |  11  |  12
```

SKILLBUILDING

B. MAP

Follow the GDP software directions for this exercise in improving keystroking accuracy.

C. DIAGNOSTIC PRACTICE: NUMBERS

If you are not using the GDP software, turn to page SB-5 and follow the directions for this activity.

D. Take two 3-minute timings. Review your speed and errors.

Goal: At least 36wpm/3'/4e

D. 3-MINUTE TIMING

```
4        Employee complaints are often viewed as a negative      10
5  power in a workforce. In fact, these complaints should        21
6  be viewed as a chance to communicate with an employee and     33
7  to improve morale. Ignoring complaints does not make them     45
8  go away. Listening to complaints objectively can help to      56
9  solve a small problem before it turns into a big one.         67
10       Often workers expect a chance to be heard by a person   78
11 who is willing to listen quite openly. That person should     90
12 recognize that the employee has concerns that need to be     101
13 discussed objectively and honestly.                          108
   |  1  |  2  |  3  |  4  |  5  |  6  |  7  |  8  |  9  |  10  |  11  |  12
```

Report 40-11 ▶

Academic Report With List

RELATIONSHIPS AT WORK
Your Name

¶ Do you believe that as long as you get your work done at the end of the day, you have had a successful day on the job? If so, you are badly mistaken. Doing the work is only half the job. The other half is relating to and working with the people around you.

TAKE A TEAM APPROACH

¶ Everything you do and every action you take affects those around you in a close working relationship. Operating as a team means thinking about others and taking actions that will help them reach their goals and achieve the goals of the company.

MAINTAIN A SPIRIT OF COOPERATION

¶ When you work in a spirit of cooperation, those around you will reflect that spirit. Your job will be easier because you will minimize resistance. It takes much more energy to resist each other than it does to cooperate and work together.

VALIDATE THE OPINIONS OF OTHERS

¶ You will find that this simple act of validation will go a long way in helping the spirit of your co-workers. Here are two simple ways to validate the opinions of others:
1. Take time to listen to the issues and accomplishments of those around you.
2. Reflect their opinions in your own words in a spirit of genuine interest. There is a saying that states, "Your success is my success." Adopt this as your motto, and you will find a great deal of satisfaction at the end of each day.

Correspondence 40-20 ▶

Business Letter in Block Style With Enclosure Notation and Envelope

Note: Omit the return address.

December 1, 20-- | Mrs. Yvonne Spillotro | 105 North Field Avenue | Edison, NJ 08837 | Dear mrs. Spillotro:

Thank you for choosing Insurance Alliance of America. Open enrollment for your insurance medical plan is scheduled to begin the first day of January. I hope it was possible for you to review the materials you received last week. Selecting the right benefit plan for you and your family can be an overwhelming task. To make this decision a little easier, I have enclosed a brochure with this letter summarizing the key features of each policy.

(Continued on next page)

Please call me if I can help in any way.

¶You might want to browse through our website at www.IAA.com for further details.

Sincerely, | Denise Broers | Customer Support | urs | enclosure

---

Table 40-15 ▶

Three-Column Boxed Table With Number Columns

✓**Progress Check**
Proofreading Check

Documents designated as Proofreading Checks serve as a check of your proofreading skill. Your goal is to have zero typographical errors when the GDP software first scores the document.

PERSONAL ASSET ACCOUNTS Your Name		
Account	**Amount**	**Interest Rate**
Interest Checking	$ 972.55	3.10%
Money Market	4,500.35	4.90%
Smart Saver	3,250.76	5.07%
Certificate of Deposit	550.00	7.41%

Presenting information in tabular format is standard business procedure today. Your keyboarding skills will help you develop effective, easy-to-understand tables.

Skills Assessment on Part 2

3-Minute Timing

```
1      From the first day of class, you have continuously    10
2   worked to improve your typing skill. You have worked hard    22
3   to increase your typing speed and accuracy. You have also    34
4   learned to format letters, memos, reports, and tables. All    46
5   of this work is quite an amazing accomplishment.    56
6      In your lessons, you have worked on learning a wide    67
7   range of word processing skills. You can expect to make    78
8   even more progress if you practice your skills regularly.    90
9   Learn as much as you can each day. Ask questions, and move    102
10  toward a new goal every day.    108
    |  1  |  2  |  3  |  4  |  5  |  6  |  7  |  8  |  9  |  10  |  11  |  12
```

Correspondence Test 2-21 ▶

Business Letter in Block Style with Enclosure Notation and Envelope

Note: Omit the return address.

Current Date | Ms. ~~Arlene~~ *Dorothy* Turner | Global Moving and Storage | 6830 Via Del Monte | San Jose, CA 95119 | Dear Ms. Turner:

¶ Thank you ~~you~~ for registering your pc Graphics software so promptly. As a registered user, you are entitled to free technical support 24 hours a day. The brochure enclosed will explain in detail how you can reach us ~~either~~ by fax, email or phone whenever you need help. Also, help is *always* available on our website at www.pcgraphics.com. All our PC Graphics users will receive our monthly newsletter, which is filled with tips on using your new software and other material we know you will be interested in ~~seeing~~ *reading*. You can also access our newest graphics online at our Web site. Please call me or send me an e mail message if you have any questions or would like to receive any additional information. Your satisfaction is our number ①priority. Sincerely | Roy Phillips | Support Technician | urs | enclosure

Report Test 2-12 ▶

Multipage Academic Report With Side Headings and Paragraph Headings

TELECOMMUTERS
Visibility at Work
Roy Phillips

¶ Have you ever wondered how to remain "visible" at work when you aren't there for most of the work week? This is a problem many telecommuters are struggling to overcome as

(Continued on next page)

more and more people do their work from home. We all know the advantages of working at home, but it may come with a heavy price unless you work smart. Here are some ways for telecommuters to increase visibility at work.

ATTEND KEY MEETINGS

¶ Make sure that you are notified by email of all key meetings so that you can be sure to be there and make your opinions and your presence known. If meeting agendas or schedules normally are distributed through office mail, make sure there is a procedure in place that distributes these important documents electronically.

COMMUNICATE WITH YOUR SUPERVISOR

¶ Don't think that there is any virtue in keeping quiet about your accomplishments. Make your accomplishments known in an assertive, regular manner. This can be done easily in several different ways.

¶ Email. Use email messages or attachments to email messages to summarize your accomplishments on a project. It would also be a good idea to send your list of work objectives for the week to your supervisor. When a project is finished, send the final documents related to the project. If a picture could help, invest in a digital camera or a scanner and attach a picture.

¶ Answering Machines and Pagers. Make it easy for your boss to contact you. Check your pager and answering machine frequently and return calls promptly. All of these techniques will help ensure your visibility when you aren't there.

Table Test 2-16 ▶

Three-Column Boxed Table With Two-Line Column Headings and Number Columns

SIENNA VILLA CONDOMINIUMS Association Fees		
Category	Average Monthly Bill	Proposed Increase
Insurance	$150	$25
Earthquake rider	75	32
Water	65	20
Landscaping	30	5

PART 3

Reports, Correspondence, and Employment Documents

OBJECTIVES

KEYBOARDING

▶ Type at least 40 words per minute on a 5-minute timing with no more than 5 errors.

LANGUAGE ARTS

▶ Refine proofreading skills and correctly use proofreaders' marks.

▶ Use punctuation and grammar correctly.

▶ Improve composing and spelling skills.

WORD PROCESSING

▶ Use the word processing commands necessary to complete the document processing activities.

DOCUMENT PROCESSING

▶ Format business and academic reports, personal-business letters, memos, modified-block style letters, and resumes.

TECHNICAL

▶ Answer at least 90 percent of the questions correctly on an objective test.

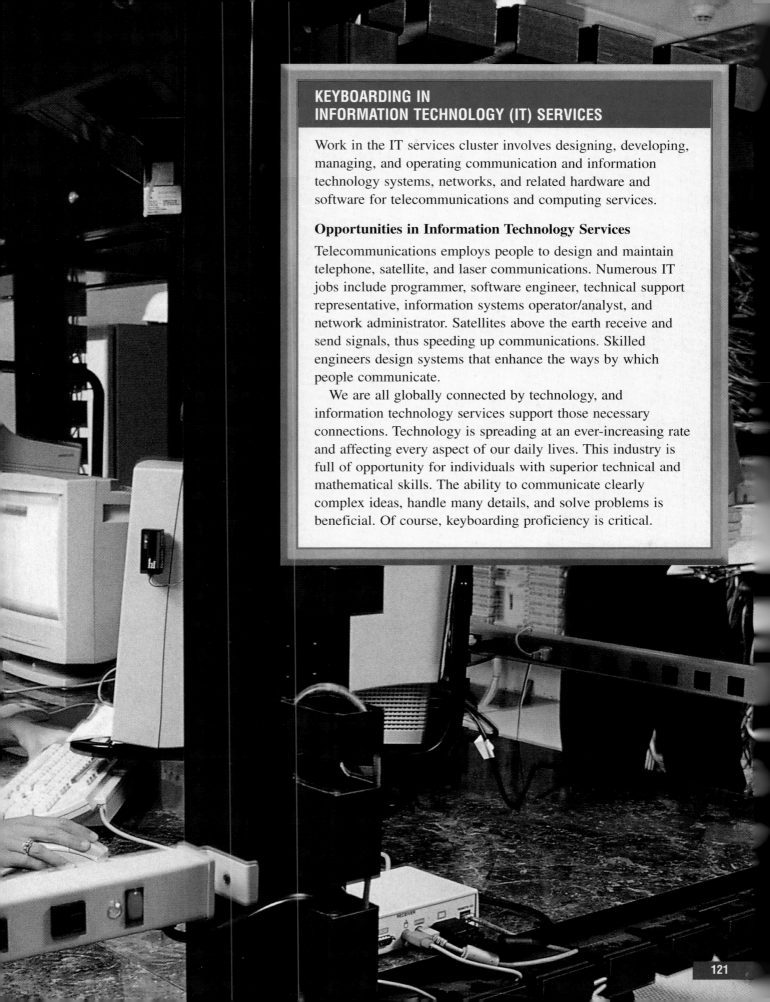

KEYBOARDING IN
INFORMATION TECHNOLOGY (IT) SERVICES

Work in the IT services cluster involves designing, developing, managing, and operating communication and information technology systems, networks, and related hardware and software for telecommunications and computing services.

Opportunities in Information Technology Services

Telecommunications employs people to design and maintain telephone, satellite, and laser communications. Numerous IT jobs include programmer, software engineer, technical support representative, information systems operator/analyst, and network administrator. Satellites above the earth receive and send signals, thus speeding up communications. Skilled engineers design systems that enhance the ways by which people communicate.

We are all globally connected by technology, and information technology services support those necessary connections. Technology is spreading at an ever-increasing rate and affecting every aspect of our daily lives. This industry is full of opportunity for individuals with superior technical and mathematical skills. The ability to communicate clearly complex ideas, handle many details, and solve problems is beneficial. Of course, keyboarding proficiency is critical.

Unit 9

Reports

Computer Generations 3

A Brief History of Computer Generations

Joshua T. Reynolds

The invention of the computer did not occur in the past two centuries; in fact, the first computer was probably the abacus, which was used about 5,000 years ago in Asia Minor. As we know them today, computers were first used just after the Second World War, around 1945. Since then, several computer advancements have occurred that make it possible to classify computer power by one of these significant advancements that can be associated with particular time periods or generations. The following paragraphs summarize the major developments that occurred in each of these generations.

First-Generation Computers

The first generation of computers generally runs from 1945 to 1956. During this time, the first vacuum tube computer, the ENIAC, was invented. The first commercial computer was called the UNIVAC, and it was used by the U.S. Census Bureau. It was also used to predict President Eisenhower's victory in the 1952 presidential election (Baker, 1998, p. 18).

Second-Generation Computers

...computers were run by transistors. These computers ...ructions for a specific function that could be stored ...o the period when COBOL and FORTRAN were used ...are industry began in this generation.

...eneration Computers

...n 1964 to 1971, and it is characterized by the use of in- ...from the previous generation. As a result of this inven- ...d more powerful (Diaz & Moore, 1999, p. 8).

Computer Generations 4

Fourth-Generation Computers

This generation is placed in the 1971 to 1999 time category. Again, computers became smaller and faster, and the Intel chip was responsible for most of the changes taking place in this 29-year period.

Enhancements in Speed

Because of the rapid miniaturization that took place with the chip, the CPU, memory, and input/output controls could now be placed on a single chip. Computers were becoming faster and faster, find they were being used in everyday items such as microwave ovens, televisions, and automobiles.

Commercial Applications

Word processing and spreadsheet applications made their debut in this generation, as did home and video game systems. Names such as Pac Man and Atari were very popular with computer users.

Fifth-Generation Computers

According to Allen, the turn of the century marks this generation, and it will be associated with artificial intelligence, spoken word instructions, and superconductor technology, which allows electricity to flow with little or no resistance (2000, p. 130).

SHOPPING FOR A HOME

(Part 1)

Buying a home is a process that many of us will go ... many other prospective buyers, we will experience ... in our working years. A home is typically the largest ... therefore deserves our careful attention.

"Most people think that the most important criterion ... The site should be on land that is well drained and fr... city zoning plan to determine if you have chosen a s... water levels. You should also check to see if the gro... considerably can cause cracks in foundations and wa...

Moreau suggests that a house survey be undertaken ...

Key problems are encroachments—trees, buil... that overlap the property line or may violate ... can be as simple as moving or removing tree...

The buying of a house is a major undertaking with a ... investigated. To ensure that the building is structural... use the services of a building inspector.

The walls, ceiling, and floors (if you have a basemen... insulation. "Both the depth and 'R' factor need to be... addition, cross braces should have been used betwe...

Check the roof carefully. Walk around the entire hou... all rooflines and angles. Are there any shingles missi...

---
[1] James Nelson, "A New Home for the Millennium," ... 27, 2000, pp. 19-24.
[2] Eva Bartlett, "Settlement Issues When Buying a N... 1999, p. 68.
[3] "Home Construction in the 21st Century," *Family ...
[4] Karen Ostrowski, "A Short Course in Buying a Ho... Publishing Company, Boston, p. 37.

Business Reports With Footnotes

GOALS:
- Improve speed and accuracy
- Refine language arts skills in using quotation marks and italics (or the underline)
- Format reports with footnotes

A. Type 2 times.

A. WARMUP

```
1      Tag #743X was attached to a black jug that was 1/3    10
2 full of a creamy liquid. Tags #914Z and #874V were both    21
3 attached to beautiful large lamps (crystal and porcelain).  33
   |  1  |  2  |  3  |  4  |  5  |  6  |  7  |  8  |  9  |  10  |  11  |  12
```

SKILLBUILDING

B. PACED PRACTICE

If you are not using the GDP software, turn to page SB-14 and follow the directions for this activity.

C. MAP

Follow the GDP software directions for this exercise in improving keystroking accuracy.

LANGUAGE ARTS

D. Study the rules at the right.

D. QUOTATION MARKS AND ITALICS (OR UNDERLINE)

RULE ▶
" direct quotation

Use quotation marks around a direct quotation.
>Harrison responded by saying, "Their decision does not affect us."
>*But:* Harrison responded by saying that their decision does not affect us.

RULE ▶
" title

Use quotation marks around the title of a newspaper or magazine article, chapter in a book, report, and similar terms.
>The most helpful article I found was "Multimedia for All."

RULE ▶
title

Italicize (or underline) the titles of books, magazines, newspapers, and other complete published works.
>Grisham's *The Brethren* was reviewed in a recent *USA Today* article.

RULE ▶
, direct quotation

Use a comma before and after a direct quotation.
>James said, "I shall return," and then left.

(Continued on next page)

Edit the sentences to correct any errors in the use of quotation marks, the underline (or italics), and a comma.

4 The interest rates were discussed in the March 1 "Tribune."
5 *The Power of e-Commerce* is an excellent chapter.
6 His reply was very short and to the point: Definitely!
7 Her title for the report was "The Internet in Action."
8 The August issue of "Newsweek" had an excellent coverage.
9 Karen interrupted by saying, That's exactly right!
10 The realtor replied "The first thing to consider is location."
11 "The margin of error is very small" said Andy.

FORMATTING

Reference Manual

If you have to format a report with endnotes instead of footnotes, study the illustration of endnotes on page R-8C and R-8D of the Reference Manual.

E. REPORTS WITH FOOTNOTES

Footnote references indicate the sources of facts or ideas used in a report. Although footnotes may be formatted in various ways, they have many characteristics in common:

1. Footnotes are indicated in the text by superior figures.
2. Footnotes are numbered consecutively throughout the report.
3. Footnotes appear at the bottom of the page on which the references appear.
4. A footnote should include the name of the author, the title of the book or article, the publisher, the place of publication, the year of publication, and the page number(s).

interrupt the speaker—don't always have a "bigger or better" one of whatever the speaker is talking about.[1] Crenshaw believes that there are some positive steps to becoming better listeners:

> One of the techniques to use is to not think about something else while the speaker is presenting his or her topic. Also, you need to be sure not to be distracted by outside noises that will disturb your concentration. Finally, learn to listen actively by taking notes and asking questions.[2]

Being a good listener is hard work. Sometimes it takes more effort to be a good listener than it does to be a good speaker. If you put these suggestions into practice, they will pay you big dividends.[3]

[1] Sarah J. Ford, "The Power of Listening," *Communications Journal*, January 1998, p. 21.
[2] Earl T. Bickham and Christopher R. Lanham, *Communications for Daily Living*, Mid-Continent Associates Press, Houston, Tex., 2000, p. 56.
[3] Regina Land, "Technological Communication," *Business Week*, November 22, 1999, p. 68.

F. LONG QUOTATIONS

A paragraph that is quoted or considered essential to a report may be highlighted or displayed by using single-spacing and indenting the paragraph 0.5 inch from both the left and right margins to make it stand out from the rest of the report.

Go To

Word Processing Manual

G. WORD PROCESSING: FOOTNOTES

Study Lesson 41 in your word processing manual. Complete all of the shaded steps while at your computer. Then format the jobs that follow.

SHOPPING FOR A HOME

(Part I)

¶ Buying a home is a proces*s* that many of us will go through in our life time. If we are like many *other* prospective buyers, we will experience this decision three or four ~~major~~ times in our working years. A home is typically the largest purchase we will make, and it deserves therefore our careful attention. ~~We must be certain to look carefully at all the information available to us.~~

¶ "Most people think that the *most* important criteria *on* in shopping for a home is its site,"[1] ~~says John Calendar.~~ The site should be on land that is well drained and free from ~~from~~ flooding ~~that can cause extensive damage.~~ Check the *Local* ~~area~~ city zoning plan to determine if you have chosen a site that is free from flooding and highwater levels ~~that can cause extensive damage.~~ You should also check to see if the ground is stable. Ground that shifts *considerably* can cause cracks in foundations and walls.

¶ Moreau suggests that a *house* ~~home~~ survey be undertaken in the early stages: Key problems are encroachments—t*r*ees, buildings, or additions to the house that overlap the property line or may violate zoning regulations. The solution can be as simple as moving or removing trees or bushes ~~from the front or back of your house.~~[2]

¶ The buying of a house is a major under taking with a long list of items that must be investigated. To ensure that the building is structurally sound, many prospective buyers use the services of a building inspector.

¶ The walls, ceiling, and floors *(if you have a basement)* need to be checked for proper insulation. "Both *the* depth and 'r' factor need to be checked for proper levels."[3] In addition, crossbraces should have been used between the beams supporting a floor.

(Continued on next page)

¶ (Carefully) check the roof. Walk around the *entire* house so that you have a clear view of all rooflines and angles. Are there any shingles missing or is there water damage?[4]

" title
[1]James Nelson, "A New Home for the Millennium," *home planning magazine*, April 27, 2000, pp. 19-24.

title
[2]Eva Bartlett, "Settlement Issues when Buying a New Home," *Home Finances,* (1999) July, p. 68.

" title
[3]"Home Construction in the 21st Century," *Family Living*, October 9, 1999, p. 75.

title
[4]Karen Ostrowski, "A Short Course in Buying a Home," *Homebuilders' Guide*, Kramer Publishing Company, Boston, p. 37.

Report 41-14

Multipage Business Report With Footnotes

! Remember to add a page number.

Open the file for Report 41-13 and make the following changes:
1. Add the final paragraph in the report:
   ¶ Finally, a thorough check should be made of the heating, cooling, and electrical systems in the home. "These features are often overlooked by prospective homeowners; nevertheless, they are as critical as any others to be examined." [5]

---

[5]Randall Evans and Marie Alexander, Home Facilities Planning, Bradshaw Publishing, Salt Lake City, Utah, 2000, p. 64.

2. Insert the footnote as indicated.
3. Change the footnote titles from italic to underline.

Keyboarding **CONNECTION**

Inedible Cookies

Is that cookie good for you? A cookie is a short text entry stored on your computer identifying your preferences to the server of the Web site you are viewing.

Certain Web sites use cookies to customize pages for return visitors. Only the information you provide or the selections you make while visiting a Web site are stored in a cookie. You can control how your browser uses cookies.

In Netscape, select Edit from the Preferences menu. Choose the Advanced category. Choose one of the options in the Cookies area. Click OK. In Internet Explorer, select Internet Options from the Tools menu. Click the Security tab. Click the zone for which you want to set the security. Move the slider up for a higher level of security or down for a lower level of security. Click OK.

YOUR TURN Access your browser's cookie policy defaults. Decide if you want to change them.

Academic Reports in APA Style

GOALS

- Type at least 36wpm/3'/3e
- Format reports in APA style
- Format author/year citations

A. Type 2 times.

A. WARMUP

```
1        The giant-size trucks, all carrying over 600 bushels,    11
2   were operating "around the clock"; quite a few of them had    23
3   dumped their boxes at Joe's during the last 18 to 20 hours.   35
    |  1  |  2  |  3  |  4  |  5  |  6  |  7  |  8  |  9  |  10  |  11  |  12
```

SKILLBUILDING

B. PROGRESSIVE PRACTICE: ALPHABET

If you are not using the GDP software, turn to page SB-7 and follow the directions for this activity.

C. Type the paragraph 2 times, using your right thumb to press the SPACE BAR in the center.

C. TECHNIQUE PRACTICE: SPACE BAR

```
4        Dale is it. Adam is there. Mark is home. Eve was lost.
5   Helen can see. Faith can knit. Gayle can fly. Hal can type.
6   Fly the kite. Swim a mile. Close the door. Lift the weight.
```

D. Take two 3-minute timings. Review your speed and errors.

Goal: At least 36wpm/3'/3e

D. 3-MINUTE TIMING

```
7        The size of their first paychecks after they finish      11
8   college seems quite high to some young men and women. They    23
9   rent a place to live that is just too expensive, or they      34
10  may buy a new car with a huge monthly payment. For some,      45
11  it takes a while to learn that there are other items in       56
12  the monthly budget.                                           60
13       Additional budget items are food, student loans, car     71
14  insurance, renters' insurance, credit card debt, health      82
15  insurance, utilities, and miscellaneous expenses. A good      93
16  goal is to put a regular amount from each paycheck into a    105
17  savings account.                                             108
    |  1  |  2  |  3  |  4  |  5  |  6  |  7  |  8  |  9  |  10  |  11  |  12
```

Reference Manual

Refer to page R-10A of the Reference Manual for additional guidance.

E. REPORTS FORMATTED IN APA STYLE

In addition to the traditional academic style, academic reports may also be formatted in APA (American Psychological Association) or MLA (Modern Language Association) style. In the APA style, format the report as follows:

1. Use 1-inch top, bottom, and side margins.
2. Center and type the title unbolded with initial capital letters for each important word.
3. Double-space the entire report.
4. Type a short title and page number in a header on all pages, flush with the right margin.
5. Indent paragraphs 0.5 inch.

top, bottom, and side margins: 1"
Double-space throughout.   A Condensed History of the Internet ← header

main heading → A Condensed History of the Internet

Karen Reynolds

The Internet has been around for over twenty years in various forms. During the past few years, however, it has experienced phenomenal growth. According to some sources, the Internet began as a military project (Rockwell, 1999). ↓1DS

sub heading → How the Internet Is Funded

According to Alexander, a great deal of support for the Internet originally came from the U.S. Federal Government (2000, p. 42). During the late 1980s, however, the use of the Internet expanded so that commercial usage became very popular. Today, the majority of Internet users are educational and research institutions, businesses, and government organizations around the globe.

F. AUTHOR/YEAR CITATIONS

Any information based on other sources and used in a report must be documented or cited. The author/year method of citation includes the source information in parentheses at the appropriate point within the text.

1. If a source has one author, give the author's last name followed by a comma and the year of publication. If a page reference of the source is needed, give the page number following the year of publication.

   Example: (Smith, 2000) or (Smith, 2000, p. 52).

2. If the author's name appears within the text, give only the year and the page number in parentheses.
3. If a source has two authors, give both last names joined by &.
4. If a source has three or more authors, give the last name of the first author followed by *et al.*

Go To

Word Processing Manual

G. WORD PROCESSING: MARGINS, HEADERS, AND FOOTERS

Study Lesson 42 in your word processing manual. Complete all of the shaded steps while at your computer. Then format the jobs that follow.

Report
42-15

Academic Report in APA Style With Author/Year Citations and Main Headings

Remember to add a page number and heading.

Computer Generations 3

A Brief History of Computer Generations

Joshua T. Reynolds

¶ The invention of the computer did not occur in the past two centuries; in fact, the first computer was probably the abacus, which was used about 5,000 years ago in Asia Minor. As we know them today, computers were first used just after the Second World War, around 1945. Since then, several computer advancements have occurred that make it possible to classify computer power by one of these significant advancements that can be associated with particular time periods or generations. The following paragraphs summarize the major developments that occurred in each of these generations.

First-Generation Computers

¶ The first generation of computers generally runs from 1945 to 1956. During this time, the first vacuum tube computer, the ENIAC, was invented. The first commercial computer was called the UNIVAC, and it was used by the U.S. Census Bureau. It was also used to predict President Eisenhower's victory in the 1952 presidential election (Baker, 1998).

Second-Generation Computers

¶ During this period, 1956 to 1963, computers were run by transistors. These computers were known for their ability to accept instructions for a specific function that could be stored within the computer's memory. This is also the period when COBOL and FORTRAN were used for computer operations. The entire software industry began in this generation.

Third-Generation Computers

¶ This computer generation ran from 1964 to 1971, and it is characterized by the use of integrated circuits to replace the transistors from the previous generation. As a result of this invention, computers became smaller, faster, and more powerful (Diaz & Moore, 1999).

(Continued on next page)

Fourth-Generation Computers

¶ This generation is placed in the 1971- to 1999-time category. Again, computers became smaller and faster, and the Intel chip was responsible for most of the changes taking place in this 29-year period. Because of the rapid miniaturization that took place with the chip, the CPU, memory, and input/output controls could now be placed on a single chip. Computers were becoming faster and faster; and they were being used in everyday items such as microwave ovens, televisions, and automobiles.

Fifth-Generation Computers

¶ According to Allen, the turn of the century marks this generation; and it will be associated with artificial intelligence, spoken word instructions, and superconductor technology, which allows electricity to flow with little or no resistance (2000, p. 130).

Report 42-16 ▶

Academic Report in APA Style With Author/Year Citations, Main Headings, and Subheadings

Open the file for Report 42-15 and make the following changes:

1. Insert a subheading into the Fourth-Generation Computers paragraph after the second sentence. Entitle it <u>Enhancements in Speed</u>.
2. Add a subheading at the end of the Fourth-Generation Computers. Entitle it <u>Commercial Applications</u>.
3. Insert the following text after the subheading "Commercial Applications":

   Word processing and spread-sheet applications made their debut in this genera-tion, as did home and video game systems. Names such as Pac Man and Atari were very popular with computer users.

Academic Reports in MLA Style

GOALS

- Improve speed and accuracy
- Refine language arts skills in composing sentences
- Format reports in MLA style

A. Type 2 times.

A. WARMUP

```
1    "Baxter & Heimark, Inc., sold 82 new vehicles (47 cars   11
2  and 35 trucks) during June," the sales manager reported.    22
3  This is 16.9% of quarterly sales, an amazing achievement!   33
   | 1 | 2 | 3 | 4 | 5 | 6 | 7 | 8 | 9 | 10 | 11 | 12
```

SKILLBUILDING

B. Take three 12-second timings on each line. The scale below the last line shows your wpm speed for a 12-second timing.

B. 12-SECOND SPEED SPRINTS

```
4  Joe must try to type as fast as he can on these four lines.
5  The screens were very clear, and the print was easy to see.
6  We will not be able to print the copy until later on today.
7  The disk will not store any of the data if it is not clean.
   I I I I 5 I I I I 10 I I I I 15 I I I I 20 I I I I 25 I I I I 30 I I I I 35 I I I I 40 I I I I 45 I I I I 50 I I I I 55 I I I I 60
```

C. PROGRESSIVE PRACTICE: NUMBERS

If you are not using the GDP software, turn to page SB-11 and follow the directions for this activity.

D. Take a 1-minute timing on the first paragraph to establish your base speed. Then take four 1-minute timings on the remaining paragraphs. As soon as you equal or exceed your base speed on one paragraph, advance to the next, more difficult paragraph.

D. SUSTAINED PRACTICE: SYLLABIC INTENSITY

```
 8      Taking care of aging parents is not a new trend. This   11
 9  issue has arisen more and more, since we are now living      22
10  longer. Companies are now trying to help out in many ways.   34

11      Help may come in many ways, ranging from financial aid   11
12  to sponsoring hospice or in-home respite care. Workers may   22
13  find it difficult to work and care for aging parents.       33

14      Why are employers so interested in elder care? Rising    11
15  interest is the result of a combination of several things.   23
16  The most notable is a marked increase in life expectancy.   35

17      Another trend is the increased participation of women,   11
18  the primary caregivers, in the workforce. Businesses are    22
19  recognizing that work and family life are intertwined.      33
    | 1 | 2 | 3 | 4 | 5 | 6 | 7 | 8 | 9 | 10 | 11 | 12
```

E. Answer each question with a complete sentence.

E. COMPOSING SENTENCES

20 What are your best traits that you will bring to your job when you graduate?
21 Would you like to work for a small company or a large company?
22 How much money will you expect to earn each month in your first job?
23 Would you like that first job to be in a small town or a large city?
24 As you begin your first job, what career goal will you have in mind?

FORMATTING

Reference Manual

Refer to page R-10C of the Reference Manual for additional guidance.

F. REPORTS FORMATTED IN MLA STYLE

To format an academic report in MLA style:

1. Use 1-inch top, bottom, and side margins.
2. Type the author's name and the page number at the right margin, 0.5 inch from the top as a header on all pages.
3. Type the heading information (your name, your instructor's name, the class name, and the date) at the left margin.
4. Type the date in military style (15 April 20--).
5. Center and type the title with upper- and lowercase letters for each important word.
6. Double-space the entire report.
7. Indent paragraphs 0.5 inch.

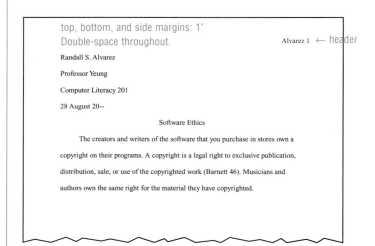

top, bottom, and side margins: 1"
Double-space throughout.   Alvarez 1 ← header

Randall S. Alvarez

Professor Yeung

Computer Literacy 201

28 August 20--

Software Ethics

The creators and writers of the software that you purchase in stores own a

copyright on their programs. A copyright is a legal right to exclusive publication,

distribution, sale, or use of the copyrighted work (Barnett 46). Musicians and

authors own the same right for the material they have copyrighted.

Campbell 1

Pamela R. Campbell
Dr. Howard Estavan
Telecommunications 315
14 September 20--

Judging a Computer System

¶ Judging the effectiveness of a computer system has taken on a new dimension in the past few years, if for no other reason than the wide range of computer systems from which the user can select. It is, therefore, important that we investigate the criteria that should be considered in making this important decision.

¶ Probably the most obvious criterion considered when one purchases a computer system is speed. The value of a computer is directly related to its speed, and a computer's speed is typically measured in megahertz (MHz). A megahertz is one million cycles per second, and many of today's microcomputers run in the range of 700-900 MHz (Kramer 173).

¶ Flexibility is especially important because of the rapid turnover of hardware and software in the computer industry. The flexibility of a computer system is important for two general reasons: to accommodate a variety of programs and to permit expandability. Hundreds and possibly thousands of software packages are available today to meet the needs of computer users. The computer you purchase must be able to accommodate this variety of software and be flexible enough to change with the increasing sophistication of software packages. Because of the substantial investment you make in a computer, you do not want to commit your resources to a computer that cannot be expanded to handle (1) newer, more powerful operating systems; (2) "memory-hungry" software packages; (3) network interfaces; and (4) additional users (Hartung and Kallock 239).

¶ A third consideration is convenience. Is it easy to learn how to operate your computer? Does the manufacturer stand by its warranty, and is it difficult to obtain repairs? How convenient is it to buy parts for your computer (such as memory boards and drives) if you want to expand your system? These questions need to be answered, and the answers should be weighed carefully before you purchase a new computer system.

David S. Swartz

Professor Arrington

Introduction to E-commerce

9 April 20--

¶ The Internet is dramatically changing the way we shop. In years past, our shopping practices consisted of driving to a local mall or department store, walking through the aisles until we found an item we wished to purchase, and then making the purchase and driving home. Today, it is becoming more common to find shoppers doing their shopping via the Internet. Shopping on the Internet brings with it some cautions that we should observe when we shop. Here are some basic rules to follow when shopping on the Internet.

¶ When you are asked to enter information on your order, do not disclose personal information unless it is needed for shipping your order to you. Be sure you know who is collecting this information, why it is needed, and how it is going to be used. Be certain that the information asked for is actually necessary for the purchase. For example, there are few instances when your password should be disclosed.

¶ You should always verify that the company from whom you are purchasing has secured the purchasing procedures. You will often be asked to enter your credit card number to complete the purchase—be certain the transfer of this information is made in a secure environment. Also, be certain you know the exact cost of the item for which you are being charged. The company from whom you are purchasing the item should have a built-in calculator so that you know at all times how much your purchase will cost you, including all necessary shipping and handling charges.

¶ Understand exactly what you should do if you encounter a problem with your purchase online. Is there an easy way to contact the company? Does the company have an email address you can use to contact a customer relations representative? Does the company's order page include a telephone number that you can call if you have questions about your order?

Report Citations

GOALS

- Type at least 37wpm/3'/3e
- Format bibliographies, references, and works-cited pages

A. Type 2 times.

A. WARMUP

```
1        The prize troops received the following extra gifts:    11
2   $20 from Larson's Bakery; $19 from Calsun, Ltd.;* $50 from    23
3   some judges; and quite a number of $5 gift certificates.     34
    | 1 | 2 | 3 | 4 | 5 | 6 | 7 | 8 | 9 | 10 | 11 | 12
```

SKILLBUILDING

PRETEST → PRACTICE → POSTTEST

PRETEST
Take a 1-minute timing.
Review your speed and
errors.

B. PRETEST: Vertical Reaches

```
4        Kim knew that her skills at the keyboard made her a     11
5   top rival for that job. About six persons had seen her race  23
6   home to see if the mail showed the company was aware of it.  34
    | 1 | 2 | 3 | 4 | 5 | 6 | 7 | 8 | 9 | 10 | 11 | 12
```

PRACTICE
Speed Emphasis:
  If you made 2 or fewer
  errors on the Pretest,
  type each *individual*
  line 2 times.
Accuracy Emphasis:
  If you made 3 or more
  errors, type each
  group of lines (as
  though it were a
  paragraph) 2 times.

C. PRACTICE: Up Reaches

```
7   se seven reset seams sedan loses eases serve used seed dose
8   ki skids kings kinks skill kitty kites kilts kite kids kick
9   rd board horde wards sword award beard third cord hard lard
```

D. PRACTICE: Down Reaches

```
10  ac races pacer backs ached acute laced facts each acre lace
11  kn knave knack knife knows knoll knots knelt knew knee knit
12  ab about abide label above abode sable abbey drab able cabs
```

POSTTEST
Repeat the Pretest
timing and compare
performance.

E. POSTTEST: Vertical Reaches

F. Take two 3-minute timings. Review your speed and errors.

Goal: At least 37wpm/3'/3e

F. 3-MINUTE TIMING

13   Every organization should have its code of ethics. A   11

14   code contains rules of conduct and moral principles that   22

15   guide the company and its employees. Some general ethics   33

16   that may be included in the code are equality, integrity,   45

17   truth, cooperativeness, and honesty.   52

18   Companies may include specific rules in the code that   63

19   relate to their type of work. For example, if specific laws   75

20   govern how they conduct business, companies may request   86

21   employees to conduct all activities in a just and lawful   97

22   manner. The code of business ethics should be equitable   108

23   for all workers.   111

| 1 | 2 | 3 | 4 | 5 | 6 | 7 | 8 | 9 | 10 | 11 | 12

FORMATTING

Reference Manual

Refer to page R-9B of the Reference Manual for additional guidance.

G. BIBLIOGRAPHIES

A bibliography is an alphabetic listing of sources typed on a separate page at the end of a report. To format a bibliography:
1. Use a 2-inch top margin for the first page.
2. Center and type the word BIBLIOGRA-PHY in all caps, 14 pt. font, and bold; then press ENTER 2 times.
3. Type the first line at the left margin and indent carryover lines 0.5 inch (a hanging indent).

4. Single-space bibliographies in business reports (with 1 blank line between entries); double-space bibliographies in academic reports.
5. Arrange book entries in this order: author(s) (last name first), title (in italics), publisher, place of publication, and year.
6. Arrange journal articles in this order: author(s) (last name first), article title (in quotation marks), journal title (in italics), volume number, issue number, date, and page.

(Continued on next page)

12 pt↓   ↓6X

hanging indent   14 pt **BIBLIOGRAPHY**

↓2X

Ferguson, Mary, *Voice Recognition Systems*, Peace Garden Printers, Grand
↓Forks, N. Dak., 2000. ↓2X

Miller, Jeffrey R., Yeung, Allen T., and Sanchez, Mary M., "Perfecting
Your Computer Speaking Voice," *PC Today*, November 30, 2000,
pp. 32-35.

"Talking to Your Computer," *Boston Globe*, February 9, 2001, p. H10.

Thomas, Anita R. <athomas@gcst.edu>, "Supporting Voice Systems,"
January 18, 2001, personal email (January 20, 2001).

"Voice Recognition Systems Leading the Industry," *VoiceSystems Home
Page*, April 17, 2000, <http://www.voicesystems.com/trends.html>
(May 15, 2000).

H. REFERENCE LIST PAGES IN APA FORMAT

Reference Manual

Refer to page R-10B
of the Reference
Manual for additional
guidance.

A reference list page also indicates sources used in a report. To format an APA reference list page:

1. Use the same margins as in the report.
2. Double-space all reference entries.
3. Center and type the word References at the top of the page.
4. Double-space the entire page.
5. Begin the reference list on a new page, continuing the page-numbering format from the report.
6. Arrange book entries in this order: author(s) (last name first), publication date in parentheses, chapter title with only the first word capitalized (no quotation marks or underline), book title (underlined or italicized), publisher's city and 2-letter state abbreviation, publisher's name.
7. Arrange periodical entries in this order: author (last name first), publication date in parentheses, article title with only the first word capitalized (no quotation marks or underline or italic), periodical title and volume number underlined or italicized, and page numbers.

(Continued on next page)

top, bottom, and side margins: 1"
Double-space throughout.

Voice Recognition 16 ← header

References

→ tab   Ferguson, M. (2000). *Voice recognition systems.* Grand Forks, ND: Peace

Garden Printers.

Miller, J. R., Yeung, A. T., & Sanchez, M. M. (2000, November 30).

Perfecting your computer speaking voice. *PC Today,* 32-35.

Talking to your computer. (2001, February 9). *Boston Globe,* p. H10.

Thomas, A. athomas@gcst.edu. "Supporting voice systems." January 18,

2001, personal email (January 20, 2001).

Voice recognition systems leading the industry (2000, April 17).

VoiceSystems Home Page. Retrieved May 15, 2000 from the World Wide Web:

http://www.voicesystems.com/trends.html.

Refer to page R-10D of the Reference Manual for additional guidance.

I. WORKS-CITED PAGES IN MLA FORMAT

A Works-Cited page is an alphabetical list of the sources used in a report formatted in MLA style. To format a list of works cited:

1. Begin the Works Cited section on a new page.
2. Use 1-inch top, bottom, and side margins.
3. Type the author's name and the page number (as a header) at the right margin, 0.5 inch from the top.
4. Center and type the words `Works Cited` in upper- and lowercase.
5. Double-space the entire page.
6. Arrange the sources alphabetically by authors' last names.
7. Begin each entry at the left margin, and indent carryover lines 0.5 inch (use a hanging indent).

(Continued on next page)

```
                                                                    Samson 9  ← header
top, bottom, and side margins: 1"
Doule-space throughout.

hanging indent                        Works Cited

         Ferguson, Mary. Voice Recognition Systems. Grand Forks: Peace Garden, 2000.

         Miller, Jeffrey R., and Mary M Sanchez. "Perfecting Your Computer Speaking

            Voice." PC Today 30 Nov. 2000: 32-35.

         "Talking to Your Computer." Boston Globe, Feb. 2001: H10.

         Thomas, Anita R. Personal email. "Supporting Voice Systems." 18 Jan. 2001.

         "Voice Recognition Systems Leading the Industry." VoiceSystems Home Page.

            17 Apr. 2000. 15 Sep. 2001.  http://www.voicesystems.com/trends.html.
```

Go To
Word Processing Manual

J. WORD PROCESSING: HANGING INDENT

Study Lesson 44 in your word processing manual. Complete all the shaded steps while at your computer. Then format the jobs that follow.

DOCUMENT PROCESSING

Report 44-19

Bibliography

BIBLIOGRAPHY

Bilanski, Charles R., "Corporate Structures in the New Millennium," *Modern Management*, Vol. 43, June 2000, pp. 43-46.

Calhoun, Josten C., *Stockholders' Guide*, Missouri Valley Press, St. Louis, 2000.

Dahlman, Leland, and Joyce C. Fahler, *Trends for Boards of Directors*, Vineyard Press, Boston, 1999.

Hammersmith Institute, *Bold Positions of the New Administration*, Hammersmith Institute Press, Baltimore, Md., 1992.

"Investing in the Corporate World," *eFinance Home Page*, March 27, 2000, http://www.efinance.com/invest/today'sworld.htm (May 18, 2000).

Polaski, James T. jpolaski@aol.com, "Summary of Investment Guide," October 10, 2000, personal email (October 13, 2000).

Report 44-20 ▶

References in
APA Style

References

Chandler, R. D., & Thompson, A. S. (1998). The evolution of America's economy in the late 1800's. Westerville, OH: Glencoe/ McGraw-Hill. Chapter 24, pp. 130-145.

Deming, W. H. (2000). Economists' guide to economic indicators. The Economic Review, XVI, 42-44.

Fortenberry, J. E., Kingston, A. E., & Worthington, S. O. (2001). The environment of business. Los Angeles: The University Press.

Meier, T. D., & Hovey, D. H. (1999). economics on the world wide web. Toronto: The Northern Press.

Tetrault, G. M. (2000). A guide for selecting economic indicators for the business entrepreneur. The Southern Economic Forecaster, 23.

Zysmanski, R. J. (2001). American capitalism and its impact on society. San Francisco: Bay Press/Area.

Report 44-21 ▶

Works Cited
in MLA Style

Works Cited

Abernathy, Thomas R. (traber@westga.edu). "Welcome to the Internet." Personal email to Helen Hynes (hhynes@westga.edu). 19 March 2000.

Benson, Lisa, et al. "E-commerce on the Net." *Online Observer*. Vol. 17. Sep. 1999: 144-146.

Cooper, Stanley. *Trends for the New Millennium*. Denver: Mountain Press, 2000. 340-352.

Lawrence, Donna, and Becky Silversmith. *Surfer's Guide to the Internet*. Atlanta: Southern Publishers, 2000.

"Starting a Business on the Internet." Jan. 2000. Online. Available: http://www.entrepreneur/startups.html. 24 May 2001.

Tidwell, Joel, and Jean Swanson. "Things You Don't Know About the Internet." *Going Online.* Vol. 23. 104-106.

Preliminary Report Pages

GOALS
- Improve speed and accuracy
- Refine language arts skills in proofreading
- Format title pages and tables of contents

A. Type 2 times.

A. WARMUP

```
 1        Did Kenny and Hazel see the first Sox ball game? I've    11
 2   heard there were 57,268 people there (a new record). Your     23
 3   home crowd was quiet when the game ended with a 4-9 loss.      34
     | 1  | 2  | 3  | 4  | 5  | 6  | 7  | 8  | 9  | 10 | 11 | 12
```

SKILLBUILDING

B. Take three 12-second timings on each line. The scale below the last line shows your wpm speed for a 12-second timing.

B. 12-SECOND SPEED SPRINTS

```
 4   Some of the new pups will be sold to the men who work here.
 5   Most of the boys and girls got to go to the fair last week.
 6   She has to take six of the top teams to the games that day.
 7   Dick said that the right way to do it is also the easy way.
     I I I I 5 I I I I 10 I I I I 15 I I I I 20 I I I I 25 I I I I 30 I I I I 35 I I I I 40 I I I I 45 I I I I 50 I I I I 55 I I I I 60
```

C. PACED PRACTICE

If you are not using the GDP software, turn to page SB-14 and follow the directions for this activity.

D. DIAGNOSTIC PRACTICE: ALPHABET

If you are not using the GDP software, turn to page SB-2 and follow the directions for this activity.

LANGUAGE ARTS

E. Study the proofreading techniques at the right.

E. PROOFREADING YOUR DOCUMENTS

Proofreading and correcting errors are essential parts of document processing. To become an expert proofreader:

1. Use the spelling feature of your word processing software to check for spelling errors; then read the copy aloud to see if it makes sense.
2. Proofread for all kinds of errors, especially repeated, missing, or transposed words; grammar and punctuation; and numbers and names.
3. Use the appropriate software command to see an entire page of your document to check for formatting errors such as line spacing, tabs, margins, and bold.

F. Compare this paragraph with the Pretest on page 135. Edit the paragraph to correct any errors.

F. PROOFREADING

8   Kim new that her skills at the key board made her a
9 top rivel for the job. About six persons had scene her race
10 home to see if the male showd the company was awarre of it.

FORMATTING

Reference Manual

Refer to page R-7B of the Reference Manual for additional guidance.

G. TITLE PAGE

Reports may have a title page, which includes information such as the report title, to whom the report is submitted, the writer's name and identification, and the date. To format a title page, follow these steps:

1. Center the page vertically.
2. Center the title in all caps and bold type, using a 14-pt. font.
3. Press ENTER 2 times; then center the subtitle in upper- and lowercase and bold type, using a 12-pt. font.
4. Press ENTER 12 times; then center the words Submitted to in regular type.
5. Press ENTER 2 times; then center the recipient's name and identification on separate lines, single-spaced.
6. Press ENTER 12 times; then center the words Prepared by in regular type.
7. Press ENTER 2 times; then center the writer's name and identification on separate lines, single-spaced.
8. Press ENTER 2 times; then center the date.

center page↓

14 pt **A TECHNOLOGY ASSESSMENT OF THE GRANTLAND CORPORATION**
↓2X

12 pt↓ **The Status of Technology in the New Millennium**
↓12X

Submitted to
↓2X

Marcia Abernathy
Regional Manager
Grantland Corporation
↓12X

Prepared by
↓2X

Timothy R. Rassmussen
District V Manager
Grantland Corporation
↓2X

March 20, 20—

H. TABLE OF CONTENTS

Reference Manual

Refer to page R-7D of the Reference Manual for additional guidance.

A table of contents is usually supplied with long reports. The table of contents identifies the major sections of a report and the page numbers where they can be found. To format a table of contents, follow these steps:

1. Use a 2-inch top margin for the first page.
2. Use a default tab of 0.5 inch on the left; set a right dot-leader tab at 6 inches.
3. Center and type the word **CONTENTS** in 14 pt. font and bold at the top margin; then press ENTER 2 times. Change to a regular font.
4. Type the major headings in all caps; double-space before and after them.
5. Indent subheadings 0.5 inch (using a default tab) and type them in upper- and lowercase and single spacing.
6. Align page numbers flush right, and type them with dot leaders—a series of periods that helps guide the reader's eye across the page to the page number on the same line.

Set left tab at 0.5; right dot-leader tab at 6.

↓6X
12 pt↓   14 pt **CONTENTS**   ↓2X

INTRODUCTION 1   ↓2X

SECURITY ON THE INTERNET 3   ↓2X

→tab Using Passwords 3
       Paying by Credit Card 4
       Keeping Your Personal Information Private 6   ↓2X

IMPLICATIONS OF E-COMMERCE 8

I. WORD PROCESSING: TAB SET—DOT LEADERS

Go To

Word Processing Manual

Study Lesson 45 in your word processing manual. Complete all of the shaded steps while at your computer. Then format the jobs that follow.

Report 45-22 ▶

Title Page

↓center page

14 pt **DISTANCE LEARNING CLASSROOMS** ↓2X

12 pt↓ **Using Technology to Reach Students
at a Distance** ↓12X

Prepared by ↓2X

Phyllis T. Black
Technology Coordinator
T-Systems Media, Inc. ↓12X

February 19, 20--

Report 45-23 ▶

Table of Contents

↓6X

CONTENTS ↓2X

Create a title page for the report below entitled LOOKING INTO THE 21ST CENTURY and a subtitle that reads Some Predictions for the New Millennium. The report is to be submitted to Alfredo Sanchez, District Manager, Millennium Concepts, Inc. The report is being prepared by Richard P. Morgan, Computer Consultant, Millennium Concepts, Inc. Use a date of May 18, 20--.

CONTENTS

Progress Check Proofreading Check

Documents designated as Proofreading Checks serve as a check of your proofreading skill. Your goal is to have zero typographical errors when the GDP software first scores the document.

LOOKING INTO THE 21ST CENTURY
Some Predictions for the New Millennium
Richard P. Morgan

¶ It is predicted that computers will alter almost every activity of our lives in the first ten years of this millennium. There is strong evidence to suggest that this prediction will soon become a reality. This paper will summarize the changes we will experience in the areas of artificial intelligence, the Internet, education, lifestyle, and health and demographics.

ARTIFICIAL INTELLIGENCE

¶ Artificial intelligence is generally described as a computer's ability to assume an intelligence similar to that of the human brain—thus, its ability to reason and make decisions based on a pre-assigned set of facts or data.[1] But many experts predict that the computer's power will not stop there. They predict that the computer will soon become much smarter than humans by a process in which "intelligent" computers create even more intelligent computers. What we learn from these computers will have a far greater impact than the combined discoveries of the microscope, telescope, and X-ray machines.

¶ It is also predicted that the power of computers will double every 18 months through the year 2010.[2] With these enhancements, robots will displace humans from farms and factories; we will travel in cars, planes, and trains that are operated solely by computers; and traveling on the interstate highways will be as safe as watching television at home.

(Continued on next page)

COMPUTERS AND THE INTERNET

¶ The Internet will continue to expand and proliferate around the world. It will develop into a telemetric system consisting of trillions of micro-processors—all linked together into a complex international network of easily accessible databases. The speed at which information is transmitted on today's Internet will be considered a "snail's pace" on tomorrow's telemetric system. It will not be unusual for computers to transmit information at gigabit speeds and higher. [3] Computer security will be "foolproof," and most business transactions will be conducted on the Net. Fewer people will travel to foreign countries to vacation since "virtual vacations" will be common-place for the Internet user.

---

[1]Peter F. Boyd, "Artificial Intelligence," *Journal of Computer Trends*, January 2001, pp. 23-24, 36.
[2]Toshida Doi, "Computer Intelligence—Better Than the Human Brain?" *Power PC Magazine*, April 2000, pp. 14-17.
[3]Melanie T. Reynolds, "AI—Tomorrow's Brainpower," March 17, 2001, http://www.businessweek.com/2001/ai.htm.

STRATEGIES FOR *Career Success*

Letter of Transmittal

A letter or memo of transmittal introduces a report or proposal. Such letters provide an overview of the report in an informal, conversational writing style.

Let the recipient know what you are sending (e.g., "Enclosed is the proposal you requested."). If you're submitting an unsolicited report, explain why you've written the report. Include the report topic and identify the person or persons who authorized the report. Recap the main points. Cite any specific information that would help your audience comprehend the material. Is it a draft?

Conclude with a note of appreciation, a willingness to discuss the report, and intended follow-up action. Will you do something? Do you want feedback? If you want the reader to act, explain what you need and provide a deadline (e.g., "Please provide your comments by July 15.").

YOUR TURN List some ways that a letter of transmittal can promote goodwill between the sender and recipient.

Correspondence

November 30, 20--

Sales Manager
Bachmann's Nursery and Landscaping
6823 Oneta Avenue
Youngstown, OH 44500-2175

Dear Sales Manager:

As you requested on the telephone, I am providing the following list of events relating to my tree problem.

1. On April 15 I purchased at your branch in Warren four silver maples for the atrium outside our Riverdale office. We also purchased four Japanese red maples at your branch in Niles later that afternoon.

2. After about three months one silver maple and one red maple had died. I phoned both the Warren and Niles branches several times on November 1, but no one returned my messages.

3. On November 8, I phoned your nursery in an attempt to have these trees replaced. Again, there was no response.

As these trees were expensive, I expect that you will either replace them or reimburse me for the cost of the trees. I shall look forward to hearing from you.

Sincerely,

Marvin L. Norgaard
Grounds Manager

Current date

Mrs. Connie Filstad
4034 Kennedy Lane
Mount Vernon, WA 98274-2340

Dear Mrs. Filstad:

We at Mirror Lake Homes believe that your selection of a SunCity town house is just the right choice for you. The SunCity was awarded three national awards the 12th of last month. You have selected one of the most popular of our six models. As you requested, a brochure of the SunCity model is enclosed. Fifty-four units in the Creekwood site in Mount Vernon, Washington, have been built since December 1999.

I am certain you will agree that the $500 earnest money you put down was a wise decision on your part, and the 6½ percent loan you received was the best available through our lending agency.

Thank you, Mrs. Filstad, for the opportunity to work with you these past few days. If you have any questions, please let us know.

Sincerely,

(Mrs.) Cheryl T. Long
Sales Director

urs
Enclosure

MEMO TO: Charles A. Cornelius, President

FROM: Alfred A. Long, Convention Director

DATE: September 8, 20--

SUBJECT: Convention Locations

As you know, this year's convention will meet in Jacksonville, Florida. It is the Executive Board's decision to rotate the convention site to each of the districts in our region. Our next three conventions will be held in the following locations:

- Mobile, Alabama
- Atlanta, Georgia
- Myrtle Beach, South Carolina

In May the Board will travel to Mobile to visit the location of our next convention site. When we return, we will draft our convention site proposal for you.

urs

Personal Titles and Complimentary Closings in Letters

GOALS

- Type at least 37wpm/3'/3e
- Format personal titles in letters
- Format complimentary closings in letters

A. Type 2 times.

A. WARMUP

```
1        B & Z requested 14 boxes at $37/box. The items they      11
2  wanted were #6 and #17. A discount of 20% would bring the       23
3  total to approximately $950. Will you verify that order?        34
   |  1  |  2  |  3  |  4  |  5  |  6  |  7  |  8  |  9  | 10  | 11  | 12
```

SKILLBUILDING

B. DIAGNOSTIC PRACTICE: NUMBERS

If you are not using the GDP software, turn to page SB-5 and follow the directions for this activity.

C. Take three 12-second timings on each line. The scale below the last line shows your wpm speed for a 12-second timing.

C. 12-SECOND SPEED SPRINTS

```
4  Nine of those new women were on time for the first session.
5  She could see that many of those old memos should be filed.
6  Forty of the men were at the game when that siren went off.
7  The line at the main hall was so long that I did not go in.
   I I I I 5 I I I I 10 I I I I 15 I I I I 20 I I I I 25 I I I I 30 I I I I 35 I I I I 40 I I I I 45 I I I I 50 I I I I 55 I I I I 60
```

Keyboarding CONNECTION

Evaluating Internet Sources

Are you sure your Internet source has valid information? Because of the broad availability of the Internet and the lack of careful review stages as are built into print publishing, you must be cautious about the dependability of information you find on the Internet. Evaluate information on the Internet by the same standards you use to evaluate other sources of information.

The best way to assure that information is valid is to get it from a reputable source. The Internet versions of established, reputable journals in medicine (e.g., *Journal of the American Medical Association*), business (e.g., *Harvard Business Review*), engineering, computer science, etc., warrant the same level of trust as the printed versions.

As you leave established, reputable Web sites, use caution. Keep in mind that anyone can publish on the Internet. For many sources, there are no editorial review safeguards in place.

YOUR TURN Search the Web for more assessment methods.

D. Take two 3-minute timings. Review your speed and errors.

Goal: At least 37wpm/3'/3e

D. 3-MINUTE TIMING

8	Now is a great time to be looking for a job. Many	10
9	employers are looking for workers who have various skills.	22
10	For example, if you have acquired good computer skills,	33
11	are experienced working with people, and are dependable,	44
12	you can find a good job. Many companies are willing to	55
13	pay top dollars to find and keep good employees.	65
14	Your first impression on a prospective employer will	76
15	be a lasting one. Your resume should list your job skills,	88
16	work experience, and your personal information. Your zeal	100
17	when you interview for a job must come through clearly.	111

| 1 | 2 | 3 | 4 | 5 | 6 | 7 | 8 | 9 | 10 | 11 | 12 |

FORMATTING

E. PERSONAL TITLES IN CORRESPONDENCE

Inside Addresses:

1. Always use a courtesy title before a person's name in the inside address of a letter; for example, *Mr., Mrs.,* or *Dr.*

   Type a person's title on the same line with the name (separated by a comma) if the title is short, or on the line below.

Personal Titles in Inside Addresses:

Mr. Frank R. Izo, Manager
Landmark Security Systems

Mrs. Joyce Mansfield
Executive Director
Tanner Hospital

Dr. Evan R. Satterfield
Manager, Duke Oil Co.

Salutations:

2. When possible, use a person's name in the salutation. The correct form for the salutation is the courtesy title and the last name. If you do not know the name of the person, use a job title or *Ladies and Gentlemen.*

Personal Titles in Salutations:

Dear Ms. North:
Dear Dr. Chapman:
Dear Mr. Wagner:
Dear Sales Manager:
Ladies and Gentlemen:

F. COMPLIMENTARY CLOSINGS IN CORRESPONDENCE

Every letter should end with a complimentary closing. Some frequently used complimentary closings are *Sincerely, Sincerely yours, Yours truly, Cordially,* and *Respectfully yours.*

In the closing lines, do not use a courtesy title before a man's name. A courtesy title may be included in a woman's typed name or her signature.

Closing Lines

Sincerely yours,

Gretchen Day

Miss Gretchen Day
Account Manager

Cordially,

(Ms.) Juanita Ponce

Juanita Ponce
Marketing Director

Yours truly,

Ben R. Cameron

Ben R. Cameron
Regional Supervisor

DOCUMENT PROCESSING

Correspondence 46-22 ►

Business Letter in Block Style With Enclosure Notation

Current Date | Mrs. Connie Filstad | 4034 Kennedy Lane | Mount Vernon, WA 98274-2340 | Dear Mrs. Filstad:

¶ We at Mirror Lake Homes believe that your selection of a SunCity townhouse is just the right choice for you. The SunCity was awarded three national awards the 12th of last month. You have selected one of the most popular of our six models. As you requested, a brochure of the SunCity model is enclosed. Fifty-four units in the Creekwood site in Mount Vernon, Washington, have been built since December 2000.

¶ I am certain you will agree that the $500 earnest money you put down was a wise decision on your part, and the 6 1/2 percent loan you received was the best available through our lending agency.

¶ Thank you, Mrs. Filstad, for the opportunity to work with you these past few days. If you have any questions, please let us know.

Sincerely, | (Mrs.) Cheryl T. Long | Sales Director | urs | Enclosure

---

Correspondence 46-23 ►

Business Letter in Block Style With Enclosure Notation

Current Date | Mr. Lawrence S. Alwich | 1800 East Hollywood Avenue | Salt Lake City, UT 84108 | Dear Mr. Alwich:

¶ Our radio station would like you to reply to our editorial about the proposed airport site that aired from Provo, Utah, on the 15th of May. Actually, you are 1 of over 27 listeners who indicated your desire for us to air your rebuttal.

¶ Of the more than 100 request letters for equal time, we selected yours because you touched on most of the relevant points of this topic.

¶ We will contact you further about taping your rebuttal on June 4. Please read the enclosed disclaimer that we would like you to sign before airing the rebuttal.

Yours truly, | Arlan T. Jensen | General Manager | urs | Enclosure

Personal-Business Letters

GOALS
- Improve speed and accuracy
- Refine language arts skills in number expression
- Format personal-business letters

A. Type 2 times.

A. WARMUP

```
1        "Rex analyzed the supply," Margie said. Based on the      11
2   results, a purchase request for 7# @ $140 (23% of what we      23
3   needed) was issued. Was Jackie surprised by this? Vi was!      34
    |  1  |  2  |  3  |  4  |  5  |  6  |  7  |  8  |  9  | 10  | 11  | 12
```

SKILLBUILDING

B. PACED PRACTICE

If you are not using the GDP software, turn to page SB-14 and follow the directions for this activity.

C. PROGRESSIVE PRACTICE: ALPHABET

If you are not using the GDP software, turn to page SB-7 and follow the directions for this activity.

LANGUAGE ARTS

D. Study the rules at the right.

D. NUMBER EXPRESSION

RULE ▶
general

In general, spell out numbers zero through ten, and use figures for numbers above ten.

> We rented two movies for tonight.
> The decision was reached after 27 precincts sent in their results.

RULE ▶
figures

Use figures for
- **Dates. (Use *st, d,* or *th* only if the day comes before the month.)**
  > The tax report is due on April 15 (*not* April 15ᵗʰ).
  > We will drive to the camp on the 23d (or *23rd* or *23ʳᵈ*) of May.
- **All numbers if two or more *related* numbers both above and below ten are used in the same sentence.**
  > Mr. Carter sent in 7 receipts, and Ms. Cantrell sent in 22.
  > *But:* The 13 accountants owned three computers each.
- **Measurements (time, money, distance, weight, and percent).**
  > The $500 statue we delivered at 7 a.m. weighed 6 pounds.
- **Mixed numbers.**
  > Our sales are up 9½ (or *9 1/2*) percent over last year.

(Continued on next page)

Edit the sentences to correct any errors in number expression.

4 On the third of June, when she turns 60, 2 of her annuities
5 will have earned an average of 10 3/4 percent.
6 Seven investors were interested in buying 2 15-unit condos
7 if they were located within fifteen miles of each other.
8 The purchase price will be $3,000,000.00 at 11 percent
9 interest; escrow will close on June 3d before five p.m.
10 The parcel weighed two pounds. She also mailed three post-
11 cards, twelve packages, and twenty-one letters on June 4.
12 The agent sent 7 ten-page letters to all the investors.

FORMATTING

E. PERSONAL-BUSINESS LETTERS

Personal-business letters are prepared by individuals to conduct their personal business. To format a personal-business letter:

1. Type the letter on plain paper or personal stationery, not letterhead.

2. Include the writer's address in the letter directly below the writer's name in the closing lines.

3. Since the writer of the letter usually types the letter, reference initials are not used.

DOCUMENT PROCESSING

Correspondence 47-24 ▶

Personal-Business Letter in Block Style With Standard Punctuation

Reference Manual

Refer to page R-3D of the Reference Manual for an illustration of a personal-business letter.

general

figures

general

figures

↓6X
Current Date ↓4X

Ms. Valarie Bledsoe, Director
City Parks and Recreation Department
7034 Renwick Avenue
Syracuse, NY 13210-0475 ↓2X

Dear Ms. Bledsoe: ↓2X

Thank you for the excellent manner in which your department accommodated our family last summer. About 120 Turners attended the reunion at Rosedale Park on August 21.

I would like to again request that Shelter 5 be reserved for our next year's family reunion on August 20, 20--. A confirmation of the date from your office will be appreciated. ↓2X

Sincerely, ↓4X

Blair R. Turner
2410 Farnham Road
Syracuse, NY 13219

Correspondence
47-25 ▶

Personal-Business
Letter in Block Style
With Standard
Punctuation

This personal-business letter is from Walter G. Halverson, who lives at 482 22d Street East, Lawrence, KS 66049. Use today's date, and supply the appropriate salutation and closing. The letter is to be sent to Mr. Robert A. Sotherden, Administrator | Glencrest Nursing Home | 2807 Crossgate Circle | Lawrence, KS 66047.

general

¶ Thanks to you and dozens of other people, the fall crafts sale at Glencrest was highly successful. I am very appreciative of the ways in which you helped. ¶ I particularly wish to thank you for transporting the display tables and chairs to Glencrest and back to the community center. Many people from the community center attended the sale and commented about how nice it was of you and your staff to support such an activity. ¶ Having a parent who is a resident of the home, I am grateful that over 20 people from the Lawrence area volunteer their services to help make life more pleasant for the residents. Please accept my special thanks to you and your staff for supporting the many activities that benefit all Glencrest residents.

Correspondence
47-26 ▶

Personal-Business
Letter in Block Style
With Standard
Punctuation

Current Date | Mr. Karl E. Davis | 5270 Rosecrans Avenue | Topeka, KS 67284 | Dear Mr. Davis:

general

¶ Your presentation at the Sand Hills Country Club was one of the most enjoyable our members have ever observed. It is always a pleasure to have professionals like you speak on ways college graduates can prepare themselves for future employment. I especially enjoyed the question-and-answer session at the conclusion of your wonderful presentation, and I received many favorable comments from other attendees as well.

¶ Our professor has suggested that we take the information you gave us and prepare a website that focuses on the key points 6 you mentioned in your speech. That way, many of our classmates can take advantage of your excellent advice when preparing for their 1st search job. We have also found

figure

at least 20 several other sources to use on the world wide web that we plan to include on in our website.

(Continued on next page)

¶ I believe this is one of the most interesting assignments I have ever been assigned, thanks to the excellent information you provided. Members of my project team are excited to see their information on our web site. The project has given other students an incentive to construct their own web sites pertaining to job searches and interviewing techniques.

¶ If you would like to view our Web site, you can do so at the following site, which will be posted by the 10th of the month: www.tamu.edu/comm/abed3600/interview.html. Again, thank you for all your excellent ideas. Sincerely, | Brian D. Benedict | 3421 Carlisle Avenue | Topeka, KS 67209

figures

Global networking connects today's business world.

Memos With Lists

GOALS
- Type at least 38wpm/3'/3e
- Format lists in correspondence

A. Type 2 times.

A. WARMUP

```
1      Three travel agencies (Jepster & Vilani, Quin & Bott,   11
2  and Zeplin & Wexter) sold the most travel tickets for the   23
3  past 12 months. They sold 785, 834, and 960 total tickets.  35
   |  1  |  2  |  3  |  4  |  5  |  6  |  7  |  8  |  9  |  10  |  11  |  12
```

SKILLBUILDING

B. DIAGNOSTIC PRACTICE: ALPHABET

If you are not using the GDP software, turn to page SB-2 and follow the directions for this activity.

C. Type each sentence on a separate line by pressing ENTER after each sentence.

C. TECHNIQUE PRACTICE: ENTER KEY

```
4  Debit the accounts. Balance your checkbook. Add the assets.
5  Take the discount. Send the statements. Compute the ratios.
6  Review the accounts. Credit the amounts. Figure the totals.
7  Prepare the statements. Send the catalog. Call the clients.
```

D. Take two 3-minute timings. Review your speed and errors.

Goal: At least 38wpm/3'/3e

D. 3-MINUTE TIMING

```
8      Many people prefer to use the Internet for shopping.    11
9  With just a simple click of the mouse, you can shop for      22
10  almost any type of product. You may purchase books, cars,   34
11  magazines, toys, furniture, boxes, and even golf clubs by   46
12  using your computer to shop online.                         53
13      The advantages of using the Internet to shop online     64
14  are numerous. First, you can shop from any place that has   76
15  access to the Internet. Second, you could compare prices    87
16  with many companies before making your purchase. Third,     98
17  you can have your purchases shipped directly to you. The    109
18  savings add up quickly.                                     114
   |  1  |  2  |  3  |  4  |  5  |  6  |  7  |  8  |  9  |  10  |  11  |  12
```

E. LISTS IN CORRESPONDENCE

To format a list in correspondence:

1. Press ENTER 2 times to insert 1 blank line above the list.
2. Type the list, unformatted, at the left margin.
3. If all of the items are 1 line long, single-space the entire list.
4. If any of the items are more than 1 line long, single-space each item in the list but insert 1 blank line between the items.
5. Press ENTER 2 times to insert 1 blank line below the list.
6. Highlight the list, and apply the number or bullet feature to the selected lines.
7. If necessary, decrease the indent to move the bullets or numbers to the left margin.

DOCUMENT PROCESSING

Correspondence ▸ 48-27

Memo With a Single-Line Bulleted List

↓6X   → tab

MEMO TO: Charles A. Cornelius, President ↓2X

FROM: Alfred A. Long, Convention Director ↓2X

DATE: September 8, 20-- ↓2X

SUBJECT: Convention Locations ↓2X

As you know, this year's convention will meet in Jacksonville, Florida. It is the Executive Board's decision to rotate the convention site to each of the districts in our region. Our next three conventions will be held in the following locations: ↓2X

- Mobile, Alabama
- Atlanta, Georgia
- Myrtle Beach, South Carolina ↓2X

In May the Board will travel to Mobile to visit the location of our next convention site. When we return, we will draft our convention site proposal for you. ↓2X

urs

**Correspondence
48-28** ▶

Memo With
a Multiline
Numbered List

MEMO TO: Marcia Davis | **FROM:** Alex Pera | **DATE:** April 9, 20-- |
SUBJECT: Program Descriptions

¶ As you requested, I have contacted the speakers for our afternoon session descriptions. All three speakers have sent me a brief description of their sessions, and they are listed in the order of presentation as follows:

1. Salon I. This session will discuss the advantages of e-commerce and its influence on the economy of the United States.
2. Salon II. This session will introduce several suggestions for enhancing your Web site.
3. Salon III. This session will discuss changes occurring in Internet access and its impact on entrepreneurial ventures.

¶ By next Monday I will send you an introduction for each speaker.

urs

**Correspondence
48-29** ▶

Memo With a
Single-Line
Bulleted List

Open the file for Correspondence 48-27 and make the following changes:

1. Change the three convention sites to Miami, Florida; Raleigh, North Carolina; and Montgomery, Alabama.

2. Change the final paragraph to indicate that the Board will travel to Miami.

STRATEGIES
FOR *Career Success*   Reducing Bias in Business Communication

Everything we do in business communication attempts to build goodwill. Bias-free language and visuals help maintain the goodwill we work so hard to create.

Bias-free language does not discriminate against people on the basis of sex, physical condition, race, age, or any other characteristic. Do not emphasize gender-specific words in your business vocabulary. Instead, incorporate gender-neutral words (e.g., chairman is chairperson) into your business communication.

Organizations that treat people fairly should also use language that treats people fairly. The law is increasingly intolerant of biased documents and hostile work environments. Practice nondiscriminatory behavior by focusing on individual merits, accomplishments, skills, and what you might share in common rather than illustrating differences. Treating every group with respect and understanding is essential to gaining loyalty and future business while cultivating harmonious relationships.

YOUR TURN   Review a document that you have recently written. Is the document bias-free?

Lesson 49

Letters With Copy Notations

GOALS
- Improve speed and accuracy
- Refine language arts skills in spelling
- Format letters with copy notations

A. Type 2 times.

A. WARMUP

```
1        "Look at them! Have you ever seen such large birds?"    11
2   When questioned later on an exam, about 80% to 90% of the    23
3   junior girls were amazed to learn that they were ospreys.    34
    |  1  |  2  |  3  |  4  |  5  |  6  |  7  |  8  |  9  |  10  |  11  |  12
```

SKILLBUILDING

B. MAP

Follow the GDP software directions for this exercise in improving keystroking accuracy.

C. Take a 1-minute timing on the first paragraph to establish your base speed. Then take four 1-minute timings on the remaining paragraphs. As soon as you equal or exceed your base speed on one paragraph, advance to the next, more difficult paragraph.

C. SUSTAINED PRACTICE: NUMBERS AND SYMBOLS

```
4        The proposed road improvement program was approved      10
5   by the county commissioners at their last meeting. There     21
6   were about ten citizens who spoke on behalf of the project.  33

7        The plan calls for blacktopping a 14-mile stretch on    11
8   County Road #2356. This is the road that is commonly called  23
9   the "roller coaster" because of all the curves and hills.    35

10       There will be 116 miles blacktopped by J & J, Inc.      10
11  (commonly referred to as the Jeremy Brothers*). J & J's      21
12  office is at 1798 30th Avenue past the 22d Street bridge.    33

13       Minor road repair costs range from $10,784 to a high    11
14  of $163,450 (39% of the total program costs). The "county    23
15  inspector" is to hold the project costs to 105% of budget!   35
    |  1  |  2  |  3  |  4  |  5  |  6  |  7  |  8  |  9  |  10  |  11  |  12
```

D. Type this list of frequently misspelled words, paying special attention to any spelling problems in each word.

D. SPELLING

16 per other receipt present provided commission international
17 service position questions following industrial maintenance
18 well absence support proposal mortgage corporate management
19 upon balance approval experience facilities recommendations
20 paid because premium procedure addition directors currently

Edit the sentences to correct any misspellings.

21 The international comission provided a list of proceedures.
22 That industrial maintainance proposal is curently in place.
23 The directers and management supported the recomendations.
24 Those present raised a question about a corperate morgage.
25 Six of the folowing persons have now given their aproval.
26 In adition, Kris has premium experience at the facilitys.

E. COPY NOTATIONS

Making file copies of all documents you prepare is a good business practice. At times you may also need copies to send to people other than the addressee of the original document.

A copy notation is typed on a document to indicate that someone else besides the addressee is receiving a copy.

1. Type the copy notation on the line below the reference initials or below the attachment or enclosure notation.

2. At the left margin, type a lowercase *c* followed by a colon.
3. Press the SPACE BAR 1 time, and type the name of the person receiving the copy.
4. If more than one person is receiving a copy, type the names on one line with a comma and space between each name.

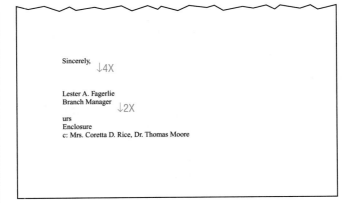

Sincerely, ↓4X

Lester A. Fagerlie
Branch Manager ↓2X

urs
Enclosure
c: Mrs. Coretta D. Rice, Dr. Thomas Moore

Correspondence 49-30 ▶

Business Letter in Block Style With Copy Notation

Current Date | Mr. and Mrs. Richard Belson | 783 Wellcourt Lane | Mount Vernon, WA 98273-4156 | Dear Mr. and Mrs. Belson:

¶ Marian Dickenson has informed me that you have several questions pertaining to the maintenance proposal that was submitted by the directors and approved by management. It is our position, based upon the procedures we provided following last week's meeting, that the proposal was submitted to corporate headquarters prior to your inquiry. Therefore, your questions should be directed to Alfred A. Long in our Seattle office.

¶ It has been our experience that inquiries such as yours will receive an immediate response because of the support you have demonstrated during other maintenance negotiations. I would recommend that you call me if you have not heard from Mr. Long by the 13th of the month. In the absence of Mr. Long's response, I am sending you a copy of other materials related to your inquiry.

¶ Thank you for your interest in this matter.

Sincerely, | Theodore A. Gardner | Sales Director | urs | c: Marian Dickenson

---

Correspondence 49-31 ▶

Business Letter in Block Style With Enclosure and Copy Notations

Open the file for Correspondence 49-30 and make the following changes:

1. Send the letter to Mr. and Mrs. George Tanner | 105 Royal Lane | Commerce, TX 75428

2. Add the following sentence to the end of the second paragraph:

    These materials are en-
    closed for your review.

3. Include an enclosure notation.

4. Send a copy of this letter to Marian Dickenson and also to Brad Chesterfield.

In a computer, each keystroke is represented by a unique combination of the numbers 0 and 1 to create ASCII Code that is used by the computer to process data into useful information.

Letters in Modified-Block Style

GOALS
- Type at least 38wpm/3'/3e
- Format letters in modified-block style

A. Type 2 times.

A. WARMUP

```
1      Mark Kara's quilts down by 25%: #489, #378, and #460.    11
2   Leave the prices as they are for the remainder of the sizes  23
3   in that section. Eleven adjoining sections will be next.     34
    | 1 | 2 | 3 | 4 | 5 | 6 | 7 | 8 | 9 | 10 | 11 | 12
```

SKILLBUILDING

PRETEST ➡ PRACTICE ➡ POSTTEST

B. PRETEST: Alternate- and One-Hand Words

PRETEST
Take a 1-minute timing. Review your speed and errors.

```
4      The chair of the trade committee served notice that    11
5   the endowment grant exceeded the budget. A million dollars  23
6   was the exact amount. The greater part might be deferred.    35
    | 1 | 2 | 3 | 4 | 5 | 6 | 7 | 8 | 9 | 10 | 11 | 12
```

C. PRACTICE: Alternate-Hand Words

PRACTICE
Speed Emphasis:
 If you made 2 or fewer errors on the Pretest, type each *indivdual* line 2 times.
Accuracy Emphasis:
 If you made 3 or more errors, type each *group* of lines (as though it were a paragraph) 2 times.

```
7   amendment turndown visible suspend visual height signs maps
8   authentic clemency dormant figment island emblem usual snap
9   shamrocks blandish problem penalty profit thrown chair form
```

D. PRACTICE: One-Hand Words

```
10   pumpkin eastward plumply barrage greater poplin trade holly
11   minikin cassette opinion seaweed created kimono union exact
12   minimum attracts reserve million scatter unhook plump defer
```

POSTTEST
Repeat the Pretest timing and compare performance.

E. POSTTEST: Alternate- and One-Hand Words

F. Take two 3-minute timings. Review your speed and errors.

Goal: At least 38wpm/3'/3e

F. 3-MINUTE TIMING

```
13        The Internet is a valuable source of information on      11
14  many topics. You can view newspapers and magazines, find        22
15  tax forms and information on how to complete them, and          33
16  even search for a job. You can also find answers to health      45
17  questions and learn about world events almost as soon as        56
18  they occur.                                                     58
19        Electronic mail is another part of the Internet that     69
20  people are using more frequently. They use email to keep        80
21  in touch with friends, family, and coworkers quickly and        91
22  inexpensively. They can write down their thoughts and send     103
23  messages just as if they were writing a letter or memo.        114
     |  1  |  2  |  3  |  4  |  5  |  6  |  7  |  8  |  9  |  10  |  11  |  12
```

FORMATTING

G. MODIFIED-BLOCK STYLE LETTERS

A modified-block style is a commonly used format for business letters. To format a modified-block style letter:

1. Clear all tabs and set a left tab at the centerpoint.
2. Press ENTER 6 times.
3. Tab to the centerpoint, and type the date of the letter.
4. Press ENTER 4 times, and type the inside address at the left margin.
5. Insert 1 blank line before and after the salutation.
6. Type the paragraphs blocked at the left margin.
7. Press ENTER 2 times after the body of the letter.
8. Tab to the centerpoint, and type the complimentary closing.
9. Press ENTER 4 times.
10. Tab to the centerpoint, and type the writer's identification.
11. Press ENTER 2 times, and type the reference initials and remaining letter parts at the left margin.

(Continued on next page)

Garner Homes
4782 Eureka Avenue
Bellingham, WA 98452
http://www.garner.com

"Putting a Roof on America"

tab to centerpoint ⟶ November 29, 20-- ↓4X

Mr. and Mrs. Arvey Gates
2308 Hannegan Road
Bellingham, WA 98226
↓2X
Dear Mr. and Mrs. Gates:
↓2X
Delores Matson, who hosted our Ridgeway open house last Saturday, has referred your unanswered questions to me. We are pleased that you are interested in a Garner home.

The usual down payment is 20 percent of the total selling price, but some lending agencies require a smaller amount in certain situations. Garner Homes is not itself involved in home financing, but we work with the financial institutions shown on the enclosed list.

Yes, the lot you prefer can accommodate a walkout basement. Delores will be in touch with you soon. We can have your new Ridgeway ready for occupancy within 90 days.
↓2X
Sincerely,
↓4X
Alfred A. Long

Alfred A. Long
Sales Director
↓2X

urs
Enclosure
c: Loan Processing Dept.

Go To

Word Processing Manual

H. WORD PROCESSING: RULER TABS AND TAB SET

Study Lesson 50 in your word processing manual. Complete all of the shaded steps while at your computer. Then format the jobs that follow.

Network administrators and information systems managers are two popular and well-paid opportunities in the Information Technology Services career cluster.

Correspondence 50-32

Business Letter in Modified-Block Style with Enclosure and Copy Notations

Reference Manual

Refer to page R-3B of the Reference Manual for additional guidance.

→ tab to centerpoint November 29, 20-- ↓4X

Mr. and Mrs. Arvey Gates
2308 Hannegan Road
Bellingham, WA 98226 ↓2X

Dear Mr. and Mrs. Gates: ↓2X

Delores Matson, who hosted our Ridgeway open house last Saturday, has referred your unanswered questions to me. We are pleased that you are interested in a Garner home.

The usual down payment is 20 percent of the total selling price, but some lending agencies require a smaller amount in certain situations. Garner Homes is not itself involved in home financing, but we work with the financial institutions shown on the enclosed list.

Yes, the lot you prefer can accommodate a walkout basement. Delores will be in touch with you soon. We can have your new Ridgeway ready for occupancy within 90 days.

→ tab to centerpoint Sincerely, ↓4X

Alfred A. Long

→ tab to centerpoint Alfred A. Long
Sales Director ↓2X

urs
Enclosure
c: Loan Processing Dept.

Correspondence
50-33 ▶

Business Letter in
Modified-Block
Style With
Numbered List

Use November 30, 20--, as the date as you format this modified-block style letter to be sent to the Sales Manager at Bachmann's Nursery and Landscaping | 6823 Oneta Avenue | Youngstown, OH 44500-2175

Dear Sales Manager:

¶ As you requested on the telephone, I am providing the following list of events relating to my tree problem.

1. On April 15, I purchased at your branch in Warren four silver maples for the atrium outside our Riverdale office. We also purchased four Japanese red maples at your branch in Niles later that afternoon.

2. After about three months, one silver maple and one red maple had died. I phoned both the Warren and Niles branches several times on November 1, but no one returned my messages.

3. On November 8, I phoned your nursery in an attempt to have these trees replaced. Again, there was no response.

¶ As these trees were expensive, I expect that you will either replace them or reimburse me for the cost of the trees. I shall look forward to hearing from you.

Sincerely, | Marvin L. Norgaard | Grounds Manager | urs

Correspondence
50-34 ▶

Business Letter in
Modified-Block
Style With
Enclosure and
Copy Notations

Current Date | Mr. Marvin L. Norgaard | 4782 Saranac Avenue | Youngstown, OH 44505-6207 | Dear Mr. Norgaard:

¶ This is in response to your recent letter.

¶ Your trees will be replaced without cost to you. We will make sure that the replacement trees will match the others you purchased in both size and color. I am enclosing a warranty for these new trees so that you can feel confident that we stand behind our product.

¶ The survival rate for trees cannot be perfect; however, we are indeed sorry that you have had to have this temporary setback.

¶ The communication breakdown with our two branch offices should not have occurred. We will take steps to ensure that this will not happen in the future. You can be confident that the appearance of your atrium will be restored and that the beauty of the new trees will add to your property's value. Thank you for shopping at Bachmann's.

Sincerely, | Mrs. Alice G. Schmidt | Co-owner | urs | Enclosure | c: Mr. George Lambrecht, Co-owner

Correspondence
50-35 ▶

Personal-Business
Letter With Bulleted
List, Enclosure, and
Copy Notations

**Progress Check
Proofreading Check**

Documents designated
as Proofreading Checks
serve as a check of your
proofreading skill. Your
goal is to have zero typographical errors when the
GDP software first scores
the document.

Current Date | Ms. Karen Shalicky | Lincoln Travel Center | 2384 Longdale Avenue | Suite 4113 | Boston, MA 02134-3489 | Dear Ms. Shalicky:

¶ I am interested in taking a cruise in one of the following regions:

- Alaska Inland Passageway
- Caribbean Islands
- Greek Isles

¶ Could you please send me some promotional materials for these cruises. My financial resources are such that I would like to limit my cruise package to $5,000 and would prefer a cruise no longer than ten days in length. I will be accompanied by my friend, Bonnie Davis, and I assume that any quotes you give me could apply to both of us.

¶ We would like to do sightseeing in some of these locations. Do you have special excursions available to passengers? I am enclosing a list of the sites we would like to visit in each of these regions.

¶ The best time for us to travel is between June 1 and June 20, and we would like you to schedule our trip around those dates. I hope to hear from you soon.

Yours truly, | Rita Wright | 678 Ardale Avenue | Milton, MA 02186-2190 | Enclosure | c: Bonnie Davis

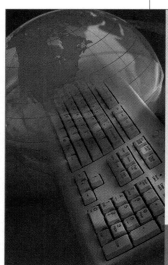

Keyboarding
CONNECTION
Avoid Email Flame Wars

Don't fan the flames! A flame is an offensive email that expresses anger, criticism, or insults. If flames are transmitted to a mailing list, they can produce a long list of flames and counter flames known as flame wars.

You may be tempted to join in, but this is a waste of everyone's time. Often the initial offense was merely a poorly worded email that a reader interpreted as an insult. There are those who intentionally send inflammatory emails called flame bait. Resist the urge to send a cutting response, and consider if the writer's intent was to provoke you.

If your reader misjudges something you wrote and becomes offended, just apologize. A timely apology can thwart a potential fire. Avoid miscommunication by watching how you word your emails.

YOUR TURN Have you ever been insulted by an email? What was your response?

Employment Documents

LESSON 51
Traditional Resumes

LESSON 52
Electronic Resumes

LESSON 53
Letters of Application

LESSON 54
Follow-Up Letters

LESSON 55
Integrated Employment Project

August 10, 20--

Personnel Director
Arlington Communications
2403 Sunset Lane
Arlington, TX 76015-3148

Dear Personnel Director:

Please consider me as an applicant for a position with Arlington Communications. My strengths have always been in the communication arts, as you can see on the enclosed resume, which lists a number of courses in English, speech, and communication technology. The two part-time jobs I held during the summer months at your company convinced me that Arlington Communications is the place where I want to work.

If you would like to interview me for any possible openings this summer or fall, please call me at 903-555-2340. I look forward to hearing from you.

ALLEN P. HUNTER

10234 Wood Sorrell Lane, Burke, VA 22015
Phone: 703-555-4902; email: aphunter@netlink.net

OBJECTIVE   To gain experience in retail sales as a foundation for a retail management position.

EDUCATION   Central High School, Burke, Virginia 22015
Graduated: May 1999

EXPERIENCE   *Computer Systems Technician, Kramer & Kramer, Inc.*
Harrisburg, VA 22807
June 1999-Present
Duties include reviewing
programs used for proce

Salesclerk, Blanchard's Departm
Richmond, VA 23218
May 1997-May 1999 (part-time)
Duties included selling
sonic cash register. Assis
monthly sales reports.

ACTIVITIES   Volunteer for Habitat for Human
Member, Computer Technicians
Senior Class President, 1999
Member, Intramural Soccer Tea
Member, Beta Club, 1996-1999

REFERENCES   References available upon reque

April 7, 20--

Ms. Kay Brewer, Personnel Director
Blanchard Computer Systems
2189 Dace Avenue
Sioux City, IA 51107

Dear Ms. Brewer:

Thank you for the opportunity of interviewing yesterday with Blanchard Computer Systems. Please express my appreciation to all of those who were involved.

The interview gave me a good feeling about the company. The positive description that you shared with me convinced me that Blanchard is indeed a company at which I would like to work. I was greatly impressed with the summary of social service programs that are sponsored by Blanchard for citizens throughout the community.

You may recall that I have had experience with all of the equipment that is used. It appears to me that my strengths in computer application software and office systems would blend in well with your company profile.

I look forward to hearing from you soon regarding your decision on the position of data records operator.

Sincerely,

Arlene F. Jefferson
1842 Amber Road
Wayne, NE 68787

Lesson 51

Traditional Resumes

GOALS

- Improve speed and accuracy
- Refine language arts skills in the use of commas
- Format traditional resumes

A. Type 2 times.

A. WARMUP

```
1      Janice had sales of over $23,000; Kathy's sales were      10
2  only $17,368 for the same quiet period. Craig agreed that     23
3  some inventory sizes were wrong and should be exchanged.       34
   | 1 | 2 | 3 | 4 | 5 | 6 | 7 | 8 | 9 | 10 | 11 | 12
```

SKILLBUILDING

B. MAP

Follow the GDP software directions for this exercise in improving keystroking accuracy.

C. Take a 1-minute timing on the first paragraph to establish your base speed. Then take four 1-minute timings on the remaining paragraphs. As soon as you equal or exceed your base speed on one paragraph, advance to the next, more difficult paragraph.

C. SUSTAINED PRACTICE: CAPITALIZATION

```
4       There are several different approaches that one can      11
5  take when considering a major purchase. Some people make      22
6  the mistake of simply going to a store and making a choice.   34

7       When one couple decided to buy a chest-type freezer,     11
8  they looked at a consumer magazine in the library. The        22
9  Sears, Amana, and General Electric were shown as best buys.   34

10      That same issue of their magazine compared electric      11
11 ranges. Jonathan and Mary Anne found that the Maytag, Magic   23
12 Chef, Amana, and Gibson were determined to be best buys.      34

13      Best buys for full-size microwave ovens were the Sharp   11
14 Carousel, Panasonic, and GoldStar Multiwave. Good midsize     23
15 models were the Frigidaire, Panasonic, and Sears Kenmore.     34
   | 1 | 2 | 3 | 4 | 5 | 6 | 7 | 8 | 9 | 10 | 11 | 12
```

D. Study the rules at the right.

D. COMMAS

RULE ▶
, date

Use a comma before and after the year in a complete date.

We will arrive on June 2, 2001, for the conference.
But: We will arrive on June <u>2</u> for the conference.

RULE ▶
, place

Use a comma before and after a state or country that follows a city (but not before a ZIP Code).

Joan moved to Vancouver, British Columbia, in May.
Send the package to Douglasville, G<u>A </u>30135, by Express Mail.
But: Send the package to Georgi<u>a </u>by Express Mail

Edit the sentences to correct any errors in the use of commas.

16 The warehouse building will be ready in September, 2001.
17 The attorney told a clerk to use June 30, 2000 as the date.
18 The report was sent to Nagoya, Japan on March 14, 1999.
19 The move to Toledo, Ohio, was scheduled for November, 2000.

FORMATTING

E. TRADITIONAL RESUMES

When you apply for a job, you may be asked to submit a resume. The purpose of a resume is to convey your qualifications for the position you are seeking. A resume should include the following:

- Personal information (name, address, telephone number, and email address).
- Your career objective (optional).
- A summary of your educational background and special training.
- Previous work experience.
- Any activities or personal achievements that relate to the position for which you are applying.
- References (optional). References should consist of at least three people who can tell a prospective employer what kind of worker you are.

Often, your resume creates the first impression you make on a prospective employer; be sure it is free of errors.

Various styles are acceptable for formatting a resume. Choose a style (or design one) that is attractive and that enables you to get all the needed information on one or two pages. The first page of a resume should start approximately 2 inches from the top of the page.

To format a traditional resume:
1. Set alignment at center.
2. Press ENTER 6 times; then center your name in 14-pt. Arial bold.
3. Press ENTER 2 times.
4. Type your street address, followed by a comma.
5. Press the SPACE BAR 1 time; then type your city, state, and ZIP code.
6. Press ENTER 1 time.
7. Type your phone number, followed by a semicolon.
8. Press the SPACE BAR 1 time; then type email: and your email address.

(Continued on next page)

9. Press ENTER 2 times.
10. Insert a table with 2 columns and 1 row. Adjust the left column to accommodate the longest entry in the left column: REFERENCES.
11. Apply a top border to the table, and press ENTER 1 time.
12. Type OBJECTIVE in bold in Row 1, Column A.
13. Move the insertion point to Column B, press ENTER 1 time, and type your objective.
14. Continue typing the entries as shown in the illustration.

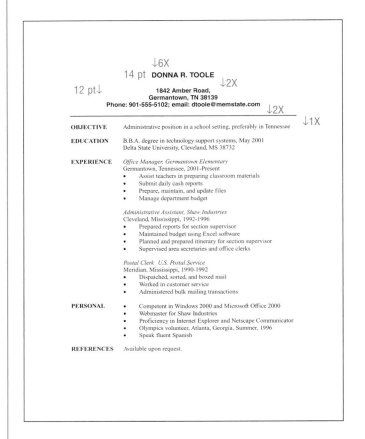

Go To

Word Processing Manual

F. WORD PROCESSING: FONTS AND TABLES—CHANGING COLUMN WIDTH

Study Lesson 51 in your word processing manual. Complete all of the shaded steps while at your computer. Then format the jobs that follow.

Report 51-27 ▶

One-Page
Traditional Resume

↓6X

14 pt **PATSY R. ROTHEL**
↓2X

12 pt↓ **2525 Hickory Ridge Drive, Plant City, FL 33567**
Phone: 813-555-0704
↓2X

↓1X

OBJECTIVE	To continue my career in computer graphics by securing a position related to graphic design ↓2X
EDUCATION	Central Florida Business College, Valrico, FL 33594 Two years of related courses in graphic design Plant City High School, Plant City, FL 33567 Graduated: May 1999
EXPERIENCE	*Graphic Designer, NetView, Inc.* Orlando, Florida October 2001-Present Designed Web pages for Internet-connected companies in central Florida. Edited page copy for Web sites. Created a database for Web-based users. *Copy Editor, The Plant City Press* Plant City, Florida May 1998-October 2001 Assisted the news editor with typing, proofreading, and editing copy for daily newspaper. Solicited subscriptions from local businesses. Conducted interviews for Citizens of the Week forum.
ACTIVITIES	Spanish Honor Society, 2001 Member, Phi Beta Lambda, 2000-2001 Newsletter Editor, *CFBC News,* 2000 President, FBLA Chapter, 1999 Treasurer, FBLA Chapter, 1998
REFERENCES	References available upon request

Open the file for Report 51-27 and make the following changes:

1. Change the name to ALLEN P. HUNTER.
2. Change the address to 10234 Wood Sorrell Lane, Burke, VA 22015
3. Change the phone number to 703-555-4902 and the email address to aphunter@netlink.net.
4. Replace the OBJECTIVE entry with the following:

   To gain experience in retail sales as a foundation for a retail management position.
5. Replace the EDUCATION entry with the following:

   Central High School, Burke, Virginia 22015 | Graduated: May 1999.
6. Change the first EXPERIENCE entry to the following:

   Computer Systems Technician, Kramer & Kramer, Inc. | Harrisburg, VA 22807 | June 1999-Present | Duties include reviewing, installing, and updating software programs used for processing legal documents.
7. Change the second EXPERIENCE entry to the following:

   Salesclerk, Blanchard's Department Store | Richmond, VA 23218 | May 1997-May 1999 (part-time) | Duties included selling sporting goods and operating Panasonic cash register. Assisted sales manager in completing monthly sales reports.
8. Change the entries for ACTIVITIES to the following:

   Volunteer for Habitat for Humanity, 2000-Present | Member, Computer Technicians Association, 2000-Present | Senior Class President, 1999 | Member, Intramural Soccer Team, 1997-1999 | Member, Beta Club, 1996-1999.

STRATEGIES FOR *Career Success*

Formatting Your Resume

The format of your resume communicates important skills—neatness and the ability to organize. Make a good first impression by following these guidelines.

Watch the spacing on your resume. A crowded resume implies you cannot summarize. Leave adequate white space between the section headings of your resume. Use different font sizes, boldface, and italics to separate and emphasize information. Font sizes should be between 10 to 14.

Print your resume on good quality 8½" × 11" white or off-white bond paper (e.g., 20-pound stock). Colored paper doesn't provide enough contrast when your resume is copied or faxed.

Proofread your resume for spelling errors and consistency of format. Ask a few friends to review it and provide feedback.

YOUR TURN Print one copy of your resume on a dark colored paper and print one copy on white paper. Photocopy each resume. Which provides the better contrast for readability?

Electronic Resumes

GOALS

- Type at least 39wpm/5′/5e
- Format an electronic resume

A. Type 2 times.

A. WARMUP

```
1        The new firm, Kulver & Zweidel, will be equipped to      11
2   handle from 1/6 to 1/4 of Martin's tax needs after they       22
3   move to the new location at 1970 Gansby, just east of Main.   34
     |  1  |  2  |  3  |  4  |  5  |  6  |  7  |  8  |  9  |  10  |  11  |  12
```

SKILLBUILDING

B. Take three 12-second timings on each line. The scale below the last line shows your wpm speed for a 12-second timing.

B. 12-SECOND SPEED SPRINTS

```
4   Pat went back to the store where he had seen the red shirt.
5   The salesclerk acted as though she had not seen him before.
6   There was a huge change when he walked into a second store.
7   Pat was met at the front door with a smile and a handshake.
    I I I I 5 I I I I 10 I I I I 15 I I I I 20 I I I I 25 I I I I 30 I I I I 35 I I I I 40 I I I I 45 I I I I 50 I I I I 55 I I I I 60
```

C. PROGRESSIVE PRACTICE: ALPHABET

If you are not using the GDP software, turn to page SB-7 and follow the directions for this activity.

Business is transacted across the world virtually instantaneously because information technologies have touched the work lives of millions of people.

D. Take two 5-minute timings. Review your speed and errors.

Goal: At least 39wpm/5'/5e

D. 5-MINUTE TIMING

8	Have you completed your education when you graduate	10
9	from high school or finish your college work? Most people	22
10	look forward to reaching milestones, such as graduation or	34
11	completing a course. Have they learned everything they will	46
12	need to know to be successful in the real world? The answer	58
13	is not so simple.	62
14	Learning continues to occur long after you leave the	73
15	classroom. No matter what job or career you pursue, you	84
16	will learn something new every day. When you investigate	95
17	new ideas, ask questions, or find a different way to do a	107
18	job, you are continuing to learn. In the process, you gain	119
19	additional experience, develop new skills, and become a	130
20	better worker.	133
21	Getting along with your peers, for example, is not	143
22	something that you learn from studying books. You learn	154
23	to be a team player when you listen to your coworkers and	166
24	share your ideas with them. Do not hesitate to acquire	177
25	new skills or to initiate new ideas. Be zealous in your	188
26	efforts to continue your education.	195

| 1 | 2 | 3 | 4 | 5 | 6 | 7 | 8 | 9 | 10 | 11 | 12 |

FORMATTING

E. ELECTRONIC RESUMES

An electronic resume is simply a resume that has been formatted for display on the World Wide Web. It can be attached to an email and sent all over the world. To format a resume for electronic display:

- Create a traditional resume, using the same guidelines you followed in Lesson 51.
- Do not use the TAB key; if you want to indent lines, use the SPACE BAR for moving characters horizontally on the page.
- Use left alignment.
- Use the default font size. Do not use any special font features (bold, italic, or underlines) or graphic features (rules, bullets, graphics, boxes, tables, or columns). To achieve a similar effect, use an asterisk (*), plus symbol (+), or capital letters.
- Use a line length of no more than 60 characters.
- Do not hyphenate words at the end of a line.
- Save the resume as a text-only file (one that has a .txt extension).

F. WORD PROCESSING: SAVING IN TEXT-ONLY FORMAT

Study Lesson 52 in your word processing manual. Complete all of the shaded steps while at your computer. Then format the jobs that follow.

DOCUMENT PROCESSING

Report 52-29

One-Page Electronic Resume

Use the model below to create an electronic resume. Observe the following points when creating the resume:
- Use a monospaced font (Courier).
- Use the SPACE BAR for indentions; use asterisks for highlighting the entries under EDUCATION, EXPERIENCE, and PERSONAL.
- Type the name, sections, and job titles in all caps.
- Save the resume as a text-only file.

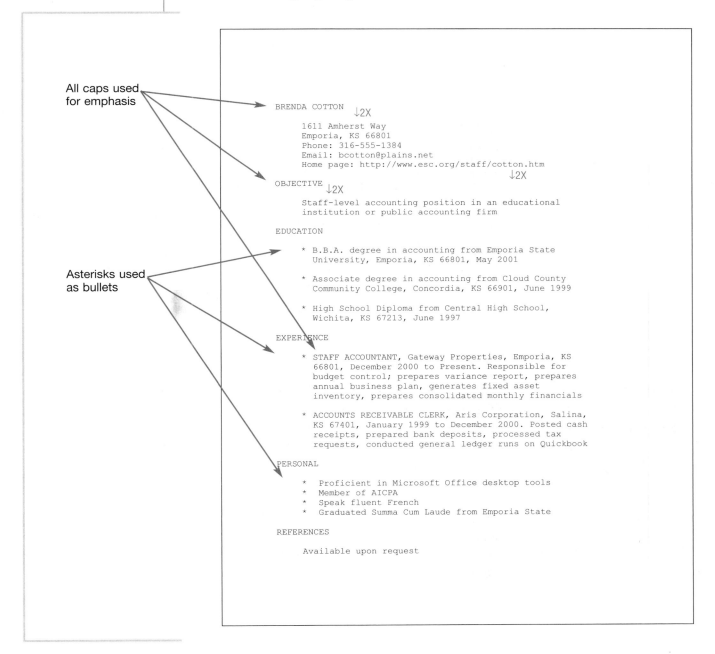

All caps used for emphasis

Asterisks used as bullets

```
BRENDA COTTON   ↓2X

      1611 Amherst Way
      Emporia, KS 66801
      Phone: 316-555-1384
      Email: bcotton@plains.net
      Home page: http://www.esc.org/staff/cotton.htm
                                        ↓2X
OBJECTIVE  ↓2X

      Staff-level accounting position in an educational
      institution or public accounting firm

EDUCATION

      * B.B.A. degree in accounting from Emporia State
        University, Emporia, KS 66801, May 2001

      * Associate degree in accounting from Cloud County
        Community College, Concordia, KS 66901, June 1999

      * High School Diploma from Central High School,
        Wichita, KS 67213, June 1997

EXPERIENCE

      * STAFF ACCOUNTANT, Gateway Properties, Emporia, KS
        66801, December 2000 to Present. Responsible for
        budget control; prepares variance report, prepares
        annual business plan, generates fixed asset
        inventory, prepares consolidated monthly financials

      * ACCOUNTS RECEIVABLE CLERK, Aris Corporation, Salina,
        KS 67401, January 1999 to December 2000. Posted cash
        receipts, prepared bank deposits, processed tax
        requests, conducted general ledger runs on Quickbook

PERSONAL

      *   Proficient in Microsoft Office desktop tools
      *   Member of AICPA
      *   Speak fluent French
      *   Graduated Summa Cum Laude from Emporia State

REFERENCES

      Available upon request
```

Report 52-30 ▶

One-Page
Electronic Resume

Open the file for Report 51-27 and make the following changes:

1. Format the traditional resume as an electronic resume.
2. Use a monospaced font (Courier).
3. Change Patsy R. Rothel's name to Sharon O. Mandrell.
4. Change the address to 247 Christine Drive | Kissimmee, FL 34744

5. Change the phone to 407-555-1389.
6. Delete the first three entries in the ACTIVITIES section.
7. Add the following entry at the end of the ACTIVITIES section:
   Track Club, 1998.
8. Save the resume as a text-only file.

Report 52-31 ▶

Two-Page Electronic
Resume

Open the file for Report 51-28 and make the following changes:

1. Format the traditional resume as an electronic resume.
2. Use a monospaced font (Courier).
3. Use the SPACE BAR for indentions.
4. Add 703.555.4924 as a fax number below the phone number.
5. Use the hyphen key and two spaces to begin the job entries in the EXPERI-ENCE section and the entries under ACTIVITIES.
6. Change the OBJECTIVE to the following:
   Retail management entry-level position with a mid-size department store.

7. Change the dates for part-time employment with Blanchard's to:
   May 1998 to May 1999.
8. Add the following experience for Mr. Hunter:
   Salesclerk, Kramer Appliances | Alexandria, VA 22310 | July 1997 to May 1998 (part-time) | Duties included creating window displays for storefront, updating Web site for Kramer Appliances.
9. Save the resume as a text-only file.

Keyboarding CONNECTION

Creating a Scannable Resume

Why create a scannable resume? Many companies electronically scan resumes and move the data to an employment database. To fill a position, managers conduct a subject search of the resumes on file and review those selected. Modify your resume's appearance so that it can be scanned.

Begin with a section that includes your name and contact information. Avoid boldface, italics, underlining, bullets, shading, and columns. Left-justify all text. Choose 10 to 14 font size for your body text. Use standard fonts (e.g., Times Roman, Arial). Use white space to separate sections of your resume.

Note the keywords used in the job postings that interest you. Include these keywords within your skills, experience, and education. Also, use noun phrases (e.g., systems analyst, sales experience, project manager).

YOUR TURN Prepare a list of keyword descriptors to summarize your skills, experience, and education.

Letters of Application

GOALS

- Improve speed and accuracy
- Refine language arts skills in composing paragraphs
- Format letters of application

A. Type 2 times.

A. WARMUP

```
1        Prices were quickly lowered (some by as much as 50%)    11
2 @ Julia's garage sale. She could see that extra sales would   23
3 not be over the 9%* she had projected to finance the prize.   35
   | 1 | 2 | 3 | 4 | 5 | 6 | 7 | 8 | 9 | 10 | 11 | 12
```

SKILLBUILDING

PRETEST ➤ PRACTICE ➤ POSTTEST

B. PRETEST: Common Letter Combinations

PRETEST
Take a 1-minute timing. Review your speed and errors.

```
4        They formed an action committee to force a motion for   11
5 a ruling on your contract case. This enabled them to comply   23
6 within the lawful time period and convey a common message.    35
   | 1 | 2 | 3 | 4 | 5 | 6 | 7 | 8 | 9 | 10 | 11 | 12
```

C. PRACTICE: Word Beginnings

PRACTICE
Speed Emphasis:
If you made 2 or fewer errors on the Pretest, type each *individual* line 2 times.
Accuracy Emphasis:
If you made 3 or more errors, type each *group* of lines (as though it were a paragraph) 2 times.

```
7 for forget formal format forces forums forked forest formed
8 per perils period perish permit person peruse perked pertly
9 com combat comedy coming commit common compel comply comets
```

D. PRACTICE: Word Endings

```
10 ing acting aiding boring buying ruling saving hiding dating
11 ble bubble dabble double enable feeble fumble tumble usable
12 ion action vision lesion nation bunion lotion motion legion
```

E. POSTTEST: Common Letter Combinations

POSTTEST
Repeat the Pretest timing and compare performance.

F. PROGRESSIVE PRACTICE: NUMBERS

If you are not using the GDP software, turn to page SB-11 and follow the directions for this activity.

G. Choose one of the phrases at the right; then compose a paragraph of three to four sentences on that topic.

G. COMPOSING PARAGRAPHS

13 My computer was working fine until it . . .
14 The Internet has helped me complete my class assignments by . . .
15 Several of us decided to take the cruise because . . .
16 I have several skills, but my best skill is . . . .

FORMATTING

Reference Manual

Refer to page R-12B of the Reference Manual for additional guidance.

H. LETTERS OF APPLICATION

A letter of application is sent along with a resume to a prospective employer. Together, the letter and the resume serve to introduce a person to the organization.

The letter of application should be no longer than one page and should include (1) the job you are applying for and how you learned of the job, (2) the highlights of your enclosed resume, and (3) a request for an interview.

DOCUMENT PROCESSING

Correspondence 53-36

Application Letter in Modified-Block Style With Enclosure Notation.

September 15, 20-- | Ms. Kay Brewer, Personel Director | Blanchard Computer Systems | 2189 Dace Ave. | Sioux City, IA 51107 | Dear Ms. Brewer:

¶ Please consider me as an applicant for the position of Data Records Operator advertized in the September 13th edition of the Sioux City Press. *ital*

¶ In May I will graduate with an A.A. degree in Systems Office from West Iowa Business College. My enclosed resume shows that I have completed courses in Excel, Access, and Microsoft word. I also have ~~significant~~ *considerable* experience in working on the internet. The skills I gained in using these software packages and in accessing the Internet will be ~~extremely~~ useful to your branch office in Sioux City.

¶ The position with your company is *very* appealing to me. If you wish to interview me for ~~the~~ *this* position, please call me at 402-555-7265. Sincerely, | Arlene F. Jefferson | 1842 Amber Road | Wayne, Ne 68787 | Enclosure

August 10, 20-- | Personnel Director | Arlington Communications | 2403 Sunset Lane | Arlington, TX 76015-3148 | Dear Personnel Director:

¶ Please consider me as an applicant for a position with Arlington Communications. My strengths have always been in the communication arts, as you can see on the enclosed resume, which lists a number of courses in English, speech, and communication technology. The two part-time jobs I held during the summer months at your company convinced me that Arlington Communications is the place where I want to work.

¶ If you would like to interview me for any possible openings this summer or fall, please call me at 903-555-2340. I look forward to hearing from you.

Sincerely, | Kenneth R. Diaz | 105 Royal Lane | Commerce, TX 75428 | Enclosure

STRATEGIES FOR *Career Success*

Writing a Job Application Letter

What's the goal of the letter that accompanies your resume? To get the interview. No two letters of application are alike.

In the opening paragraph, state your purpose (e.g., the position applied for, how you became aware of it, etc.).

In the middle section, sell yourself. Convince the reader that you are the best match for the job. If you respond to a job posting, match your qualifications to the job description. If you send an unsolicited letter, specify how the employer will benefit from your qualifications. Also, refer to your resume.

In the closing paragraph, show confidence in your abilities (e.g., "I'm certain I can meet your needs for a …"). Then state a specific time you will call to schedule an interview.

YOUR TURN Obtain a job description for which you believe you are qualified. List the job requirements, then list your qualifications that match.

Follow-Up Letters

GOALS:

- Type at least 39wpm/5'/5e
- Format follow-up letters

A. Type 2 times.

A. WARMUP

```
1        Quite a night! All sixty senior citizens (including      11
2   the handicapped) really enjoyed that play. Over 3/4 of the    23
3   tickets were sold; most had been sold by Frank's workers.     35
    | 1  | 2  | 3  | 4  | 5  | 6  | 7  | 8  | 9  | 10 | 11 | 12
```

SKILLBUILDING

B. DIAGNOSTIC PRACTICE: ALPHABET

If you are not using the GDP software, turn to page SB-2 and follow the directions for this activity.

The keyboard is still the most commonly used input device, facilitating the interaction between a computer and a user.

C. Take two 5-minute timings. Review your speed and errors.

Goal: At least 39wpm/5'/5e

C. 5-MINUTE TIMING

```
 4        In the past, typing was a skill that was used only by    11
 5   those who were secretaries, students, and office workers.      23
 6   High school students who were preparing to go to college       34
 7   often took typing classes so they could type their college     46
 8   research papers easily. Often students who wanted to be        57
 9   hired for office jobs or secretaries would take advanced       68
10   courses in typing.                                             72
11        With the invention of word processors and advances in     83
12   computer technology, people are recognizing that they need     95
13   keyboarding skills. From the top executive to the customer    107
14   service representative, everyone needs to be able to use a    119
15   computer keyboard. Workers in almost any kind of business     131
16   use their keyboarding skills to perform their daily tasks.    143
17        Employers are looking for skilled workers who can key    154
18   at a steady speed and with accuracy. People who can type      165
19   documents accurately and enter data quickly are needed for    177
20   many types of careers. Skills in keyboarding are valuable     189
21   assets for many types of jobs.                                195
     |  1  |  2  |  3  |  4  |  5  |  6  |  7  |  8  |  9  |  10  |  11  |  12
```

FORMATTING

D. FOLLOW-UP LETTERS

As soon as possible after your interview (preferably the next day), you should send a follow-up letter to the person who conducted your interview. In the letter you should:

- Use a positive tone.
- Thank the person who conducted the interview.
- Mention some specific information you learned during the interview.
- Highlight your particular strengths.
- Restate your interest in working for that organization and mention that you look forward to a favorable decision.

Correspondence 54-38

Follow-Up Letter in Block Style

September 12, 20-- | Ms. Carole Rothchild | Personnel Director | Arlington Communications | 2403 Sunset Lane | Arlington, TX 76015-3148 | Dear Ms. Rothchild:

¶ It was a real pleasure meeting with you yesterday and learning of the wonderful career opportunities at Arlington Communications. I enjoyed meeting all the people, especially those working in the Publications Division. Thank you for taking the time to tell me about the interesting start-up history of the company and its location in Arlington.

¶ I believe my experience and job skills match nicely with those you are seeking for a desktop publishing individual, and this position is exactly what I have been looking for. You may recall that I have had experience with all of the equipment and software that are used in your office.

¶ Please let me hear from you when you have made your decision on this position. I am very much interested in joining the professional staff at Arlington Communications.

Sincerely yours, | Kenneth R. Diaz | 105 Royal Lane | Commerce, TX 75428

Correspondence 54-39

Follow-Up Letter in Modified-Block Style

April 7, 20-- | Ms. Kay Brewer, Personnel Director | Blanchard Computer Systems | 2189 Dace Avenue | Sioux City, IA 51107 | Dear Ms. Brewer:

¶ Thanks for the opportunity of interviewing with Blanchard computer Systems yesterday. Please express my appreciation to all of those who were involved.

¶ The interview gave me a very good feeling about the company. The description that you shared me with convinced me that blanchard is in deed a company at which I would like to work. I was greatly impressed with the summary of social service programs for citizens throughout the community that are sponsored by Blanchard.

(Continued on next page)

¶ You may recall that I have had experience with all of the equipment that is used. It appears to me that *my* strengths in ~~software~~ application soft ware *computer* *and office systems* would blend in well with your ~~company~~ profile.

¶ I look forward to hearing you from soon regarding you*r* decision on the position of data records operator.

Sincerely, | Arlene F. Jefferson | 1842 Amber Road | Wayne, NE 68787

Correspondence 54-40 ▶

Follow-Up Letter in Modified-Block Style

Open the file for Correspondence 54-39, and make the following changes:

- Change the date of the letter to August 7, 20--.
- Send the letter to Mr. William E. Boyd | Personnel Director | Hawkeye Computers, Inc. | 5604 Melrose Avenue | Sioux City, IA 51105.
- Replace "Blanchard Computer Systems" with Hawkeye Computers in

both the first and the second paragraphs.
- Change "yesterday" in the first paragraph to August 5.
- Change the complimentary closing to Yours truly.
- Change "data records operator" to technology support assistant in the final paragraph.

STRATEGIES FOR *Career Success*

Interview Thank-You Letter

Expressing your appreciation is a very important follow-up step in your job search. Send a thank-you letter or email within 24 hours after your interview.

In the opening paragraph, thank the interviewer for taking time to meet with you. Make a positive statement about the company or interview feature (e.g., meeting potential coworkers).

In the middle paragraph, close the sale. Address any qualifications you neglected. Turn around an interview weakness (e.g., reconsider your statement that you wouldn't travel). Strengthen your relationship with the interviewer (e.g., refer the interviewer to a good article on a topic in which he/she expressed interest).

In the closing paragraph, ask to be notified when the decision is made. A thank-you letter ensures your last impression is a positive one.

YOUR TURN After your next interview, send a thank-you letter that effectively closes the sale.

Integrated Employment Project

GOALS:
- Improve speed and accuracy
- Refine language arts skills in proofreading
- Format employment documents

A. Type 2 times.

A. WARMUP

```
1      Lex was quite pleased with his travel plans; the trip    11
2  to Bozeman was on Flight #578 on July 30, and the return is   23
3  on August 12 on Flight #643. The ticket will cost $1,090.     34
   |  1  |  2  |  3  |  4  |  5  |  6  |  7  |  8  |  9  | 10  | 11  | 12
```

SKILLBUILDING

B. Type the columns 2 times. Press TAB to move from column to column.

B. TECHNIQUE PRACTICE: TAB

```
4  J. Barnes      P. Varanth     S. Childers    M. Christenson
5  F. Gilsrud     J. Benson      D. Bates       M. Jordan
6  B. Harringer   J. Suksi       J. Lee         P. North
7  V. Hill        A. Budinger    T. Gonyer      S. Kravolec
```

C. PACED PRACTICE

If you are not using the GDP software, turn to page SB-14 and follow the directions for this activity.

LANGUAGE ARTS

D. Edit this paragraph to correct any typing or formatting errors.

D. PROOFREADING

```
8       The Smith were please to learn from their insurance
9   agent that the covrage ona $50,000 life insurance policy
10  policy would be increased by $ 20,000 at no extra cost.

11  The continued to pay the same premum, not knowing that the
12  cash value of there original policy was being taped each
13  month to pay an addition premium for hte new coverage.
```

In this unit you have learned how to prepare a resume, an application letter, and a follow-up letter—all of which are frequently used by job applicants. You will now use these skills in preparing the documents necessary to apply for the job described in the newspaper ad illustrated below.

Desktop Publisher

NetJobs, a worldwide leader in employment and job searches, has an immediate opening for a desktop publisher. This person will work in the ad production and Web page design office.

This is an entry-level position within the Advertising Department in our San Francisco office. Applicant must have experience in using Word, FrontPage, and PageMaker. Creative ability and typing skills are a must. Candidate must be able to work in a fast-paced team environment and be highly self-motivated.

Excellent company benefits are available, and they include a comprehensive medical and dental program, disability insurance, and a credit union.

If interested, send a letter of application and resume to:

Ms. Danielle E. Rose
HRM Department
NetJobs, Inc.
9350 Kramer Avenue
San Francisco, CA 94101

NetJobs is an Equal Opportunity Employer

Report
55-32

Resume

Prepare a resume for yourself as though you are applying for the job described in the ad above. Use actual data in the resume. Assume that you have just graduated from a postsecondary program. Include school-related activities, courses you have completed, and any part-time or full-time work experience you may have acquired. Make the resume as realistic as possible, and provide as much information as you can about your background.

Correspondence
55-41

Application Letter in Block Style

Prepare an application letter to apply for the position described in the ad. Date your letter March 10. Emphasize the skills you have acquired during your years in school and while working in any part-time or full-time positions. Use Correspondence 53-37 (page 179) as a guide for your letter.

Assume that your interview was held on March 25 and that you would very much like to work for NetJobs. It is now the day after your interview. Prepare a follow-up letter expressing your positive thoughts about working for NetJobs. Use Correspondence 54-39 (page 182) as a guide for your letter.

Current Date | Mr. Blair N. Scarborough | Wyatt Insurance Agency | 2834 International Blvd. | Fort Worth, TX 76390 | Dear Mr. Scarborough:

¶ My advisor, Dr. Bonnie Allworth, mentioned to me that you have an opening for a computer specialist in your Denton office. I would like to be considered as an applicant for that position.

¶ My extensive training and experience in using various software programs are ideal for the position you have open. As a student at Texas State University, I won two national awards in computer programming competition. Also, as my enclosed resume indicates, I have completed several computer courses that uniquely qualify me for the computer specialist position at Wyatt Insurance Agency.

¶ At Texas State University, I took an active leadership role as president of the local chapter of Phi Beta Lambda. In my junior year I was treasurer of my campus fraternity, and during my senior year I was elected class president. These activities have provided me with valuable leadership and teamwork skills that I hope to demonstrate at Wyatt.

¶ I am very interested in working for Wyatt Insurance Company. I will telephone your office later this week to arrange an interview with you at your convenience. If you would like to speak to me prior to that time, please telephone me at my home number, 901-555-3203, after 5 p.m. or email me at pmcclean@stu.edu.

Sincerely, | Pat R. McClean | 894 Cremans Avenue | Fort Worth, TX 76384 | Enclosure

✓ **Progress Check**
Proofreading Check

Documents designated
as Proofreading Checks
serve as a check of your
proofreading skill. Your
goal is to have zero typographical errors when the
GDP software first scores
the document.

Assume that you have interviewed for the position mentioned in the previous letter and that you would now like to send a follow-up letter to Mr. Blair N. Scarborough, thanking him for the interview. Use the address, salutation, and closing lines shown in Correspondence 55-43 to create the follow-up letter below:

Current Date | [Address and salutation from Correspondence 55-43]

¶ Thank you for the time you spent with me, *yesterday* telling me about the Computer Specialist position with Wyatt. My interview with you reafirmed my interest in working for Wyatt.

¶ I was very impresed with work done in your Information Processing department. The hardware and software you use for writing computer code and the people working in that department are very apealing to me.

¶ I believe my particular background and skills blend perfectly with ~~the~~ *this* position. I hope to hear from you by the end of next week for a ~~positive~~ decision on my employment. Thank you *again* for bringing me in for the interview.

STRATEGIES FOR *Career Success*

Looking for a Job

Don't waste time! Start your job search early. Scan the Help Wanted section in major Sunday newspapers for job descriptions and salaries. The Internet provides electronic access to worldwide job listings. If you are interested in a particular company, access its home page.

Ask a reference librarian for handbooks (e.g., *Occupational Outlook Handbook*), government publications (e.g., *Federal Career Opportunities*), and journals or magazines in your field. Visit your college placement office. Sign up for interviews with companies that visit your campus.

Talk with people in your field to get advice. Look for an internship or join a professional organization in your field. Attend local chapter meetings to network with people in your chosen profession.

Taking the initiative in your job search will pay off!

YOUR TURN Visit the Internet site for the National Business Employment Weekly (http://www.cweb.com/NBEW/welcome.html), which provides more than 45,000 national and international job listings online.

Skillbuilding and In-Basket Review

MEMO TO: Blanche O. Pruitt

FROM: Kevin Hite

DATE: Current Date

SUBJECT: District Meetings

As you know, each year we rotate the location of our district meetings to each of our regional offices. This year our meeting will be held in your region, preferably in Albuquerque. Would you please contact the hotels in Albuquerque and select a suitable site for this year's meeting, which will be held on March 7 and 8.

We decided at our last regional manager's meeting that this year's meeting would highlight our Internet sales campaign. Specifically, we want to focus on the following issues:

e design to attract a higher percentage of the mar-

erce procedures so that our order processing routine
Web visitor?

e page to encourage visitors to view a greater per-

ade arrangements for our meeting site. I look for-
rch.

Current Date

Mr. Brandon T. Wright
District Manager
206 S. Rock Road
Wichita, KS 67210

Dear Mr. Wright:

Several of our service representatives have indicated
clients are becoming increasingly more interested i
ating their insurance carriers. All-City has prided its
service record with its policyholders, and the servic
shared this record with prospective customers. How
characteristics about All-City are also shared with th

Please be sure that your representatives share the fo
potential customers:

• Our claims are handled quickly and with a mini
• Our ratio of number of policies to number of cor
• No disciplinary actions have been taken against
• We conduct our business directly with our custo
  Internet assistance if requested.

Please share this information with your service repre
dated information on our services is provided on ou
policyholders' use.

Sincerely,

Ellen B. Boldt
Executive Vice President

urs

Current Date

Ms. Rolanda L. Farmer
203 Grand Avenue
Bozeman, MT 59715

Dear Ms. Farmer:

Your order for Internet service has been processed, and you can enjoy surfing the Web immediately!

As a customer of Global Communications, you will enjoy several benefits:

1. You will receive 24/7 customer service when using our service hotline at 1-800-555-3888.

2. You will be protected by E-Protect, Global's virus protection software. This software is updated weekly, and you can download weekly updates at www.global.net.

3. You will receive 10 Mbytes of Web page space.

4. You will receive automated credit card billing, as requested.

A complete listing of all our services is enclosed for your perusal.

Thank you for joining Global Communications. Please email us at www.global.net if you have any questions, or call us on our service hotline. We expect the coming months of providing Internet service to you to be a very enjoyable experience for both of us.

Sincerely,

Tedra M. Hester
New Accounts Manager

urs
Enclosure

In-Basket Review (Insurance)

GOALS:
- Type at least 40wpm/5'/5e
- Format insurance documents

A. Type 2 times.

A. WARMUP

```
1        Kyu Choi jumped at the opportunity to assume 40% of      11
2   the ownership of your restaurant. Alverox & Choi Chinese      22
3   Cuisine will be opening quite soon at 1528 Waysata Street.    34
    |  1  |  2  |  3  |  4  |  5  |  6  |  7  |  8  |  9  |  10  |  11  |  12
```

SKILLBUILDING

B. DIAGNOSTIC PRACTICE: NUMBERS

If you are not using the GDP software, turn to page SB-5 and follow the directions for this activity.

C. Take three 12-second timings on each line. The scale below the last line shows your wpm speed for a 12-second timing.

C. 12-SECOND SPEED SPRINTS

```
4   Kay Sue is on her way to that new show to take some photos.
5   Most of the ones who go may not be able to make it on time.
6   When they got to their seats, they were glad they had come.
7   Both men and women might take some of their pets with them.
    I I I I I 5 I I I I 10 I I I I 15 I I I I 20 I I I I 25 I I I I 30 I I I I 35 I I I I 40 I I I I 45 I I I I 50 I I I I 55 I I I I 60
```

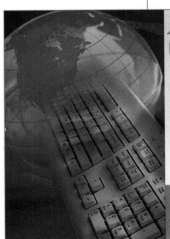

Keyboarding CONNECTION

Creating an Email Signature File

Creating a signature file saves you time and adds a personal touch to your email messages! A signature file is a tag of information at the end of your email. It may include your signature, a small graphic, address, phone number, or quotation. The signature file appears on every email message you send. Use the following guidelines to create a signature file.

Open your email software. Open the menu item that allows you to create a signature file. Type the information you want to include in your signature file. Close the file.

YOUR TURN

Create a signature file. Then address an email to yourself. Type "Test" in the Subject box. In the body, type "This is a test of the signature file." Send the email. Open the test email and locate your signature file at the bottom of the email message.

D. Take two 5-minute timings. Review your speed and errors.

Goal: At least 40wpm/5'/5e

D. 5-MINUTE TIMING

8	When you first begin choosing a career, you should	10
9	assess your personal abilities and interests. Do you have	22
10	a natural aptitude in a certain area? Do you have special	34
11	interests or hobbies that you would like to develop into	45
12	a career? Do you enjoy working with other people, or do	56
13	you like to work independently? Would you like to work in	68
14	a large office, or do you prefer to work outdoors? These	79
15	questions are important to consider when you are thinking	91
16	about your career.	95
17	Your quest to find the perfect career will be more	105
18	successful if you try to maximize the opportunities that	116
19	are available. For example, you might consider working	127
20	with an organization that offers you career counseling. A	139
21	career counselor is trained to help you determine your	150
22	aptitudes and interests. You may contact people who work	161
23	in a career that interests you and ask to shadow them on	172
24	their jobs and ask them questions. You may find an online	184
25	service to assist in finding an interesting career that	198
26	is just right for you.	200

| 1 | 2 | 3 | 4 | 5 | 6 | 7 | 8 | 9 | 10 | 11 | 12 |

DOCUMENT PROCESSING

Correspondence 56-45

Business Letter With Bulleted List

Situation: You are employed in the office of All-City Insurance of Columbia, Missouri. Their offices are located at 17 North Eighth Street, Columbia, MO 65201-7272. All-City handles auto, home, and life insurance coverage in Iowa, Kansas, and Missouri. You work for Ellen B. Boldt, executive vice president. Ms. Boldt prefers the block-style letter and *Sincerely* as the complimentary closing. When you create correspondence in this unit, the word processing program will automatically insert the letterhead information.

Current Date | Mr. Brandon T. Wright | District Manager | 206 S. Rock Road | Wichita, KS 67210 | Dear Mr. Wright:

¶ Several of our service representatives have indicated on our Web-site chat room that new clients are becoming increasingly more interested in the

(Continued on next page)

criteria to consider when evaluating their insurance carriers. All-City has prided itself in years past on its reputable service record with its policyholders, and the service representatives have undoubtedly shared this record with prospective customers. However, we want to be certain that other characteristics about All-City are also shared with these potential policyholders.

¶ Please be sure that your representatives share the following service characteristics with potential customers:

- Our claims are handled quickly and with a minimum of "red tape."
- Our ratio of number of policies to number of complaints is the lowest in the industry.
- No disciplinary actions have been taken against All-City in the past 50 years.

¶ Please share this information with your service representatives and inform them that updated information on our services is provided on our home page for their use or for their policyholders' use.

Provide suitable closing lines.

Correspondence 56-46 ▶

Memo With Bulleted List and Enclosure Notation

Ms. Boldt has dictated the following memo for you to transcribe. As you can see, there are several rough-draft changes that you will have to make to the memo.

MEMO TO: Sheila Parsons, Training Director

FROM: Ellen B. Boldt, Executive Vice President

DATE: October 17, 20--

SUBJECT: Training seminar

¶ Our new agent training seminar will be held on March 10, and we plan this again year as we have in the past to conduct separate sessions for auto and life insurance policies. You will be in charge of the auto insurance seminars and Victor Samuels will conduct the life insurance seminars.

(Continued on next page)

¶ I expect that this years' auto insurance seminars will present our 6 basic coverage areas using the latest presentation demo software for the following:

- Bodily injury liability
- Medical payments or personal injury protection
- Property damage liability
- Collision
- Comprehensive
- Uninsured Motorist

We are the market leaders in bodily injury liability and property damage liability coverages. Therefore, you should plan to spend at least one-half of your presentation discussing our strengths in these coverages. You might want to include in your presentation the fact that our coverages in these areas have more than surpassed those of our competitors for the past 7 years, or so.

¶ Use Table 1 that is enclosed to be sure that we use accurate figures for discussing our liability limits for each of the coverages specified for Iowa, Kansas, and missouri. Separate comparisons are also included for Alaska, Arizona, Virginia, and Wyoming.

urs | Enclosure

Prepare Table 56-17 on a full sheet of paper as an enclosure for the memo to Ms. Parsons.

Table 56-17 ▶

Three-Column Boxed Table

State	**Insurance Requirements**	**Minimum Liability**
Iowa	Bodily Injury & Property Damage Liability	20/40/10
Kansas	Bodily Injury & Property Damage Liability, Personal Injury Protection	15/30/10
Missouri	Bodily Injury & Property Damage Liability, Uninsured Motorist, Underinsured Motorist	25/50/15
Alaska	Bodily Injury & Property Damage Liability	20/40/10
Arizona	Bodily Injury & Property Damage Liability	20/40/10
Virginia	Bodily Injury & Property Damage Liability, Uninsured Motorist	25/5/20
Wyoming	Bodily Injury & Property Damage Liability	25/50/20

LIABILITY LIMITS (For Selected States)

In-Basket Review (Hospitality)

GOALS

- Improve speed and accuracy
- Refine language arts skills in number expression and in the use of the hyphen
- Format hospitality documents

A. Type 2 times.

A. WARMUP

```
1        Dexter gave an ultimatum: Quit driving on the lawn or    11
2  I will call the police. A fine of $100 (or even more) may    23
3  be levied against Kyle, who lives at 2469 Zaine in Joplin.   35
   | 1 | 2 | 3 | 4 | 5 | 6 | 7 | 8 | 9 | 10 | 11 | 12
```

SKILLBUILDING

B. PROGRESSIVE PRACTICE: ALPHABET

If you are not using the GDP software, turn to page SB-7 and follow the directions for this activity.

C. PACED PRACTICE

If you are not using the GDP software, turn to page SB-14 and follow the directions for this activity.

LANGUAGE ARTS

D. Study the rules at the right.

D. NUMBER EXPRESSION AND HYPHENATION

RULE ▶
 # word

Spell out

- **A number used as the first word of a sentence.**
  Seventy-five people attended the conference in San Diego.
- **The shorter of two adjacent numbers.**
  We have ordered 3 two-pound cakes and one 5-pound cake for the reception.
- **The words *million* and *billion* in even amounts (do not use decimals with even amounts).**
  A $5 ticket can win $28 million in this month's lottery.
- **Fractions.**
  Almost one-half of the audience responded to the question.

Note: When fractions and the numbers twenty-one through ninety-nine are spelled out, they should be hyphenated.

(Continued on next page)

Hyphenate compound numbers between twenty-one and ninety-nine and fractions that are expressed as words.

Twenty-nine recommendations were approved by at least three-fourths of the members.

Edit the sentences to correct any errors in number expression.

4 Seven investors were interested in buying 2 15-unit condos.
5 The purchase price for the buildings will be $3,000,000.00 each, which is 1/2 the total.
6 The computers were mailed in 5 40-pound boxes for 2/3 of the price paid yesterday.
7 Our food chains sold seventeen million hamburgers last year.
8 I can sell nearly one-half of all the tickets at the gate on November 13.
9 14 banks are located within 5 miles of the city center.
10 We must place our mailing pieces in 8 twenty-pound bags for the mail clerk.
11 I don't believe more than 1/4 of the drivers have insurance.

DOCUMENT PROCESSING

Situation: Today is August 21, and you are employed in the office of Suite Retreat, a group of vacation resorts in Naples, Florida. Your employer, the general manager, is Mr. Aaron Hynes. Mr. Hynes is attending a meeting in Miami and has left the following jobs for you to complete.

Table 57-18 ▶

Four-Column Open Table

SUITE RETREAT PROPERTIES
Selected Beach Rentals

Property	Rooms	Rental Rate In Season	Rental Rate Off Season
Carriage House	4	$3,500	$2,400
Ocean Breeze	5	3,850	2,700
Naples Hideaway	5	2,750	2,100
Princeton Palace	4	3,200	2,550
Seville Landings	6	4,250	3,100
The Vanderbilt	5	3,475	2,575
Westover Estates	6	5,250	4,150

Correspondence
57-47

Business Letter in
Modified-Block Style
With Enclosure and
Copy Notations

word

word

≡ number

Current Date | Mr. Leland Dutt | 243 Worth Street | Raleigh, NC 27603 | Dear Mr. Dutt:

¶ We were pleased to hear of your interest in renting one of our prime beach units in Naples, Florida. I have enclosed a listing of all our current properties in the Naples area. We have 14 two-bedroom rentals, 15 three-bedroom rentals, and 10 four-bedroom rentals. Five of our three-bedroom units have already been rented for this season; one-half of the other thirty-four units are still available.

¶ Let me review a few of the particulars of each unit with you. Our Carriage House and Naples Hideaway have Gulf Coast views and garage facilities. The Ocean Breeze and Princeton have lake views and tennis courts. The Seville, Vanderbilt, and Westover have a Gulf Coast view and a private golf course.

¶ If you plan to rent one of our units, please be sure to notify us by writing or by calling our toll-free number at 1-800-555-1348.

Sincerely, | Aaron Hynes | General Manager | urs | Enclosure | c: Theresa McDonald, Celeste Binghamton

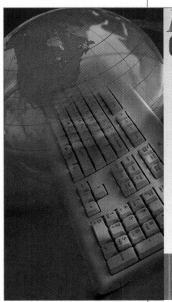

Keyboarding CONNECTION   Finding Business Information on the Internet

To begin research on a business-related topic, try one of the following sites:

Business Resources on the Web (*www.cio.com/WebMaster/lm_resources.html*) provides links to Cable News Network (CNN) Business News, the Wall Street Journal Money and Investing Update, and other news sources. It includes information about careers, Electronic Data Interchange (EDI) and the Internet, general business sources, training, marketing, and resources for entrepreneurs.

Business Administration Internet Resources (*www.acad.sunytccc.edu/library/busman.htm*) provides links to news and financial market updates, the Securities & Exchange Commission (SEC), Thomas Register, U.S. Census Bureau, U.S. Economic and Labor Statistics, and World Bank reports.

Selected Business Resources on the Web (*www.uwrf.edu/library/business.html*) provides information about marketing, finance, small business, business law, international business, stock markets, and a link to the Small Business Administration.

YOUR TURN   Access one of the business information sites listed above and explore its offerings.

Report 57-33 ▶

Business Report
With Bulleted List

Mr. Hynes has recently purchased a fishing resort on Lake Okeechobee, Florida, and plans to open it on September 1. Type the following report and send it to the *Naples Press* so that it will appear in this Sunday's special *Travel and Tourism* section. Use a standard business format to prepare the report.

FISHING PARADISE SCHEDULED TO OPEN | **Suite Retreat** | **Naples, Florida**

INTRODUCTION

¶ Suite Retreat is celebrating the grand opening of its newest fishing resort, Kamp Kellogg, located on the northwest corner of Lake Okeechobee, on the banks of the Kissimmee River. The reservation desk will open on September 1 to reserve your cabin at our beautiful resort. You can reach reservations via the Internet by logging on to our Web site at http://www.kellogg.com.

¶ **Accommodations.** Whether you're looking for deluxe accommodations or rustic surroundings, Kamp Kellogg has it all. You have a choice of rustic cabins nestled in the woods or large chalets overlooking Lake Okeechobee. If you enjoy an evening of relaxation, each cabin includes a gazebo, out near the water's edge, that is screened in for a perfect evening of comfort.

¶ **Amenities.** Your lodging choice includes full kitchens for those who want to do your own cooking, or you can order a full meal through our catering service. Each unit has a game room with a large-screen television, VCR, videotapes, and computer workstation with Internet connectivity. Outside the sliding glass door is a covered deck, equipped with a barbecue grill and hot tub.

LAKE OKEECHOBEE

¶ Lake Okeechobee lies geographically in the center of the state of Florida. The name "Okeechobee" was given to the lake by the Seminole Indians, and it means "big water." Lake Okeechobee is the largest freshwater lake in the United States occurring in one state. It is approximately 37 miles long and 30 miles wide, with an average depth of almost 10 feet. The lake produces more bass over 8 pounds than any lake in the United States. It is famous for bass, crappie, and bluegill fishing. Several species of wildlife also thrive around the lake such as the bald eagle, blue heron, egret, white ibis, sand hill crane, turkey vulture, owl, alligator, bobcat, turkey, and panther.

PRICING INFORMATION

¶ We are offering a special introductory rate of $250 through November 1. This rate includes the following:

- Two-night stay for a family of four
- Two half days of fishing
- One USCG licensed fishing guide
- Tackle and bait

¶ A full refund will be made if the fishing excursion is cancelled because of inclement weather or failure of equipment (boat, trailer, or vehicle). If only a partial day of fishing was completed, one-half of the charges will be refunded.

word

word

word

- number

In-Basket Review (Retail)

GOALS:
- Type at least 40wpm/5'/5e
- Format retail documents

A. Type 2 times.

A. WARMUP

```
1        Do you think 1/3 of the contents of the five quart-        11
2  sized boxes would be about right? I do! If not, they can        22
3  adjust the portions by adding 6 or 7 gallons of warm water.     34
   | 1  | 2  | 3  | 4  | 5  | 6  | 7  | 8  | 9  | 10  | 11  | 12
```

SKILLBUILDING

B. DIAGNOSTIC PRACTICE: ALPHABET

If you are not using the GDP software, turn to page SB-2 and follow the directions for this activity.

C. Type each line 2 times. Change every singular noun to a plural noun, and change every plural noun to a singular noun.

C. TECHNIQUE PRACTICE: CONCENTRATION

```
4  Debit the accounts. Balance your checkbook. Add the assets.
5  Take the discount. Send the statements. Compute the ratios.
6  Review the accounts. Credit the amounts. Figure the totals.
7  Prepare the statements. Send the catalog. Call the clients.
```

Keyboarding ability is critical to success in working with a computer system.

D. Take two 5-minute timings. Review your speed and errors.

Goal: At least 40wpm/5'/5e

D. 5-MINUTE TIMING

8	Most employees receive a job performance appraisal at	11
9	least once a year. Managers are responsible for conducting	23
10	these reviews. While the performance review is important,	35
11	either party may not anticipate this meeting eagerly. Many	47
12	times employees and managers look upon these meetings as a	59
13	time to discuss everything the employee has done wrong in	71
14	the last year. This negative approach adds to stress and	82
15	tension between the employee and management. In the long	93
16	run, work productivity suffers and everyone is affected.	104
17	Managers must learn new ways for conducting positive	115
18	performance appraisals. Appraisal meetings should begin	126
19	with recalling the contributions the employee has made to	138
20	the organization in the past year. Positive comments may	149
21	include coming to work on time, working well with others,	161
22	and being willing to pitch in whenever needed. The areas	172
23	for improvement may be discussed next. The employee should	184
24	be given the opportunity to ask questions or to write a	195
25	response to the appraisal.	200

| 1 | 2 | 3 | 4 | 5 | 6 | 7 | 8 | 9 | 10 | 11 | 12 |

DOCUMENT PROCESSING

Situation: You are employed as an administrative assistant for Sports 'R Us, a retailer for sports equipment and clothing in Denver, Colorado. Your employer is Mr. Kevin Hite, marketing director for Sports 'R Us. Upon arriving at your office on Monday morning, you notice that Mr. Hite has left several jobs that need to be completed for his signature. He prefers a block letter style in his correspondence and uses *Sincerely* as the complimentary close.

Correspondence 58-48 ▶

Business Letter in Block Style With Copy Notations

Current Date | Mr. Alex R. Chaney, Principal | Madison Heights High School | 1839 East Colfax Avenue | Denver, CO 80212 | Dear Mr. Chaney:
¶ Thank you for your invitation to advertise on your school's Web site. We were delighted to have the opportunity to sponsor last week's Marathon Mile at Madison Heights High School and hope that all the participants enjoyed the competition and spectator activities.
¶ This week my office staff will be putting together a Web page that we would like to display on the Web space you have so generously provided. It is my understanding that the Web site will remain online throughout this school year. We will be certain to maintain it on a regular basis so that our products and prices always remain current.

(Continued on next page)

Add the closing lines to Mr. Hite's letter. Send copies of this letter to Ardele Stevens, Jennifer Smits, and Randall Campbellton.

¶ The Marathon Mile has certainly become one of the county's most popular school events. We look forward to the opportunity of cosponsoring next year's Marathon Mile at Madison Heights.

Correspondence ▶
58-49

Memo With Numbered List

MEMO TO: Blanche O. Pruitt | **FROM:** Kevin Hite | **DATE:** Current Date | **SUBJECT:** District Meetings

¶ As you know, each year we rotate the location of our district meetings to each of our regional offices. This year our meeting will be held in your region, preferably in Albuquerque. Would you please contact the hotels in Albuquerque and select a suitable site for this year's meeting, which will be held on March 7 and 8.

¶ We decided at our last regional manager's meeting that this year's meeting would highlight our Internet sales campaign. Specifically, we want to focus on the following issues:

1. How can we improve our Web page design to attract a higher percentage of the market?
2. How can we improve our e-commerce procedures so that our order-processing routine is easier and faster for the average Web visitor?
3. What links can we add to our home page to encourage visitors to view a greater percentage of our product line?

¶ Please let me know when you have made arrangements for our meeting site. I look forward to meeting with all of you in March. | urs

Table ▶
58-19

Three-Column Boxed Table

WEEKLY BICYCLE SPECIALS February 13, 20--		
Model	**Price**	**Special Features**
Comanche	$270	15" Y-frame; 18-speed drivetrain; adjustable seat
Cyclone	375	Our lightest bike; preassembled; wired blue color
Duster	480	Front suspension fork; semislick tires; 24-speed
Trail Blazer	725	Titanium frame; aluminum seatpost; two bottle mounts

In-Basket Review (Nonprofit)

GOALS
- Improve speed and accuracy
- Refine language arts skills in spelling
- Format government documents

A. Type 2 times.

A. WARMUP

```
1      Crowne and Metzner, Inc., employees* joined with 68     11
2  youngsters to repair the brick homes of 13 elderly persons;   23
3  several became very well acquainted with six of the owners.   35
   |  1  |  2  |  3  |  4  |  5  |  6  |  7  |  8  |  9  |  10  |  11  |  12
```

SKILLBUILDING

B. MAP

Follow the GDP software directions for this exercise in improving keystroking accuracy.

C. Take a 1-minute timing on the first paragraph to establish your base speed. Then take four 1-minute timings on the remaining paragraphs. As soon as you equal or exceed your base speed on one paragraph, advance to the next, more difficult paragraph.

C. SUSTAINED PRACTICE: PUNCTUATION

```
4       The men in the warehouse were having a very difficult    11
5   time keeping track of that inventory. Things began to go      22
6   much more smoothly for them when they got the new computer.   34

7       Whenever something was shipped out, a computer entry      11
8   was made to show the changes. They always knew exactly what   23
9   merchandise was in stock; they also knew what to order.       34

10      Management was pleased with that improvement. "We          10
11  should have made the change years ago," said the supervisor   22
12  to the plant manager, who was in full agreement with him.     34

13      This is just one example (among many) of how the work     11
14  areas can be improved. Workers' suggestions are listened      22
15  to by alert, expert managers. Their jobs are better, too.     33
    |  1  |  2  |  3  |  4  |  5  |  6  |  7  |  8  |  9  |  10  |  11  |  12
```

D. Type this list of frequently misspelled words, paying special attention to any spelling problems in each word.

D. SPELLING

16 development determine enclosed complete members recent site
17 permanent personal facility medical library however purpose
18 representative implementation electrical discussed eligible
19 organization performance minimum discuss expense areas next
20 professional arrangements separate changes reason field pay

Edit the sentences to correct any misspellings.

21 Members of the medicle and profesional group discussed it.
22 The development of the seperate cite will be completed.
23 A recent representive said the libary facility may be next.
24 A perpose of the electricle organization is to get changes.
25 However, the implimentation of changes will be permenant.
26 Arrangments for the enclosed eligable expenses are listed.

| 1 | 2 | 3 | 4 | 5 | 6 | 7 | 8 | 9 | 10 | 11 | 12 |

DOCUMENT PROCESSING

Situation: Today is October 10. You work for Quick Trip, a ride-share company located in Windsor, Connecticut.

Your company is a nonprofit commuter company that provides the following services: move people to and from work, conduct parking studies, match people with available rides, and publish a commuter ride-share weekly report.

Your job responsibilities include preparing reports that summarize weekly commuter news, typing correspondence to advertise and promote Quick Trip's services, and communicating with area commuters who subscribe to Quick Trip's services.

Today, you must (1) prepare a report that summarizes services offered by Quick Trip, and (2) create a table that lists new additions to the weekly report.

Report 59-34

Business Report With Bulleted List and Footnotes

QUICK TRIP
Windsor's Premier Ride- Share

INTRODUCTION

¶ If you're tired of driving that one- to two hour commute into Connecticut's busy metropolitan areas, then let us take that burden ~~on for you.~~ *off your shoulders.* Quick Trip, the metro's premier ride-share company, is a convenient, economical way to get to & from work. All you have to do is get on board!

(Continued on next page)

Costs of Commuting

¶ A recent article showed that commuting just 15 miles each way can cost a minimum of $1,200 per year; sharing the ride with some one else can cut your commuting expenses in half.[1] In addition to the cost of gas, you must also figure in other costs of transportation such as maintenance on your vehicle, insurance premiums, depreciation, and finance charges.[2] When you consider all these costs, ride-sharing takes on a whole new significance. You should also consider how you are helping the traffic congestion and air pollution problems by ride-sharing. And don't forget about the possibility of being involved in an accident. Finally you can reduce stress by ride-sharing because you can choose to leave the driving to someone else.

RESERVATIONS AND BENEFITS

¶ If you want to reserve a seat on a Quick Trip route, just call one of our professional service representatives at 1.800.555.Trip. Our representatives in the field have information on routes, schedules, rides availability, and other benefits. For example, we have an E-ride available for you if there is an emergency that requires you to get home immediately. Here are some special benefits with Quick Trip:

- A free commute for every 500 commuting miles.
- Separate insurance and medical coverage.
- Flexible payment policies.
- A free commute for every 500 commuting miles.
- Full insurance coverage.
- Flexible payment policies.
- Week-to-week or month-to-month commitments.
- Weekly commuter bulletin to update available rides and riders.
- 4 free taxi rides home per year in the event of illness or personal emergency.

SERVICE AREAS

¶ Quick Trip serves the cities of Plainville, Rocky Hill, Manchester, Windsor, New Haven, and Suffield. Next month we will open routes to Avon, Glastonbury,

(Continued on next page)

Durham, and Middletown. In all, we have over 300 regular routes state wide, and service is expanding monthly. Easy access is guaranteed with all our routes. To view our entire service area, go to our web site, http://www.quicktrip.com, and link to the Quick Trip regional service map area. The map details all our routes, highlights specific pickup points, and identifies our regional service facilities. Visit our site today and become a ride-share enthusiast!

---

[1]Erica Sommers, "Ride-Sharing for the Environment," *Environmental Planning*, February 21, 2000, p. 18.

[2]Joshua R. Blake, *Cleaning Up America*, New Haven Publishing, Manchester, Connecticut, 2001, p. 138.

Table 59-20 ▶

Four-Column Boxed Table

QUICK TRIP COMMUTER BULLETIN *For the Week of October 12*			
From	*To*	*Name*	*Telephone*
Manchester	Rocky Hill	S. Baskin	860-555-5581
Manchester	Windsor	E. Lindholm	203-555-4684
Manchester	Suffield	P. Mack	860-555-4322
New Haven	Plainville	I. Thompson	203-555-1249
Rocky Hill	Windsor	J. Kiczuk	860-555-1842
Suffield	Manchester	M. Duprey	203-555-9339
Suffield	New Haven	B. Huehner	203-555-0442
Suffield	New Haven	M. Mac	203-555-1844
Windsor	Manchester	L. Smith	203-555-8893
Windsor	Rocky Hill	R. McCaffrey	203-555-7782

Lesson 60

In-Basket Review (Manufacturing)

GOALS
- Type at least 40wpm/5′/5e
- Format manufacturing documents

A. Type 2 times.

A. WARMUP

1   "Fay's #6 report shows increases of @ 2,649 and 3,779   11
2 units," the proud CEO announced. Mrs. Bailey's reaction was   23
3 quite amazing as 80 jobs were validated with checked boxes.   35

  | 1 | 2 | 3 | 4 | 5 | 6 | 7 | 8 | 9 | 10 | 11 | 12

SKILLBUILDING

PRETEST → PRACTICE → POSTTEST

B. PRETEST: Close Reaches

PRETEST
Take a 1-minute timing. Review your speed and errors.

4   Sally took the coins from the pocket of her blouse   10
5 and traded them for seventy different coins. Anyone could   22
6 see that Myrtle looked funny when extra coins were traded.   34

  | 1 | 2 | 3 | 4 | 5 | 6 | 7 | 8 | 9 | 10 | 11 | 12

C. PRACTICE: Adjacent Keys

PRACTICE
Speed Emphasis:
If you made 2 or fewer errors on the Pretest, type each *individual* line 2 times.
Accuracy Emphasis:
If you made 3 or more errors, type each *group* of lines (as though it were a paragraph) 2 times.

7 as asked asset based basis class least visas ease fast mass
8 we weary wedge weigh towel jewel fewer dwell wear weed week
9 rt birth dirty earth heart north alert worth dart port tort

D. PRACTICE: Consecutive Fingers

10 sw swamp swift swoop sweet swear swank swirl swap sway swim
11 gr grade grace angry agree group gross gripe grow gram grab
12 ol older olive solid extol spool fools stole bolt cold cool

E. POSTTEST: Close Reaches

POSTTEST
Repeat the Pretest timing and compare performance.

F. Take two 5-minute timings. Review your speed and errors.

Goal: At least 40wpm/5'/3e

F. 5-MINUTE TIMING

```
13    Information technology is among the fastest growing    11
14  fields of employment as well as one of the most rapidly    22
15  changing fields. Educational institutions are attempting   33
16  to prepare students to be specialists in a workplace that  45
17  will continue to be challenging and will need to change    56
18  quickly as advances are made in technology.                65
19    People who wish to work in the field of information      76
20  technology need to know all about the systems with which   87
21  they work. Network administrators, for example, often take 99
22  courses to certify that they have a strong knowledge of    110
23  networking hardware. Specialists must know about specific  122
24  equipment and have an understanding of how the software    133
25  works with the hardware.                                   138
26    Candidates seeking to pass the certification exams       148
27  must have the zeal and the determination to satisfy all of 160
28  the requirements. They know that it will not be long before 172
29  the current systems will be upgraded or new software will  183
30  be released. They will learn the new systems and review    195
31  the certification process again.                           200
    | 1 | 2 | 3 | 4 | 5 | 6 | 7 | 8 | 9 | 10 | 11 | 12
```

DOCUMENT PROCESSING

Situation: You are an administrative assistant, and you work for Disk Drives, Etc. in Phoenix, Arizona. Your supervisor is Mr. Vance Gibson, sales and marketing director. Mr. Gibson has asked you to prepare the following documents for him while he is in a staff meeting this morning. The letter is to be prepared for his signature, the table will be enclosed with the letter, and he will initial the memo before sending it out this afternoon.

Correspondence 60-50 ▶

Business Letter in Block Style With Bulleted List, Enclosure, and Copy Notations

September 13, 20-- | Ms. Tina C. Bennett | 1387 Rim Drive | Flagstaff, AZ 86001-3111 | Dear Ms. Bennett:

¶ We were pleased to see that you have used our Web site at www.tosabi.com to inquire about our online catalog. We specialize in computer drives of all types: CD-ROM, DVD, Zip, Jaz, floppy, and hard drives. I have enclosed a listing of our most popular CD-ROM writers that will appear online next week in our catalog. As a new customer, we invite you to visit our catalog and place your order at these special prices.

(Continued on next page)

¶ Our online customers receive the same privileges as our hard-copy catalog shoppers. These online privileges include:

- no shipping charges.
- toll-free customer support line.
- discounts on ten or more purchases.
- 90-day warranties [parts and labor] on all purchases.

¶ We look forward to many years of doing business with you. Please email me at vgibson@tosabi.net if you have any questions or would like additional information.

Sincerely, | Vance Gibson | Sales and Marketing Director | urs | Enclosure | c: S. Halley, W. Matson

Table 60-21 ▶

Four-Column Boxed Table

CD-ROM WRITERS (Effective Dates September 18-23)			
Model No.	Part No.	Price	Specifications
460RW	841120	$199	4x Speed Write, 16x Speed Read, CD recording software
2600E	841111	235	4x Speed Write, 24x Speed Read, 4x Speed Rewrite, stores up to 650 MB per disk
9282E	841415	415	Rewritable. 4x Speed Write, 8x Speed Read, Direct CD software
8428S	842013	595	Rewritable. 8x Speed Write, 24x Speed Read, 2x Speed Erase, Direct CD software
93422R	841712	658	Rewritable. 4x Speed Write, 6x Speed Read, 2x Speed Rewrite, Direct CD software, CDR-DJ

Correspondence 60-51 ▶

Memo With Numbered List

MEMO TO: Claudia Crenshaw | Publications Department | **FROM:** Vance Gibson | Sales and Marketing Director | **DATE:** September 13, 20-- | **SUBJECT:** Ad in the *Arizona Daily Sun*

¶ Claudia, please include the following criteria in our ad that will run in the *Arizona Daily Sun* this Sunday:

1. Quarter-page ad
2. Run-time: 2 weeks
3. Location: Business Section as well as Classified Section
4. Contact: Include telephone, fax, and email numbers

¶ This is our first ad piece in the *Sun* since we ran that special promotion last March. Let's add some graphics to make this one an "eye-catcher." | urs

Correspondence
60-52 ▶

Business Letter in
Modified-Block Style
with Numbered
List and Enclosure
Notation

Current Date | Ms. Rolanda L. Farmer | 203 Grand Avenue | Bozeman, MT 59715 | Dear Ms. Farmer:

¶ Your order for Internet service has been processed, and you can enjoy surfing the Web immediately!

¶ As a customer of Global Communications, you will enjoy several benefits:

1. You will receive 24/7 customer service when using our service hotline at 1-800-555-3888.
2. You will be protected by E-Protect, Global's virus protection software. This software is updated weekly, and you can download weekly updates at www.global.net.
3. You will receive 10 Mbytes of Web page space.
4. You will receive automated credit card billing, as requested.

¶ A complete listing of all our services is enclosed for your perusal.

¶ Thank you for joining Global Communications. Please email us at www.global.net if you have any questions, or call us on our service hotline. We expect the coming months of providing Internet service to you to be a very enjoyable experience for both of us.

Sincerely, | Tedra M. Hester | New Accounts Manager | urs | Enclosure

Many careers, including Web designers, Web masters, and programmers, are associated with the Internet.

**Progress Check
Proofreading Check**

Documents designated
as Proofreading Checks
serve as a check of your
proofreading skill. Your
goal is to have zero typographical errors when the
GDP software first scores
the document.

CUSTOMER SERVICES (Effective May 1, 20--)		
Service	**Description/Comments**	**Representative**
24/7 Service	Call 1-800-555-3888; wait time is usually less than 1 minute.	M. R. Milton, mrmilton@global.net
Virus-Protection Service	E-Protect software is down-loaded automatically to your computer when service is installed.	W. N. Gauthier, wngauth@global.net
Web Space	10 Mbytes Web page space is standard; an additional 10 Mbytes can be obtained on an as-needed basis.	M. J. Bohannon, mjbohan@global.net
Credit Card Billing	When requested by the customer, your monthly bill is automatically sent to a credit card of your choice.	L. T. Matthews, ltmatt@global.net

STRATEGIES
FOR *Career Success*   ## Successful Interviewing Techniques

The interview is a useful tool for researching information. Here are some steps to effective interviewing.

Conduct preliminary research so you can ask intelligent questions and make efficient use of the interview time. Prepare a list of questions (e.g., an interview script) to use in the interview. Make sure the questions are open-ended, unbiased, and geared toward gathering insights you can't gain through reading. Be prepared to take notes, listen actively, and ask follow-up questions, as needed.

Greet the interviewee by name and thank him or her for taking time to talk with you. Explain why you are interested in interviewing him or her. Stay within the scheduled time limits. In closing the interview, thank the interviewee again, and ask if you can get in touch if other questions come to mind.

YOUR TURN Prepare a list of questions you might use in interviewing someone concerning the current U.S. immigration policies.

Skills Assessment on Part 3

1	People are the most valuable assets of a company.	10
2	Excellent firms know that having well-qualified employees	22
3	is an important step to ensure the success of the company.	34
4	Managers play a huge part in determining how successful a	46
5	company will be when they provide a work environment that	58
6	encourages teams of people to work together to achieve a	69
7	common goal. When people realize they are being encouraged	81
8	to work toward achieving their own goals as well as the	92
9	goals of the company, they may respond by working to their	104
10	highest potential with enthusiasm.	111
11	Supervisors and managers need to show that they value	122
12	the contributions their employees make to the success of	133
13	the company. People thrive on compliments that show their	145
14	work is appreciated. They like to be rewarded in some way	157
15	when they have done an exceptional job. When supervisors	168
16	and managers are successful in motivating the employees	179
17	to work to their full potential, the company will grow and	191
18	prosper. The result is that every person wins.	200

| 1 | 2 | 3 | 4 | 5 | 6 | 7 | 8 | 9 | 10 | 11 | 12

Correspondence Test 3-53

Business Letter in Block Style With Bulleted List and Copy Notations

Current Date | Mr. Anthony Gillespie | Goddard Properties | 1808 Augusta Court | Lexington, KY 40505-2838 | Dear Mr. Gillespie:

¶ Let me introduce myself. I am committee chair of a group that monitors development projects in Lexington, Kentucky. It was brought to my attention that your proposal to construct 100 three- and four-bedroom homes was approved by the city council last night. As a resident in a neighboring community, I wish to share with you the stipulations

(Continued on next page)

Add an envelope to the letter, and omit the return address.

we would like you to incorporate into your development project:

- *The new homes should have no less than 2,700 square feet of living space.*
- *All structures should have brick frontage.*
- *No external, unattached buildings should be constructed.*

¶ Following these stipulations will ensure that your homes adhere to our community building codes. Sincerely, | Dora H. Hayes | Committee Chair | urs |
c: S. Benefield, T. Grace

MEMO TO: Curtis Hollaubaugh, Jr.
FROM: Elaine H. Nugent
DATE: June 26, 20--
SUBJECT: Desktop Publishing Certificate

¶ Our DTP certificate seminar will be held in St. Louis on August 14. Upon request of last year's participants, we want to be sure to include the following topics:

- Integrated Computer Applications
- Advanced Desktop Publishing
- Introduction to Computer Graphics
- Graphic Design I and II

¶ These were the four most popular topics at last year's seminar. Let's use a brochure design similar to the one we used at the Denver meeting in 1999. A copy of that brochure is attached for you to review. | urs | Attachment

Report ▶
Test 3-35

Business Report
With Footnotes,
Side Headings, and
Paragraph Headings

AIR POLLUTION

INTRODUCTION

¶ When we hear about pollution, we tend to think of smog, traffic congestion, acid rain, and other pollutant-related terms. However, we also need to consider the air we breathe as we work. We need to be concerned about indoor air because it can affect the health, comfort, and productivity of workers.[1]

¶ **Strategies to Improve Air Quality.** The three basic approaches to improving air quality include the use of air pressure to keep the pollutants "at bay," the use of ventilation systems to remove the pollutants, or the use of filters to clean the air. The pollutants can appear in various forms but are typically biological contaminants, chemical pollutants, or particles.

¶ **Pollutant Descriptions.** Biological contaminants can include viruses, molds, bacteria, dust mites, pollen, and water spills. These contaminants cause allergic reactions that trigger asthma attacks for an estimated 16 million Americans.[2] Chemical pollutants include tobacco smoke and accidental chemical spills. Particles include such pollutants as dust and dirt from drywall, carpets, copying machines, and printing operations. [3]

MANAGERS' RESPONSIBILITIES

¶ Office managers should help by reviewing records pertaining to air conditioning and ventilation systems. They should also provide training sessions for employees to learn about maintaining clean air. Finally, they should keep a record of reported health complaints related to polluted air and aid in resolving these complaints.

AIR QUALITY IS A TEAM EFFORT

¶ All workers can have a positive impact on improving the quality of air they breathe. For example, simply making sure that air vents and grilles are not blocked will help improve the quality of air. People who smoke should do so only in areas designated as smoking areas for employees.

---

[1]Karen Scheid, "Pollution at Work," *Los Angeles Times*, May 4, 2001, p. C8.
[2]"Dirty Air in Today's Offices," *Air America's Home Page*, March 12, 2001, http:www.airamerica.com/dirty.htm (May 13, 2001).
[3]Carlos Sanchez, *Pollutants in America*, Southwest Press, Albuquerque, 2000.

PART 4

Advanced Formatting

OBJECTIVES

KEYBOARDING

▶ Type at least 43 words per minute on a 5-minute timing with no more than 5 errors.

LANGUAGE ARTS

▶ Refine proofreading skills and correctly use proofreaders' marks.

▶ Use capitals, punctuation, and grammar correctly.

▶ Improve composing and spelling skills.

▶ Recognize subject/verb agreement.

WORD PROCESSING

▶ Use the word processing commands necessary to complete the document processing activities.

DOCUMENT PROCESSING

▶ Format reports, multipage letters, multipage memos, and tables.

TECHNICAL

▶ Answer at least 90 percent of the questions correctly on an objective test.

KEYBOARDING IN ARTS, AUDIO, VIDEO TECHNOLOGY, AND COMMUNICATIONS SERVICES

Occupations in this cluster deal with organizing and communicating information to the public in various forms and media. This cluster includes jobs in radio and television broadcasting, journalism, motion pictures, the recording industry, the performing arts, multimedia publishing, and the entertainment services. Work as a book editor, computer artist, technical writer, radio announcer, news correspondent, and camera operator are just a few jobs within this cluster.

Qualifications and Skills

Strong oral and written communication skills and technical skills are necessary for anyone in communications and media. Without a doubt, enhancing keyboarding skill is extremely advantageous.

Working in the media requires creativity, talent, and accurate use of language. In journalism, being observant, thinking clearly, and seeing the significance of events are all of utmost importance. Announcers must have exceptional voices, excellent speaking skills, and a unique style. The ability to work under pressure is important in all areas of media.

Unit 13
Skill Refinement

LESSON 61
Skillbuilding and Report Review

LESSON 62
Skillbuilding and Letter Review

LESSON 63
Skillbuilding, Memo, and Email Review

LESSON 64
Skillbuilding and Table Review

LESSON 65
Skillbuilding and Employment Document Review

2

SKILLS THAT A LEADER NEEDS

A good leader must have the prerequisite skills if he or she is to be effective in business. Many textbook and business journal writers have used various terms to describe these skills. Quible lists such skills as characteristics. They are "getting others to cooperate, delegating responsibilities, understanding subordinates, and using fairness."[2] However, Quible also discusses human relations, teaching, coaching, and communications as special skills that a leader should possess. These skills are often acquired on the job with the assistance of mentors within the firm.

PROBLEM SOLVING

Dealing with problems is a delicate business. On the one hand, leaders do not want to anger anyone, especially union personnel, by being too harsh. On the other hand, they must confront problems head-on. Leaders should first make a special effort to identify clearly the real problem. Second, they should pinpoint the individual factors that may be causing the problem. Finally, they should take definite steps to correct the problem.

Organizational Behavior, 2nd ed., Allyn and Bacon, Boston,

gement: An Introduction, 4th ed., Prentice-Hall, Englewood

LEADERSHIP SKILLS NEEDED IN BUSINESS

Sally Rodriguez

Leadership skills are needed now more than ever in business and industry if our nation is to maintain a leading role in the business world of tomorrow. With the advent of a common European community without boundaries, the Asian influence throughout the world, and the development of a common North American business community, we must have leaders with vision and the appropriate skills for meeting the challenges of the new, very technical century.

Each of the new skills that a successful leader needs is discussed in the following pages.

LEADERSHIP

Leadership has been defined in a variety of of an individual when he or she is directing the acti goal."[1]

A successful leader is one who is committed and services, for improving the firm's market positi her employees. A leader possesses a value system th Leaders who make decisions affecting the firm, em liefs that influence decision-making.

MEMO TO: Frank Janowicz, Ticket Manager

FROM: Sam Steele, Executive Director

DATE: March 1, 20--

SUBJECT: Ticket Sales Campaign

We tentatively have scheduled 114 concerts for Orchestra Hall for the calendar year beginning September 1, 20--. The attached list shows the new season ticket prices for the main floor, mezzanine, balcony, and gallery.

These prices are grouped in 11 different concert categories, which reflect the varied classical tastes of our patrons. These groupings also consider preferences for day of the week, time of day, and season of the year.

Please see me at 3 p.m. on March 10 so that we can review our ticket sales campaign. Last year's season ticket holders have had ample time to renew their subscriptions; we must now concentrate on attracting new season subscribers. I shall look forward to reviewing your plans on the tenth.

urs
Attachment

Skillbuilding and Report Review

GOALS

- Improve speed and accuracy
- Refine language arts skills in the use of commas
- Format reports

A. Type 2 times.

A. WARMUP

```
1      A queen quickly adjusted 12 blinds as the bright sun    11
2   blazed down from the sky; she then paced through the 19    22
3   rooms (all very large) next to the castle for 38 minutes.  33
    |  1  |  2  |  3  |  4  |  5  |  6  |  7  |  8  |  9  |  10  |  11  |  12
```

SKILLBUILDING

B. Take three 12-second timings on each line. The scale below the last line shows your wpm speed for a 12-second timing.

B. 12-SECOND SPEED SPRINTS

```
4   Most of those autos on the road had only one or two people.
5   Those boys and girls did the right thing by doing the work.
6   Some of the men ran to the gym to work out with their kids.
7   All of the new male workers were given a tour of the plant.
  | | | | 5 | | | | 10 | | | | 15 | | | | 20 | | | | 25 | | | | 30 | | | | 35 | | | | 40 | | | | 45 | | | | 50 | | | | 55 | | | | 60
```

C. DIAGNOSTIC PRACTICE: ALPHABET

If you are not using the GDP software, turn to page SB-2 and follow the directions for this activity.

LANGUAGE ARTS

D. Study the rules at the right.

D. COMMAS

RULE ▶
, series

Use a comma between each item in a series of three or more.
> We need to order paper, toner, and font cartridges for the printer.
> They saved their work, exited their program, and turned off their computers when they finished.

Note: Do not use a comma after the last item in a series.

RULE ▶
, transitional expression

Use a comma before and after a transitional expression or independent comment.
> It is critical, therefore, that we finish the project on time.
> Our present projections, you must admit, are inadequate.
> *But:* You must admit our present projections are inadequate.

Note: Examples of transitional expressions and independent comments are *in addition to, therefore, however, on the other hand, as a matter of fact,* and *unfortunately.*

Edit the sentences to correct any errors in the use of the comma.

8 The lawyer the bank and the courthouse received copies.
9 The closing was delayed therefore for more than an hour.
10 The abstract deed and contract were all three in order.
11 Ms. Sperry's flight was delayed however for two hours.
12 Happily the drinks snacks and napkins arrived on time.
13 This offer I think will be unacceptable to the board.

DOCUMENT PROCESSING

Report 61-36

Business Report

,transitional expression

Go To
Word Processing Manual Review:
L. 21–24: *All*
L. 23: Bold
L. 26: Alignment and Font Size

Reference Manual
Review:
R-8A: Report in Business Style

, series

UTI EMPLOYEE TRAINING PROGRAMS

Your Name, **Training Coordinator**

¶ Various training techniques are used in business and industry to update employees acquire new skills and to assist them in acquiring new skills. It should be no surprise, therefore, that conscientious employees are eager to participate in training programs. Some of the various effective techniques that United Transportation Inc. (UTI) uses in its training programs are described below discussed in this report.

ON-THE-JOB TRAINING AND LECTURES

¶ Two of the most frequently used and highly effective training methods are on-the-job training and lectures.

¶ **On-the-Job Training.** On the job training saves time and money by enabling permitting individuals to train at the workplace. This method lets the trainer uses the workstation in place of a classroom. While there are many benefits from this type of experience, on-the-job training does require careful coordination to insure that learning objectives are achieved.

¶ **Lectures.** Lectures are often used because they are a low-cost method of instruction training. Lectures which require little action on the part of the trainer, may not be effective when introducing employees to new techniques and work programs.

CONFERENCES

¶ In the a conference method of instruction, small groups of employees are taught by a conference director, manager, or outside consultant. This Conferences provide method of instruction results in considerable give-and-take between the director and the employees. For learning to occur, the director trainer must be skilled in the use of interactive techniques.

(Continued on next page)

DISTANCE EDUCATION

¶ A growing segment of UTI's training is now delivered on-line via the internet. Some of these courses, called distance education (DE), are designed and managed by UTI itself, but an increasing number are designed and managed by ~~form~~ independent vendors, such as educational institutions and management-consulting firms. These on-line courses are not only cost-effective, but also permit the trainee to complete the course at a time that is convenient for ~~them~~ him or her.

¶ The UTI Training Department estimates that within five years, 80% or more of its training modules will be delivered on-line, at a projected annual cost savings of at least $575,000 ~~dollars~~.

Report 61-37 ▶

Multipage Academic Report With Footnotes

Go To

Word Processing Manual Review:
L. 27: Page Numbering and Page Break
L. 29: Line Spacing
L. 35: Italics
L.41: Footnotes

Reference Manual

Review:
R-8C and
R-8D: Report in Academic Style

,series

,transitional expression

LEADERSHIP SKILLS NEEDED IN BUSINESS
Sally Rodriguez

Leadership skills are needed now more than ever in business and industry if our nation is to maintain a leading role in the business world of tomorrow. With the advent of a common European community without boundaries, the Asian influence throughout the world, and the development of a common North American business community, we must have leaders with vision and the appropriate skills for meeting the challenges of the new, very technical century.

Each of the new skills that a successful leader needs is discussed in the following pages.

LEADERSHIP

Leadership has been defined in a variety of ways. One definition is "the behavior of an individual when he or she is directing the activities of a group toward a shared goal."[1]

A successful leader is one who is committed to ideas—ideas for future products and services, for improving the firm's market position, and for the well-being of his or her employees. A leader possesses a value system that is ethically and morally sound. Leaders who make decisions affecting the firm, employees, and society have a set of beliefs that influence decision-making.

SKILLS THAT A LEADER NEEDS

A good leader must have the prerequisite skills if he or she is to be effective in business. Many textbook and business journal writers have used various terms to describe these skills. Quible lists such skills as characteristics. They are "getting others to cooperate, delegating responsibilities, understanding subordinates, and using fairness."[2] However, Quible also

(Continued on next page)

,series

discusses human relations, teaching, coaching, and communications as special skills that a leader *should* possess. These skills are often acquired on the job with the assistance of mentors within the firm.

PROBLEM SOLVING

,transitional expression

,transitional expression

,transitional expression

Dealing with problems is a delicate business. On the one hand, leaders do not want to anger anyone, especially union personnel, by being too harsh. On the other hand, they must confront problems head-on. Leaders should first make a special effort to identify clearly the *real* problem. Second, they should pinpoint the individual factors that may be causing the problem. Finally, they should take definite steps to correct the problem.

[1]Judith R. Gordon, *A Diagnostic Approach to Organizational Behavior,* 2nd ed., Allyn and Bacon, Boston, 1997, p. 393.

[2]Zane K. Quible, *Administrative Office Management: An Introduction,* 4th ed., Prentice-Hall, Englewood Cliffs, N.J., 1996, pp. 212-216.

Report 61-38 ▶

Multipage Business Report With Footnote

Open the file for Report 61-37 and make the following changes.

1. Change the report from academic style to business style.
2. Assume that you wrote the report, and change the byline accordingly.
3. Delete the third paragraph. Note that this results in the elimination of the first footnote.
4. Add a fourth side heading, THE LEADER AS TEACHER. Then add the following paragraph:

   Those who are in leadership positions often assume that workers learn how to perform a job simply by doing it without guidance. The real leader plans well-structured orientation sessions for new workers and does the same for all workers whenever there is new technology to be learned or when there is a change in policy or procedure.

   (**Note:** If necessary, force a page break to prevent the new side heading from appearing at the bottom of the first page.)
5. Finally, add a footnote at the end of the paragraph you inserted in Step 4:

   Ahmed Bazarak, "The Leader as Teacher," *The Manager's Newsletter,* July 18, 2001, pp. 14-17.

Skillbuilding and Letter Review

GOALS

- Type at least 40wpm/5'/5e
- Format business letters and personal-business letters

A. Type 2 times.

A. WARMUP

```
1      Quist & Zenk's sales were exactly $247,650; but the      10
2  cost of goods sold was $174,280 (70.37%). The profit made    22
3  was small after other, extensive expenses were subtracted.   34
   |  1  |  2  |  3  |  4  |  5  |  6  |  7  |  8  |  9  |  10  |  11  |  12
```

SKILLBUILDING

B. MAP

Follow the GDP software directions for this exercise in improving keystroking accuracy.

C. PACED PRACTICE

If you are not using the GDP software, turn to page SB-14 and follow the directions for this activity.

STRATEGIES FOR *Career Success*

Corrective Feedback

Sometime in your career, you will give someone corrective feedback. You can use positive communication to do this and not appear to criticize the person.

Here are some things you should not do. Do not correct the person in front of others. Avoid giving feedback when you are angry. Stay away from personal comments (e.g., "That idea will get us nowhere!"). Do not diminish a person's enthusiasm (e.g., "We've never done that before, and we're not starting now.").

Here are some things you should do. Listen to the person's side of the situation. Express yourself in a positive way (e.g., "You're getting much closer."). Be specific about what the person can do to correct the situation. Follow up within a short time and identify all progress.

YOUR TURN Think about the last time you received corrective feedback. Did the person giving you feedback use techniques to create a positive outcome?

D. Take two 5-minute timings. Review your speed and errors.

Goal: At least 40wpm/5'/5e

D. 5-MINUTE TIMING

4 Many computer users are quite familiar with software 11
5 commands. However, many users do not know the importance 22
6 of system software. System software controls the operation 34
7 of computer hardware. 38
8 The operating system is one type of system software. 49
9 It manages the operations of a computer and functions as 60
10 the interface between the user, application software, and 72
11 computer hardware. Application software includes the word 84
12 processing, spreadsheet, and database software. Computer 95
13 hardware includes the mouse, keyboard, printer, and disk 106
14 drives. A computer must have an operating system to work. 118
15 Windows is a popular operating system. It allows the user 130
16 to click icons and issue commands to move within screens 141
17 called windows. 144
18 Another type of system software is utility software. 155
19 Utility programs perform specific tasks. Utilities manage 167
20 resources. File conversion, file compression, backup, and 179
21 virus protection are examples of utility programs. These 190
22 programs are analyzed in many computer magazines. 200

| 1 | 2 | 3 | 4 | 5 | 6 | 7 | 8 | 9 | 10 | 11 | 12 |

DOCUMENT PROCESSING

Correspondence 62-55

Personal-Business Letter in Block Style

Reference Manual

Review:
R-3D: Personal-Business Letter

October 1, 20-- | Dr. Anthony L. Robbins | 2345 South Main Street | Bowling Green, OH 43402 | Dear Anthony:

¶ Thank you for your letter of September 25 in which you inquired about my trip to New York City. Your letter brought back a lot of memories of those days when I was one of your students.

¶ I plan to leave on October 15 for a two-week business and vacation trip to the city. While at Columbia University, I will be conducting a workshop on the utilization of voice-activated equipment.

¶ My work at Columbia will be completed on October 22, after which I plan to attend a number of plays, visit the Metropolitan Museum of Art, and take one of the sightseeing tours of the city.

¶ If you and your wife would care to join me on October 22, please let me know. I would be most happy to make reservations at the hotel for you and to purchase theater tickets. Why don't you consider joining me in the "Big Apple."

Sincerely, | Bryan Goldberg | 320 South Summit Street | Toledo, OH 43604

Correspondence
62-56

Business Letter in
Modified-Block Style

Go To

**Word
Processing
Manual
Review:**
L. 50: Ruler Tabs and
Tab Sets

Reference Manual

Review:
R-3B: Business
Letter in Modified-
Block Style

June 3, 20--

Director of Product Development

Hampton Associates, Inc.

830 Market St.

San Francisco, Ca 94103-1925

Dear Director of Product Development:

¶ I recently read an article in <u>Business Week</u> concerning how computer buyers can make standards happen. It was a very interesting article. The article indicates that if customers demand standard products when they purchase computers, participate in standard-setting groups, and band together with other customers, they will do better in the long run. Have you had customer groups assist you or provide you with information on the adoption of more computer standards? These standards include industry-wide interfaces, a mix and match of computer gear and programs, and building the best system for each application utilized?

¶ I would appreciate any data that you might furnish for me with regard to customers and your firm working together to set past or future standards.

Sincerely yours,

Alice Karns

Vice President

urs

Correspondence
62-57

Business Letter in
Block Style

Go To

**Word
Processing
Manual
Review:**
L. 33: Envelopes

Reference Manual

Review pages
R-3A and **R-6A** of the
Reference Manual.

Revise Correspondence 62-56, making the following changes:
1. Change the letter to block style.
2. Change the date to June 5, 20--.
3. Send the letter to Ms. Heidi M. Fischer at Gramstad Brothers, Inc., located at 5417 Harbord Drive in Oakland, CA 94618.
4. Change the salutation.
5. Combine the second and third paragraphs into one paragraph.
6. Add the following text as a new third paragraph:
   Some of my colleagues and I would like to get involved with others in an effort to make desired changes. I am confident that there are others around the Bay area that feel the same way.
7. Prepare an envelope for the letter.

Lesson 63

Skillbuilding, Memo, and Email Review

GOALS
- Improve speed and accuracy
- Refine language arts skills in composing paragraphs
- Format memos and an email message

A. Type 2 times.

A. WARMUP

```
1      "When is the quarterly jury report due?" asked Glenn.    11
2  He had faxed forms* to 64 of the 135 prospective jurors.     22
3  Only about one dozen of 596 citizens could not be located.   34
   | 1 | 2 | 3 | 4 | 5 | 6 | 7 | 8 | 9 | 10 | 11 | 12
```

SKILLBUILDING

PPP

PRETEST → PRACTICE → POSTTEST

B. PRETEST: Discrimination Practice

PRETEST
Take a 1-minute timing. Review your speed and errors.

```
4      The entire trip on a large train was better than we     11
5  had hoped. Polite police looked out for both the young and   23
6  old. One unit was outnumbered by herds of frolicking deer.   35
   | 1 | 2 | 3 | 4 | 5 | 6 | 7 | 8 | 9 | 10 | 11 | 12
```

C. PRACTICE: Left Hand

PRACTICE
Speed Emphasis:
If you made no more than 1 error on the Pretest, type each *individual* line 2 times.
Accuracy Emphasis:
If you made 2 or more errors, type each *group* of lines (as though it were a paragraph) 2 times.

```
7  rtr trip trot sport train alert courts assert tragic truest
8  asa mass salt usage cased cease astute dashed masked castle
9  rer rear rest overt rerun older before entire surest better
```

D. PRACTICE: Right Hand

```
10  mnm menu numb hymns unmet manly mental namely manner number
11  pop post coop opera pools opens polite proper police oppose
12  iui unit quit fruit suits built medium guided helium podium
```

E. POSTTEST: Discrimination Practice

POSTTEST
Repeat the Pretest timing and compare performance.

F. PROGRESSIVE PRACTICE: ALPHABET

If you are not using the GDP software, turn to page SB-7 and follow the directions for this activity.

G. **COMPOSING: PARAGRAPH**

Read through the paragraphs in the 5-minute timing in Lesson 62. Compose a paragraph to include the type of operating system, application software, and utility programs loaded on the computers used in your keyboarding class.

DOCUMENT PROCESSING

Correspondence 63-58 ▶

Memo With Attachment

Reference Manual

Review: R-4D: Memo

 Do not indent paragraphs in a memo.

 Remember to type your reference initials.

MEMO TO: Frank Janowicz, Ticket Manager | **FROM**: Sam Steele, Executive Director | **DATE**: March 1, 20-- | **SUBJECT**: Ticket Sales Campaign

¶ We tentatively have scheduled 114 concerts for Orchestra Hall for the calendar year beginning September 1, 20--. The attached list shows the new season ticket prices for the main floor, mezzanine, balcony, and gallery.

¶ These prices are grouped in 11 different concert categories, which reflect the varied classical tastes of our patrons. These groupings also consider preferences for day of the week, time of day, and season of the year.

¶ Please see me at 3 p.m. on March 10 so that we can review our ticket sales campaign. Last year's season ticket holders have had ample time to renew their subscriptions; we must now concentrate on attracting new season subscribers. I shall look forward to reviewing your plans on the tenth.

urs | Attachment

Correspondence 63-59 ▶

Email Message

Go To

Word Processing Manual Review: L. 25: Email a Document

Reference Manual

Review: R-5C: Email Message in Internet Explorer, or **R-5D:** Email Message in Netscape Navigator

gpeters@ssw.com | Request for Information | Mr. Peters:

¶ Please send information and prices on the security software you recently advertised in *PC Magazine.*

¶ We are interested in implementing a new security program for the personal computers in our main office and would like to study the specifications and features your system provides.

¶ Thank you for your assistance.

C. H. Cox

MEMO TO: Edo Dorati, Cabaret pops Conductor
FROM: Sam Steele, Executive Director
DATE: March 2, 20--
Subject: Erving Berlin Concert

Our Patron Advisory Program Committiee recomments inits their attached letter that the Erving Berlin concert begin with some pre-World War I hits, followed by music from the '20s and '30s. Favorites from this era are hit songs from Music Box Review, Puttin' on The Ritz, and Follow the the Fleet. After the intermission the committee suggest songs from the '40s and '50s, hits from Annie get Your Gun, Call me Madam, Easter parade. A planning meeting has been scheduled for you, Dolly Carpenter (the Rehearsals Coordinator), and me on Mar. 9 at 10 A.M. at Orchestra Hall. I shall look forward to seeing you then.

urs

Attachment

c: Dolly Carpenter

MEMO TO: Dolly Carpenter, Rehearsals Coordinator
FROM: Sam Steele, Executive Director
DATE: March 3, 20--
SUBJECT: Summer Cabaret Pops Concerts

We are pleased that you will be our rehearsals coordinator for this summer's Cabaret Pops concerts. The five biweekly concerts will run from June 13 through August 8.

As the concert schedule is much lighter during the summer months, I am quite confident that you will be able to use the Orchestra Hall stage for all rehearsals. This is the preference of Edo Dorati, who will be the conductor for this year's Cabaret Pops concerts.

I look forward to seeing you on June 1.

Skillbuilding and Table Review

GOALS

- Type at least 40wpm/5'/5e
- Format tables

A. Type 2 times.

A. WARMUP

```
1      There were two big questions: (1) Would both have to      11
2  be present to pick up the license? and (2) Is a blood test    23
3  required? Jeff and Faye were quite dizzy with excitement.     34
   |  1  |  2  |  3  |  4  |  5  |  6  |  7  |  8  |  9  |  10  |  11  |  12
```

SKILLBUILDING

B. PROGRESSIVE PRACTICE: NUMBERS

If you are not using the GDP software, turn to page SB-11 and follow the directions for this activity.

C. SUSTAINED PRACTICE: ALTERNATE-HAND WORDS

C. Take a 1-minute timing on the first paragraph to establish your base speed. Then take four 1-minute timings on the remaining paragraphs. As soon as you equal or exceed your base speed on one paragraph, advance to the next, more difficult paragraph.

```
4       The town council decided to shape its destiny when a     11
5  rich landowner lent a hand by proposing to chair the audit    23
6  committee. He will be a good chairman, and eight civic        34
7  club members will work to amend some troublesome policies.    46

8       One problem relates to the change in profit for many     11
9  of the firms in the city. As giant property taxes do not      22
10 relate to income, they wish to make those taxes go down.      33
11 The result means increases in their sales or income taxes.    45

12      All eight members of the town council now agree that     11
13 it is time to join with other cities throughout the state     23
14 in lobbying with the state legislature to bring about the     35
15 needed change. The right balance in taxes is the goal.        46

16      The mayor pointed out that it is not only business       10
17 property owners who would be affected. Homeowners should      22
18 see a decrease in property taxes, and renters might see       33
19 lower rents, as taxes on rental property would be lowered.    45
   |  1  |  2  |  3  |  4  |  5  |  6  |  7  |  8  |  9  |  10  |  11  |  12
```

D. Take two 5-minute timings. Review your speed and errors.

Goal: At least 40wpm/5'/5e

D. 5-MINUTE TIMING

20   The computer has changed the way you do many things   11

21 in the office today. Jobs that used to take many hours to   23

22 complete now can be done in less time. A quick review of   34

23 ways in which your computer can streamline your work may be   45

24 in order.   47

25   Most computer programs include various wizards that   57

26 will help you through any project. You can use a stored   68

27 template, or you can create your own style. You do not   79

28 need to write your thoughts in longhand on paper before   90

29 you type them. Composing and revising documents as you   101

30 type them will save you lots of time.   109

31   Your computer is valuable for more than just writing   120

32 letters, however. Using various software applications, you   132

33 can create multimedia presentations that dazzle. You can   143

34 also build databases for sorting and storing all types of   155

35 data, format spreadsheets, create personal calendars and   166

36 colorful charts, and perform calculations. You can even   177

37 create stationery and publish newsletters. It is exciting   189

38 to consider all the possibilities for using computers.   200

| 1 | 2 | 3 | 4 | 5 | 6 | 7 | 8 | 9 | 10 | 11 | 12 |

DOCUMENT PROCESSING

Table 64-23 ▶

Three-Column Boxed Table

Go To

Word Processing Manual Review:
L. 36: Table—Create; AutoFit to Contents
L. 37: Table—Merge Cells
L. 38: Center a Table Horizontally and Center Page
L. 39: Table—Align Text in a Column

Reference Manual

Review:
R-13A: Boxed Table

$700 COMPOUNDED ANNUALLY FOR 7 YEARS AT 7 PERCENT		
Beginning of Year	**Interest**	**Value**
First	$00.00	$ 700.00
Second	49.00	749.00
Third	52.43	801.43
Fourth	56.10	857.53
Fifth	60.03	917.56
Sixth	64.23	981.79
Seventh	68.72	1,050.51
Eighth	78.68	1,129.19

Table
64-24 ▶

Three-Column
Open Table

Go To

**Word
Processing
Manual
Review:**
L. 37: Tables—
Borders

Reference Manual

Review:
R-13B: Open Table

1. Center the table vertically.
2. Create a table with 3 columns and 9 rows.
3. Center the column headings and type in upper- and lowercase and bold.
4. Automatically adjust the column widths for all columns.
5. Merge the cells in Row 1.
6. Center and type the title in all caps and bold. Press ENTER 1 time.
7. Center and type the subtitle in upper- and lowercase and bold.
8. Press ENTER 1 time after typing the subtitle.
9. Center the table horizontally.

SALES CONFERENCES
All Sessions at Regional Offices

Date	City	Leader
October 7	Boston	D. G. Gorham
October 17	Baltimore	James B. Brunner
October 24	Miami	Becky Taylor
November 3	Dallas	Rodney R. Nordstein
November 10	Minneapolis	Joanne Miles-Tyrell
November 17	Denver	Becky Taylor
November 26	Los Angeles	Rodney R. Nordstein

Table
64-25 ▶

Three-Column
Ruled Table

Reference Manual

Review:
R-13C: Ruled Table

SECOND HALF-YEAR SALES
Ending December 31, 20--

Month	Sales Quotas ($)	Actual Sales ($)
July	335,400	350,620
August	370,750	296,230
September	374,510	425,110
October	390,270	390,110
November	375,890	368,290
December	360,470	378,690
TOTAL	2,207,290	2,209,050

Lesson 65

Skillbuilding and Employment Document Review

GOALS
- Improve speed and accuracy
- Refine language arts skills in proofreading
- Format employment documents

A. Type 2 times.

A. WARMUP

```
 1        Only 6 of the 18 competitors weighed more than 149#.      11
 2   All Big Five matches were scheduled in Gym #3. Amazingly,      23
 3   about 1/3 of the #1 Jaguars were picked to acquire titles.     35
     | 1  | 2  | 3  | 4  | 5  | 6  | 7  | 8  | 9  | 10 | 11 | 12
```

SKILLBUILDING

B. TECHNIQUE PRACTICE: BACKSPACE KEY

Type each word as shown until you reach the backspace sign (←). Then backspace 1 time and replace the previously typed character with the one shown.

First Letter
Middle Letter
Last Letter

```
 4  h←fall s←dash h←lead k←heel p←cage b←rare d←bark l←date t←sold
 5  has←lf far←te mak←de roo←am do←ive fas←ce war←ve wee←ak yok←lk
 6  sale←t they←m helm←d wall←k pals←e milk←d told←l quip←t main←l
```

LANGUAGE ARTS

C. Compare this paragraph with the fourth paragraph of Report 61-37 on page 217. Edit the paragraph to correct any errors.

C. PROOFREADING

```
 7        A successful leader is one who is commited to ideas-
 8   ideas for future product and services for improving the
 9   firms market position, and for the wellbeing of his or her
10   employes. A leeder possesses a value system that is
11   ethicly and morally sound. leaders who make decisions
12   effecting the firm, employees, and society, have set of
13   beliefs that influence decision-making.
```

Report 65-39 ▶

Traditional Resume

Go To

Word Processing Manual Review:
L. 51: Fonts

Reference Manual

Review:
R-12A: Resume

Follow these steps to format this resume correctly:

1. Set alignment at center.
2. Press ENTER 6 times; then center the name in 14-pt. Arial bold.
3. Press ENTER 2 times. Switch to 12-pt. font.
4. Type the street address, followed by a comma.
5. Press the SPACE BAR 1 time; then type the city, state, and ZIP code.
6. Press ENTER 1 time.
7. Type the phone number, followed by a semicolon.
8. Press the SPACE BAR 1 time; then type email: and the email address.
9. Press ENTER 2 times.
10. Create an open table with 2 columns and 4 rows. Set alignment to left.
11. Apply a top border to the table, and press ENTER 1 time.
12. Type OBJECTIVE in bold in Row 1, Column A.
13. Tab to Column B, press ENTER 1 time, and type your objective.
14. Continue typing the entries in each column as shown. Automatically adjust column widths when finished.

TIMOTHY J. ROBINSON

5816 Foxfire Road, Lawton, OK 73501
Phone: 405-555-3039; email: trobin@lcc.edu

EDUCATION	Lawton Community College, Lawton, Oklahoma Associate in Business degree, Office Systems, June 1998 Specialization in computer application software (Microsoft Word, Excel, Access), business communication, and office systems management.
	Frederick High School, Frederick, Oklahoma Graduated: May 1996
EXPERIENCE	*Computer Systems Technician*, September 1996-Present Selkirk & Associates, Lawton, Oklahoma Duties include installing and updating computer software programs throughout the firm.
	Secretary II, July 1994-August 1996 (part-time) Kittredge Insurance Agency, Frederick, Oklahoma Duties included typing and word processing while reporting to the administrative assistant to the owner.
ACTIVITIES	College Choir, 1996-1998 Business Students Club, 1996-1998 (Secretary, 1997-1998) Varsity Basketball, 1996-1998 Intramural Soccer, 1996-1998
REFERENCES	References available upon request.

Current Date | Mrs. Denise F. Klenzman | Director of Human Resources | Cole Enterprises | 3714 Crestmont Avenue | Norman, OK 73069 | Dear Mrs. Klenzman:

¶ Please consider me an applicant for the position of Computer Systems Coordinator with your firm. I became aware of the ~~new~~ position through a friend who is an employee at Cole Enterprises. I have been employed at Selkirk & Associates since graduating from high school in 1996. During this time I have also earned an Assoc. in Business degree at Lawton Community College. The resume enclosed shows that I have had several courses in computer application soft ware and office systems. I am confident that my educational ~~experience~~ background and my computer systems experience make me highly qualified for the position with your firm. You may call me for an interview at 405-555-~~4572~~ 3039.

Sincerely yours, | Timothy J. Robinson | 5816 Foxfire Road | Lawton, OK 73501 | Enclosure

Correspondence 65-63 ▶

Follow-Up Letter in Block Style

☑ **Progress Check Proofreading Check**

Documents designated as Proofreading Checks serve as a check of your proofreading skill. Your goal is to have zero typographical errors when the GDP software first scores the document.

Current Date | Mrs. Denise F. Klenzman | Director of Human Resources | Cole Enterprises | 3714 Crestmont Avenue | Norman, OK 73069

Dear Mrs. Klenzman:

¶ Thank you for the opportunity to meet with you yesterday and to learn of the exciting career opportunities at Cole Enterprises. It was inspiring for me to learn about future plans for your forward-looking company.

¶ I am confident that my education and my experience qualify me in a special way for your position of computer systems coordinator. I am familiar with all of your present equipment and software.

¶ I would very much like to join the professional staff at Cole Enterprises. Please let me know when you have made your decision.

Sincerely yours, | Timothy J. Robinson | 5816 Foxfire Road | Lawton, OK 73501

LESSON 66
Itineraries

LESSON 67
Agendas and Minutes of Meetings

LESSON 68
Procedures Manual

LESSON 69
Reports Formatted in Columns

LESSON 70
Report Review

Presentation Software Guide   Cartwright Services, Page 2

FORMATTING SLIDES

Once you have written you presentation, you can place your key points on slides using presentation software. Follow these steps to prepare your presentation slides.

* Select a template or background that is appropriate for every slide.
* Select a layout such as text copy, bulleted or numbered lists, etc.
* Use the edit, copy, and paste commands to add text to your presentation slides.

FORMATTING THE PRESENTATION

After you finish preparing the slides for your presentation, you may want to change the method by which each slide appears on the screen or the way individual points are displayed on the screen. In presentation software, moving from one slide to another is known as transition. Transition is accomplished by following these steps:

* Select those slides you want to control by the transition method.
* Select a transition method such as Cover Right or Wipe Left.
* Run through the slide show to determine whether or not you are satisfied with the transition.

Slide presentations can also be formatted so that each point you make on an individual slide appears individually on the screen. To structure your slides this way, follow these steps:

* Select those slides to be controlled by a build effect.
* ... Fly From Left.
* ... to determine whether or not you are satisfied with

... of a slide, and it can be added easily to selected ...resentation. Several clip art images are included in ...e of them can be used in slides that you prepare. If ...lip art images from other packages. To insert a clip ...age, follow these steps:

* ...t the clip art to appear.
* ... image.
* ...e clip art library.
* ...rect location on the slide.
* ...e if it is to appear on all slides.

CALIFORNIA PLANNING MEETING

Itinerary for Nancy Perkins

July 8-10, 20--

MONDAY, JULY 8

2:45 p.m.-4:05 p.m.   Flight from Houston to Los Angeles; United Flight 834; seat 10C; nonstop

TUESDAY, JULY 9

10 a.m.-11:15 a.m.   Flight from Los Ang...
                          seat 4A; nonstop

WEDNESDAY, JULY 10

7 p.m.-11:15 p.m.   Flight from Sacramen...
                         7B; nonstop; dinner

NOTES

1. Adam Broderick, chief engineer for Natural Gas... Los Angeles.
2. 2. At 7 p.m. on July 8, you will have dinner with... the Hollywood & Vine Restaurant.
3. You will have a 9 a.m. tour of the wastewater tr... Wednesday, July 10.
4. At 12 noon on Wednesday, July 10, you will ha... at J. C. Crawford's. Topic: Senate Bill 4501-68...

PERFORMING SUCCESSFULLY

Ginger Nichols

We have been involved in giving performances since our very early years when we played a part in a class play or participated in competitive sporting events at our school. The most terrifying part of each performance was probably the fear that we would "freeze" when it came our turn to perform. Whenever we find ourselves in this predicament, the best thing to do is to accept that fear and to learn to let it work for us, not against us. We need to recognize that nervousness or fear may set in during our performance. Then, when it does happen (if it does), we will be ready to cope with it and overcome it.

If you forget some of your lines in a recitation, try to remember other lines and recite them. Doing so may help those forgotten lines to "pop back" into your memory so that you put them in at a later time, if possible.

You always want to leave your audience with the idea that you have given them something worthwhile that they can use or apply to their own lives. For maximum impact on your audience and to make sure that they remember what you say, use audiovisual aids to reinforce your message. Remember, however, that audiovisual aids are nothing more than aids. The real message should come in the words you choose when giving your presentation.

Study your speech well; even rehearse it if necessary. However, do not practice it to the extent that it appears that you are merely reading what is written down on the paper in front of you. Much of your personality should be exhibited while you are giving your speech. If you are an enthusiastic, friendly person who converses well with people face-to-face, then that same persona should be evident during your speech. A good piece of advice is to just go out there and be yourself—you will be much more comfortable by doing so, and your audience will relate to you better than if you try to exhibit a different personality when at the podium.

No matter how rapidly you speak in general, slow down when you are in front of a group. The fact that you are nervous can cause your speech rate to increase. The best way to slow down your speaking is to breathe deeply. Doing so also causes your nervous system to relax, allowing you to proceed with your speech calmly.

Finally, possibly the best advice for giving a successful speech is to be prepared. You will be more confident if you are thoroughly prepared. Do your research, rehearse your speech, and make notes where you want to give emphasis or use an audiovisual aid.

Lesson 66

Itineraries

A. Type 2 times.

A. WARMUP

```
1      Had Phil been given a quiz on a subject that had been    11
2   reviewed by Max and Kay? Frank scored 89 on that quiz; Sue   23
3   scored 93 (*math only). Both tests were taken on 10/25/01.    35
       | 1  | 2  | 3  | 4  | 5  | 6  | 7  | 8  | 9  | 10 | 11 | 12
```

SKILLBUILDING

B. Take three 12-second timings on each line. The scale below the last line shows your wpm speed for a 12-second timing.

B. 12-SECOND SPEED SPRINTS

```
4   This is not the person who is my first choice for this job.
5   The day was bright as the sun shone on the clear blue lake.
6   All of you should take a long walk when the sun sets today.
7   This line has many easy words in it to type your very best.
    I I I I 5 I I I I 10 I I I I 15 I I I I 20 I I I I 25 I I I I 30 I I I I 35 I I I I 40 I I I I 45 I I I I 50 I I I I 55 I I I I 60
```

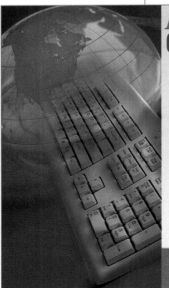

Keyboarding CONNECTION

Observing Netiquette

Netiquette is proper conduct for email users. It shows courtesy and professionalism and conveys a good impression of you and your company. Since email is nearest to speech, it is the most informal of business documents.

Check your email daily. Try to answer it the same day it arrives. Don't let it accumulate in your mailbox; you risk offending the sender. Use regular capitalization. All caps indicate SHOUTING; all lowercase letters convey immaturity. Most readers tolerate an infrequent typo, but if your message is filled with errors, you appear unprofessional. Use your spell checker, and don't overwhelm people with unnecessary emails. Use discretion. Make sure the information is relevant to each email recipient.

Be considerate. Be professional. Anything you write can wind up in your personnel file. Email that critiques another person can be forwarded to him or her without your knowledge.

YOUR TURN Review your next email message for use of netiquette.

C. Take two 5-minute timings. Review your speed and errors.

Goal: At least 41wpm/5'/5e

C. 5-MINUTE TIMING

8   Making a successful presentation to an audience is a   11
9   skill that is absolutely essential in your career. The   22
10 art of speaking before a group requires planning and very   34
11 hard work. Although each speaker makes preparation in a   45
12 different manner, a speaker should follow certain rules.   56
13   As the speaker, you are quite visible to people in   66
14 the audience. Therefore, you must make an effort to make   77
15 a good first impression. Walking to the podium to speak,   88
16 you give your audience an opportunity to notice your neat   100
17 appearance, good posture, and confident manner. You will   111
18 improve the quality of your voice by standing up straight   123
19 and holding your shoulders back and stomach in.   133
20   As you talk, use your eyes, face, and hands to help   144
21 you connect with your listeners. Maintain eye contact by   155
22 just moving your eyes over the group without focusing on   166
23 any one person. Use hand movements and facial expressions   178
24 to convey meanings to your audience. By utilizing these   189
25 techniques you will improve your speaking skills and your   201
26 efforts will be noted.   205

| 1 | 2 | 3 | 4 | 5 | 6 | 7 | 8 | 9 | 10 | 11 | 12

FORMATTING

D. ITINERARIES

An itinerary is a proposed outline of a trip that provides a traveler with information such as flight times and numbers, meeting times, travel dates, and room reservations. An itinerary may also include notes of special interest to the traveler.

Report 66-40 ▶

Itinerary

Reference Manual

Review:
R-11C: Itinerary

Follow these steps to format Report 66-40.
1. Press ENTER 6 times to leave an approximate two-inch top margin.
2. Insert a 2-column, 10-row open table.
3. Merge Row 1 for the main heading and subheading. Remember to insert a blank line between each of the headings and after the date information.
4. Move to Row 2, Column A and type the date; then press Enter 1 time.
5. Move to Row 3 and type the time in Column A. Then type the corresponding information for this time in Column B. Remember to insert a hard return after the final line in Column B.
6. Move to Row 4 and repeat steps 4 and 5 until all dates, times, and entries have been completed. (Do not insert a hard return at the end of the final itinerary entry.)

↓6X

14 pt **PORTLAND SALES MEETING** ↓2X

12 pt↓ **Itinerary for Arlene Gilsdorf** ↓2X

March 12-18, 20-- ↓2X

THURSDAY, MARCH 12 ↓2X

5:10 p.m.-5:55 p.m.   Flight from Detroit to Minneapolis; Northwest 83 (Phone: 800-555-1222); e-ticket; Seat 8D; nonstop ↓2X

6:30 p.m.-8:06 p.m.   Flight from Minneapolis to Portland; Northwest 2363; e-ticket; Seat 15C; nonstop; dinner ↓2X

SUNDAY, MARCH 15

10:35 a.m.-12:22 p.m.   Flight from Portland to Los Angeles; United Airlines 360; e-ticket; Seat 15F; nonstop; breakfast

TUESDAY, MARCH 17

8 a.m.-9:22 a.m.   Flight from San Francisco to Los Angeles; United Airlines 748; e-ticket; Seat 10D; nonstop; snack

WEDNESDAY, MARCH 18

3:40 p.m.-5:50 p.m.   Flight from Los Angeles to Detroit; Southwest 327; e-ticket; Seat 17D; nonstop; snack

INTERCO SEMINAR
Itinerary for Mrs. Helen Kyslowsky
September 25-29, 20--

WEDNESDAY, SEPTEMBER 25

6:50 p.m.-9:10 p.m. *Flight from Columbus to Boston;*
America West 2053;
Seat 13 F; nonstop

FRIDAY, SEPTEMBER 27

9 a.m.-10:17 a.m. *Flight from Boston to New York City;*
US Airways 454; Seat 10 D; nonstop

SUNDAY, SEPTEMBER 29

2:07 p.m.-4:18 p.m. *Flight from New York City to Columbus;*
US Airways 324; Seat 9A; nonstop

CALIFORNIA PLANNING MEETING | **Itinerary for Nancy Perkins** | **July 8-10, 20--** | **MONDAY, JULY 8** | Leave at 2:45 p.m. and arrive at 4:05 p.m. Houston to Los Angeles; United Flight 834; Seat 10C; nonstop; | Marriott (310-555-1014) King-sized bed; nonsmoking room; late arrival guaranteed (Reservation No. 45STX78 | **TUESDAY, JULY 9** | Leave at 10 a.m. and arrive at 11:15 a.m. Los Angeles to Sacramento; American Flight 206; Seat 4A; nonstop | **WEDNESDAY, JULY 10** | Leave at 7 p.m. and arrive at 11:15 p.m. Sacramento to Houston; United Flight 307; Seat 7B; nonstop; dinner

Lesson 67

Agendas and Minutes of Meetings

GOALS

- Improve speed and accuracy
- Refine language arts skills in the use of hyphens, abbreviations, and agreement
- Format agendas and minutes of meetings

A. Type 2 times.

A. WARMUP

```
1      Rex Yantz was calm before quitting his job at the zoo     11
2  on 7/10/00. On 8/23/00 he applied for a job at Vance &       22
3  Walton, "specialists" in corporate law and bankruptcies.     33
   |  1  |  2  |  3  |  4  |  5  |  6  |  7  |  8  |  9  |  10  |  11  |  12
```

SKILLBUILDING

B. DIAGNOSTIC PRACTICE: ALPHABET

If you are not using the GDP software, turn to page SB-2 and follow the directions for this activity.

C. DIAGNOSTIC PRACTICE: NUMBERS

If you are not using the GDP software, turn to page SB-5 and follow the directions for this activity.

LANGUAGE ARTS

D. Study the rules at the right.

D. HYPHENS

RULE ▶
-compound adjective

Hyphenate compound adjectives that come before a noun (unless the first word is an adverb ending in -ly).

> We reviewed an up-to-date report on Wednesday.
> *But:* The report was up to date.
> *But:* We reviewed the highly rated report.

Note: A compound adjective is two or more words that function as a unit to describe a noun.

E. AGREEMENT

RULE ▶
agreement singular
agreement plural

Use singular verbs and pronouns with singular subjects; use plural verbs and pronouns with plural subjects.

> I was happy with my performance.
> Janet and Phoenix were happy with their performance.
> Among the items discussed were our raises and benefits.

F. ABBREVIATIONS

In general business writing, do not abbreviate common words (such as *dept.* or *pkg.*), compass points, units of measure, or the names of months, days of the week, cities, or states (except in addresses).

Almost one-half of the audience indicated they were at least 5 feet 8 inches tall.

Note: Do not insert a comma between the parts of a single measurement.

Edit the sentences to correct any errors in grammar.

4   The Queens visited Hickory to look at four bedroom homes.
5   Cindy Wallace has a part time job after school.
6   The accountants was extremely busy from March through April.
7   Lydia and Margaret were invited to present their report.
8   The portfolio include several technology stocks.
9   The planning committee will meet on Tue., Sept. 26.
10   Please credit the acct. for the amt. of $55.48.
11   The mgr. said the org. will move its headquarters to NC.

FORMATTING

G. AGENDAS

An agenda is a list of topics to be discussed at a meeting. It may also include a formal program of a meeting consisting of times, rooms, speakers, and other related information. Follow these steps to format an agenda:

1. Press ENTER 6 times to leave an approximate 2-inch top margin.
2. Center and type the name of the company or committee in all caps, bold, and 14 points.
3. Press ENTER 2 times, and center and type Meeting Agenda in upper-and lowercase, bold, and 12 points.
4. Press ENTER 2 times, and center and type the date in upper- and lowercase, bold, and 12 points.
5. Press ENTER 2 times, and change the line spacing to double.
6. Type the first item in the agenda. Number each item using the numbering command.

Remember to position the numbers at the left margin.

↓6X
14 pt   **ALLIANCE CORPORATION STAFF MEETING**

12 pt↓   **Meeting Agenda**
↓2X
November 17, 20--
↓2X
1. Approval of minutes of October 15 meeting
↓2X
2. Progress reports of new district offices

3. Discussion of attendance at the National Hardware Association's meeting

4. Multimedia installation update: B. Harris

5. Annual fund drive: T. Henderson

H. MINUTES OF MEETINGS

Minutes of a meeting are a record of items discussed during a meeting. To format meeting minutes, follow these steps:

1. Press ENTER 6 times to leave an approximate 2-inch top margin.
2. Create an open, two-column table that has enough rows to accommodate all of the given information.
3. Merge Row 1 for the main heading, subheading, and date. Format the main heading and subheadings appropriately. (Remember to insert a blank line between each of the headings and after the date information.)
4. Type side headings in all caps and bold.
5. Type all corresponding information in Column B. Remember to insert a hard return after the final line in all Column B entries.
6. Continue typing the minutes as shown in the illustration. Manually adjust column width as needed. Do not insert a hard return at the end of the final minutes entry.

↓6X

14 pt **PLANNING COMMITTEE**

12 pt↓ **Minutes of the Meeting**
↓2X
February 10, 20—
↓2X

ATTENDANCE   The Planning Committee meeting was called to order at 1 p.m. on February 10, 20--, by Michelle North, chairperson. Members present were Cal Anderson, L. T. Braddock, Lisa Samson, Sharon Owens, and J. R. Sterns.
↓2X
OLD BUSINESS   The committee reviewed bids for the purchase of a new computer for the Cheyenne office. We will accept the lower of two bids that have been submitted.

NEW BUSINESS   The committee reviewed a proposal for a new complex in Helena. After much discussion, the committee agreed to contact the Helena county clerk's office to get information on zoning ordinances.

ADJOURNMENT   The meeting was adjourned at 2:45 p.m. The next meeting is scheduled for March 22 in Room 16.
↓2X
Respectfully submitted,
↓4X
L. T. Braddock

L. T. Braddock, Secretary

Go To

Word Processing Manual

I. WORD PROCESSING: HYPHENATION

Study Lesson 67 in your word processing manual. Complete all of the shaded steps while at your computer. Then format the jobs that follow.

Report 67-43 ▶

Agenda

Go To

Word Processing Manual Review:
L. 28: Bullets and Numbering

Reference Manual

Review:
R-11A: Meeting Agenda

↓6X
14 pt **ALLIANCE CORPORATION STAFF MEETING** ↓2X

12 pt↓ **Meeting Agenda** ↓2X

November 17, 20-- ↓2X

1. Approval of minutes of October 15 meeting ↓2X

2. Progress reports of new district offices

3. Discussion of attendance at the National Hardware Association's annual meeting

4. Multimedia installation update: B. Harris

5. Annual fund drive: T. Henderson

Report 67-44 ▶

Agenda

APEX MULTIMEDIA CORPORATION
Meeting Agenda
October 13, 20--

1. Call to order
2. Approval of minutes of September 10 meeting
3. Progress reports on Sherman contract
   (Julia Adams)
4. Upgrading of 8.0 presentation media
5. CD-ROM *development program (Ray Sanchez)*
6. Internet configuration (JoAnn Hubbard)
7. Adjournment

Report ▶
67-45

Minutes of a
Meeting

Turn on hyphenation,
if needed.

↓6X

14 pt **PLANNING COMMITTEE** ↓2X

12 pt↓ **Minutes of the Meeting** ↓2X

February 10, 20-- ↓2X

ATTENDANCE	The Planning Committee meeting was called to order at 1 p.m. on February 10, 20--, by Michelle North, chairperson. Members present were Cal Anderson, L. T. Braddock, Lisa Samson, Sharon Owens, and J. R. Sterns. ↓2X
OLD BUSINESS	The committee reviewed bids for the purchase of a new computer for the Cheyenne office. We will accept the lower of two bids that have been submitted.
NEW BUSINESS	The committee reviewed a proposal for a new complex in Helena. After much discussion, the committee agreed to contact the Helena county clerk's office to get information on zoning ordinances.
ADJOURNMENT	The meeting was adjourned at 2:45 p.m. The next meeting is scheduled for March 22 in Room 16. ↓2X

Respectfully submitted, ↓4X

L. T. Braddock, Secretary

PERSONNEL COMMITTEE

Minutes of the Meeting

May 14, 20--

ATTENDENCE   A ~special~ meeting of the Personnel Committee was held ~on May 14, 20--,~ in the office of Mr. Cameron. ~All~ Members present were

(Continued on next page)

except Richard Dixon, who was repre-sented by Monica Zick man. The meeting was called to order at 2 p. m.

Old Business A copy of the survey is attached. Eighty-eight employees participated in a survey that had been completed by Andrea Fields. The minutes of the last monthly meeting were read.

NEW BUSINESS Ms. ~~Samuels~~ *Daniels* discussed the need for planning a campaign for job applicants *letting* about vacancies *know* occur *that* within the company. Frank Lundquist will draft a fl*y*er to be sent to the Park view *ital* sentinel. Programs for the N P A convention to be held in Des Moines were distributed to all members. Each committee member ~~were~~ *was* asked to distribute copies to *all* employees in his or her department.

ADJOURN *MENT* The meeting was adjourned at 3:25 *p*.m. The next meeting has been scheduled for July 10 in the conference center.

Respectfully submitted,

Brandon Stinson, Secretary

Procedures Manual

GOALS
- Type at least 41wpm/5'/5e
- Format a procedures manual

A. Type 2 times.

A. WARMUP

```
1      Zach sharpened the ax for Quinn just to help him win    10
2   the $100 tree-cutting event to be held in Kildeer on May 8   23
3   (if it doesn't rain). The prize will be $250--fantastic!    34
    |  1  |  2  |  3  |  4  |  5  |  6  |  7  |  8  |  9  |  10  |  11  |  12
```

SKILLBUILDING

B. MAP

Follow the GDP software directions for this exercise in improving keystroking accuracy.

C. Take two 5-minute timings. Review your speed and errors.

Goal: At least 41wpm/5'/5e

C. 5-MINUTE TIMING

```
4       Ergonomics is the science of adapting today's office    11
5    environment to the human body so that the productivity,     22
6    health, and safety of employees is at the optimal level.    33
7    Physical issues, such as proper body posture and support,   45
8    adjustable office furniture, and adequate lighting are      55
9    studied to make recommendations for office environments.    67
10      Office equipment should be adjusted to ensure safety     78
11   and health of the workers. Place the monitor at a distance  90
12   that will allow the eyes to relax. Adjust the lighting and  102
13   the monitor position to reduce the glare. Lower or raise    113
14   the keyboard so that the wrists are straight. Place the     124
15   mouse at the same level next to the keyboard.               133
16      Chair height should allow the feet to rest on the        143
17   floor and allow the legs to move freely. The height of      154
18   the chair can be adjusted if the height of the keyboard is  166
19   not flexible. Remember to walk around the office plaza at   178
20   regular intervals to provide relief for the body.           188
21      When office personnel are comfortable and healthy,       198
22   they will improve their productivity.                       205
    |  1  |  2  |  3  |  4  |  5  |  6  |  7  |  8  |  9  |  10  |  11  |  12
```

D. PROCEDURES MANUAL

Organizations often prepare procedures manuals to assist employees in identifying the steps or methods they must follow to accomplish particular tasks. To format a procedures manual:

1. Type the manual as a single-spaced report.
2. Place a header on every page except the first page. The header may include such items as the title of the manual (at the left margin) and the company name and page number (at the right margin).
3. Place a footer on every page including the first page. The footer may include the same information as the header or it may identify the content of that page (for example, "Training Program").

Employees' Manual   Chandler Industries, Page 7

The purpose of this procedures manual is to assist managers who are responsible for developing training programs for new employees who have been hired in any of the seven regional branches of Chandler Industries. The basic content of this training program is outlined in the following paragraphs. ↓2X

INTRODUCTION ↓2X

This section identifies specific ways the manual should be used at Chandler Industries as well as the content of the manual. Answers are provided to the following questions: ↓2X

1. Where does the training manual fit within the training program?
2. For whom is the manual designed, and what does it contain?
3. How should the manual be used?
4. Can the manual be used in a classroom setting?
5. Can the manual be used as self-paced instructional material?
6. Can study guides accompany the manual? ↓2X

PROGRAM PHILOSOPHY AND GOALS ↓2X

This section reveals the nature of the training program. The statements below provide the context for all courses within Chandler Industries. The focus of the section is as follows: ↓2X

- Why does this program exist, and who benefits from it?
- What company needs are satisfied by this program?
- What goals, tasks, and competencies are satisfied by this program?
- What specific skills does this training program develop?

Training Program

DOCUMENT PROCESSING

Report 68-47

Procedures Manual

1. Turn on hyphenation.
2. In page numbering, change the page number to start at page 7, then create a header as follows: Type `Employees' Manual` at the left margin. Type `Chandler Industries, Page 7` aligned at the right margin.
3. Create a footer by typing `Training Program` in italic and aligned at the left margin.
4. Type the following portion of a procedures manual.

Go To

Word Processing Manual Review:
L. 27: Page Numbering
L. 42: Headers and Footers

Employees' Manual   Chandler Industries, Page 7

¶ The purpose of this procedures manual is to assist managers who are responsible for developing training programs for new employees who have been hired in any of the seven regional branches of Chandler Industries. The basic content of this training program is outlined in the following paragraphs.

(Continued on next page)

INTRODUCTION

¶ This section identifies specific ways the manual should be used at Chandler Industries as well as the content of the manual. Answers are provided to the following questions:

1. Where does the training manual fit within the training program?
2. For whom is the manual designed, and what does it contain?
3. How should the manual be used?
4. Can the manual be used in a classroom setting?
5. Can the manual be used as self-paced instructional material?
6. Can study guides accompany the manual?

PROGRAM PHILOSOPHY AND GOALS

¶ This section reveals the nature of the training program. The statements below provide the context for all courses within Chandler Industries. The focus of the section is as follows:

- Why does this program exist, and who benefits from it?
- What company needs are satisfied by this program?
- What goals, tasks, and competencies are satisfied by this program?
- What specific skills does this training program develop?

Training Program

Remember to single-space the entire list if all items in the list are one line long.

Report 68-48

Procedures Manual

Remember to insert a blank line between items in a multiline list in a single-spaced document.

1. In page numbering, change the page number to start at page 2.
2. Create a header as follows:
   Type `Presentation Software Guide` at the left margin. Type `Cartwright Services, Page 2` aligned at the right margin.
3. Type `FORMATTING` as a footer at the left margin.

Presentation Software Guide   Cartwright Services, Page 2

FORMATTING SLIDES

¶ Once you have written your presentation, you can place your key points on slides using presentation software. Follow these steps to prepare your presentation slides.

- Select a template or background that is appropriate for every slide.
- Select a layout such as text copy, bulleted or numbered lists, etc.
- Use the edit, copy, and paste commands to add text to your presentation slides.

FORMATTING THE PRESENTATION

¶ After you finish preparing the slides for your presentation, you may want to change the method by which each slide appears on the screen or the way individual points are displayed on the screen. In presentation software, moving from one slide to another is known as transition. Transition is accomplished by following these steps:

- Select those slides you want to control by the transition method.
- Select a transition method such as Cover Right or Wipe Left.
- Run through the slide show to determine whether or not you are satisfied with the transition.

(Continued on next page)

¶ Slide presentations can also be formatted so that each point you make on an individual slide appears individually on the screen. To structure your slides this way, follow these steps:
- Select those slides to be controlled by a build effect.
- Select a build effect style such as Fly From Left.
- Run through the slide show again to determine whether or not you are satisfied with the build effect.

Report 68-49 ▶

Procedures Manual

1. Open the file for Report 68-48.
2. Add the following sections to the end of the report.

ADDING CLIP ART

¶ Clipart can enhances the appearance of a slide, and it can be easily added to selected slides or to every other slide in your presentation. Several clip art images are included in this presentation package, and any one of them can be used in slides that you prepare. If you choose, however, you can insert clip art images from other packages. To insert a clip art image from your presentation package, follow these steps:

- Select the slide on which you want the clip art to appear.
- Click the icon for adding a clip art image. This icon is found on the menu bar.
- Select the image from the software clip art library. The slide can come and size and move it to its new location from the presentation package or you can retrieve it from another clip art package.
- Size and move the image to its correct location on the presentation slide.
- Copy the image to the master slide if it is to appear on all slides.

¶ You can also change the appearance of the clip art image by (1) changing the colors used in the image; (2) flipping the image so that its horizontal or vertical position is reversed (mirror image); (3) changing the contrast or brightness of the image; and (4) cropping the image so that unwanted sections are eliminated from view.

Reports Formatted in Columns

GOALS

- Improve speed and accuracy
- Refine language arts skills in spelling
- Format magazine articles

A. Type 2 times.

A. WARMUP

```
1        On 12/30/00 Jim gave Alex and Pam a quiz--it was quite    11
2   difficult! Neither scored higher than 82%; their average       22
3   was 79. They should retake the quiz by the 4th or 5th.         32
    |  1  |  2  |  3  |  4  |  5  |  6  |  7  |  8  |  9  | 10  | 11  | 12
```

SKILLBUILDING

B. PACED PRACTICE

If you are not using the GDP software, turn to page SB-14 and follow the directions for this activity.

PRETEST ➡ PRACTICE ➡ POSTTEST

C. PRETEST: Horizontal Reaches

PRETEST
Take a 1-minute timing. Review your speed and errors.

```
4        Four famous adults gazed at a wren on our farm gate.      11
5   A group of gawking writers wrote facts about an additional     23
6   upward gain in wildlife numbers on their supply of pads.       34
    |  1  |  2  |  3  |  4  |  5  |  6  |  7  |  8  |  9  | 10  | 11  | 12
```

D. PRACTICE: In Reaches

PRACTICE
Speed Emphasis:
If you made no more than 1 error on the Pretest, type each *individual* line 2 times.
Accuracy Emphasis:
If you made 2 or more errors, type each *group* of lines (as though it were a paragraph) 2 times.

```
7   wr wrap wren wreak wrist wrote writer unwrap writhe wreaths
8   ou pout ours ounce cough fouls output detour ousted coupons
9   ad adds dead adult ready blade advice fading admits adheres
```

E. PRACTICE: Out Reaches

```
10  fa fact farm faith sofas fakes faulty unfair famous defames
11  up upon soup upset group upper upturn supply uplift upsurge
12  ga gate gave cigar gains legal gazing legacy gawked garbage
```

POSTTEST
Repeat the Pretest timing and compare performance.

F. POSTTEST: Horizontal Reaches

G. Type this list of frequently misspelled words, paying special attention to any spelling problems in each word.

G. SPELLING

13 personnel information its procedures their committee system
14 receive employees which education services opportunity area
15 financial appropriate interest received production contract
16 important through necessary customer employee further there
17 property account approximately general control division our

Edit the sentences to correct any misspellings.

18 The revised systom was adopted by the finantial division.
19 Four employes want to serve on the new property commitee.
20 Approximatly ten proceedures were included in the contract.
21 Further informasion will be recieved from the customers.
22 Their was much interest shown by the production personal.
23 The services in that aria are necesary for needed control.

H. MAGAZINE ARTICLES

Magazine articles can be formatted as two-column reports. Follow these steps:

1. Press ENTER 6 times to leave an approximate 2-inch top margin on page 1.
2. Use single spacing and justified alignment; then turn on hyphenation.
3. Create a header to print on all pages except page 1 to identify the author's name and the page number at the top right of every page. Use only the author's last name and the page number in the header (for example, Mysweski 2).
4. Center and type the article title in all caps, bold, and 14 points.
5. Press ENTER 2 times; then center and type the byline in upper- and lower-case, bold, and 12 points.
6. Press ENTER 2 times and change to left-alignment. Then type the article single-spaced in a two-column format.
7. Insert 1 blank line before and after all headings.

MEMBER BUYING SERVICES

Brenda T. Mysweski

↓6X
14 pt **MEMBER BUYING SERVICES** ↓2X
12 pt **Brenda T. Mysweski** ↓2X

Policyholders of AICA (and their dependents) are eligible for a wide range of discount services. These services provide you with a variety of items you can purchase, from automobiles to computers to jewelry. Here are some examples of the merchandise and services that are available to all AICA members. ↓2X

AUTO PRICING ↓2X

You can order the most sophisticated auto information guide on the market. The guide will give you information on retail prices, vehicle specifications, safety equipment, and factory-option packages. ↓2X

When you are ready to place your order for an automobile, a team of company experts will work with you and with the prospective dealer to ensure that you are getting the best possible price through a network of nationwide dealers. You are guaranteed to get the best price for the automobile you have chosen.

Once you have purchased your automobile, AICA will provide your insurance needs. Discounts on policy rates are provided for completion of a driver-training program, for installed antitheft devices, and for installed passive restraint systems such as air bags.

Finally, we can make your purchase decision an easy one by always providing a low-rate finance plan for you. You can be certain that you are getting the most competitive interest rate for the purchase of your automobile when you finance with AICA.

CAR RENTAL DISCOUNTS

When you need to rent an automobile while traveling, special rates and discounts are available to you from five of the largest car rental agencies, and you'll never find better prices!

Mysweski 2

MERCHANDISE BUYING

Each quarter a buying services catalog will be sent to you. This catalog includes a variety of items that can be purchased through AICA. Through the catalog you can purchase jewelry, furniture, sports equipment, electronics, appliances, and computers. To place an order, all you have to do is call AICA toll-free at 1-800-555-3838. Your order will arrive within 10 to 15 days.

Go To

Word Processing Manual

I. WORD PROCESSING: COLUMNS

Study Lesson 69 in your word processing manual. Complete all of the shaded steps while at your computer. Then format the jobs that follow.

DOCUMENT PROCESSING

Report 69-50

Magazine Article in Two Columns

MEMBER BUYING SERVICES | **Brenda T. Mysweski**

¶ Policyholders of AICA (and their dependents) are eligible for a wide range of discount services. These services provide you with a variety of items you can purchase, from automobiles to computers to jewelry. Here are some examples of the merchandise and services that are available to all AICA members.

AUTO PRICING

¶ You can order the most sophisticated auto information guide on the market. The guide will give you information on retail prices, vehicle specifications, safety equipment, and factory-option packages.

¶ When you are ready to place your order for an automobile, a team of company experts will work with you and with the prospective dealer to ensure that you are getting the best possible price through a network of nationwide dealers. You are guaranteed to get the best price for the automobile you have chosen.

(Continued on next page)

¶ Once you have purchased your automobile, AICA will provide all your insurance needs. Discounts on policy rates are provided for completion of a driver-training program, for installed antitheft devices, and for installed passive restraint systems such as air bags.

¶ Finally, we can make your purchase decision an easy one by always providing a low-rate finance plan for you. You can be certain that you are getting the most competitive interest rate for the purchase of your automobile when you finance with AICA.

CAR RENTAL DISCOUNTS

¶ When you need to rent an automobile while traveling, special rates are available to you from five of the largest car rental agencies.

ROAD AND TRAVEL SERVICES

¶ You can enjoy the security of emergency road service through the AICA Road and Travel Plan. This plan also includes discounts on hotels and motels.

¶ As an AICA traveler, you can take advantage of our exclusive discounts and bonuses on cruises and tours. Our travel plan provides daily and weekend trips to over 100 destinations. Take advantage of this wonderful opportunity to let AICA serve all your travel needs.

MERCHANDISE BUYING

¶ Each quarter a buying services catalog will be sent to you. This catalog includes a variety of items that can be purchased through AICA—and you'll never find better prices! Through the catalog you can purchase jewelry, furniture, sports equipment, electronics, appliances, and computers. To place an order, all you have to do is call AICA toll-free at 1-800-555-3838. Your order will arrive within 10 to 15 days.

Report 69-51 ▶

Magazine Article in Two Columns

INTERVIEW TECHNIQUES | By Paul Sanford

The interview process enables a company to gather information about you that was not provided on your resume or application form. This information may includes such items as your career goals, appearance, personality, poise, attitudes, and ability to express yourself verbally.

APPEARANCE

There are several things you should keep in mind when going to an interview. You should plan your wardrobe carefully because first impressions are lasting ones when you walk into the interviewer's office. If you are not quite certain about what you should wear, dress conservatively. Whatever you choose, be sure that your clothing is clean, neat, and comfortable. You should

(Continued on next page)

also pay attention to important details such as clean hair, shined shoes, well-groomed nails, and appropriate jewelry and other accessories.

MEETING THE INTERVIEWER

Be sure to arrive at the interview site a few minutes early. Stand when you meet the interviewer ~~for the first time.~~ If ~~a handshake is~~ the interviewer offered s to shake hands, shake hands in a confident, firm manner. It is also a good idea not to smoke or chew gum during the interview.

THE INTERVIEW PROCESS

Maintain ~~good~~ direct eye contact with the interviewer when you respond to his or her questions. Listen intently to everything that is said. Be aware of ~~the~~ any movements you make with your eyes, your hands, and other parts of your body during the interview. Too much movement may be a signal to the interviewer that you are nervous, that you lack confidence, or that you are not certain of your answers.

During the interview ~~process,~~ the interviewer will judge not only what you say but also how you say it. As you ~~speak,~~ answer questions you will be judged on grammar, articulation, vocabulary, and tone of voice. The nonverbal skills that may ~~be~~ the interviewer judged are your attitude, enthusiasm, listening abilities, and promptness in responding to questions.

ENDING THE INTERVIEW

Let the interviewer determine when it is time to close the interview. When this time arrives, ask the interviewer when he or she expects to make a decision on hiring for this position and when you ~~can~~ may expect to hear about the job. Thank the interviewer for taking the time to meet with you, and express a ~~positive~~ desire to work for the company.

After the interview, send a follow-up letter to remind the interviewer of your name and your continued interest in the company. Let that person know how to contact you by providing a telephone number where you can be reached, either at home or at your current work location.

Report 69-52 ▶

Magazine Article
in Two Columns

Go To

**Word
Processing
Manual
Review:**
L. 30:
Cut/Copy/Paste

Open the file for Report 69-50 and make the following changes:

1. Make yourself the author of the article.
2. Make the MERCHANDISE BUYING section the second paragraph in the article.
3. Add the following section to the end of the article:

MISCELLANEOUS SERVICES | In addition to the above services, AICA provides permanent life insurance, pension plan funding, cash management, and credit card programs. At your request, detailed catalogs will be sent to you that explain each of these services.

Careers in the publishing field require excellent keyboarding skills.

Report Review

A. Type 2 times.

A. WARMUP

```
1        Felix Quayle sat in Seat #14 when he won the jackpot;    11
2   Van Gill sat in Seat #23 but did not win a prize. Do you      22
3   think Row 19 (Seats #1560 and #1782) will be lucky for me?    34
    |  1  |  2  |  3  |  4  |  5  |  6  |  7  |  8  |  9  |  10  |  11  |  12
```

SKILLBUILDING

B. PROGRESSIVE PRACTICE: ALPHABET

If you are not using the GDP software, turn to page SB-7 and follow the directions for this activity.

C. SUSTAINED PRACTICE: ROUGH DRAFT

C. Take a 1-minute timing on the first paragraph to establish your base speed. Then take four 1-minute timings on the remaining paragraphs. As soon as you equal or exceed your base speed on one paragraph, advance to the next, more difficult paragraph.

```
4         The possibility of aging and not being able to live as    11
5   independently as we want to is a prospect that no one wants     23
6   to recognize. One resource designed to counter some of the     35
7   negative realities of aging is called the Handyman Project.    47

                      program
8         This type of project helps support elders and disabled   12
                                                ir
9   residents in their efforts to maintain the homes. As the       24
                              e       m
10  name implies, "handy" volunters per for minor home repairs     36
                       e
11  such as tightning leaky faucets and fixing broken windows.     48

          s
12  Other type of work include: (painting, plumbing, yard          11
                                                          i
13  work, and carpentery. The volunteers are all as diversfied     23
              k                                    e       o
14  as the word itself. You may find a retire working next too     35
                           assisting    c
15  an executive or a student helping a lisensed electrician.      47
```

(Continued on next page)

16   Their back grunds may vary, but that they share is the   11

17   ~~hope~~ *desire* to put their capabilities to good use. Volunters ~~take~~ *find*   23

18   a high level of personal satisfaction after ~~doing~~ *finishing* a job   35

19   *and* ~~but~~ spending time with *an elder who really needs the help.*   47

| 1 | 2 | 3 | 4 | 5 | 6 | 7 | 8 | 9 | 10 | 11 | 12 |

D. TECHNIQUE PRACTICE: SHIFT/CAPS LOCK

20   RHONDA KORDICH was promoted on APRIL 1 to SENIOR

21   SECRETARY. The SOLD sign replaced the FOR SALE sign at

22   1904 ELM DRIVE. The trip to DULUTH was on INTERSTATE 35.

E. Take two 5-minute timings. Review your speed and errors.

Goal: 41wpm/5′/5e

E. 5-MINUTE TIMING

23   In most offices, many products that are used daily   10

24   are made of materials that can be recycled. Amazingly,   21

25   items made of glass, steel, aluminum, plastics, and paper   33

26   can be recycled to make many products that we need. Also,   45

27   the recycling process can help save our environment.   56

28   Some unique examples of the process of recycling the   67

29   items we throw away regularly are listed here. Used coffee   79

30   filters can be recycled to make soles for new shoes. Many   91

31   pieces of paper that are thrown away every day can be used   103

32   to make tissue paper and paper towels. Most plastics that   115

33   are used in soda bottles can be recycled for car interiors   127

34   and insulation for jackets. Used light bulbs and similar   138

35   glass products can be used to resurface streets.   148

36   Look around the room in which you are working. If you   159

37   are not already participating in a recycling program, you   171

38   may want to recycle some items that you no longer need.   182

39   Items such as paper, aluminum cans, and file folders can   193

40   be collected quickly. What additional items can you add?   205

| 1 | 2 | 3 | 4 | 5 | 6 | 7 | 8 | 9 | 10 | 11 | 12 |

Report 70-53 ▶

Agenda

Crandall First National Bank | Meeting Agenda | May 15, 20--

1. Call to Order
2. Approval of minutes of April 16 17 meeting
3. (Mortgage loans (J. William Hokes))
4. Installment loans (Lorraine Hagen))
5. Series EE bonds (Joni Ellickson)
6. Club memberships (Louise Abbey)
7. Certificates of deposit (~~Louise Abbey~~) Robert Hunt
8. Closing remarks
9. Adjournment

Report 70-54 ▶

Minutes of a Meeting

LITTLETON WATER COLOUR SOCIETY

Minutes of Meeting

Oct. 23, 20--

CALL TO ORDER The meeting was called to order by Sandra Garvy at 8 p.m. in the Littleton library conference room.

OLD BUSINESS Susan Firtz furnished each member with a list of artists and the names of the watercolor paintings each artist is entering in the Fall Arts Fair.

NEW BUSINESS John Cahmpion informed members that a new supply of canvas and oil paint arrived. Members can check out any items ~~they need~~ to begin their winter projects. Winter Fair will be held December 14. at the Expo

He reminded everyone that

ADJOURNMENT The meeting was adjourned at 9:45 p.m. The next meeting ~~is~~ will be held November 12.

Respectfully submitted,

Catherine Argetes

Type the article in two columns and balance the columns.

✔ **Progress Check**
Proofreading Check

Documents designated as Proofreading Checks serve as a check of your proofreading skill. Your goal is to have zero typographical errors when the GDP software first scores the document.

PERFORMING SUCCESSFULLY
Ginger Nichols

¶ We have been involved in giving performances since our very early years when we played a part in a class play or participated in competitive sporting events at our school. The most terrifying part of each performance was probably the fear that we would "freeze" when it came our turn to perform. Whenever we find ourselves in this predicament, the best thing to do is to accept that fear and to learn to let it work for us, not against us. We need to recognize that nervousness or fear may set in during our performance. Then, when it does happen (if it does), we will be ready to cope with it and overcome it.

¶ If you forget some of your lines in a recitation, try to remember other lines and recite them. Doing so may help those forgotten lines to "pop back" into your memory so that you put them in at a later time, if possible.

¶ You always want to leave your audience with the idea that you have given them something worthwhile that they can use or apply to their own lives. For maximum impact on your audience and to make sure that they remember what you say, use audiovisual aids to reinforce your message. Remember, however, that audiovisual aids are nothing more than aids. The real message should come in the words you choose when giving your presentation.

¶ Study your speech well; even rehearse it if necessary. However, do not practice it to the extent that it appears that you are merely reading what is written down on the paper in front of you. Much of your personality should be exhibited while you are giving your speech. If you are an enthusiastic, friendly person who converses well with people face-to-face, then that same persona should be evident during your speech. A good piece of advice is to just go out there and be yourself—you will be much more comfortable by doing so, and your audience will relate to you better than if you try to exhibit a different personality when at the podium.

¶ No matter how rapidly you speak in general, slow down when you are in front of a group. The fact that you are nervous can cause your speech rate to increase. The best way to slow down your speaking is to breathe deeply. Doing so also causes your nervous system to relax, allowing you to proceed with your speech calmly.

¶ Finally, possibly the best advice for giving a successful speech is to be prepared. You will be more confident if you are thoroughly prepared. Do your research, rehearse your speech, and make notes where you want to give emphasis or use an audiovisual aid.

November 8, 20--

CONFIDENTIAL

Mrs. Katie Hollister
11426 Prairie View Road
Kearney, NE 68847

Dear Mrs. Hollister:

Subject: Site for New Elementary School

As you are aware, your 160-acre farm, located in the
Tyro township, is a part of Independent School Dist
schools occupies 2 acres and is adjoined by an 8-acr
planning stages for a fourth elementary school. As y
District 17 Board has directed me to initiate discuss
acres of land.

Please call me at your convenience to arrange a mee
and me. I look forward to our discussions.

Yours truly,

Irvin J. Hagg
Superintendent

urs
c: District 17 Board

March 1, 20--

Mr. Rodney Graae
Thompson Corporation
42 Harris Court
Trenton, NJ 08648

Dear Mr. Graae:

We are indeed interested in designing a new corporate logo and the corresponding
stationery for your fine corporation. As I indicated in our recent telephone conversation,
we have a design staff that has won many national awards for letterhead form design, and
we consider it an honor to be contacted by you.

Within a month, we will submit several basic designs to you and your board of directors.
At that time, please feel free to make any comments and suggestions that will help us
finalize a design. Here is a modified price list for the printed stationery:

	Cost
00 sheets)	$ 80.00
s (1,000 cards)	39.50
res (1,000 sheets)	219.30
	92.00

can be of further service.

MEMO TO: All Employees

FROM: Adrienne Barzanov

DATE: March 2, 20--

SUBJECT: New Building Site

We have consulted with several architects and have finalized plans to build a new
administrative center at 6400 Easton Plaza. This memo provides general information
about plans for the center's exterior and interior development.

EXTERIOR PLANS

Exterior plans will maintain the historical integrity and beauty of the surrounding area
and reflect the architecture of other buildings in the office park. Landscaping plans
include a nature preserve, a picnic area, and a small pond.

INTERIOR PLANS FOR STAFF

Staff will be located within the new facility as follows:

1. Accounting will be located on the first floor in the west wing.

2. Sales and marketing will be located on the first floor in the east wing. All staff will be
   grouped according to product line.

3. All other staff will be located on the second floor. Exact locations will be determined
   at a later date.

INTERIOR PLANS FOR SPECIAL FACILITIES

Conference rooms will be located in the center of the building on the first floor to provide
easy access for everyone. All rooms will be equipped with state-of-the-art technology.

Our new center will also include a full-service cafeteria, a copy center, a library, an
athletic center, and an on-site day care center.

Construction of the new center will begin when we obtain the necessary permits.

Multipage Letters

GOALS

- Improve speed and accuracy
- Refine language arts skills in the use of commas
- Format multipage letters

A. Type 2 times.

A. WARMUP

```
1        We were quite dazzled when the plumber drove up in a      11
2   C-150 pickup truck! She was joined by 26 young people (all     23
3   students) who gazed intently as she welded six of the rods.    35
   |  1  |  2  |  3  |  4  |  5  |  6  |  7  |  8  |  9  |  10  |  11  |  12
```

SKILLBUILDING

B. Take three 12-second timings on each line. The scale below the last line shows your wpm speed for a 12-second timing.

B. 12-SECOND SPEED SPRINTS

```
4   Pam knew that five girls in the other car were on the team.
5   The women drove eight blue autos when they made some trips.
6   All the girls in four other autos may go on the same trips.
7   Spring is the time of the year when they have a lot of pep.
   I I I I 5 I I I I 10 I I I I 15 I I I I 20 I I I I 25 I I I I 30 I I I I 35 I I I I 40 I I I I 45 I I I I 50 I I I I 55 I I I I 60
```

LANGUAGE ARTS

C. Study the rules at the right.

C. COMMAS

RULE ▶
,nonessential expression

Use a comma before and after a nonessential expression.
> Andre, who was there, can verify the statement.
> *But:* Anyone who was there can verify the statement.
> Van's first book, *Crisis of Management*, was not discussed.
> Van's book *Crisis of Management* was not discussed.

Note: A nonessential expression is a group of words that may be omitted without changing the basic meaning of the sentence. Always examine the noun or pronoun that comes before the expression to determine whether the noun needs the expression to complete its meaning. If it does, the expression is *essential* and does *not* take a comma.

RULE ▶
,adjacent adjective

Use a comma between two adjacent adjectives that modify the same noun.
> We need an intelligent, enthusiastic individual for this job.
> *But:* Please order a new bulletin board for our main conference room.

Note: Do not use a comma after the second adjective. Also, do not use a comma if the first adjective modifies the combined idea of the second adjective and the noun (for example, *bulletin board* and *conference room* in the second example).

Edit the sentences by inserting any needed punctuation.

8 The school president Mr. Roberts will address the students.
9 The fall planning meeting which is held in Charlotte has been canceled.
10 Students planning to take the certification test must register for the orientation class.
11 The sleek luxury car is scheduled for delivery next week.
12 Margaret brought her reliable trustworthy laptop to the meeting.
13 A stamped addressed envelope should be included with the survey.

FORMATTING

D. MULTIPAGE LETTERS

To format a multipage letter:
1. Type the first page on letterhead stationery and continuing pages on plain paper that matches the letterhead.
2. Insert a page number at the top right of the second and succeeding pages.

> 2
>
> A copy of the formal complaint is enclosed for your review. I shall call you in about a week to arrange a time and place for our meeting.
>
> I have never been involved with anything like this before. Any help that you give me will be appreciated.
>
> Sincerely,
>
> Ms. Jeanne M. Hoover
> Attorney-at-Law
>
> urs
> Enclosure

DOCUMENT PROCESSING

Correspondence 71-64

Multipage Business Letter in Modified-Block Style With Enclosure Notation

Reference Manual

Review:
R-5A and R-5B:
Multipage Business Letter

October 16, 20-- | Miss Florence B. Glashan | Attorney-at-Law | 2406 Shadows Glade | Dayton, OH 45426-0348 | Dear Miss Glashan: |

¶ It was good to meet you at the convention for trial attorneys in Detroit last week. In addition to the interesting program highlights of the regular sessions, I find that the informal discussions with people like you are an added plus at these meetings. Your contribution to the program was very beneficial to me.

¶ You may recall that I told you I had just been appointed by the court to defend a woman here in Dayton who has been charged with embezzling large sums of money from her previous employer. The defendant had been employed at a large department store for more than 25 years. Because of her valuable years of experience in accounting with the store, she was in charge of accounts receivable at the store. Her previous employer, the plaintiff in the case, claims that she embezzled $18,634 in 1997; $39,072 in 1998; and $27,045 in 1999.

(Continued on next page)

¶ I feel that it is my responsibility to represent my client and to provide the best defense possible. I recall that you mentioned that you had represented defendants in similar cases in previous years. As I prepare for this defense, perhaps you might help me in the following ways:

1. Please send me the appropriate citations for all similar trials in which you participated.

2. Also, please provide me with any other case citations that you think might be helpful to me in this case.

3. Arrange to meet with me soon so that I can benefit from your experience as I prepare for the trial.

¶ A copy of the formal complaint is enclosed for your review. I shall call you in about a week to arrange a time and place for our meeting. Please let me know if there is additional information that would be helpful in preparing for this case.

¶ I have never been involved with anything like this before. Any help that you give me will be appreciated. I shall look forward to working with you.

Sincerely, | Ms. Jeanne M. Hoover | Attorney-at-Law | urs | Enclosure

---

Use the numbering command for the numbered list.

Remember to insert a blank line before and after the list and between each item in a multiline list.

Correspondence 71-65

Multipage Business Letter in Block Style With Copy Notation

April 3, 20-- | Mr. Michael Mc Ginty | District Manager | Starr & Morgan Company | One DuPont circle | Washington, DC 20036-2133 |

Dear Mike:

¶ It was good to see you at our sales conference *in Reston, Virginia,* last week. Your winning the "golden apple" award for the most sales for the *year* was well deserved. When you first became part of our sales team, you showed great enthusiasm for your job immediately. There is no doubt *in my mind* that Starr & Morgan *Company* is very well represented in the metro Washington area. We particularly want to commend you for obtaining the Westminster Account. Acquiring this account has been a major objective for a number of years. None of our company's *other* sales representatives have been able to *accomplish* this feat. Just the idea of a new account of over $500,000 is quite mind-boggling. How did you do it? Did you:

1. spend considerable time with the President, Mr. Arch Davis, or the Director of Purchasing, Ms. Betsy Matin?

2. Conduct a series of hands-on workshops for the employees and managers?

3. Develop a special marketing campaign for Westminster itself or use a regular campaign model? *and customize it for Westminster*

4. Combine various strategies in your efforts to obtain this ~~important~~ account?

(Continued on next page)

¶ ~~Can you~~ *Please* let me know what approaches ~~were~~ *you* used to make this sale?

Successes of this nature do not happen without a lot of hard work. You are

to be commended for putting forth your best efforts to sign the account.

¶ If ~~it~~ *we* can be arranged *time*, a ~~presentation by you~~ at our ~~next~~ sales ~~conference~~ *annual meeting, we*
like to have you make a presentation to our *They*
would ~~seem very appropriate. The other~~ sales representatives would benefit
greatly having you share *annual* *held*
~~much~~ from your success story. Our ~~next~~ meeting will be in late September in

Richmond, Virginia. Again, co*n*gratulations on ~~your receipt of~~ *receiving* this *prestigious* award.

All of us here in the home office are [pleased/greatly] with the performance
our sales
of our entire sales team. Indications are that this will be a year when records
will be *again*
~~are~~ broken and we will be in the media spotlight.

Sincerely yours, | Robert D. Miley | (Pres.) | urs | c: R. Olson, Director of

Sales

Correspondence 71-66

Multipage Business Letter in Modified-Block Style With Enclosure Notation

Open the file for Correspondence 71-64 and make the following changes:

1. Change the addressee to Ms. Cynthia Barnes, Attorney-at-Law.
2. Change the office address to:
   ```
   4066 Quarry Estates
   Dayton, OH 45429-1362
   ```
3. Change the salutation and header as needed.
4. Add this sentence at the end of the second paragraph:
   ```
   The defendant is also being
   accused of embezzling
   $35,680 in 2000.
   ```

Special Letter Features

GOALS

- Type at least 42wpm/5'/5e
- Format special letter features

A. Type 2 times.

A. WARMUP

```
 1        Six citizens from 14ᵗʰ Avenue East joined 83 other      10
 2   residents to discuss the #794 proposal* for a new swimming   23
 3   pool. Barry Kelm quoted numbers about current pool usage.     34
     | 1  | 2  | 3  | 4  | 5  | 6  | 7  | 8  | 9  | 10 | 11 | 12
```

SKILLBUILDING

B. DIAGNOSTIC PRACTICE: ALPHABET

If you are not using the GDP software, turn to page SB-2 and follow the directions for this activity.

C. MAP

Follow the GDP software directions for this exercise in improving keystroking accuracy.

STRATEGIES FOR *Career Success*

Audience Analysis

Knowing your audience is fundamental to the success of any message. Ask the following questions to help identify your audience.

What is your relationship to your audience? Are they familiar—people with whom you work or people unknown? The latter will prompt you to conduct some research to better communicate your purpose. What is the attitude of your audience? Are they hostile or receptive to your message? How will your message benefit them? What is your anticipated response? Asking these questions first can help prevent message mishap later.

When writing to a diverse audience, direct your message to the primary audience. These key decision makers will make a decision or act on the basis of your message. Determine the level of detail, organization, formality, and use of technical terms and theory.

YOUR TURN Compose a thank you email to a friend. How would it differ from an interview thank you letter?

D. Take two 5-minute timings. Review your speed and errors.

Goal: At least 42wpm/5'/5e

D. 5-MINUTE TIMING

4 Imagine that you have just finished college, and you 11

5 are starting a job in the field of human resources. What 22

6 are the major qualities you will need to perfect to become 34

7 successful in your position? While human resource experts 46

8 display a variety of skills, workers in this field must be 58

9 competent in their abilities to connect with clients and 69

10 have the knowledge to counsel them through crises. 79

11 Connecting is the process of building good relations 90

12 with people in an organization. When connecting with an 101

13 employee, several things are important. The main goal is 112

14 to determine the needs of the employee and to work toward 124

15 meeting those needs. The end result should be acceptable 135

16 to both the company and the employee. 143

17 Another goal is to establish open communication with 154

18 employees. To communicate freely, they must feel they can 166

19 trust other people. They must be allowed to express their 178

20 opinions without fear of being criticized. People who help 190

21 to resolve issues that affect their coworkers contribute 201

22 significantly to creating a good environment. 210

| 1 | 2 | 3 | 4 | 5 | 6 | 7 | 8 | 9 | 10 | 11 | 12

A career in the design engineering field requires creativity and keyboarding skill.

E. MULTIPLE ADDRESSES

Often a letter may be sent to two or more people at the same address or to different addresses:

1. If a letter is addressed to two people at the same address, type each name on a separate line above the same inside address.
2. If a letter is addressed to two people at different addresses, type each name and address, one under the other. Press ENTER 2 times between the addresses.
3. If a letter is addressed to three or more people, type the names and addresses side by side, with one at the left margin and another beginning at the center-point. Insert 1 blank line before typing the third name and address.

November 19, 20-- ↓4X

Dr. Albert Russell, Professor
Department of English
Appalachian State University
Boone, NC 28608 ↓2X

Dr. Kay Smith, Professor
Director of Business
Grove City College
Grove City, PA 16127 ↓2X

Dear Dr. Russell and Dr. Smith:

F. ON-ARRIVAL NOTATIONS

On-arrival notations (such as *Confidential*) should be typed on the second line below the date, at the left margin. Type the notation in all caps. Press ENTER 2 times to begin the inside address.

November 19, 20-- ↓2X

CONFIDENTIAL ↓2X

Mr. and Mrs. Earl Walters
3408 Washington Boulevard
New Tripoli, PA 18066 ↓2X

Dear Mr. and Mrs. Walters:

G. SUBJECT LINES

A *subject* line indicates what a letter is about. Type the subject line below the salutation at the left margin, preceded and followed by 1 blank line. (The term *Re* or *In re* may be used in place of *Subject*.)

November 19, 20-- ↓4X

Mr. and Mrs. Earl Walters
3408 Washington Boulevard
New Tripoli, PA 18066 ↓2X

Dear Mr. and Mrs. Walters: ↓2X

Subject: Insurance Enrollment ↓2X

We are pleased to be able to offer you enrollment in our insurance program.

Go To

Word Processing Manual

H. WORD PROCESSING: SORT

Study Lesson 72 in your word processing manual. Complete all of the shaded steps while at your computer. Then format the jobs that follow.

DOCUMENT PROCESSING

Correspondence 72-67 ▶

Business Letter in Block Style With Subject Line and Copy Notation

November 8, 20--

CONFIDENTIAL

Mrs. Katie Hollister

11426 Prairie View Rd.

Kearney, NE 68847

Dear Mrs. Hollister:

Subject: Site For New ~~Elementary~~ School

¶ As you are aware, your 160-acre farm, located in the northeast quarter ~~northeast~~ of Section 25 in Tyro township, is a part of independent School District 17. Each of our three elementary schools occupies ~~two~~ 2 acres and is adjoined by an 8-acre park. We are now in the early planning stages for a ~~third~~ fourth elementary school. As your large farm is centrally located, the District 17 Board has directed me to initiate discussions with you for the purchase of 10 acres of land.

(Continued on next page)

¶ I look forward to our discussions. Please call me at your convenience to arrange a meeting with you and/or your attorney and me.

Yours truly,

Irvin J. Hagg

Superintendent

urs

c: District 17 Board

Correspondence 72-68 ▶

Multipage Business Letter in Block Style With Multiple Addresses

Sort each bulleted list in the letter in ascending order.

October 4, 20-- | Ms. Deborah Campbell Wallace | 7835 Virginia Avenue Northwest | Washington, DC 20037 | Mr. Thomas E. Campbell | 3725 Stevens Road Southeast | Washington, DC 20020 | Dear Ms. Wallace and Mr. Campbell:

¶ We received your letter requesting instructions for transferring stock. The most common stock transfer situations are provided below. Determine which type of transfer you require and select the instructions that apply to your stock transfer.

- Name change
- Transferring shares to another individual(s)
- Transfers involving a deceased shareholder (individual ownership)
- Transfers involving a deceased shareholder (multiple owners)
- Transfers involving a minor
- Transfers involving a trust
- Transfers involving a power of attorney

¶ Every transfer requires a letter of instruction specifying how you want your shares transferred. The following items are required for all types of transfers:

- Name and address of new owner(s)
- Social security number or tax payer identification number
- Preferred form of ownership (i.e., joint tenants, tenants in common, etc.)
- Indicate total shares that are being transferred
- Sign and date the form

¶ Please be sure to submit all required documentation and note that all documents submitted become part of the permanent record of transfer and will not be returned.

(Continued on next page)

¶ All transfers must have your signature(s) guaranteed by a financial institution participating in the Medallion Signature Guarantee Program.

¶ If you need additional information, you may visit our Web site for step-by-step instructions or you may call one of our customer service representatives at our toll-free number.

Sincerely, | William J. Shawley | Shareholder Services | urs

Correspondence 72-69 ▶

Personal-Business Letter in Block Style With Subject Line

! Format book titles in italic instead of underlining.

November 17, 20--

Dr. Arif Gureshi
8726 East Ridge Drive
Morehead, KY 40351-7268
Dear Dr. Gureshi:
Subject: *The Middle East in the Year 2005* Book Discussion
¶ Your new book, *The Middle East in the Year 2005*, has gotten excellent reviews. The citizens of Morehead are pleased that a respected member of one of our local colleges is receiving national attention.
¶ Our book discussion group in Morehead, composed of members of the AAUW (American Association of University Women), has selected your book for discussion at our May meeting. We would very much like you to be a participant; your attendance at the meeting would be a real highlight.
¶ I shall call you next week. Our members are hoping that you will be able to attend and that an acceptable date can be arranged.
Sincerely,

Theresa A. Gorski
2901 Garfield Court
Morehead, KY 40351-2687

More Special Letter Features

GOALS
- Improve speed and accuracy
- Refine language arts skills in composing paragraphs
- Format letters with special features

A. Type 2 times.

A. WARMUP

```
1      The 83 Lions Club members raised $6,690 (95% of the      11
2  requested sum) to resurface the tennis courts. Gayle was      22
3  amazed when sixteen jolly members picked up over 10% more.    34
   |  1  |  2  |  3  |  4  |  5  |  6  |  7  |  8  |  9  | 10 | 11 | 12
```

SKILLBUILDING

B. PACED PRACTICE

If you are not using the GDP software, turn to page SB-14 and follow the directions for this activity.

PPP

PRETEST → PRACTICE → POSTTEST

C. PRETEST: Vertical Reaches

PRETEST
Take a 1-minute timing. Review your speed and errors.

```
4      The scents in the trunk scared the rest of the drama     11
5  class. One judge drank juice and ate pecans as the cranky    23
6  coach scolded the best junior and bought the pink dresses.   35
   |  1  |  2  |  3  |  4  |  5  |  6  |  7  |  8  |  9  | 10 | 11 | 12
```

D. PRACTICE: Up Reaches

PRACTICE
Speed Emphasis:
If you made no more than 1 error on the Pretest, type each *individual* line 2 times.
Accuracy Emphasis:
If you made 2 or more errors, type each *group* of lines (as though it were a paragraph) 2 times.

```
7  dr draft drank dryer drain drama dread dream drag drew drug
8  ju judge juice jumpy junks juror julep jumbo judo jump just
9  es essay nests tests less dress acres makes uses best rest
```

E. PRACTICE: Down Reaches

```
10  ca cable caddy cargo scare decay yucca pecan cage calm case
11  nk ankle blank crank blink think trunk brink bank junk sink
12  sc scale scalp scene scent scold scoop scope scan scar disc
```

F. POSTTEST: Vertical Reaches

POSTTEST
Repeat the Pretest timing and compare performance.

G. COMPOSING: PARAGRAPH

Compose a paragraph expressing your opinion on whether or not it is safe to make purchases online. Include precautions and potential dangers.

FORMATTING

H. TABLES WITHIN DOCUMENTS

To format a table that is part of a letter, memo, or report:

1. In a single-spaced document, press ENTER 2 times before and 1 time after the table. Be sure you are outside the table structure before pressing ENTER 1 time.
2. In a double-spaced document, press ENTER 1 time before and after the table.
3. Single-space the body of the table.
4. Adjust the column widths, and center the table within the margins of the document.
5. Never split a table between two pages. If a table will not fit at the bottom of the page on which it is first mentioned, place it at the top of the next page.

MEMO TO: Leo Guthrie

FROM: Paul Forester

DATE: January 10, 20--

SUBJECT: Sales Comparison

Listed below are the sales totals for the last two quarters. Please review the information before our staff meeting on Friday.

↓2X

SALES SUMMARY December 31, 20--		
↓1X Region	Third Quarter	Fourth Quarter
Northeast	456,321	512,980
Southeast	335,765	375,112
Northwest	425,666	457,034
Southwest	388,546	410,478

↓1X

Come to the meeting prepared to discuss plans for the upcoming sales promotions that will take place in our district.

I. COMPANY NAME IN CLOSING LINES

Some business firms show the company name in the closing lines of a letter. The company name is typed in all caps on the second line below the complimentary closing, followed by 3 blank lines before the writer's name.

Thank you for inviting me to participate in the discussion concerning this issue.
↓2X
Sincerely yours, ↓2X
HENDERSON AND SONS, INC. ↓4X

Mark Henderson, President ↓2X

urs

J. BLIND COPY NOTATION

A blind copy (bc:) notation is used when the addressee is not intended to know that one or more other persons are being sent a copy of the letter. Type the bc notation on the file copy at the left margin on the second line after the last item in the letter.

   When preparing a letter with a blind copy, print one copy of the letter; then add the blind copy notation and print another.

Thank you for inviting me to participate in the discussion concerning this issue.

Sincerely yours, ↓4X

Mark Henderson
President ↓2X

urs ↓2X
bc: Mary Stevenson

K. DELIVERY NOTATION

Type a delivery notation on the line below the enclosure notation (if used) or on the line below the reference initials. A delivery notation comes before a copy notation.

Sincerely yours, ↓4X

Mark Henderson
President ↓2X

urs
Enclosure
By fax
c: Mary Stevenson

L. POSTSCRIPT

If a postscript is added to a letter, it is typed as the last item in the letter, preceded by 1 blank line. If a blind copy notation and postscript are used, the bc: notation follows the postscript.

urs
Enclosure ↓2X

PS: You will be reimbursed for all expenses. Complete an expense report and submit it to your supervisor. ↓2X

bc: Mary Stevenson

Go To

Word Processing Manual

M. WORD PROCESSING: SHADING

Study Lesson 73 in your word processing manual. Complete all of the shaded steps while at your computer. Then format the jobs that follow.

Correspondence 73-70 ▶

Business Letter in Block Style With Open Table and Delivery and Blind Copy Notations

Automatically adjust the column widths and center the table horizontally.

March 1, 20-- | Ms. Maureen Testa | Austin Communications | 37 Pittsburgh Road | Franklin, PA 16323 | Dear Ms. Testa:

¶ We are indeed interested in designing a new corporate logo and the corresponding stationery for your fine company. As I indicated in our recent telephone conversation, we have a design staff that has won many national awards for letterhead form design, and we consider it an honor to be contacted by you.

¶ Within a couple of weeks, we will submit to you and your committee several basic designs. Based on your evaluation and suggestions, we can go from there. Here is a modified price list for the printed stationery:

Stationery	Cost
Letterhead (500 sheets)	$ 80.00
Business cards (1,000 cards)	39.50
Coated brochures (1,000 sheets)	219.30
Envelopes	92.00

¶ In the meantime, please call me if we can be of further service. Sincerely yours, | Samantha A. Steele | General Manager | urs | By fax | bc: Design Department

Correspondence 73-71 ▶

Business Letter in Block Style with Boxed Table and Delivery and Blind Copy Notations

Apply 15% shading to the first row of the table.

Open the file for Correspondence 73-70 from Ms. Steele and make the following changes:
1. Send the letter to Mr. Rodney Graae | Thompson Corporation | 42 Harris Court | Trenton, NJ 08648
2. Change the word "company" in the first paragraph to corporation.
3. Revise the first two sentences of the second paragraph to say:

Within a month, we will submit several basic designs to you and your board of directors. At that time, please feel free to make any comments and suggestions that will help us finalize a design.

4. Change the table to a boxed table.

Correspondence 73-72 ▶

Multipage Business Letter in Modified-Block Style With Enclosure, Delivery, and Postscript Notations

Current Date | Master Gyms, Inc. | 4201 Castine Court | Raleigh, NC 27613-5981 | Ladies and Gentlemen:

¶ We have 494 apartments at Fountain Ridge. As the recreation coordinator, I have concerns not only about the leisure-time activities of our residents but also about the health and physical fitness of the more than 1,100 people who call Fountain Ridge home.

(Continued on next page)

¶ Our recreation facilities are excellent. In addition to our two outdoor tennis courts and swimming pool, we also have the following indoor facilities: two racquetball courts, swimming pool, whirlpool bath, sauna, steam room, and two billiard tables. However, we have no workout equipment.

¶ During the next few months we will be equipping a new gymnasium. The dimensions of the gym are shown on the enclosed sketch. There will be exercise bicycles, treadmills, and rowing machines. In addition, we would like to install a muscle-toning machine that includes features such as the following: leg press, chest press, shoulder press, arm pull, leg pull, arm lift, leg lift, and sit-up board.

¶ The needs and interests of our residents are varied. Some residents will take full advantage of the equipment we have suggested for the gymnasium. However, many of our residents have expressed interests in an indoor track for walking; others would like to add a track for running. We hope to accommodate as many of the suggestions as we feel are feasible.

¶ The population of the residents in the Fountain Ridge complex consists of a mixture of young and middle-age adult couples as well as single residents. Some of the couples have children who would be old enough to enjoy the facilities. Therefore, safety and durability of the equipment are very important considerations. In addition, we would like to continue to develop our complex in a way that would invite family participation in our recreational activities.

¶ Do you have a sales representative serving this area who could meet with me within a week or ten days? As an alternative, perhaps you have some brochures, including prices, that could be sent to me.

Sincerely yours, | FOUNTAIN RIDGE | Rosa Bailey-Judd | Recreation Coordinator | urs | Enclosure | By fax | PS: Please send a current catalog and price list immediately so that we can prepare for our meeting with the sales representative.

Opportunities in television production studios require keyboarding skill.

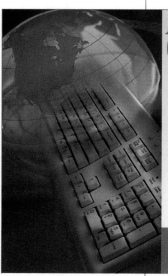

Multipage Memos With Tables

GOALS
- Type at least 42wpm/5′/5e
- Format multipage memos with tables

A. Type 2 times.

A. WARMUP

1   Over 270 cars were backed up near the Baxter & Meintz   11
2 building after an 18-wheeler jackknifed at an icy junction.   23
3 About 1/3 to 1/2 of the cars were required to use a detour.   35

| 1 | 2 | 3 | 4 | 5 | 6 | 7 | 8 | 9 | 10 | 11 | 12 |

SKILLBUILDING

B. PROGRESSIVE PRACTICE: ALPHABET

If you are not using the GDP software, turn to page SB-7 and follow the directions for this activity.

C. PROGRESSIVE PRACTICE: NUMBERS

If you are not using the GDP software, turn to page SB-11 and follow the directions for this activity.

Keyboarding CONNECTION   Virus and Spam Prevention

Use caution when opening email attachments or downloading files from the Internet. Only download files from reliable Web sites. Do not open files attached to an email from an unknown source. Also question files attached to a known source. Some viruses replicate themselves and are sent through email without users' knowledge.

Delete any email with an odd subject, a chain email, or electronic junk mail, commonly known as spam. If you're given the opportunity to unsubscribe from a spammer's list, think twice. Your reply will stop the messages on a reputable mailing list but may incite disreputable list marketers.

To protect against lost data, back up your files on a regular basis. Then you will be prepared if a virus infects your computer. New viruses are discovered daily so update your anti-virus software regularly.

YOUR TURN   How do you handle junk mail via post? Do you notice similarities when dealing with spam?

D. Take two 5-minute timings. Review your speed and errors.

Goal: At least 42wpm/5'/5e

D. 5-MINUTE TIMING

4   Biometric security is used by government agencies   10
5   and businesses to identify users who access the computer   21
6   systems. Using a technique of biometric technology, the   32
7   identity of the user is established. When a user attempts   44
8   to access the system, the technology is used to search the   56
9   database for a match. Authentication requires the user to   68
10 provide a name or personal identification number.   78
11 Four basic steps are used in biometric technology.   88
12 First, the images are captured. Then, the features are   99
13 extracted and converted to a template. Finally, data is   110
14 matched for authentication.   116
15 In biometric scanning, images of the fingers, hand,   127
16 face, or the eye are captured. The unique patterns that   138
17 exclusively identify the person in an image are extracted,   150
18 converted to a template, and stored as data. Scans of the   162
19 retina and iris recognition are most accurate and reliable   174
20 methods of biometric technology. The blood vessels in the   186
21 back zone of the eye show unique patterns, and the iris of   198
22 the eye provides accurate details that identify the person.   210

| 1 | 2 | 3 | 4 | 5 | 6 | 7 | 8 | 9 | 10 | 11 | 12 |

FORMATTING

Go To

Word Processing Manual

E. WORD PROCESSING: FIND AND REPLACE

Study Lesson 74 in your word processing manual. Complete all of the shaded steps while at your computer. Then format the jobs that follow.

DOCUMENT PROCESSING

Correspondence 74-73

Multipage Memo With Open Table With Postscript Notation

MEMO TO: L. B. Chinn, Station Manager | **FROM**: Mitzi Grenell, News Director | **DATE**: May 5, 20-- | **SUBJECT**: FCC European Trip

¶ As you requested, this memo is being sent to you as one in a series to keep you informed about my upcoming trip to Europe. I have been invited by the Federal Communications Commission to participate in a study of television news in European countries. The invitation came from Jill Andrews, FCC vice-chair; and I am, of course, delighted to take part in this challenging project.

(Continued on next page)

¶ One function of this study will be to compare the news in countries that have a long history of free-access broadcasting with the programming in newly democratic countries. I have been assigned to lead a study group to six European countries to gather firsthand information on this topic. We will be visiting England, France, Germany, Poland, Romania, and Latvia from August 24 through September 3. In addition to me, our group will consist of the following members:

Arkady Gromov	News Director National Public Radio	Washington, DC
Manuel Cruz	Executive Editor *Miami Herald*	Miami, FL
Katherine Grant	Station Manager WPQR-TV	Boston, MA
Richard Logan	Operations Manager Cable News System	New York, NY

¶ Our initial plans are to spend at least one full day in each of the countries, meeting with the news staff of one or two of the major networks, touring their facilities, viewing recent broadcasts, and becoming familiar with their general operations.

¶ If you need to contact me during my absence, Barbara Brooks, our liaison at the Federal Communications Commission (1919 M Street, NW, Washington, DC 20554; phone: 202-555-3894), will be able to provide a location and phone number.

¶ Arrangements will be made with several different staff members in the News Department to handle my responsibilities here at Channel 5 while I am gone. Dave Gislason will be the contact person for the department. As you can imagine, this is an exciting time for me. Thank you for supporting the project.

| urs | PS: Thanks also for suggesting that this trip be combined with a vacation. My husband and I have discussed the possibility of his joining me for a two-week tour of the Scandinavian countries after the FCC trip has been completed. I shall let you know what our plans are by the end of May.

Correspondence 74-74 ▶

Multipage Memo With Open Table and Postscript Notation

Open the file for Correspondence 74-73 and make the following changes:

1. Jill Andrews has just been promoted to FCC chair.
2. Finland has been added as a seventh country.
3. The trip has been extended through September 5.
4. Each occurrence of news (lowercase) has to be changed to news programming. (Do not replace News.)
5. Reggie Jordan, Staff Assistant, FCC, Washington, DC, will replace Manuel Cruz on the trip.
6. Gil Friesen will replace Dave Gislason as contact person.

MEMO TO: Terri Hackworth, Manager

FROM: Rosa Bailey, Judd, Recreation Coordinator

DATE: *April 14, 20--*

SUBJECT: Fitness room

The new Fitness Room will be ready for use in about ① month. Your

leadership in bringing thsi about is sincerely appreciated. After ~~much~~ *extensive*

investigation (much reading and several interviews), I likely will be requesting

approval soon to purchase the *following* equipment:

No.	Type
4	exercise bicycles
2 ~~1~~	treadmill*s*
1	muscle-toner*ing* machine

Three other types of equipment wer*e* considered seriously, but those listed

above enable users to reach objectives with out excessive cost. I am not

quite ready to recommend the specific brands or the suppiers for these

machines. As we expect that there will be very heavy usage, we are

concerned with dur*a*bility, warranties, and the available*ility* of dependable service

personnel. Thanks again for your full support and cooperation with this

project.

urs

Lesson 75

Memo Reports

GOALS
- Improve speed and accuracy
- Format memo reports

A. Type 2 times.

A. WARMUP

```
1      The sizable judge asked three questions: "What's the      11
2 best time of the day for you to be in court? Can you leave     23
3 your job at exactly 4 p.m.? If not, 5 p.m. or 7 p.m.?"         34
   |  1  |  2  |  3  |  4  |  5  |  6  |  7  |  8  |  9  |  10  |  11  |  12
```

SKILLBUILDING

B. Take a 1-minute timing on the first paragraph to establish your base speed. Then take four 1-minute timings on the remaining paragraphs. As soon as you equal or exceed your base speed on one paragraph, advance to the next, more difficult paragraph.

B. SUSTAINED PRACTICE: SYLLABIC INTENSITY

```
4      Each of us has several bills to be paid on a monthly      11
5 basis. For most of us, a checkbook is the tool that we use     23
6 to take care of this chore. However, in this electronic        34
7 age, other ways of doing this have received rave reviews.      45

8      You will likely be surprised to learn that the most       11
9 basic way and the cheapest way to pay bills electronically     23
10 involves the use of a Touch-Tone phone. The time required     35
11 is approximately a third of that used when writing checks.    47

12      Several banking institutions offer or plan to offer      11
13 screen phones as a method for paying bills. It is possible    22
14 to buy securities, make transfers, and determine account      34
15 balances. You will save time by using a Touch-Tone phone.     45

16      A third type of electronic bill processing involves      10
17 using a microcomputer and a modem. Software programs have     21
18 on-screen checkbooks linked to bill-paying applications.      34
19 Other microcomputers use on-line services through a modem.    46
   |  1  |  2  |  3  |  4  |  5  |  6  |  7  |  8  |  9  |  10  |  11  |  12
```

C. TECHNIQUE PRACTICE: SPACE BAR

```
20      We will all go to the race if I win my event today.
21 Do you think that I will be able to finish the race at the
22 front of the pack, or do you think there are lots of very
23 fast runners out there who surely can finish ahead of me?
```

LANGUAGE ARTS

D. Edit this paragraph to correct any typing or formatting errors.

D. PROOFREADING: EDITING

24   Many home computer user like the challenge of haveing
25 the latest in both hardware and software technology. Their
26 are those however, who's needs likely can be satisfied at
27 a very low costs. A used 486-chip personnel computer with
28 color monitor and keyboard might be your's for under $ 300.
29 Check out th Yellow Page, or visit a used-computer store.

FORMATTING

E. REPORT HEADINGS IN MEMOS

There are times when a memo report is used rather than preparing a cover memo to accompany a report. The documents are combined into one, and headings are formatted as they are in a report.

DOCUMENT PROCESSING

Report 75-56 ▶

Memo Report

Reference Manual

Review:
R-9C: Memo Report

MEMO TO: All Employees | **FROM:** Franklin Coates, Director | **DATE:** February 24, 20-- | **SUBJECT:** Security System

¶ Beginning March 1, we will install a new security access system. Complete installation should occur by the end of March. The system will include new magnetic card readers at all entrances. It will also provide a more secure working environment, especially in the evenings and on weekends. Entrances will lock and unlock automatically each day during working hours. Please carefully read and follow the detailed instructions for using the new system.

RECEIVING A NEW ACCESS CARD

¶ Once the new system is installed, you will need a new access identification card to enter the building during nonworking hours. Human Resources will begin taking pictures for new cards during the week of March 20. When you are called, report immediately. The cards will be issued as soon as they are ready. To receive your new card, you must turn in your old one.

(Continued on next page)

ENTERING THE BUILDING

¶ Entrances will automatically unlock each working day at 8 a.m and lock at 5 p.m. To enter the building during nonworking hours, slide your access identification card (with the magnetic strip facing left) through the card reader at the right of the entrance door. When the green light comes on, open the door. Do not hold the door open longer than 30 seconds.

¶ Once you enter the building during nonworking hours, please proceed immediately to the front desk and sign in. Record in the log book your name, department, extension number, and arrival time.

LEAVING THE BUILDING

¶ Before leaving the building, you must sign out. Please record your departure time beside your name. Do not use the special latch handle to open the door, or the alarm will sound. Instead, use the push bar. Once you have opened the door, do not let it remain open longer than 30 seconds, or the alarm will sound. If you accidentally set off the alarm, return to the front desk and call the security company (the telephone number is at the top of the log book). Be prepared to provide them with your name, extension number, and access card number.

¶ At times you may need to have the door held open for extended periods of time during nonbusiness hours. In these situations, please make arrangements with Building Maintenance by calling extension 4444.

¶ If you have questions about our new security access system and procedures, please contact me.

Report 75-57 ▶

Memo Report

Mr. Coates has asked you to revise Report 75-56 as follows:
1. Use February 25 as the date.
2. Change "nonworking" to nonbusiness throughout the report.

3. Add the following sentence at the end of the second paragraph:
   `New employees will be asked for a special form, to be provided by their supervisors.`
4. Change "Building Maintenance" to Building Security.

MEMO TO: All Employees
FROM: Adrienne Barzanov
DATE: March 2, 20--
SUBJECT: New Building Site

¶ We have consulted with several architects and have finalized plans to build a new administrative center at 6400 Easton Plaza. This memo provides general information about plans for the center's exterior and interior development.

EXTERIOR PLANS

¶ Exterior plans will maintain the historical integrity and beauty of the surrounding area and reflect the architecture of other buildings in the office park. Landscaping plans include a nature preserve, a picnic area, and a small pond.

INTERIOR PLANS FOR STAFF

¶ Staff will be located within the new facility as follows:

1. Accounting will be located on the first floor in the west wing.
2. Sales and marketing will be located on the first floor in the east wing. All staff will be grouped according to product line.
3. All other staff will be located on the second floor. Exact locations will be determined at a later date.

INTERIOR PLANS FOR SPECIAL FACILITIES

¶ Conference rooms will be located in the center of the building on the first floor to provide easy access for everyone. All rooms will be equipped with state-of-the-art technology.

¶ Our new center will also include a full-service cafeteria, a copy center, a library, an athletic center, and an on-site day care center.

¶ Construction of the new center will begin when we obtain the necessary permits.

Unit 16

Tables

LESSON 76
Tables With Footnotes or Source Notes

LESSON 77
Tables With Braced Column Headings

LESSON 78
Tables Formatted Sideways

LESSON 79
Multipage Tables

LESSON 80
Using Predesigned Table Formats

CITY BANK
Interest Rates Schedule
Effective Date: Current Date

	Interest Rate	APY*
Value Checking	No Interest	
City Checking	2.00%	2.02%
Prestige Checking	2.00%	2.02%
Golden Checking	3.00%	3.05%
Regular Savings	2.50%	2.53%
Young Savers	2.50%	2.53%
Christmas Club	2.50%	2.53%
Money Market – Tier I	4.16%	4.25%
Money Market – Tier II	4.40%	4.50%
Money Market – Tier III	4.64%	4.75%
Money Market – Tier IV	4.88%	5.00%
	5.75%	5.75%
	6.35%	6.50%
	6.82%	7.00%
	7.06%	7.25%
	6.82%	7.00%

Percentage Yield

CITY BANK
Interest Rates Schedule
Effective Date: Curr

	Inte	No
Value Checking		
City Checking		
Prestige Checking		
Golden Checking		
Regular Savings		
Young Savers		
Christmas Club		
Money Market – Tier I		
Money Market – Tier II		
Money Market – Tier III		
Money Market – Tier IV		
CD – 91 day		
CD – 6 month		
CD – 1 year		
CD – 2 year		
CD – 3 year		

CUSTOMER DATABASE INFORMATION
(Ohio District)
August 31, 20—

Customer	Address	City	ZIP	Telephone No.	Item	Stock No.
Westphal, Darlene	3309 Aaron Place Street	Kenton	44426	419-555-2384	Pentium Computer	4-238-CW
Roanne, Dennis	20604 Lucile Road South	Columbus	43230	614-555-2074	Laser Printer	3-895-LP
Byrnes, Carl	322 West Lyons Road	Mansfield	44902	216-555-2002	Laser Printer	3-895-LP
Dawson, Cynthia	5914 Bay Oaks Place	Chillicothe	45601	614-555-1399	Color Ink-Jet Printer	2-550-CIJ
Graupmann, Meg	10386 Power Drive	Steubenville	43952	614-555-7821	Pentium Computer	4-238-CW
Neusome, Jo	Box 365	Youngstown	44502	216-555-3885	Pentium Computer	4-238-CW
Shapiro, Tony	6823 Creekwood Drive	Columbus	43085	614-555-2934	Pentium Computer	4-238-CW
Garand, Lisa	26044 Manzano Court	Youngstown	44505	216-555-1777	Flatbed Color Scanner	6-882-CSC
Parker, Tom	936 Eastwind Drive	Cleveland	44121	216-555-2839	Laser Printer	3-895-LP

Tables With Footnotes or Source Notes

GOALS

- Type at least 43wpm/5′/5e
- Change text direction
- Insert or delete rows or columns

A. Type 2 times.

A. WARMUP

```
1        Order #Z391 must be processed "quickly" and exactly        11
2   as specified! In January several orders were sent out by        22
3   mistake; regrettably, one order worth $5,680 was canceled.      34
    |  1  |  2  |  3  |  4  |  5  |  6  |  7  |  8  |  9  |  10  |  11  |  12
```

SKILLBUILDING

B. Take three 12-second timings on each line. The scale below the last line shows your wpm speed for a 12-second timing.

B. 12-SECOND SPEED SPRINTS

```
4   You paid for the ruby that she owned when he was just five.
5   Toby wishes to thank all eight of the girls for their time.
6   Yale is a very fine place to learn about the world of work.
7   She has a theory that the icy roads will cause a bad wreck.
    I I I I 5 I I I I 10 I I I I 15 I I I I 20 I I I I 25 I I I I 30 I I I I 35 I I I I 40 I I I I 45 I I I I 50 I I I I 55 I I I I 60
```

C. DIAGNOSTIC PRACTICE: ALPHABET

If you are not using the GDP software, turn to page SB-2 and follow the directions for this activity.

STRATEGIES FOR Career Success

Cellular Phone Manners Matter

Mind your cell phone manners! While the cellular phone allows you to keep in touch with your boss, coworkers, and clients, it also requires you to consider your communication etiquette. One of the worst violations of etiquette and safety is driving and talking at the same time. It is much safer to pull off the road to make a call.

Consider others when you use the cellular phone in a public place (e.g., a restaurant). If you use the phone in public, talk quietly and watch what you say. Cellular phones in meetings can distract others; some companies prohibit them in business meetings.

Since cellular phone use is costlier than a traditional phone, when you call a cell phone user, keep your message brief.

YOUR TURN Observe cellular phone users in a public place. Are they mindful of others when they use their phones?

D. Take two 5-minute timings. Review your speed and errors.

Goal: At least 43wpm/5′/5e

D. 5-MINUTE TIMING

8	Several years ago many corporations in the business	11
9	world adopted a policy called casual Friday. This trend	22
10	enabled employees to dress down each Friday. Employers	33
11	distributed guidelines for appropriate casual clothing.	44
12	Advocates for casual Friday justified the change by citing	56
13	increased productivity and better employee morale.	66
14	A controversy regarding the casual Friday policy is	78
15	being addressed currently. Many businesses are questioning	90
16	the effect of casual dress on productivity. Studies are	101
17	being analyzed to determine if casual dress has an adverse	113
18	affect on the attitudes of employees toward attendance,	124
19	tardiness, and professional image.	131
20	Apparently some managers believe that workers are	141
21	not following the guidelines. The managers want to adopt	152
22	stricter standards for an acceptable dress code that would	164
23	prohibit employees from appearing too relaxed when they	175
24	report for work. Some employees with concerns about the	186
25	casual dress code are suggesting that Friday should be a	197
26	day to dress up for the office. They intend to foster a	208
27	more productive office environment.	215

| 1 | 2 | 3 | 4 | 5 | 6 | 7 | 8 | 9 | 10 | 11 | 12 |

FORMATTING

Reference Manual

Refer to pages R-8A and R-13A of the Reference Manual.

E. TABLES WITH FOOTNOTES OR SOURCE NOTES

To format tables with footnotes:
1. Include a separator row for the footnote reference at the bottom when you are creating the table structure.
2. Select the cells in the bottom row and merge the cells.
3. Type an asterisk (or another symbol) at the appropriate point within the table to indicate that there is a footnote.
4. Type the footnote.

Word Processing Manual

F. WORD PROCESSING: TABLE—TEXT DIRECTION, AND TABLE— INSERT OR DELETE ROWS OR COLUMNS

Study Lesson 76 in your word processing manual. Complete all of the shaded steps while at your computer. Then format the jobs that follow.

DOCUMENT PROCESSING

Table 76-26

Seven-Column Boxed Table With Table Note
Your completed table will look different from the one shown.

1. Center the table vertically.
2. Create a boxed table with 7 columns and 6 rows, and type the table.
3. Merge cells in Row 6 for the table note.
4. Right-align the text in the number columns.
Note: Do not change the left alignment of the column headings.

(Continued on next page)

5. Bold Row 1 and Column A, excluding the table note.
6. Select Row 1 and change the text direction to display vertically top-to-bottom.
7. Drag down on the bottom border of Row 1 until the column headings dis-

play in one continuous line without wrapping.
8. Automatically adjust the column widths for all columns.
9. Center the table horizontally.

Account Number	Blue Sierra Letterhead	Italian Renaissance Letterhead	Sonoma Desert Letterhead	Watercolor Wash Letterhead	Sandstone Marble Letterhead	Greek Acropolis Letterhead
GV-11	3,500	500	750	1,000	250	1,250
GV-29	2,500	250	250	500	500	250
GV-37	750	1,000	500	2,500	250	2,500
GV-10	250	500	1,000	250	1,500	250
Note: This information is subject to change.						

Table 76-27

Seven-Column Boxed Table

Open the file for Table 76-26 and make the following changes:
1. Delete the table note row.
2. Delete Column G.
3. Insert a column to the left of Column B.
4. Insert a row above Row 3. Type: GV-72 | 1,250 | 500 | 1,000 | 250 | 750 | 2,000
5. Type: French Patina Letterhead | 750 | 1,250 | 250 | 1,000 | 500
6. Right-align the text in the numbers columns as needed.
7. Apply 10% shading to Row 1.

Table 76-28

Six-Column Boxed Table With Source Note

1. Center the table vertically.
2. Create a boxed table with 5 columns and 6 rows, and type the table.
3. Merge cells in Row 6 for the source note.
4. Right-align the text in the number columns.
   Note: Do not change the left alignment of the column headings
5. Select Row 1 and change the text direction to display vertically top-to-bottom.
6. Drag down on the bottom border of Row 1 until the column headings display in one continuous line without wrapping.
7. Automatically adjust the column widths for all columns.
8. Center the table horizontally.

Office Supply Account	LED Laser Printer	Internal Fax Modem	Cash Management System	Plain-paper Laser Fax
OE-9	$405	$181	$199	$249
DD-7	395	150	205	234
US-2	410	125	183	252
OB-1	420	167	179	245
Source: March invoices				

Tables With Braced Column Headings

GOALS
- Improve speed and accuracy
- Refine language arts skills in capitalization
- Format braced headings in tables

A. Type 2 times.

A. WARMUP

1   Six citizens from 14th Avenue East joined 83 other   10
2 residents to discuss the #794 proposal* for a new swimming   22
3 pool. Barry Kelm quoted numbers about current pool usage.   33
   | 1 | 2 | 3 | 4 | 5 | 6 | 7 | 8 | 9 | 10 | 11 | 12

SKILLBUILDING

B. DIAGNOSTIC PRACTICE: NUMBERS

If you are not using the GDP software, turn to page SB-5 and follow the directions for this activity.

C. MAP

Follow the GDP software directions for this exercise in improving keystroking accuracy.

LANGUAGE ARTS

D. Study the rules at the right.

D. CAPITALIZATION

RULE ▶
≡ noun #

Capitalize nouns followed by a number or letter (except for the nouns *line, note, page, paragraph,* and *size*).
    Please read Chapter 5, which begins on page 94.

RULE ▶
≡ compass point

Capitalize compass points (such as *north, south,* or *northeast*) only when they designate definite regions.
    From Montana we drove <u>south</u> to reach the Southwest.

Edit the sentences to correct any errors in capitalization.

4 The marketing manager had a reservation on flight 505 to Atlanta.
5 Please order two model 6M printers.
6 The desktop publishing seminar will be held in Room 101.
7 Study pages 120-230 for the unit test.
8 Please contact all representatives in the northern states.
9 Have you visited the city of Pittsburgh?
10 The population of the south continues to increase.

E. BRACED COLUMN HEADINGS

A braced column heading is a heading that applies to more than one column (for example, *Retirement Account* in the table shown below):

1. To create a braced column heading, position the insertion point where you want the braced heading to appear.

2. Merge the cells to create space for the braced heading.
3. Center the braced column headings over the columns.

DOCUMENT PROCESSING

Table 77-29 ▶

Six-Column Boxed Table With Braced Column Headings

1. Center the table vertically.
2. Create a boxed table with 6 columns and 6 rows.
3. Center and type the braced and regular column headings in upper- and lower-case and bold.
4. Block column headings and right-align the text in columns containing numbers.
5. Follow the standard table format.
6. Merge cells and columns as necessary.

INSURED ACCOUNT DEPOSITS For Melanie and Frank Bush					
First World Savings		**Individual Account**		**Retirement Account**	
Month	**Branch**	**M. Bush**	**F. Bush**	**M. Bush**	**F. Bush**
January	Reseda	$5,500	$2,350	$2,000	$10,000
February	Valencia	7,950	5,700	5,500	4,300
March	Van Nuys	2,400	7,300	9,300	2,550

Table 77-30 ▶

Four-Column Boxed Table With Braced Column Headings

1. Center the table vertically.
2. Create a boxed table with 4 columns and 6 rows.
3. Center and type the braced and regular column headings in upper- and lower-case and bold; right-align the number columns.
4. Follow the standard table format.
5. Merge cells as necessary.

CINEPLEX VIDEOS Sales Trends			
Western Region		**Total Sales**	
State	**Manager**	**Last Year**	**This Year**
California	George Lucas	$1,956,250	$2,135,433
Nevada	Marjorie Matheson	859,435	1,231,332
Washington	Valerie Harper	737,498	831,352

Open the file for Table 77-30 and make the following changes.

1. Change the column heading "Western Region" to Eastern Region.
2. Change the state names to New York | New Jersey | Delaware.
3. Change the manager's names to Robert DeLuca | Doris Lynch | Megan Bennett.
4. Change last year's amounts to $2,052,659 | 534,958 | 894,211.
5. Change this year's amounts to $3,345,312 | 2,311,478 | 925,138.

Excellent keyboarding skills are among the many qualifications required for an exciting career in television news reporting.

Tables Formatted Sideways

GOALS
- Type at least 43wpm/5'/5e
- Format tables in landscape orientation

A. Type 2 times.

A. WARMUP

```
1      This week order a monitor with a resolution of 1280 x   11
2   1024 that supports an optimal refresh rate from V & Q Inc.  23
3   It will cost $573* (*a 9% savings) if ordered before July!  35
   |  1  |  2  |  3  |  4  |  5  |  6  |  7  |  8  |  9  |  10  |  11  |  12
```

SKILLBUILDING

B. PACED PRACTICE

If you are not using the GDP software, turn to page SB-14 and follow the directions for this activity.

Keyboarding CONNECTION   Finding People on the Internet

Remember that long-lost friend from high school? Well, he or she may not be lost for long if you use the Internet's assistance. It is easy to search for a person on the Net by following a few simple steps.

Access a search engine. Click hyperlinks pertaining to finding people such as People Finder or People Search. Enter the information requested about the person, and press the Search button.

Conduct a search for Web sites where you can also find email addresses. Enter the information about the person you are seeking. Click the Search button. Your search should list any names and email addresses that match the name you entered.

YOUR TURN   Access a search engine and try to locate the address of a high school friend.

C. Take two 5-minute timings. Review your speed and errors.

Goal: At least 43wpm/5′/5e

C. 5-MINUTE TIMING

4 Virtual office workers conduct their work in settings 11
5 having different requirements from the ordinary workplace. 23
6 They may rely extensively on telecommuting to transmit and 35
7 access data to and from corporate offices. They often use 47
8 a company Website, which is protected by a password, for 58
9 electronic communication. By connecting to the site, they 70
10 can use services such as office support and Web research. 82
11 Access to the Internet, telephones, and fax lines 92
12 are among the basic tools required for the virtual office. 104
13 To succeed in the virtual office environment, workers must 116
14 be competent and very organized, work well without being 127
15 supervised, and be skilled in effective time management. 138
16 Coping skills for virtual office workers may include 149
17 maintaining a good balance between work and personal life, 161
18 preserving contact with office coworkers and customers, 172
19 solving hardware and software problems, and scheduling 183
20 vacations. Home office workers may also have to deal with 195
21 feelings of being isolated and distracted. Many workers, 206
22 however, enjoy the nontraditional job setting. 215

| 1 | 2 | 3 | 4 | 5 | 6 | 7 | 8 | 9 | 10 | 11 | 12

FORMATTING

D. WORD PROCESSING: PAGE ORIENTATION

Go To
Word Processing Manual

Study Lesson 78 in your word processing manual. Complete all of the shaded steps while at your computer. Then format the jobs that follow.

DOCUMENT PROCESSING

Table 78-32

Seven-Column Boxed Table in Landscape

1. Format the table in landscape orientation.
2. Set 0.5-inch side margins for the page.
3. Create a boxed table with 7 columns and 11 rows.
4. Type the following column headings in bold:

Customer | Address | City | ZIP | Telephone No. | Item | Stock No.

5. In Column A, type the customer's last name followed by a comma; then type the first name.

(Continued on next page)

CUSTOMER DATABASE INFORMATION

(Ohio District)

August 31, 20---

~~Maria~~ *Darlene* Westphal | 3309 aaron Place ~~Avenue~~ *Street* | Kenton | 44426 | 419-555-2384 | Pentium computer | 4-238-cw

Dennis Roanne | 20604 Lucile Rd. South | Columbus | 43230 | 614-555-2074 | laser printer | 3-895-LP

Carl Byrnes | 322 W. Lyons Road | Mansfield | 44902 | 216-555-2002 | ~~Color~~ Laser Printer | 3-895-LP

Cynthia Dawson | 5914 Bay Oaks Place | Chilicothe | 45610 | 614-555-1399 | Color Ink-Jet Printer | 2-550-cij

Meg Graupmann | 10386 power Dr. | Steubenville | 43952 | 614-555-7821 | Pentium Computer | 4-238-CW

Jo Neusome | Box 365 | Youngstown | 44502 | 216-555-3885 | Pentium computer | 4-238-CW

Tony Shapiro | 6823 Creekwood ~~Lane~~ *Drive* | Columbus | 43085 | 614-555-2934 | Pentium Computer | ~~5 987 PC~~ *4-238-CW*

Lisa Garand | 26044 Manzano Court | Youngstown | 44505 | 216-555-1777 | FlatBed Color Scanner | 6-8820-CSC

Tom Parker | 936 East wind Drive | Cleveland | 44121 | 216-555-2839 | Lasser Printer | 3-895-LP

Table 78-33 ▶

Seven-Column Boxed Table in Landscape

Open the file for Table 78-32, and make the following changes:
1. Change the date to August 19, 20--.
2. Sort the table alphabetically by the customers' last names.

3. Change the font for the column headings to Arial Narrow, and shade the headings with a 10% fill.

1. Create a boxed table using landscape orientation.
2. Use 1-inch margins for top, bottom, left, and right margins.
3. Center the table vertically and horizontally.
4. Center-align headings, and apply standard table format.
5. Insert a row above Row 1.
6. Type REGIONAL SALES OFFICES in bold and uppercase. Center the heading.
7. Type General Information as a subtitle for the table.

REGIONAL SALES OFFICES
General Information

Region	Street Address	City	State	ZIP	Telephone	Fax
East	8787 Orion Place	Columbus	OH	43240-4027	614-555-4951	614-555-4999
Mid-Continent	1415 Elbridge Payne Road	Chesterfield	MO	63017-8522	636-555-9940	636-555-9034
Southeast	3100 Breckinridge Boulevard	Duluth	GA	30096	770-555-7007	770-555-7422
West	21600 Oxnard Street	Woodland Hills	CA	91367	818-555-2675	818-555-2697

Multipage Tables

GOALS

- Improve speed and accuracy
- Refine language arts skills in spelling
- Format multipage tables

A. Type 2 times.

A. WARMUP

```
1        Please request this key item by June: an XYZ 2000        10
2 motherboard with 512-MB RAM. I don't expect delivery until      22
3 7/5; I realize this is a "great" investment for the money!      34
   | 1 | 2 | 3 | 4 | 5 | 6 | 7 | 8 | 9 | 10 | 11 | 12
```

SKILLBUILDING

PRETEST → PRACTICE → POSTTEST

B. PRETEST: Alternate- and One-Hand Words

PRETEST
Take a 1-minute timing. Review your speed and errors.

```
4        They both blame the fight on the visitor. The girl       10
5 had no right to imply that the proxy was brave enough to        21
6 draw you into the unholy case. The union will reward you.       32
   | 1 | 2 | 3 | 4 | 5 | 6 | 7 | 8 | 9 | 10 | 11 | 12
```

C. PRACTICE: Alternate-Hand Words

PRACTICE
Speed Emphasis:
If you made no more than 1 error on the Pretest, type each *individual* line 2 times.
Accuracy Emphasis:
If you made 2 or more errors, type each *group* of lines (as though it were a paragraph) 2 times.

```
7 also angle field bushel ancient emblem panel sight fish big
8 both blame fight formal element handle proxy signs girl and
9 city chair giant island visitor profit right their laid cut
```

D. PRACTICE: One-Hand Words

```
10 acts hilly award uphill average poplin refer jolly adds him
11 area jumpy based homily baggage you'll serve union beat ink
12 case brave extra limply greater unholy wages imply draw you
```

E. POSTTEST: Alternate- and One-Hand Words

POSTTEST
Repeat the Pretest timing and compare performance.

F. PROGRESSIVE PRACTICE: ALPHABET

If you are not using the GDP software, turn to page SB-7 and follow the directions for this activity.

G. Type this list of frequently misspelled words, paying special attention to any spelling problems in each word.

G. SPELLING

13 assistance compliance initial limited corporation technical
14 operating sufficient operation incorporated writing current
15 advice together prepared recommend appreciated cannot based
16 benefit completing analysis probably projects before annual
17 issue attention location association participation proposed

Edit the sentences to correct any misspellings.

18 The complience by the corporation was sufficient to pass.
19 I cannot reccomend the project based on the expert advise.
20 The location of the proposed annual meeting was an issue.
21 Your assistance in completeing the project is appreciated.
22 Together we prepared an analysis of their current operation.
23 The writing was incorporated in the initial asociation bid.

FORMATTING

H. MULTIPAGE TABLES

Tables should generally be formatted to fit on one page. However, if a table extends to another page, follow these formatting rules:

1. Repeat the column headings at the top of each new page.
2. Number all pages in the upper right-hand corner.

1

75 TALLEST MOUNTAINS OF NORTH AMERICA
(Ranked by Height in Feet)

Name	Place	Rank	Height
McKinley	Alaska	1	20,320
Logan	Yukon	2	19,850
Pico de Orizaba	Mexico	3	18,555
St. Elias	Alaska/Yukon	4	18,008
Popocatepetl	Mexico	5	17,930
Foraker	Alaska	6	17,400
Iztaccihuatl	Mexico	7	17,343
Lucania	Yukon	8	17,147
King	Yukon	9	16,971
Steele	Yukon	10	16,644
Bona	Alaska	11	16,550
Blackburn	Alaska	12	16,390
Kennedy	Alaska	13	16,286
Sanford	Alaska	14	16,237
Vancouver	Alaska/Yukon	15	15,979
South Buttress	Alaska	16	15,885
Wood	Yukon	16	15,885
Churchill	Alaska	18	15,638
Fairweather	Alaska/British Columbia	19	15,300
Zinantecatl (Toluca)	Mexico	20	15,016
Hubbard	Alaska/Yukon	21	15,015
Bear	Alaska	22	14,831
Walsh	Yukon	23	14,780
East Buttress	Alaska	24	14,730
Matlalcueyetl	Mexico	25	14,636
Hunter	Alaska	26	14,573
Alverstone	Alaska/Yukon	27	14,565
Browne Tower	Alaska	28	14,530
Whitney	California	29	14,494
Elbert	Colorado	30	14,433
Massive	Colorado	31	14,421
Harvard	Colorado	32	14,420
Rainier	Washington	33	14,410
University Peak	Alaska	33	14,410
Williamson	California	35	14,375
La Plata Peak	Colorado	36	14,361
Blanca Peak	Colorado	37	14,345
Uncompahgre Peak	Colorado	38	14,309
Crestone Peak	Colorado	39	14,294

2

75 TALLEST MOUNTAINS OF NORTH AMERICA
(Ranked by Height in Feet)

Name	Place	Rank	Height
Lincoln	Colorado	40	14,286
Grays Peak	Colorado	41	14,270
Antero	Colorado	42	14,269
Torreys Peak	Colorado	43	14,267
Castle Peak	Colorado	44	14,265
Quandary Peak	Colorado	44	14,265
Evans	Colorado	46	14,264
Longs Peak	Colorado	47	14,255
McArthur	Yukon	48	14,253
Wilson	Colorado	49	14,246
White Mt. Peak	California	49	14,246
North Palisade	California	51	14,242
Cameron	Colorado	52	14,238
Shavano	Colorado	53	14,229
Belford	Colorado	54	14,197
Princeton	Colorado	54	14,197
Crestone Needle	Colorado	54	14,197
Yale	Colorado	57	14,196
Bross	Colorado	58	14,172
Kit Carson	Colorado	59	14,165
Wrangell	Alaska	60	14,163
Shasta	California	61	14,162
El Diente Peak	Colorado	62	14,159
Point Success	Washington	63	14,158
Maroon Peak	Colorado	64	14,156
Tabeguache	Colorado	65	14,155
Oxford	Colorado	66	14,153
Sill	California	66	14,153
Sneffels	Colorado	68	14,150
Democrat	Colorado	69	14,148
Capitol Peak	Colorado	70	14,130
Liberty Cap	Washington	71	14,112
Pikes Peak	Colorado	72	14,110
Snowmass	Colorado	73	14,092
Russell	California	74	14,088
Eolus	Colorado	75	14,083

I. WORD PROCESSING: REPEATING TABLE HEADING ROWS

Study Lesson 79 in your word processing manual. Complete all of the shaded steps while at your computer. Then format the jobs that follow.

DOCUMENT PROCESSING

Table 79-35

Multipage Four-Column Boxed Table

Follow these steps to create a multipage table:
1. Create a boxed table with 4 columns and 79 rows.
2. Type the table as shown.
3. Include column headings on all pages.
4. Apply 10% shading to the column headings row.
5. Number the pages in upper right-hand corner.

1

75 TALLEST MOUNTAINS OF NORTH AMERICA
(Ranked by Height in Feet)

Name	Place	Rank	Height
McKinley	Alaska	1	20,320
Logan	Yukon	2	19,850
Pico de Orizaba	Mexico	3	18,555
St. Elias	Alaska/Yukon	4	18,008
Popocatepetl	Mexico	5	17,930
Foraker	Alaska	6	17,400
Iztaccihuatl	Mexico	7	17,343
Lucania	Yukon	8	17,147
King	Yukon	9	16,971
Steele	Yukon	10	16,644
Bona	Alaska	11	16,550
Blackburn	Alaska	12	16,390
Kennedy	Alaska	13	16,286
Sanford	Alaska	14	16,237
Vancouver	Alaska/Yukon	15	15,979
South Buttress	Alaska	16	15,885
Wood	Yukon	16	15,885
Churchill	Alaska	18	15,638
Fairweather	Alaska/British Columbia	19	15,300
Zinantecatl (Toluca)	Mexico	20	15,016
Hubbard	Alaska/Yukon	21	15,015
Bear	Alaska	22	14,831
Walsh	Yukon	23	14,780
East Buttress	Alaska	24	14,730
Matlalcueyetl	Mexico	25	14,636
Hunter	Alaska	26	14,573
Alverstone	Alaska/Yukon	27	14,565
Browne Tower	Alaska	28	14,530
Whitney	California	29	14,494
Elbert	Colorado	30	14,433
Massive	Colorado	31	14,421
Harvard	Colorado	32	14,420
Rainier	Washington	33	14,410
University Peak	Alaska	33	14,410
Williamson	California	35	14,375
La Plata Peak	Colorado	36	14,361
Blanca Peak	Colorado	37	14,345
Uncompahgre Peak	Colorado	38	14,309
Crestone Peak	Colorado	39	14,294

2

75 TALLEST MOUNTAINS OF NORTH AMERICA
(Ranked by Height in Feet)

Name	Place	Rank	Height
Lincoln	Colorado	40	14,286
Grays Peak	Colorado	41	14,270
Antero	Colorado	42	14,269
Torreys Peak	Colorado	43	14,267
Castle Peak	Colorado	44	14,265
Quandary Peak	Colorado	44	14,265
Evans	Colorado	46	14,264
Longs Peak	Colorado	47	14,255
McArthur	Yukon	48	14,253
Wilson	Colorado	49	14,246
White Mt. Peak	California	49	14,246
North Palisade	California	51	14,242
Cameron	Colorado	52	14,238
Shavano	Colorado	53	14,229
Belford	Colorado	54	14,197
Princeton	Colorado	54	14,197
Crestone Needle	Colorado	54	14,197
Yale	Colorado	57	14,196
Bross	Colorado	58	14,172
Kit Carson	Colorado	59	14,165
Wrangell	Alaska	60	14,163
Shasta	California	61	14,162
El Diente Peak	Colorado	62	14,159
Point Success	Washington	63	14,158
Maroon Peak	Colorado	64	14,156
Tabegauche	Colorado	65	14,155
Oxford	Colorado	66	14,153
Sill	California	66	14,153
Sneffels	Colorado	68	14,150
Democrat	Colorado	69	14,148
Capitol Peak	Colorado	70	14,130
Liberty Cap	Washington	71	14,112
Pikes Peak	Colorado	72	14,110
Snowmass	Colorado	73	14,092
Russell	California	74	14,088
Eolus	Colorado	75	14,083

Table
79-36 ▶

Multipage
Four-Column
Boxed Table

Open the file for Table 79-35, and make the following changes:
1. Sort the table alphabetically by state in ascending order.

2. Delete the subtitle (Ranked by Height in Feet).

Table
79-37 ▶

Five-Column Boxed
Table in Landscape

Follow these steps to create a boxed table:
1. Use landscape orientation.
2. Create a boxed table with 5 columns and 7 rows.
3. Type the table as shown.
4. Apply 10% shading to the heading row.
5. Apply 100% shading (black) to the title row.

INVESTMENT SUMMARY				
Limited Partnership	Date of Issue	Initial Cost	Annual Dividend*	Owner
HS Properties	January 2001	$ 50,000	$ 6,066	Alpha Association
Northern Lumber	May 2001	50,000	8,750	CXT Corporation
ST1	February 2001	50,000	7,500	Smith & Sons, Incorporated
ST2	December 2001	100,000	12,250	Q and S Company

*Annual dividends based on current market analysis.

Using Predesigned Table Formats

GOALS

- Type at least 43wpm/5'/5e
- Format tables using TableAutoFormat

A. Type 2 times.

A. WARMUP

1   "Just when can we expect to realize a profit of 5% or   11
2 more?" This kind of question will be important to 2/3 of   22
3 the shareholders; they own over 89% of the prime holdings.   34

| 1 | 2 | 3 | 4 | 5 | 6 | 7 | 8 | 9 | 10 | 11 | 12

SKILLBUILDING

B. Take a 1-minute timing on the first paragraph to establish your base speed. Then take four 1-minute timings on the remaining paragraphs. As soon as you equal or exceed your base speed on one paragraph, advance to the next, more difficult paragraph.

B. SUSTAINED PRACTICE: NUMBERS AND SYMBOLS

4   There is a need at this time to communicate our new   11
5 pricing guidelines to our franchise outlets. In addition,   23
6 they must be made aware of inventory implications. They   34
7 will then be in a position to have a successful operation.   46

8   Franchise operators could be requested to use either   11
9 a 20% or a 30% markup. A $50 item would be marked to sell   23
10 for either $60 or $65. Depending on future prospects for   34
11 sales, half of the articles would be priced at each level.   46

12   Ms. Aagard's suggestion is to assign items in Groups   11
13 #1470, #2830, and #4560 to the 20% category. The Series 77   23
14 items* would be in the 30% markup category except for the   35
15 items with a base rate under $100. What is your reaction?   46

16   Mr. Chavez's recommendation is to assign a 30% markup   11
17 to Groups #3890, #5290, #6480, and #7180. About 1/4 of the   22
18 remainder (except for soft goods) would also be in the 30%   34
19 category. Groups #8340 and #9560 would have a 20% markup.   46

| 1 | 2 | 3 | 4 | 5 | 6 | 7 | 8 | 9 | 10 | 11 | 12

C. Type each sentence on a separate line by pressing ENTER after each sentence.

C. TECHNIQUE PRACTICE: ENTER KEY

20   Start a business. See the banker. Rent a building.
21 Check state codes. Check city codes. Get needed licenses.
22 Contact suppliers. Call utility companies. Buy furniture.
23 Hire the employees. Open the doors. Hope for customers.

D. Take two 5-minute timings. Review your speed and errors.

Goal: At least 43wpm/5'/5e

D. 5-MINUTE TIMING

24 Finding a job may be more difficult today with the 10

25 rapid changes in technology. Students just entering the 21

26 workforce must complete specialized classes to compete for 33

27 the new technology jobs. However, completing a course of 44

28 study does not guarantee employment. 51

29 A candidate who is ready for employment must build 61

30 a resume and prepare for the interview process. A resume 72

31 is a written statement of you and your qualifications. When 84

32 you have completed your resume, you are ready to market 95

33 yourself to prospective employers. 102

34 After you have scheduled an interview appointment 112

35 with a potential employer, take time to become familiar 123

36 with the job and the company. Research the products or 134

37 services the company provides. Make a list of questions 145

38 to ask during the interview. Plan to wear clothing that is 157

39 appropriate for the company you are visiting. 166

40 During the interview, be prepared to answer questions 177

41 that relate to travel, relocation, your goals, strengths 188

42 and weaknesses, and why you should be hired. After the 199

43 interview, express your interest in the job and thanks for 211

44 the time to interview. 215

| 1 | 2 | 3 | 4 | 5 | 6 | 7 | 8 | 9 | 10 | 11 | 12

FORMATTING

Go To

Word Processing Manual

E. WORD PROCESSING: TABLE—AUTOFORMAT

Study Lesson 80 in your word processing manual. Complete all the shaded steps while at your computer. Then format the jobs that follow.

Table 80-38 ▶

Three-Column Table

1. Change the orientation to landscape and, create a table with 3 columns and 18 rows.
2. Apply the 3D effects 3 Table AutoFormat—or one of your choice.
3. Remove bold formatting from the last line, if necessary.

CITY BANK Interest Rates Schedule Effective Date: [Current Date]		
	Interest Rate	APY
Value Checking	0.00%	0.00%
City Checking	2.00%	2.02%
Prestige Checking	2.00%	2.02%
Golden Checking	3.00%	3.05%
Regular Savings	2.50%	2.53%
Young Savers	2.50%	2.53%
Christmas Club	2.50%	2.53%
Money Market—Tier I	4.16%	4.25%
Money Market—Tier II	4.40%	4.50%
Money Market—Tier III	4.64%	4.75%
Money Market—Tier IV	4.88%	5.00%
CD—91 day	5.75%	5.75%
CD—6 month	6.35%	6.50%
CD—1 year	6.82%	7.00%
CD—2 year	7.06%	7.25%
CD—3 year	7.15%	7.50%

Table 80-39 ▶

Three-Column Table With Table Note

Open the file for Table 80-38 and make the following changes:
1. Change the orientation to portrait.
2. Add 1 blank row between Golden Checking and Regular Savings.
3. Add 1 blank row between Christmas Club and Money Market—Tier I.
4. Add 1 blank row between Money Market—Tier IV and CD—91 day.
5. Merge the cells in the inserted rows.
6. Apply a Table AutoFormat of your choice.
7. Type an * after APY.
8. Insert 1 blank row at the bottom of the table and type *APY=Annual Percentage Yield.

Table
80-40 ►

Four-Column Table

Follow these steps to create a table using Table AutoFormat.

1. Create the following table in default format.

2. Apply the Contemporary Table Auto-Format option—or one of your choice.

BUILDING DIRECTORY Paulding Meeting Facility			
No.	Room Name	Seating	Square Feet
102	Alabama	35	400
104	Colorado	150	1,600
106	Delaware	25	350
108	Georgia	50	600
202	Montana	35	400
204	Nevada	50	600
206	New Jersey	300	3,200
208	Pennsylvania	350	3,600

Architectural designers use their keyboarding skills continually.

Skills Assessment on Part 4

5-Minute Timing

1	Many business firms and agencies are publishing their	11
2	own publications by using various software packages that	22
3	are available today. These packages have been created to	33
4	enable persons with limited knowledge to design pages very	45
5	easily. The big challenge, however, is for the person to	56
6	design the pages effectively so that the reader will read	68
7	the pages. After all, the main reason for investing time	79
8	and money in the publication is to read the articles.	90
9	Designing pages that are easy to read is not as easy	101
10	as it seems. For example, a reader may be confused if a	112
11	page has too many headlines and stories. However, a reader	124
12	may prefer to read fewer headlines with longer articles	135
13	that are printed in larger type.	142
14	Desktop publishers need a few good tools to interest	153
15	readers. A good plan to capture attention is to place the	165
16	most important articles at the top of the first page and	176
17	the less important stories on the inside pages. Listings	187
18	and subheadings are excellent tools to guide the reader	198
19	through the pages. Also, pictures and graphics are good	209
20	tools for capturing attention.	215

| 1 | 2 | 3 | 4 | 5 | 6 | 7 | 8 | 9 | 10 | 11 | 12

Correspondence Test 4-76

Memo Report
With Four-Column
Boxed Table

MEMO

^TO: All employees

FROM: Paula Sullivan

Date: January 15, 20--

SUBJECT: Capital Communication Co.

Capital Communication Co. (CCC) operates the fourth largest network in the U.S. In addition, CCC owns 8 television stations, 3 radio stations, and 4 newspapers.

HISTORY

CCC was started in 1962 by a subsidiary of Heartland Publications as a public ^service network. It began with three radio stations and added both radio and television stations until it went public in 1956. In 1987 it merged with Pacific

(Continued on next page)

Media Company and added 4 newspapers. CCC's largest *news*paper, *The San Antonio* ~~Times~~, won a pulitzer Prize for *feature* writing last year.

EARNINGS With sales of $4.9 billion ~~dollars~~ for the most recent 12-month period and *a net* income of $486 million, *CCC* ~~it~~ continues to lead the "buy" list of most stock brokers. The *following* table shows a break down of ~~its~~ *CCC's* earnings.

CAPITAL COMMUNICATION COMPANY				Sales (in Billions
Company	Last Year	This Year	Next Year*	
Radio	#1.3	$1.4	$1.4	
Television	$1.8	$2.10	$2.2	
Newspapers	$1.4	$1.5	$2.0	
*Projected				

Correspondence ▶ Test 4-77

Business Letter in Block Style With Blind Copy and Postscript Notations

Current Date | Mr. Owen F. Austin | 1734 Perry Street | Flint, MI 48504 | Dear Mr. Austin:

¶ I am sorry that time constraints shortened our telephone conversation yesterday. Given the circumstances as you presented them, you would be wise to consider drafting a General Durable Power of Attorney as described in Section 495 of the new act.

¶ A Power of Attorney, under the old law, is effective only up to the time that a person is disabled or incompetent. Now the General Durable Power of Attorney, under the new statute, will remain in effect until a person either revokes it or passes away.

¶ The new law will be very helpful to many elderly and infirm people. Sincerely yours, | C. F. Storden | Attorney-at-Law | urs | PS: You may want to discuss this matter with your children before calling my office for an appointment. | bc: Peggy Austin, Walter Austin

Four-Column
Boxed Table

Add 20% shading to
the title row and 10%
shading to column
headings and total
rows.

AMERICAN TRADE (As a Percentage of Total)			
Exports		**Imports**	
Canada	22	Japan	20
Japan	12	Canada	19
Mexico	7	Mexico	6
United Kingdom	6	Germany	5
Germany	5	Taiwan	5
South Korea	4	South Korea	4
Other Countries	44	Other Countries	41
TOTAL	100	TOTAL	100

PART 5

Specialized Applications

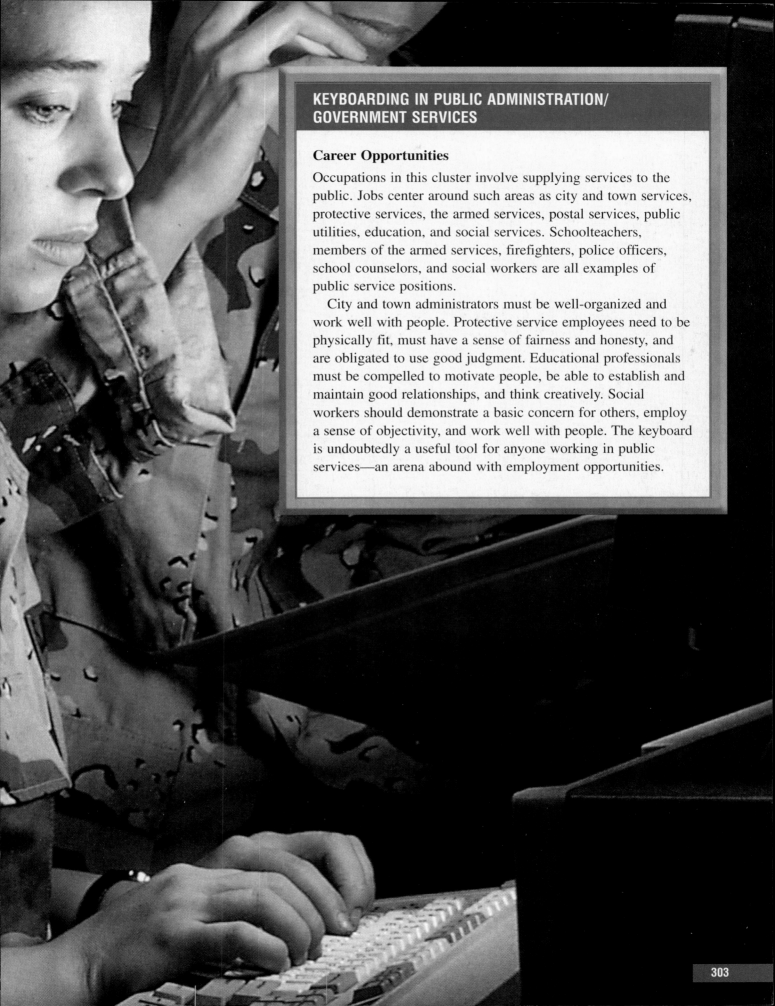

KEYBOARDING IN PUBLIC ADMINISTRATION/ GOVERNMENT SERVICES

Career Opportunities

Occupations in this cluster involve supplying services to the public. Jobs center around such areas as city and town services, protective services, the armed services, postal services, public utilities, education, and social services. Schoolteachers, members of the armed services, firefighters, police officers, school counselors, and social workers are all examples of public service positions.

City and town administrators must be well-organized and work well with people. Protective service employees need to be physically fit, must have a sense of fairness and honesty, and are obligated to use good judgment. Educational professionals must be compelled to motivate people, be able to establish and maintain good relationships, and think creatively. Social workers should demonstrate a basic concern for others, employ a sense of objectivity, and work well with people. The keyboard is undoubtedly a useful tool for anyone working in public services—an arena abound with employment opportunities.

Formal Report Project

LESSON 81
Formal Report Project

LESSON 84
Formal Report Project

LESSON 82
Formal Report Project

LESSON 85
Formal Report Project

LESSON 83
Formal Report Project

CONTENTS

INTERCULTURAL SEMINARS AT DOMESTIC
AND INTERNATIONAL SITES

Submitted to

Jordan D. Sylvester,
Human Resources De

Prepared by

Anthony Willia
St. Cloud Technical

February 12, 20

TABLE 2. FOREIGN-CITY SEMINARS

City	First Seminar	Second Seminar
Melbourne	May 2-4	July 5-7
Rio de Janeiro	May 9-11	July 11-13
Beijing	May 16-18	July 18-20
Hamburg	May 23-25	July 25-27
Tokyo	June 6-8	August 1-3
Warsaw	June 13-15	August 8-10
Oslo	June 20-22	August 15-17
Madrid	June 27-29	August 22-24

Formal Report Project

GOALS

- Improve speed and accuracy
- Refine language arts skills in grammar
- Format a formal report

A. Type 2 times.

A. WARMUP

```
1     The jalopy quivered as it crossed over the 1/5-mile    11
2  long bridge on Route 267 about 14 miles south @ Granite    22
3  Falls. The axle on Richard's truck broke as he whizzed by.  34
   |  1  |  2  |  3  |  4  |  5  |  6  |  7  |  8  |  9  |  10  |  11  |  12
```

SKILLBUILDING

B. MAP

Follow the GDP software directions for this exercise in improving keystroking accuracy.

C. Take a 1-minute timing on the first paragraph to establish your base speed. Then take four 1-minute timings on the remaining paragraphs. As soon as you equal or exceed your base speed on one paragraph, advance to the next, more difficult paragraph.

C. SUSTAINED PRACTICE: CAPITALIZATION

```
4      A visit to Europe is a vacation that many people dream  11
5  of doing. There are many countries to visit and hundreds of  23
6  sites to see if you can spend at least four weeks on the    34
7  continent. A trip to Europe is one you will never forget.   45

8      If you decide to visit Europe, the months of June and   11
9  July would probably be the prettiest, but they would also   23
10 be the busiest. England, France, and Germany are popular    34
11 countries to visit; Spain is popular for Americans as well. 46

12     In England you will want to visit St. Paul's Cathedral  11
13 and Big Ben. And, of course, when you are in England, you   23
14 do not want to pass up the opportunity to see Buckingham     34
15 Palace. Plan on staying a few days to see all the sites.    45

16     France certainly is a highlight of any European visit.  11
17 Paris offers many sites such as the Arc de Triomphe, the    22
18 Louvre, the Eiffel Tower, and the Gothic Cathedral of Notre 34
19 Dame. Other cities to visit are Nice, Lyon, and Versailles. 46
   |  1  |  2  |  3  |  4  |  5  |  6  |  7  |  8  |  9  |  10  |  11  |  12
```

D. Study the rules at the right.

D. AGREEMENT

RULE ▶
agreement pronouns

Some pronouns (*anybody, each, either, everybody, everyone, much, neither, no one, nobody,* and *one*) are always singular and take a singular verb. Other pronouns (*all, any, more, most, none,* and *some*) may be singular or plural, depending on the noun to which they refer.

<u>Each</u> of the employees <u>has</u> finished <u>his or her</u> task.
<u>Much</u> <u>remains</u> to be done.
<u>Most</u> of the pie <u>was</u> eaten, but <u>most</u> of the cookies <u>were</u> left.

RULE ▶
agreement intervening words

Disregard any intervening words that come between the subject and verb when establishing agreement.

The <u>box</u> containing the books and pencils <u>has</u> not been found.
<u>Alex</u>, accompanied by Tricia, <u>is</u> attending the conference and taking <u>his</u> computer.

Edit the sentences to correct any errors in grammar.

20 Everybody who signed up for the trip are to be at Building 16.
21 All the tourists are sending cards to us from their hotels.
22 Everyone on the trip, including spouses, have been having fun.
23 Some of the postcards from their vacations are not arriving.
24 Two of the sales reps from Region 4 were given cash bonuses.
25 The fastest runner from all five teams are receiving a trophy.

FORMATTING

Go To

Word Processing Manual

E. WORD PROCESSING: STYLES

Study Lesson 81 in your word processing manual. Complete all of the shaded steps while at your computer. Then format the job that follows.

DOCUMENT PROCESSING

Report 81-59 ▶

Multipage Business Report

Reference Manual
▶ Refer to Reference Manual pages R-8A and R-8B to review the correct format for business reports.

The business report that starts in this lesson is continued through Lesson 85. Use the following guidelines to format the report:

1. Create a style named Report Title for the title of the report. The title is to be formatted in all caps, bold, and 14 points.
2. Create a style named Subtitle for the subtitle, byline, and date at the beginning of the report. This information is to be formatted in upper- and lowercase, bold, and 12 points.
3. Create a style named Side for the side headings. Side headings are to be formatted in all caps, bold, and 12 points.
4. Create a style named Paragraph for the paragraph headings. Paragraph

headings are to be formatted in upper- and lowercase, bold, and 12 points.
5. Create a header for all pages except the first page. Use 10-point Arial italic font. Type Human Resources Department at the left margin. At the right margin, type Page followed by 1 space, and insert automatic page numbering. Add a bottom border/line.

Note: The same instructions for adding a border to a table apply to adding a border to a header. Click F̲ormat, Bo̲rders and Shading, and then click Ho̲rizontal Line. Refer to Lesson 37 in the Word Manual for additional instruction.

INTERCULTURAL SEMINARS AT DOMESTIC AND INTERNATIONAL SITES

Jordan D. Sylvester, Director

Human Resources Department

February 12, 20--

INTRODUCTION

¶ The marketing department has been ~~doing~~ conducting surveys of our world wide offices, foreign customers, and prospective foreign customers over the last several months. Information received through the use of mailed questionnaires has made us aware of an urgent need to improve our communication skills as we conduct our operations at the international level.

THE PROBLEM

¶ Some incidents have been reported to us in which we have failed to negotiate contracts with foreign customers and prospective foreign customers because of serious break downs in communication. ~~Very few~~ Some of these setbacks have been the result of conscious negative acts on the part of our employees. However, The main culprit seems to be lack of awareness of cultural differences and a lack of appreciation for the nuances that reflect these cultural differences. Indeed there are almost unlimited possibilities for misunderstandings, insults, miscues, and avenues for people of good intent to miscommunicate.

INTERCULTURAL SEMINARS

¶ Three-day seminars designed to improve intercultural communication skills will be held at regional sites in the U. S. and in foreign cities where we have offices:

- Beijing
- Hamburg
- Madrid
- Melbourne

(Continued on next page)

- Oslo

- Rio de Janeiro

- Tokyo

- Warsaw

agreement intervening words

¶ It will be our inten*t* that all employees who have direct contact with people from other countries will participate in these seminars over a four-month period.

¶ It would be unreasonable to assume that a small team of people from our company would have the breadth *of knowledge* needed to conduct these seminars in ⑧ foreign countries. However, Christin Zapoola, Terrence Mazlowski, and Nadene Andropolis have agreed to work together as the coordinating team

agreement pronouns

for this effort. Each of these individuals has worked over the past ② months with the managers of our international offices as well as natives in specific countries to formulate a preliminary plan for these in-service programs. *Their*

agreement pronouns

~~There~~ plan will utilize the expertise of our employees who have had negotiating experience in each country and who have knowledge of *local* customs as demonstrated by natives. We are confident that through this team approach, everyone will gain an understanding of problems *only* not from the position of our company but also from the perspective of those with whom they conduct business.

Save this unfinished report. You will resume work on it in Lesson 82.

Formal Report Project

GOALS
- Type at least 44wpm/5′/5e
- Format a formal report

A. Type 2 times.

A. WARMUP

```
 1        The path will be covered by approximately 30 pieces     11
 2   of slate from Quarry #19. Schreiner & Zimmer (the general     23
 3   contractor) took the joint bid of $638, including delivery.   35
```
| 1 | 2 | 3 | 4 | 5 | 6 | 7 | 8 | 9 | 10 | 11 | 12

SKILLBUILDING

B. Take three 12-second timings on each line. The scale below the last line shows your wpm speed for a 12-second timing.

B. 12-SECOND SPEED SPRINTS

```
 4   There are many things to think about if you buy a used car.
 5   Two of the main things are its age and the number of miles.
 6   Take the car for a test drive in town and on the open road.
 7   Pay a fee to an auto expert who will check it over for you.
```
5 10 15 20 25 30 35 40 45 50 55 60

C. PROGRESSIVE PRACTICE: ALPHABET

If you are not using the GDP software, turn to page SB-7 and follow the directions for this activity.

STRATEGIES FOR *Career Success*

Letter of Complaint

Is poor product or bad service getting you down? By writing a concise, rational letter of complaint, you have the possibility of the reader honoring your request.

In the first paragraph, give a precise description of the product or service (e.g., model, serial #). Include a general statement of the problem (e.g., "It is not working properly."). In the middle section, provide the details of what went wrong (e.g., when it happened, what failed). Refer to copies of invoices, checks, etc. Describe how you were inconvenienced, with details about time and money lost. State what you want (e.g., refund, repair, replace). In the closing paragraph, ask for a timely response to the complaint (e.g., "Please resolve this problem within the next two weeks.").

YOUR TURN Think about the last time that you experienced poor product or service. Did you write a letter of complaint?

D. Take two 5-minute timings. Review your speed and errors.

Goal: At least 44wpm/5'/5e

D. 5-MINUTE TIMING

8   Critical thinking is a skill that can be learned and   11
9   applied to many life situations. Many definitions are used   23
10 to describe critical thinking skill. The common theme that   35
11 is expressed in these definitions is associated with using   47
12 cognitive skill. With this skill, the person thinks with a   59
13 purpose in mind and usually directs his or her thoughts   70
14 toward goals. The person looks at a situation and decides   82
15 rationally what to believe or not believe. In critical   93
16 thinking, the goal is to achieve understanding, evaluate   104
17 viewpoints, and solve problems. After evaluating all the   115
18 elements of the problem, a decision is made based on the   126
19 evidence and concrete findings. Emotions, prejudices, and   138
20 biases should not sway the final outcome.   146
21 Critical thinking is useful in reading, speaking,   156
22 writing, and listening. A critical thinker asks pertinent   168
23 questions and looks for new solutions. He or she listens   179
24 carefully to others and gives feedback. A critical thinker   191
25 zealously searches out the truth and willingly accepts   202
26 change when new facts are presented. Critical thinking is   213
27 very important for solving problems.   220

| 1 | 2 | 3 | 4 | 5 | 6 | 7 | 8 | 9 | 10 | 11 | 12 |

DOCUMENT PROCESSING

Report 81-59 ▶

(Continued)

Continue working on Multipage Business Report 81-59.

INSTRUCTIONAL APPROACH

¶ Connors and Saggett suggest a framework of instruction with the following: *three components*

1. The cognitive component includes information about communicating with people *of other cultures*.

2. The *a*ffective component is the area in which attention is given to attitudes, emotions, and resulting behaviors as they are *a*ffected by human interaction in a multicultural environment.

(Continued on next page)

3. The experiential component is the "hands-on" element ~~which~~ *that* suggests different possibilities. Others have found that the use of simulations is a natural for this type of experience. The writing of letters, memos, and reports to persons in other cultures also provides beneficial learning experiences. In addition, the use of tutors can be very helpful to workers unfamiliar with a particular culture.[1]

SEMINAR CONTENT

¶ The cognitive, affective, and experiential ~~frames~~ *components* would be applied as appropriate for each of the topics included. The coordinating team members have utilized the resources available to them at our (3) local universities. Most colleges and universities now provide instruction in international communication. While the content at times is integrated into several business administration courses, there has been a trend in recent years to provide a course ~~or courses~~ specifically designed for business interaction in an intercultural setting. The very nature of this type of study makes it very difficult to segment the broad topical areas, as all elements are so closely intertwined. However, the tentative seminar plan is to cover the content as described below.

¶ The seminars must reflect the broad involvement of our international operations. There is a need for many workers in our domestic offices to develop an appreciation of the intercultural challenge. This is true not only for those in the marketing and sales areas. Those in our Finance Department and our Legal Department are *increasingly* involved not only with foreign companies but also with huge multinational corporations that, at times, are as large as or larger than the biggest companies in the ~~entire~~ United States.

¶ Zapoola, Mazlowski, and Andropolis suggest the following as tentative instructional topics:[2]

---

[1] James C. Connors and Paul T. Saggett, "Communicating With World Cultures," *World of Business*, April 2000, pp. 25-28.

[2] Christin Zapoola, Terrence Mazlowski, and Nadene Andropolis, *Conducting Intercultural Seminars*, Northeast Publishing, Boston, Mass., 2001.

(Continued on next page)

Reference Manual

Review the format for placing a table in a report on page R-8B of the Reference Manual.

TABLE 1. SEMINAR TOPICS	
Instructional Topic	**Time**
Body Movements _Positions and_	2 hours
Concept of Culture	⁴3̸ hours
Language	2 hours
Conflict Resolution	3 hours
Intimacy in Relationships	3 hours
Male/female Roles	²3̸ hours
Punctuality, Time, and Space	2 hours
Religion, Values, and ethics	4 hours

¶ **Body Positions and Movements.** Body language, that is, facial expressions, gestures, and body movements, conveys messages about attitude and may be interpreted differently by people in _different_ cultures. For example, firm handshakes are the norm in the U.S.; loose handshakes are the custom in some other countries. The way we stand, sit, and hold our arms may convey different messages in different cultural settings.

¶ **Concept of culture.** This session will be an over view of the various cultures in which we conduct our business affairs. Perreault identifies the need for varied marketing strategies within the different economic, political, and cultural environments:

> International marketing is complicated because these environ-
> ments—in particular, the cultural environment—often consist of
> elements _un_ familiar to american marketing executives. A further
> complication is the tendency for people to use their own cultural
> values as a frame of reference when in a foreign environment.[3]

Case studies will be reviewed that are considered classics in the field of international communication. _In addition,_ Summaries of some of our own successes and failures will be reported.

Save this unfinished report. You will resume work on it in Lesson 83.

---

[3]William D. Perreault, "The World Is Our Market," _E-Market USA Home Page_, January 2001, http://www.emarket.com/newstoday.htm (March 18, 20--).

Formal Report Project

GOALS

- Improve speed and accuracy
- Refine language arts skills in composing
- Format a formal report

A. Type 2 times.

A. WARMUP

```
1        The 16 young farmers (only 50% over 30 years of age)     11
2   gathered in Room 209 to begin discussing the earthquake       22
3   threat; an extra door prize was given as a "joke present."     34
    | 1  | 2  | 3  | 4  | 5  | 6  | 7  | 8  | 9  | 10 | 11 | 12
```

SKILLBUILDING

PRETEST → PRACTICE → POSTTEST

B. PRETEST: Common Letter Combinations

PRETEST
Take a 1-minute timing. Review your speed and errors.

```
4        The insurance agent read the report before giving it     11
5   to your deputy director. This weekly action showed that        22
6   the agent really knew the actual input on a daily basis.       33
    | 1  | 2  | 3  | 4  | 5  | 6  | 7  | 8  | 9  | 10 | 11 | 12
```

C. PRACTICE: Word Beginnings

PRACTICE
Speed Emphasis:
If you made no more than 1 error on the Pretest, type each *individual* line 2 times.
Accuracy Emphasis:
If you made 2 or more errors, type each *group* of lines (as though it were a paragraph) 2 times.

```
7  re- repel renew remit relax refer ready react really reveal
8  in- inept inert inset input infer index incur inches insert
9  be- bears beams beach below being began befit beauty beside
```

D. PRACTICE: Word Endings

```
10 -ly truly madly lowly early daily apply hilly simply weekly
11 -ed sized hired dated cited based acted added opened showed
12 -nt plant meant giant front event count agent amount fluent
```

E. POSTTEST: Common Letter Combinations

POSTTEST
Repeat the Pretest timing and compare performance.

F. PROGRESSIVE PRACTICE: NUMBERS

If you are not using the GDP software, turn to page SB-11 and follow the directions for this activity.

G. COMPOSING A DOCUMENT

Compose a one-page document in which you describe how you can use the Styles command in a resume you are preparing for a job search. You might include features such as fonts, font sizes, indentations, spacing, etc., to control the appearance of your resume. Use default margins, double spacing, and two paragraphs in your document. Provide a title, and type your name at the top of the document.

In paragraph 1, you could include information on using styles for those items you want to highlight in your resume such as (1) your name and address at the top of the resume, (2) the section headings that often run down the left side of the resume, and (3) any bullets you want to include for items that contain multiple entries.

In paragraph 2, you could include a brief discussion on (1) the margins to use for your resume, (2) line spacing to use for individual entries, and (3) line spacing to use between entries.

A brief summary statement should be included to emphasize the importance of proofreading your document and the need for accuracy in a resume.

FORMATTING

Go To

Word
Processing
Manual

H. WORD PROCESSING: INSERT CLIP ART AND FILES

Study Lesson 83 in your word processing manual. Complete all of the shaded steps while at your computer. Then format the job that follows.

DOCUMENT PROCESSING

**Report
81-59** ▶

(Continued)

Continue working on
Report 81-59.

Insert "conversation.wmf" from the People category in the Microsoft Clip Art Gallery (or insert a similar piece of clip art).

Set the clip art at a size of 1-inch square, and place it at the right margin at the beginning of the **Language** paragraph.

¶ **Conflict Resolution.** Whether in negotiating a contract, working together to remedy product quality issues, or resolving contract interpretations, the need for tact and skill is particularly important in the foreign setting. Many of the seminar topics discussed above have implications in the area of conflict resolution. While every effort should be made to prevent conflict, there is a need for guidance in resolving disagreements in foreign cultures.

¶ **Intimacy in Relationships.** The degree of physical contact that is acceptable varies considerably. Hugs and kisses are the standard, even in the business office, in some countries. By contrast, the act of touching a person is considered an extreme invasion of privacy in other places. The use of first names may or may not be acceptable. To ask a personal question is extremely offensive in some cultures. While socializing with business clients is to be expected in some countries, that would be highly inappropriate in others. These are only a few of the relationship concerns that will be explored.

¶ **Language.** It is obvious that language differences play a major part in business miscommunication. Whenever there is an interpreter or a written translation involved, the chances for error are increased. There are over 3,000 languages used on the earth. Just as with English, there are not only

(Continued on next page)

grammar rules but also varied meanings as words are both spoken and written. Even with the English language, there are differences in usage between the English used in the United States and that used in England. Although English is the language usually used in international communication, the topics identified in Table 1 above illustrate the complexity of communicating accurately; and the problem continues to grow. For example, literal translations of American advertising and labeling have sometimes resulted in negative feelings toward products. As world trade increases, so does the need for American businesses to understand the complexities of cultural differences. Ober offers this excellent example:

> Businesspeople in both Asian and Latin American countries tend to favor long negotiations and slow deliberations. They exchange pleasantries at some length before getting down to business. Likewise, many non-Western cultures use the silent intervals for contemplation, whereas businesspeople from North America tend to have little tolerance for silence in business negotiations. As a result, North Americans may rush in and offer compromises and counterproposals that would have been unnecessary if they had shown more patience.[4]

¶ A good sense of humor is an asset not only in our personal lives but also in the business environment. However, it probably should be avoided in multicultural settings because the possibilities for misinterpretation are compounded. Do not use humor that makes fun of a particular individual, group, or culture. Remember that what may appear to be humorous to you may have a negative connotation in another culture.

¶ **Male/Female Roles.** There are major contrasts in the ways male and female roles are perceived in different cultures. The right to vote is still withheld from women in countries all over the world. Opportunities for female employment in the business environment vary considerably. Pay differentials for men and women continue to exist even when they are performing the same tasks. Opportunities for advancement for men and women often are not the same.

¶ **Punctuality, Time, and Space.** A meeting that is scheduled for 9 a.m. likely will start on time in the United States, but in some other cultures the meeting may not start until 9:30 or even 10 o'clock. Punctuality and time concepts vary with the customs and practices of each country. Patience really can be a virtue.

¶ There is also the element of space—the distance one stands from someone when engaged in conversation. If a person stands farther away than usual, this may signal a feeling of indifference or even a negative feeling. Standing too close is a sign of inappropriate familiarity. However, it should be recognized that different cultures require a variety of space for business exchanges to take place. In the United States, that space is typically from three to five feet, but in the Middle East and in Latin American countries, this distance is considered too far.

---

[4]Scot Ober, *Contemporary Business Communication*, 3rd ed., Houghton-Mifflin Company, Boston, 1998, p. 49.

Insert "alarmclock. gif" from the Web Bullets and Buttons category in the Microsoft Clip Art Gallery (or insert a similar piece of clip art).

Set the clip art at a size of 1-inch square, and place it at the right margin at the beginning of the **Punctuality, Time, and Space** paragraph.

Save this unfinished report. You will resume work on it in Lesson 84.

Lesson 84

Formal Report Project

GOALS

- Type at least 44wpm/5′/5e
- Format a formal report

A. Type 2 times.

A. WARMUP

```
1        The new schedule* has the Lynx at their home park on      11
2  July 27 with the zany Waverley Blackhawks. The Lynx scored      23
3  five fourth-quarter goals in their last game to win 8 to 4!     35
   |  1  |  2  |  3  |  4  |  5  |  6  |  7  |  8  |  9  |  10  |  11  |  12
```

SKILLBUILDING

B. DIAGNOSTIC PRACTICE: ALPHABET

If you are not using the GDP software, turn to page SB-2 and follow the directions for this activity.

Careers in the public administration/government services career cluster offer many opportunities to use keyboarding skills, at times in unconventional locations.

C. Take two 5-minute timings. Review your speed and errors.

Goal: At least 44wpm/5'/5e

C. 5-MINUTE TIMING

4   Proofreading skill is developed with practice. You   10

5 may want to master several techniques that will help you   21

6 develop and improve your proofreading skills.   30

7   In order to be a successful proofreader, you will   40

8 want to schedule time to read through the completed job   51

9 several times. At the first reading, check your work to   62

10 see if the margins are correct and the page numbers are in   74

11 the right places. Determine if the spacing and font styles   86

12 are correct. With each reading, zone in on a specific type   98

13 of error. If possible, read your work out loud and only   109

14 read one word at a time. You may find that placing a ruler   121

15 under each line as you read it will give your eyes a more   133

16 manageable amount of text to read.   140

17   At the next reading, ascertain that the content of   150

18 the document follows a logical order. If cited works are   161

19 included, be sure the citations are in the proper format   172

20 with complete and accurate data. Check to be sure that all   184

21 the basic rules of grammar, spelling, and punctuation have   196

22 been followed. Proofread your document when you are fresh   208

23 and alert. Remember, proofreading takes time and patience.   220

| 1 | 2 | 3 | 4 | 5 | 6 | 7 | 8 | 9 | 10 | 11 | 12 |

Keyboarding CONNECTION

Sending Email Attachments

Your email program will tell you if an attachment has been sent, but the attachment may arrive in unusable or partially usable form. Often the sender and recipient need to use the same or compatible software to open and use each other's documents, especially if the files contain visuals, records, or spreadsheets.

Send a test email by attaching a test document and ask your receiver to send you one in return. If the test fails with a word processing document, open your word processor, and save the document again as a text file. You may lose some formatting (indents, bold, bullets), but any email program, as well as any word processor, can usually read the file.

YOUR TURN   Open a word processing file. Save it as a text file. Open the text file in your word processor. What formatting has changed? Send both files to yourself as email attachments. Open them and note any changes.

Table 84-42 ▶

Three-Column
Boxed Table

TABLE 2. FOREIGN-CITY SEMINARS		
City	First Seminar	Second Seminar
Melbourne	May 2-4	July 5-7
Rio de Janeiro	May 9-11	July 11-13
Beijing	May 16-18	July 18-20
Hamburg	May 23-25	July 25-27
Tokyo	June 6-8	August 1-3
Warsaw	June 13-15	August 8-10
Oslo	June 20-22	August 15-17
Madrid	June 27-29	August 22-24

Report 81-59 ▶

(Continued)

Continue working on
Report 81-59.

¶ **Religion, Values, and Ethics.** While we can recognize the difficult challenge presented by language differences, this category (religion, values, and ethics) is in some ways the area that can bring about the most serious breakdowns in relations with those from other cultures.

• The very nature of religious beliefs suggests that this is a delicate area for those involved in business transactions in foreign countries. Also, religious beliefs affect the consumption of certain products throughout the world. Examples are tobacco, liquor, pork, and coffee.

• Values are a reflection of religious beliefs for most people. We often hear references to right and wrong as applied to the ideals and customs of a society. Values relate to a range of topics, and they may pertain to areas such as cleanliness, education, health care, and criminal justice.

• Ethics can be considered as standards of conduct that reflect moral beliefs as applied to both one's personal life and one's business life. Camp and Satterwhite suggest a definition for ethical behavior and the use of a code of ethics within the business environment:

Being ethical means being honest, fair, and objective in all forms of communication. The true test of being ethical is to work toward the good of all rather than towards the good of a specialized group at the expense of some other group. Some organizations and companies develop a written code of ethics so employees and customers or clients have a written record of the philosophy of the group. A code of ethics states the goals of the group in terms of how the business operates and how it treats customers and competitors.[5]

---

[5]Sue C. Camp and Marilyn L. Satterwhite, *College English & Communication*, Glencoe/McGraw-Hill Book Company, New York, 1998, p. 53.

Insert "world.wmf" from the Maps category in the Microsoft Clip Art Gallery (or insert a similar piece of clip art).

Set the clip art at a size of 1-inch square, and place it at the right margin at the beginning of the first paragraph.

TENTATIVE SEMINAR SCHEDULE

¶ As indicated earlier, it is our intent that all employees who have direct contact with people in other cultures will participate in these seminars. For that reason there will be two identical three-day seminars scheduled at each foreign site. Only selected employees in our regional sites in the United States will participate. These people have been tentatively identified on the basis of the extent of their involvement with persons from other countries.

¶ As all employees in our foreign offices will participate, a decision has been made to schedule these seminars through the summer. A tentative schedule for these seminars is shown in Table 2.

(Insert Table 84-42 here)

The Marketing Department is to be commended for calling our attention to the seriousness of our international communication problem. Christin Zapoola, Terrence Maslowski, and Nadene Andropolis also deserve our sincere thanks for their planning efforts for our intercultural communication seminars. As can be seen, special attention is being given to the seminar topics for these in-service programs. Efforts are also being made to identify instructors and resource persons who will develop instructional strategies that will be effective, interesting, and well received by the participants. These seminars will help significantly in increasing our market share in the international market.

Save this unfinished report. You will resume work on it in Lesson 85.

Lesson 85

Formal Report Project

GOALS
- Improve speed and accuracy
- Refine language arts skills in proofreading
- Format a formal report

A. Type 2 times.

A. WARMUP

```
1      Bev ordered the following: 24 #794 napkin boxes, 48      11
2   #265B quarts of ketchup, and 72 reams of 20-lb white print   23
3   paper. Did you receive the prize jalapeno peppers we sent?   35
    |  1  |  2  |  3  |  4  |  5  |  6  |  7  |  8  |  9  | 10 | 11 | 12
```

SKILLBUILDING

B. Type the columns 2 times. Press TAB to move from column to column.

B. TECHNIQUE PRACTICE: TAB

```
4  M. A. Barnes    Julie Herden    Lynn Masica    Don Trueblood
5  Nathan Favor    Brett Irvin     Lisa O'Keefe   Matthew Utbert
6  Lee Chinn       Rick Kenwood    J. E. Perry    Jill Voss-Walin
7  Xavier Saxon    Lance King      Chad Quinn     Robin Yager
```

C. PACED PRACTICE

If you are not using the GDP software, turn to page SB-14 and follow the directions for this activity.

LANGUAGE ARTS

D. Compare this paragraph with lines 4-7 on page 305.

D. PROOFREADING

```
8      A visitt to Europe is a vacation that many people dreem
9   of takking. There are many countrys to visit and hundreds
10  of sights to see if you can spend at least for weeks on the
11  continnent. A trip too Europe is one you will never forget.
```

Report 85-60

Title Page

Create a title page for Report 81-59 as a separate document. Use the copy in the illustration.

↓Center page

14 pt **INTERCULTURAL SEMINARS AT DOMESTIC AND INTERNATIONAL SITES** ↓12X

12 pt↓ Submitted to ↓2X

Jordan D. Sylvester, Director
Human Resources Department ↓12X

Prepared by ↓2X

Your Name ↓2X

February 12, 20--

Report 85-61

Table of Contents

Create a Table of Contents page for Report 81-59. Use the following guidelines to prepare the Table of Contents page:
1. Type the entries using the side and paragraph headings from the report.
2. Type the side headings in all caps; type the paragraph headings in upper- and lowercase.
3. Paragraph headings are indented 0.5 inch from the left margin.
4. Do not include the header on the Table of Contents page.
5. Use the page numbers from your report to complete each entry in the Table of Contents page.

(Continued on next page)

Use the model for reference to format the Table of Contents. Refer to your report to prepare the Table of Contents.

↓6X

14 pt **CONTENTS** ↓2X

Report 85-62 ▶

Bibliography

Reference Manual

Refer to page R-9B of the Reference Manual to format the Bibliography page.

Spell-check your report for errors. Proofread it for omitted or repeated words, errors that form a new word, and formatting errors.

Create a Bibliography for Report 81-59 as a separate document. Study the illustration below. Use the footnote references plus the following entry for the Bibliography page: Locker, Kitty O., *Business and* *Administrative Communication,* 4th ed., Irwin McGraw-Hill Book Company, New York, 1997. Remember that bibliographic entries are arranged alphabetically by last name of the author.

↓6X

BIBLIOGRAPHY ↓2X

hanging indent

Camp, Sue C., and Satterwhite, Marilyn L., *College English & Communication,*
0.5" Glencoe/McGraw-Hill Book Company, New York, 1998, p. 53. ↓2X

Connors, James C., and Saggett, Paul T., "Communicating With World Cultures," *World of Business,* April 2000, pp. 25-28.

Locker, Kitty O., *Business and Administrative Communication,* 4th ed., Irwin McGraw-Hill Book Company, New York, 1997.

✔ **Progress Check**
Proofreading Check

Documents designated as Proofreading Checks serve as a check of your proofreading skill. Your goal is to have zero typographical errors when the GDP software first scores the document.

Finalize the report project:
• Proofread all the pages for format and typing errors.
• Assemble the pages in this order: title page, table of contents, body, bibliography, and a blank page for a back cover sheet.
• Staple the report at three places along the left edge.

INTERNATIONAL FORMATTING

LESSON 86
International Formatting (Canada)

LESSON 87
International Formatting (Mexico)

LESSON 88
International Formatting (France)

LESSON 89
International Formatting (Germany)

LESSON 90
International Formatting (Japan)

Current Date

Mr. Henry R. Defforey
Human Resources Director
Gemey Techtronics
Avenue Raymond Poincore
75116 Paris
FRANCE

Dear Mr. Defforey:

I am pleased that we will be involved in an employee exchange this coming year. As we discussed earlier, the exchange of our 26 production employees will benefit both

...through the various units of our production
...ials division right on through our shipping
...ed rotation plan for you to review. Included in the
...ve discussed at our last meeting. Please review the
...hanges you wish to make. You can email me at
...u wish to speak to me directly, you can call

...this coming year. As soon as we have agreed on
...s for all affected employees. I know that
...ticipating this collaborative effort.

MEXICO TRAVEL DEST...

Most Popular Attrac...

Current Date

INTRODUCTION

In the past decade, Mexico national parks have become p...
the Americas, Europe, and Asia. As a result, an increasing...
made for travel brochures and maps from our Visitors...
few weeks, we will be publishing several new broch...
these requests.

Brochures. The brochures will include a detailed d...
information on beginning and ending visitation sch...
popular photography locations. Brochures will be p...
locations:

Area	Site
Northern	Cumbres de Majalca
Northern	Cumbres de Monterrey
Northern	Sierra del Pinacate
Middle	El Rosario
Middle	El Tepozteco
Middle	Iztaccihuatl y Popocatepetl
Middle	Malinche
Southern	Bonampak/Yaxchilan Monuments
Southern	Chichen Itza
Southern	Dzibilchaltun
Southern	Sian Káan Biosphere Reserve

Maps. Maps will be drawn for the locations above,...
visitors from the nearest cities to the tourist attractio...
stations will be highlighted, and approximate walki...
maps. Individual maps will be prepared for each ar...
as well as a comprehensive map for all three visitor...

We will also be placing materials on our National...
(http://www.tourism.dfmexcity.mx.parks.html). Ple...
you wish to promote to Señor Garcia, Public Relati...
operational within the next 30 days.

Current Date

Ms. Sharla D. Enterline
Project Coordinator
Carroll Technology
8723 Hill Avenue
Bowling Green, KY 42823

Dear Ms. Enterline:

The following information is being sent to assist you with Japanese mailing rules. As a service to your employees, I am providing the following summary of these rules.

A Japanese mailing address consists of the name, street address, town, city, prefecture, postal code, and country. The illustration below shows an example of an envelope addressed to a citizen of Japan.

Address Items	Address Example
Name	Mr. Yoshifumi Uda
Street Address, Town (first address)	1-17, Akai-cho
City, Prefecture (second address), Postal Code	Minato-Ku, Tokyo 108-8005
JAPAN	JAPAN

Please email me if you have questions about mailing rules in Japan. You can reach me at shiroshi@tadashi.jp.com.

Very sincerely,

S. Hiroshi
Shipping Department

urs
c: K. Tachikawa

International Formatting (Canada)

GOALS
- Type at least 45wpm/5'/5e
- Format international documents

A. Type 2 times.

A. WARMUP

```
 1        The lynx at the zoo fought wildly and had to be moved    11
 2   quickly to a new cage (#248-I or #357-II). These adjoining    23
 3   cages place the lynx (all of them) into individual areas.     34
     |  1  |  2  |  3  |  4  |  5  |  6  |  7  |  8  |  9  |  10  |  11  |  12
```

SKILLBUILDING

B. DIAGNOSTIC PRACTICE: NUMBERS

If you are not using the GDP software, turn to page SB-5 and follow the directions for this activity.

C. Take three 12-second timings on each line. The scale below the last line shows your wpm speed for a 12-second timing.

C. 12-SECOND SPEED SPRINTS

```
 4   The auto will now have to turn off on the lane to the lake.
 5   Mark must type these lines fast and press for a high speed.
 6   We had a lunch at the lake and went for a walk in the park.
 7   Take this disk to have it fixed by the end of your workday.
     I I I I 5 I I I I 10 I I I I 15 I I I I 20 I I I I 25 I I I I 30 I I I I 35 I I I I 40 I I I I 45 I I I I 50 I I I I 55 I I I I 60
```

Conduct business across the world with keyboarding skills.

D. Take two 5-minute timings. Review your speed and errors.

Goal: At least 45wpm/5'/5e

D. 5-MINUTE TIMING

8   During good economic times businesses have trouble   10

9 finding and retaining skilled workers. As a result, some   21

10 companies may offer exceptional benefit packages to their   33

11 employees. Benefit packages can include such items as life   45

12 insurance, profit sharing, sick leave, paid vacation and   56

13 holidays, and flextime.   61

14   The concept of flextime was introduced to the work   71

15 force many years ago. Companies adopted this policy for a   83

16 variety of reasons. Among the reasons for flexible work   94

17 schedules are relieving traffic congestion, attracting   105

18 women back into the workforce, and helping the employees   116

19 meet family needs and responsibilities.   124

20   Organizations can manage flexible scheduling in many   135

21 ways. Employees may have flexible arrival and departure   146

22 times. This policy allows people who like to work early in   158

23 the day to start early and end early in the afternoon, and   170

24 vice versa. Other companies may allow their employees to   181

25 work extended hours for four days and then have three days   193

26 off. This type of benefit has been quite beneficial to   204

27 workers and companies. Companies have found that workers   215

28 are usually more productive and have fewer absences.   225

| 1 | 2 | 3 | 4 | 5 | 6 | 7 | 8 | 9 | 10 | 11 | 12 |

Keyboarding CONNECTION   Effective Teleconferencing for Meetings

Teleconferencing is a useful way to conduct meetings with businesspersons across the globe. To make the best use of teleconference meetings, follow these guidelines.

Since sound quality varies greatly, use the best equipment available. Allow individual participants enough time to use their technology. Participants should select a conference leader and alternate that leadership. Distribute agendas to everyone in advance, possibly via email.

Be sensitive to time zone differences. Since it is possible someone will experience an inconvenient time, consider rotating the times of the meetings. Assign someone to prepare and email to the participants a brief summary covering the main discussion topics and action items of the teleconference.

YOUR TURN   List what you think are the advantages and disadvantages of conducting meetings via teleconference.

E. METRIC PAPER SIZE

Paper size for correspondence in the United States is typically 8.5 × 11 inches. However, correspondence in many foreign countries is often formatted on metric-sized paper. The most popular of these is called A4 paper, and it measures 210 × 297 millimeters—approximately 8.25 × 11.75 inches.

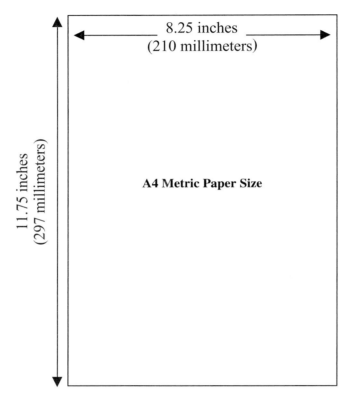

A4 Metric Paper Size

8.25 inches (210 millimeters)

11.75 inches (297 millimeters)

F. METRIC ENVELOPE SIZE

A standard large envelope (No. 10) measures 9.5 × 4.125 inches. A large envelope for metric size paper is called DL, and it measures 110 × 220 millimeters—approximately 4.33 inches by 8.67 inches. The metric envelope is not as deep as a No. 10 envelope, but it is slightly wider.

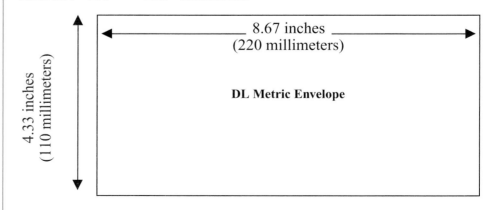

DL Metric Envelope

8.67 inches (220 millimeters)

4.33 inches (110 millimeters)

G. INTERNATIONAL ADDRESSES IN LETTERS

International addressing is becoming more common with the advent and popularity of Internet communications. International addresses frequently require slight modifications to the address lines, such as the addition of special codes, abbreviations, and capitalization. Examples of these modifications are illustrated below.

Canada Address Example:

8437 Dixie Road ← Street Address [street number followed by street name]

Brampton, ON L6T 5P6 ← City/Province/Postal Code [1 space between first 3 and last 3 characters]

CANADA ← Country Name [typed in all capitals]

Mexico Address Example:

AV. Chapultepec 28 ← Street Address [street name followed by street number]

06724 MEXICO D.F. ← Postal Code/City [postal code and city name; "MEXICO D.F." denotes Mexico City]

MEXICO ← Country Name [typed in all capitals]

France Address Example:

14, RUE ROYALE ← Street Address [street number followed by a comma, then street name]

75008 PARIS ← Postal Code/City [postal code and city name]

FRANCE ← Country Name [typed in all capitals]

Germany Address Example:

MANNESMANNUFER 2 ← Street Address

D-40213 DUESSELDORF ← Postal Code/City [Postal code and city name]

GERMANY ← Country Name [typed in all capitals]

Japan Address Example:

10-1, TORANOMON 2-CHOME ← Division of the City

MINATO-KU TOKYO 105-8436 ← Additional Division of the City, plus the City Name and Postal Code

JAPAN ← Country Name [typed in all capitals]

Go To
Word Processing Manual

H. WORD PROCESSING: PAPER SIZE

Study Lesson 86 in your word processing manual. Complete all of the shaded steps while at your computer. Then format the jobs that follow.

Situation: You work for World-Tech Industries, an international computer manufacturer, and are employed in their Vancouver, Canada, office. Your customer base consists primarily of companies located in northwestern states of the United States, but you also maintain several accounts with Canadian firms in Western Canada.

With your Canadian customers, you prepare written communications on A4 metric paper because Canadian corporations use A4 letterhead and DL metric envelopes. You also adhere to Canadian mailing guidelines by using two-letter province codes and postal codes. Prepare the following correspondence, which appears in your in-basket for today.

Correspondence 86-78 ▶

Business Letter in Modified-Block With Copy and Postscript Notations

Current Date | Mr. Alec R. Cousins | Manager, Computer Services | Columbia Enterprises, Ltd. | 338 Dunsmuir Street | Vancouver, BC V4B 5R9 | CANADA | Dear Mr. Cousins:

¶ Thank you for your recent computer order. As you requested, we have added the DVD drives to the 50 computers. There will be no extra charge for exchanging the DVD drives for the ZIP drives that come standard with the C-420 model you ordered.

¶ Your order will be shipped 10 business days from the date of your order. Our order processing and shipping departments are online, and you can check the progress of your order by going to www.worldtech.com and clicking on Customer Orders.

¶ We look forward to the opportunity to serve your computer needs for many years to come.

Sincerely, | Sharon T. Yates | Sales Manager | urs | c: T. D. Mourieux, P. M. Phillips | PS: The special software you ordered with your computers will be installed at our factory, ready for your use when your computers arrive.

Table 86-43 ▶

Five-Column Boxed Table in Landscape

Prepare Table 86-42 on A4 paper, in landscape orientation. **Note:** Entries are arranged by kilometers from Vancouver, British Columbia.

CUSTOMER SHIPPING ADDRESSES AND DISTANCE
(Distance Appears in Kilometers from Vancouver—"As the Crow Flies")

Name	Address	City/Province	Postal Code	Kilometers
Francis Stevens	17820 Attwood Road	Prince George, BC	V2N 653	520
Helene Abrams	269 Acadia Drive, SE	Calgary, AB	T2J 0A6	673
Connie Visocki	39 Blackburn Drive, SW	Edmonton, AB	T6W 1C5	817
Clarence Brewer	157 Caribou Street, E.	Moose Jaw, SK	S6H 0R4	1,266
Christine Osborn	P.O. Box 613	The Pas, MB	R9A 1K7	1,597
Andrew Svenson	14 Island Drive	Flin Flon, MB	R8A 058	1,850
Gary Fitzpatrick	635 Agnes Street	Winnipeg, MB	R3E 1X8	1,869
Lazo Aida	P.O. Box 1016	Churchill, MB	R0B 0E0	2,152

Table 86-44 ▶

Five-Column
Boxed Table
in Landscape

Open the file for Table 86-43 and make the following changes:

1. Rearrange the entries in Column A so that they appear as follows: (last name, comma, first name)

2. Rearrange the entries in the table, placing them in alphabetical order by the last name of the customer.

Keyboarding skills can be a very important part of your job—anywhere and anytime.

Lesson 87

International Formatting (Mexico)

GOALS
- Improve speed and accuracy
- Refine language arts skills in the use of abbreviations
- Format international documents

A. Type 2 times.

A. WARMUP

```
1        On 4/25/00 Jamie exercised by "power walking" on the      11
2   athletic tracks. She also zipped along the city's favorite    23
3   route (Polk Street & Bell Avenue). It was a quick walk!       34
    |  1  |  2  |  3  |  4  |  5  |  6  |  7  |  8  |  9  |  10  |  11  |  12
```

SKILLBUILDING

B. PROGRESSIVE PRACTICE: ALPHABET

If you are not using the GDP software, turn to page SB-7 and follow the directions for this activity.

C. Type the paragraph 2 times, concentrating on each letter typed.

C. TECHNIQUE PRACTICE: CONCENTRATION

```
4        El uso de la bicicleta es muy popular en Barranquilla.
5   Cuando el tiempo es bueno a toda la gente joven le gusta ir
6   a pasear en bicicletas. Me gusta ir a montar en bicicleta,
7   especialmente cuando hace sol y el tiempo es agradable.
```

LANGUAGE ARTS

D. Study the rules at the right.

D. ABBREVIATIONS

RULE ▶
abbreviate measure

In technical writing, on forms, and in tables, abbreviate units of measure when they occur frequently. Do not use periods.

    14 oz   5 ft 10 in   50 mph   2 yrs 10 mo

RULE ▶
abbreviate lowercase

In most lowercase abbreviations made up of single initials, use a period after each initial but no internal spaces.

a.m.	p.m.	i.e.	e.g.	e.o.m.
Exceptions:	mph	mpg	wpm	

RULE ▶
abbreviate ≡

In most all-capital abbreviations made up of single initials, do not use periods or internal spaces.

OSHA	PBS	NBEA	WWW	VCR	MBA
Exceptions:	U.S.A.	A.A.	B.S.	Ph.D.	P.O.
	B.C.	A.D.			

Edit the sentences to correct any errors in the use of abbreviations.

8 A mixture of 25 lb of cement and 100 lb of gravel was used.
9 The desk height must be reduced from 2 ft. 6 in. to 2 ft 4 in.
10 The 11 a. m. meeting was changed to 1 p. m. because of a conflict.
11 The eom statement was published over the Internet on the W.W.W.
12 She enlisted in the U.S.M.C. after she received her MBA degree.
13 His Ph. D. dissertation deals with the early history of NATO.

FORMATTING

E. INTERNATIONAL URLs

Uniform Resource Locators (URLs) identify a site on the World Wide Web where specific information can be found. In international URLs, an abbreviation for a country is often included in the URL, as shown below.

Country	Uniform Resource Locator (URL)
Canada	http://www.pearlson.animate.chap2.ca
France	http://www.education.grad.up.fr
Germany	http://www.mercedes.de
Japan	http://www.sushi.co.jp
Mexico	http://www.reloj.baja.mx

F. WORD PROCESSING: INSERT SYMBOL

Special symbols are used frequently in foreign languages to provide readers with a special accent that must be used to pronounce words correctly. Some examples of special accent symbols used in Mexico in the Spanish language are shown below.

Symbol	Spanish Word	English Translation
ñ	Señor, Señorita	Mr., Mrs
í	el río	river
ó	adiós	goodbye

Correspondence 87-79 ▶

Email Message

Send an email message to Medina Noriega (mnoriega@riobravo.net), with a subject as follows: New Manufacturing Plants. Type an appropriate greeting for Mr. Noriega and a closing and signature line for yourself. Type the body as shown below. Proofread your email message for typing, spelling, and formatting errors.

¶ As you know, sales in our international divisions have been accelerating since the advent of our new Jefe automobile. As a result, several new manufacturing plants will open in the next eight years. The first five of these plants will open in France and Germany.

¶ To market our new manufacturing plants and promote the Jefe, our Marketing Division is planning to open new Web sites on the Jefe home page. The following links will be added to advertise our plant expansion:

abbreviate lowercase

Bordeaux, France: http://www.bordeaux.fr.jefe.new.html
Toulouse, France: http://www.toulouse.fr.jefe.new.html
Grenoble, France: http://www.grenoble.fr.jefe.new.html
Hamburg, Germany: http://www.hamburg.de.jefe.new.html
Stuttgart, Germany: http://www.stuttgart.de.jefe.new.html

¶ You will be notified when the Web sites go online. Until then, plan to work with your Marketing Division personnel to implement the marketing plan we discussed at our meeting last month (i.e., the Henderson Proposal). When the sites go online, we hope to maximize our exposure on the WWW. If they are as successful as we believe they will be, our promotional campaign may also be implemented at our plants in Piedras Negras, Morelia, and Cancun.

abbreviate ≡

Business Report
With Four-Column
Table

Type the report on
A4-size paper.

Type the copy at the
right in table format,
inserting the table into
the report.

abbreviate measure

Accent symbol used in
Sian Káan

MEXICO TRAVEL DESTINATIONS
Most Popular Attractions
(Current Date)

INTRODUCTION

¶ In the past decade, Mexico national parks have become popular tourist sites for visitors from the Americas, Europe, and Asia. As a result, an increasing number of requests have been made for travel brochures and maps from our Visitors' Bureau. Therefore, in the next few weeks, we will be publishing several new brochures and maps to accommodate these requests.

¶ Brochures. The brochures will include a detailed description of the site, providing information on beginning and ending visitation schedules, highlights of the site, and popular photography locations. Brochures will be prepared on the following sites and locations:

Area	Site	Location	Top 10 Ranking
Northern	Cumbres de Majalca	Chihuahua	2 yrs
Northern	Cumbres de Monterrey	Nuevo Leon	2 yrs
Northern	Sierra del Pinacate	Mexicali	4 yrs
Middle	El Rosario	Mexico City	1 yr
Middle	El Tepozteco	Morelos	10 yrs
Middle	Iztaccihuatl y Popocatepetl	Morelos	10 yrs
Middle	Malinche	Puebla	3 yrs
Southern	Bonampak/Yaxchilan Monuments	Chiapas	7 yrs
Southern	Chichen Itza	Merida	15 yrs
Southern	Dzibilchaltun	Yucatan	5 yrs
Southern	Sian Káan Biosphere Reserve	Quintana Roo	4 yrs

(Continued on next page)

¶ Maps. Maps will be drawn for the locations above, with detailed inserts to guide visitors from the nearest cities to the tourist attractions. Walking trails and resting stations will be highlighted, and approximate walking times will be noted on the maps. Individual maps will be prepared for each area (northern, middle, and southern) as well as a comprehensive map for all three visitor areas.

¶ We will also be placing materials on our National Parks Web site (http://www.tourism.dfmexcity.mx.parks.html). Please send any advertising pieces you wish to promote to Señor Garcia, Public Relations Director. These sites will be operational within the next 30 days.

Accent symbol used in Señor

The keyboard connects us to the world.

International Formatting (France)

GOALS

- Type at least 45wpm/5′/5e
- Format international documents

A. Type 2 times.

A. WARMUP

1   On May 4, 2000, Kaye gave a dazzling talk on graphics; 11
2 it was quite fantastic! She is also writing an excellent   22
3 book about graphics with text. It might sell for $23.85.   33

   | 1 | 2 | 3 | 4 | 5 | 6 | 7 | 8 | 9 | 10 | 11 | 12

SKILLBUILDING

B. DIAGNOSTIC PRACTICE: ALPHABET

If you are not using the GDP software, turn to page SB-2 and follow the directions for this activity.

C. PACED PRACTICE

If you are not using the GDP software, turn to page SB-14 and follow the directions for this activity.

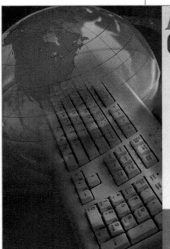

Keyboarding CONNECTION Protecting Your Files With Anti-Virus Programs

A virus is a computer program intentionally written to contaminate your computer system. Viruses can enter your system from files downloaded from the Internet or can be acquired from infected files sent to you via email, diskette, or other storage media.

You can protect your computer by purchasing an anti-virus program. These programs periodically scan your computer system for viruses. They also scan files that you bring into the system. Some anti-virus manufacturers allow you to download a trial copy of their software from their Web site. You can try the software for a few days before you decide if you want to buy it.

If you want to visit anti-virus sites to find out what they have to offer, search for ***anti-virus software*** on your search engine.

YOUR TURN From your browser, access *www.thefreesite.com/antivirus.htm* for a listing and overview of some free anti-virus software.

D. Take two 5-minute timings. Review your speed and errors.

Goal: At least 45wm/5'5e

D. 5-MINUTE TIMING

4	Technology surrounds us. It is everywhere you look.	10
5	People use their cell phones to have conversations just	21
6	about anywhere. They carry their pagers so that they can	32
7	be reached at any time. Everyone, from busy executives to	44
8	the college students, has become accustomed to always being	56
9	available, at all hours, day or night.	64
10	In recent years, busy travelers have become used to	74
11	using their laptops everywhere. They use computer ports	86
12	in airports, hotel rooms and lobbies, and even taxis. The	98
13	technology allows the busy traveler to have access to the	110
14	Internet while on the go. Using the laptop, the user can	121
15	access the latest weather report, sports scores, and news,	133
16	almost as soon as they happen.	139
17	Using the latest technology, you can keep up with	149
18	your work and maintain contact with your office. You can	160
19	even access your bank accounts and pay bills while waiting	172
20	in traffic. Also, if you are in an unfamiliar area, you can	184
21	locate a restaurant or call for directions. The technology	196
22	options that have become available to almost everyone are	208
23	quite amazing. We are living in a small world that seems	219
24	to be getting smaller each day.	225

| 1 | 2 | 3 | 4 | 5 | 6 | 7 | 8 | 9 | 10 | 11 | 12 |

FORMATTING

E. DAY/MONTH/YEAR FORMAT

In international correspondence, the date line is often formatted as follows: day, month, year. Thus, the first line of a letter to a foreign recipient may appear as shown in the illustration.

12 April 20--

Mr. James E. Burillon
Sales Director
Avian Industries
14, Rue Royale
75008 Paris
FRANCE

Dear Mr. Burillon:

F. DOT-STYLE TELEPHONE NUMBERS

Telephone numbers in the United States use a format that places hyphens after the area code and after the 3-digit prefix for a 7-digit telephone number. Another format for displaying telephone numbers used in many countries is to replace the hyphens with periods. Examples of this format are as follows: 701.555.4832 or 818.555.3424.

G. INTERNATIONAL TELEPHONE ACCESS CODES

International phone numbers require a series of special access codes. Each country is assigned a unique access code. Some of the more common access codes are displayed in the table below. Note that the United States and Canada share the same access code: 1. (**Note:** An access code of "011" is used for calls made from the United States or Canada to other countries. For calls made from other countries to the United States or Canada, the access code is "1.")

When listing a United States telephone number in a document going to an international address, precede the access code with a plus sign. For example, if a telephone number in Boston was listed in a document being sent to a foreign address, it would appear as follows: "+1.617.555.8923."

Country	Access Code	Country	Access Code
Canada	1	Taiwan	886
Japan	81	Germany	49
Denmark	45	United Kingdom	44
Mexico	52	Italy	39
France	33	United States	1

DOCUMENT PROCESSING

Correspondence 88-80

Business Letter in Block Style With Enclosure and Copy Notations

Type the letter on A4-size paper.

Current Date (use day/month/year format) | Mr. Henry R. Defforey | Human Resources Director | Gemey Techtronics | Avenue Raymond Poincore | 75116 Paris | FRANCE | Dear Mr. Defforey:

¶ I am pleased that we will be involved in an employee exchange this coming year. As we discussed earlier, the exchange of our 26 production employees will benefit both companies.

¶ We plan to rotate all 26 employees through the various units of our production process, starting from the raw materials division right on through our shipping operations. I have enclosed a projected rotation plan for you to review. Included in the plan are all the employee rotations we discussed at our last meeting. Please review the plan and email me if there are any changes you wish to make. You can email me at ssouthern@techgroup.com, or, if you wish to speak to me directly, you can call +1.214.555.9090.

(Continued on next page)

¶ I look forward to working with you this coming year. As soon as we have agreed on the rotation plan, we can make copies for all affected employees. I know that everyone from our end is eagerly anticipating this collaborative effort.

Sincerely, | Sheila T. Southern | Human Resources Manager | urs | Enclosure | c: T. Lambeer, S. Gouet

Table 88-45 ▶

Three-Column Boxed Table

Type the table on A4-size paper.

Apply 20% shading to the column headings.

ROTATION PLAN		
Tech-Group Inc. and Gemey Techtronics		
Department	**Rotation Start Date**	**Rotation End Date**
Raw Materials	3 July 20--	August 11 20--
Board assembly	14 August 20--	22 September 20--
Drive and Assembly	25 Sept. 20--	3 November 20--
Power Unit	6 November 20--	15 December 20--
Testing & Evaluation	18 December 20--	2 Feburary 20--
Shiping	5 Feb. 20--	16 March 20--

Correspondence 88-81 ▶

Email Message

Send an email message to Henry R. Defforey (hdefforey@techtron.com) with a subject as follows: Rotation Plan Revision. Type an appropriate greeting for Mr. Defforey and a closing and signature line for yourself. Type the body as shown below. Proofread your email message for typing, spelling, and formatting errors.

¶ I am sending you this email to alert you to a change we must make in the rotation plan I sent you last week. We will have to refit several of our board assembly production unit relay systems during the week of 14 August through 18 August. To avoid significantly altering the remaining rotation plan, I would like to suggest that we use one-half of the drive assembly rotation period to complete the board assembly rotation. ¶ Please respond to my email as soon as possible so that we can make whatever changes are necessary.

International Formatting (Germany)

GOALS

- Improve speed and accuracy
- Refine language arts skills in spelling
- Format international documents

A. Type 2 times.

A. WARMUP

```
1      Did Jacqueline get 62% of the vote in the election on    11
2  9/04/00? I think Buzz* (*Kelly) voted for her at 7:35 p.m.   23
3  that evening, and she was really excited when Jackie won.    34
   |  1  |  2  |  3  |  4  |  5  |  6  |  7  |  8  |  9  |  10  |  11  |  12
```

SKILLBUILDING

B. MAP

Follow the GDP software directions for this exercise in improving keystroking accuracy.

C. Take a 1-minute timing on the first paragraph to establish your base speed. Then take four 1-minute timings on the remaining paragraphs. As soon as you equal or exceed your base speed on one paragraph, advance to the next, more difficult paragraph.

C. SUSTAINED PRACTICE: PUNCTUATION

```
4       One of the strengths you must have if you are going to   11
5  be a success in business is good writing skills. You must    23
6  practice your writing skills every day if you want them to   35
7  improve. Perfection of writing skills takes much practice.   47

8       You must always strive to write clearly, concisely,     11
9  and accurately. Remember always that your writing can be     22
10 examined by more people than just the one to whom you have   34
11 written. It's often looked at by other readers as well.      45

12      You want to be sure that your letters always convey a    11
13 positive, helpful attitude. Don't forget, you represent      23
14 more than yourself when you write--you also represent your   35
15 company! This is an important, useful rule to remember.      46

16      Try to stay away from negative words like "can't" or    11
17 "won't." Readers also do not like phrases such as "because   23
18 of company policies" or "due to unforeseen circumstances."   35
19 Using these words and phrases never helps resolve problems.  47
   |  1  |  2  |  3  |  4  |  5  |  6  |  7  |  8  |  9  |  10  |  11  |  12
```

D. Type this list of frequently misspelled words, paying special attention to any spelling problems in each word.

D. SPELLING

20 means valve entry patient officer similar expenses industry
21 quality judgment academic provisions previously cooperation
22 foreign closing indicated secretary especially construction
23 monitoring assessment continuing registration manufacturing
24 products policies capacity presently accordance implemented

Edit the sentences to correct any misspellings.

25 Every company offiser will have simaler expenses next week.
26 In my judgement, we must insist on co-operation from all.
27 My secretery said that she traveled to a foriegn country.
28 We must continue monitering the progress for assesment.
29 The new policeis must be implimented for all products.

FORMATTING

E. METRIC UNITS OF MEASUREMENT

The metric unit of measurement was devised in 1670. It is based on units of 10 and is used by almost every nation in the world. The five common measurements in the metric system are length, area, volume, weight, and temperature. The table below shows a comparison of the basic units of measure used in the metric and U.S. systems.

Metric Unit	Metric Units of Measure	U.S. Units of Measure
Length	millimeter, centimeter, meter, kilometer	inch, foot, yard, mile
Area	square centimeter, square meter, hectare	square inch, square foot, square yard
Volume	cubic centimeter, cubic decimeter, cubic meter, liter, hectoliter	cubic inch, cubic foot, fluid ounce, pint, gallon
Weight	milligram, gram, kilogram, tonne	ounce, pound, ton
Temperature	Celsius	Fahrenheit

Correspondence 89-82 ▶

Email Message

Send an email message to Klaus Neuberger (kneuberger@deutschecomp. de.com) with a subject as follows: Metric Conversions. Type an appropriate greeting for Mr. Neuberger and a closing and signature line for yourself. Type the body as shown below. Proofread your email message for typing, spelling, and formatting errors.

¶ The total conversion of our processing plant in Wiesbaden to a metric system is now only six months away. To prepare our employees who will be transferring to the Wiesbaden plant, I would like you to send me the brief summary report we completed for plant supervisors when we were planning for the conversion last year.

¶ The metric system will be quite foreign to many of our younger employees who were not involved in the planning stages of the conversion, and the summary report will give them a head start on metrication before their transfer.

¶ Call me on Thursday morning (+1.702.555.1839) so that we can discuss the Frankfurt plant closing. As you recall, the operations at that plant will be transferred to Wiesbaden in July; we need to monitor that operation closely until the transfer has been completed.

Correspondence 89-83 ▶

Business Letter in Block Style

Type the letter on A4-size paper.

Current Date (use day/month/year format) | Ms. Geraldine Sommer | Marketing Department | Deutsch Lebensmittel, Inc. | Mannesmannufer 2 | D-40213 Duesseldorf | GERMANY | Dear Ms. Sommer:

¶ Student's first and last name has asked that I send a copy of the summary report on metrics that we completed last year. As you recall, I sent you that report previously to share with the new employees at our Stuttgart plant.

¶ If you wish, you can email me the disk copy that accompanied the report, and my secretary will run a hard copy from my office.

Sincerely, | Klaus Neuberger | Human Resources Manager | trl

Report ▶
89-64

Multipage Report In
Business Style

Type the report on
A4 size paper.

Insert "bd05089. wmf"
from the Academic
category in the
Microsoft Clip Art
Gallery or insert a similar
piece of clip art.
Change the clip art
height to 1.16 inches;
place it at the left
margin at the beginning
of the first paragraph.

METRIC SUMMARY REPORT
July 30, 20--

¶ The metric system was devised by Gabriel Mouton, a French man, in 1607. It is a system based on units of 10 and is considered by some *many* to be more accurate and easier to use than the imperial system of measure used in the United States. When it was first defined, a meter was considered to be 1/10,000,000 of the distance from the Pole to the Equator.

¶ The most common metric measurements are for length, *area,* volume, weight, and temperature. For our wiesbaden plant, the most crucial measurements for new employees from the U.S. will be volume and weight. Comparisons between these two measures appear in Table 1 (comparing volume measures) and Table 2 (comparing weight measures).

Table 1. METRIC/U.S. COMPARISONS FOR VOLUME

Metric Unit	Metric Measure	U.S. Measure
Cubic Centimeter	1 cubic centimeter	0.061 cubic inches
Cubic Decimeter	1,000 cubic centimeters	0.053 cubic ft
Cubic Meter	1,000 cubic decimeters	1.31 cubic yards
Liter	1 cubic decimeter	1.76 pints
Hectoliter	100 Liters	21.99 gal *gallons*

Table 2. METRIC/U.S. COMPARISONS FOR WEIGHT

Metric Unit	Metric Measure	U.S. Measure
Miligram	1 milligram	0.015 grain
gram	1,000 milligrams	0.035 ounces
Kilogram	1,000 grams	2.205 lbs *pounds*
Tonne	1,000 kilograms	0.984 tons

(Continued on next page)

¶ Employees will quickly adapt to the metric system when they use it daily. *on a basis* Although we encourage all employees to make calculations in the metric system, it may be helpful for the first few days if they are aware of the conversion factors involved in comparing the ② measurement systems. The following conversions may therefore be helpful to them:

- Multiply inches by 2.45 to get centimeters
- Multiply feet by 0.305 to get meters
- Multiply miles by 1.6 to get kilometers
- Divide lbs. by 2.2 to get kilograms
- Multiply ounces by 28 to get grams
- Multiply fluid ounces by 30 to get milliliters
- Multiply gallons by 3.8 to get liters

¶ More detailed conversions and metric information can be obtained by visiting the web site for the U.S. metric association at http://lamar.colostate.edu/~hillger/.

The keyboard is an integral component in the growth of our global economy.

International Formatting (Japan)

GOALS
- Type at least 45wpm/5'/5e
- Format international documents

A. Type 2 times.

A. WARMUP

```
1       James used a dozen of Harold's power trucks to quickly   11
2   move over 17 large boxes on 11/30/00. I think these trucks   23
3   (just the diesels) may need maintenance work on 3/24/01.     34
    |  1  |  2  |  3  |  4  |  5  |  6  |  7  |  8  |  9  |  10  |  11  |  12
```

SKILLBUILDING

PRETEST ➞ PRACTICE ➞ POSTTEST

B. PRETEST: Close Reaches

PRETEST
Take a 1-minute timing. Review your speed and errors.

```
4       Uncle Bert chased a fast, weary fox into the weeds of   11
5   the swamp. He hoped to grab the old gray fox under the       22
6   bridge with a rope as he darted swiftly from his cold lair.  34
    |  1  |  2  |  3  |  4  |  5  |  6  |  7  |  8  |  9  |  10  |  11  |  12
```

C. PRACTICE: Adjacent Keys

PRACTICE
Speed Emphasis:
If you made no more than 1 error on the Pretest, type each *individual* line 2 times.
Accuracy Emphasis:
If you made 2 or more errors, type each *group* of lines (as though it were a paragraph) 2 times.

```
7   as asked asset based basis class least visas ease fast mass
8   op opera roped topaz adopt scope troop shops open hope drop
9   we weary wedge weigh towed jewel fewer dwell wear weed week
```

D. PRACTICE: Consecutive Fingers

```
10  sw swamp swift swoop sweet swear swank swirl swap sway swim
11  un uncle under undue unfit bunch begun funny unit aunt junk
12  gr grade grace angry agree group gross gripe grow gram grab
```

POSTTEST
Repeat the Pretest timing and compare performance.

E. POSTTEST: Close Reaches

F. Take two 5-minute timings. Review your speed and errors.

Goal: At least 45wpm/5′/5e

F. 5-MINUTE TIMING

```
13    Anyone with a supervisory position will occasionally     11
14  have to deal with a problem employee. Learning to deal      22
15  positively with this type of worker can benefit everyone    33
16  within the organization. As a manager, you should address   45
17  the problem as soon as you become aware of it. However, if  57
18  you are extremely upset, it may be best to wait until you   69
19  calm down and have time to plan what you will say. Avoid    80
20  using an approach based on reaction, which can often be     91
21  ineffective and too emotional. Speaking too quickly and     102
22  without thinking may bring unwanted consequences.           112
23    When you talk to the employee, be sure you get to        122
24  the real issue. Present the facts and tell the employee     133
25  exactly what he or she is doing wrong on the job. Do not    144
26  express your own personal opinion. You need to present a    155
27  positive and mutually fair solution to the employee in      166
28  order to solve the problem. At the end of the meeting, ask  178
29  the employee to explain the problem to you and the changes  190
30  that are necessary. By following this procedure, you know   202
31  that everyone understands what is happening. Set up a time  214
32  to meet in a few weeks to follow up with the employee.      225
```
| 1 | 2 | 3 | 4 | 5 | 6 | 7 | 8 | 9 | 10 | 11 | 12

DOCUMENT PROCESSING

Correspondence 90-84 ▶

Business Letter in Block Style With Copy Notations

Type the letter on A4-size paper.

Current Date (use day/month/year format) | Mr. Kouji Tachikawa | Chief Technology Officer | Tadashi Corporation | 7-1, Shiba 5-Chome | Minato-Ku, Tokyo 108-8001 | JAPAN | Dear Mr. Tachikawa:
¶ It is a distinct pleasure to learn that we will be working together to develop the training manual to be used in our joint venture. Your company has long been known for its excellence in developing instructional materials, and Carroll Technology is pleased to play a collaborative part with you in this venture.
¶ Our development teams have been working with their counterparts in Tadashi over the past several weeks. Your suggestion that we pool our personnel resources was indeed an excellent one that will give us a head start in the development stage.

(Continued on next page)

¶ If I may make one suggestion, I believe it would be helpful for the personnel in our mailing and shipping department to have a better understanding of the labeling procedures used in Japan for distributing the training manuals. Could you please send me some information that might be helpful in this regard? I will do the same for you by sending you the labeling procedures used at Carroll Technology.

Sincerely | Sharla D. Enterline | Project Coordinator | urs | c: Mr. R. Akiyama, Mr. S. Hiroshi, Mr. C. Brandenburger

---

Correspondence 90-85 ▶

Email Message

Send an email message to Sharla Enterline (senterline@carroll.com) with a subject as follows: Labeling Procedures. Type a greeting for Ms. Enterline and a closing and signature line for yourself. Type the following copy as the body.

¶ It is my pleasure to inform you that Mr. S. Hiroshi will be forwarding to your office a summary of the package labeling procedures used at Tadashi Inc. Employees from many different foreign countries have used these procedures to help them understand mailing requirements in Japan.

¶ After receiving the procedures, feel free to email Mr. Hiroshi with any questions you may have. You can reach him at shiroshi@tadashi.jp.com. If you prefer, you can call Mr. Hiroshi at +81.3.3454313.

Correspondence 90-86 ▶

Business Letter in Block Style With Illustration and Copy Notation

Type the letter on A4-size paper.

Military dates should have a 0 inserted before the date if it is the 1st through the 9th of the month.

Current Date (use day/month/year format) | Ms. Sharla D. Enterline | Project Coordinator | Carroll Technology | 8723 Hill Avenue | Bowling Green, KY 42823 | Dear Ms. Enterline:

¶ The following information is being sent to asist you with Japanese mailing rules. As a service to your employees, I am providing the following summary of these rules.

¶ A Japanese mailing address consists mainly of the name, street address, town, city, prefecture, postal, code and country. The illustration below shows an example of an envelope addressed to a citizen of Japan.

(Continued on next page)

Address Items	Address Example
Name	Mr. Yoshifumi Uda
~~St.~~ *Street* Address, Town (1st) address)	1-17, Akai-cho
City, Prefecture (2d) address), *Postal* ^Code	Minato-Ku, Tokyo 108-8005
JAPAN	JAPAN

¶Please ~~E~~mail me if you have questions about mailing rules in japan. You can reach me at shiroshi@tadashi.jp.com.

Very sincerely, | S. Hiroshi | Shipping (Dept.) | urs | c: K. Tachikawa

Table 90-46 ▶

Two-Column Boxed Table

JAPANESE POSTAL CODE REGULATIONS Prepared by Student Name	
Postal Code Rule	**Example**
The first line of a Japanese address can be used for the addressee's name.	Mr. Takashi Imaizumi Mr. Kazuki Terada
The second line may include a street name or building number.	Kifune 3-402 (this represents building 402 on the 3rd street within the Kifune neighborhood)
The third line represents the city and prefecture (an area within the city).	Meito-ku, Nagoya 112-3844 Minato-Ku, Tokyo 105-8436
The fourth line can be used to identify the country to where the document or package is being mailed.	JAPAN

Correspondence 90-87 ▶

Business Letter in Block Style With Enclosure Notation

Type the letter on A4-size paper.

☑ **Progress Check Proofreading Check**

Documents designated as Proofreading Checks serve as a check of your proofreading skill. Your goal is to have zero typographical errors when the GDP software first scores the document.

Current Date | Mr. Fujio Okuda | Sales Manager | Naruto Publishing Company | 7-35, Kitashinagawa 6-Chome | Shinagawa-Ku, Tokyo 141-0001 | JAPAN | Dear Mr. Okuda:

¶ We are pleased to have this opportunity for two of our computer textbooks to be translated into Japanese and for you to do the same for two of your textbooks in the computer area. As we agreed at our meeting in Takasaki last week, sales for both of our book companies should improve substantially with these translations.

¶ I am enclosing with this letter the first three units of *Computer Essentials* so that your editors can begin the translation process. We will do the same here at Globe Publishing when your first three units from *Global Computers* arrive in Chicago.

¶ Should your editorial staff have any questions during the translation, they can email me at shaddock@globe.com or telephone me at +1.402.555.3848.

Sincerely, | Shannon Haddock | Editorial Director | urs | Enclosure

Medical Office Applications

LESSON 91
Medical Office Applications

LESSON 92
Medical Office Applications

LESSON 93
Medical Office Applications

LESSON 94
Medical Office Applications

LESSON 95
Medical Office Applications

MEMO TO: Dr. Charlene T. Gutierrez
Director of Plastic Surgery

FROM: Dr. Alec Pera

DATE: Current Date

SUBJECT: Mr. Owensby's Surgery

On February 28 I visited with Mr. Bryan Owensby to discuss his options relative to the muscle transfer we plan to complete following radiation treatment. Mr. Owensby is a 53-year-old male who has had multiple lesions recently excised.

Mr. Owensby is aware that our goal is to provide healthy tissue that could tolerate the radiation treatment he would need to destroy the malignant cells on his upper thigh. At this time, we plan to complete a skin graft from the contralateral thigh to provide the healthy tissue for radiation treatment. I believe this will give Mr. Owensby the best opportunity for early healing.

A free tissue transfer was also discussed, and this may be an option if the contralateral graft is unsuccessful. Mr. Owensby understands the risks and complications of either method. Scheduling is pending jointly through our offices. Thank you for this opportunity to participate in Mr. Owensby's care.

urs
c: Dr. Taiwo Owakoniro, Dr. Lewis Sethna, Dr. Monica Stevens

INSTRUCTIONS FOR RECOVERING FROM KNEE SURGERY
Dr. Alec Pera, M.D.

Current Date

Specific procedures should be followed by patients who are recovering from knee surgery. Depending on the particular surgery that was performed, post-operative needs of patients with knee replacements vary greatly. Healthy, young individuals may require only a few therapy sessions to recover from their surgery completely. Older individuals with no family or friends to help them at home may need special assistance or equipment to aid their mobility. Some patients may benefit from a short stay in a rehabilitation facility. To enhance the rate of recovery, patients should identify and address any special needs that may be required before their operation.

To promote full recovery, Pacific Medical has developed a coordinated pathway of physical and occupational therapy for patients' use. Patient Rehabilitation and Therapy Service (PRTS) and Pacific Medical have collaborated ... quence of procedures to follow.

Prior to your surgery, we recommend that you:

1. Determine any special equipment that will be re...

2. Learn correct techniques for performing day-to-... out of bed, driving your automobile, taking show... up and down stairs.

3. Learn what exercises will help facilitate your rec...

After surgery, patients must participate in physical t...

• Extend their knee straight or bend it past 90 degr...

• Place weight on their knee to ensure that they ha... their weight.

• Use the knee without discomfort (this may take ...

DESCRIPTIONS AND TREATMENTS OF ADULT BRAIN TUMORS	
Tony Simta	
Type of Tumor	**Description/Treatment**
Astrocytomas	Tumors that start in brain cells. Treatment includes surgery, chemotherapy, and radiation.
Brain Stem Gliomas	Tumors located in the bottom part of the brain that connects to the spinal cord. Treatment includes radiation and biological therapy.
Cerebellar Astrocytomas	Tumors that occur in the area of the brain called the cerebellum. Treatment is similar to that for Astrocytomas.
Craniopharyngiomas	Tumors that occur near the pituitary gland. Treatment includes surgery and radiation.
Oligodendroglial	Tumors that begin in brain cells that provide support and nourishment for the cells that transmit nerve impulses. Treatment includes surgery, chemotherapy, and radiation.

Medical Office Applications

GOALS

- Improve speed and accuracy
- Refine language arts skills in punctuation
- Format medical office documents

A. Type 2 times.

A. WARMUP

```
 1       The taxes* were quickly adjusted upward by 20 percent    11
 2  because of the improvements to her house (built in 1901).     23
 3  A proposed law might not penalize good homeowners like her.   35
    |  1  |  2  |  3  |  4  |  5  |  6  |  7  |  8  |  9  | 10  | 11  | 12
```

SKILLBUILDING

B. MAP

Follow the GDP software directions for this exercise in improving keystroking accuracy.

C. Take a 1-minute timing on the first paragraph to establish your base speed. Then take four 1-minute timings on the remaining paragraphs. As soon as you equal or exceed your base speed on one paragraph, advance to the next, more difficult paragraph.

C. SUSTAINED PRACTICE: ALTERNATE-HAND WORDS

```
 4       A downturn in world fuel prices signals a lower profit   11
 5  for giant oil firms. In fact, most downtown firms might       22
 6  see the usual sign of tight credit and other problems. The    34
 7  city must get down to business and make plans in the fall.    46

 8       The hungry turkeys ate eight bushels of corn that were   11
 9  given to them by our next door neighbors. They also drank     22
10  the eight bowls of water that were left in the yard. All in   34
11  all, the birds caused quite a bit of chaos early that day.    46

12       A debate on what to do about that extra acreage in the   11
13  desert dragged on for four hours. One problem is what the     23
14  effect may be of moving the ancient ruins to a much safer     35
15  place. City officials must always protect our environment.    47

16       Molly was dressed in a plain pink dress at the annual    11
17  meeting that was taking place at the hotel in Tempe later     23
18  that last week in September. The agenda included four very    35
19  controversial topics that have often generated much debate.   47
    |  1  |  2  |  3  |  4  |  5  |  6  |  7  |  8  |  9  | 10  | 11  | 12
```

D. Study the rules at the right.

D. PUNCTUATION

RULE ▶
: explanatory material

Use a colon to introduce explanatory material that follows an independent clause.

The computer satisfies three criteria: speed, cost, and power.

But: The computer satisfies the three criteria of speed, cost, and power.

Remember this: only one coupon is allowed per customer.

Note: An independent clause can stand alone as a complete sentence. Do not capitalize the word following the colon.

RULE ▶
. polite request

Use a period to end a sentence that is a polite request.

Will you please call me if I can be of further assistance.

Note: Consider a sentence a polite request if you expect the reader to respond by doing as you ask rather than by giving a yes-or-no answer.

Edit the sentences to correct any errors in punctuation.

20 We need the following items, pens, pencils, and paper.
21 May I suggest that you send the report by Tuesday?
22 These are some of your colleagues: Bill, Mary, and Ann.
23 Would you please pay my bills when I am on vacation?
24 Our flag is these three colors; red, white, and blue.
25 Would you please start my car to warm it up for me.

DOCUMENT PROCESSING

Situation: You work for a temporary agency in Eugene, Oregon. This week you are employed by McKenzie-Willamette Hospital, 1460 G Street, Springfield, OR 97477. For the next five days you will be working in various units within the hospital: Admissions Office, Billing Office, Dermatology, Oncology, and Surgery.

Your administrative assignments require you to format various documents such as letters, memos, medical reports, surgery reports, visitation reports, doctors' reports, etc.

You will spend today in the Admissions Office at McKenzie-Willamette. Complete the jobs that have been assigned to you in the order in which they appear below.

Proofread your work carefully and check for spelling, punctuation, grammar, and formatting errors so that your documents are mailable and free of errors.

**Correspondence ▶
91-88**

Block Style Letter
With Enclosure
Notation

: explanatory material

Current Date | Ms. Nancy J. Dodson | 3727 Harris Street | Eugene, OR 97405-4246 | Dear Ms. Dodson:

¶ Thank you for contacting us and considering us as your primary care provider. We are confident that you will be pleased with our services and our patient care, and we look forward to many years of serving your health needs.

¶ Now that you have made your final selection, we would like you to complete the enclosed Patient Information Form and send it back to us at your earliest convenience. As you can see, the form asks mostly for personal information so that we can contact you or your employer if necessary. In addition, the form requests the following information: the name, address, and telephone number of your insurance company, and your insurance policy number.

(Continued on next page)

¶ Again, welcome to McKenzie-Willamette! If there is any additional information we can provide about our services, do not hesitate to call us at 555-2300 or email us at mckenzie@pacific.net.
Sincerely, | Lucille R. Medford | Office Manager | urs | Enclosure

Table 91-47 ▶

Three-Column Table With Shaded Cells

Remember to hold down the CTRL key as you press TAB to position the words (Last), (First), and (Initial) correctly in the table.

Create a patient information form, using the illustration below and these guidelines:

1. Create a table with 3 columns and 13 rows.
2. Merge cells in selected rows to provide room for each individual entry.
3. Insert 1 blank line above and below the centered section headings.
4. Merge three cells into two cells in Rows 2, 5, 8, and 13.
5. Use the ENTER key to increase the depth of each row.
6. Use default Tab settings to type the "Last/First/Initial" entries in Row 1.
7. Use Arial, 12 pt. for the entire table.
8. Use 10% shading for the centered section heading cells.

Patient Information		
Name: (Last) (First) (Initial)		Birth Date:
Address:		
City:	State:	ZIP:
Phone:	Social Security Number:	
Employer Information		
Employer:		
Address:		Phone:
City:	State:	ZIP:
Insurance Information		
Name of Company:		
Address:		
Phone:	Policy Number:	

: explanatory material

. polite request

MEMO TO: *Dr. Abraham Kramer*
FROM: *Paula Campbell*
DATE: *Current Date*
SUBJECT: *Radiology Lab Closing*

¶ *Next week the Radiology Lab in Building D will be closed for repairs. I realize that this is the week you were going to take a group of interns from McKenzie-Willamette to see our new equipment.*

¶ *I have arranged to have the Radiology Lab in Building C open for you to use so that you do not have to postpone the meeting with the interns. I am sending over a passkey for the lab with security. The passkey will open three doors: main entry, hall entry, lab door.*

¶ *Would you please give me a call on Ext. 75 if this lab substitution is not satisfactory with you.*

urs

c: Dr. Arnold, Dr. Kazinofski

Laptop computers are becoming more widely used in the office setting because of the flexibility they offer to employees for working at home and traveling on business.

Medical Office Applications

GOALS
- Type at least 46wpm/5′/5e
- Format medical office documents

A. Type 2 times.

A. WARMUP

```
 1        Missy examined these items: the #4261 oil painting, a      11
 2  Bowes & Elkjer porcelain vase, and the 86-piece collection       23
 3  of glazed antique pitchers. There were 337 people present.       35
    |  1  |  2  |  3  |  4  |  5  |  6  |  7  |  8  |  9  |  10  |  11  |  12
```

SKILLBUILDING

B. Take three 12-second timings on each line. The scale below the last line shows your wpm speed for a 12-second timing.

B. 12-SECOND SPEED SPRINTS

```
 4  Their home is on a lake that is right south of the prairie.
 5  They have a boat and motor and spend a lot of time fishing.
 6  Kay caught so many fish that she gave some to the old lady.
 7  She was so pleased that a young girl would do this for her.
    I I I I 5 I I I I 10 I I I I 15 I I I I 20 I I I I 25 I I I I 30 I I I I 35 I I I I 40 I I I I 45 I I I I 50 I I I I 55 I I I I 60
```

C. PROGRESSIVE PRACTICE: ALPHABET

If you are not using the GDP software, turn to page SB-7 and follow the directions for this activity.

STRATEGIES FOR Career Success

Business Communication

There are five components to the communication process, whether written or oral.

The **sender** is the person who initiates the communication process. The **message** is the information that needs to be communicated (e.g., There will be a meeting at…). The **channel** is the method for transmitting the message (e.g., email, letter, memo, orally). The **audience** is the person(s) who receives the message. **Feedback** is the response given to the sender by the audience that enables the sender to determine if the message was received as intended.

The most effective communication within companies must flow, not only downward but also upward.

YOUR TURN

Suppose you send a memo to 20 people in your department announcing a meeting to discuss your company's new policy on flex time. Who is the sender? What is the message? What is the channel you use to transmit the message? Who is the audience? What is the ultimate feedback?

D. Take two 5-minute timings. Review your speed and errors.

Goal: At least 46wpm/5'/5e

D. 5-MINUTE TIMING

8   The first impression you make on a job interview will   11

9 be a lasting one, and you will want it to be favorable. A   23

10 safe choice is to dress conservatively. If you have time,   35

11 find out what people who are currently employed at this   46

12 company wear to work. You can acquire this information by   58

13 simply calling the human resources office. Or, you could   69

14 observe what the current employees are wearing when you   80

15 pick up a job application from the company.   89

16   As you plan the details of your appearance before   99

17 your job interview, be cognizant of all the details. You   110

18 will want to present a neat and clean appearance. Your   121

19 clothing should be clean and neatly pressed. Your hair and   133

20 your nails should be neatly groomed, and your shoes should   145

21 be clean and polished. You should use only a small amount   157

22 of perfume or cologne and wear only basic jewelry. Plan to   169

23 arrive for the appointment in time to make a final check   180

24 of your appearance before your interview.   188

25   Your appearance may not be the sole factor that will   199

26 secure the job, but it will help you make a positive first   211

27 impression. Remember to dress for the position you would   222

28 like rather than the position you have.   230

| 1 | 2 | 3 | 4 | 5 | 6 | 7 | 8 | 9 | 10 | 11 | 12 |

DOCUMENT PROCESSING

Report 92-65

Multipage Business Report

This is now Day 2 in your temporary work assignment at McKenzie-Willamette Hospital. Today you are assigned to the Billing Office, where you will complete documents related to the activities in that office. Your first assignment is to prepare a report describing the billing process at McKenzie-Willamette.

MCKENZIE-WILLAMETTE BILLING PROCESS

Student's Name

Current Date

Determining Fees

¶ Fees that a physician charges for services should be fair both to the patients that are under his or her care as well as to the medical profession.

A doctors' fees should be based on the following criteria:

(Continued on next page)

- the amount of time involved in providing ~~the~~ service.
- the level of skill required in providing the service.
- the degree of expertise required to interpret the results of the service provided.

¶ Fees should be identified in a fee schedule that lists procedures performed and the charges assessed for those procedures. The fee schedule should be made available to patients if (it's) requested. If patients inquire ~~as to~~ about the amount of the fee, an estimate should be given to the patient. In all instances, this estimate should be made available to the patient before treatment begins.

RECORDING TRANSACTIONS

¶ A record of all patient visits must be maintained. A charge slip should be used to record all procedures. The charge slip includes information such as a checklist of all procedures; a checklist of all diagnoses; space for additional information; and an area for all previous charges, payments, and balances. As the doctor performs procedures, annotations and changes are made to the charge slip so that it is ~~always~~ kept current. The charge slip should be attached to the patient's chart. When all procedures have been completed, a copy of the charge slip is sent to the patient to indicate the charges incurred during the patient's visit.

MAKING PAYMENT ARRANGEMENTS

¶ A patient's bill can be paid by one of the following methods:
- A patient can pay the bill by cash or check at the conclusion of the visit.
- A patient can pay fixed amounts of the bill at ~~any~~ designated times, weekly or monthly.
- A bill (statement) can be sent to the patient at the conclusion of the visit.
- A bill can be sent to the Health Insurance Carrier.

COLLECTING OVERDUE ACCOUNTS

¶ There are a number of reasons why a patient might not pay a bill. Whatever the reason, however, steps must be taken to collect delinquent accounts. Depending on the number of days the account has been overdue, here are some suggestions for steps that can be taken to collect payment:

(Continued on next page)

1. Attach a reminder when the bill is sent if payment is over ~~thirty~~ ³⁰ days overdue (this is the usual grace period given to accounts).

2. If payment is not received after the reminder is sent, it may be necessary to call the patient to request payment.

3. The next step would be to attach a personal note to a statement that is over due, possibly as long as 60 days.

4. Make one further attempt to telephone the patient for payment.

5. Send a collection letter for payment. The letter should be friendly but firm. Remind the patient that the account is overdue. Offer to assist the patient in making payments on a fixed schedule by establishing a payment plan. Leave your telephone number so the patient can call you if there are any questions that need to be answered regarding the bill.

6. The final alternative in collecting an unpaid bill is to turn over the account to a collection agency or go to court for legal action. This is a costly step for both caregivers and patients, and it should be used only as a last resort.

Table 92-48 ▶

Five-Column Boxed Table

Press the SPACE BAR 10 times between the phone number and the email address.

STATEMENT

WENDY NEWMAN, M.D.
McKenzie-Willamette Hospital
1460 G Street
Springfield, OR 97477
Phone: 541-555-2300   Email: mckenzie@pacific.net

Patient: Marion W. Fleming
Address: 852 East 26th Avenue
City/State/ZIP: Eugene, OR 97405-4104

Date	Description	Charge	Payment	Balance
3/18/01	EKG	185.00	50.00	135.00
3/18/01	Laboratory Work	125.00	25.00	100.00
3/19/01	X-Ray	85.00	0.00	85.00
3/21/01	Cholesterol Check	75.00	25.00	50.00
3/21/01	Laboratory Work	80.00	25.00	55.00
Total Due				**425.00**

Medical Office Applications

GOALS

- Improve speed and accuracy
- Refine language arts skills in composing
- Format medical office documents

A. Type 2 times.

A. WARMUP

```
1        Did you hear the excellent quartet of junior cadets?    11
2   Everybody in that crowd (estimated at over 500) applauded    23
3   "with gusto." The sizable crowd filled the 3/4-acre park.    34
    | 1 | 2 | 3 | 4 | 5 | 6 | 7 | 8 | 9 | 10 | 11 | 12
```

SKILLBUILDING

PRETEST → PRACTICE → POSTTEST

B. PRETEST: Discrimination Practice

PRETEST
Take a 1-minute timing. Review your speed and errors.

```
4        Did the new clerk join the golf team? James indicated    11
5   to me that Patricia invited her prior to last Wednesday. He   23
6   believes she must give you a verbal commitment at once.       34
    | 1 | 2 | 3 | 4 | 5 | 6 | 7 | 8 | 9 | 10 | 11 | 12
```

C. PRACTICE: Left Hand

PRACTICE
Speed Emphasis:
If you made no more than 1 error on the Pretest, type each *individual* line 2 times.
Accuracy Emphasis:
If you made 2 or more errors, type each *group* of lines (as though it were a paragraph) 2 times.

```
7   vbv bevy verb bevel vibes breve viable braves verbal beaver
8   wew went week weans weigh weave wedges thawed weaker beware
9   ded dent need deals moved ceded heeded debate edging define
```

D. PRACTICE: Right Hand

```
10  klk kale look kilts lakes knoll likely kettle kernel lacked
11  uyu buys your gummy dusty young unduly tryout uneasy jaunty
12  oio oils roil toils onion point oriole soiled ration joined
```

E. POSTTEST: Discrimination Practice

POSTTEST
Repeat the Pretest timing and compare performance.

F. PROGRESSIVE PRACTICE: NUMBERS

If you are not using the GDP software, turn to page SB-11 and follow the directions for this activity.

G. COMPOSING AN EMAIL MESSAGE

Compose an email message to your employer (Dr. Natalie Benson—nbenson@docmed.com), informing Dr. Benson of the appointments you have scheduled for Tuesday, April 17, 20--. The first appointment is with James Mitchell, who is coming for his annual physical—make this appointment at 9 a.m. The second appointment is with Karen McDaniels, who is going to have her blood pressure and cholesterol checked. She will see Dr. Benson at 10 a.m. The final appointment is with Mary Ann Bradley, who will see the doctor about flu symptoms. Be sure you use an appropriate signature line in your closing. Print but do not save or send this email message.

DOCUMENT PROCESSING

Correspondence 93-90 ▶

Business Letter in Modified-Block With Enclosure and Postscript Notations

This is the third day of your temporary assignment, and it is the first experience you will gain working in a specialty area—the Dermatology Unit. Dermatology is a branch of science dealing with the skin and its structure, functions, and diseases.

Current Date | Dr. Stanley G. Streisand | 110 Sunset Drive | Professor of Medical Science | Hillside Medical College | Eugene, OR 97403-2120 | Dear Dr. Streisand:

¶ Thank you for the invitation to address the students in your medical science class on the topic of dermatology. As you know, this is my specialty; I am especially interested in the topic of skin rashes and their causes and treatments.

¶ I recognize that your students are beginning medical school students, so my presentation will focus on a very general talk about dermatology. I am enclosing a copy of a paper I presented at the AMA meeting in San Francisco last week that I think would be appropriate for your students. The audience at my AMA presentation was primarily first-year nursing students who were interested in a general background of the more common types of skin rashes.

¶ Please send me a copy of your program with directions on how to reach your classroom on the day of my presentation. I look forward to meeting with your students.

Sincerely yours, | Angela Miller, M.D. | urs | Enclosure | PS: Please let me know how many students you have in your class so I can prepare an adequate number of handouts for them.

COMMON SKIN RASHES
(Their Causes and Cures)
Dr. Stanley G. Streisand

¶ Skin rashes are caused by many different things. They are often recognized by symptoms of reddening, itching, blistering, dryness, or scabbing of the skin. Some of the more common ailments that fall into the category of skin rashes are dermatitis, eczema, and psoriasis. This paper will discuss these three common types of skin rashes.

DERMATITIS

¶ Dermatitis is often referred to as *contact dermatitis*. Some of the more common substances that cause dermatitis are soaps, rubber, jewelry, plants, household and industrial chemicals, cosmetics, and perfumes. Contact dermatitis is further classified as either *allergic contact dermatitis* or *irritant contact dermatitis*.

¶ *Allergic Contact Dermatitis.* This skin rash occurs after contact is made with certain substances, called allergens. The rash occurs as a reaction of the body's immune system to expel the allergen from your skin. Some common allergens are metals in jewelry, cosmetics, and rubber boots.

¶ *Irritant Contact Dermatitis.* This skin rash does not require exposure to an allergen but can develop when you come in contact with certain substances—skin cleansers, detergents, solvents, and oils.

Instead of underlining a word, use italic.

(Continued on next page)

ECZEMA

¶ Eczema, also known as atopic dermatitis, causes the skin to appear red and blotchy all over. The disease occurs at any age but mainly from infancy to childhood. It affects about 3 percent of the United States population. There are two types of eczema–atopic eczema and hand eczema.

¶ Atopic Eczema. This form of eczema is caused by the house dust mite, by heat, by contact with woolen clothing, by detergents, and by stress.

¶ Hand Eczema. Hand eczema is caused by sensitive skin, too much exposure to wet work, detergents, oils, and greases.

PSORIASIS

¶ Psoriasis is a chronic skin disease characterized by inflammation and skin scaling. This disease affects about 5.5 million people in the United States. It occurs in all age groups and affects both men and women. When psoriasis develops, patches of skin redden and become covered with scales. The skin then cracks and may cause severe irritation in places like the elbows, knees, face, scalp, and lower back.

¶ It is believed that psoriasis is a disorder of the immune system in which there are not enough white blood cells to help protect the body against infection and diseases of this type.

Medical Office Applications

GOALS

- Type at least 46wpm/5′/5e
- Format a formal report

A. Type 2 times.

A. WARMUP

```
1        Mr. Baxter will move to 1749 Larkin Street; his old      11
2   home is in Gray's Woods, just east of the corner of Parson    23
3   and 167th Avenue. The house sizes are quite different!        34
    |  1  |  2  |  3  |  4  |  5  |  6  |  7  |  8  |  9  |  10 |  11 |  12
```

SKILLBUILDING

B. DIAGNOSTIC PRACTICE: ALPHABET

If you are not using the GDP software, turn to page SB-2 and follow the directions for this activity.

A career in pharmacy requires fast and accurate keyboarding skills.

C. Take two 5-minute timings. Review your speed and errors.

Goal: At least 46wpm/5'/5e

C. 5-MINUTE TIMING

```
 4       Innovative technology may bring new problems for our      10
 5   homes and businesses. The use and overuse of cell phones      21
 6   is causing many people to look at the etiquette of cell       32
 7   phone usage. Are there times and places where a cell phone    44
 8   should not be used?                                           48
 9       People want to be able to stay in touch, no matter        58
10   where they are or what they are doing. However, in some       69
11   places cell phone usage is inappropriate or simply not        80
12   allowed. For example, you would not want a ringing cell       91
13   phone to disrupt the entire production if you are enjoying   103
14   a concert or play. As a consideration to everyone in the    114
15   audience, the management may make an announcement asking     125
16   audience members to turn off their cell phones or pagers     136
17   before the production begins. Making this request gives      147
18   everyone the opportunity to enjoy the show.                  156
19       Often you see someone driving a car while talking on     167
20   a cell phone. Talking on the phone while you are driving     178
21   is not a good idea. When you are talking on the phone and    190
22   not concentrating on driving, you may cause an accident.     201
23   Driving a vehicle in traffic deserves your full attention.   213
24   Be cognizant of this fact, and do not use your cell phone    225
25   when driving your vehicle.                                   230
     | 1 | 2 | 3 | 4 | 5 | 6 | 7 | 8 | 9 | 10 | 11 | 12
```

DOCUMENT PROCESSING

Table 94-49 ▶

Two-Column Open Table

This is the Day 4 of your temporary assignment. Today you are working in the Oncology Unit. Oncology is a branch of science dealing with the study of tumors.

DESCRIPTIONS AND TREATMENTS OF ADULT BRAIN TUMORS

Type of Tumor	Description/Treatment
Astrocytomas	Tumors that start in brain cells. Treatment includes surgery, chemotherapy, and radiation.

(Continued on next page)

Brain Stem Gliomas	Tumors located in the bottom part of the brain that connects to the spinal cord. Treatment includes radiation and biological therapy.
Cerebellar Astrocytomas	Tumors that occur in the area of the brain called the cerebellum. Treatment is similar to that for Astrocytomas.
Craniopharyngiomas	Tumors that occur near the pituitary gland. Treatment includes surgery and radiation.
Oligodendroglial	Tumors that begin in brain cells that provide support and nourishment for the cells that transmit nerve impulses. Treatment includes surgery, chemotherapy, and radiation.

Correspondence 94-91 ▶

Business Letter in Block Style With Subject Line

Current Date | Dr. Samuel Abbott | Sacred Heart Medical Center | 267 Ferry Street | Eugene, OR 97401-2409 | Dear Sam: | Subject: Paul R. Williams

¶ On March 3 I examined Mr. Williams and discovered a Stage 1A, Cleaved B cell follicular lymphoma in the left inguinal region. I conducted a surgical excision and recommended radiation therapy. Mr. Williams completed his radiation therapy four weeks ago and feels well at this time. He has no complaints, his appetite and energy are normal, and he looks good. His weight is down five pounds upon my recommendation four weeks ago that he lose some excess weight.

¶ There are no abdominal or inguinal lymph nodes to his scrotal sac exam. There are, however, three to four millimeter nodes in the right inguinal region that appear totally unchanged from his original exam on March 3. His lungs are clear, his heartbeat is regular, the liver and spleen are not enlarged, and there are no palpable masses.

¶ It appears to me that Mr. Williams has recovered satisfactorily from his radiation therapy. He has requested a second opinion, and I am therefore recommending that he make an appointment with you at his earliest convenience. We will prepare a referral for Mr. Williams and forward it to your office in a day or two.

Sincerely, | Donna Stensland, M.D. | urs

Table 94-50 ▶

Two-Column Boxed Table

Open the file for Table 94-49 and make the following changes:
1. Change the format to a boxed table.
2. Shade the cells in Row 2 at 10 percent.
3. Remove the extra hard return at the bottom of each cell.
4. Change the bottom border style in Row 2 to a double line.
5. After the title, press the ENTER key 2 times; then type your name.

Lesson 95

Medical Office Applications

GOALS
- Improve speed and accuracy
- Refine language arts skills in proofreading
- Format medical office documents

A. Type 2 times.

A. WARMUP

```
1      The extra black vacuum cleaners with the large-sized      11
2   grips were just lowered to $160 from $240 (a 33 1/3% mark-    23
3   down). Jay's #57 quilts were marked down to $98 from $108.    35
```
| 1 | 2 | 3 | 4 | 5 | 6 | 7 | 8 | 9 | 10 | 11 | 12

SKILLBUILDING

B. Type each word as shown until you reach the backspace sign (←). Then backspace 1 time and replace the previously typed character with the character shown. For example, if you see "hi←at," type "hi," backspace 1 time, and then type "at," resulting in the word "hat." *Technique Tip:* Press the BACKSPACE key with the sem finger, without looking at your keyboard.

B. TECHNIQUE PRACTICE: BACKSPACE KEY

```
4   p←cat c←tab b←peg p←but p←tie m←say t←car s←tea s←mad f←car
5   di←ye be←ag ge←um ri←ob mu←ad pa←it ca←rt fa←it fa←in pa←od
6   ham←d any←t new←t was←r sea←t mad←t gag←p tab←r tax←p ant←d
7   cheat←p scalp←e charm←t peace←h chart←m trace←k hub←t bib←t
```

C. PACED PRACTICE

If you are not using the GDP software, turn to page SB-14 and follow the directions for this activity.

LANGUAGE ARTS

D. Edit this paragraph to correct any keyboarding or formatting errors.

D. PROOFREADING

```
8       Suprising as it may seem, their has been a good deal
9    of interest in comunicating with a computer thruogh the
10   human voice for about fourty years. Researchers haev spent
11   millions ofdollars in hteir efforts to improve voice input
12   tecknology. It is likly that in the next decade we will
13   see many use ful applications in busness and in education.
```

Table 95-51 ▶

Two-Column Boxed Table

This is the final day of your five-day temporary assignment, and today you are working in the Surgery Unit. The specialty within this unit is knee surgery. Your first assignment is to create a table displaying various medical terms and their definitions.

MEDICAL TERMS AND THEIR DEFINITIONS

Student's Name

Current Date

Adenopathy	Swelling or morbid enlargement of the lymph nodes
Auscultation	Listening to sounds made by the various body structures as a diagnostic method
Cholecystectomy	Surgical removal of the gall bladder
Enterostomies	Incisions into the intestines that produce a small hole in the abdomen which through the intestines are emptied
Femur	The long bone of the thigh
Fibroperitoneal	Related to the tissue that lines the abdominal cavity which and covers most of the viscera
Laparoscopic	A minimally invasive surgical technique using a fiber optic instrument
Hemostasis	The arrest of bleeding
Laparotomy	incision into the loin
Trocars	Instruments for withdrawing fluid from a cavity

INSTRUCTIONS FOR RECOVERING FROM KNEE SURGERY
Dr. Alec Pera, M.D.

Current Date

¶ Specific procedures should be followed by patients who are recovering from knee surgery. Depending on the particular surgery that was performed, post-operative needs of patients with knee replacements vary greatly. Healthy, young individuals may require only a few therapy sessions to recover from their surgery completely. Older individuals with no family or friends to help them at home may need special assistance or equipment to aid their mobility. Some patients may benefit from a short stay in a rehabilitation facility. To enhance the rate of recovery, patients should identify and address any special needs that may be required before their operation.

¶ To promote full recovery, Pacific Medical has developed a coordinated pathway of physical and occupational therapy for patients' use. Patient Rehabilitation and Therapy Service (PRTS) and Pacific Medical have collaborated on recommending a specific sequence of procedures to follow.

¶ Prior to your surgery, we recommend that you:

1. Determine any special equipment that will be required to promote your recovery.
2. Learn correct techniques for performing day-to-day activities such as getting in and out of bed, driving your automobile, taking showers, getting up from a seat, and going up and down stairs.
3. Learn what exercises will help facilitate your recovery.

¶ After surgery, patients must participate in physical therapy to ensure that they can:

- Extend their knee straight or bend it past 90 degrees.
- Place weight on their knee to ensure that they have the strength and stability to hold their weight.
- Use the knee without discomfort (this may take several months).

Send an email message to Dr. Sandra Lockhart (slockhart@sacredheart.com), with a subject as follows: Patient File for P. R. Walden. Type an appropriate greeting for Dr. Lockhart and a closing and signa-ture line for yourself. Type the body as shown below. Proofread your email message for typing, spelling, and formatting errors.

Mr. Walden came in today with a crusted lesion in his back. Lesion was removed using 1% Xylocaine with Epinephrine loc. Wound was closed with 4.0 nylon sutures. Stitches should be removed in approximately 10 days. Sutures should be kept dry for 3 days. Mr. Walden is to call if he has questions or if problems arise.

Correspondence
95-93

Memo With
Copy Notation

✓ **Progress Check
Proofreading Check**

Documents designated as Proofreading Checks serve as a check of your proofreading skill. Your goal is to have zero typo-graphical errors when the GDP software first scores the document.

Dr. Charlene T. Gutierrez, Director of Plastic Surgery, was asked to assist Dr. Alec Pera with surgery on Bryan Owensby. After an office visit with Mr. Owensby, Dr. Gutierrez dictated the following memo to Dr. Pera. Use the current date and a subject of *Mr. Owensby's Surgery*.

On Friday I visited with Mr. Bryan Owensby to discuss his options relative to the muscle transfer we plan to complete following radiation treatment. Mr. Owensby is a 53-year-old male who has had multiple lesions recently excised.

¶ Mr. Owensby is aware that our goal is to provide healthy tissue that could tolerate the radiation treatment he would need to destroy the malignant cells on his upper thigh. At this time, we plan to complete a skin graft from the contralateral thigh to provide the healthy tissue for radiation treatment. I believe this will give Mr. Owensby the best opportunity for early healing.

¶ A free tissue transfer was also discussed, and this may be an option if the contralateral graft is unsuccessful. Mr. Owensby understands the risks and complications of either method. Scheduling is pending jointly through our offices. Thank you for this opportunity to participate in Mr. Owensby's care.

urs | c: Dr. Taiwo Owakoniro, Dr. Lewis Sethna, Dr. Monica Stevens

Unit 20

Legal Office Applications

```
1   STATE OF KANSAS                    IN DISTRICT COURT
2
3   COUNTY OF DOUGLAS                  NORTHEAST JUDICIAL DISTRICT
4
5   PEOPLE'S BANK            )
6   607 New Hampshire Street )          NO._____
7   Lawrence, KS 66044-2243 )
8                           )
9              Plaintiff,   )
10                          )          SUMMONS
11      - vs -              )
12                          )
13  JOHN COUZINS and GLORIA )
14  COUZINS, Defendants.    )
15
16  THE STATE OF KANSAS TO THE ABOVE-NAMED DEFENDANTS:
17
18      You are hereby summoned and required to appear and defend against the
19  Complaint in this action, which is hereby served upon you by serving upon the undersigned
20  an Answer or other proper response within twenty (20) days after the service of the
21  Summons and Complaint upon you, exclusive of the day of service.
22      If you fail to do so, judgment by defa
23  demanded in the Complaint.
24
25      SIGNED this _____ day of Decem
26
27
28                          Ann
29                          Attorn
30                          806 K
31                          Lawre
32                          Teleph
33                          Attorn
```

```
LAST WILL AND TESTAMENT
1                           OF
2                    MATTHEW R. HENRY
3
4
5       I, MATTHEW R. HENRY, residing in Corvallis, Oregon, do hereby make and
6   declare this to be my Last Will and Testament, hereby revoking any and all former Wills and
7   Codicils by me at any time heretofore made.
8
9                        ARTICLE I
10
11      This will is made in Oregon and shall be governed, construed, and administered
12  according to Oregon law, even though subject to probate or administered elsewhere. The
13  Oregon laws applied shall not include any principles or laws relating to conflicts or choice of
14  laws.
15
16                       ARTICLE II
17
18      Whenever used herein, words importing the singular shall include the plural and
19  words importing the masculine shall include the feminine and neuter, and vice versa, unless
20  the context otherwise requires.
21
22                       ARTICLE III
23
24      I am married and my wife's name is Karen E. Henry. All references hereinafter
25  made to "wife" or "spouse" shall refer to her and no other; and if she is not my legal wife at
26  the time of my death, then she shall be deemed for the purpose of this, my last Will and
27  Testament, to have predeceased me. I was formerly married to Donna Henry, who is now
28  deceased. There were three (3) children born of my marriage to Donna Henry. The names of
29  those children are as follows: Judy Parsons, Wayne Henry, and Randy Henry.
30
31                       ARTICLE IV
32
        Except as may otherwise be provided hereunder in this
        me, I devise to my spouse all my interest in household
        apparel, art objects, collections, jewelry, and similar
        ional equipment; all other tangible property for personal
        me and any vacation property that I may own or reside in
        s; any motor vehicles that I may own on the date of my
        on all such property.

                         ARTICLE V

        Survive. Except as may be otherwise provided in this
        urvive me, I devise the property described above in this
        y children who survive me, to be divided among them as
```

```
                                        Page 2 of 2

1   they shall agree, or in the absence of such agreement, as my Personal Representative shall
2   determine, which determination shall be conclusive.
3
4                        ARTICLE VI
5
6       If any beneficiary named or described in this Will fails to survive me for 120
7   hours, all the provisions in this Will for the benefit of such deceased beneficiary shall lapse,
8   and this Will shall be construed as though the fact were that he or she predeceased me.
9
10                       ARTICLE VII
11
12      All estate, inheritance, transfer, succession, and any other taxes plus interest and
13  penalties thereon (death taxes) that become payable by reason of my death upon property
14  passing under this instrument shall be paid out of the residue of my estate without
15  reimbursement from the recipient and without apportionment. All death taxes upon property
16  not passing under this instrument shall be apportioned in the manner provided by law.
17
18      IN WITNESS WHEREOF, I have hereunto affixed my hand and seal this
19  _____ day of _____, 20--.
20
21
22                MATTHEW R. HENRY                    Testator
23
24      The foregoing instrument, consisting of TWO (2) pages (this page included), was
25  on this _____ day of _____m 2999m subscribed on each page and at the
26  end thereof by Matthew R. Henry, the above-named Testator and by him signed, sealed,
27  published and declared to be his Last Will, in the presence of us, and each of us, who
28  thereupon, at his request, in his presence, and in the presence of each other, have hereunto
29  subscribed our names as attesting witnesses thereto.
30
31  _____ residing at _____
32
33  _____ residing at _____
```

Legal Office Applications

GOALS

- Type at least 47wpm/5'/5e
- Format legal office applications

A. Type 2 times.

A. WARMUP

```
1      Marshal bought five chances for the contest. He won      11
2  six prizes and was given a check for $2,350--these prizes    23
3  are equal to 1/4th of Jill's winnings for all of last year.  35
   |  1  |  2  |  3  |  4  |  5  |  6  |  7  |  8  |  9  | 10 | 11 | 12
```

SKILLBUILDING

B. DIAGNOSTIC PRACTICE: NUMBERS

If you are not using the GDP software, turn to page SB-5 and follow the directions for this activity.

C. Take three 12-second timings on each line. The scale below the last line shows your wpm speed for a 12-second timing.

C. 12-SECOND SPEED SPRINTS

```
4  They saw the sun shine through after days and days of rain.
5  She hopes to get a much higher math score on the next test.
6  Jo did not study for the math exam she took late last week.
7  This time he spent at least ten days studying for the test.
   | | | | 5 | | | | 10 | | | | 15 | | | | 20 | | | | 25 | | | | 30 | | | | 35 | | | | 40 | | | | 45 | | | | 50 | | | | 55 | | | | 60
```

Keyboarding CONNECTION

Capturing an Image From the Internet

Would you like to copy an image or graphic from the Internet? It's easy!

Point to the image or graphic and press the right mouse button. When the shortcut menu appears, choose Save Picture As (or Save Image As). The Save Picture dialog displays. Select the appropriate drive and name the file if necessary. Click Save. The image is usually saved with a .gif, .jpg, or .bmp file extension. To insert the image into a Word document, choose Picture from the Insert menu, and select From File. Locate the file, and click Insert.

YOUR TURN Conduct a Web search and locate an image or graphic to save. Right-click the image, and choose Save Picture As; name the file; and save the image. Insert the image into a word processing document.

D. Take two 5-minute timings. Review your speed and errors.

Goal: At least 47wpm/5′/5e

D. 5-MINUTE TIMING

8   Many businesses across the country are adopting a   10
9   new trend called business casual. Depending on the type of   22
10 organization for which you work, business casual can have   34
11 various interpretations. Most corporations allow their   45
12 employees to dress down a notch from what was expected   56
13 previously. If people wore suits and ties previously, then   68
14 the business casual code would allow them to eliminate   79
15 wearing ties and suit jackets. It is quite necessary for   90
16 businesses to formulate dress code guidelines for their   101
17 employees to follow when business casual is introduced.   112
18 Surveys of various companies show mixed results when   123
19 employees are given the option of dressing more casually.   135
20 Some companies feel business casual is a perk that works   146
21 for employees. However, other companies report that job   157
22 productivity rates decrease when workers are allowed to   168
23 dress down.   170
24 When you feel good about the way you look, you will   181
25 show this attitude in your performance. If your company   192
26 has adopted a business casual dress code, you must keep in   204
27 mind that business casual does not mean that you can dress   216
28 in a sloppy manner. A neat appearance and good grooming   227
29 always enhance a business casual look.   235

| 1 | 2 | 3 | 4 | 5 | 6 | 7 | 8 | 9 | 10 | 11 | 12

FORMATTING

E. LEGAL DOCUMENTS

Legal documents are typed on either 8½-inch by 14-inch legal paper or 8½-inch by 11-inch standard paper. Many firms today use standard paper for their legal documents.

Legal cap, vertical rules running from top to bottom on a page, have been used for years to identify the left and right margins of legal documents. Whether or not legal cap is used, the left margin is typi-cally set at 1.25 inches and the right margin maintains a default 1.0 inch. The top and bottom margins in a legal document are usually set at 1 inch but may vary from firm to firm.

It is also common practice to number the lines in a legal document to enable an attorney to make reference to particular lines or sections in the document.

(Continued on next page)

Pages in a legal document are often numbered as *"Page 1 of 7"* to indicate the total number of pages in the document. Paragraphs are usually indented from 0.5 inch to 1.0 inch. Full justification is frequently used.

Legal documents come in numerous formats such as affidavits, wills, deeds, summons, indictments, etc. The illustration below shows a sample of an affidavit. An affidavit is a written statement made under oath.

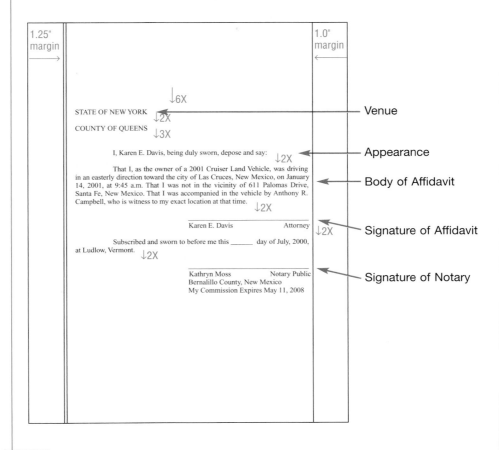

1.25" margin	1.0" margin
↓6X	
STATE OF NEW YORK ↓2X	← Venue
COUNTY OF QUEENS ↓3X	
I, Karen E. Davis, being duly sworn, depose and say: ↓2X	← Appearance
That I, as the owner of a 2001 Cruiser Land Vehicle, was driving in an easterly direction toward the city of Las Cruces, New Mexico, on January 14, 2001, at 9:45 a.m. That I was not in the vicinity of 611 Palomas Drive, Santa Fe, New Mexico. That I was accompanied in the vehicle by Anthony R. Campbell, who is witness to my exact location at that time. ↓2X	← Body of Affidavit
Karen E. Davis Attorney ↓2X	← Signature of Affidavit
Subscribed and sworn to before me this _____ day of July, 2000, at Ludlow, Vermont. ↓2X	
Kathryn Moss Notary Public Bernalillo County, New Mexico My Commission Expires May 11, 2008	← Signature of Notary

Go To
Word Processing Manual

F. WORD PROCESSING: LINE NUMBERING

Study Lesson 96 in your word processing manual. Complete all of the shaded steps while at your computer. Then format the jobs that follow.

DOCUMENT PROCESSING

Report 96-68

Affidavit of Possession

Insert line numbering for all lines.

Indent paragraphs 1 inch.

1   **AFFIDAVIT OF POSSESSION** ↓1DS

2

3 STATE OF VERMONT ↓1DS

4

5 COUNTY OF WINDSOR ↓1DS

6   1"

7 ¶   Eric Wesley, being first duly sworn, deposes and says: ↓1DS

8   1"

9 ¶   That he is an adult person and is a resident of Windsor County,

10 Vermont, and that his mailing address is P.O. Box 801, Ludlow, VT 05149.

(Continued on next page)

11   That he knows and is well acquainted with the history,
12 ownership and occupancy of the following-described property situated in
13 Windsor County, Vermont, to-wit:
14   All that part of the Southeast Quarter of the Northeast Quarter
15 of Section Nine (9), Township Seventy-two (72), further described as
16 follows: Beginning at the Northeast corner of said Southeast Quarter of the
17 Northeast Quarter; thence South along the East line of said quarter 1000.00
18 feet; thence west 575.00 feet; thence North 200.00 feet; thence West 204.00
19 feet; thence North 800.00 feet; thence East 979.00 feet.
20   That the record title holder in fee simple of the above property is
21 Eric Wesley, a single person; that he is presently in possession of the above-
22 described premises;
23   That ownership of the aforesaid property is based upon an
24 unbroken chain of title through immediate and remote grantors by deed of
25 conveyance which has been recorded for a period of more than twenty-one
26 (21) years, to-wit: Since August 21, 1943, at 2 a.m.;
27   That the owner(s) and his predecessors in title to the
28 aforementioned property have had open, actual, adverse, notorious and
29 continuous possession against all persons and have paid taxes in open and
30 adverse possession for more than twenty-one (21) years; and
31   That the purpose of this Affidavit of Possession is to show proof of
32 ownership by providing and recording evidence of possession for marketable
33 title as required by the Marketable Record Title Act of the State of Vermont.
34   DATED this _____ day of August, 20--, at Ludlow, Vermont.

35 ↓1DS

36   3" Tab

37 ————————————————→ ——————————————————————

38   Blake Crawford   Attorney-at-Law

39

40 Subscribed and sworn to before me this _____ day of August, 20--. ↓1DS

41   3" Tab

42 ————————————————→ ——————————————————————

43   Shirley Blakely   Notary Public

44   Windsor County, Vermont

45   My Commission Expires July 17, 2008

Underscore is 6 characters wide.

Underscore starts at a left tab of 3.0 inches and ends at the right margin.

Underscore starts at a left tab of 3.0 inches and ends at the right margin.

Correspondence 96-94 ▶

Business Letter in Block Style With Enclosure and Copy Notations

Current Date | Mr. Eric Wesley | P.O. Box 801 | Ludlow, VT 05149 | Dear Mr. Wesley:

¶ Enclosed is your copy of the Affidavit of Possession that was filed on your behalf with the Windsor County Courthouse.

¶ As you can see, only the Southeast Quarter of your property was included in the affidavit. We will have to file an additional affidavit if you want to add the Northwest Quarter as well as your Franklin County properties. All affidavits must be completed prior to your property being advertised in the *Windsor News.*

¶ I will be out of the office all of next week. If you have questions, please call my associate, Emily Waters.

Sincerely, | Blake Crawford | urs | Enclosure | c: Marvin Steele, Beverley Perez

Legal Office Applications

GOALS

- Improve speed and accuracy
- Refine language arts skills in the use of punctuation
- Format legal office applications

A. Type 2 times.

A. WARMUP

```
1      Jacqueline kept prize #2490 instead of #3761 because     11
2  it was worth 58.5% more value. That was a great prize! Last  23
3  year the law firm of Adams & Day donated all grand prizes.   34
   |  1  |  2  |  3  |  4  |  5  |  6  |  7  |  8  |  9  |  10  |  11  |  12
```

SKILLBUILDING

B. PROGRESSIVE PRACTICE: ALPHABET

If you are not using the GDP software, turn to page SB-7 and follow the directions for this activity.

C. PACED PRACTICE

If you are not using the GDP software, turn to page SB-14 and follow the directions for this activity.

LANGUAGE ARTS

D. Study the rules at the right.

D. SEMICOLONS

RULE ▶
; no conjunction

Use a semicolon to separate two closely related independent clauses that are not connected by a conjunction (such as *and, but,* or *nor*).

Management favored the vote; stockholders did not.

But: Management favored the vot**e,** but stockholders did not.

RULE ▶
; series

Use a semicolon to separate three or more items in a series if any of the items already contain commas.

Staff meetings were held on Thursday, May 7; Monday, June 7; and Friday, June 12.

Note: Be sure to insert the semicolon between (not within) the items in a series.

Edit the sentences to correct any errors in the use of semicolons.

```
4  Paul will travel to Madrid, Spain; Lisbon, Portugal, and
5  Nice, France.
6  Mary's gift arrived yesterday, Margie's did not.
7  Bring your textbook to class; I'll return it tomorrow.
8  The best days for the visit are Monday, May 10, Tuesday,
9  May 18, and Wednesday, May 26.
10 Jan is the president; Peter is the vice president.
```

Insert line numbers for all lines.

Underscore is 6 characters wide.

A warranty deed is one in which a seller warrants (or guarantees) that he or she has full ownership of the property with the right to sell it. The seller also guarantees all rights of the property to the buyer.

WARRANTY DEED ↓1DS

1" tab →   **THIS INDENTURE,** Made this ——— day of October, 20--, between **Thomas J. Wallace**, **Grantor,** whether one or more, and **Barbara Denman, Grantee,** whether one or more, whose post office address is 315 Clark Avenue, Ames IA 50010-3314. ↓2X

WITNESSETH, for and in consideration of the sum of **SEVENTY-FIVE THOUSAND and 00/100 DOLLARS ($75,000),** Grantor does hereby **GRANT** to Grantee, all of the following real property lying and being in the County of Story, State of Iowa, and described as follows, to-wit:

Lots Seventeen (17) and Eighteen (18), Block Seventy-three (73), Original Townsite of Ames, Iowa, **SUBJECT TO** easements, special or improvement taxes and assessments, mineral conveyances, rights-of-way and reservations of record.

(THIS DEED IS IN FULFILLMENT OF THAT CERTAIN CONTRACT FOR DEED ENTERED INTO BY AND BETWEEN THE SAME PARTIES ON THE DATE HEREOF.)

And the said Grantor for himself, his heirs, executors and administrators, does covenant with the Grantee that he is well seized in fee of the land and premises aforesaid and has good right to sell and convey the same in manner and form aforesaid: that the same are free from all encumbrances, except installments of special assessments or assessments for special improvements which have not been certified to the County Treasurer for collection, and the above granted lands and premises in the possession of said Grantee, against all persons lawfully claiming or to claim the whole or any part thereof, the said Grantor will warrant and defend.

WITNESS, the hand of the Grantor.

3" tab

————————————————————

Thomas J. Wallace ↓2X

(Continued on next page)

STATE OF IOWA ↓2X

County of Story ↓2X

On this _____ day of October, 20--, before me, a notary public within and for said County and State, personally appeared Thomas J. Wallace, to me known to be the person described in and who executed the within and foregoing instrument and acknowledged to me that he executed the same as his free act and deed. ↓2X

3-inch tab

Boyd H. Fraser   Notary Public
Story County, Iowa
My Commission Expires June 15, 2008

Table 97-52

Two-Column Boxed Table

WARRANTY DEED TERMINOLOGY *State of Iowa*	
Term	*Definition*
Appurtenance	Something attached to the land
Consideration	The value of the property
Escrow	A system of document transfer in which the document is given to a third party to hold until the conditions of the agreement have been met
Grantee	The person who is buying the property
Grantor	The person who owns the property
Mortgage	The pledging of property as security for a loan
Tenement	Something that can be possessed, such as land or a building
Warranty Deed	A deed in which the seller forever guarantees clear title to the land

; no conjunction

; series

; no conjunction

Send an email message to David Barinowski, (dbarinowski@legal.com) with a subject as follows: Foreclosure Property. Type a closing and signature line for yourself. Type the body as shown below. Proofread your email message for typing, spelling, and formatting errors. Print but do not save or send this email message.

¶ David, you might recall last week that I indicated there might be some foreclosure property available and that it would be auctioned at the Story ^County^ Courthouse. On September 9, 3 properties in southern Story county will be auctioned as foreclosures. These properties are located adjacent to the lots you purchased last year. I know that you would be interested in expanding your lot size with this purchase. Specifically, they are located in Spring Township, Lot 23; Aiken Township, Lot 17; and Andrews Township, Lot 9.

¶ I expect these properties will sell for around $36,000 each; their excellent location may force the bidding into the $40,000 ^or $50,000^ range. If you cannot be present for the auction but would like to place a bid on the properties, please let me know so that I can act on your behalf as your agent. If you ~~want~~ ^elect^ to do this, send me the bidding range you wish to present for each of the ^P^roperties or for all 3 as one combined property. I need confirmation from you no later than September ^7^ so that I can register ^as^ your agent to present your bid.

Keyboarding skills are essential for any career in the legal field.

Legal Office Applications

GOALS
- Type at least 47wpm/5'/5e
- Format legal office applications

A. Type 2 times.

A. WARMUP

```
1      Janet bought dozens of disks (5 or 6) to store her      10
2  article, "The Internet Sanctions." She quickly sent it to   23
3  her editor, Max Pavlow, on the 18th or 19th of September.   34
   | 1 | 2 | 3 | 4 | 5 | 6 | 7 | 8 | 9 | 10 | 11 | 12
```

SKILLBUILDING

B. DIAGNOSTIC PRACTICE: ALPHABET

If you are not using the GDP software, turn to page SB-2 and follow the directions for this activity.

C. Type the paragraph 2 times, concentrating on each letter typed.

C. TECHNIQUE PRACTICE: SHIFT/CAPS LOCK

```
4      Raymond and Karen must travel through TENNESSEE and
5  KENTUCKY on TUESDAY and WEDNESDAY. Raymond will speak in
6  NASHVILLE on the topic of COMPUTER AWARENESS; Karen will
7  speak in LOUISVILLE, and her talk is on INTERNET ACCESS.
```

STRATEGIES FOR *Career Success*   Enhance Your Presentation With Visual Aids

Visual aids capture people's attention while increasing their retention. Use visual aids to present an outline of your presentation, explain detailed technical or numeric information, and summarize your key points.

Be selective. Don't bombard your audience with visuals. Your visual aids should support and clarify your verbal presentation. Consider the size of your audience and the size of the room before selecting your visuals. Audiences have little patience for visuals that are too small to read. Types of visual aids are overhead transparencies, slides, photographs, flip charts, maps, flowcharts, posters, handouts, and computer graphics including tables, graphs, and charts.

Limit the amount of information on a visual. Use simple graphics. Continue displaying the current visual until you are ready to discuss the next one. Always keep the projector or overhead on.

YOUR TURN In what ways would your visual aids differ if your audience had 10 people or 110?

D. Take two 5-minute timings. Review your speed and errors.

Goal: At least 47wpm/5′/5e

D. 5-MINUTE TIMING

8   From the time you start attending school, you begin   10

9 to develop the skills in making friends and getting along   23

10 with people. These skills are used throughout your life   34

11 journey. If you want to be successful in any business or   45

12 career, you can't be a loner. You must learn skills for   56

13 working successfully with people from all cultures.   66

14   In a corporation, people use their unique skills   76

15 to work as a team in order to accomplish their goals. Like   88

16 a finely tuned orchestra or a football team, all members   99

17 must work together to achieve the desired objective. If a   111

18 person does not work efficiently within the group, then   122

19 other team members may have to work harder to compensate   133

20 so that the effort of the team will not fall short.   143

21   Working with others allows you the opportunity to   153

22 learn from other people. You may also learn some things   164

23 about yourself. To get along with your coworkers, you may   176

24 have to overlook the personal faults of others. Everyone   187

25 has faults, and your faults may be just as disconcerting   198

26 to other people as their faults are to you. Your ability   209

27 to work with people will enhance your quest for career   220

28 advancement. You can expect amazing results when you work   232

29 with your team.   235

| 1 | 2 | 3 | 4 | 5 | 6 | 7 | 8 | 9 | 10 | 11 | 12 |

Lawyers, as well as other professionals, find a laptop computer a valuable resource while traveling on business.

**Report
98-70** ►

Summons

A summons is a document that notifies a defendant that a lawsuit has been filed and an appearance must be made before the court, at a specified time, to answer the charges.

Insert line numbers for all lines.

Underscore is 6 characters wide.

Use a right tab setting of 2.25" for the closing parentheses of the venue information.

STATE OF KANSAS ↓2X   **IN DISTRICT COURT**

COUNTY OF DOUGLAS ↓2X   **NORTHEAST JUDICIAL DISTRICT**

PEOPLE'S BANK   )   **NO._____**
607 New Hampshire Street   )
Lawrence, KS 66044-2243   ) ↓2X
)
                          Plaintiff,) ↓2X   **SUMMONS**
)
          - vs -   )
)
) ↓2X
JOHN COUZINS and GLORIA)
COUZINS, Defendants.   ) ↓2X

THE STATE OF KANSAS TO THE ABOVE-NAMED DEFENDANTS: ↓2X

Tab at 1"
_____, You are hereby summoned and required to appear and defend against the Complaint in this action, which is hereby served upon you by serving upon the undersigned an Answer or other proper response within twenty (20) days after the service of the Summons and Complaint upon you, exclusive of the day of service.

          If you fail to do so, judgment by default will be taken against you for the relief demanded in the Complaint. ↓2X

                    SIGNED this _____ day of December, 20--. ↓2X

Tab at 3"
_____ | _____

                                             Ann Barfield
                                             Attorney at Law
                                             806 Kentucky St.
                                             Lawrence KS 66044-2648
                                             Telephone: (785) 555-8226
                                             Attorney for Plaintiff

MEMO TO: Raymond Ruzi

FROM: Charlotte Libretto

DATE: Current Date

SUBJECT: Client listing

¶ As you requested, I am ~~now~~ enclosing an up-to-date new client list for our Atlanta area clients. This list is curent [r] as of ~~last~~ [this] week, and it includes clients in the counties of Carroll, Cobb, Douglas, Fulton, and paulding. Please note that the [total] billing hours are [also] shown in this list.

¶ Douglas and ~~Cobb~~ [Fulton] counties represent the greatest number of clients over all, although this list doesn't [# not] reveal the total number of clients per county. Just in the past quarter, these two counties represented nearly ~~eighty~~ [80] (%) of our client base. Cobb County clients do not represent a sizable percentage of our client base, but the opening of ~~three~~ [two] new law offices in that county will most certainly generate considerable [new] business in the coming months.

¶ We will send you an updated list bi-weekly. The ~~next~~ list will most certainly show substantial gains in Cobb County, and we expect business in Douglas and Fulton counties to continue growing because of the [tremendous] growth in the area West of Atlanta. If you have any questions about any of our new clients, please call our main office at 770-555-1843.

urs | Enclosure | c: Blair Kiplan

Much of the work done in a legal office is transcribed by administrative support staff.

Table
98-53

Four-Column
Boxed Table

CLIENT LIST Current Date			
Name	**Address**	**County**	**Billing Hours**
Gary Baxter	128 Holly St.	Douglas	25
Carroll Bryan	323 Newnan St.	Carroll	28
Margie Coulon	301 Bradley St.	Paulding	15
Thomas Henry	2900 Shady Grove	Cobb	22
Debra Johnson	215 Griffin Dr.	Cobb	34
Sean Lowe	156 Cypress Circle	Fulton	10
Luther Nicholson	6703 Burns Rd.	Paulding	12
Pearl Nix	106 Alice Lane	Douglas	18
James Presley	622 North Ave.	Carroll	23
Janie Ramey	1202 Park St.	Fulton	32
Heather Sanders	248 Lakeshore Dr.	Cobb	12
Thomas Tarpley	2950 Chapel Hill Rd.	Douglas	29
Vickie Thomas	4821 Hope Rd.	Carroll	9
Jack West	111 Pierce St.	Fulton	18
Ray Young	108 Waverly Way	Douglas	30
Tong Zhen	286 Laurel Terrace	Paulding	35

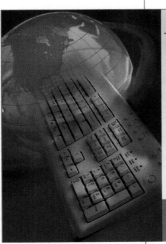

Keyboarding CONNECTION

Coping With Spam

Have you received heaps of unsolicited email, commonly known as spam? Everyone wants to get rid of those irritating online sales pitches. Contrary to popular advice, however, there is not much you can do about them. You can make use of various filters, but they aren't foolproof.

If you end up on a spammer's list and receive a courteous email asking you to reply if you wish to be removed from the list, DO NOT REPLY. The spammer may take your reply as someone who's reading the mail, and you may be put on the hot list. The best action is to try to avoid divulging your email address to spam. Most importantly, use an alternate account if posting to any kind of online forum.

YOUR TURN How do you deal with postal "junk mail" that you receive? Are there similarities in dealing with spam?

Lesson 99

Legal Office Applications

GOALS

- Improve speed and accuracy
- Refine language arts skills in spelling
- Format legal office applications

A. Type 2 times.

A. WARMUP

```
1       Zeke sharpened his ax so that he could quite easily    11
2   saw through 15 very large pine trees. Each load will sell   23
3   for $175 (to Blake & James Inc.) at next Friday's auction.  35
    |  1  |  2  |  3  |  4  |  5  |  6  |  7  |  8  |  9  |  10  |  11  |  12
```

SKILLBUILDING

B. MAP

Follow the GDP software directions for this exercise in improving keystroking accuracy.

C. Take a 1-minute timing on the first paragraph to establish your base speed. Then take four 1-minute timings on the remaining paragraphs. As soon as you equal or exceed your base speed on one paragraph, advance to the next, more difficult paragraph.

C. SUSTAINED PRACTICE: ROUGH DRAFT

```
4       The pattern of employment in our country is undergoing   11
5   some major changes. Companies are slowly decreasing their    23
6   permanent staff to just a core group of managers and other   35
7   high-powered people and are using temporaries for the rest.  47

8       This trend is creating an accordion aftermath in many    11
9   firms: the ability to expand and contract as the time or     23
                                                        and
10  the balance sheets dictate. Have this range of flexibility   35
                              Having
11  would be a key ingredient in the competative fight to come.  47
    will                                        i

12      All of these changes would make it tough for all unions  11
                            will                    the
13  to stay a float. They do not have a satisfactory method of   23
                                                  o
14  organizing such employes. Unions can try to change in to     35
                         e          could             
15  social agendeis, providing aid to members outside of work.   47

16      Such services as elder or child care, counseling, debt   11
17  managment, and even health care maybe of great asistance     23
          e                            #            s
18  as employers find it more and more dificult to offer these   35
                                       f
19  benfits. Unions may find their niche by filling this gap.    47
       e
    |  1  |  2  |  3  |  4  |  5  |  6  |  7  |  8  |  9  |  10  |  11  |  12
```

D. Type this list of frequently misspelled words, paying special attention to any spelling problems in each word.

D. SPELLING

20 distribution executive extension requested specific carried
21 recommended alternative programs access budget issued seize
22 objectives indicated calendar family could these until your
23 administrative accommodate possibility students fiscal past
24 transportation employee's categories summary offered estate

Edit the sentences to correct any misspellings.

25 The execitive requested an extention on spicific programs.
26 I have recomended alternive programs for early next week.
27 These objectives were indacated for the new calender year.
28 These passed administrative goals will accomodate the team.
29 These catagories could be included in the employee summery.

DOCUMENT PROCESSING

Report 99-71

Last Will and Testament

Add line numbers to entire document; restart line numbering on the second page.

Add page number for page 2 in this format: Page 2 of 2.

Use a 1-inch tab for new paragraphs.

Press ENTER 2 times before and after the Articles.

A last will and testament is a legal document stating how a person wants his or her property distributed after death.

LAST WILL AND TESTAMENT
OF
MATTHEW R. HENRY

I, **MATTHEW R. HENRY**, residing in Corvallis, Oregon, do hereby make and declare this to be my Last Will and Testament, hereby revoking any and all former Wills and Codicils by me at any time heretofore made.

ARTICLE I

This will is made in Oregon and shall be governed, construed, and administered according to Oregon law, even though subject to probate or administered elsewhere. The Oregon laws applied shall not include any principles or laws relating to conflicts or choice of laws.

ARTICLE II

Whenever used herein, words importing the singular shall include the plural and words importing the masculine shall include the feminine and neuter, and vice versa, unless the context otherwise requires.

(Continued on next page)

ARTICLE III

I am married and my wife's name is Karen E. Henry. All references hereinafter made to "wife" or "spouse" shall refer to her and no other; and if she is not my legal wife at the time of my death, then she shall be deemed for the purpose of this, my last Will and Testament, to have predeceased me. I was formerly married to Donna Henry, who is now deceased. There were three (3) children born of my marriage to Donna Henry. The names of those children are as follows: Judy Parsons, Wayne Henry, and Randy Henry.

ARTICLE IV

<u>If My Spouse Survives</u>. Except as may otherwise be provided hereunder in this Article IV, if my spouse survives me, I devise to my spouse all my interest in household furniture and furnishings, books, apparel, art objects, collections, jewelry, and similar personal effects; sporting and recreational equipment; all other tangible property for personal use; all other like contents of my home and any vacation property that I may own or reside in on the date of my death; all animals; any motor vehicles that I may own on the date of my death; and any unexpired insurance on all such property.

ARTICLE V

<u>If My Spouse Does Not Survive</u>. Except as may be otherwise provided in this Article IV, if my spouse does not survive me, I devise the property described above in this Article (except motor vehicles) to my children who survive me, to be divided among them as they shall agree, or in the absence of such agreement, as my Personal Representative shall determine, which determination shall be conclusive.

ARTICLE VI

If any beneficiary named or described in this Will fails to survive me for 120 hours, all the provisions in this Will for the benefit of such deceased beneficiary shall lapse, and this Will shall be construed as though the fact were that he or she predeceased me.

ARTICLE VII

All estate, inheritance, transfer, succession, and any other taxes plus interest and penalties thereon (death taxes) that become payable by reason of my death upon property passing under this instrument shall be paid out of the residue of my estate without reimbursement from the recipient and without apportionment. All death taxes upon property not passing under this instrument shall be apportioned in the manner provided by law.

(Continued on next page)

The first underscore is 6 characters wide; the second underscore is 20 characters wide.

Set left tab at 3.0 inches for signature line; set right tab for "Testator."

Each underscore is 25 characters wide.

IN WITNESS WHEREOF, I have hereunto affixed my hand and seal this _____ day of _____, 20--.

_____

MATTHEW R. HENRY   Testator

The foregoing instrument, consisting of TWO (2) pages (this page included), was on this _____ day of _____, 20--, subscribed on each page and at the end thereof by Matthew R. Henry, the above-named Testator and by him signed, sealed, published and declared to be his Last Will, in the presence of us, and each of us, who thereupon, at his request, in his presence, and in the presence of each other, have hereunto subscribed our names as attesting witnesses thereto.

_____ residing at _____

_____ residing at _____

Correspondence 99-97 ▶

Business Letter in Block Style with Subject Line, Bulleted List, Enclosure, and Copy Notations

Current Date | Mr. Matthew R. Henry | 768 Southwest Adams Avenue | Corvallis, OR 97333-4523 | Dear Mr. Henry: | Subject: Will Provisions ¶ Your last will and testament has been drafted and is enclosed for your review. Please review it carefully for any specific omissions or deletions. ¶ Although your will has been drafted as you indicated, there are still a couple of alternative inclusions that I would recommend.

• Do you wish to include a fiduciary powers summary in the will?
• What division of estate do you wish to include for your family?

¶ These inclusions could be rather comprehensive. Therefore, could we schedule a meeting for next Tuesday to accommodate these changes? Please call my administrative assistant so she can put you on my calendar. Sincerely, | Andrea L. Grainger | Attorney-at-Law | urs | Enclosure | c: T. Carter, S. Rohrer, A. Winchester

Legal Office Applications

GOALS

- Type at least 47wpm/5'/5e
- Format legal office applications

A. Type 2 times.

A. WARMUP

1   Val Lopez and Jack Drew quickly bought six tickets for   11
2 Sam's $24,600 collector's auto (a 1957 Chevrolet). Over the   23
3 past month, its value increased by 1.5%. That is fantastic!   35
  | 1 | 2 | 3 | 4 | 5 | 6 | 7 | 8 | 9 | 10 | 11 | 12

SKILLBUILDING

PRETEST ➡ PRACTICE ➡ POSTTEST

B. PRETEST: Horizontal Reaches

PRETEST
Take a 1-minute timing. Review your speed and errors.

4   Bart enjoyed his royal blue race car. He bragged about   11
5 how he learned to push for those speed spurts that helped   23
6 him win those races. The car had a lot of get-up-and-go.   34
  | 1 | 2 | 3 | 4 | 5 | 6 | 7 | 8 | 9 | 10 | 11 | 12

C. PRACTICE: In Reaches

PRACTICE
Speed Emphasis:
  If you made no more than 1 error on the Pretest, type each *individual* line 2 times.
Accuracy Emphasis:
  If you made 2 or more errors, type each *group* of lines (as though it were a paragraph) 2 times.

7 oy toy ahoy ploy loyal coyly royal enjoy decoy annoy deploy
8 ar fare arch mart march farms scars spear barns learn radar
9 pu pull push puts pulse spurt purge spuds pushy spurs pupil

D. PRACTICE: Out Reaches

10 ge gear gets ages getup raged geese lunge pages cagey forge
11 da dare date data dance adage dazed sedan daubs cedar daily
12 hi high hick hill hinge chief hires ethic hiked chili hitch

POSTTEST
Repeat the Pretest timing and compare performance.

E. POSTTEST: Horizontal Reaches

F. Take two 5-minute timings. Review your speed and errors.

Goal: At least 47wpm/5'/5e

F. 5-MINUTE TIMING

13	Company loyalty may be a thing of the past. A worker	11
14	who stayed and worked for one corporation for thirty or	22
15	more years is a rarity these days. People are moving to	33
16	different jobs at a faster pace than in the past. Changing	45
17	jobs many times over a career no longer carries the stigma	57
18	of the past. People are looking for new challenges.	67
19	Workers who change jobs are able to market their	77
20	skills and get significant salary increases. Hopping from	89
21	job to job can pay amazing dividends for some careers.	100
22	Corporations are quite willing to offer higher salaries	111
23	and more perks to attract the most talented people. People	123
24	who are changing jobs frequently have the experience and	134
25	knowledge that other companies are willing to employ.	145
26	The opportunity to change jobs is available not only	156
27	to younger workers but also to the older workers who are	167
28	well into their careers. For example, computer technology	179
29	is currently experiencing a boom. The Internet industry	190
30	has placed a high demand for computer programmers. People	202
31	with experience in this area can request higher salaries.	214
32	A company may even offer additional benefits in order to	225
33	attract experienced workers with great credentials.	235

| 1 | 2 | 3 | 4 | 5 | 6 | 7 | 8 | 9 | 10 | 11 | 12

STRATEGIES FOR *Career Success*

Letter of Resignation

When you plan to leave a job, you should write a resignation letter, memo, or email to your supervisor and send a copy to Human Resources. Follow these guidelines to write an effective resignation.

Start a resignation letter positively, regardless of why you are leaving. Include how you benefited from working for the company, or compliment your coworkers.

In the middle section, state why you are leaving. Provide an objective, factual explanation and avoid accusations. Your resignation becomes part of your permanent company record. If it is hostile, it could backfire on you when you need references. Stipulate the date your resignation becomes effective (provide at least a two-week notice).

End the letter of resignation with a closing of goodwill (e.g., "I wish all of you the best in the future.").

YOUR TURN List the benefits of NOT "burning your bridges" (showing anger or bitterness) in your letter of resignation.

Report 100-72 ▶

Complaint

Review the format of a summons in Lesson 98 before typing the introductory lines in the complaint.

COMPLAINT is aligned at the right on the same line as – vs-.

Use a right tab setting of 2.31" for the closing parentheses of the venue information.

Press ENTER 2 times before each Roman numeral.

All Roman numerals are centered between the margins.

A complaint is the initial document filed with a court by a plaintiff to begin an adversarial or action at law proceeding. A judgment is the decision of the court.

STATE OF NORTH DAKOTA   **IN DISTRICT COURT**

COUNTY OF WALSH   **NORTHEAST JUDICIAL DISTRICT**

WALSH COUNTY BANK	)	**NO.** _____
170 Main Street	)	
Adams, ND 58210	)	
	)	
Plaintiff,)		
	)	
- vs -	)	**COMPLAINT**
	)	
KENNEDY FARMERS, INC.	)	
JAMES D. KENNEDY and	)	
CAROL KENNEDY, Defendants)		

PLAINTIFF FOR ITS CAUSE OF ACTION AND COMPLAINT AGAINST THE DEFENDANTS, COMPLAINS, ALLEGES AND SHOWS TO THE COURT:

I.

That defendants owe plaintiff $5,685.00, plus interest and charges, under the terms of a promissory note executed April 10, 20--, a copy of which is attached hereto and incorporated by reference as "Exhibit A."

II.

That defendants have not, upon due demand, satisfied their obligation under the terms of the promissory note.

III.

That Kennedy Farmers, Inc., is a North Dakota for-profit corporation duly organized under the corporate laws of the State of North Dakota.

IV.

That the registered agent of Kennedy Farmers, Inc., is James D. Kennedy.

V.

That James D. Kennedy executed a Commercial Guaranty for the note dated April 10, 20--, a copy of which is attached hereto and incorporated herein by reference as "Exhibit B."

(Continued on next page)

VI.

That the indebtedness was the renewal of a prior promissory note executed by Kennedy Farmers, Inc., to Walsh County Bank on June 17, 20--, which was in the original principal amount of $6,685.00, a copy of which is attached hereto and incorporated by reference as "Exhibit C."

VII.

That Carol Kennedy executed a Commercial Guaranty on the prior promissory note No. 7249, and the Commercial Guaranty provides that the guaranty extends to " . . . all renewals of, extensions of, modifications of, refinancings of, consolidations of, and substitutions for the promissory note or agreement." A copy of that Commercial Guaranty is attached hereto and incorporated hereby by reference as "Exhibit D."

VIII.

That James D. Kennedy and Carol Kennedy are personally liable for the amount of the debt, as is the corporation, Kennedy Farmers, Inc.

WHEREFORE, PLAINTIFF DEMANDS JUDGMENT AGAINST THE DEFENDANTS, AND EACH OF THEM, AS FOLLOWS:

1. For the amount of $3,585.00, plus interest on that amount from and after April 10, 20--, at the rate of 10.75% per annum; and for its costs, late charges, and disbursements in this action;
2. For such other and further relief as the Court may deem appropriate.

SIGNED this _____ day of December, 20--.

_____

Harold E. Jensen
Attorney at Law
405 1st Street
Adams, ND 58210
Telephone: (701) 555-4832
Attorney for Plaintiff

Be sure to use bold type in selected words and phrases of the complaint.

Numbered items are indented to the same point as the paragraphs.

Set a left tab at 3.0 inches for the signature lines and attorney description.

A Judgment uses the same format as a Complaint, shown in Report 100-72 on pages 388–389.

Be sure to use bold type in selected words of the judgment.

Use a right tab setting of 2.88" for the closing parentheses of the venue information.

Format all-caps text in bold.

STATE OF ARIZONA

COUNTY OF MARICOPA

IN DISTRICT COURT

CENTRAL JUDICIAL DISTRICT

CIVIL NO. 43-89-D-00145

Timothy Barnes d/b/a Barnes Computers)
1651 West Baseline Road)
Tempe, AZ 85283)
)
Plaintiff,)
)
- vs -)
)
Maricopa Hospital Association)
d/b/a Maricopa Nursing Care)
Defendant)

JUDGMENT

¶ The defendant, Maricopa Hospital Association, d/b/a Maricopa Nursing Care, having been regularly served with process, and having failed to appear and answer the plaintiff's Complaint filed herein, and the default of said defendant having been duly entered, and it appearing that said defendant is not an infant nor an incompetent person, and an affidavit of nonmilitary service having been filed herein, and it appearing by the affidavits of plaintiff that plaintiff is entitled to judgment herein,

¶ IT IS THEREFORE ORDERED AND ADJUDGED, that the plaintiff have and recover from the defendant, Maricopa Hospital Association d/b/a Maricopa Nursing Care, the sum of $8,000.00 plus interest thereon from and after August 10, 20--, until paid, together with costs in the sum of $252.75.

¶ SIGNED this _____ day of _____, 20___.

_____
Clerk of the District Court

✔ **Progress Check**
Proofreading Check

Documents designated as Proofreading Checks serve as a check of your proofreading skill. Your goal is to have zero typographical errors when the GDP software first scores the document.

The first underscore is 6 characters wide; the second underscore is 20 characters wide.

AFFIDAVIT OF POSSESSION

STATE OF OREGON

COUNTY OF LINN

¶ I, MARILYN T. HUGGINS, being first duly sworn, depose and say:
¶ That I am the petitioner in the above-entitled suit.
¶ That the respondent, RICHARD M. HUGGINS, and I are the parents of BENJAMIN T. HUGGINS. That BENJAMIN T. HUGGINS is currently residing exclusively with me. Respondent is currently residing away from the home at 1529 South Oak Street, Albany, Oregon. That I am a fit and proper person to have immediate and temporary custody of BENJAMIN T. HUGGINS.
¶ I believe that these pending dissolution proceedings will aggravate this situation; therefore, I believe that it is necessary and appropriate for the Court to issue an Order restraining and enjoining respondent from physically or verbally abusing or harassing me or our child in any way.

¶ Subscribed and sworn to before me this _____ day of
_____, 20--.

_____
Notary Public for Oregon
My commmission expires: 1/7/20--

Legal teams frequently work together on documentation review, using the keyboard to track revisions.

Skills Assessment on Part 5

5-Minute Timing

1　　　When you submit your resume to apply for a job, you　　10

2　want your resume to be noticed. Here are some things you　　22

3　can do to make certain your resume receives the attention　　34

4　it deserves.　　36

5　　　First, be neat. Review the resume to make sure there　　47

6　are no spelling or typographical errors. Check your resume　　59

7　for correct grammar. Remember, this document will make the　　71

8　first impression with a potential employer; you want the　　82

9　document to represent you in the best way. Use white paper　　94

10　of good quality to print your resume.　　102

11　　　Second, try to be creative. Make your resume unique.　　113

12　A potential employer may be looking for specific criteria　　125

13　when he or she scans the elements of your resume. Be sure　　137

14　to provide information that explains exactly what skills　　148

15　you have acquired in positions you have held in the past.　　160

16　Avoid using the buzzwords that everyone else uses.　　170

17　　　Finally, state a career objective on your resume.　　180

18　Some experts suggest that by stating a career objective,　　191

19　you are showing a career path. Others think that stating　　202

20　a career objective may limit many job possibilities. If　　213

21　you state a career objective, make sure the objective is　　224

22　in line with the specific job for which you are applying.　　235

| 1 | 2 | 3 | 4 | 5 | 6 | 7 | 8 | 9 | 10 | 11 | 12

Current Date (use day/month/year format) | Mr. Antoine Lauvergeon | Marketing Director | Alatel Inc. | 54 Rue la Boetie | 75382 Paris cedex 08 | France | Dear Mr. Lauvergeon:

¶ As we predicted, our jefe effort marketing was a tremendous success in the 5 new plants opened last Spring in France and Germany. In fact, sales at those two plants have surpassed our Switzerland and Italy sales over the same period. Much of this sucess is due to your timely marketing campaign that was conducted during the first quarter. Congratulations to you and your staff on this fine effort.

Because of this positive experience, we have decided to expand our promotional campaign at our plants in Negras Piedras, Morelia, and Cancun. Would you please put together a proposal for these plants and send it to me by the end of next week. We are excited about this oportunity and look forward to recieving your proposal.

¶ Again, nice work on the France and Germany promotion effort.

Sincerely, | Harold Deforey | V.P., Marketing | c: Mari Lynn Somnolet, James Lafforgue

HEMATOLOGY REPORT

Name ―――――――――――――――――――――― **Doctor** ――――――――――――――――――――

Test Results ――――――――――――――――――――――――――――――――――

―― WBC   ―― Glucose
―― Hemoglobin   ―― Cholesterol
―― PMN   ―― BUN
―― Bands   ―― Calcium
―― Lymphs   ―― Phosphorous
―― Mono   ―― Bilirubin
―― Eos   ―― Uric acid
―― Baso   ―― Alkaline phosphatase
―― Platelets   ―― Albumin
―― Thyroid   ―― Protein, total

Productivity for the voluminous research involved in the legal profession is enhanced by the use of a keyboard.

Use a right tab setting of 2.18" for the closing parentheses of the venue information.

STATE OF NEBRASKA	**IN DISTRICT COURT**
COUNTY OF WAYNE	**NORTHEAST JUDICIAL DISTRICT**

PAUL C. CREWS   )
610 Thorman St   )
Wayne, NE 68787   )
)
            Plaintiff,)
)
      - vs -   )
)
ANGELINA WASHINGTON)
          Defendant.)

NO.———

SUMMONS

THE STATE OF NEBRASKA TO THE ABOVE-NAMED DEFENDANT:

You are hereby required to appear and defend the complaint filed against you in the above-entitled action within thirty (30) days from the date of service of this summons upon you, and in case of your failure to do so, for want thereof, plaintiff(s) will apply to the court for the relief demanded in the complaint.

SIGNED this ——— day of May, 20--

_____

Jeremy Richfield
Attorney at Law
Box 148
Wayne, NE 68787
Telephone: (402) 555-3832
Attorney for Plaintiff

PART 6

Using and Designing Business Documents

OBJECTIVES

KEYBOARDING

▶ Type at least 50 words per minute on a 5-minute timing with no more than 5 errors.

LANGUAGE ARTS

▶ Refine proofreading skills and correctly use proofreaders' marks.

▶ Use capitals, punctuation, and grammar correctly.

▶ Improve composing and spelling skills.

▶ Recognize subject/verb agreement.

WORD PROCESSING

▶ Use the word processing commands necessary to complete the document processing activities.

DOCUMENT PROCESSING

▶ Design office forms, office publications, and Web pages.

TECHNICAL

▶ Answer at least 90 percent of the questions correctly on an objective test.

KEYBOARDING IN WHOLESALE/RETAIL SALES AND SERVICES

Occupations in this cluster involve planning, managing and performing wholesaling and retailing services and related marketing and distribution support services including merchandise/product management and promotion. Types of jobs within this sector include purchasing agent and buyer, sales manager, wholesaler, retail store owner, market research analyst, broker, salesperson, and package designer.

Personality characteristics are more important in marketing and sales occupations than in almost any other line of work. People who work in this area should be outgoing, enthusiastic, persuasive, and receptive to new ideas. Keyboarding skills are essential for anyone venturing into marketing and distribution. Success in sales takes initiative, energy, self-confidence, and self-discipline.

Job Outlook

Wholesale/retail sales and services offer numerous employment opportunities because people are constantly purchasing new products and replacing old ones. The field of design is teeming with job possibilities for those who are self-disciplined, creative problem-solvers, and have an eye for color and design.

Using and Designing Office Forms

 **From the Desk of James Kirkland**

 From the Desk of James Kirkland

☐ Urgent
☐ Do Today
☐ Follow-up

☐ Urgent
☐ Do Today
☐ Follow-up

 **From the Desk of James Kirkland**

 **From the Desk of James Kirkland**

☐ Urgent
☐ Do Today
☐ Follow-up

☐ Urgent
☐ Do Today
☐ Follow-up

Memorandum

To: Gloria Hernandez, Vice President

CC: Roy Phillips, Marketing Manager

From: Naoe Okubo, Senior Graphics Artist

Date: Current Date

Re: Web Site Redesign

I have finished evaluating the five Web design firms who made formal presentations to our Web site team last week. The two finalists are Global Web Resources and CompuTek International. Their portfolios and presentations were very impressive. I believe either firm would be an excellent choice. Mr. Phillips agrees with this assessment.

I have arranged for a formal presentation to our key executives for Wednesday afternoon of next week in our corporate dining room. We will have a luncheon first followed by the presentations. I have also attached key information from the portfolios of both firms as well as details of Wednesday's meeting. Please let me know if you need any further information.

urs

Attachment

1

WINTER SPORTS

2820 Cerrillos Road • Santa Fe, NM 87505 • 505-555-3496 • www.wintersports.com

Using Correspondence Templates

GOALS
- Improve speed and accuracy
- Refine language arts skills in grammar
- Format correspondence using a template

A. Type 2 times.

A. WARMUP

```
1    The secretary made a reservation on Flight #847; it      11
2  departs at exactly 3:05 on July 6. A sizable number of     22
3  key executives (about 1/2) requested seats in Rows G to M. 34
   | 1 | 2 | 3 | 4 | 5 | 6 | 7 | 8 | 9 | 10 | 11 | 12
```

SKILLBUILDING

B. Take three 12-second timings on each line. The scale below the last line shows your wpm speed for a 12-second timing.

B. 12-SECOND SPEED SPRINTS

```
4  Bob will lend all the keys to you if you will fix the leak.
5  Ruth wanted to thank you for all of the work you did today.
6  Both of the books will have to be sent to her by next week.
7  Dick paid her half of the money when she signed the papers.
   I I I I 5 I I I I 10 I I I I 15 I I I I 20 I I I I 25 I I I I 30 I I I I 35 I I I I 40 I I I I 45 I I I I 50 I I I I 55 I I I I 60
```

C. PROGRESSIVE PRACTICE: ALPHABET

If you are not using the GDP software, turn to page SB-7 and follow the directions for this activity.

D. PROGRESSIVE PRACTICE: NUMBERS

If you are not using the GDP software, turn to page SB-11 and follow the directions for this activity.

LANGUAGE ARTS

E. Study the rules at the right.

E. ADJECTIVES AND ADVERBS AND AGREEMENT

RULE ▶
, adjective/adverb

Use comparative adjectives and adverbs (-*er, more,* and *less*) when referring to two nouns or pronouns; use superlative adjectives and adverbs (-*est, most,* and *least*) when referring to more than two.

The <u>shorter</u> of the <u>two</u> training sessions is the <u>more</u> helpful one.
The <u>longest</u> of the <u>three</u> training sessions is the <u>least</u> helpful one.

If two subjects are joined by *or, either/or, neither/nor,* or *not only/but also,* make the verb agree with the subject nearer to the verb.

Neither the coach nor the <u>players</u> <u>are</u> at home.

Not only the coach but also the <u>referee</u> <u>is</u> at home.

But: <u>Both</u> the coach and the referee <u>are</u> at home.

Edit the sentences to correct any errors in grammar.

8 Of the three printers, the faster one was the most expensive.
9 Of the two phones purchased, the first one is the better model.
10 The quietest of the five printers is also the less expensive.
11 Not only the manager but also the employees wants to attend.
12 Neither the printer nor the monitors is in working order.
13 Either Mr. Cortez or his assistants have to sign the order.
14 Coffee or soft drinks is available for the afternoon session.
15 Not only the manual but also the software were mailed.

FORMATTING

F. FILLING IN FORMS

Many business forms can be created by using templates that are provided within word processing software. When a template is opened, a generic form is displayed on the screen. Specific information that is appropriate for that form may then be added.

Template forms contain data fields that correspond to blank sections on printed forms. For example, a memo template may include the guide words *To:*, *CC:*, *From:*, *Date:*, and *Re*: for the subject. Templates are usually designed so that

you can replace data in fields easily by clicking in the field and typing or by selecting the information you want to replace and typing. Built-in styles are also readily available.

You can customize a generic template by filling in repetitive information (such as the company name and telephone number) and save it as a new template. Then each time you open that newly created template, the customized information appears automatically.

Go To

Word Processing Manual

G. WORD PROCESSING: CORRESPONDENCE TEMPLATES

Study Lesson 101 in your word processing manual. Complete all of the shaded steps while at your computer. Then format the jobs that follow.

DOCUMENT PROCESSING

Form 101-1 ▶

Memo Template

Note: You may want to read and print the information in the template before deleting it.

1. Select the first memo template listed in your word processing software.
2. Follow the directions on the template to type the information for this memo using the built-in styles as needed.
3. Use the default style for the current date.
4. Type the rest of the information in the copy shown on the next page.

(Continued on next page)

To: Naoe Okubo, Senior Graphics Artist

CC: ~~Mr.~~ Roy Phillips, Marketing Manager

From: Gloria Hernandez, Vice President

Date: Current Date

Re: Website Redesign

¶ Our web site needs a complete redesign and reorganization. I know this assignment ~~is~~ *will be* a major challenge, and I have full confidence in your ~~skill~~ *experience* and ability. Within the next week, ~~you should~~ *please* contact 5 web design firms and make arrangements for a formal presentation to you and your staff. ~~Please~~ invite Roy Phillips and his staff in Marketing as well. When you have chosen the two best candidates, submit your findings to *our* key executives in a *formal* presentation. The better of the two will then be chosen.

¶ Because our web site is ~~crucial~~ *critical* to our sales and marketing efforts, you must make this assignment a top priority. If you need temporary help to support you in your efforts, let me know. Thank you for your continued good work, Naoe. I look forward to ~~your~~ *the* presentation and your recom*m*endations.

urs

adjective/adverb

adjective/adverb

Form 101-2 ▶

Letter Template With Enclosure Notation

1. Select the first letter template listed in your word processing software.
2. Follow the template directions to type the information for this letter using the built-in styles as needed.
   Note: There is no company slogan.
3. The company name is `Global Web Resources`.
4. Type each line of the return address on a separate line similar to the inside address on the letter.

The return address is as follows:
   `575 Eighth Avenue, Suite 1104`
   `New York, NY 10018`
   `212-555-3495`
   `www.globalwebresources.com`

5. Use the default spacing provided by the template between the date and the inside address.
6. Type the rest of the information into the template as indicated in the copy below using standard business letter format for a block-style letter.

Current Date | Naoe Okubo | Contempo Fashions | 22802 Soledad Canyon | Santa Clarita, CA 91355 | Dear Ms Okubo:

¶ Thank you for your request for more information on Web page design, layout, and graphics. I have enclosed some brochures that address some of your questions.

¶ Ms. Ina Phillips is our senior account manager in your area. Either her staff members or Ms. Phillips is going to schedule an appointment with you and your staff for a formal presentation of our design portfolios this week. The best way to answer your questions and to help you reach a decision is to

agreement nearer noun

(Continued on next page)

have you see examples of some of the Web sites we have developed for other clients in the fashion industry. I know you will be impressed by the creativity and innovative concepts that Global Web Resources is known for in this business.

¶ If you would like a preview now, please go to www.globalwebresources.com and click the link entitled Professional Images to see some of our best designs. Again, thank you for your interest in our services.

Sincerely, | Linda Vigil | Vice President | urs | Enclosures

adjective/adverb

Form 101-3 ▶

Memo Template With Attachment Notation

agreement nearer noun

Select the first memo template listed in your word processing software.

To: Roy Phillips, Marketing Manager | **CC:** Gloria Hernandez, Vice President | **From:** Naoe Okubo, Senior Graphics Artist | **Date:** Current Date | **Re:** Web Site Redesign

¶ I have contacted five Web design firms for formal presentations in our executive boardroom. A schedule of the meeting dates and times is attached. Because Ms. Hernandez has indicated that this assignment is to take top priority, not only current projects but also future work is to be put on hold. If you need any temporary help with any projects in progress, let me know.

¶ The Web design firms that have been scheduled are very innovative and creative. The presentations should be exciting. Ask your staff to prepare for the meeting by visiting the Web sites and doing some research on each company. Please forward this memo to the members of your staff.

urs | Attachment

Keyboarding CONNECTION

Transferring Text From a Web Page

Have you ever wished you could copy the text from a Web page? You can!

To select the desired text to copy, click in front of the text and drag to the end of it. (If the text won't highlight, try to click at the end of the desired text and drag backwards.) To copy the Web text, from the Edit menu, select Copy. Open your word processing document. Position the cursor where you want to paste the text. From the Edit menu of the word processor, select Paste. The text appears in the word processing document.

When you copy text information from the Web, you must cite the source in your word processing document by giving the URL (Web page address), Web page name, and author, if given.

YOUR TURN Open a Web page. Copy some text and paste it in a word processing document.

Using Report Templates

GOALS

- Type at least 48wpm/5'/5e
- Format reports using a template

A. Type 2 times.

A. WARMUP

```
1        I am glad the office measures just 15 x 23* (*feet)      11
2   because the carpet is quite expensive! At $64/yard, we        21
3   can't afford any mistakes; contact v&zcarpets@mail.com.        33
    |  1  |  2  |  3  |  4  |  5  |  6  |  7  |  8  |  9  |  10  |  11  |  12
```

SKILLBUILDING

B. PACED PRACTICE

If you are not using the GDP software, turn to page SB-14 and follow the directions for this activity.

Careers in wholesale businesses use keyboard input to get products to customers quickly and efficiently.

C. Take two 5-minute timings. Review your speed and errors.

Goal: At least 48wpm/5'/5e

C. 5-MINUTE TIMING

4   In their quest to complete school and enter the job   11

5 market, students will discover quickly that they have more   23

6 to learn about office politics. At the beginning of their   35

7 careers, students become acquainted with the importance of   47

8 power, the office grapevine, and building relationships.   58

9   Power can be defined as the possession of control or   69

10 command over others. In any type of business there are two   81

11 types of power, formal and informal. The people listed in   93

12 the company directory in positions of authority have the   104

13 formal power. Support personnel, such as secretaries and   115

14 office assistants, have informal power.   123

15   Students understand quickly the importance of the   133

16 grapevine in office politics. Sometimes the grapevine is   144

17 portrayed as gossip, and workers need to determine that   155

18 this type of information could be harmful. However, the   166

19 grapevine can be a good source for learning procedures for   178

20 working within the organization; this type of information   190

21 is vital for career success.   196

22   Building good relationships with coworkers is also   206

23 important. Successful workers assist others in becoming a   218

24 part of the team. They realize that working together will   230

25 develop a strong team spirit that gets things done.   240

| 1 | 2 | 3 | 4 | 5 | 6 | 7 | 8 | 9 | 10 | 11 | 12

FORMATTING

Word Processing Manual

D. WORD PROCESSING: REPORT TEMPLATES

Study Lesson 102 in your word processing manual. Complete all of the shaded steps while at your computer. Then format the jobs that follow.

Form 102-4 ►

Report Template

Note: You may want to read and print the information in the template before deleting it.

1. Select the first report template listed in your word processing software.
2. Type the information for this report using the built-in template styles as needed.
3. On the title page, type the following address:

   575 Eighth Avenue, Suite 1104
   New York, NY 10018
   212-555-3495
   www.globalwebresources.com.

4. The company name is Global Web Resources.
5. The title is Web Design Proposal.
6. The subtitle is Strategies for the Online Presence of Contempo Fashions.
7. Use the same title and subtitle on the second page of the report.
8. Type the rest of the information into the template as indicated in the copy below.

Introduction

¶ Two major issues need to be addressed in terms of the website design for Contempo Fashions. The site's most obvious weakness is its lack of unity. The content seems to be out of sync with the design. This division is definitely noticeable to the casual observer.

¶ Often those in charge of content don't have any background in html or coding of any kind, and feel locked into the current design because they simply don't know what their options are. Those in charge of the design can get caught up in trying to create an attractive page that doesn't really effectively work with the content. Global Web Resources is in the business of providing workable solutions to address both needs.

Content Issues

¶ The content is the first and most important element in a web site. If the content is not effective, it doesn't matter how attractive the design is because no one will bother to read beyond the first page or even the first line. Spelling and grammar must be checked with meticulos care. The credibility of your company is at stake. The readability of the web site can be dramatically improved. Headings, subheadings, bullets, and numbers are critical in making your pages readable. Visitors to your site scan for major headings and want to move quickly and efficiently to any items of interest. Visual separation between paragraphs is also critical for readability. The use of

(Continued on next page)

whitespace created by inserting blank lines between paragraphs is generally more effective than indenting paragraphs. Short lines and short pages make readers want to look at your site pages rather than avoid them.

Design Issues

¶ The design of the web site is done well overall. Appropriate fonts, colors, and art were used in a manner that complements the image of Contempo Fashions. The site navigation is intuitive and easy to use. However, the design is dated and needs a new look.

¶ The 2 groups that are now managing the site must be given guidance in working together to produce a unified site that is both attractive and effective. The goals of the design group and those in charge of content must be brought into alignment in order to make the content work within the context of the current design. Global Web Resources has a web design solution that will bring the needs of both groups into alignment. Your redesigned site will be visually appealing, informative, and intuitive to the visitor. We look forward to our meeting this week.

Form 102-5 ▶
Report Template

Open the file for Form 102-4 and make the following changes:

1. On the title page, change the address as follows:

   ```
   8502 N. Ashley Street
   Tampa, FL 33604
   813-555-1205
   www.CTI.com.
   ```

2. The company name is CompuTek International.
3. Change the report title both on the title page and on the first page of the report to Web Site Proposal.
4. Change the report subtitle both on the title page and on the first page of the report to Content and Design Recommendations for Contempo Fashions.
5. Delete the second paragraph under the heading "Introduction."
6. Delete the second paragraph under the heading "Content Issues."
7. Delete the last paragraph of the report.

8. Move the insertion point to the end of the first paragraph under the heading "Design Issues," and press ENTER 1 time.
9. Use the Heading 1 style to add the heading Solutions.
10. Move to the end of the report, and add the following paragraphs.
    Paragraph 1:

    ```
    Your Web site should always
    have new and updated con-
    tent so that your visitors
    will have good reason to
    return. If you continue
    with your current Web site
    plan, the maintenance of
    your site will become a
    major responsibility.
    Hundreds of files will need
    to be maintained whenever
    you want to make a funda-
    mental change to your site.
    ```

(Continued on next page)

The best approach is to let your writers post new content themselves without having to worry about design issues. This is accomplished through a database-driven Web site.

Paragraph 2:
Building a database-driven Web site requires a great deal of technical expertise and tools such as scripting languages and relational database software. Your operating system must be compatible with these languages and databases. Server-side programming is also critical here. CompuTek International would build a database-driven site design and host the site to minimize technical troubleshooting issues. We look forward to our meeting this week.

A career in the exciting and ever-changing fashion industry demands an eye for color and design as well as keyboarding skills.

Designing Letterheads

GOALS
- Improve speed and accuracy
- Refine language arts skills in composing
- Design letterheads

A. Type 2 times.

A. WARMUP

```
1       Does Quentin know if 1/2 of the January order will be      11
2   ready? At 5:30 about 46% of the orders still hadn't been       22
3   mailed! Mr. Gray expects a very sizable loss this month.       33
    |  1  |  2  |  3  |  4  |  5  |  6  |  7  |  8  |  9  |  10  |  11  |  12
```

SKILLBUILDING

B. DIAGNOSTIC PRACTICE: ALPHABET

If you are not using the GDP software, turn to page SB-2 and follow the directions for this activity.

C. These paragraphs are made up of very short words, requiring the frequent use of the SPACE BAR. Do not pause before or after pressing the SPACE BAR. Type the paragraph 2 times.

C. TECHNIQUE PRACTICE: SPACE BAR

```
4       He had the car in the shop and knew that the cost for
5   the work might be high. If the bill for the work was to be
6   more than he could pay, he knew that he would skip it. It
7   did not make any sense to put more money into the old car.
8       If you are near the old shop, come in to see if you can
9   pay the bill at that time. If you are not able to pay it at
10  that time, you can come back to see us when you are able.
```

LANGUAGE ARTS

D. COMPOSING A MEMO

Compose the body of a memo to explain basic design guidelines. Refer to page 409—Section E, Designing a Form—frequently. Use the following suggestions for composing each paragraph:

Paragraph 1. Explain that a simple, balanced design is essential and that typefaces, attributes, and sizes should be limited.

Paragraph 2. Explain that white space should be used to make text easier to read and graphics easier to see.

Paragraph 3. Explain that word processing software is a powerful tool that makes experimenting easy.

E. DESIGNING A FORM

Use the following guidelines to design an attractive, effective form:

1. Keep all elements of your design simple and balanced.
2. Limit the number of typefaces (fonts), attributes (bold, italics, etc.), and sizes. Using two typefaces is a good rule of thumb.
3. Use white space liberally to separate and open up text and graphics.
4. Use different alignments (left, center, right, and full) to add interest and emphasis.
5. Experiment and change—word processing software makes both easy to do.

Go To

Word Processing Manual

F. WORD PROCESSING: SMALL CAPS AND TEXT BOXES

Study Lesson 103 in your word processing manual. Complete all of the shaded steps while at your computer. Then format the jobs that follow.

DOCUMENT PROCESSING

Form 103-6 ▶

Letterhead Form

Note: When creating, sizing, or positioning a text box, switch to a whole-page view. When typing text, switch to a page-width view or larger as desired. As you add information to the text box, adjust the size of the text box as needed.

1. Change the left and right margins to 0.25 inch, and press ENTER 2 times.
2. Apply a border to the bottom of the second blank line.
3. Insert a picture of an elementary school or kindergarten.
4. Drag and size the picture so that it looks like the one in the illustration.
5. Create a text box about the size and in the same position as the one in the illustration to hold the business name.
6. Remove the line around the text box, and change the fill to none.
7. Change to Arial 18 point small caps, and center and type Tutor Time.
8. Change the font color as desired to coordinate with the picture.
9. Create a text box about the size and in the same position as the one in the illustration to hold the address of the business.
10. Remove the line around the text box, and change the fill to none.
11. Change the font to Arial 10 point, and right-align and type the lines of the address:

       4219 Richmond Ave., Suite 205
       Houston, TX 77027
       713-555-7337
       www.tutortime.com

(Continued on next page)

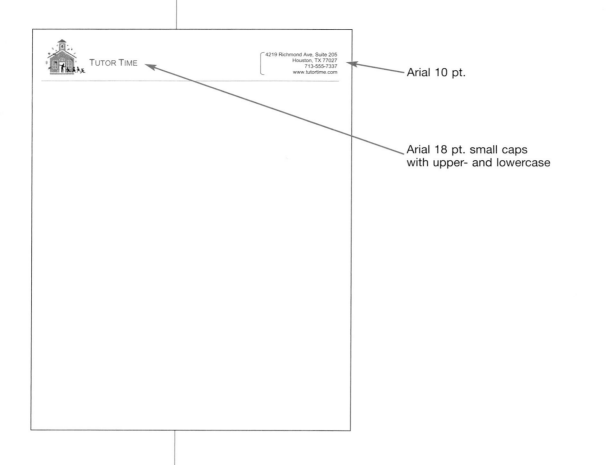

TUTOR TIME

4219 Richmond Ave, Suite 205
Houston, TX 77027
713-555-7337
www.tutortime.com

Arial 10 pt.

Arial 18 pt. small caps
with upper- and lowercase

Letterhead Form

1. Press ENTER 2 times, and insert a picture of your favorite winter sport.
2. Drag and size the picture so that it looks like the one in the illustration.
3. Create a text box about the size and in the same position as the one in the illustration to hold the name of the business.
4. Remove the line around the text box, and change the fill to none.
5. Change to Times New Roman 24 point small caps, and type Winter Sports with upper- and lowercase.
6. Change the font color of the business name to coordinate with one of the colors in the picture.
7. Create a text box about the size and in the same position as the one in the illustration to hold the address of the business.

8. Change the font to Times New Roman 10 point and center and type the lines of the address:
   2820 Cerillos Road
   Santa Fe, NM 87505
   505-555-3496
   www.wintersports.com.
9. Insert a diamond-shaped symbol between each item in the address block as shown in the illustration. Insert 1 space before and after the symbol.
10. Add a fill to the textbox to coordinate with one of the colors in the picture.

(Continued on next page)

Times New Roman 24 pt. small caps
with upper- and lowercase

Times New Roman 10 pt.

WINTER SPORTS

2820 Cerillos Road ◆ Santa Fe, NM 87505 ◆ 505-555-3496 ◆ www.wintersports.com

Form 103-8 ▶

Letterhead Form

1. Create a letterhead design of your own—for you personally, for your school, or for a business.
2. Insert at least one picture that enhances the theme of the letterhead.

3. Remember to include complete information in the address block.
4. Try using other fonts that you have not yet applied—experiment with point sizes and attributes.

STRATEGIES FOR *Career Success*

Designing the Page for Readability

A well-designed document is appealing to the eye, easy to read, and shows you are professional and competent. Follow these simple guidelines to increase the readability of your documents.

Use white space (e.g., empty space) to make material easier to read by separating it from the other text. Side margins should be equal. Create white space by varying paragraph length. The first and last paragraphs should be short—three to five typed lines.

Use bulleted or numbered lists to emphasize material. Lists are normally indented on the left. Make sure all the items in the list are grammatically parallel in structure. Use headings to introduce new material. Use full caps sparingly. Consider desktop publishing software to visually enhance your document. Remember to balance graphics, lists and text.

YOUR TURN Review a document you have recently written. What page design and format techniques did you use to make the document more readable?

Designing Notepads

GOALS

- Type at least 48wpm/5'/5e
- Design notepads

A. Type 2 times.

A. WARMUP

```
1        This series* (*6 films, 28 minutes) by J Zeller goes      11
2 beyond the "basics" of computers. Viewers keep requesting       23
3 an extension on the dates; this includes 3/2, 5/5, and 8/9.   35
   |  1  |  2  |  3  |  4  |  5  |  6  |  7  |  8  |  9  |  10  |  11  |  12
```

SKILLBUILDING

B. MAP

Follow the GDP software directions for this exercise in improving keystroking accuracy.

Retail sales management opportunities require excellent keyboarding skills in the day-to-day business operation.

C. Take two 5-minute timings. Review your speed and errors.

Goal: At least 48wpm/5'/5e

C. 5-MINUTE TIMING

```
 4      Employers are always searching for people who have        10
 5  saleable skills. Having saleable skills makes you unique      21
 6  and desirable as an employee. Developing skills such as       32
 7  tenacity, a good sense of humor, positive attitude, ability   44
 8  to get along with coworkers, a pleasing personality, and      55
 9  the ability to manage your time and prioritize your work      66
10  could help you find a good job.                               72
11      A tenacious person is persistent and maintains strong     83
12  work habits. He or she does not give up on any task easily    95
13  and always expects to complete the assigned tasks.           105
14      A good sense of humor and a positive attitude are two    116
15  traits that can help a person advance on the job. Although   128
16  there are times to be serious at work, sometimes you have    140
17  to look at things humorously. If you maintain a positive     151
18  attitude, other workers will like working with you.          162
19      When you acquire the skills to manage your time and      172
20  prioritize your work, you will be successful in anything     183
21  you try to do. When you are given an assignment, ask for     195
22  guidelines so that you will know what needs to be done and   207
23  in what order. Then try to complete the assignment in a      218
24  timely fashion. The skills may be difficult to learn, but    230
25  you will be glad you can manage your time and work.          240
    |  1  |  2  |  3  |  4  |  5  |  6  |  7  |  8  |  9  |  10  |  11  |  12
```

FORMATTING

Go To
Word Processing Manual

D. WORD PROCESSING: PRINT OPTIONS

Study Lesson 104 in your word processing manual. Complete all of the shaded steps while at your computer. Then format the jobs that follow.

Form 104-9 ▶

Notepad Form

Many ink jet printers do not print beyond the bottom half inch on a sheet of paper. Keep this in mind when positioning objects at the bottom of a page.

1. Press ENTER 2 times, and insert a picture of an office desk or some picture related to an office notepad.
2. Drag and size the picture so that it looks similar to the one in the illustration.
3. Create a text box about the size and in the same position as the one in the illustration to hold the words "From the Desk of Your Name."
4. Remove the line around the text box, and change the fill to none.
5. Change to Arial Bold 36 point, and center and type From the Desk of Your Name inside the text box.
6. Create a text box about the size and in the same position as the one in the illustration to hold the checkbox list at the bottom of the notepad.
7. Remove the line around the text box, and change the fill to none.

8. Insert a checkbox symbol using Wingdings Italic 28 point. Space 1 time.
9. Change to Arial Italic 28 point, type Urgent inside the text box, and press ENTER 1 time.
10. Repeat Steps 8 and 9 for the remaining lines in the checkbox list, adding the words Do Today and Follow-up.
11. Change to a whole-page view, and select and copy the entire document.
12. Move to the end of the document and insert 3 hard page breaks to create 3 additional blank pages.
13. Paste the copied document into each of the 3 newly created pages.
14. Use the print option to print 4 pages per sheet on 8.5- by 11-inch paper.

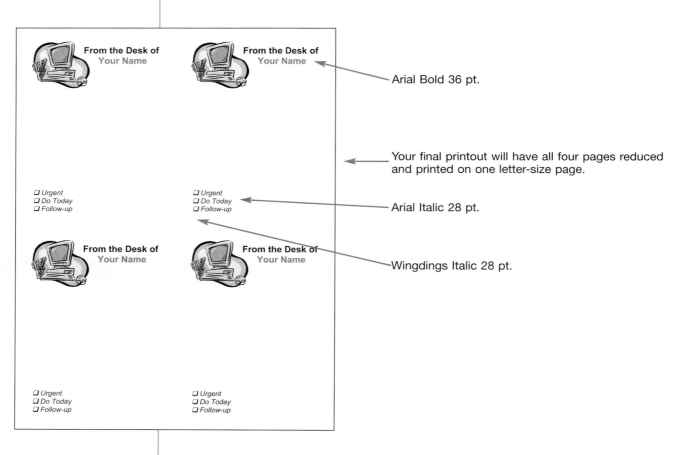

From the Desk of
Your Name — Arial Bold 36 pt.

Your final printout will have all four pages reduced and printed on one letter-size page.

❑ Urgent
❑ Do Today — Arial Italic 28 pt.
❑ Follow-up

Wingdings Italic 28 pt.

Form ▶
104-10

Notepad Form

1. Press ENTER 2 times, and insert a picture of an office desk or some picture related to a musical note or a personalized office note.
2. Drag and size the picture so that it looks similar to the one in the illustration.
3. Create a text box about the size and in the same position as the one in the illustration to hold the words "Just a Note to Say."
4. Remove the line around the text box, and change the fill to none.
5. Change to a script font of your choice in 48 point bold and italic.
6. Center and type Just a Note to Say followed by 1 space and 3 periods with 1 space after each period except the last.

7. Create a text box about the size and in the same position as the one in the illustration to hold the words at the bottom of the notepad.
8. Change to the same script font used in the first text box in 36 point, and center and type From the Desk of Your Name inside the text box.
9. Change to a whole-page view, and select and copy the entire document.
10. Move to the end of the document, and insert 3 hard page breaks to create 3 additional blank pages.
11. Paste the copied document into each of the 3 newly created pages.
12. Use the print option to print 4 pages per sheet on 8.5- by 11-inch paper.

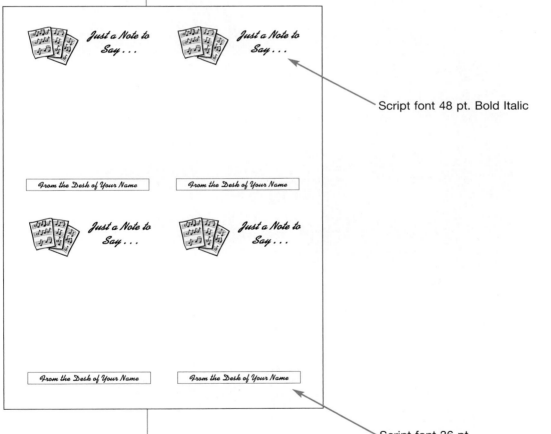

Script font 48 pt. Bold Italic

Script font 36 pt.

1. Create a notepad design of your own—for you personally, for your school, or for a business.
2. Insert at least one picture that enhances the theme of the notepad.

3. Insert at least one text box with a fill.
4. Try using other fonts that you have not yet applied. Experiment with point sizes and attributes.

Careers in retail sales and service may use scanning input for some tasks, but the keyboard is a necessary component to complete business transactions.

Designing Miscellaneous Office Forms

GOALS
- Improve speed and accuracy
- Refine language arts skills in proofreading
- Design miscellaneous office forms

A. Type 2 times.

A. WARMUP

```
1        Item #876 won't be ordered until 9/10. Did you gather    11
2 all requests and input them exactly as they appeared? Zack      23
3 will never be satisfied until he contacts jack@orders.com.      35
  | 1 | 2 | 3 | 4 | 5 | 6 | 7 | 8 | 9 | 10 | 11 | 12
```

SKILLBUILDING

PRETEST → PRACTICE → POSTTEST

B. PRETEST: Vertical Reaches

PRETEST
Take a 1-minute timing. Review your speed and errors.

```
4        The man knelt on the lawn and used a knife with skill    11
5 to raise the valve away from the brace. His back ached in       23
6 vain as he crawled over the knoll to fix the flawed valve.      35
  | 1 | 2 | 3 | 4 | 5 | 6 | 7 | 8 | 9 | 10 | 11 | 12
```

C. PRACTICE: Up Reaches

PRACTICE
Speed Emphasis:
If you made no more than 1 error on the Pretest, type each *individual* line 2 times.
Accuracy Emphasis:
If you made 2 or more errors, type each *group* of lines (as though it were a paragraph) 2 times.

```
7 aw away award crawl straw drawn sawed drawl await flaw lawn
8 se self sense raise these prose abuse users serve send seem
9 ki kind kites skill skier skims skips skits kilts king skid
```

D. PRACTICE: Down Reaches

```
10 ac ache track paced brace races facts crack acute back aces
11 kn knob knife kneel knows knack knelt known knoll knot knew
12 va vain vague value valve evade naval rival avail vats vase
```

POSTTEST
Repeat the Pretest timing and compare performance.

E. POSTTEST: Discrimination Practice

F. SUSTAINED PRACTICE: SYLLABIC INTENSITY

13	People continue to rent autos for personal use or for	11
14	their work, and the car-rental business continues to grow.	23
15	When you rent a car, look carefully at the insurance cost.	35
16	You might also have to pay a mileage charge for the car.	46
17	It is likely that a good deal of insurance coverage is	11
18	part of the standard rental cost. But you might be urged	22
19	to procure extra medical, property, and collision coverage.	34
20	If you accept, be ready to see your rental charge increase.	46
21	Perhaps this is not necessary, as you may already have	11
22	the kind of protection you want in a policy that you have	23
23	at the present time. By reviewing your own auto insurance	35
24	policy, you may easily save a significant amount of money.	47
25	Paying mileage charges could result in a really large	11
26	bill. This is especially evident when the trips planned	22
27	involve destinations that are many miles apart. Complete a	34
28	total review of traveling plans before making a decision.	45

LANGUAGE ARTS

G. Compare these lines with lines 25-28 in the Sustained Practice drill above. Edit the lines to correct any errors.

G. PROOFREADING

29	Paying milage charges could result in a very large
30	bill. This is especially evident when the trips planned
31	involve destinations that are manymiles apart. complete a
32	total review of traveling plans before making a decsion.

DOCUMENT PROCESSING

Form 105-12

Directory Form

1. Change the page orientation to landscape.
2. Change the top margin to 2.3 inches and the remaining margins to 0.75 inch.
3. Press ENTER 1 time.
4. Create a boxed table with 4 columns and 17 rows.
5. Select the entire table and change the font to Arial Bold 18 point.
6. Type these column headings in Row 1: Name | Department | Phone Number | Email Address. Change the alignment in the row to center.
7. Move to the top of the document, and insert a picture associated with a directory in the same position as the one in the illustration.
8. Insert a text box about the size and in the same position as the one in the illustration to hold the heading.
9. Change to Arial 48 point, and center and type Directory at a Glance inside the text box.
10. Remove the line around the text box, and change the fill to none.
11. Add shading to the cells in Row 1 of the boxed table, using a color that complements the picture.

(Continued on next page)

Directory at a Glance

Arial 48 pt.

Name	Department	Phone Number	Email Address

Arial Bold 18 pt.

Form 105-13 ►

Sign-In Form

1. Change the top margin to 2 inches and the remaining margins to 0.75 inch.
2. Create a boxed table with 4 columns and 29 rows.
3. Select Row 1 and change the font to Arial Bold 18 point.
4. Type these column headings in Row 1: Name | Time In | Doctor's Name | Purpose. Change the alignment in the row to center.
5. Adjust the column widths manually so they appear similar to the illustration.
6. Select Rows 2-29 and change the font to Arial Bold 12 point.
7. Insert a text box about the size and in the same position as the one in the illustration to hold the name of the medical group.
8. Change to Times New Roman 48 point, and center and type Facey Medical Group.
9. Remove the line around the text box, and change the fill to none.
10. Insert a picture of an office desk or some clip art related to an office notepad.
11. Create a text box about the size and in the same position as the one in the illustration to hold the date line.
12. Change to Arial Bold 12 point, and type Date: followed by a series of underlines to form a signature line similar to the one in the illustration.
13. Remove the fill and the lines around the text box.
14. Create a text box about the size and in the same position as the one in the illustration to hold the names of the doctors.
15. Change to Times New Roman Italic 12 point, and type the following doctors' names in a bulleted list:
    Dr. Mary Chavez
    Dr. Irving K. Levine
    Dr. Evelyn Jones
16. Remove the line around the text box, and change the fill to none.
17. Change the font color of the words on the form as desired to coordinate with the picture.

(Continued on next page)

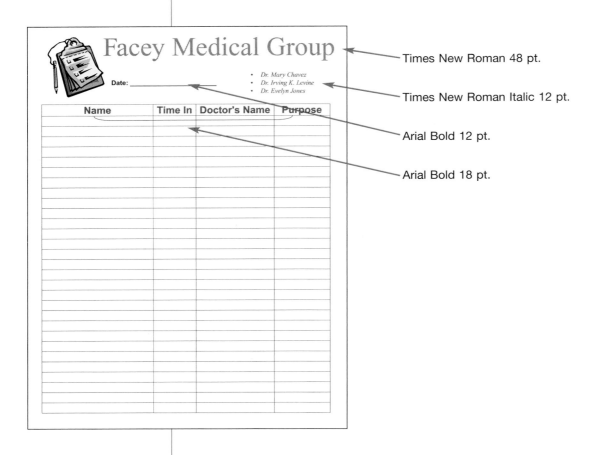

Facey Medical Group → Times New Roman 48 pt.

Date: _____

- Dr. Mary Chavez
- Dr. Irving K. Levine
- Dr. Evelyn Jones

→ Times New Roman Italic 12 pt.

→ Arial Bold 12 pt.

→ Arial Bold 18 pt.

Name	Time In	Doctor's Name	Purpose

**Form ▶
105-14**

Memo Template With
Attachment Notation

Select the first memo
template listed in your
word processing
software.

**✓ Progress Check
Proofreading Check**

Documents designated
as Proofreading Checks
serve as a check of your
proofreading skill. Your
goal is to have zero typographical errors when the
GDP software first scores
the document.

To: Gloria Hernandez, Vice President | **CC:** Roy Phillips, Marketing Manager | **From:** Naoe Okubo, Senior Graphics Artist | **Date:** Current Date | **Re:** Web Site Redesign

¶ I have finished evaluating the five Web design firms who made formal presentations to our Web site team last week. The two finalists are Global Web Resources and CompuTek International. Their portfolios and presentations were very impressive. I believe either firm would be an excellent choice. Mr. Phillips agrees with this assessment.

¶ I have arranged for a formal presentation to our key executives for Wednesday afternoon of next week in our corporate dining room. We will have a luncheon first followed by the presentations. I have also attached key information from the portfolios of both firms as well as details of Wednesday's meeting. Please let me know if you need any further information.

urs | Attachment

Designing Office Publications

LESSON 106
Designing Cover Pages

LESSON 107
Designing Announcements and Flyers

LESSON 108
Designing Newsletters: A

LESSON 109
Designing Newsletters: B

LESSON 110
Designing Newsletters: C

The Traveler's Connection
A Newsletter From E-Travel.com

Volume 9, Issue No. 5 — Spring 20--

In This Issue:
A Few Tips for the Smart Traveler, Page 1
Planning Your Travel Online, Page 1
Focus on Dallas-Fort Worth, Page 2
Texas Tidbits, Page 2
Thistle Hill, Page 2

A Few Tips for the Smart Traveler

We all have visions of the perfect vacation. They usually include a beautiful hotel, a comfortable room, great food, and wonderful entertainment. Unfortunately, sometimes our vision doesn't exactly align itself with reality, and our dream has suddenly turned into a nightmare. You can avoid this situation if you will do some smart advance planning.

Here are some smart travel tips that can turn your dream vacation into a reality:

- Do your homework. Your best bet is to find out all you can about your destination before you do anything else. Find a good travel agent, do your own research on the Internet, and buy some good travel books on your destination in your favorite bookstore.

- Carry medications and other essentials with you. To avoid a disaster, carry everything you can't function without in the event that your luggage is lost. This would inc lude medications, money, tickets, toiletries, visas, passports, eyeglasses, and anything else you can think of that is irreplaceable in the course of a day or two.

- Buy travel insurance. If you are taking an expensive vacation and are not completely sure you can make it, buying travel insurance is a wise expenditure. Many people today have children and aging parents whose needs are unpredictable.

- Confirm all reservations. Be sure that all your reservations including hotels, cars, and entertainment are confirmed and that you have the different confirmation numbers and phone numbers written down. Nothing can ruin a trip faster than finding out that you don't' have a place to sleep or suitable transportation. You will find that if you take these tips to heart, your vac ation will be just as wonderful as you imagined!

Planning Your Travel Online

The Internet has opened up a wealth of information that used to be the domain of individual travel agencies. If you have a computer and Internet access, you can make reservations, buy tickets, book entertainment packages, and do any number of other things.

Save hours of time and lots of money by using the Internet wisely when you plan your travel. You can shop for the best airline rates and even name your own price if you are flexible in your travel plans.

Several good books are available to help you use the Internet for your travel plans. Please check our web site at www.TTC.com for suggested books.

Page 1

Focus on Dallas-Fort Worth

This month's focus is on the Dallas-Fort Worth area.

THE AIRPORT
The Dallas-Fort Worth International Airport is 17 miles from the business districts of each town. The

LOVE FIELD
Love Field is a $10 to $15 taxi ride from downtown Dallas. The phone number is 214-555-6073.

Love Field is the hub of Western Airlines, which offers service within Texas, to many cities in the surrounding states, and, with stops, to destinations as far away as Chicago.

BETWEEN THE AIRPORT AND TOWN
It costs around $30 to get to downtown Dallas by taxi from the Dallas-Fort Worth International Airport. It is about $25 to downtown Fort Worth.

Cheaper bus and van service is also available. Please check our web site at

Although this is the world's second busiest airport, it is surprisingly easy to use. However, the transportation between terminals is slow.

Texas Tidbits

- To receive mail while traveling in Dallas, have it sent c/o General Delivery at the city's main post office.
- Most businesses open between 8 a.m. and 10 a.m. and close around 6 p.m. Many are also open on weekends.
- Banks operate weekdays from 9 a.m. until 2 or 3 p.m., and some are also open on Saturday mornings.
- Post offices are open weekdays from 8 a.m. to 5 p.m. and Saturday mornings.
- At traffic lights, it's legal to make a right turn on a red light except when there is a sign at the intersection stating that such a turn is not   permitted. Of course, come to a full stop first and make sure

Your Guide to Online Banking

Account	ATM Card	Check Writing	Monthly Fee
Regular Checking	None	Unlimited	$ 9.00
Interest Checking	Express Card	Unlimited	10.00
Basic Checking	Express Card	Unlimited	4.50
Student Checking	Express Card	Unlimited	3.00
Note: Fees may apply to telephone banking calls and the use of the ATM Express Card.			

Lesson 106

Designing Cover Pages

GOALS
- Type at least 49wpm/5'/5e
- Design cover pages

A. Type 2 times.

A. WARMUP

```
1        Buzz told us that Flight #7864 got into Phoenix just      11
2  3 minutes before Vick's! This is quite remarkable when        22
3  you realize that we never planned for such a "coincidence."    34
   | 1 | 2 | 3 | 4 | 5 | 6 | 7 | 8 | 9 | 10 | 11 | 12
```

SKILLBUILDING

B. PROGRESSIVE PRACTICE: ALPHABET

If you are not using the GDP software, turn to page SB-7 and follow the directions for this activity.

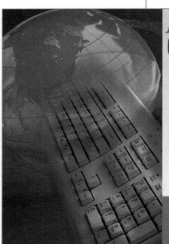

Keyboarding CONNECTION

Searching the Yellow Pages

Do you find the Yellow Pages of your phone directory handy? Try the Internet as an alternate source. Many of the Web's search engines have a Yellow Pages feature that is quite useful.

You can use the Yellow Pages feature to search for mailing addresses and phone numbers of businesses and organizations. The Yellow Pages link appears in most leading Internet search engines. These search engines may also provide a map of the location of the business or organization.

The Yellow Pages feature of a search engine is like having all the phone directories in the United States at your fingertips.

YOUR TURN Click the Yellow Pages feature on one of your favorite search engines. Search for a business in your city by name and then by category. Did you retrieve the address and phone number of the business using both search methods?

C. Take two 5-minute timings. Review your speed and errors.

Goal: At least 49wpm/5′/5e

C. 5-MINUTE TIMING

4 Are women better at some jobs than men? In one recent 11

5 study, researchers found that women might be better sales 23

6 managers. Women are better suited for organizations that 34

7 have a collaborative style of management. The study found 46

8 other interesting tendencies among women managers. 56

9 Females were able to build sales teams that had more 67

10 commitment to company goals. They could motivate, direct, 79

11 evaluate, and reward their sales force better than their 90

12 male counterparts. The study found that the managers were 102

13 able to reduce stress levels by working closely with their 114

14 teams, and workers were more satisfied with their jobs and 126

15 happier with their pay. Staff turnover was also reduced. 137

16 The team building and nurturing skills of female sales 148

17 managers may be what some companies need to be successful. 160

18 This study also compared sales in companies using 170

19 controls based on behavior with sales in companies using 181

20 controls based on outcome. Companies with sales based on 192

21 behavior want to make sales, but they also want to acquire 204

22 closer relationships with their customers. However, in 215

23 companies using controls based on outcomes, sales reps are 227

24 not given exact directions by their managers, and they are 239

25 usually paid only commissions. 245

| 1 | 2 | 3 | 4 | 5 | 6 | 7 | 8 | 9 | 10 | 11 | 12 |

FORMATTING

Go To

Word Processing Manual

D. WORD PROCESSING: WORD ART

Study Lesson 106 in your word processing manual. Complete all of the shaded steps while at your computer. Then format the jobs that follow.

DOCUMENT PROCESSING

Report 106-76

Cover Page

To ensure that your document is scored properly, you will insert 2 spaces at the beginning of the document.

1. Press the SPACE BAR 2 times, and insert a picture related to vision or reading.
2. Drag and size the picture so that it looks similar to the one in the illustration.

3. Insert word art about the size and in the same position as the one at the top of the illustration with the words Preferred Optical Vision Plan in 2 lines as shown. Use the default font.

(Continued on next page)

4. Choose a style and color to coordinate with the picture.
5. Create a text box about the size and in the same position as the one at the bottom of the illustration to hold the directory information.
6. Remove the line around the text box, and change the fill to none.
7. Change to Arial Bold 20 point, center and type `Directory of Participating Vision Care Specialists` in 2 lines as shown in the illustration, and press ENTER 2 times.

8. Change to Arial 16 point, center, and type `for all salaried employees of the San Francisco Community College District` in 2 lines as shown in the illustration, and press ENTER 2 times.
9. Change to Arial 18 point, center, and type `September 20--`.
10. Change any of the font colors to coordinate with the picture as desired.

Preferred Optical

Vision Plan

Arial Bold 20 pt.

**Directory of
Participating Vision Care Specialists**

Arial 16 pt.

for all salaried employees of the
San Francisco Community College District

Arial 18 pt.

September 20--

**Report
106-77**

Cover Page

1. Press the SPACE BAR 2 times, and insert a picture related to dining.
2. Drag and size the picture so that it looks similar to the one in the illustration on page 425.
3. Insert word art about the size and in the same position as the one at the top of the illustration with the words `Sonoma County's Dining Guide` in 2 lines as shown.
4. Choose a style and color for the word art to coordinate with the picture, and use the default font.

5. Create a text box about the size and in the same position as the one at the bottom of the illustration to hold the bulleted list.
6. Remove the line around the text box, and change the fill to none.
7. Change to Arial Bold 24 point, and type the following list unformatted (without bullets):
   `Fine Dining`
   `Midrange`
   `Bargain`
8. Apply bullets to the list.

(Continued on next page)

9. Create a text box about the size and in the same position as the one at the bottom of the illustration to hold the date.
10. Add a line around the text box, and change the fill to a color that coordinates with the picture.
11. Change to Arial Bold Italic 26 point, and type Summer 20--.
12. Change any of the font colors to coordinate with the picture as desired.

Sonoma County's
Dining Guide

Arial Bold 24 pt.

• **Fine Dining**
• **Midrange**
• **Bargain**

Arial Bold Italic 26 pt.

Summer 20--

Report ▶ 106-78

Cover Page

1. Create a cover page design of your own to be used as the insert for a view binder that holds information for one of your courses.
2. Insert at least one picture related to the subject of the course.
3. Insert at least one text box with a fill.
4. Insert some word art.
5. Change any of the font colors to coordinate with the picture or word art as desired.

Designing Announcements and Flyers

GOALS
- Improve speed and accuracy
- Refine language arts skills in grammar
- Design announcements and flyers

A. Type 2 times.

A. WARMUP

```
1        Does Quentin know if 1/2 of the January order will be      11
2   ready? At 5:30 about 46% of the orders still hadn't been        22
3   mailed! Mr. Gray expects a very sizable loss this month.        33
     |  1  |  2  |  3  |  4  |  5  |  6  |  7  |  8  |  9  |  10  |  11  |  12
```

SKILLBUILDING

B. Take three 12-second timings on each line. The scale below the last line shows your wpm speed for a 12-second timing.

B. 12-SECOND SPEED SPRINTS

```
4   Rico will rush to tidy the big room that held the supplies.
5   Yale is a very fine school that has some very strict rules.
6   Helen will audit the books of one civic leader in the city.
7   The man had a name that was hard for the small girl to say.
      I I I I 5 I I I I 10 I I I I 15 I I I I 20 I I I I 25 I I I I 30 I I I I 35 I I I I 40 I I I I 45 I I I I 50 I I I I 55 I I I I 60
```

C. Type each sentence on a separate line by pressing ENTER after each sentence. Type 2 times.

C. TECHNIQUE PRACTICE: ENTER

```
8    Decorate the room. Attend the seminar. Go to the theater.
9    Watch the inauguration. Go to the rally. See the recital.
10   Run in the marathon. Bake the bread. Vacuum the bedrooms.
11   Visit the nursing home. Sell the ticket. Drive the truck.
```

D. DIAGNOSTIC PRACTICE: ALPHABET

If you are not using the GDP software, turn to page SB-2 and follow the directions for this activity.

LANGUAGE ARTS

E. Study the rules at the right.

E. PRONOUNS

RULE ▶
nominative pronoun

Use nominative pronouns (such as *I, he, she, we, they,* and *who*) as subjects of a sentence or clause.

The programmer and <u>he</u> are reviewing the code.

Barb is a person <u>who</u> can do the job.

(Continued on next page)

Use objective pronouns (such as *me, him, her, us, them,* and *whom*) as objects of a sentence, clause, or phrase.

The code was reviewed by the programmer and <u>him</u>.
Barb is the type of person <u>whom</u> we can trust.

Edit the sentences to correct any errors in the use of pronouns.

12 We hope they will take all of them to the concert tomorrow.
13 John gave the gift to she on Monday; her was very pleased.
14 If them do not hurry, Mary will not finish her work on time.
15 The book was proofread by her; the changes were made by he.
16 It is up to them to give us all the pages they read today.
17 Me cannot assure they that it will not rain for the picnic.

FORMATTING

Go To

Word Processing Manual

F. WORD PROCESSING: TABLE—MOVE

Study Lesson 107 in your word processing manual. Complete all of the shaded steps while at your computer. Then format the jobs that follow.

DOCUMENT PROCESSING

Report 107-79

Announcement

1. Change the left and right margins to 0.5 inch.
2. Press the SPACE BAR 2 times, and insert a picture associated with a large city.
3. Drag and size the picture so that it looks similar to the one in the illustration.
4. Create a text box about the size and in the same position as the one at the top of the illustration to hold the welcoming message.
5. Remove the line around the text box, and change the fill to none.
6. Change to Arial 28 point, center, and type The Hotel Cosmopolitan in 2 lines as shown in the illustration, and press ENTER 1 time.
7. Change to Arial 22 point, and center and type welcomes.
8. Insert word art about the size and in the same position as the one at the top of the illustration with the words NBEA Conference Attendees.
9. Drag and size the word art so that it looks similar to the word art shown in the illustration.
10. Change the word art font for readability if desired.
11. Choose a style and color for the word art to coordinate with the picture.
12. Insert a boxed table with 3 columns and 7 rows, and drag it into position as shown in the illustration.
13. Change to Times New Roman Bold 20 point, and type the centered column headings.
14. Change to Times New Roman 20 point, and type the left-aligned column entries.
15. Type the information in Column C in 2 lines as shown.
16. Merge the cells in Row 7, change to Times New Roman 16 point, and type the information as shown.
17. Automatically adjust the column width for all entries, and drag the table into position again.
18. Add a shading color to the first and last row to coordinate with the word art and picture.

(Continued on next page)

Event	Time	Location
President's Welcome	8:30-9:30 a.m.	Mezzanine Ballroom B
Internet Training	10-11:30 a.m.	First Floor Cityscape Room
NBEA Luncheon	12-1 p.m.	Mezzanine Grand Ballroom
Computer Workshops	1-3 p.m.	First Floor Rooms A, B, and D
Research Sessions*	3-5:30 p.m.	Third Floor Rooms 1, 3, and 5

nominative pronoun
nominative pronoun
objective pronoun
nominative and objective pronouns

*President's Note: I encourage anyone who is interested to attend our research sessions this afternoon. Dr. Roy Phillips, who will be the facilitator, is excellent. Both of us are available to answer group questions during the session, or you may direct individual questions to either him or me after the session.

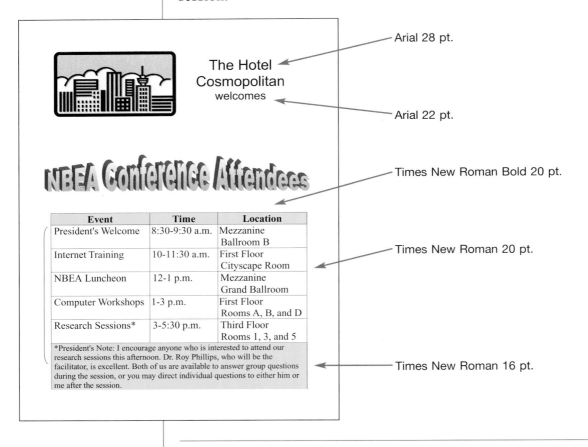

Report 107-80

Flyer

1. Press the SPACE BAR 2 times, and insert a picture associated with the summer season.
2. Drag and size the picture so that it looks similar to the one shown in the illustration.
3. Insert word art about the size and in the same position as the one at the top of the illustration with the words `Summerset Homes`.
4. Choose a style and color for the word art to coordinate with the picture.

(Continued on next page)

5. Create a text box about the size and in the same position as the one in the middle of the illustration to hold the message.
6. Remove the line around the text box, and change the fill to none.
7. Change to Arial 28 point; center and type Summerset Homes proudly invites you to the grand opening of our newest group of single-family homes! as shown in the illustration.
8. Create a text box about the size and in the same position as the one at the bottom of the illustration to hold the address information.
9. Remove the line around the text box, and add a fill using a color to coordinate with the word art and the fill.

10. Change to Arial 12 point; center and type as shown in the illustration:
    Summerset Homes
    520 SW Harbor Way
    Portland, OR 97201
    800-555-2649
    www.Summerset.com
11. Insert a star-shaped symbol between each item in the address block as shown in the illustration.
12. Insert 2 spaces before and after the star-shaped symbol.
13. Insert a boxed table with 3 columns and 5 rows, and drag it into position as shown in the illustration.
14. Change to Times New Roman 22 point, and type the column entries.
15. Automatically adjust the column width for all entries, and drag the table into position again.

Shadow Pines	1,235 sq. ft.	$209,990
Ocean View	1,495 sq. ft.	223,990
Country Meadow	1,759 sq. ft.	265,990
Desert Breeze	2,042 sq. ft.	295,990
Valley Oasis	2,537 sq. ft.	322,990

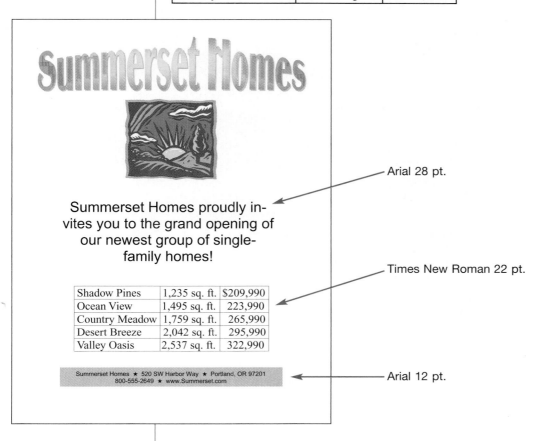

Arial 28 pt.

Times New Roman 22 pt.

Arial 12 pt.

1. Create an announcement or flyer design of your own for an upcoming event at work or on campus.
2. Press the SPACE BAR 2 times and insert at least one picture related to the topic of the announcement or flyer.
3. Insert at least one text box with a fill.

4. Insert some word art.
5. Apply color to your fonts to coordinate with the picture or word art.
6. Insert a table that contains information related to the topic of the flyer or announcement.

The demand for multimedia products has created many opportunities in sales careers, all requiring the use of keyboarding skills.

Designing Newsletters: A

GOALS

- Type at least 49wpm/5'/5e
- Design newsletters

A. Type 2 times.

A. WARMUP

```
1       Does Pamela know if Region 29* (*Ventura) has met the    11
2  sales quota? Their exact target zone is just not clear;       22
3  they don't have to submit their totals until 4:30 on 5/7.     33
   | 1 | 2 | 3 | 4 | 5 | 6 | 7 | 8 | 9 | 10 | 11 | 12
```

SKILLBUILDING

B. PACED PRACTICE

If you are not using the GDP software, turn to page SB-14 and follow the directions for this activity.

STRATEGIES FOR *Career Success*

Managing Business Phone Time

The average American spends an hour a day on the phone. Phone calls can be extremely distracting from necessary tasks. Time is spent taking the call and following up after the call. You can take steps to reduce wasted time on the phone.

When you make an outgoing call, organize the topics you want to discuss. Have all the materials you need: pencils, paper, order forms, etc. When you take an incoming call, answer it promptly. Identify yourself. It is common to answer the phone with your first and last name (e.g., "Mary Smith speaking." or "Mary Smith").

Limit social conversation; it wastes time. Give concise answers to questions. At the end of the call, summarize the points made. End the conversation politely.

YOUR TURN Keep a log of your time on the phone for one day. What is your average conversation time? What can you do to reduce your average phone conversation time?

C. Take two 5-minute timings. Review your speed and errors.

Goal: At least 49wpm/5'/5e

C. 5-MINUTE TIMING

4 The personal use of computers and the Internet in the   11
5 workplace has contributed some new issues for employers   22
6 and employees. Are employees entitled to privacy in the   33
7 workplace? Do employers have a right to monitor workers   44
8 who are using company computers for personal use? Should   55
9 employers impose restrictions regarding Internet activity   67
10 and email use to protect their businesses?   75

11 Employers should scrutinize the Internet sites and   85
12 chat rooms that workers may be accessing on company time.   97
13 Also, employers may want to check on their workers during   109
14 office hours to determine if they are using their time   120
15 effectively on the job. Employers have a right to expect   131
16 high levels of productivity from their employees during   142
17 office hours. Employees should realize that excessively   153
18 using company computers for personal email messages and   164
19 Internet activity is not acceptable.   171

20 The company policy on personal computer usage should   182
21 be explained to all employees. Employees must understand   193
22 that the surveillance of their computer usage is required   205
23 in order to protect the business from possible lawsuits.   216
24 Employees should be given the opportunity to ask questions   228
25 to make sure they understand the penalties they may incur   240
26 if they violate the policy.   245

| 1 | 2 | 3 | 4 | 5 | 6 | 7 | 8 | 9 | 10 | 11 | 12 |

FORMATTING

D. NEWSLETTER DESIGN

Newsletters are an excellent forum for communicating information on a wide range of subjects. A well-planned newsletter will employ all the basic principles of good design. However, because newsletters usually include information on a wide variety of topics, they are generally more complex in their layout.

Most newsletters have the following elements in common: mastheads, main headings and subheadings, text arranged in flowing newspaper-column format using various column widths to add interest, text boxes to emphasize and summarize, pictures to draw readers' attention and interest to a topic, and a variety of borders and fills.

The design of a multipage newsletter must look consistent from one page to the next. This consistency provides unity to the newsletter design and is often achieved through the use of headers and footers.

Report 108-82

Newsletter

Reminder: You will finish the newsletter in Lessons 109 and 110.

Follow these steps to create the masthead and footer for the first page of the newsletter shown on page 421.

1. Set all margins at 0.75 inch.
2. Create an open table with 2 columns and 2 rows. Drag the middle column border to the left so the first column is about 1.75 inches wide.
3. Right-align Column B.
4. In Column B, Row 1, change to Times New Roman Bold 48 point, and type The Traveler's Connection.
5. Press ENTER 1 time, change to Arial Bold 14 point, and type A Newsletter From E-Travel.com.

6. Move to Column A, Row 2, and type Volume 9, Issue No. 5.
7. Move to Column B, Row 2, and type Spring 20--.
8. Apply borders to the top and bottom of Row 2.
9. In Column A, Row 1, insert a picture associated with world travel.
10. Drag and size the picture so that it looks similar to the one shown in the illustration.
11. Insert a footer, and center and type Page followed by 1 space.
12. Insert a page number field and close the footer.

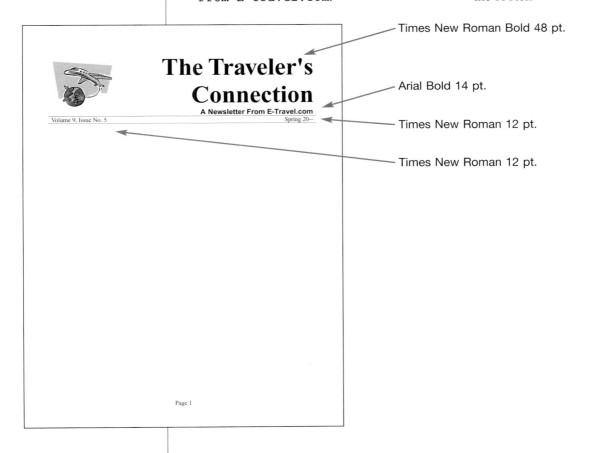

Times New Roman Bold 48 pt.

Arial Bold 14 pt.

Times New Roman 12 pt.

Times New Roman 12 pt.

The Traveler's Connection
A Newsletter From E-Travel.com
Volume 9, Issue No. 5   Spring 20--

Page 1

Report 108-83

Newsletter

1. Create a newsletter masthead of your own related to travel and similar to the one in Report 108-82.

2. Use any picture that enhances the purpose of your travel newsletter.

Lesson 109

Designing Newsletters: B

GOALS
- Improve speed and accuracy
- Refine language arts skills in spelling
- Design newsletters

A. Type 2 times.

A. WARMUP

```
1        Approximately 90% of the weekly budget was just used    11
2   to buy equipment. A very sizable amount totaling $12,654     22
3   was spent on "necessities" as requested by the department!   34
    | 1  | 2  | 3  | 4  | 5  | 6  | 7  | 8  | 9  | 10 | 11 | 12
```

SKILLBUILDING

PRETEST → PRACTICE → POSTTEST

B. PRETEST: Alternate- and One-Hand Words

PRETEST
Take a 1-minute timing. Review your speed and errors.

```
4        A great auditor is eager to spend a minimum of eighty   11
5   hours to amend a problem. If he assessed a penalty that      22
6   exceeded the usual fee, I reserve the right to correct it.   34
    | 1  | 2  | 3  | 4  | 5  | 6  | 7  | 8  | 9  | 10 | 11 | 12
```

C. PRACTICE: Alternate-Hand Words

PRACTICE
Speed Emphasis:
If you made no more than 1 error on the Pretest, type each *individual* line 2 times.
Accuracy Emphasis:
If you made 2 or more errors, type each *group* of lines (as though it were a paragraph) 2 times.

```
7   also amend maps thrown blame city problem panel formal down
8   snap rigid lens social visit with penalty right height half
9   chap usual such enrich shape dish auditor spend eighty kept
```

D. PRACTICE: One-Hand Words

```
10  was only great pupil regret uphill scatter homonym assessed
11  bed join water nylon target pompon savages minimum exceeded
12  age hook eager union teased limply reserve opinion attracts
```

POSTTEST
Repeat the Pretest timing and compare performance.

E. POSTTEST: Alternate- and One-Hand Words

F. SUSTAINED PRACTICE: NUMBERS AND SYMBOLS

13	Shopping in the comfort and convenience of your own	11
14	living room has never been more popular than it is right	22
15	now. Shopping clubs abound on cable channels. You could	33
16	buy anything from exotic pets to computers by mail order.	44
17	Sometimes you can find discounts as high as 20% off	11
18	the retail price; for example, a printer that sells for	22
19	$565 might be discounted 20% and be sold for $452. You	33
20	should always investigate quality before buying anything.	44
21	Sometimes hidden charges are involved; for example,	11
22	a printer costing $475.50 that promises a discount of 12%	23
23	($57.06) has a net price of $418.44. However, if charges	34
24	for shipping range from 12% to 15%, you did not save money.	46
25	You must also check for errors. Several errors have	11
26	been noted so far: Invoice #223, #789, #273, and #904 had	23
27	errors totaling $21.35, $43.44, $79.23, and $91.23 for a	34
28	grand total of $235.25. As always, let the buyer beware.	45

LANGUAGE ARTS

G. SPELLING

29	operations health individual considered expenditures vendor
30	beginning internal pursuant president union written develop
31	hours enclosing situation function including standard shown
32	engineering payable suggested participants providing orders
33	toward nays total without paragraph meetings different vice

34	The participents in the different meetings voted for hours.
35	The presdent of the union is working toward a resolution.
36	The health of each individal must be seriously considered.
37	Engineering has suggested providing orders for the vendor.
38	One expanditure has been written off as part of oparations.
39	He is inclosing the accounts payible record as shown today.

Report 109-84 ▶

Newsletter (continued)

 Reminder: You will finish the newsletter in Lesson 110.

Open the file for Report 108-82 shown on page 433. Follow these steps to create the second page of the newsletter shown on page 421.

1. Move outside the table below Column A and press ENTER 2 times.
2. Insert File 109, and turn on automatic hyphenation.
3. Carefully place your insertion point in front of the second blank line under the masthead, and select all the newly inserted text including 1 blank line below the last line of text.
4. Create 3 columns with a line between columns.
5. Select the following headings in the newsletter, and change the font to Arial 24 point:
   ```
   A Few Tips for the Smart
      Traveler
   Planning Your Travel Online
   Focus on Dallas-Fort Worth
   ```
6. Select the following subheadings in the newsletter and bold them:
   ```
   THE AIRPORT
   LOVE FIELD
   BETWEEN THE AIRPORT AND TOWN
   ```
7. Place your insertion point in front of the second blank line under the masthead.
8. Insert a table with 1 column and 1 row.
9. Change to Arial 12 point, and type In This Issue:.

10. Change to Times New Roman Italic 12 point, and type the following lines:
    ```
    A Few Tips for the Smart
       Traveler, Page 1
    Planning Your Travel
       Online, Page 1
    Focus on Dallas-Fort
       Worth, Page 2
    Texas Tidbits, Page 2
    Thistle Hill, Page 2
    ```
11. Add a shading color to the table to coordinate with the picture in the masthead.
12. Insert a picture in the space above each of the bulleted items in the first article on the first page of the newsletter. The pictures should be associated in some way with the topic in each of the bulleted items.
13. Drag and size the pictures so that they look similar to the ones shown in the illustration.
14. Place your insertion point in the blank line above the heading "Planning Your Online Travel," and apply a top border.
15. Place your insertion point in the blank line above the heading "Focus on Dallas-Fort Worth," and apply a top border.

(Continued on next page)

The Traveler's Connection

A Newsletter From E-Travel.com

Volume 9, Issue No. 5   Spring 20--

Arial 12 pt.

Times New Roman Italic 12 pt.

A Few Tips for the Smart Traveler

We all have visions of the perfect vacation. They usually include a beautiful hotel, a comfortable room, great food, and wonderful entertainment. Unfortunately, sometimes our vision doesn't exactly align itself with reality, and our dream has suddenly turned into a nightmare. You can avoid this situation if you do some smart advance planning.

Here are some smart travel tips that can turn your dream vacation into a reality:

- Do your homework. Your best bet is to find out all you can about your destination before you do anything else. Find a good travel agent, do your own research on the Internet, and buy some good travel books on your destination in your favorite bookstore.

- Carry medications and other essentials with you. To avoid a disaster, carry everything you can't function without in the event that your luggage is lost. These items would include medications, money, tickets, toiletries, visas, passports, eyeglasses, and anything else you can think of that is irreplaceable in the course of a day or two.

- Buy travel insurance. If you are taking an expensive vacation and are not completely sure you can make it, buying travel insurance is a wise expenditure. Many people today have children and aging parents whose needs are unpredictable.

- Confirm all reservations. Be sure that all your reservations, including hotels, cars, and entertainment, are confirmed and that you have the different confirmation numbers and phone numbers written down. Nothing can ruin a trip faster than finding out that you don't have a place to sleep or suitable transportation.

You will find that if you take these tips to heart, your vacation will be just as wonderful as you imagined!

Arial 24 pt.

Planning Your Travel Online

The Internet has opened up a wealth of information that used to be the domain of individual travel agencies. If you have a computer and Internet access, you can make reservations, buy tickets, book entertainment packages, and do any number of other things.

Arial 24 pt.

Page 1

Save hours of time and lots of money by using the Internet wisely when you plan your travel. You can shop for the best airline rates and even name your own price if you are flexible in your travel plans.

Several good books are available to help you use the Internet for your travel plans. Please check our Web site at www.TTC.com for suggested books.

Focus on Dallas-Fort Worth

This month's focus is on the Dallas-Fort Worth area.

THE AIRPORT

The Dallas-Fort Worth International Airport is 17 miles from the business districts of each town. The phone number is 214-555-8888.

Although this is the world's second busiest airport, it is surprisingly easy to use. However, the transportation between terminals is slow.

LOVE FIELD

Love Field is a $10 to $15 taxi ride from downtown Dallas. The phone number is 214-555-6073.

Love Field is the hub of Western Airlines, which offers service within Texas, to many cities in the surrounding states, and, with stops, to destinations as far away as Chicago.

BETWEEN THE AIRPORT AND TOWN

It costs around $30 to get to downtown Dallas by taxi from the Dallas-Fort Worth International Airport. It is about $25 to downtown Fort Worth.

Cheaper bus and van service is also available. Please check our Web site at www.TTC.com. for details.

Arial 24 pt.

Page 2

1. Open the file for Report 108-82 with the newsletter masthead you created.
2. Follow the steps for Report 109-84, and then delete everything on the second page of the newsletter.

3. Change the information in the contents text box at the top of the first column, insert a picture at the end of the last column of the newsletter to balance the page, and move any pictures around as needed.

Planning a trip online is fun, easy, and requires the use of your keyboarding skills.

Designing Newsletters: C

GOALS

- Type at least 49wpm/5'/5e
- Design newsletters

A. Type 2 times.

A. WARMUP

```
1        At exactly 8:30 a.m., Quigley & Co. will host a wide      11
2   variety of chat room discussions; send email to chat@QC.com. 23
3   Organizational skills will be the topics in Rooms K5 and J6. 35
    |  1  |  2  |  3  |  4  |  5  |  6  |  7  |  8  |  9  | 10  | 11  | 12
```

SKILLBUILDING

B. DIAGNOSTIC PRACTICE: NUMBERS

If you are not using the GDP software, turn to page SB-5 and follow the directions for this activity.

C. MAP

Follow the GDP software directions for this exercise in improving keystroking accuracy.

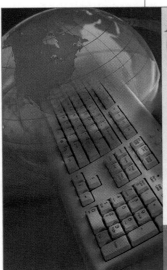

Keyboarding CONNECTION

Effective Email Management

Are you bombarded with email? Take a few simple steps to manage email more efficiently and reduce wasted time.

Create separate accounts for receiving messages that require your direct attention. Keep your mailbox clean by deleting messages you no longer use. Create folders to organize messages you need to keep (e.g., folders for separate projects).

If you receive numerous email messages, consider purchasing an email manager. Email manager programs help you manage multiple email accounts, find messages using powerful search functions, and notify you when you receive a message from a specified person.

Keep backups of important files. Be cautious of email from people you do not know. Check your email on a regular basis to avoid buildup of messages.

YOUR TURN Review the current organization of your email. List ways you can improve the management of your email.

D. Take two 5-minute timings. Review your speed and errors.

Goal: At least 49wpm/5'/5e

D. 5-MINUTE TIMING

4 　　When the rate of unemployment is very low, jobs are　11

5 easier to find. Although you may find a job easily, what　22

6 can you do to make sure your job is one you will enjoy?　33

7 Here are some suggestions to help you.　41

8 　　First, be certain you receive a job description when　52

9 you are hired. The job description should list all of the　64

10 requirements of the job and the details of what you will　75

11 be expected to do.　79

12 　　Second, you should receive some type of orientation　90

13 to your job and the company. During orientation, you will　102

14 fill out various tax forms, benefit forms, and insurance　113

15 papers. You may view a video that will help you learn more　125

16 about the company and available benefits.　133

17 　　Third, when you start your training, you should take　144

18 notes, pay attention, and ask questions. You should also　155

19 have your trainer check your work for a period of time to　167

20 be sure you are performing your duties correctly. If your　179

21 tasks are complex, you can break them down into smaller　190

22 parts so you can remember all parts of the job.　199

23 　　Finally, when you know your job requirements, chart　210

24 your work each day. Concentrate on being part of the team.　222

25 Be zealous in striving to work beyond the expectations of　234

26 your supervisor. Then, you will achieve job satisfaction.　245

| 1 | 2 | 3 | 4 | 5 | 6 | 7 | 8 | 9 | 10 | 11 | 12 |

DOCUMENT PROCESSING

Report 110-86 ▶

Newsletter (continued)

Open the file for Report 109-84 shown on page 436. Follow these steps to finish creating the newsletter shown on page 441.

1. Place your insertion point directly in front of the first blank line underneath the last line of text in the newsletter.
2. Insert File 110A.
3. Insert a picture in the space to the right of the heading "Focus on Dallas-Fort Worth" on the second page of the newsletter. The pictures should be associated with the concept of focusing on a subject or associated with Texas.
4. Drag and size the picture so that it looks similar to the one shown in the illustration.
5. Insert word art, about the size and in the same position as the word art at the top of the bulleted list on the second page of the newsletter, with the words Texas Tidbits.
6. Choose a style and color for the word art to coordinate with the newsletter.
7. Insert a picture at the bottom of the second page in the space to the left of the information on "Thistle Hill." The

(Continued on next page)

If your printer or computer memory is limited, try previewing the document before you print, and then print only one page at a time.

picture should be associated with the information about Thistle Hill or with Texas.

8. Drag and size the picture so that it looks similar to the one shown in the illustration.

9. Create a text box about the size and in the same position as the one at the bottom of the newsletter to hold the information about Thistle Hill.

10. Insert File 110B and adjust the size of the text box as needed.

11. Add a fill color or fill effect to the text box to coordinate with the picture to the left of the text box.

12. Create a text box about the size and in the same position as the one at the bottom of the newsletter to hold the information about tours.

13. Change to Times New Roman Bold 12 point, and center and type For tour information, call 817-555-2663.

14. Remove the lines around the text box, and change the fill to none.

15. The first page of the newsletter should look like the illustration below.

16. The second page of the newsletter should look like the illustration on page 442.

The Traveler's Connection

A Newsletter From E-Travel.com

Volume 9, Issue No. 5   Spring 20--

In This Issue:
A Few Tips for the Smart Traveler, Page 1
Planning Your Travel Online, Page 1
Focus on Dallas-Fort Worth, Page 2
Texas Tidbits, Page 2
Thistle Hill, Page 2

A Few Tips for the Smart Traveler

We all have visions of the perfect vacation. They usually include a beautiful hotel, a comfortable room, great food, and wonderful entertainment. Unfortunately, sometimes our vision doesn't exactly align itself with reality, and our dream has suddenly turned into a nightmare. You can avoid this situation if you do some smart advance planning.

Here are some smart travel tips that can turn your dream vacation into a reality:

• Do your homework. Your best bet is to find out all you can about your desti-

nation before you do anything else. Find a good travel agent, do your own research on the Internet, and buy some good travel books on your destination in your favorite bookstore.

• Carry medications and other essentials with you. To avoid a disaster, carry everything you can't function without in the event that your luggage is lost. These items would include medications, money, tickets, toiletries, visas, passports, eyeglasses, and anything else you can think of that is irreplaceable in the course of a day or two.

• Buy travel insurance. If you are taking an expensive vacation and are not completely sure you can make it, buying travel insurance is a wise expenditure. Many people today have children and aging parents whose needs are unpredictable.

• Confirm all reservations. Be sure that all your reservations, including hotels, cars, and entertainment, are confirmed and that you have the different confirmation numbers and phone numbers written down. Nothing can ruin a trip faster than finding out that you don't have a place to sleep or suitable transportation.

You will find that if you take these tips to heart, your vacation will be just as wonderful as you imagined!

Planning Your Travel Online

The Internet has opened up a wealth of information that used to be the domain of individual travel agencies. If you have a computer and Internet access, you can make reservations, buy tickets, book entertainment packages, and do any number of other things.

Page 1

(Continued on next page)

Save hours of time and lots of money by using the Internet wisely when you plan your travel. You can shop for the best airline rates and even name your own price if you are flexible in your travel plans.

Several good books are available to help you use the Internet for your travel plans. Please check our web site at www.TTC.com for suggested books.

Focus on Dallas-Fort Worth

This month's focus is on the Dallas-Fort Worth area.

THE AIRPORT

The Dallas-Fort Worth International Airport is 17 miles from the business districts of each town. The phone number is 214-555-8888.

Although this is the world's second busiest airport, it is surprisingly easy to use. However, the transportation between terminals is slow.

LOVE FIELD

Love Field is a $10 to $15 taxi ride from downtown Dallas. The phone number is 214-555-6073.

Love Field is the hub of Western Airlines, which offers service within Texas, to many cities in the surrounding states, and, with stops, to destinations as far away as Chicago.

BETWEEN THE AIRPORT AND TOWN

It costs around $30 to get to downtown Dallas by taxi from the Dallas-Fort Worth International Airport. It is about $25 to downtown Fort Worth.

Cheaper bus and van service is also available. Please check our web site at www.TTC.com. for details.

Texas Tidbits

- To receive mail while traveling in Dallas, have it sent c/o General Delivery at the city's main post office.
- Most businesses open between 8 a.m. and 10 a.m. and close around 6 p.m. Many are also open on weekends.
- Banks operate weekdays from 9 a.m. until 2 or 3 p.m., and some are also open on Saturday mornings.
- Post offices are open weekdays from 8 a.m. to 5 p.m. and Saturday mornings.
- At traffic lights, it's legal to make a right turn on a red light except when there is a sign at the intersection stating that such a turn is *not* permitted. Of course, come to a full stop first and make sure no traffic is coming.

Thistle Hill

In 1903, cattle baron William T. Waggoner built his daughter this three-story mansion as a wedding present. The house was built in a wealthy neighborhood known as Quality Hill. This Georgian Revival-style mansion has been restored to its 1912 condition and is listed in the National Register.

It is located today on Pennsylvania Avenue near the hospital district. It cost about $38,000 when the nearly 11,000-square-foot, red brick structure was built back in 1903. The house was used for lavish dinners and parties to entertain many of Fort Worth's powerful and elite. It was often referred to as the "honeymoon cottage" and was restored in the 1970s.

For tour information, call 817-555-2663

Page 2

Times New Roman Bold 12 pt.

Report 110-87 ▶

Flyer

✓ Progress Check Proofreading Check

Documents designated as Proofreading Checks serve as a check of your proofreading skill. Your goal is to have zero typographical errors when the GDP software first scores the document.

1. Press the SPACE BAR 2 times, and insert a picture related to a globe.
2. Drag and size the picture so that it looks similar to the one shown in the illustration.
3. Insert word art about the size and in the same position as the one at the top of the illustration, with the words Global Savings & Loan.
4. Choose a style and color for the word art to coordinate with the picture.
5. Create a text box with no lines and fill and about the size and in the same position as the one shown at the middle of the illustration.
6. Change to Times New Roman 48 point, and center and type Your Guide to Online Banking in 2 lines as shown.
7. Insert a boxed table with 4 columns and 6 rows, and drag it into position as shown in the illustration.
8. Change to Arial Bold 18 point, and type the one- and two-column headings in Row 1 aligned as shown.
9. Move to Row 2, change to Times New Roman 20 point, and type the left-aligned column entries as shown.
10. Right-align the information in Column D, and add spaces after the dollar sign to align the dollar sign just to the left of the widest entry below it.
11. Merge the cells in Row 6, change to Times New Roman 14 point, and type the information as shown.
12. Adjust the column widths manually as shown.
13. Add a shading color to the first and last row to coordinate with the word art and picture.

(Continued on next page)

↓1X Account	↓1X ATM Card	Check Writing	Monthly Fee
Regular Checking	None	Unlimited	$ 9.00
Interest Checking	Express Card	Unlimited	10.00
Basic Checking	Express Card	Unlimited	4.50
Student Checking	Express Card	Unlimited	3.00
Note: Fees may apply to telephone banking calls and the use of the ATM Express Card.			

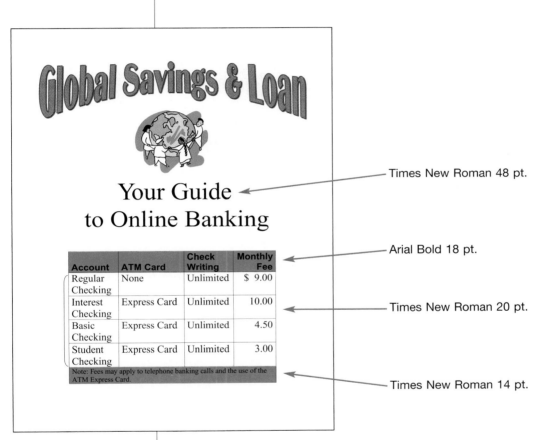

Times New Roman 48 pt.

Arial Bold 18 pt.

Times New Roman 20 pt.

Times New Roman 14 pt.

Designing Web Pages

In The Game

5779 Del Monte Drive
Santa Rosa, CA 95409
888-555-7897
email@InTheGame.com

Main | Contact Us

Contact Us

If there is any sporting good item or apparel item related to baseball and softball, soccer, track and field, or gymnastics that you can't find on our site, we want to hear from you.

Email
Send us an email message now at email@InTheGame.com

Call Us
Call us toll free at 888-555-7897.

Snail Mail
rite to us at the address below:

In the Game
Del Monte Drive
Rosa, CA 95409

In The Game

5779 Del Monte Drive
Santa Rosa, CA 95409
888-555-7897
email@InTheGame.com

Main | Contact Us

Welcome to In The Game, your online supplier specializing in sporting goods for baseball and softball, soccer, track and field, and gymnastics. We can offer you quality products at low prices delivered to you fast!

Baseball and Softball
If you can't wait to play ball, you'll love what we have to offer you. Our line of gear includes automated batting cages, pitching machines, batting tees and radar guns. We sell apparel such as caps, jerseys, a

Soccer
If scoring goals is on the top of your list, you have all types of soccer equipment and clothir

Track and Field
Is running your game? We have batons, cross blocks, starting pistols, stop watches, and mo

Gymnastics
You'll flip for our line of clothing, fan wear, training aids are first quality.

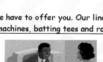

The Virtual Assistant
901 S. Rainbow, Suite 1
Las Vegas, Nevada 89145
888-555-3499
email@TVA.com

Home | Services | Fees | References

Do you need a skilled assistant who works tirelessly on your documents, doesn't need any office space, and gives your work that personal touch? The Virtual Assistant is a professional document processing and design service that will help create the professional image your business demands.

You don't get a second chance at a first impression. The graphics experts in our word processing and desktop publishing departments will make sure your documents look gorgeous. Our editors, who have completed a series of rigorous courses in business English and business communications, will make sure they are letter perfect. Please browse around our site for details.

Word Processing
- Correspondence
- Reports
- Proposals
- Manuals

Layout Editing
- In-house Styles
- Custom Styles
- Master Documents
- Table of Contents
- Indexes

Desktop Publishing
- Newsletters
- Brochures
- Letterheads
- Resumes

Copy Editing
- Proofreading
- Technical Editing
- Grammar Checking
- Writing Style

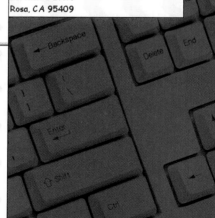

Creating, Saving, and Viewing Web Pages

GOALS

- Improve speed and accuracy
- Refine language arts skills in capitalization
- Create, save, and view web pages

A. Type 2 times.

A. WARMUP

```
1      The taxes* were quickly adjusted upward by 20 percent   11
2  because of the improvements to her house (built in 1901).   23
3  A proposed law will not penalize good homeowners like this. 35
   |  1  |  2  |  3  |  4  |  5  |  6  |  7  |  8  |  9  |  10  |  11  |  12
```

SKILLBUILDING

B. Take three 12-second timings on each line. The scale below the last line shows your wpm speed for a 12-second timing.

B. 12-SECOND SPEED SPRINTS

```
4  Their home is on a lake that is just east of her old house.
5  He has an old boat that is in bad need of a good paint job.
6  He got so many fish that she gave some to the nice old man.
7  She was so nice that it was easy for him to help her drive.
   I I I I 5 I I I I 10 I I I I 15 I I I I 20 I I I I 25 I I I I 30 I I I I 35 I I I I 40 I I I I 45 I I I I 50 I I I I 55 I I I I 60
```

C. PROGRESSIVE PRACTICE: ALPHABET

If you are not using the GDP software, turn to page SB-7 and follow the directions for this activity.

D. PROGRESSIVE PRACTICE: NUMBERS

If you are not using the GDP software, turn to page SB-11 and follow the directions for this activity.

LANGUAGE ARTS

E. Study the rules at the right.

E. CAPITALIZATION

RULE ▶
≡ organization

Capitalize common organizational terms (such as *advertising department* and *finance committee*) only when they are the actual names of the units in the writer's own organization and when they are preceded by the word *the*.

The report from the Advertising Department is due today.
But: Our <u>a</u>dvertising <u>d</u>epartment will submit its report today.

(Continued on next page)

Capitalize the names of specific course titles but not the names of subjects or areas of study.

I have enrolled in Accounting 201 and will also take the marketing course.

Edit the sentences to correct any errors in capitalization.

8 Our advertising department consistently delivers quality work.
9 The Finance Committee must submit the report by noon today.
10 I think I am going to pass keyboarding 1 with flying colors.
11 The marketing department must approve the proposal first.
12 A class in Business Communications would be very helpful.
13 To take Math 102, you must have taken a beginning math course.

---

12 ▾ B I *FORMATTING*

F. BASIC PARTS OF A WEB PAGE

LAYOUT VIEW. Working view of a Web page in a word processor with certain elements, such as table gridlines, visible.

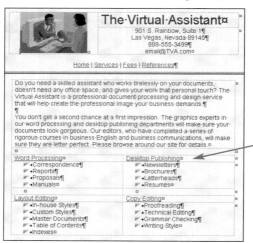

BROWSER VIEW. Final view of a Web page as displayed in a browser; text and tables wrap to fit window; table gridlines are invisible. Different browser views may vary.

FRAMES PAGE. A Web page divided into independent sections or frames, each displaying a different Web page.

HEADER FRAME. Displays the same information at the top of every page of the Web site.

MAIN FRAME. Displays content of different Web pages each time a page hyperlink is clicked.

HYPERLINKS. Are clicked to move from one page or place on a page to another within a Web site.

G. WEB SITE DESIGN GUIDELINES

Follow these guidelines to design effective Web sites:

- Plan appropriate, specific content first. Define the purpose of the site, and make a list of what visitors need to know.
- Organize the content into logical groups and subgroups similar to an outline in a report.
- Plan the main page (usually called a home page), which should identify the business and its services.
- Plan and test the site navigation. Hyperlinks help visitors jump from one spot or page to another.

- Plan the content and design details of specific pages, and use tables to position information.
- Design an appropriate, attractive visual theme with consistent design elements on each page to unify your site. Many programs come with a gallery of attractive themes with unified design elements and eye-catching color schemes.
- Use graphics to enhance your page, but use them sparingly because they increase download times.
- Use color to create a mood, attract attention, and categorize information.

Go To

Word
Processing
Manual

H. WEB PAGE—SAVING AND VIEWING

Study Lesson 111 in your word processing manual. Complete all of the shaded steps while at your computer. Then format the jobs that follow.

DOCUMENT PROCESSING

**Report
111-88**

Web Site

Computers that run the UNIX operating system generally use the html extension for the home page of a Web site. Personal computers that run Windows or Macintosh operating systems usually use the htm extension. If you are planning on publishing the Web site you create on a commercial server, you should ask your host server which extension is required.

≡ organization

≡ course

Follow these steps to create the main page of the Web site named *main.htm*:

1. GDP will automatically open a blank document. Save it as a Web page named *main.htm*.
2. Create an open table with 2 columns and 7 rows. Note: Refer to the layout view on page 446 for the placement of information within rows.
3. Merge the cells in Row 1, and type the information in the first row as shown below.

4. Move to Row 3, and continue typing the rest of the table as shown on page 446, leaving Row 2 and Row 4 empty.
5. View the Web page in a browser (if one is available), and compare this view with the layout view in your word processor.

Do you need a skilled assistant who works tirelessly on your documents, doesn't need any office space, and gives your work that personal touch? The Virtual Assistant is a professional document processing and design service that will help create the professional image your business demands.

You don't get a second chance at a first impression. The graphics experts in our word processing and desktop publishing departments will make sure your documents look gorgeous. Our editors, who have completed a series of rigorous courses in business English and business communications, will make sure your documents are letter perfect. Please browse around our site for details.

(Continued on next page)

Word Processing	Desktop Publishing
Correspondence	Newsletters
Reports	Brochures
Proposals	Letterheads
Manuals	Resumes

Layout Editing	Copy Editing
In-house Styles	Proofreading
Custom Styles	Technical Editing
Master Documents	Grammar Checking
Table of Contents	Writing Style
Indexes	

! Reminder: You will finish building the Web site in Lessons 112 through 115.

Report 111-89

Your Web Site

Plan and write the content for a Web site for a business of your own to include a main page and three related pages very similar to the project in this unit. You may want to look at the Web site for Report 115-100 on pages 465-466 for ideas.

1. GDP will automatically open a blank document. Save it as *my main.htm*.

2. Create an open table with 2 columns and 7 rows, and type the information for this main page inside the table similar to Report 115-100.

3. View the Web page in a browser (if one is available), and compare it with the layout view in your word processor.

STRATEGIES for *Career Success*

Types of Interviews

Most employers conduct two or three interviews before making a job offer. The first interview, held at the company or conducted by phone, is usually a screening interview. This determines if you are qualified for the job.

The next set of interviews is more selective. At the company, you might have a panel interview with several interviewers who ask directed, prepared questions; or you might have an open-ended interview that is relatively unstructured. Interviewing by video teleconference is another possibility.

No matter what type of interview you encounter, the outcome will be better if you have enthusiasm for the job, match your qualifications to the company's needs, ask relevant questions, and listen well.

YOUR TURN Visit career Web sites for articles on preparing for job interviews as well as information on employers, resumes, job searches, etc.

Creating Frames

GOALS

- Type at least 50wpm/5'/5e
- Create frames

A. Type 2 times.

A. WARMUP

```
1        Missy examined these items: the #426 oil painting, a    11
2   Bowes & Elkjer porcelain vase, and the 86-piece collection   23
3   of glazed antique pitchers. There were 337 people present.   35
    |  1  |  2  |  3  |  4  |  5  |  6  |  7  |  8  |  9  |  10  |  11  |  12
```

SKILLBUILDING

B. PACED PRACTICE

If you are not using the GDP software, turn to page SB-14 and follow the directions for this activity.

Keyboarding skills are essential in the retail sales and services industry.

C. Take two 5-minute timings. Review your speed and errors.

Goal: At least 50wpm/5'/5e

C. 5-MINUTE TIMING

4   Employers want the people who work for them to have   11

5   many qualities of good character. Character is defined as   23

6   a distinguishing feature of a person or thing. Character   34

7   may be what you are remembered for or why you remember   45

8   someone else. What are some of the traits associated with   57

9   good character? Respect, honesty, trustworthiness, caring, 69

10 leadership, responsibility, attitude, tolerance, fairness, 81

11 and citizenship are a few traits.   88

12   All people should have respect for themselves and for   99

13 others. If you respect people, you have a high regard for 111

14 the way they conduct themselves in all aspects of life.   122

15 However, before you can respect others, you need to have   133

16 respect for yourself.   137

17   Honesty and trustworthiness are similar traits. In   147

18 business dealings, people expect honesty and will admire   158

19 people who have this quality. They like to build business 170

20 relationships with companies whose employees are honest   181

21 and trustworthy.   184

22   Your attitude is reflected in the way you act toward   195

23 other people or in the way you speak to them. You can make 206

24 great strides in advancing your career by taking a look at 219

25 the way you interact with people. You may want to take a   230

26 closer look at some character traits you want to improve. 242

27 The improvements in life will amaze you.   250

| 1 | 2 | 3 | 4 | 5 | 6 | 7 | 8 | 9 | 10 | 11 | 12

FORMATTING

D. WEB PAGE FRAMES

Refer to the illustration of a frames page shown on page 446.

A frame is a defined section on a Web page that divides it into two or more windows. Frames organize and link the pages in a Web site and make navigation easy and seamless. A frames page is usually the opening page in a Web site.

The header frame displays the same information consistently at the top of every page. The design and content of the header frame varies but commonly includes identifying information, a related picture, and navigational hyperlinks.

The main frame displays the individual pages of the Web site when a hyperlink is clicked. The home page is usually the first page displayed in the main frame. Using a header frame in conjunction with a main frame and navigational hyperlinks helps the user change pages easily and unifies the Web site.

Go To

Word Processing Manual

E. WEB PAGE—FRAMES

Study Lesson 112 in your word processing manual. Complete all of the shaded steps while at your computer. Then format the jobs that follow.

DOCUMENT PROCESSING

Report 112-90 ►

Web Site (continued)

Some Internet Service Providers use an extension of .htm and some use. html. You must name your Web page to conform to the requirements of your ISP.

Follow these steps to finish the main page and create a frames page for this Web site named *index.html*:

1. Open the file for Report 111-88, named *main.htm*.
2. Horizontally center the table on this page.
3. Insert a header frame above the main page to create a frames page, and drag the bottom border of the frame to adjust the frame size if necessary.
4. Create an open table with 2 rows and 2 columns inside the header frame, and center it horizontally.
5. In Column B, Row 1, center and type The Virtual Assistant.
6. In Column B, Row 2, center and type these lines:

   901 S. Rainbow, Suite 1
   Las Vegas, Nevada 89145
   888-555-3499
   email@TVA.com

7. Merge the cells in Column A, and insert a picture with an office theme.
8. Resize the picture proportionately until it is about 2 inches wide, and center the picture.
9. Move the insertion point under the table in the top frame, and press ENTER 1 time.
10. Type the following line centered using the pipe symbol, with one space before and after it, as shown:

    Home | Services | Fees | References

    Note: The pipe symbol (|) is above the backslash symbol on most keyboards.
11. Resize the header frame as shown by dragging on the bottom border.
12. Save the frames page and name it *index.html*.
13. View the Web page in a browser.

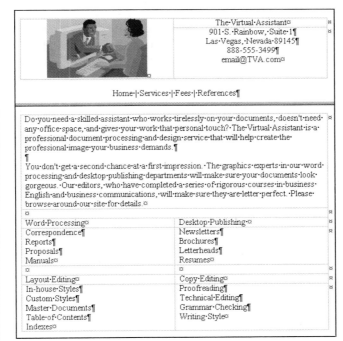

Layout View of Frames Page

(Continued on next page)

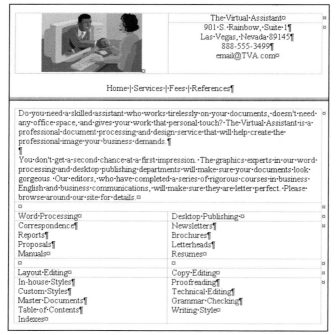

Browser View of Frames Page

Report 112-91 ▶

Your Web Site (continued)

Follow these steps to finish your main page (*my index.htm*) and create a frames page for your Web site named *index.htm*:

1. Open the file for Report 111-89, named *my main.htm*.
2. Horizontally center the table on the page.
3. Insert a header frame above the main page to create a frames page, and drag the bottom border of the frame to adjust the frame size if necessary.
4. Create an open table with 2 rows and 2 columns inside the header frame, and center it horizontally.
5. In Column B, Row 1, center and type the name of the Web site.
6. In Column B, Row 2, center and type the mailing address and email address of the Web site.
7. Merge the cells in Column A, and insert a picture related to the Web site business.
8. Resize the picture as needed, and align the picture as needed.
9. Move the insertion point under the table in the top frame, and press ENTER 1 time.
10. Type the following line centered, using the pipe symbol with one space before and after it as shown:

    Home | Services | Fees | References

    Note: The pipe symbol (|) is above the backslash symbol on most keyboards.
11. Resize the header frame as shown by dragging on the bottom border.
12. Save the frames page, and name it *my index.htm*.
13. View the Web page in a browser.

Creating and Saving More Web Pages

GOALS

- Improve speed and accuracy
- Refine language arts skills in composing
- Create and save more Web pages

A. Type 2 times.

A. WARMUP

```
1        Did you hear the excellent quartet of junior cadets?     11
2  Everybody in the crowd (estimated at over 500) applauded      22
3  "with gusto." The sizable crowd filled the 3/4-acre park.     33
   | 1 | 2 | 3 | 4 | 5 | 6 | 7 | 8 | 9 | 10 | 11 | 12
```

SKILLBUILDING

B. DIAGNOSTIC PRACTICE: ALPHABET

If you are not using the GDP software, turn to page SB-2 and follow the directions for this activity.

C. Type the columns 2 times. Press TAB to move from column to column.

C. TECHNIQUE PRACTICE: TAB KEY

```
4  T. Waters      L. Vigil      S. Zimmerly    D. Colwell    C. Foster
5  M. Goldbach    R. Hempker    G. Beckert     M. Kinsey     A. Lucero
6  C. Maclean     J. Nichols    I. Ohlsen      R. Parlee     S. Quale
7  J. Rondeau     G. Snowden    Y. Tokita      C. Upton      C. Vaughn
```

LANGUAGE ARTS

D. COMPOSING A PERSONAL-BUSINESS LETTER

Compose a two-paragraph personal-business letter that summarizes the content of the Web site design guidelines on page 447. Address the letter to your instructor; provide a suitable inside address and salutation for your letter. Also, provide a complimentary closing and sign the letter yourself.

In the letter, discuss the following:

Paragraph 1. Describe how to plan an effective Web site.
Paragraph 2. Describe how to design an effective Web site.

Report 113-92

Web Site (continued)

Follow these steps to create a new page for the Web site named *fees.htm*:

1. Type Fees centered on the first line, and press ENTER 2 times.
2. Create an open table with 1 cell, and center it horizontally.
3. Type the information as shown below inside the table.
4. View the Web page in a browser.

The Virtual Assistant strives to work within your organization's budget. We will review your individual needs and tailor the pricing to fit your project. We welcome the opportunity to provide an individual estimate. Be assured that our prices are extremely competitive. Here are some general guidelines regarding our fees: ¶

¶

We typically charge by the hour or by the page, depending upon the job. ¶
Most fees are based on the length of the document and the amount of editing deemed necessary. ¶
We offer substantial discounts for volume work and repeat clients. ¶
A surcharge is added for rush jobs. ¶
Payment for services rendered should be made by credit card, check, or money order. ¶

¶

For a copy of our current rate guide, please send an email message to rateguide@TVA.com. ¶

Fees¶
¶

The·Virtual·Assistant·strives·to·work·within·your·organization's·budget.·We·will·review·your·individual·needs·and·tailor·the·pricing·to·fit·your·project.·We·welcome·the·opportunity·to·provide·an·individual·estimate.·Be·assured·that·our·prices·are·extremely·competitive.·Here·are·some·general·guidelines·regarding·our·fees·¶
¶
We·typically·charge·by·the·hour·or·by·the·page,·depending·upon·the·job.¶
Most·fees·are·based·on·the·length·of·the·document·and·the·amount·of·editing·deemed·necessary.¶
We·offer·substantial·discounts·for·volume·work·and·repeat·clients.¶
A·surcharge·is·added·for·rush·jobs.
Payment·for·services·rendered·should·be·made·by·credit·card,·check,·or·money·order.¶
¶
For·a·copy·of·our·current·rate·guide,·please·send·an·email·message·to·rateguide@TVA.com.¤
¶

Layout View of Fees Page

Follow these steps to create a new page for the Web site named *references.htm*:

1. Type References centered on the first line, and press ENTER 2 times.
2. Create an open table with 1 cell, and center it horizontally.
3. Type the information below inside the table.
4. View the Web page in a browser.

↓2X

I've been in a highly successful business for over 10 years and attribute much of that success to the skilled professionals at The Virtual Assistant. I am always confident that my work will go out error free. They are top-notch professionals and can work for my team anytime! ↓2X

Mike Rashid
Network Engineer
Denver, Colorado ↓4X

The documents produced by The Virtual Assistant are impeccable! I can count on professional, reliable, competent, and efficient service without question. It is so easy to send documents back and forth via the Internet, and we all know that time is money. I highly recommend TVA for any of your word processing needs. ↓2X

Nancy Shipley
Attorney at Law
Chicago, Illinois ↓4X

As the president of a dynamic company with tremendous growth potential, I have to be concerned with my image in the business world and with the bottom line. I have counted on the services of The Virtual Assistant for the past five years, and I have always been thrilled with their reliability and consistency. I particularly like the discounts we enjoy as a repeat customer. ↓2X

I have worked closely with Kevin Nguyen, who now has a sixth sense about my needs. He can always anticipate my thoughts and can substitute the right meaning when it is necessary. I would be lost without Kevin and TVA. I wouldn't trust my documents or my image to anyone else!! ↓2X

Debbie Matte, President
New Millennium Designs
Orlando, Florida ↓2X

(Continued on next page)

Layout View of References Page

Report
113-94

Your Web Site
(continued)

Follow these steps to create a new page for the Web site named *my fees.htm* similar to Report 113-92:
1. Type Fees centered on the first line, and press ENTER 2 times.
2. Create an open table with 1 cell, and center it horizontally.
3. Type content similar to Report 113-92.
4. View the Web page in a browser.

Report
113-95

Your Web Site
(continued)

Follow these steps to create a new page for the Web site named *my references.htm* similar to Report 113-93:
1. Type References centered on the first line, and press ENTER 2 times.
2. Create an open table with 1 cell, and center it horizontally.
3. Type the information for the 3 references inside the table similar to Report 113-93.
4. View the Web page in a browser.

Creating Web Pages With Hyperlinks

GOALS

- Type at least 50wpm/5′/5e
- Create hyperlinks

A. Type 2 times.

A. WARMUP

```
1        This series* (*6 films, 28 minutes) by J. Zeller goes   11
2     beyond the "basics" of computers. Viewers keep requesting   23
3     an extension on the dates; this includes 3/2, 5/5, and 8/9.  35
      |  1  |  2  |  3  |  4  |  5  |  6  |  7  |  8  |  9  |  10  |  11  |  12
```

SKILLBUILDING

B. MAP

Follow the GDP software directions for this exercise in improving keystroking accuracy.

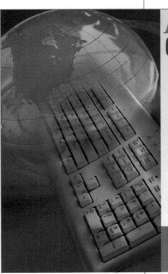

Keyboarding CONNECTION

Using Hypertext

Do you know how to surf the Web? It's easy! The Web contains pages, which are blocks of text, visuals, sound, or animation. Hypertext is a technique where certain words in the text of a Web page are highlighted, underlined, or colored differently from the other words. These colored or highlighted words link to other pages on the Web.

When you point to one of these hyperlinks and click the mouse button, the page connected to that word is displayed. Therefore, one page on the Web can link to many other pages. Hypertext pages do not have to be read in any specific order.

Hypertext enables you to connect and retrieve Web pages from computer networks worldwide. With hypertext, you can point and click or surf your way all over the Web.

YOUR TURN Open a page on the Web. Surf the Web using the hyperlinks displayed on the page.

C. Take two 5-minute timings. Review your speed and errors.

Goal: At least 50wpm/5'/5e

C. 5-MINUTE TIMING

4   Before you apply for jobs, you will want to do some   11

5 detective work. First, choose the company for which you   22

6 want to work and then use the Internet to find out about   33

7 the company. If you find a Web site for the organization,   45

8 then you can learn about the company, its hiring policies,   57

9 available jobs, and how to apply for a job opening.   67

10   When you are researching a company, you want to learn   78

11 about the history of the company. You may be able to find   90

12 out how stock analysts expect the company stock to perform   102

13 in the coming months if the company is publicly held.   113

14   When you find a job opening for which you wish to   123

15 apply, read carefully to see what type of work experience   135

16 and education the company requires for the job. When you   146

17 prepare your resume, emphasize your qualifications based   157

18 on the requirements listed for the job. If the person who   169

19 should receive job inquiries is not listed, contact the   180

20 company by phone or email to get a name. Personalize your   192

21 cover letter and resume, if possible.   200

22   The information you find in your research will be very   211

23 helpful during the interview with a representative of the   223

24 company. Ask intelligent questions and speak confidently   234

25 about the position. Emphasize how your skills would be   245

26 valuable to the company.   250

| 1 | 2 | 3 | 4 | 5 | 6 | 7 | 8 | 9 | 10 | 11 | 12

FORMATTING

D. HYPERLINKS

Hyperlinks are powerful navigational tools that are critical to the overall plan and design of a Web site. When clicked, they move a visitor from one page or one location on a page to another.

When you create a hyperlink, you must indicate the target. The hyperlink can point to the same page, to a different page, to another site, or perhaps to an email address. You can assign a hyperlink to a word, a group of words, or a picture.

The presence of a text hyperlink is usually indicated by underlined text with a different color from the rest of the words on the page. Also, the mouse pointer changes to a hand shape when hovering over a hyperlink.

E. WEB PAGE—HYPERLINKS

Study Lesson 114 in your word processing manual. Complete all of the shaded
steps while at your computer. Then format
the jobs that follow.

DOCUMENT PROCESSING

Report 114-96

Web Site
(continued)

Follow these steps to create a new page
for the Web site named *services.htm*:
1. Type Services centered on the first
line, and press ENTER 2 times.
2. Create an open table with 1 cell, and
center it horizontally.

3. Type the information as shown below
inside the table.
4. View the Web page in a browser.

Word Processing ¶
We prepare documents with a professional look for correspondence of all
types as well as reports, proposals, manuals, etc. ¶
Desktop Publishing ¶
Our professional design specialists will create newsletters, brochures,
letterheads, etc., that are sure to capture your imagination. ¶
Layout Editing ¶
Our layout editors will transform your documents using in-house styles or
custom styles. For your longer projects, they are experts at building master
documents that include a cover page, table of contents, and index. ¶
Copy Editing ¶
Our copy editors will make sure that your document content is perfect.
Proofreading, grammar, and writing style will all be checked so that your
ideas are expressed clearly and effectively.

Layout View of Services Page

Follow these steps to create hyperlinks for the frames page:

1. Open the file for Report 112-90 (*index.html*), the frames page.
2. Create four text hyperlinks for each of the four words in the header frame as follows:

   Home, opens *main.htm*
   Services opens *services.htm*
   Fees opens *fees.htm*
   References opens *references.htm*

3. Create the hyperlinks so that the corresponding target document will display in the main fame below the header frame.
4. Create a hyperlink for each of the four headings on the main page (*Word Processing, Desktop Publishing*, etc.) to open *services.htm*.
5. View the Web page in a browser.

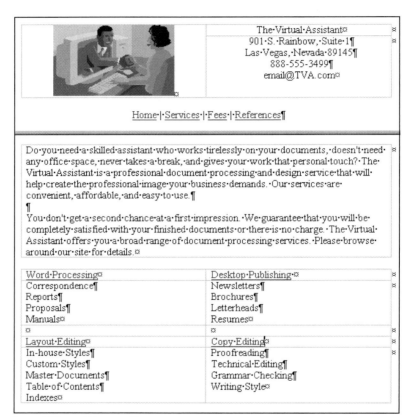

Layout View of Frames Page

(Continued on next page)

The Virtual Assistant
901 S. Rainbow, Suite 1
Las Vegas, Nevada 89145
888-555-3499
email@TVA.com

Home | Services | Fees | References

Do you need a skilled assistant who works tirelessly on your documents, doesn't need any office space, never takes a break, and gives your work that personal touch? The Virtual Assistant is a professional document processing and design service that will help create the professional image your business demands. Our services are convenient, affordable, and easy to use.

You don't get a second chance at a first impression. We guarantee that you will be completely satisfied with your finished documents or there is no charge. The Virtual Assistant offers you a broad range of document processing services. Please browse around our site for details.

Word Processing	Desktop Publishing
Correspondence	Newsletters
Reports	Brochures
Proposals	Letterheads
Manuals	Resumes

Layout Editing	Copy Editing
In-house Styles	Proofreading
Custom Styles	Technical Editing
Master Documents	Grammar Checking
Table of Contents	Writing Style
Indexes	

Browser View of Frames Page

Report 114-98

Your Web Site (continued)

Follow these steps to create the final page for your Web site named *my services.htm*:
1. Type Services centered on the first line, and press ENTER 2 times.
2. Create an open table with 1 cell, and center it horizontally.

3. Inside the table, type four headings followed by one or two sentences each describing the services of your business.
4. View the Web page in a browser.

Report 114-99

Your Web Site (continued)

Follow these steps to finish your Web site.
1. Open the file for Report 112-91 (*my index.htm*), the frames page.
2. Create four text hyperlinks for each of the four words in the header frame as follows:
    Home, opens *my main.htm*
    Services opens *my services.htm*
    Fees opens *my fees.htm*
    References opens *my references.htm*

3. Create the hyperlinks so that the corresponding target document will display in the main fame below the header frame.
4. Create a hyperlink for each of the four headings on the main page to open *my services.htm*.
5. View the Web page in a browser.

Lesson 115

Formatting Web Pages

GOALS
- Improve speed and accuracy
- Refine language arts skills in proofreading
- Format Web pages

A. Type 2 times.

A. WARMUP

```
1       Contact bxvacuum@clean.com to order the large-sized    11
2   grips. They were just lowered to $160 from $240 (a 33 1/3%   23
3   markdown). Jay's #55 quilts were reduced to $88 from $99.    34
    |  1  |  2  |  3  |  4  |  5  |  6  |  7  |  8  |  9  |  10 |  11 |  12
```

SKILLBUILDING

PPP

PRETEST → PRACTICE → POSTTEST

B. PRETEST: Common Letter Combinations

PRETEST
Take a 1-minute timing. Review your speed and errors.

```
4       He did mention that they are sending a lawful taping    11
5   of the comedy format to a performing combo. A motion to     22
6   commit a useful option forced a fusion of forty persons.    33
    |  1  |  2  |  3  |  4  |  5  |  6  |  7  |  8  |  9  |  10 |  11 |  12
```

C. PRACTICE: Word Beginnings

PRACTICE
Speed Emphasis:
If you made no more than 1 error on the Pretest, type each *individual* line twice.
Accuracy Emphasis:
If you made 3 or more errors, type each *group* of lines (as though it were a paragraph) 2 times.

```
7   for forty forth format former forget forest forearm forbear
8   per peril perky period permit person peruse perform persist
9   com combo comic combat commit common combed compose complex
```

D. PRACTICE: Word Endings

```
10  ing doing mixing living filing taping sending biking hiding
11  ion onion nation lotion motion option mention fusion legion
12  ful awful useful joyful earful lawful helpful sinful armful
```

POSTTEST
Repeat the Pretest timing and compare performance.

E. POSTTEST: Common Letter Combinations

F. SUSTAINED PRACTICE: CAPITALIZATION

13   Even though he was only about thirty years old, Jason   11
14 knew that it was not too soon to begin thinking about his   23
15 retirement. He soon found out that there were many things   35
16 involved in his plans for an early and long retirement.   46

17   Even without considering the uncertainty of social   10
18 security, Jason knew that he should plan his career moves   22
19 so that he would have a strong company retirement plan. He   34
20 realized that he should have an Individual Retirement Plan.   46

21   When he became aware that The Longman Company, the   10
22 firm that employed him, would match his contributions to a   22
23 supplemental retirement account, he began saving even more.   34
24 He used the Payroll Department funds from the Goplin Group.   46

25   He also learned that The Longman Company retirement   11
26 plan, his Individual Retirement Plan, and his supplemental   23
27 retirement account are all deferred savings. With those   34
28 tax-dollar savings, Jason bought New Venture Group mutuals.   46

LANGUAGE ARTS

G. PROOFREADING

29   The idea and practise of sharing risk originated in
30 antiquetry. Many years ago, Chinese merchants deviced an
31 injenious way of protecting themselves against the chance
32 of a financialy ruinous accadent in the dangerous river
33 along the trade routtes when they were delivring goods.

FORMATTING

H. MORE WEB SITE DESIGN GUIDELINES

Follow these guidelines to design effective Web sites:

- Experiment with the themes that come with most programs.
- If you use a theme, experiment with the embedded styles that can be applied to titles, headings, subheadings, etc., for design consistency.

- Choose a consistent look for headings and subheadings, including font size, color, and alignment, for design unity.
- Use color to establish moods: black is somber; white is clean, organized, or sterile; bright colors are energetic, but may be hard to read. Experiment and use your judgment.

I. WEB PAGE—DESIGN THEMES

Study Lesson 115 in your word processing manual. Complete all of the shaded steps while at your computer. Then format the jobs that follow.

DOCUMENT PROCESSING

Report 115-100 ▶

Web Site (continued)

Follow these steps to format the Web site:

1. Open the file for Report 114-97 (*index.htm*), the frames page.
2. Apply a design theme to the main frame that coordinates with the picture in the frame on top.
3. Jump to *services.htm* and apply the same design theme to this page.
4. Apply a Heading 2 style to the first line, and center the line.
5. Add a bullet to each sentence under each heading beginning with the heading "Word Processing."
6. Apply a Heading 3 style to each heading beginning with the heading "Word Processing."
7. Jump to *fees.htm* and apply the same design theme to this page as used in Step 2.
8. Apply a Heading 2 style to the first line, and center the line.
9. Add a bullet to each sentence under the first paragraph except for the last sentence on the page.
10. Insert a horizontal line after the last bulleted item.
11. Jump to *references.htm* and apply the same design theme to this page as used in Step 2.
12. Apply a Heading 2 style to the first line, and center the line.
13. Place the insertion point in front of the first blank line in the table, and insert a horizontal line.
14. Place the insertion point in front of the second blank line between each reference, and insert a horizontal line.
15. Place the insertion point in front of the second blank line under the last reference, and insert a horizontal line.
16. Change any styles, fonts, or colors as desired.
17. View your finished Web site in a browser.

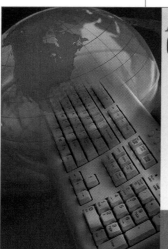

Keyboarding CONNECTION

Choosing a Different Home Page

You don't have to start at the same home page every time you use your browser. You can change the browser's home page to start at one of your favorite Web pages. Here's how to do it.

In Netscape, go to the chosen page and select Preferences from the Edit menu. Click the Navigator category in the Preferences dialog box. Click the Use Current Page button in the "Home page" area. Choose Home Page in the "Navigator starts with" area. Click OK.

In Internet Explorer, from the chosen page, select Internet Options from the Tools menu. Click the General tab, and then click the Use Current button in the "Home page" area. Click OK.

YOUR TURN Using your browser, access a favorite Web page. Make it your browser's home page.

(Continued on next page)

The Virtual Assistant

901 S. Rainbow, Suite 1
Las Vegas, Nevada 89145
888-555-3499
email@TVA.com

Home | Services | Fees | References

Do you need a skilled assistant who works tirelessly on your documents, doesn't need any office space, never takes a break, and gives your work that personal touch? The Virtual Assistant is a professional document processing and design service that will help create the professional image your business demands. Our services are convenient, affordable, and easy to use.

You don't get a second chance at a first impression. We guarantee that you will be completely satisfied with your finished documents or there is no charge. The Virtual Assistant offers you a broad range of document processing services. Please browse around our site for details.

Word Processing
- Correspondence
- Reports
- Proposals
- Manuals

Desktop Publishing
- Newsletters
- Brochures
- Letterheads
- Resumes

Layout Editing
- In-house Styles
- Custom Styles
- Master Documents
- Table of Contents
- Indexes

Copy Editing
- Proofreading
- Technical Editing
- Grammar Checking
- Writing Style

The Virtual Assistant

901 S. Rainbow, Suite 1
Las Vegas, Nevada 89145
888-555-3499
email@TVA.com

Home | Services | Fees | References

Services

Word Processing
- We prepare documents with a professional look for correspondence of all types as well as reports, proposals, manuals, etc.

Desktop Publishing
- Our professional design specialists will create newsletters, brochures, letterheads, etc., that are sure to capture your imagination.

Layout Editing
- Our layout editors will transform your documents using in-house styles or custom styles. For your longer projects, they are experts at building master documents that include a cover page, table of contents, and index.

Copy Editing
- Our copy editors will make sure that your document content is perfect. Proofreading, grammar, and writing style will all be checked so that your ideas are expressed clearly and effectively.

(Continued on next page)

The Virtual Assistant

901 S. Rainbow, Suite 1
Las Vegas, Nevada 89145
888-555-3499
email@TVA.com

Home | Services | Fees | References

Fees

The Virtual Assistant strives to work within your organization's budget. We will review your individual needs and tailor the pricing to fit your project. We welcome the opportunity to provide an individual estimate. Be assured that our prices are extremely competitive. Here are some general guidelines regarding our fees:

- We typically charge by the hour or by the page, depending upon the job.
- Most fees are based on the length of the document and the amount of editing deemed necessary.
- We offer substantial discounts for volume work and repeat clients.
- A surcharge is added for rush jobs.
- Payment for services rendered should be made by credit card, check, or money order.

For a copy of our current rate guide, please send
an email message to rateguide@TVA.com.

The Virtual Assistant

901 S. Rainbow, Suite 1
Las Vegas, Nevada 89145
888-555-3499
email@TVA.com

Home | Services | Fees | References

References

I've been in a highly successful business for over 10 years and attribute much of that success to the skilled professionals at The Virtual Assistant. I am always confident that my work will go out error free. They are top-notch professionals and can work for my team anytime!

Mike Rashid
Network Engineer
Denver, Colorado

The documents produced by The Virtual Assistant are impeccable! I can count on professional, reliable, competent, and efficient service without question. It is so easy to send documents back and forth via the Internet, and we all know that time is money. I highly recommend TVC for any of your word processing needs.

Nancy Shipley
Attorney at Law
Chicago, Illinois

Follow these steps to create this Web site:

1. GDP will automatically open a blank document. Save it as a Web page named *main page.htm*.
2. Insert File 115A.
3. Insert a header frame above the main page to create a frames page. Save the frames page as *index page.htm*.
4. Insert File 115B.
5. Insert a picture related to sports in the open cell in Column A.
6. Resize the picture proportionately until it is about 2 inches wide, and center the picture.
7. Click outside the table when you have finished.
8. Create a text hyperlink in the header frame for the word "Main" so that the target document, *main page.htm*, will display in the main frame.
9. Create a text hyperlink in the header frame for the words "Contact Us" so that the target document, *contact us.htm*, will display in the main frame.
10. Apply a design theme to the header frame and both pages in the main frame that coordinates with the picture in the header frame.
11. Move to the header frame, and apply a Heading 1 style to the business name *In The Game*.
12. Move to *main page.htm* in the main frame, and apply a Heading 2 style to each of the four headings (*Baseball and Softball, Soccer, Track and Field,* and *Gymnastics*) on the main page.
13. Move to the *contact us.htm* in the main frame.
14. Apply a Heading 2 style to the title "Contact Us" at the top of the page, and center the title if needed.
15. Apply a Heading 3 style to each of the three headings (*Email, Call Us,* and *Snail Mail*) on the page.
16. Resize the header frame as shown below by dragging the bottom border.
17. Save the frames page again.
18. View the Web page in a browser.

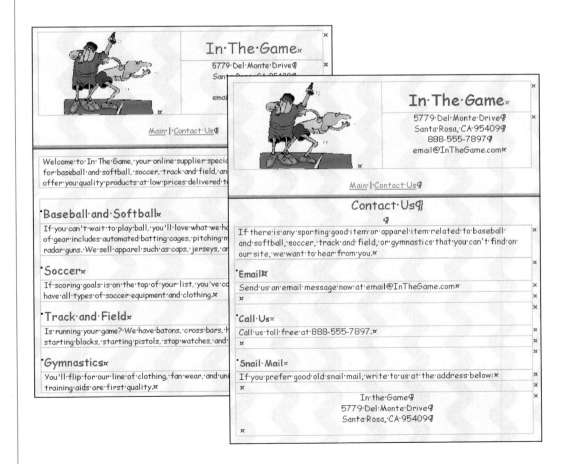

Unit 24
Skillbuilding and In-Basket Review

LESSON 116
In-Basket Review (Insurance)

LESSON 117
In-Basket Review (Hospitality)

LESSON 118
In-Basket Review (Retail)

LESSON 119
In-Basket Review (Government)

LESSON 120
In-Basket Review (Manufacturing)

Suite Retreat
3539 Shell Basket Lane
Sanibel Island, Florida 33957
941-555-3422
email@SuiteRetreat.com

Home | Suites

Are you ready to experience a private beach retreat with warm waters, endless white sand, and blue skies? The personnel at Suite Retreat are at your service and will make sure your stay is a pleasurable one.

Suite Retreat is hidden away on a private beach on the Gulf of Mexico at the end of a secluded country road. You will feel the soothing effects of our lush, tropical surroundings and charming cottage suites the moment you enter our winding drive. Each suite is beautifully decorated and appointed with marble baths and private whirlpools for ~~~~ ~~~~ r further details on our suites.

~~~~ ~~~~ recreation during your stay, we have a ~~~~ ~~~~ h the property:

~~~~ ~~~~ ennis courts

~~~~ ~~~~ g, you will find a small golf course and ~~~~ ~~~~ walking distance about a half mile

All-City, Inc.
17 N. 8ᵗʰ Street ◆ Columbia, MO 65201 ◆ 800-555-9981 ◆ www.ACI.com

Insuring you at home and a~~~~

SRU Sunwear

Sports 'R Us
3939 Townsgate Drive
San Diego, CA 92130
www.SRU.com

In-Basket Review (Insurance)

GOALS

- Type at least 50wpm/5'/5e
- Format insurance documents

A. Type 2 times.

A. WARMUP

```
1        He realized that exactly 10% of the budget ($62,475)     11
2   was questionable. Several key people reviewed it; most of      23
3   them wanted to reject about 1/3 of the proposed line items!    35
    |  1  |  2  |  3  |  4  |  5  |  6  |  7  |  8  |  9  |  10  |  11  |  12
```

SKILLBUILDING

B. PROGRESSIVE PRACTICE: ALPHABET

If you are not using the GDP software, turn to page SB-7 and follow the directions for this activity.

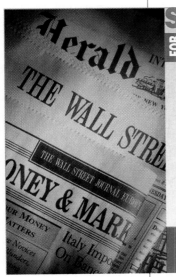

STRATEGIES FOR *Career Success*

Managing Group Conflict

Not all team members have the same opinion or approach to solving a problem. Before a group can reach an agreement, conflicts must be addressed and expressed openly. Follow these steps to manage group conflict.

Take everyone's feelings and opinions seriously. Don't be afraid to disagree. Offer and accept constructive criticism. Find points of agreement. When the group makes a decision, support it fully.

Be a good listener. Take notes, maintain eye contact, restate what you hear, and listen for the emotions behind the words. Try to view the situation through the other person's eyes. Don't jump to conclusions. Ask non-threatening questions to clarify meaning, and listen without interrupting. Most group conflicts don't get resolved until everyone feels he or she has had a chance to be heard.

YOUR TURN When is the last time you had a conflict with a coworker? What did you do about it? What was the result?

C. Take two 5-minute timings. Review your speed and errors.

Goal: At least 50wpm/5'/5e

C. 5-MINUTE TIMING

4	Several factors should be considered before you buy	11
5	a new printer for your computer. First, decide how you will	23
6	use the new printer. If you plan to use the printer for	34
7	composing letters or reports, you may want to shop for an	46
8	ink jet printer that is reasonably priced and capable of	57
9	doing general tasks. If you are purchasing the printer for	69
10	office use, you may wish to shop for a printer that prints	81
11	documents more quickly and of exceptional quality. Finally,	93
12	if you plan to use a digital camera with the printer, you	105
13	will want a printer that is designed to print documents of	117
14	photo quality.	120
15	Resolution, speed, and paper handling are some other	131
16	factors you should consider when you purchase a printer.	142
17	Resolution refers to how sharp the image appears on the	153
18	paper. With printers producing a higher resolution, the	164
19	imaging gives a higher quality output. You will see this	175
20	amazing difference in imaging when you compare samples of	187
21	print from various types of printers.	195
22	If you expect to print long documents, then you will	206
23	want to look for a reliable printer with a feed tray that	218
24	holds large amounts of paper. The more expensive printers	230
25	are usually faster printers. After assessing your printer	241
26	needs, you are ready to make your purchase.	250

| 1 | 2 | 3 | 4 | 5 | 6 | 7 | 8 | 9 | 10 | 11 | 12 |

DOCUMENT PROCESSING

Form 116-15

Letter Template With Enclosure Notation

Use the first letter template in your word processing software.

Situation: You are employed in the office of All-City, Inc., an insurance company in Columbia, Missouri. Their offices are located at 17 N. 8th Street, Columbia, MO 65201, and their phone number is 800-555-9981. All City, Inc., handles auto, home, and life insurance coverage. The Web site address is www.ACI.com.

Mr. Greg Scher, executive vice president, has written the letter shown on page 471 using the current date. You are to type it using a correspondence template. He prefers block-style letters with *Sincerely* as his complimentary closing and uses his title in the writer's identification. The letter should be addressed to Ms. Thelma Day, 731 Broad Street, Newark, NJ 07102, and you should use standard punctuation. This letter includes two enclosures. The company slogan is "Insuring you at home and around the world."

¶ Your recent letter was filled with excellent questions, Ms. Day, and I am more than happy to answer them for you.

¶ All City, Inc., handles auto, home, and life insurance coverage for you and your family. However, since you are primarily interested in auto insurance, I have enclosed a brochure with the details and a table with required minimum coverage for the states you mentioned.

¶ ACI's automobile policy combines both mandatory and optional coverages in one package. This policy can be tailored to meet your individual needs so that you end up with a policy that provides comprehensive protection. However, the best way for you to understand fully what we can offer you is to schedule a meeting at your convenience.

¶ Ms. Elena Ortega will be calling you in the next day or two to arrange an appointment after you have had a chance to review the enclosed materials. We also have an excellent Web site at ACI.com filled with helpful information. Again, thank you for your inquiry, Ms. Day.

Table 116-55 ▶

Three-Column Boxed Table

The boxed table below is to be enclosed with the letter when it is sent to Ms. Day.

STATE MINIMUM COVERAGE REQUIREMENTS		
Minimum Limits	**State**	**Required Coverage**
25/50/10	NY	Bodily Injury and Property Damage Liability, Personal Injury Protection, Uninsured Motorist
15/30/5	NJ	Bodily Injury and Property Damage Liability, Personal Injury Protection, Uninsured Motorist
15/30/5	PA	Bodily Injury and Property Damage Liability, Medical Payments
20/40/10	CT	Bodily Injury and Property Damage Liability, Uninsured and Underinsured Motorist

Mr. Scher has sketched out a letterhead form, and he would like you to design the finished letterhead for All-City, Inc.

Insert a decorative image.

Identify our company, including our Web site.

Insert our company slogan with a border above it.

In-Basket Review (Hospitality)

GOALS

- Improve speed and accuracy
- Refine language arts skills in word usage
- Format documents used in the hospitality industry

A. Type 2 times.

A. WARMUP

```
1      The executive meeting won't begin until 8:15; please      11
2   contact just the key people at zfnet@mail.com. Did Kay say   23
3   that quite a group* (*234) is expected by 9 o'clock today?   35
    |  1  |  2  |  3  |  4  |  5  |  6  |  7  |  8  |  9  |  10  |  11  |  12
```

SKILLBUILDING

B. Take three 12-second timings on each line. The scale below the last line shows your wpm speed for a 12-second timing.

B. 12-SECOND SPEED SPRINTS

```
4   Half of the space was going to be used for seven new desks.
5   She will soon know if all their goals have been met or not.
6   You must learn to focus on each one of your jobs every day.
7   The group will meet in the new suite that is down the hall.
    I I I I 5 I I I I 10 I I I I 15 I I I I 20 I I I I 25 I I I I 30 I I I I 35 I I I I 40 I I I I 45 I I I I 50 I I I I 55 I I I I 60
```

C. Type line 8. Then type lines 9-11 (as a paragraph), reading the words from right to left. Type 2 times.

C. TECHNIQUE PRACTICE: CONCENTRATION

```
8       When typing, always strive for complete concentration.
9   concentration. complete for strive always typing, When
10  errors. your on down cut may rate typing your in decrease A
11  errors. of number the reduce to rate reading your down Slow
```

D. DIAGNOSTIC PRACTICE: ALPHABET

If you are not using the GDP software, turn to page SB-2 and follow the directions for this activity.

E. Study the rules at the right.

E. WORD USAGE

> RULE ▶
> accept/except

Accept means "to agree to"; *except* means "to leave out."

All employees <u>except</u> the maintenance staff should <u>accept</u> the agreement.

> RULE ▶
> affect/effect

Affect is most often used as a verb meaning "to influence"; *effect* is most often used as a noun meaning "result."

The ruling will <u>affect</u> our domestic operations but will have no <u>effect</u> on Asian operations.

> RULE ▶
> farther/further

Farther refers to distance; *further* refers to extent or degree.

The <u>farther</u> we drove, the <u>further</u> agitated he became.

> RULE ▶
> personal/personnel

Personal means "private"; *personnel* means "employees."

All <u>personnel</u> agreed not to use email for <u>personal</u> business.

> RULE ▶
> principal/principle

Principal means "primary"; *principle* means "rule."

The <u>principle</u> of fairness is our <u>principal</u> means of dealing with customers.

Edit the sentences to correct any errors in word usage.

12 The company cannot accept any collect calls, except for his.
13 The affect of the speech was dramatic; everyone was affected.
14 Further discussion by office personal was not appropriate.
15 Comments made during any meeting should never be personal.
16 If the meeting is held any further away, no one will attend.
17 The principle reason for the decision was to save money.
18 Office ethics is a basic principle that should be practiced.
19 He cannot except the fact that the job was delegated to Jack.
20 Any further effects on office personnel will be evaluated.

DOCUMENT PROCESSING

Situation: You are employed at the office of Suite Retreat, a group of vacation cottage-style suites in Sanibel, Florida. The office and suites are located at 3539 Shell Basket Lane, Sanibel Island, Florida 33957. The phone number is 941-555-3422, and the email address is email@SuiteRetreat.com.

Ms. Maxwell, your boss, has asked you to redesign the home page for Suite Retreat. She has written a description of Suite Retreat that she wants you to use in the main frame. The header frame should include identifying information and a picture that will capture the feeling of a carefree beach vacation spot. The theme and styles you choose for the header and main frame should reflect this same image.

Begin by creating the file for Web page 117-102 named *main suite.htm*. Create the main page first by typing the information inside a one-row centered open table, followed by the frames page, and save the frames page as *index suite.htm*.

(Continued on next page)

Report
117-102 ▶

Web Site

personal/personnel

affect/effect

personal/personnel
farther/further

farther/further

¶ Are you ready to experience a private beach retreat with warm waters, endless white sand, and blue skies? The personnel at Suite Retreat are at your service and will make sure your stay is a pleasurable one.

¶ Suite Retreat is hidden away on a private beach on the Gulf of Mexico at the end of a secluded country road. You will feel the soothing effects of our lush, tropical surroundings and charming cottage suites the moment you enter our winding drive. Each suite is beautifully decorated and appointed with marble baths and private whirlpools for your personal use. Click here for further details on our suites.

¶ If you are interested in a little recreation during your stay, we have a variety of activities available on the property:

- shuffleboard courts and tennis courts
- bicycles and kayaks
- swimming and shelling

¶ If you enjoy golf and fine dining, you will find a small golf course and excellent seafood within easy walking distance about a half mile farther down the beach.

STRATEGIES
Career Success
What to Exclude From Your Resume

What items should you remove from your resume? Don't list salary demands. If the job posting requires a salary history, create a separate page listing the salaries for each position you've held. If the job posting wants your salary requirements, in the application letter state, "Salary expectation is in the range…", and provide a range (usually a $5000 range).

Exclude personal information such as race, gender, health status, age, marital status, religious preference, political preference, national origin, and physical characteristics (e.g., height, weight). Do not provide your Social Security number or your photograph.

Exceptions to listing personal information do exist. For example, if you are applying for a job at a political party's headquarters and you are a member of that party, listing your party affiliation might be important to your potential employer.

YOUR TURN Review your resume. Have you included any personal information? If yes, does it serve a purpose for being in your resume?

Ms. Maxwell has asked you to continue building the Web site by opening the frames page (index suite.htm) and adding two hyperlinks at the bottom of the header frame named "home" and "suites." These hyperlinks should point to the main page (main suite.htm) and a second page named *suites.htm*, which has already been created and includes details on the suite rates.

She also wants you to add a hyperlink on the main page on the word *here* in the last sentence of the second paragraph to link to the second page. After you create these hyperlinks, she wants you to add formatting, themes, etc., to the second page.

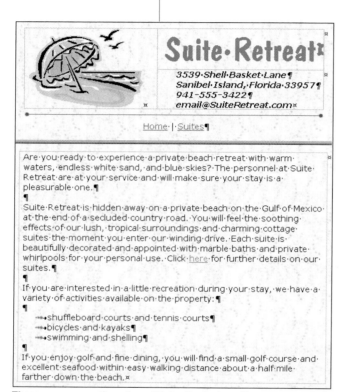

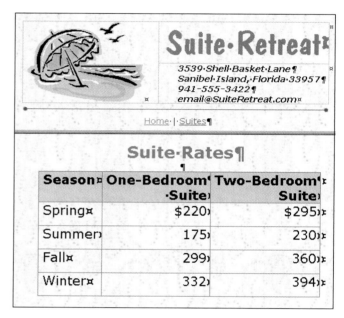

These are suggestions for a Web site design. Use your own judgment in the layout and design of the Web site.

In-Basket Review (Retail)

GOALS

- Type at least 50wpm/5′/5e
- To format retail documents

A. Type 2 times.

A. WARMUP

```
1       Does Pamela know if Region 29* (*Ventura) has met the    11
2  sales quota? Their exact target zone is just not clear;       22
3  they don't have to submit their totals until 4:30 on 5/7.     33
   |  1  |  2  |  3  |  4  |  5  |  6  |  7  |  8  |  9  |  10  |  11  |  12
```

SKILLBUILDING

B. PACED PRACTICE

If you are not using the GDP software, turn to page SB-14 and follow the directions for this activity.

State-of-the-art technology is readily available to consumers at retail stores. Success in retail sales takes initiative, energy, self-confidence, and keyboarding skills.

C. Take two 5-minute timings. Review your speed and errors.

Goal: At least 50wpm/5'/5e

C. 5-MINUTE TIMING

4   Job sharing is a current concept that many employers   11

5 are using to keep valued workers. People are finding a   22

6 variety of reasons for preferring not to work full time.   33

7 Here are some tips on how to approach your employer if you   45

8 would like to try job sharing.   51

9   First, check your company handbook for an official   61

10 policy regarding this concept. If there is no policy that   73

11 prohibits the concept, then try to enlist a coworker who   84

12 would like to job share and help you in writing a proposal   96

13 for job sharing.   99

14   Next, define your needs and objectives. Develop a   109

15 work schedule that will meet your personal and monetary   120

16 needs. Be sure to include adequate time to get the work   131

17 done. If you want to work from home occasionally, be sure   143

18 to indicate your preference. You may find it quite useful   155

19 to maintain a journal of your job responsibilities, noting   167

20 how much time is devoted to each task.   175

21   Your plan also should include information about the   186

22 logistics of your proposal. Determine how you will deal   197

23 with unexpected and crisis situations.   205

24   Finally, time your presentation so there will be no   216

25 unnecessary interruptions. Be organized, persistent, and   227

26 professional in your presentation. Prepare to be successful   239

27 by compiling clearly defined ideas to support your plan.   250

| 1 | 2 | 3 | 4 | 5 | 6 | 7 | 8 | 9 | 10 | 11 | 12

DOCUMENT PROCESSING

Form 118-17 ▶

Memo Template

Use the first memo template in your word processing software.

Situation: Today is January 5. You are employed as an administrative assistant to Kelley O'Brian. Ms. O'Brian is Vice President of Marketing for Sports 'R Us, a retailer for sports equipment and clothing in San Diego, California at 3939 Townsgate Drive, San Diego, CA 92130. The Web site is www.SRU.com.

The company is in the midst of launching a brand new line of women's sportswear for the beach. Ms. O'Brian has written the memo below to Hitochi Morimoto, President of Sports 'R Us, with a copy to Barbara Warrick, Vice President of Sales. You are to type the memo, using a memo template. The subject of the memo is SRU Sunwear Ad Campaign.

(Continued on next page)

¶ I am pleased to tell you that we are in the final stages of our ad campaign to launch our newest line of women's beach sportswear named SRU Sunwear. We are just about to sign Cindy Bloom to serve as our spokesperson and featured model in our magazine ad campaign.

¶ I have scheduled a meeting for next week so that you can meet Cindy and see a representative sampling of our exciting new sportswear line. My staff members will also be ready with a presentation for our ad campaign, which will focus on the practicality and smart good looks of our newest beachwear. I have attached an agenda for your review.

¶ Our company has always been known for the value and quality of our sportswear. This line is based on a smaller emerging brand that will save our customers money while still maintaining the high quality they have come to expect. I look forward to our meeting next week.

Report 118-104 ►

Agenda

The meeting agenda entitled SRU SUN-WEAR AD CAMPAIGN shown below is to be attached to the memo when it is sent to Mr. Morimoto. The meeting will be held January 12, 20--, at 11 a.m.

Call to order
Approval of minutes of December 20 meeting
Introduction of Cindy Bloom
Progress report on the status of the ad campaign
Presentation of the ad campaign
Presentation of some samples from the new sportswear line
Announcements
Miscellaneous
Adjournment

Ms. O'Brian has sketched out a cover page for the ad campaign report and would like you to design the finished cover page for the SRU Sunwear line of beach apparel. The report will be distributed at the meeting.

*Insert some word art
with the name of our
sportswear line.*

*Insert a picture
related to our new
line of beach
sportswear.*

*Identify our company and our
address, including our Web site.*

In-Basket Review (Government)

GOALS
- Improve speed and accuracy
- Refine language arts skills in spelling
- Format government documents

A. Type 2 times.

A. WARMUP

```
1     Turner & Finch will charge us $10,234 to complete the    11
2  job. Do they realize that they quoted us an initial fee of  23
3  exactly $9,876? Kelly will call them very soon to verify.    34
   | 1 | 2 | 3 | 4 | 5 | 6 | 7 | 8 | 9 | 10 | 11 | 12
```

SKILLBUILDING

PRETEST → PRACTICE → POSTTEST

B. PRETEST: Close Reaches

PRETEST
Take a 1-minute timing. Review your speed and errors.

```
4     Sadly, the same essay was used to oppose and deny the   11
5  phony felony charge. After the weapon was located in his   22
6  pocket, the jury was left to cast the joint ballot anyway.  34
   | 1 | 2 | 3 | 4 | 5 | 6 | 7 | 8 | 9 | 10 | 11 | 12
```

C. PRACTICE: Adjacent Keys

PRACTICE
Speed Emphasis:
If you made no more than 1 error on the Pretest, type each *individual* line 2 times.
Accuracy Emphasis:
If you made 2 or more errors, type each *group* of lines (as though it were a paragraph) 2 times.

```
7  po post spot pours vapor poker powder oppose weapon pockets
8  sa sash same usage essay sadly safety dosage sample sailing
9  oi oily join point voice doing choice boiled egoist loiters
```

D. PRACTICE: Conscecutive Fingers

```
10 ft left soft often after shift gifted crafts thrift uplifts
11 ny onyx deny nylon vinyl phony anyway skinny felony canyons
12 lo loss solo loser flood color locate floral ballot loaders
```

E. POSTTEST: Close Reaches

POSTTEST
Repeat the Pretest timing and compare performance.

F. Take a 1-minute timing on the first paragraph to establish your base speed. Then take four 1-minute timings on the remaining paragraphs. As soon as you equal or exceed your base speed on one paragraph, advance to the next, more difficult paragraph.

F. SUSTAINED PRACTICE: PUNCTUATION

13   Have you ever noticed that a good laugh every now and   11
14 then really makes you feel better? Research has shown that   23
15 laughter can have a very healing effect on our bodies. It   35
16 is an excellent way to relieve tension and stress all over.   47

17   When you laugh, your heart beats faster, you breathe   11
18 deeper, and you exercise your lungs. When you laugh, your   23
19 body produces endorphins--a natural painkiller that gives   35
20 you a sense of euphoria that is very powerful and pleasant.   47

21   Someone said, "Laugh in the face of adversity." As it   11
22 happens, this is first-rate advice. It's a great way to   22
23 cope with life's trials and tribulations; it's also a good   34
24 way to raise other people's spirits and relieve tension.   45

25   Finding "humor" in any situation takes practice--try   11
26 to make it a full-time habit. We're all looking for ways   22
27 to relieve stress. Any exercise--jogging, tennis, biking,   34
28 swimming, or golfing--is a proven remedy for "the blues."   45

LANGUAGE ARTS

G. Type these frequently misspelled words, paying special attention to any spelling problems in each word.

G. SPELLING

29 practice continue regular entitled course resolution assist
30 weeks preparation purposes referred communication potential
31 environmental specifications original contractor associated
32 principal systems client excellent estimated administration
33 responsibility mentioned utilized materials criteria campus

Edit the sentences to correct any misspellings.

34 It is the responsability of the administration to assist.
35 The principle client prepared the excellent specifications.
36 He mentioned that the critiria for the decision were clear.
37 The contractor associated with the project referred them.
38 He estamated that the potential for resolution was great.
39 I was told that weeks of reguler practice were required.

Words shown in a different color are spelling words from the language arts activities.

Situation: You work as an administrative assistant for Ruth McBride. She is Research Director for Ride Share, a free government-funded commuter service in Chicago that informs people about commuting alternatives.

Ms. McBride has left the letter below in your in-basket to be sent to Mr. Jason Davis, Executive Director for Canadian CarShare, which is located at 1233 West 3rd Ave., Vancouver, BC V6J 1K1 in Canada. When communicating with Canadian firms, use A4 metric size paper and adhere to Canadian mailing guidelines.

Ms. McBride prefers a block-style letter with standard punctuation, uses *Sincerely* as the complimentary close, and likes her business title typed below her name in a letter closing. Use the current date, and add this postscript notation at the end of the letter:

```
Any statistics you might
choose to include on the
environmental impact
associated with car sharing
in your Web site at
http://www.carshare.ca would
be very helpful.
```

¶ Ride Share is a government funded commuter service whose mission is to inform our citizens about commuting alternatives in the Chicago area. My responsibility is to gather as many facts as possible regarding the regular practice of car sharing in Canada.

¶ As I understand this concept, a car share client could conceivably mix and match alternative modes of transportation and also have exclusive use of a reserved car for a fixed period of time. For example, a commuter could arrive at work on a train, pick up a reserved car at a nearby parking lot to run errands at lunch, return the car an hour later, and then continue home perhaps using a van pool or bus. The commuter would pay about 20 to 40 cents a kilometer along with some monthly membership fees.

¶ If you can tell me which cities have successfully utilized car sharing in Canada since it was first introduced and why, I can begin preparation for a proposal for a car sharing pilot project as a potential commuter alternative here in the Chicago area.

Correspondence 119-100 ▶

Business Letter in Block Style With Postscript Notation

Open the file for Correspondence 119-99. Ms. McBride would like you to send the same letter to Mr. Frans Zimmerly, Executive Director of Europa CarShare at Siesmayerstrasse 23, 60323 Frankfurt, GERMANY. When communicating with German firms, use A4 metric size paper and adhere to German mailing guidelines.

Find and replace all instances of Canada with Germany. Use the current date (use day/month/year format), and add this postscript at the end of the letter:

```
Any statistics you might
choose to fax to me at
+1.217.782.5553 regarding
the environmental impact
associated with car sharing
in Germany would be very
helpful.
```

Correspondence 119-101 ▶

Email Message

Send the email message below to Ms. McBride (mcbride@commerce.state.il.us). The subject line is Car Sharing. Type an appropriate greeting for Ms. McBride and a closing and signature line for yourself.

¶ I sent the two letters to the executive directors of CarShare as you requested. I will follow up in a week with phone calls and email messages as follows:

¶ Mr. Jason Davis

+1.604.877.5555

jdavis@carshare.ubc.ca

¶ Mr. Frans Zimmerly

+49.30.20304-0

fzimmerly@carshare.de

¶ I found some statistics about car sharing that might be useful. Car sharing was first introduced in Quebec City in 1994 and now has about 1,200 users in six Canadian cities. About 90,000 car share commuters are located worldwide, with about half of them in Europe.

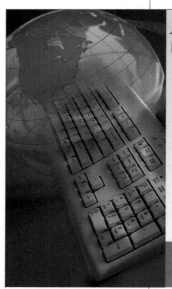

Keyboarding CONNECTION

Email Privacy

How private are your email messages? Although there has been a lot of discussion about hacking and Internet security, email may be more secure than your phone or postal mail. In fact, most new-generation email programs have some kind of encryption built in.

It is not hackers who are the most likely to read your email. It is anyone with access to your incoming mail server or your computer. If your computer and incoming server are at work, then you can assume that your supervisor can read your email. In some companies, it is a normal practice to monitor employees' email. Therefore, you should not send email from work that you wouldn't want anyone there to read.

If you are serious about email privacy, you may want to examine other encryption methods. Different products are available to ensure that your email is only read by the intended recipient(s).

YOUR TURN Perform a keyword search, using a search engine (e.g., *www.altavista.com*), for information on different products that are available to protect your email privacy.

In-Basket Review (Manufacturing)

GOALS

- Type at least 50wpm/5′/5e
- Format manufacturing documents

A. Type 2 times.

A. WARMUP

```
1        Order extra color cartridges very soon! G & K Supply    11
2  just announced a 15% discount on orders for the following     23
3  cartridges: QB728 and ZM 436* (*for the ink-jet printers).    35
   | 1 | 2 | 3 | 4 | 5 | 6 | 7 | 8 | 9 | 10 | 11 | 12
```

SKILLBUILDING

B. DIAGNOSTIC PRACTICE: NUMBERS

If you are not using the GDP software, turn to page SB-5 and follow the directions for this activity.

C. MAP

Follow the GDP software directions for this exercise in improving keystroking accuracy.

Fast and accurate keyboarding skills are critical in providing service to people who are traveling.

D. Take two 5-minute timings. Review your speed and errors.

Goal: At least 50wpm/5'/5e

D. 5-MINUTE TIMING

4	With modern technology, it is possible to work at a	11
5	job full time and never leave your home. You can set up a	22
6	home office with a phone line, fax machine, and a computer	34
7	system. Before choosing to work at home, however, you will	46
8	want to examine carefully your reasons for working at home.	58
9	Some people think about working at home so they can	69
10	have more time to spend with their families. Other people	81
11	like to have more flexibility in their work schedule. They	93
12	are looking for the opportunity to enjoy a better quality	105
13	of life or to participate in other activities.	114
14	There are some factors to consider before you make	124
15	the decision to work at home. You will want to consider	135
16	the ultimate cost of benefits that you may give up if you	147
17	change your place of work. You will want to check with	158
18	your employer to see if you are entitled to paid vacation	170
19	days and health insurance or to make contributions to your	181
20	retirement plan. Another factor to consider is the limited	193
21	contact with peers.	197
22	Before making the ultimate decision to work at home,	208
23	develop some realistic expectations of how you will spend	220
24	each day. Although you can organize your work to fit your	232
25	schedule, you will find the real challenge is to determine	244
26	a routine that works for you.	250

| 1 | 2 | 3 | 4 | 5 | 6 | 7 | 8 | 9 | 10 | 11 | 12 |

DOCUMENT PROCESSING

Situation: You work as an administrative assistant for Melanie Stone at MedPro Manufacturing, one of the largest medical diagnostic equipment manufacturers in the world. The home office is located in Arden, North Carolina, with branch offices located worldwide.

Your boss has left a business report in your in-basket for you to format and type. The title of the report is MedPro Manufacturing. The subtitle of the report is Vision, Innovation, and Partnership. Use the current date after the subtitle.

(Continued on next page)

Introduction

¶ Med Pro Manufacturing is ① of the largest medical diagnostic equipment manufacturers in the world. We have been in business for almost ~~eighty~~ 80 years and our company has a solid reputation for quality and reliability in all our manufacturing processes. We take great pride in our ~~current~~ state-of-the-art manufacturing facilitise because we realize that doctors' reputations and patients' lives depend on the quality and reliability of our products and medical supplies.

VISION

¶ MedPro's vision for the New Millennium is to continue the manufacturing of circuit boards, light sources, fiber optic light guides, and scanning engines. We have in place a stringent quality management process so that our customers are guaranteed a superior product at a competitive price. Because of these high standards, ~~we have~~ our company has attained the most current ISO Certification. We have reduced consistently our manufacturing cycles without sacrificing quality.

INNOVATION

¶ Everyone at MedPro from those on the manufacturing floor to those in the presidents office, is committed to the continuation of the research and development of innovative products and ~~state-of-the-art~~ high-tech manufacturing processes.

Products. Our electronic stethoscope system combined a revolutionary acoustic technology and teamed it with the power of a computer to produce extraordinary results in doctors offices. We specialize in innovative products for ~~kids~~ children. Our autorefractor has allowed optometrists and ophthalmologists to perform an objective refraction on children ~~that is~~ faster and easier than ever before. We are committed to the continuous development of innovative products like these.

Manufacturing processes. Our fiber optic light guides and scanning engines are ② more examples of how MedPro is committed to innovation in the manufacturing process ~~as well~~. Our computer controlled manufacturing

(Continued on next page)

and CAD/ECAD equipment helps us to control precisely the manufacturing of all our medical equipment. These same innovative processes have helped us reduce our costs and reduce our manufacturing cycle.

PARTNERSHIP

¶ One of the most effective ways to ensure success is to develop partnerships with other innovative businesses that have the same commitment to high standards and are leaders in their respective fields. Our team work and collaboration with our partners have helped us to establish an international presence and reputation. ¶ Our website can be found at http://medpro.com, and it is filled with a wealth of excellent information. All details of our products, services, employees, contact information, etc., can be found there. We look forward to your business.

Correspondence 120-102 ▶

Multipage Business Letter in Block Style With Three-Column Boxed Table

✔ **Progress Check Proofreading Check**

Documents designated as Proofreading Checks serve as a check of your proofreading skill. Your goal is to have zero typographical errors when the GDP software first scores the document.

A letter that includes a table has also been left in your in-basket to be typed with the current date (use day/month/year format). The letter is to be sent to Mrs. Carmen Tamashiro, Associate Director for Medical Relief International, which is located at 3-5-1 Kanda Jinbo-cho, Chiyoda-ku Tokyo 101, Japan. The subject line is Relief Medical Supplies. When communicating with Japanese firms, you are to use A4 metric size paper and adhere to Japanese mailing guidelines.

Ms. Stone, Public Relations Director, prefers a block-style letter with standard punctuation and likes to use a predesigned format for tables. She prefers *Sincerely* as the complimentary close, uses the company name in the closing, and likes her business title typed below her name in the closing. She does not use a courtesy title.

¶ Med Pro Manufacturing is happy to send our tenth shipment of relief medical supplies to be distributed as needed to the people of Japan who have been devastated by recent earthquakes and other natural disasters.

(Continued on next page)

¶ Our previous shipments to Japan have amounted to well over $1 million worth of medical supplies such as antibiotics, surgical supplies, catheters, packs, crutches, splints, braces, and slings. Med Pro Manufacturing usually sends medical goods and equipment exclusively; however, some of the earlier shipments have also included basic survival supplies. Our employees have helped us in our efforts to gather hundreds of tents, sleeping bags, blankets, flashlights, coats, socks, gloves, and all-weather apparel.
¶ Several international branches of our company would also like to offer their help if you need it. The table below includes all the pertinent information:

Address	Email	Telephone
Marie Desaulnier 4, rue Galvani Massy, F-91745 FRANCE	medpro.com@email.fr	+33.1.64531515
Frank Liberman Mittlerer Pfad 9 D-70499 Stuttgart GERMANY	medpro.com@email.de	+49.711.8871624
Manny Yamamoto 16-13, 2-chome Hongo Tokyo 113-0033 JAPAN	medpro.com@email.jp	+81.3.38138841

¶ If I can offer you any further assistance or information, please don't hesitate to contact me at +1.704.555.8945.

Skills Assessment on Part 6

5-Minute Timing

1	The potential to reach your career goals has never	10
2	been better. The person who will advance in a career is	21
3	the one who will make the bold moves to follow his or her	33
4	dreams. He or she will have the required attributes of	44
5	initiative and motivation to put forth maximum efforts	55
6	in order to realize a fulfilling career.	63
7	If you want to get ahead in the highly competitive	73
8	business world today, you need a personal coach or mentor	85
9	who is experienced in motivating people who want to reach	97
10	their potential. You may be afraid to go after your dream	109
11	career because you are afraid of failure. Your personal	120
12	mentor will help you to minimize any problems you incur.	131
13	He or she will encourage you to strive for more.	141
14	When you decide to work with a professional coach,	151
15	you are investing in yourself. You can trust your coach to	163
16	work with you through the entire process of expanding your	175
17	horizons until you reach your goal. When you think you	186
18	have reached your limit, your coach will make suggestions	198
19	for additional improvement. He or she will present the	209
20	strategies you can use to be successful. Your coach will	220
21	guide you in making the critical decisions for advancing	231
22	your career. The final decision to improve your skills	242
22	and become successful is yours, however.	250

| 1 | 2 | 3 | 4 | 5 | 6 | 7 | 8 | 9 | 10 | 11 | 12 |

Form
Test 6-18 ▶

Memo Template With
Attachment Notation

Select the first memo
template listed in your
word processing
software.

To: Michael Lani, Human Resources Director | **CC:** Armando Lopez, President | **From:** Charlene Morimoto, Committee Chairperson | **Date:** Current Date | **Re:** Turkey Trot Fun Run Fundraiser

¶ It's time once again for our annual Turkey Trot Fun Run, in which all proceeds are donated to the Read-2-Learn literacy program for inner-city youth. Since 1980, our Read-2-Learn Committee has donated over $150,000 to this very worthy cause, and we have every intention of raising at least $8,000 in this Fun Run on Thanksgiving Day, but we need your help.

¶ As our director of human resources, you are in a unique position to help us raise funds. If you could encourage each of our employees to donate $20 to sponsor one runner in this event, we would easily meet our goals this year. Last year we had over 400 sponsored runners.

(Continued on next page)

¶ The Read-2-Learn program is specifically targeted at the inner-city elementary students in our neighborhood in their quest for basic literacy skills. Our business is located in a rich, multicultural urban neighborhood that is in desperate need of this type of program. I have attached a brochure that explains all details of this reading program and an event flyer. If you need additional copies, please let me know. Also, please visit our Web site at http://www.turkeytrot.org for further details.

¶ urs | Attachments

Report Test 6-107 ▶

Web Page

1. Save a new, unnamed document as a Web page and name it *main read.htm*.
2. Create a centered, boxed table with 2 columns and 4 rows.
3. Type this information in the open table as shown in the illustration.
4. Insert a picture related to reading and size it approximately as shown. Apply a coordinated design theme.
5. Insert horizontal lines in Rows 2 and 4. Change any styles, fonts, or colors as desired.

Read-2-Learn

A Youth Literacy Program of the Los Angeles Public Library

Our mission is to provide instructions in the basic literacy skills of reading and writing for elementary school children. Read-2-Learn offers participants free tutoring and a variety of other support services. Our volunteer tutors have been trained and will be matched with students to provide optimal conditions for learning and practicing basic reading and writing skills. The learner's interests and needs are always considered first.

This literacy program is funded by the Los Angeles Public Library; government grants; special events; and contributions from corporations, foundations and individuals. Our services include the following:

- Free individualized tutoring
- A resource library including books, tapes, games, and manuals
- Basic computer literacy instruction
- Small group or one-on-one instruction for learners
- Ongoing evaluation and instructional support with a reading specialist
- Referrals to other literacy programs

(Continued on next page)

Read-2-Learn

*A Youth Literacy Program of the
Los Angeles Public Library*

Our mission is to provide instructions in the basic literacy skills of reading and writing for elementary school children. Read-2-Learn offers participants free tutoring and a variety of other support services. Our volunteer tutors have been trained and will be matched with students to provide optimal conditions for learning and practicing basic reading and writing skills. The learner's interests and needs are always considered first.

This literacy program is funded by the Los Angeles Public Library; government grants; special events; and contributions from corporations, foundations, and individuals. Our services include the following:

- Free individualized tutoring
- A resource library including books, tapes, games, and manuals
- Basic computer literacy instruction
- Small group or one-on-one instruction for learners
- Ongoing evaluation and instructional support with a reading specialist
- Referrals to other literacy programs

**Report
Test 6-108** ▶

Flyer

Press the SPACE BAR 2 times, and create the flyer as shown in the illustration.

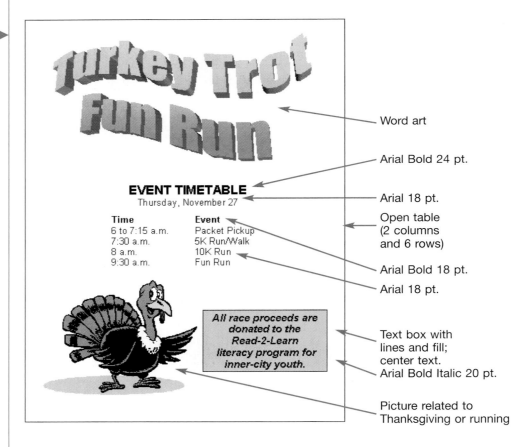

Word art

Arial Bold 24 pt.

Arial 18 pt.

Open table
(2 columns
and 6 rows)

Arial Bold 18 pt.

Arial 18 pt.

Text box with
lines and fill;
center text.
Arial Bold Italic 20 pt.

Picture related to
Thanksgiving or running

(Continued on next page)

Type this information in the open table and text box as shown in the flyer illustration.

EVENT TIMETABLE
Thursday, November 27

Time	Event
6 to 7:15 a.m.	Packet Pickup
7:30 a.m.	5K Run/Walk
8 a.m.	10K Run
9:30 a.m.	Fun Run

All race proceeds are donated to the Read-2-Learn literacy program for inner-city youth.

. . . Your keyboarding skills—just the beginning . . .

SKILLBUILDING

Diagnostic Practice: Alphabet

The Diagnostic Practice: Alphabet program is designed to diagnose and then correct your keystroking errors. You may use this program at any time throughout the course after completing Lesson 9.

Directions

1. Type one of the three Pretest/Posttest paragraphs 1 time, pushing *moderately* for speed. Review your errors.
2. Note your results—the number of errors you made on each key and your total number of errors. For example, if you typed *rhe* for *the,* you would count 1 error on the letter *t.*
3. For any letter on which you made 2 or more errors, select the corresponding drill lines and type the lines 2 times. If you made only 1 error, type the drill 1 time.
4. If you made no errors on the Pretest/Posttest paragraph, type one 3-line set of the Troublesome Pairs on page SB-4.
5. Finally, retype the same Pretest/Posttest, and compare your performance with your Pretest.

PRETEST/POSTTEST

Paragraph 1

    Sylvia and Julia made six quilts that were sold at the bazaar. Several kinds of new craft projects were judged to be quite complex and were given five kinds of prizes. Most sizable quarterly taxes were backed by both boys and girls.

Paragraph 2

    Jacob and Zeke Koufax quietly enjoyed jazz music on my new jukebox. The six or seven pieces of exquisite equipment helped both create lovely music by Richard Wagner; I picked five very quaint waltzes from Gregg Ward's jazz recordings.

Paragraph 3

    A quiet girl seized the black vase and gave it to five judges who examined it carefully. Two quickly gave it high marks. Forty people in the adjoining zone were quite vexed at some lazy judges who were lax about keeping on schedule.

PRACTICE: Individual Reaches

Note that each letter drill provides practice in typing that letter combination with as many other letters as possible. For example, in the A drill, the first word (Isaac) practices *aa,* the second word (badge) practices *ba,* the third word (carry) practices *ca,* and so on, through *za* in Zaire.

```
aa Isaac badge carry dared eager faced gains habit dials AA
aa jaunt kayak label mamma Nancy oasis paint Qatar rapid AA
aa safer taken guard vague waves exact yacht Zaire Aaron AA

bb about ebbed ebony rugby fiber elbow amber unbar oboes BB
bb arbor cubic oxbow maybe abate abbot debit libel album BB
bb embed obeys urban tubes Sybil above lobby webby bribe BB

cc acted occur recap icing ulcer emcee uncle ocean force CC
cc scale itchy bucks excel Joyce acute yucca decal micro CC
cc mulch McCoy incur octet birch scrub latch couch cycle CC
```

```
dd admit daddy edict Magda ideal older index oddly order DD
dd outdo udder crowd Floyd adapt added Edith Idaho folds DD
dd under modem sword misdo fudge rowdy Lydia adept buddy DD

ee aegis beach cents dense eerie fence germs hence piece EE
ee jewel keyed leads media nerve poems penny reach seize EE
ee teach guest verse Wendy Xerox years zesty aerie begin EE

ff after defer offer jiffy gulfs infer often dwarf cuffs FF
ff awful afoul refer affix edify Wolfe infra aloof scarf FF
ff bluff afoot defer daffy fifty sulfa softy surfs stuff FF

gg again edges egged soggy igloo Elgin angel ogled Marge GG
gg outgo auger pygmy agape Edgar Egypt buggy light bulge GG
gg singe doggy organ bugle agree hedge began baggy Niger GG

hh ahead abhor chili Nehru ghost Elihu khaki Lhasa unhat HH
hh aloha phony myrrh shale Ethan while yahoo choir jihad HH
hh ghoul Khmer Delhi hoard photo rhino shake think while HH

ii aired bides cider dices eight fifth vigil highs radii II
ii jiffy kinds lives mired niece oiled piped rigid siren II
ii tired build visit wider exist yield aimed binds cigar II

jj major eject fjord Ouija enjoy Cajun Fijis Benjy bijou JJ
jj banjo jabot jacks jaded jails Japan jaunt jazzy jeans JJ
jj jeeps jeers jelly jerks jibed jiffy jilts joint joker JJ

kk Akron locks vodka peeks mikes sulky links okras larks KK
kk skins Yukon hawks tykes makes socks seeks hiker sulks KK
kk tanks Tokyo jerky pesky nukes gawks maker ducks cheek KK

ll alarm blame clank idled elope flame glows Chloe Iliad LL
ll ankle Lloyd inlet olive plane burly sleet atlas Tulsa LL
ll yowls axles nylon alone blunt claim idler elite flute LL

mm among adman demit pigmy times calms comma unman omits MM
mm armor smell umber axmen lymph gizmo amass admit demon MM
mm dogma imply films mommy omits armed smear bumpy adman MM

nn ankle Abner envoy gnome Johns input knife kilns hymns NN
nn Donna onion apnea angle snore undid owned cynic angle NN
nn entry gnash inset knoll nanny onset barns sneer unfit NN

oo aorta bolts coats dolls peony fouls goofs hoped iotas OO
oo jolts kooky loins moral noise poled Roger soaks total OO
oo quote voter would Saxon yo-yo zones bombs colts doles OO

pp apple epoch flips alpha ample input droop puppy sharp PP
pp spunk soups expel typed April Epsom slips helps empty PP
pp unpin optic peppy corps spite upset types apply creep PP
```

```
qq Iraqi equal pique roque squad tuque aquae equip toque QQ
qq squab squat squid squaw quail qualm quart queen quell QQ
qq query quest quick quiet quilt quirk quota quote quoth QQ

rr array bring crave drive erode freak grain three irate RR
rr kraft honor orate Barry tramp urges liver wrote lyric RR
rr rears armor broth crown drawl erect freer grade throw RR

ss ashen bombs specs binds bares leafs bangs sighs issue SS
ss necks mills teams turns solos stops stirs dress diets SS
ss usury Slavs stows abyss asked stabs cords mares beefs SS

tt attic debts pacts width Ethel often eight itchy alter TT
tt until motto optic earth stops petty couth newts extra TT
tt myths Aztec atone doubt facts veldt ether sight Italy TT

uu audio bumps cured dumps deuce fuels gulps huffy opium UU
uu junta kudos lulls mumps nudge outdo purer ruler super UU
uu tulip revue exult yucca azure auger burns curve duels UU

vv avows event ivory elves envoy overt larva mauve savvy VV
vv avant every rivet Elvis anvil coves curvy divvy avert VV
vv evict given valve ovens serve paves evade wives hover VV

ww awash bwana dwarf brews Gwenn schwa kiwis Elwin unwed WW
ww owner Irwin sweet twins byway awake dwell pewee tower WW
ww Erwin swims twirl awful dwelt Dewey owlet swamp twine WW

xx axiom exile fixed Bronx toxin Sioux Exxon pyxie axman XX
xx exert fixes foxes oxbow beaux calyx maxim exact sixth XX
xx proxy taxes excel mixed boxer axing Texas sixty epoxy XX

yy maybe bylaw cynic dying eying unify gypsy hypos Benjy YY
yy Tokyo hilly rummy Ronny loyal pygmy diary Syria types YY
yy buyer vying Wyatt epoxy crazy kayak ready cycle bawdy YY

zz azure Czech adzes bezel dizzy Franz froze Liszt ritzy ZZ
zz abuzz tizzy hazed czars maize Ginza oozes blitz fuzzy ZZ
zz jazzy mazes mezzo sized woozy Hertz fizzy Hazel Gomez ZZ
```

PRACTICE: Troublesome Pairs

```
B/V Beverly believes Bob behaved very bravely in Beaverton.
F/G Griffin goofed in figuring their gifted golfer's score.
H/J Joseph joshed with Judith when John jogged to Johnetta.

M/N Many women managed to move among the mounds of masonry.
O/P A pollster polled a population in Phoenix by telephone.
Q/A Quincy acquired one quality quartz ring at the banquet.

U/Y Buy your supply of gifts during your busy July journey.
X/C The exemptions exceed the expert's wildest expectation.
Z/A Liza gazed as four lazy zebras zigzagged near a gazebo.
```

Diagnostic Practice: Numbers

The Diagnostic Practice: Numbers program is designed to diagnose and then correct your keystroking errors. You may use this program at any time throughout the course after completing Lesson 14.

Directions

1. Type one of the three Pretest/Posttest paragraphs 1 time, pushing *moderately* for speed. Review your errors.
2. Note your results—the number of errors you made on each key and your total number of errors. For example, if you type *24* for *25,* you would count 1 error on the number *5.*
3. For any number on which you made 2 or more errors, select the corresponding drill lines and type the drills 2 times. If you made only 1 error, type the drill 1 time.
4. If you made no errors on the Pretest/Posttest paragraph, type 1 set of the drills that contain all numbers on page SB-6.
5. Finally, retype the same Pretest/Posttest, and compare your performance with your Pretest.

PRETEST/POSTTEST

Paragraph 1

The statement dated May 24, 1995, listed 56 clamps; 14 batteries; 160 hammers; 358 screwdrivers; 1,208 pliers; and 2,475 files. The invoice numbered 379 showed 387 hoes, 406 rakes, 92 lawn mowers, 63 tillers, and 807 more lawn items.

Paragraph 2

My inventory records dated May 31, 1994, revealed that we had 458 pints; 2,069 quarts; and 8,774 gallons of paint. We had 2,053 brushes; 568 scrapers; 12,063 wallpaper rolls; 897 knives; 5,692 mixers; 480 ladders; and 371 step stools.

Paragraph 3

Almost 270 hot meals were delivered to the 15 shut-ins in April, 260 in May, and 280 in June. Several workers had volunteered 7,534 hours in 1996; 6,348 hours in 1995; 5,438 in 1994; and 6,277 in 1993. About 80 people were involved.

PRACTICE: Individual Reaches

1 aq aq1 aq1qa 111 ants 101 aunts 131 apples 171 animals a1
They got 11 answers correct for the 11 questions in BE 121.
Those 11 adults loaded the 711 animals between 1 and 2 p.m.
All 111 agreed that 21 of those 31 are worthy of the honor.

2 sw sw2 sw2ws 222 sets 242 steps 226 salads 252 saddles s2
The 272 summer tourists saw the 22 soldiers and 32 sailors.
Your September 2 date was all right for 292 of 322 persons.
The 22 surgeons said 221 of those 225 operations went well.

3 de de3 de3ed 333 dots 303 drops 313 demons 393 dollars d3
Bus 333 departed at 3 p.m. with the 43 dentists and 5 boys.
She left 33 dolls and 73 decoys at 353 West Addison Street.
The 13 doctors helped some of the 33 druggists in Room 336.

4 fr fr4 fr4rf 444 fans 844 farms 444 fishes 644 fiddles f4
My 44 friends bought 84 farms and sold over 144 franchises.
She sold 44 fish and 440 beef dinners for $9.40 per dinner.
The '54 Ford had only 40,434 fairly smooth miles by July 4.

5 fr fr5 fr5rf 555 furs 655 foxes 555 flares 455 fingers f5
They now own 155 restaurants, 45 food stores, and 55 farms.
They ordered 45, 55, 65, and 75 yards of that new material.
Flight 855 flew over Farmington at 5:50 p.m. on December 5.

6 jy jy6 jy6yj 666 jets 266 jeeps 666 jewels 866 jaguars j6
Purchase orders numbered 6667 and 6668 were sent yesterday.
Those 66 jazz players played for 46 juveniles in Room 6966.
The 6 judges reviewed the 66 journals on November 16 or 26.

7 ju ju7 ju7uj 777 jays 377 jokes 777 joists 577 juniors j7
The 17 jets carried 977 jocular passengers above 77 cities.
Those 277 jumping beans went to 77 junior scouts on May 17.
The 7 jockeys rode 77 jumpy horses between March 17 and 27.

8 ki ki8 ki8ik 888 keys 488 kites 888 knives 788 kittens k8
My 8 kennels housed 83 dogs, 28 kids, and 88 other animals.
The 18 kind ladies tied 88 knots in the 880 pieces of rope.
The 8 men saw 88 kelp bass, 38 kingfish, and 98 king crabs.

9 lo lo9 lo9ol 999 lads 599 larks 999 ladies 699 leaders 19
All 999 leaves fell from the 9 large oaks at 389 Largemont.
The 99 linemen put 399 large rolls of tape on for 19 games.
Those 99 lawyers put 899 legal-size sheets in the 19 limos.

0 ;p ;p0 ;p0p; 100 pens 900 pages 200 pandas 800 pencils ;0
There were 1,000 people who lived in the 300 private homes.
The 10 party stores are open from 1:00 p.m. until 9:00 p.m.
They edited 500 pages in 1 book and 1,000 pages in 2 books.

All numbers   ala s2s d3d f4f f5f j6j j7j k8k 191 ;0; Add 6 and 8 and 29.
That 349-page script called for 10 actors and 18 actresses.
The check for $50 was sent to 705 Garfield Street, not 507.
The 14 researchers asked the 469 Californians 23 questions.

All numbers   ala s2s d3d f4f f5f j6j j7j k8k 191 ;0; Add 3 and 4 and 70.
They built 1,200 houses on the 345-acre site by the canyon.
Her research showed that gold was at 397 in September 1994.
For $868 extra, they bought 15 new books and 62 used books.

All numbers   ala s2s d3d f4f f5f j6j j7j k8k 191 ;0; Add 5 and 7 and 68.
A bank auditor arrived on May 26, 1994, and left on May 30.
The 4 owners open the stores from 9:30 a.m. until 6:00 p.m.
After 1,374 miles on the bus, she must then drive 185 more.

SKILLBUILDING

Progressive Practice: Alphabet

This skillbuilding routine contains a series of 30-second timings that range from 16wpm to 104wpm. The first time you use these timings, take a 1-minute timing on the Entry Timing paragraph. Note your speed.

Select a passage that is 2 words per minute higher than your current speed.

Then take six 30-second timings on the passage.

Your goal each time is to complete the passage within 30 seconds with no errors. When you have achieved your goal, move on to the next passage and repeat the procedure.

Entry Timing

```
        Bev was very lucky when she found extra quality in the      11
home she was buying. She quietly told the builder that she          23
was extremely satisfied with the work done on her new home.         35
The builder said she can move into her new house next week.         47
|  1  |  2  |  3  |  4  |  5  |  6  |  7  |  8  |  9  |  10 |  11 |  12
```

16wpm The author is the creator of a document.

18wpm Open means to access a previously saved file.

20wpm A byte represents one character to every computer.

22wpm A mouse may be used when running Windows on a computer.

24wpm Soft copy is text that is displayed on your computer screen.

26wpm Memory is the part of the word processor that stores information.

28wpm A menu is a list of choices to direct the operator through a function.

30wpm A sheet feeder is a device that will insert sheets of paper into a printer.

32wpm An icon is a small picture that illustrates a function or an object in software.

34wpm A window is a rectangular area with borders that displays the contents of open files.

36wpm To execute means to perform an action specified by an operator or by the computer program.

38wpm Output is the result of a word processing operation. It can be either printed or magnetic form.

40wpm Format refers to the physical features which affect the appearance and arrangement of your document.

42wpm

A font is a style of type of one size or kind which includes all letters, numbers, and punctuation marks.

44wpm

Ergonomics is the science of adapting working conditions or equipment to meet the physical needs of employees.

46wpm

Home position is the starting position of a document; it is typically the upper left corner of the display monitor.

48wpm

The mouse may be used to change the size of a window and to move a window to a different location on the display screen.

50wpm

An optical scanner is a device that can read text and enter it into a word processor without the need to type the data again.

52wpm

Hardware refers to the physical equipment used, such as the central processing unit, display screen, keyboard, printer, or drives.

54wpm

A peripheral device is any piece of equipment that will extend the capabilities of a computer system but is not required for operation.

56wpm

A split screen displays two or more different images at the same time; it can, for example, display two different pages of a legal document.

58wpm

When using Windows, it's possible to place several programs on a screen and to change the size of a window or to change its position on a screen.

60wpm

With the click of a mouse, one can use a Button Bar or a toolbar for fast access to features that are frequently applied when using a Windows program.

62wpm

An active window can be reduced to an icon when you use Windows, enabling you to double-click another icon to open a new window for formatting and editing.

64wpm

Turnaround time is the length of time needed for a document to be keyboarded, edited, proofread, corrected if required, printed, and returned to the originator.

66wpm

A local area network is a system that uses cable or another means to allow high-speed communication among many kinds of electronic equipment within particular areas.

68wpm

To search and replace means to direct the word processor to locate a character, word, or group of words wherever it occurs in the document and replace it with newer text.

70wpm
Indexing is the ability of a word processor to accumulate a list of words that appear in a document, including page numbers, and then print a revised list in alphabetic order.

72wpm
When a program needs information from you, a dialog box will appear on the desktop. Once the dialog box appears, you must identify the option you desire and then choose that option.

74wpm
A facsimile is an exact copy of a document, and it is also a process by which images, such as typed letters, graphs, and signatures, are scanned, transmitted, and then printed on paper.

76wpm
Compatibility refers to the ability of a computer to share information with another computer or to communicate with some other apparatus. It can be accomplished by using hardware or software.

78wpm
Some operators like to personalize their desktops when they use Windows by making various changes. For example, they can change their screen colors and the pointer so that they will have more fun.

80wpm
Wraparound is the ability of a word processor to move words from one line to another line and from one page to the next page as a result of inserting and deleting text or changing the size of margins.

82wpm
It is possible when using Windows to evaluate the contents of different directories on the screen at the very same time. You can then choose to copy or move a particular file from one directory to another.

84wpm
List processing is a capability of a word processor to keep lists of data that can be updated and sorted in alphabetic or numeric order. A list can also be added to any document that is stored in one's computer.

86wpm
A computer is a wondrous device, which accepts data that are input and then processes the data and produces output. The computer performs its work by using one or more stored programs, which provide the instructions.

88wpm
The configuration is the components that make up your word processing system. Mainly systems include a keyboard that is used for entering data, a central processing unit, at least one disk drive, a monitor, and a printer.

90wpm

Help for Windows can be used whenever you see a Help button in a dialog box or on a menu bar. Once you finish reading about a topic that you have selected, you will see a list of some related topics from which you can choose.

92wpm

When you want to look at the contents of two windows when using Windows, you will want to reduce the window size. Do this by pointing to a border or a corner of a window and dragging it until the window is the size that you want.

94wpm

Scrolling means to display a large quantity of text by rolling it horizontally or vertically past the display screen. As the text disappears from the top section of the monitor, new text will appear at the bottom section of the monitor.

96wpm

The Windows Print Manager is used to install and configure printers, join network printers, and monitor the printing of documents. Windows requires that a default printer be identified, but you can change the designation of it at any point.

98wpm

A stop code is a command that makes a printer pause while it is printing to permit an operator to insert text, change the font style, or change the kind of paper in the printer. To resume printing, the operator must use a special key or command.

100wpm

A computerized message system is a class of electronic mail that enables any operator to key a message on any computer terminal and have the message stored for later retrieval by the recipient, who can then display the message on his or her terminal.

102wpm

Many different graphics software programs have been brought on the market in recent years. These programs can be very powerful in helping with a business presentation. If there is any need to share data, using one of these programs could be quite helpful.

104wpm

Voice mail has become an essential service that many people in the business world use. This enables anyone who places a call to your phone to leave a message if you cannot answer it at that time. This special feature helps lots of workers to be more productive.

Progressive Practice: Numbers

This skillbuilding routine contains a series of 30-second timings that range from 16wpm to 80wpm. The first time you use these timings, take a 1-minute timing on the Entry Timing paragraph. Note your speed.

Select a passage that is 4 to 6 words per minute *lower* than your current alphabetic speed. (The reason for selecting a lower speed goal is that sentences with numbers are more difficult to type.) Take six 30-second timings on the passage.

Your goal each time is to complete the passage within 30 seconds with no errors. When you have achieved your goal, move on to the next passage and repeat the procedure.

Entry Timing

Their bags were filled with 10 sets of jars, 23 cookie   11
cutters, 4 baking pans, 6 coffee mugs, 25 plates, 9 dessert   23
plates, 7 soup bowls, 125 recipe cards, and 8 recipe boxes.   35
They delivered these 217 items to 20487 Mountain Boulevard.   47

| 1 | 2 | 3 | 4 | 5 | 6 | 7 | 8 | 9 | 10 | 11 | 12

16wpm There were now 21 children in Room 2110.

18wpm Fewer than 12 of the 121 boxes arrived today.

20wpm Maybe 12 of the 21 applicants met all 15 criteria.

22wpm There were 34 letters addressed to 434 West Cranbrooke.

24wpm Jane reported that there were 434 freshmen and 43 transfers.

26wpm The principal assigned 3 of those 4 students to Room 343 at noon.

28wpm Only 1 or 2 of the 34 latest invoices were more than 1 page in length.

30wpm They met 11 of the 12 players who received awards from 3 of the 4 trainers.

32wpm Those 5 vans carried 46 passengers on the first trip and 65 on the next 3 trips.

34wpm We first saw 3 and then 4 beautiful eagles on Route 65 at 5 a.m. on Tuesday, June 12.

36wpm The 16 companies produced 51 of the 62 records that received awards for 3 of 4 categories.

38wpm The 12 trucks hauled the 87 cows and 65 horses to the farm, which was about 21 miles northeast.

40wpm

She moved from 87 Bayview Drive to 657 Cole Street and then 3 blocks south to 412 Gulbranson Avenue.

42wpm

My 7 or 8 buyers ordered 7 dozen in sizes 5 and 6 after the 14 to 32 percent discounts had been bestowed.

44wpm

There were 34 men and 121 women waiting in line at the gates for the 65 to 87 tickets to the Cape Cod concert.

46wpm

Steve had listed 5 or 6 items on Purchase Order 241 when he saw that Purchase Requisition 87 contained 3 or 4 more.

48wpm

Your items numbered 278 will sell for about 90 percent of the value of the 16 items that have code numbers shown as 435.

50wpm

The managers stated that 98 of those 750 randomly selected new valves had about 264 defects, far exceeding the usual 31 norm.

52wpm

Half of the 625 volunteers received over 90 percent of the charity pledges. Approximately 83 of the 147 agencies will have funds.

54wpm

Merico hired 94 part-time workers to help the 378 full-time employees during the 62-day period when sales go up by 150 percent or more.

56wpm

Kaye only hit 1 for 4 in the first 29 games after an 8-game streak in which she batted 3 for 4. She then hit at a .570 average for 6 games.

58wpm

The mail carrier delivered 98 letters during the week to 734 Oak Street and also took 52 letters to 610 Faulkner Road as he returned on Route 58.

60wpm

Pat said that about 1 in 5 of the 379 swimmers had a chance of being among the top 20. The best 6 of those 48 divers will receive the 16 best awards.

62wpm

It rained from 3 to 6 inches, and 18 of those 20 farmers were fearful that 4 to 7 inches more would flood about 95 acres along 3 miles of the new Route 78.

64wpm

Those 7 sacks weighed 48 pounds, more than the 30 pounds that I had thought. All 24 believe the 92-pound bag is at least 15 or 16 pounds above its true weight.

66wpm

They bought 7 of the 8 options for 54 of the 63 vehicles last month. They now own over 120 dump trucks for use in 9 of the 15 new regions in the big 20-county area.

68wpm

Andy was 8 or 9 years old when they moved to 632 Glendale Street away from the 1700 block of Horseshoe Lane, which is about 45 miles directly west of Boca Raton, FL 33434.

70wpm

Doug had read 575 pages in the 760-page book by March 30; Darlene had read only 468 pages. Darlene has read 29 of those optional books since October 19, and Doug has read 18.

72wpm

That school district has 985 elementary students, 507 middle school students, and 463 high school students; the total of 1,955 is 54, or 2.84 percent, over last year's grand total.

74wpm

Attendance at last year's meeting was 10,835. The goal for this year is to have 11,764 people. This will enable us to plan for an increase of 929 participants, a rise of 8.57 percent.

76wpm

John's firm has 158 stores, located in 109 cities in the West. The company employs 3,540 males and 2,624 females, a total of 6,164 employees. About 4,750 of those employees work part-time.

78wpm

Memberships were as follows: 98 members in the Drama Guild, 90 members in Zeta Tau, 82 members in Theta Phi, 75 in the Bowling Club, and 136 in the Ski Club. This meant that 481 joined a group.

80wpm

The association had 684 members from the South, 830 members from the North, 1,023 members from the East, and 751 from the West. The total membership was 3,288; these numbers increased by 9.8 percent.

Paced Practice

The Paced Practice skillbuilding routine builds speed and accuracy in short, easy steps by using individualized goals and immediate feedback. You may use this program at any time after completing Lesson 9.

This section contains a series of 2-minute timings for speeds ranging from 16wpm to 96wpm. The first time you use these timings, take the 1-minute Entry Timing.

Select a passage that is 2wpm higher than your current typing speed. Then use this two-stage practice pattern to achieve each speed goal: (1) concentrate on speed, and (2) work on accuracy.

Speed Goal. To determine your speed goal, take three 2-minute timings in total. Your goal each time is to complete the passage in 2 minutes without regard to errors. When you have achieved your speed goal, work on accuracy.

Accuracy Goal. To type accurately, you need to slow down—just a bit. Therefore, to reach your accuracy goal, drop back 2wpm to the previous passage. Take consecutive timings on this passage until you can complete the passage in 2 minutes with no more than 2 errors.

For example, if you achieved a speed goal of 54wpm, you should then work on an accuracy goal of 52wpm. When you have achieved 52wpm for accuracy, move up 4wpm (for example, to the 56-wpm passage) and work for speed again.

Entry Timing

If you can dream it, you can live it. Follow your | 10
bliss. There are many careers, from the mundane to the | 21
exotic to the sublime. Start your career planning now. | 32
Prepare for the future by exploring your talents, skills, | 43
and interests.

| 1 | 2 | 3 | 4 | 5 | 6 | 7 | 8 | 9 | 10 | 11 | 12

16wpm

Your future is now. Seize each day. After you have explored your personal interests, study the sixteen career clusters for a broad range of job possibilities.

18wpm

While exploring various job options, think about what a job means to you. A job can mean something you do simply to earn money or something you find more rewarding and challenging.

20wpm

If you have a job you enjoy, work means more than just receiving wages. It means using your talents, being among people with like interests, making a contribution, and gaining a sense of satisfaction.

22wpm

What is the difference between a job and a career? Think carefully. A job is work that people do for money. A career is a sequence of related jobs built on a foundation of interests, knowledge, training, and experiences.

24wpm

Learn more about the world of work by looking at the sixteen career clusters. Most jobs are included in one of the clusters that have been organized by the government. During your exploration of careers, list the clusters that interest you.

26wpm

Once you identify your career clusters of interest, look at the jobs within each cluster. Find out what skills and aptitudes are needed, what education and training are required, what the work environment is like, and what is the possibility for advancements.

28wpm

Use your career center and school or public libraries to research career choices. Search the Internet. Consult with professionals for another perspective of a specific career. As you gather information about career options, you may discover other interesting career possibilities.

30wpm

Gain insights into a career by becoming a volunteer, participating in an internship, or working a part-time or temporary job within a chosen field. You will become more familiar with a specific job while developing your skills. You'll gain valuable experience, whether you choose that career or not.

32wpm

Whichever path you choose, strive for a high level of pride in yourself and your work. Your image is affected by what you believe other people think of you as well as by how you view yourself. Evaluate your level of confidence in yourself. If you have self-doubts, begin to build up your self-confidence and self-esteem.

34wpm

Self-esteem is essential for a positive attitude, and a positive attitude is essential for success in the world of work. While you cannot control everything that happens at work, you can control how you react. Your attitude matters. Becoming more confident and cultivating positive thoughts can bring you power in your life and on the job.

36wpm

Several factors lead to success on the job. People who have studied the factors say that it is the personal traits that often determine who is promoted or who is not. One of the finest traits a person can possess is the trait of being likable. Being likable means a person is honest, courteous, loyal, thoughtful, pleasant, kind, and most assuredly, positive.

38wpm

If you are likable, probably you relate well with others. Your kindness serves you well in the workplace. Developing good interpersonal relationships with coworkers will make work more enjoyable. After all, think of all the hours you will spend together. By showing that you are willing to collaborate with your coworkers, most likely you will receive their cooperation in return.

40wpm

Cooperation begins on the first day of your new job. When you work for a company, you become part of the team. Meeting people and learning new skills can be exciting. For some people, however, any new situation can trigger anxiety. The best advice is to remain calm, do your job to the best of your ability, learn the workplace policies, be flexible, avoid being too critical, and always be positive.

SKILLBUILDING

42wpm

When you begin a new job, even if you have recently received your college diploma, chances are you will start at the bottom of the organizational chart. Each of us has to start somewhere. But don't despair. With hard work and determination, soon you will be climbing up the corporate ladder. If you are clever, you will embrace even the most tedious tasks, take everything in stride, and use every opportunity to learn.

44wpm

If you think learning is restricted to the confines of an academic institution, think again. You have plenty to learn on the job, even if it is a job for which you have been trained. As a new worker, you won't be expected to know everything. When necessary, do not hesitate to ask your employer questions. Learn all you can about your job and the company. Use the new information to enhance your job performance and to prepare for success.

46wpm

Begin every valuable workday by prioritizing all your tasks. Decide which tasks must be done immediately and which can wait. List the most important tasks first; then determine the order in which each task must be done. After you complete a task, triumphantly cross it off your priority list. Do not procrastinate; that is, don't put off work you should do. If a task needs to be done, do it. You will be on top of your task list if you use your time wisely.

48wpm

Prevent the telephone from controlling your time by learning to manage your business phone calls. Phone calls can be extremely distracting from necessary tasks. When making an outgoing call, organize the topics you want to discuss. Gather needed materials such as pencils, papers, and files. Set a time limit, and stick to business. Give concise answers, summarize the points discussed, and end the conversation politely. Efficient telephone usage will help you manage your time.

50wpm

As with anything, practice makes perfect, but along the way, we all make mistakes. The difference between the successful people and those who are less successful is not that the successful people make fewer mistakes. It's that they don't give up. Instead of letting mistakes bring them down, they use their mistakes as opportunities to grow. If you make a mistake, be patient with yourself. You might be able to fix your mistake. Look for more opportunities for success to be just around the corner.

52wpm

Be patient with yourself when handling problems and accepting criticism. Handling criticism gracefully and maturely may be a challenge. Still, it is vital in the workplace. Criticism presented in a way that can help you learn and grow is constructive criticism. When you see criticism as helpful, it's easier to handle. Believe it or not, there are some employees who welcome criticism. It teaches them better ways to succeed on the job. Strive to improve how you accept constructive criticism, and embrace your growth.

54wpm

People experience continuous growth during a career. Goal setting is a helpful tool along any career path. Some people believe that goals provide the motivation needed to get to the place they want to be. Setting goals encourages greater achievements. The higher we set our goals, the greater the effort we will need to reach these goals. Each time we reach a target or come closer to a goal, we see an increase in our confidence and our performance, leading to greater accomplishments. And the cycle continues to spiral onward and upward.

56wpm

One goal we should all strive for is punctuality. When employees are tardy or absent from the workplace, it costs the company money. If you are frequently tardy or absent, others have to do their own work and cover for you. If you are absent often, your peers will begin to resent you, causing everyone stress in the department. Being late and missing work can damage the relationship with your manager and have a negative effect on your career. To avoid these potential problems, develop a personal plan to assure that you arrive every day on time or early.

58wpm

Holding a job is a major part of being an adult. Some people begin their work careers as adolescents. From the beginning, various work habits are developed that are as crucial to success as the actual job skills and knowledge that a person brings to the job. What traits are expected of workers? What do employers look for when they evaluate their employees? Important personal traits include being confident, cooperative, positive and dependable. If you are organized, enthusiastic, and understanding, you have many of the qualities that employers value most in their employees.

60wpm

Being dependable is a desirable trait. When a project must be completed by a specific time, a manager will be reassured to know that reliable workers are going to meet the deadline. Workers who are dependable learn to utilize their time to achieve maximum results. Dependable workers can always be counted on, have good attendance records, are well prepared, and arrive on time ready to work. If a company wants to meet its goals, it must have a team of responsible and dependable workers. You, your coworkers, your supervisors, and your managers are all team members, working to reach common goals.

62wpm

The ability to organize is an important quality for the employee who wishes[1] to display good work habits. The worker should have the ability to plan the work[2] that needs to be completed and then be able to execute the plan in a timely[3] manner. An employer requires a competent worker to be well organized. If an[4] office worker is efficient, he or she handles requests swiftly and deals with[5] correspondence without delay. The organized worker does not allow work to accumulate[6] on the desk. Also, the organized office worker returns all phone calls[7] immediately and makes lists of the activities that need to be done each day.[8]

64wpm

Efficiency is another work habit that is desired. An efficient worker completes[1] a task quickly and begins work on the next project eagerly. He or she thinks about ways[2] to save steps and time. For example, an efficient worker may plan a single[3] trip to the copier with several copying jobs rather than multiple trips to do[4] each separate job. Being efficient also means having the required supplies to[5] successfully complete each job. An efficient employee zips along on each project[6], uses time wisely, and stays focused on the present task. With careful and thorough[7] planning, a worker who is efficient can accomplish more tasks in less time.[8]

66wpm

Cooperation is another ideal work habit. As previously mentioned, cooperation begins[1] on the first day on the job. Cooperation is thinking of all team members when making[2] a decision. A person who cooperates is willing to do what is necessary for[3] the good of the whole group. For you to be a team player, it is essential that you take[4] extra steps to cooperate. Cooperation may mean being a good sport if you are asked[5] to do something you would rather not do. It may mean you have to correct a mistake[6] made by another person in the office. If every employee has the interests of[7] the company at heart and works well as a team player, then cooperation is at work.[8]

68wpm

Enthusiasm is still another work trait that is eagerly sought after by employers. Being enthusiastic means that a person has lots of positive energy. This is reflected in actions toward your work, coworkers, and employer. It has been noted that eagerness can be catching. If workers show they are eager to attempt any project, they will not only achieve the highest praise but will also be considered for career advancement. How much enthusiasm do you show at the workplace? Do you encourage people or complain to people? There will always be plenty of good jobs for employees who are known to have a wealth of zeal and a positive approach to the projects that they are assigned.

70wpm

Understanding is also a preferred work habit for every excellent worker. In today's world, virtually all business includes both men and women of different religions, races, cultures, work ethic, abilities, aptitudes, and attitudes. You'll interact with various types of people as customers, coworkers, and owners. Treat everyone fairly, openly, and honestly. Any type of prejudice is hurtful, offensive, and unacceptable. Prejudice cannot be tolerated in the office. Each employee must try to understand and accept everyone's differences. Because so many diverse groups of people work side by side in the workplace, it is essential that all coworkers maintain a high degree of mutual understanding.

72wpm

It can be concluded that certain work habits or traits can play a major role in determining the success of an employee. Most managers would be quick to agree on the importance of these traits. It is most probable that these habits would be evaluated on performance appraisal forms. Promotions, pay increases, new responsibilities, and your future with the company may be based on these evaluations. You should request regular job performance evaluations even if your company does not conduct them. This feedback will improve your job performance and career development by helping you grow. If you continually look for ways to improve your work habits and skills, then you will enjoy success in the workplace and beyond.

74wpm

You can be certain that no matter where you work, you will use some form of computer technology. Almost every business is dependent upon computers. Companies use such devices as voice mail, fax machines, cellular phones, and electronic schedules. Technology helps to accomplish work quickly and efficiently. A result of this rapidly changing technology is globalization, which is the establishment of worldwide communication links between people. Our world is becoming a smaller, global village. We must expand our thinking beyond the office walls. We must become aware of what happens in other parts of the world. Those events may directly affect you and your workplace. The more you know, the more valuable you will become to the company.

76wpm

Technological advancements are affecting every aspect of our lives. For example, the advent of the Internet has changed how we receive and send information. It is the world's largest information network. The Internet is often called the information superhighway because it is a vast network of computers that connect people and resources worldwide. It is an exciting medium to help you access the latest information. You can even learn about companies by visiting their Web sites. Without any doubt, we are all globally connected, and information technology services support those necessary connections. This industry offers many different employment opportunities. Keep in mind that proficiency in keyboarding is beneficial in this field and in other fields.

SKILLBUILDING

78wpm

It is amazing to discover the many careers in which keyboarding skill is necessary today, and the use of the computer keyboard by executive chefs is a prime example. The chefs in major restaurants must prepare parts or all of the meals served while directing the work of a staff of chefs, cooks, and other kitchen staff. The computer has become a necessary tool for a variety of tasks, including tracking inventories of food supplies. By observing which items are favorites and which items are not requested, the chef can calculate food requirements, order food, and supervise the food purchases. Additionally, the computer has proven to be a very practical tool for such tasks as planning budgets, preparing purchase orders for vendors, creating menus, and printing out reports.

80wpm

Advanced technology has opened the doors to a wider variety of amazing new products and services to sell. It seems the more complex the products, the higher the price of the products, or the greater the sales commission, the stiffer the competition. Selling these technical products requires detailed product knowledge, good verbal skills, smooth sales rapport, and proficient keyboarding skills. Business favors people with special training. For example, a pharmacy company may prefer a person with knowledge in chemistry to sell its products. Selling is for people who thrive on challenges and changes in products and services. Sales is appealing to people who enjoy using their powers of persuasion to make the sales. The potential for good earnings is very high for the well-trained salesperson.

82wpm

As you travel about in your sales job or type a report at the office or create Friday night's pasta special for your five-star restaurant, always remember to put safety first. Accidents happen, but they don't have to happen regularly or to have such serious consequences. Accidents cost businesses billions of dollars annually in medical expenses, lost wages, and insurance claims. A part of your job is to make certain you're not one of the millions of people injured on the job every year. You may believe you work in a safe place, but accidents occur in all types of businesses. A few careless people cause most accidents, so ensure your safety on the job. Safety doesn't just happen. Safety is the result of the careful awareness of many people who plan and put into action a safety program that benefits everyone.

84wpm

In today's market, you need more than the necessary skills or the personal qualities described above to exceed in the workplace. Employers also expect their employees to have ethics. Ethics are the principles of conduct governing an individual or a group. Employees who work ethically do not lie, cheat, or steal. They are honest and fair in their dealings with others. Employees who act ethically build a good reputation for themselves and their company. They are known to be dependable and trustworthy. Unethical behavior can have a spiraling effect. A single act can do a lot of damage. Even if you haven't held a job yet, you have had experience with ethical problems. Life is full of many opportunities to behave ethically. Do the right thing when faced with a decision. The ethics you practice today will carry over to your workplace.

86wpm

Now that you know what is expected of you on the job, how do you make sure you will get the job? Almost everyone has experienced the interview process for a job. For some, the interview is a traumatic event, but it doesn't have to be stressful. Preparation is the key. Research the company for which you are seeking employment. Formulate a list of questions. Your interview provides you the opportunity to interview the organization. Don't go empty-handed. Take a portfolio of items with you. Include copies of your resume with a list of three or more professional references, your academic transcript, and your certificates and licenses. Be sure to wear appropriate business attire. The outcome of the interview will be positive if you have enthusiasm for the job, match your qualifications to the company's needs, ask relevant questions, and listen clearly.

88wpm

How can you be the strongest candidate for the job? Be sure that your skills in reading, writing, mathematics, speaking, and listening are solid. These basic skills will help you listen well and communicate clearly, not only during a job interview, but also at your workplace. The exchange of information between senders and receivers is called communication. It doesn't matter which occupation you choose; you will spend most of your career using these basic skills to communicate with others. You will use the basic skills as tools to gain information, solve problems, and share ideas. You will use these skills to meet the needs of your customers. The majority of jobs available during the next century will be in the industries that will require direct customer contacts. Your success will be based upon your ability to communicate effectively with customers and coworkers.

90wpm

Writing effectively can help you gain a competitive edge in your job search and throughout your career. Most of us have had occasion to write business letters whether to apply for a job, to comment on a product or service, or to place an order. Often it seems easy to sit and let our thoughts flow freely. In other cases, we seem to struggle to find the proper wording while trying to express our thoughts in exactly the right way. Writing skill can improve with practice. Implement the following principles to develop your writing skill. Try to use language that you would be comfortable using in person. Use words that are simple, direct, kind, confident, and professional. When possible, use words that emphasize the positive side. Remember to proofread your work. Well-organized thoughts and proper grammar, spelling, and punctuation show the reader that you care about the quality of your work.

92wpm

Listening is an essential skill of the communication process. It is crucial for learning, getting along, and forming relationships. Do you think you are an active or passive listener? Listening is not a passive activity. Conversely, active listening is hearing what is being said and interpreting its meaning. Active listening makes you a more effective communicator because you react to what you have heard. Study the following steps to increase your listening skills. Do not cut people off; let them develop their ideas before you speak. If a message is vague, write down your questions or comments, and wait for the entire presentation or discussion to be finished. Reduce personal and environmental distractions by focusing on the message. Keep an open mind. Be attentive and maintain eye contact whenever possible. By developing these basic communication skills, you will become more confident and more effective.

94wpm

Speaking is also a form of communication. In the world of work, speaking is an important way in which to share information. Regardless of whether you are speaking to an audience of one or one hundred, you will want to make sure that your listeners get your message. Be clear about your purpose, your audience, and your subject. A purpose is the overall goal or reason for speaking. An audience is anyone who receives information. The subject is the main topic or key idea. Research your subject. Using specific facts and examples will give you credibility. As you speak, be brief and direct. Progress logically from point to point. Speak slowly and pronounce clearly all your words. Do people understand what you say or ask you to repeat what you've said? Is the sound of your voice friendly and pleasant or shrill and off-putting? These factors influence how your message is received. A good idea is worthless if you can't communicate it.

96wpm

Developing a career is a process. You have looked at your interests, values, skills, aptitudes, and attitudes. Your exploration into the world of work has begun. The journey doesn't stop here, for the present is the perfect place to start thinking about the future. It's where you begin to take steps toward your goals. It's where you can really make a difference. As you set personal and career goals, remember the importance of small steps. Each step toward a personal goal or career goal is a small victory. That feeling of success encourages you to take other small steps. Each step builds onto the next. Continue exploring your personal world as well as the world you share with others. Expect the best as you go forward. Expect a happy life. Expect loving relationships. Expect success in life. Expect fulfilling and satisfying work in a job you truly love. Last but not least, expect that you have something special to offer the world, because you do.

Supplementary Timings

**Supplementary
Timing 1**

All problem solving, whether personal or academic, 10
involves decision making. You make decisions in order to 21
solve problems. On occasion, problems occur as a result of 33
decisions you have made. For example, you may decide to 44
smoke, but later in life, you face the problem of nicotine 56
addiction. You may decide not to study mathematics and 67
science because you think that they are too difficult. 78
Because of this choice, many career opportunities will be 90
closed to you. There is a consequence for every action. Do 102
you see that events in your life do not just happen, but 113
that they are the result of your choices and decisions? 124

How can you prepare your mind for problem solving? A 135
positive attitude is a great start. Indeed, your attitude 147
affects the way in which you solve a problem or make a 158
decision. Approach your studies, such as science and math 170
courses, with a positive and inquisitive attitude. Try to 182
perceive academic problems as puzzles to solve rather than 192
homework to avoid. 198

Critical thinking is a method of problem solving that 209
involves decoding, analyzing, reasoning, evaluating, and 220
processing information. It is fundamental for successful 231
problem solving. Critical thinking is a willingness to 242
explore, probe, question, and search for answers. Problems 254
may not always be solved on the first try. Don't give up. 266
Try, try again. Finding a solution takes sustained effort. 278
Use critical thinking skills to achieve success in today's 290
fast-paced and highly competitive world of business. 300

| 1 | 2 | 3 | 4 | 5 | 6 | 7 | 8 | 9 | 10 | 11 | 12 |

For many, the Internet is an important resource in 10
their private and professional lives. The Internet provides 22
quick access to countless Web sites that contain news, 33
products, games, entertainment, and many other types of 44
information. The Web pages on these sites can be designed, 56
authored, and posted by anyone, anywhere around the world. 68
Utilize critical thinking when reviewing all Web sites. 79

Just because something is stated on the radio, printed 90
in the newspaper, or shown on television doesn't mean that 102
it's true, real, accurate, or correct. This applies to 113
information found on the Internet as well. Don't fall into 125
the trap of believing that if it's on the Net, it must be 137
true. A wise user of the Internet thinks critically about 149
data found on the Net and evaluates this material before 160
using it. 162

When evaluating a new Web site, think about who, what, 173
how, when, and where. Who refers to the author of the Web 185
site. The author may be a business, an organization, or a 197
person. What refers to the validity of the data. Can this 209
data be verified by a reputable source? How refers to the 221
viewpoint of the author. Is the data presented without 232
prejudice? When refers to the time frame of the data. Is 244
this recent data? Where refers to the source of the data. 256
Is this data from an accurate source? By answering these 267
critical questions, you will learn more about the accuracy 279
and dependability of a Web site. As you surf the Net, be 290
very cautious. Anyone can publish on the Internet. 300

| 1 | 2 | 3 | 4 | 5 | 6 | 7 | 8 | 9 | 10 | 11 | 12

Supplementary Timing 3

Office employees perform a variety of tasks during 10
their workday. These tasks vary from handling telephone 21
calls to forwarding personal messages, from sending short 33
email messages to compiling complex office reports, and 44
from writing simple letters to assembling detailed letters 56
with tables, graphics, and imported data. Office workers 67
are a fundamental part of a company's structure. 77

The office worker uses critical thinking in order to 88
accomplish a wide array of daily tasks. Some of the tasks 100
are more urgent than other tasks and should be completed 111
first. Some tasks take only a short time, while others take 123
a lot more time. Some tasks demand a quick response, while 135
others may be attended as time permits or even postponed 147
until the future. Some of the tasks require input from 158
coworkers or managers. Whether a job is simple or complex, 170
big or small, the office worker must decide what is to be 182
tackled first by determining the priority of each task. 193

When setting priorities, critical thinking skills are 204
essential. The office worker evaluates each aspect of the 216
task. It is a good idea to identify the size of the task, 228
determine its complexity, estimate its effort, judge its 239
importance, and set its deadline. Once the office worker 250
assesses each task that is to be finished within a certain 262
period of time, then the priority for completing all tasks 274
can be set. Critical thinking skills, if applied well, 285
can save the employer money or, if executed poorly, can 296
cost the employer. 300

| 1 | 2 | 3 | 4 | 5 | 6 | 7 | 8 | 9 | 10 | 11 | 12

SKILLBUILDING

Each day business managers make choices that keep 10
businesses running smoothly, skillfully, and profitably. 21
Each decision regarding staff, finances, operations, and 32
resources often needs to be quick and precise. To develop 44
sound decisions, managers must use critical thinking. They 56
gather all the essential facts so that they can make good, 68
well-informed choices. After making a decision, skilled 79
managers review their thinking process. Over time, they 90
refine their critical thinking skills. When they encounter 102
similar problems, they use their prior experiences to help 114
them solve problems with ease and in less time. 124

What type of decisions do you think managers make that 135
involve critical thinking? Human Resources managers decide 147
who to employ, what to pay a new employee, and where to 158
place a new worker. In addition, Human Resources managers 170
should be unbiased negotiators, resolving conflict between 182
other employees. Office managers purchase copy machines, 194
computers, software, and office supplies. Finance officers 206
prepare precise, timely financial statements. Top managers 218
control business policies, appoint mid-level managers, and 230
assess the success of the business. Plant supervisors set 242
schedules, gauge work quality, and evaluate workers. Sales 254
managers study all of the new sales trends, as well as 265
provide sales training and promotion materials. 275

Most managers use critical thinking to make wise, well 286
thought-out decisions. They carefully check their facts, 297
analyze these facts, and make a final judgment based upon 309
these facts. They should also be able to clearly discern 320
fact from fiction. Through trial and error, managers learn 332
their own ways of solving problems and finding the most 343
effective and creative solutions. 350

| 1 | 2 | 3 | 4 | 5 | 6 | 7 | 8 | 9 | 10 | 11 | 12

Supplementary Timing 5

In most classes, teachers want students to analyze 10
situations, draw conclusions, and solve problems. Each 21
of these tasks requires students to use thinking skills. 32
How do students acquire these skills? What is the process 44
students follow to develop thinking skills? 53

During the early years of life, students learn words 63
and then combine these words into sentences. From there, 74
they learn to declare ideas, share thoughts, and express 85
feelings. Students learn numbers and simple math concepts. 97
They may learn to read musical notes, to keep rhythm, to 108
sing songs, and to recognize many popular and classical 119
pieces of music. Students learn colors, identify shapes, 130
and begin drawing. During the early years, students learn 142
the basic problem-solving models. 149

One way to solve problems and apply thinking skills 159
is to use the scientific approach. This approach requires 171
the student to state the problem to be solved, gather all 183
the facts about the problem, analyze the problem, and pose 195
viable solutions. Throughout this process, teachers ask 206
questions that force students to expand their thinking 217
skills. Teachers may ask questions such as these: Did you 229
clearly state the problem? Did you get all the facts? Did 241
you get the facts from the right place? Did you assume 252
anything? Did you pose other possible solutions? Did you 263
keep an open mind to all solutions? Did you let your bias 275
come into play? Did you listen to others who might have 286
insights? Did you dig deep enough? Does the solution make 298
sense to you? 301

This simple four-step process for solving problems 311
gives students a model to use for school, for work, and 322
for life. While the process may not be used to solve every 334
problem, it does provide a starting point to begin using 345
critical thinking skills. 350

| 1 | 2 | 3 | 4 | 5 | 6 | 7 | 8 | 9 | 10 | 11 | 12 |

SKILLBUILDING

**Supplementary
Timing 6**

A major goal for nearly all educators is to teach 10
critical thinking skills to a class. Critical thinking, 21
which is the process of reasonably or logically deciding 32
what to do or believe, involves the ability to compare and 44
contrast, resolve problems, make decisions, analyze and 55
evaluate, and combine and transfer knowledge. These skills 67
benefit the student who eventually becomes a part of the 78
workforce. Whether a person is in a corporate setting, a 89
small business, or self-employed, the business environment 101
of today is highly competitive and skilled employees are in 113
great demand. 116

One factor in achieving success in the workforce is 127
having the ability to deal with the varied demands of the 139
fast-paced business world. Required skills are insightful 150
decision making, creative problem solving, and earnest 162
communication among diverse groups. These groups could be 174
employees, management, employers, investors, customers, 185
or clients. 187

In school, we learn the details of critical thinking. 198
This knowledge extends far beyond the boundaries of the 209
classroom. It lasts a lifetime. We use critical thinking 220
throughout our daily lives. We constantly analyze and 231
evaluate music, movies, conversations, fashion, magazine 242
or newspaper articles, and television programs. We all had 254
experience using critical thinking skills before we even 265
knew what they were. So keep on learning, growing, and 276
experimenting. The classroom is the perfect setting for 287
exploration. Take this opportunity to see how others solve 299
problems, give each other feedback, and try out new ideas 311
in a safe environment. 316

A person who has learned critical thinking skills is 327
equipped with the essential skills for achieving success 338
in today's workforce. There are always new goals to reach. 350

| 1 | 2 | 3 | 4 | 5 | 6 | 7 | 8 | 9 | 10 | 11 | 12

Supplementary Timing 7

Use your unique creativity when applying critical 10
thinking skills. One of the first steps in unlocking your 22
creativity is to realize that you have control over your 33
thinking; it doesn't control you. Creativity is using new 45
or different methods to solve problems. Many inventions 56
involved a breakthrough in traditional thinking, and the 67
result was an amazing experience. For example, Einstein 78
broke with tradition by trying lots of obscure formulas 89
that changed scientific thought. Your attitude can form 100
mental blocks that keep you from being creative. When you 112
free your mind, the rest will follow. 120

Do your best to unleash your mind's innate creativity. 131
Turn problems into puzzles. When you think of a task as a 143
puzzle, a challenge, or a game instead of a difficult 154
problem, you open your mind and encourage your creative 165
side to operate. Creative ideas often come when you are 176
having fun and are involved in an unrelated activity. 187
You will find that when your defenses are down, your brain 199
is relaxed and your subconscious is alive, then creative 210
thoughts can flow. 214

Habit often restricts you from trying new approaches 225
to problem solving. Remember, there is usually more than 237
one solution. Empty your mind of the idea of only one way 249
of looking at a problem and strive to see situations in a 261
fresh, new way. How many times have you told yourself that 273
you must follow the rules and perform tasks in a certain 284
way? If you want to be creative, look at things in a new 295
way, break the pattern, explore new options, and challenge 307
the rules. If you are facing a difficult problem and can't 319
seem to find a solution, take a quick walk or relax for 330
a few minutes; then go back to the problem renewed. When 341
working on homework or taking a test, always work the 352
easiest problems first. Success builds success. 362

A sense of humor is key to being creative. Silly and 373
irrelevant ideas can lead to inventive solutions. Humor 384
generates ideas, puts you in a creative state of mind, 395
and makes work exciting! 400

| 1 | 2 | 3 | 4 | 5 | 6 | 7 | 8 | 9 | 10 | 11 | 12 |

Keyboarding is a popular business course for many 10
students. The major objectives of a keyboarding course are 22
to develop touch control of the keyboard and proper typing 34
techniques, build basic speed and accuracy, and provide 45
practice in applying those basic skills to the formatting 57
of letters, reports, tables, memos, and other kinds of 68
personal and business communications. In the early part of 80
a keyboarding course, students learn to stroke by touch 91
using specific techniques. They learn to hit the keys in a 103
quick and accurate way. After the keys are learned and 114
practiced, students move into producing documents of all 125
sizes and types for personal and vocational use. 135

When first learning keyboarding, there are certain 145
parameters, guidelines, and exercises to follow. There are 157
rules intended to help you learn and eventually master the 169
keyboard. Creating documents requires students to apply 180
critical thinking. What format or layout should be used? 191
What font and font size would be best? Are all the words 202
spelled correctly? Does the document look neat? Are the 213
figures accurate? Are punctuation and grammar correct? 224

There is a lot to learn in the world of keyboarding. 235
Be persistent, patient, and gentle with yourself. Allow 246
failure in class and on the job; that's how we learn. It's 258
okay to admit mistakes. Mistakes are stepping stones for 269
growth and creativity. Being creative has a lot to do with 281
risk-taking and courage. It takes courage to explore new 292
ways of thinking and to risk looking different, being 303
silly and impractical, and even being wrong. Your path to 315
creativity is such a vital component of your critical 326
thinking skills. Allow your creative thoughts to flow 337
freely when producing each of your keyboarding tasks. 348

Keyboarding skill and personal creativity are valuable 359
attributes for life and on the job. The worker who can see 371
situations and problems in a fresh way, reason logically, 383
explore options, and come up with inventive ideas is sure 395
to be a valuable employee. 400

| 1 | 2 | 3 | 4 | 5 | 6 | 7 | 8 | 9 | 10 | 11 | 12

Supplementary Timing 9

One of the most important decisions we all have to   10
face is choosing a career. The possibilities can appear   21
overwhelming. Fear not! Your critical thinking skills will   33
save you! Start your career planning today. Begin with   44
self-assessment. What are your interests? Do you enjoy   55
working indoors or outdoors? Do you prefer working with   66
numbers or with words? Are you the independent type or   77
would you rather work with a group? What are your favorite   89
academic studies? Think about these questions and then   100
create a list of your interests, skills, aptitudes, and   111
values. What you discover about yourself will help you in   123
finding the career that is right for you.   131

After you have explored your personal interests, look   142
at the sixteen career clusters for a wide range of job   153
prospects. Most jobs are included in one of these clusters   165
that have been organized by the government. During your   176
exploration, make a note of the clusters that interest you   188
and investigate these clusters.   194

Gather as much information as possible by using all   205
available resources. Scan the Help Wanted section in the   216
major Sunday newspapers for job descriptions and salaries.   228
Search the Net. The Internet provides electronic access to   240
worldwide job listings. If you want to know more about a   251
specific company, access its home page. Go to your college   263
placement office. Sign up for interviews with companies   274
that visit your campus. Visit your local school or county   286
library and ask the reference librarian for occupational   297
handbooks. Talk with people in your field of interest to   308
ask questions and get advice. Attend chapter meetings of   319
professional organizations to network with people working   331
in your chosen profession. Volunteer, intern, or work a   342
part-time or temporary job within your career choice for   353
valuable, first-hand insight. Taking an initiative in your   365
job search will pay off.   370

A career search requires the use of critical thinking   381
skills. These skills will help you to choose the career   392
that will match your skills and talents.   400

| 1 | 2 | 3 | 4 | 5 | 6 | 7 | 8 | 9 | 10 | 11 | 12 |

Ten-Key Numeric Keypad

GOAL:
● To control the ten-key numeric keypad keys.

Some computer keyboards have a separate ten-key numeric keypad located to the right of the alphanumeric keyboard. The arrangement of the keypad enables you to type numbers more rapidly than using the top row of the alphanumeric keyboard.

To input numbers using the ten-key numeric keypad, you must activate the Num Lock (Numeric Lock) key. Usually, an indicator light signals that the Num Lock is activated.

On the keypad, 4, 5, and 6 are the home keys. Place your fingers on the keypad home row as follows:

▶ First finger (J finger) on 4
▶ Second finger (K finger) on 5
▶ Third finger (L finger) on 6

The keypad keys are controlled as follows:

▶ First finger controls 1, 4, and 7
▶ Second finger controls 2, 5, and 8
▶ Third finger controls 3, 6, 9, and decimal point

▶ Right thumb controls 0
▶ Fourth finger controls ENTER

Since different computers have different arrangements of ten-key numeric keypads, study the arrangement of your keypad. The illustration shows the most common arrangement. If your keypad is arranged differently from the illustration, check with your instructor for the correct placement of your fingers on the keypad.

NEW KEYS

A. Use the first finger to control the 4 key, the second finger to control the 5 key, and the third finger to control the 6 key.

Keep your eyes on the copy.

Before beginning, check to be sure the Num Lock Key is activated.

Type first column from top to bottom. Next, type the second column; then type the third column. Press ENTER after typing the final digit of each number.

A. THE `4`, `5`, AND `6` KEYS

444	456	454
555	654	464
666	445	546
455	446	564
466	554	654
544	556	645
566	664	666
644	665	555
655	456	444
456	654	456

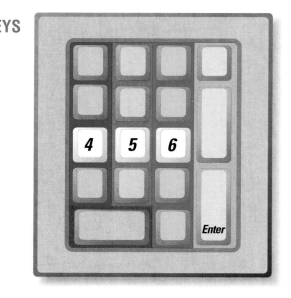

B. Use the 4 finger to control the 7 key, the 5 finger to control the 8 key, and the 6 finger to control the 9 key.

Keep your eyes on the copy.

Press ENTER after typing the final digit of each number.

B. THE 7, 8, AND 9 KEYS

474	585	696
747	858	969
774	885	996
447	558	669
744	855	966
477	588	699
444	555	666
747	858	969
774	885	996
747	858	969

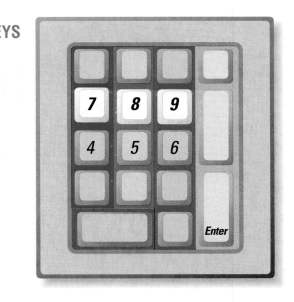

C. Use the 4 finger to control the 1 key, the 5 finger to control the 2 key, and the 6 finger to control the 3 key.

Keep your eyes on the copy.

Press ENTER after typing the final digit of each number.

C. THE 1, 2, AND 3 KEYS

444	555	666
111	222	333
144	225	336
441	552	663
144	255	366
411	522	633
444	555	666
414	525	636
141	252	363
411	525	636

D. Use the right thumb to control the 0 key.

Keep your eyes on the copy.

Press ENTER after typing the final digit of each number.

D. THE 0 KEY

404	470	502
505	580	603
606	690	140
707	410	250
808	520	360
909	630	701
101	407	802
202	508	903
303	609	405
505	401	506

E. Use the 6 finger to control the decimal key.

Keep your eyes on the copy.

Press ENTER after typing the final digit of each number.

E. THE . KEY

4.5	7.8	1.2
6.5	9.8	3.2
4.4	7.7	1.1
4.4	7.7	1.1
5.5	8.8	2.2
5.5	8.8	2.2
6.6	9.9	3.3
6.5	9.9	3.3
4.5	7.8	1.2
6.5	8.9	1.3